THE

GREAT

DEPRESSION

AND

THE NEW DEAL

A seven volume series reproducing nearly one hundred and fifty of the most important articles on all aspects of the Great Depression

Edited with introductions by

Melvyn Dubofsky
State University of New York at Binghamton

Stephen Burwood
Alfred University

A GARLAND SERIES

THE
GREAT DEPRESSION
AND THE
NEW DEAL

2

LABOR

Edited with an introduction by

Melvyn Dubofsky
and
Stephen Burwood

GARLAND PUBLISHING, INC.
NEW YORK & LONDON
1990

Library of Congress Cataloging-in-Publication Data

Labor : selected articles on workers and unions during the Great Depression /
edited, with an introduction, by Melvyn Dubofsky and Stephen Burwood.
p. cm. — (The Great Depression and the New Deal ; 2)
Includes bibliographical references.
ISBN 0-8240-0894-4 (alk. paper)
1. Working class—United States—History—20th century. 2. Trade unions—United
States—History—20th century. 3. Depressions—1929—United States. 4. New Deal,
1933–1939. I. Dubofsky, Melvyn.
II. Burwood, Stephen. III. Series.
HD8072.L217 1990
331.88'0973'09043—dc20   89-71389

Printed on acid-free, 250-year-life paper
Manufactured in the United States of America

CONTENTS

INTRODUCTION

N o decade in United States history has been more fraught with drama and change for American workers and their unions than that of the 1930s. The Great Depression cut like a giant scythe through the ranks of workers, leaving nearly a third of the labor force without jobs and income at the depth of the contraction in the winter of 1932–33. Despite sometimes dramatic improvements in the level of employment during the next six years, mass joblessness remained the reality for working people until the outbreak of World War II. As a consequence of unemployment, millions of Americans lost their homes, automobiles, lesser possessions, and dreams of a better future. For the first time in American history, new entrants to the labor force could not expect to improve on the situation of their parents and elders. For working people, then, the Great Depression brought misery, disillusionment, and faded hopes.

The reforms associated with the New Deal of Franklin D. Roosevelt, however, stimulated workers to act forcefully in order to transform disillusionment into hope, frustration into achievement, and failure into success. From 1933 through 1937 workers rebelled against the circumstances of their lives and sought to grasp a share of power from those who had heretofore dominated them. Massive waves of strikes flowed across the country and its major industries in the years 1934 and 1937. A labor movement that had fallen on hard times between 1922 and 1929 and then nearly expired in the early years of the depression rejuvenated itself during the New Deal. Part of the labor militancy had been generated by what the historian Irving Bernstein and others have characterized as the New Deal revolution in labor law. Another part of the militancy cascaded directly from the activities and interests of workers who were no longer willing to subjugate their needs and desires to the whims of others with more power. Whatever the source of the new labor militancy, masses of American workers acted to transform everyday work practices on the factory floor, the distribution of power between employers and employees, and the structure of national political parties. For the first time in United States history, trade unions wrested recognition and collective bargaining agreements from such corporate giants of mass-production industry as General Motors, U.S. Steel, General Electric, and Westinghouse. The number of union members soared from under three million in early 1933 to more than eight million by 1939, and this despite the fact that the labor movement had split into two hostile and competitive federations in the years 1935–36, the old and established American Federation of Labor (AFL) and the insurgent Congress of Industrial Organizations (CIO). In fact, labor's own civil war seemed to revitalize unionism rather than weaken it. Along with the resurgence of trade unionism came a political reawakening among workers. In many smaller industrial cities and also such larger ones as Detroit and Akron, workers built their own political organizations and grasped for a full share of local power. More often than not, however, the political reawakening of American labor made itself felt within the Democratic party. Between 1936 and 1944 workers proved the most loyal of Roosevelt Democrats, and the political analyst and pollster Samuel Lubell concluded in the aftermath of the election of 1940 that never before had class lines become so salient and evident in national elections.

The New Deal's impact on American workers has been the object of enormous scholarly attention during the past quarter of a century. The articles and essays in this volume provide readers with a sampling of the best contemporary scholarship on the subject of the New Deal and workers. We have chosen the selections with an eye to reprinting the best of the older and more traditional approaches to labor history as exemplified in the articles by Sidney Fine as well as the finest of the newer, innovative techniques in the discipline as embodied in the work of Steve Fraser, Daniel Nelson, and Robert Zieger. The articles in this volume also span the gamut from general interpretations by David Brody, Christopher Tomlins, and Melvyn Dubofsky to case studies of specific communities, economic sectors, and institutions by John Barnard, Jeremy Egolf, Daniel Leab, and others.

Chapter V

THE CIO ERA, 1935–55
SUMNER M. ROSEN

Resolved, that the CIO reaffirms the position which it
has consistently maintained from the beginning in opposition to any and all forms of discrimination between one
worker and another based upon considerations of race,
creed, color, or nationality . . . and that the CIO con-
demns the policies of many employers of discriminating
in their hiring and other employment conditions against
Negroes. . . .
>   Adopted at the 1941 Convention of the CIO

Negro workers, join the CIO union in your industry. The
CIO welcomes you. It gives you strength to win justice
and fair play. The CIO unites you with fellow workers
of all races and all creeds in the common struggle for
freedom, for democracy, for a better life.
>   *"The CIO and the Negro Worker—Together*
>   *for Victory,"* CIO publication no. 63

Most people who remember the CIO would probably
describe its position on race in language similar to these
quotations. The CIO is remembered for its militancy on
the burning questions of its era, and the question of racial
discrimination was one key to the politics of that period.
CIO leaders and literature espoused and elaborated a whole
range of progressive attitudes—on taxes, employment policy,
social security, planning, health, education, and many more
—and racial justice was a necessary, central element in that
series. CIO literature was aimed directly at Negro workers.
"The CIO and the Negro Worker" boasted of CIO actions
and statements attacking discrimination and attacked the

1

craft unions for their racial practices.[1] Other CIO publications dealt vigorously and directly with the problems of racism and prejudice. Southern policies and politicians were excoriated; denial of the right to vote in the South was the subject of CIO wrath and resolution; anti-lynch and anti-poll laws were supported, as was a federal FEPC. The CIO's Committee to Abolish Racial Discrimination—later the Committee on Civil Rights—was headed by such men as George Weaver and chaired through much of its life by James Carey; by 1944 there were eighty-five committees at the state and local level.[2] Affiliated unions had, in many cases, similar committees in operation.

None could doubt the political or rhetorical commitment. But rhetoric is not always an accurate gauge of reality. To what extent did the performance of the CIO and its affiliated unions translate these sentiments into practice, on the job and in the union hall? To what extent could they? How was the commitment to fight racism translated into bargaining and hiring concessions from employers, the government, and affiliated unions? An examination of these and other questions is necessary to assess the degree to which the CIO affected the rights of Negro workers, and the relationship between Negroes and the labor movement as a whole.

A few summary observations, elaborated in the body of this essay, may convey the results of such an assessment.

1. The CIO commitment to racial equality, while unquestionable, was pursued more through CIO influence in the general political process than through direct action. CIO strength supported such progressive measures as were adopted—such as the wartime FEPC—but did not, and probably could not, either innovate or decisively shape any of them.
2. CIO affiliates varied considerably in their devotion to eliminating racial barriers to hiring, promotion, and equal treatment on the job. Some lagged behind the leader-

ship; a few forged well ahead. The latter were not the largest or strongest unions in the CIO.

3. Most advances secured by Negro industrial workers during the CIO's lifetime were due to dominant economic forces, specifically the acute and prolonged labor shortage which prevailed during the Second World War. CIO affiliates gladly capitalized on these conditions to secure concessions for Negro workers from employers; AFL affiliates were in many cases far more resistant to these forces, and did not generally welcome the threat that they posed to traditional racial patterns and practices. Nevertheless, CIO practices altered those of AFL unions, often to a considerable extent.

4. By the time of the AFL-CIO merger the CIO had largely abandoned any vigorous commitment to an improvement in the position of Negroes through direct union action, either in collective bargaining or by internal reform. It did not seriously fight to implant CIO standards of union conduct in the merged organization.

It might be well to consider the last of these points first. In 1955 many people were disappointed that the CIO did not wage a stronger fight to exorcize the racist taint from the merged organization. In part, this failure reflected its relative weakness vis-à-vis the AFL, as well as the fact that merger was as necessary to prevent CIO splits as to save both organizations from a rising tide of public and political opposition to labor unions. However, the CIO seems to have deliberately avoided a fight, against the wishes of some of its leaders. There was no open opposition to the terms of the merger from the floor at the last CIO convention except on this issue. Michael Quill, President of the Transport Workers, delivered a strong and emotional speech on the first day of the convention, arguing that the proposed constitution of the merged organization contained no binding language on the racial practices of affiliates; he also attacked the general posture of the CIO for apparently accepting submergence in the new structure, and

190

3

for having failed to fight for principles in the premerger negotiations. But this was clearly a minority position. Quill, while a member of the Executive Committee of the CIO, was not a major power in the organization and had few allies willing to jeopardize such autonomy as the CIO had been able to salvage. In the debate he was supported by only one delegate, a Negro from the United Packinghouse Workers of America; in the vote the UPWA delegation supported the official position. President Walter Reuther's rebuttal dealt not with the merits of Quill's case, but with Quill's alleged failure to have stated it during the merger negotiations, which, as a member of the Executive Committee, he could have done. Earlier, in his opening speech, Reuther had praised the new constitution's racial provisions:

> I believe that we will demonstrate, before the gavel adjourns the united labor convention, in a very tangible way that we intend to give meaning and a purpose to the constitutional declarations against discrimination for racial reasons.

The Civil Rights Committee, in its convention report, expressed similar sentiments, but in more circumspect language:

> When this constitution is analyzed, it is evident that this principle [of equality] is protected to the extent that can be defined in a labor constitution for a voluntary federation of labor unions.

This deference to the traditional AFL position tended to negate the committee's assertion that the racial clauses of the new constitution were "stronger than the present CIO constitution."

The near-unanimity was more apparent than real. Clearly many were disturbed at the concessions that necessity seemed to have imposed on the CIO, and it seemed for a time that James Carey might speak for them on this aspect of the merger agreement. For the founding convention of the

AFL-CIO, Carey prepared—but never delivered—a speech that sounded the traditional CIO position. It called on the new Federation to emulate some specific CIO practices such as prohibiting any state or city-wide affiliate from meeting in segregated facilities; it also called for a vigorous civil rights committee, comparable to that which he had chaired in the CIO, with a broad mandate to enforce the constitutional standards. Carey's failure to deliver his speech was a case of discretion serving as the better part of valor, but given his commitment to racial equality, it must have required considerable persuasion to induce him merely to place it in the record. It is worth noting, in passing, that Thurgood Marshall, who addressed the founding convention for the NAACP—presumably a CIO nominee—never mentioned the problem of union racial practices.

The causes of the decline of CIO strength relating to the AFL in the decade preceding merger need not detain us here. What is important is that they demonstrated the degree to which the CIO depended on forces outside itself —in the economy and in the political apparatus—to achieve the kind of change in the economic status of Negro workers to which it was deeply committed in principle. When these forces were favorable, the CIO could defy the AFL and successfully prove that it could deliver, at least to a degree, those improvements which had never had real meaning for the AFL or most of its affiliates. But when these forces lost strength, particularly in political life, defiance became a hollow and possibly a dangerous gesture.

In effect, the AFL won the real victory, whatever the new constitution seemed to promise. Five years after the merger, the formation of the Negro American Labor Council by more than one thousand Negroes active in labor unions seemed to mark the final recognition of this victory by those most directly affected; the presence at the opening meeting of Walter Reuther and the conspicuous absence of George Meany was an ironic accent to this phase of history. Ray Marshall had pointed out that neither Reuther nor

Carey voted to exclude from the new Federation either of the two railroad brotherhoods—the Firemen and Trainmen—which retained racial bars in their constitutions; only A. Philip Randolph voiced his objections, as he had been doing for many years.[3]

The truth was that the most important reasons for the typical CIO policies and attitudes on race had lost most of their significance by the time of the merger. For one thing, the appeal to Negroes had been an important element in organizing some of the key industries on which CIO strength was based, but the organizing drive had spent itself. Indeed, CIO numbers were ebbing in the early 1950s; there were no great new fields to conquer except—as in the South—those in which the unions had been virtually checkmated and had largely abandoned their organizing efforts. Thus the need to speak with a clear voice on the race question in order to win the support of unorganized Negro workers in target industries no longer existed. Secondly, the political climate that had done so much to foster a Negro-CIO alliance had altered dramatically. The heart of the New Deal Democratic Party had been the CIO and the Negro organizations. Their common work had yielded significant gains to both, especially in terms of prestige and influence within party circles. Each needed and worked with the other, extended courtesies to the other, and used its influence for the benefit of the other when needed. In national discussion the two spoke largely with one voice, and they reaped concrete political rewards. However, even before the Eisenhower period began, it was apparent that the center of power had moved elsewhere. Increasingly, both the CIO and the Negro leadership began to define their interests in new and different terms. For the CIO, merger with the AFL became increasingly the center of attention, leading to an inevitable emphasis of those policies, such as militancy on the race question, that had most sharply marked its differences with the AFL. In this way the alliance with such Negro organizations as the NAACP and the Urban

193

6

League began to acquire an increasingly formal and rhetorical character, without the substance of past commitment. The Negro groups, too, began to seek influence where it mattered, to place greater emphasis on governmental and business pressure than on the support of the CIO. While the good relations between these organizations never ceased, much of the real meaning of their mutual support slowly eroded. By the time of the merger there was little save nostalgia to put in the way of the CIO's capitulation.

From the very beginning the CIO appeared to the American Communist Party to offer the avenue to mass organization that the Party had sought in vain by various other routes since its formation. The Party had always stressed the importance of the Negro masses for the revolutionary future it foresaw. Its role in the CIO and constituent unions was bound to bring the question into prominence once the actual mass organization of industrial workers had begun. James W. Ford, long a Party spokesman on Negro questions, emphasized the importance of the CIO to the Party's hopes in the presidential campaign of 1936, and it was a dominant theme in party planning through the CIO's early years.[4] The earlier, sterile definition of the Negro question as one of national identity gave way to this more pragmatic and promising strategy.[5]

The part that Communists played in the CIO has been described in detail.[6] The times were ripe for an active role, and Party members achieved considerable influence within the CIO itself, and important—often dominant—positions within constituent unions. This influence persisted until the painful, protracted, but ultimately successful effort to eliminate it that went on from 1948 to 1950. Its effects on the struggle for Negro rights during this period fall into three phases.

I. In the organizing period prior to the war, the CIO enrolled hundreds of thousands of Negroes; nobody knows the exact number. In many cases the unions encountered

194

7

suspicion and apathy among these workers who had long been short-changed and discriminated against by organized labor.[7] The early sit-down strikes in Detroit were carried out with virtually no Negro participation.[8] But wherever Negro workers formed a significant fraction of the labor force, intensive, persistent efforts were expended to secure their support. This was true whether Communists played a subordinate role or held the key positions of leadership. CIO organizers, both Communist and non-Communist, brought unionism to many thousands of Negro workers. The distinctive feature of the efforts of the Communist organizers was to secure the maximum possible influence for Party members and supporters, a strategy which is no surprise.

Where the Communists were in control, Negroes who received support for leadership positions were generally men who would respond to Party influence. Where Communists did not control, they often sought to elevate to a principle the election of Negroes to leadership positions, making of this question an issue on which to build support among the Negro workers. The most celebrated instance was the concerted campaign to put a Negro on the Executive Board of the UAW, an effort which, though it failed, worked as a chronically divisive factor in the immediate prewar years of that union's life. Similar in purpose was the use of the issue within local unions as the basis for mobilizing support for Party-backed "fractions," a basic Communist technique of organization.[9] In many cases, of course, the goal of placing Negroes in leadership positions was a logical element in the major organizing task in which the unions were engaged, but such consistency was often not the deciding factor for those who wanted to further Party fortunes. Even where an effort to raise the question of Negro leadership roles was likely to hurt rather than help the union cause, it was still emphasized.

What the Party sought in those years was to achieve the greatest possible influence within the unions; its appeal to

195

8

Negro workers was calculated to secure and consolidate that influence. Party organs stressed the importance of the new unions to the economic liberation of Negro workers. A Party pamphlet in 1938[10] argued that the advance of Negroes resulted from "the alliance of the Negro people with the progressive sections of the white population"; among these:

> Most important . . . has been the advance made on the economic field. The advent of the CIO and the great advance of militant trade unionism has doubtlessly been a prime factor in breaking down Jim Crow bars and practices in the trade unions, resulting in the participation en masse of Negro industrial workers, on the basis of equality, in the trade union movement of the country.

Clearly the Communists expected and intended their role in the CIO to provide them with a secure and significant position from which to mobilize Negro workers around Party goals and programs.

II. Whatever the timetable for achieving this goal might have been, the Second World War altered matters considerably and, as it turned out, permanently. The Party and its supporters opposed American involvement in the early years of the war, but Hitler's attack on the Soviet Union in June 1941 reversed that position. The war was henceforth characterized as a holy crusade and its successful prosecution became the overriding priority. While Communist literature continued to stress the necessity of rooting out racial injustice, the emphasis changed. In the name of furthering the war effort Negroes were denied their right to full participation in that effort.[11] Labor leaders were judged not on their racial attitudes but on their devotion to the war effort, and Foster was harshly critical of John L. Lewis, once a Party favorite, for his failure in that regard. Party spokesmen criticized Adam Clayton Powell for his insistence that Negro grievances receive attention.[12] This new tendency reached its climax in the *Daily Worker's* harsh denunciation of A. Philip Randolph for organizing

196

9

the March on Washington Movement that led to the establishment of the Fair Employment Practices Commission.[13] Ben Davis, dismissing a shameful incident involving the medical neglect of some Negro soldiers, wrote:

> The U. S. General Staff has on many occasions . . . proved that they deserve the full confidence of the Negro people. . . . We cannot temporarily stop the war until all questions of discrimination are ironed out.[14]

The Party abandoned its work in the South and, in effect, its commitment to Negro equality.

This was an important and fateful step. The CIO, in contrast, continued its pressure to improve the economic status of Negro workers and used its influence within the government vigorously. CIO leaders argued that the promotion of racial equality was a necessary war measure, but they continued to stress the moral imperatives involved. They also understood that wartime prosperity offered the most favorable setting in which to improve the economic and legal welfare of Negroes. When the Communists downgraded the issue of Negro rights, the first meaningful differences between the two groups began to become clear, presaging the later open struggle. Union strength continued to grow during the war, and Communists inside the CIO unions grew with it. But the stage was set for a new phase in the relationship.

III. The postwar period saw the decline of Communist influence. Many factors contributed to this decline, predominantly the onset of the cold war. As pressure to purge its ranks mounted within and upon the CIO, the Party and its supporters fought to hold their positions. This effort largely depended on the reaction of the Negro workers. In some cases their response made the difference between success and failure. Kampelman states that the inability of the National Maritime Union to take over the Marine Cooks and Stewards after the latter was expelled from the CIO was due to Negro loyalty to the MCS, based on its solid achievements in improving the economic

197

welfare of Negro workers in that branch of the maritime industry:

> The Negroes in the stewards' department on vessels from West Coast ports were since 1947 the source of some of the strongest union support. Negroes became increasingly common on the ships' rosters of stewards. Many Negroes entered the union and received jobs at a time when jobs were denied them by other shipping unions on the West Coast. The MCS made much of the fact that it was the only organization on the West Coast that came to their aid as a union. The union leadership insisted that any anti-MCS talk was in fact anti-Negro union talk. The union leadership saw to it that Negroes entered into the ranks of the leaders. For this reason the NMU was unable to use the issue of Communism successfully in its efforts to undermine the MCS.[15]

Unfortunately for those who fought against expulsion from the CIO, this had not been the general rule in those unions where the struggle took place. The Party's wartime position had been a strategic error which contributed to the downfall of those union leaders who, later, became the targets of the anti-Communist struggle within the CIO.

The Party made further errors. For a short time after the war its position on the Negro question consisted of a militant revival of prewar demands. In the face of declining employment in the war industries, the Party held that Negroes needed and deserved special treatment including super-seniority systems to protect them from layoff.[16] Such demands found a favorable reception among some Negroes,[17] but there was little opportunity to put them into practice except in a few smaller unions.[18] While the bulk of the CIO unions did not take this position—rightly or wrongly —the Party was unable to dramatize the difference effectively to the mass of Negro workers. Before the effort to do so had really gotten under way, the Communist position on the Negro question shifted; the replacement of Earl Browder by William Z. Foster saw a return to the old pre-CIO approach, stressing Negro nationalism and all but

11

abandoning the pragmatic, influence-building strategy of the immediate prewar period. Added to this was a near-hysterical witch hunt for "white chauvinists" within the Party, a desperate and divisive expenditure of energy that served only to divide the Party, isolate the trade unionists within it, and confuse and alienate precisely those Negro masses on whom the Party's fate rested. From 1946 to 1953 this rigid and perplexing purgation continued, weakening the Party and rendering it even less capable of effectively countering the attack that had been launched by those whom Foster called the "Social-Democratic leaders" of the CIO.[19]

It is worth noting that the CIO did not immediately take up the challenge of declining Negro economic opportunity in postwar period. The CIO's entire political position had been greatly altered by the war, and its capacity for bold initiatives weakened. The postwar strike wave had evoked a public reaction that put the unions on the defensive, a position from which, in fact, they never succeeded in extricating themselves. There were more pressing matters to worry about than the problems of Negro workers. Testifying for the CIO about these problems before a Senate Committee in 1947, Walter Reuther said:

> No single institution such as the CIO . . . can do more than fight a holding action until the community moves through law to guarantee basic freedoms.[20]

In fairness, one must observe that this approach has not significantly changed in the intervening years.

Yet the Communists could not withstand the challenge; after a bitter struggle the CIO acted to expel or to "cleanse" virtually all the unions in which Communist influence had been significant. The CIO itself was so deeply enmeshed in this struggle that, in these critical years, it had little energy to spare for other things, including the development and application of an effective strategy for dealing with the economic problems of Negro workers. And, to the extent that the unions expelled had been the more militant

199

12

and devoted advocates of racial justice, the cause itself lost much of its meaning and appeal. The unions under attack had sought vigorously—but ineffectively—to label as racists all those CIO leaders who had become their enemies. But in one of the ironies of this history, those unions that survived the purge with their identities preserved were largely unions with few Negro members.[21]

The net effect of American Communism on the racial practices and achievements of American unions in this period is ambiguous. Clearly the Party's role inside the CIO was to strengthen the rhetorical and political commitment to racial equality, to participate effectively in organizing many Negro workers, and to single out for special attention the problems, grievances, and ambitions of Negro workers in individual CIO unions. These were positive contributions. They took place almost entirely during the early phases of the CIO's life. During the war the Party uncritically subordinated Negro needs to the war effort, thus abandoning a cause that urgently needed intensive work—as it still does. The postwar period saw the Party struggling, weakly and unsuccessfully, to preserve its mass base; in this struggle the needs of Negro workers were brought in primarily for tactical purposes. The struggle itself constituted a massive and tragic diversion of union effort from the real problems of the society and the economy, and thus represents a serious setback to progress in the welfare of Negro workers, which had begun so auspiciously with the formation of the CIO.

It is necessary to recognize the reality of Negro gains during the period under review, and to assess them as carefully as possible. These gains were real. Many opportunities long denied were at last realized; many barriers of long standing were at last broken down. The data show important increases in Negro industrial employment and income. They also show that these gains were not uniform, but varied by industry, occupation, and area.

In 1939 the median income of nonwhite wage and salary

earners was 41 per cent of that of whites; by 1950 it had risen to 60 per cent.[22] Negro wages rose, on the average, faster than white wages during this period. A significant upward shift occurred in the occupational distribution of Negroes, reflecting the large migration from the rural South to industrial areas, and the penetration of Negroes into occupations where manpower shortages were acute. The percentage of male Negro workers in white-collar and professional jobs rose from 5.6 per cent in 1940 to 7.2 per cent in 1950; craftsmen and operatives rose from 16.6 per cent of the total in 1940 to 28.8 per cent in 1950.[23] Along with large numbers of white workers, many Negroes achieved middle-class standards of employment and income.

Robert Weaver's study[24] showed that a large part of this change, the most important since the Civil War, occurred between 1942 and 1945. Negro employment in the war industries studied rose in that period from 5.8 per cent to 8.2 per cent. In iron and steel foundries, where Negroes had always been an important part of the labor force, the Negro share of total employment exceeded 25 per cent in 1945. In other industries important but not spectacular rises were observed in this short period, so that at the end of the war Negro workers constituted an important fraction—ranging from 5 to 13 per cent in most cases—of the dozen or so key war industries. At the same time, Weaver points out, a large share of the total of one and a half million Negro war workers was concentrated in a relatively small number of geographic areas where labor shortages were especially acute,[25] and this period saw virtually no change in the proportion of Negroes occupying professional, managerial, or sales jobs.[26] Retrogression also occurred. The introduction of the diesel engine in railroads made it possible for the Brotherhood of Locomotive Firemen and Enginemen, between 1937 and 1943, "to achieve an objective it had been seeking for over fifty years—namely, the perfection of a plan to eliminate Negro firemen."[27] CIO unions were not immune to racist resistance; even the United Electrical Workers, which took effective initiative

14

in some places to open doors to Negro workers, was forced to accede to resistance from a Pennsylvania local, while the United Steelworkers and the Marine and Shipbuilding Workers met strong rank-and-file resistance to efforts to break down racial barriers.[28] Resistance was of course strongest in the South, and even the tight labor markets of the war years did not, on the whole, open the doors of opportunity to Negro workers in skills and occupations historically closed to them.[29]

These and other facts support the view that, even at the most propitious moments, the power and willingness of unions deliberately to alter hiring and promotional patterns are limited. Though there are exceptions, the dominant pattern is one of accommodation to the prevailing pattern of employment as it has been historically determined by the employers. In some industries, such as iron, steel, and coal mining, Negroes have long been employed in jobs at relatively skilled levels. In these cases the unions accepted and built on the pattern they found, adopting non-racist policies which, whatever their secondary motivation, were calculated to achieve and maintain organizational success. The United Mine Workers and the United Steelworkers both represent this pattern. Both have long and honorable traditions of racial equality; these have their roots in employment patterns that preceded the unions' presence. But the Textile Workers Union, although squarely in the CIO tradition of racial equality, found itself forced to accept Southern patterns of segregation in hiring and assignment as the price of survival in the South.[30]

In the auto industry, Weaver points out, the prevailing employment pattern, confining Negroes to unskilled and foundry work, did not begin to alter until conversion to war production was actually under way.[31] Here the United Auto Workers put its weight squarely in support of equal opportunity and at length—after painful and protracted negotiations—these policies prevailed. Hitherto the union, whatever its desires, found itself with no option but to accept the patterns established in the past. This was, in-

202

15

deed, the general picture in American industry. What differentiated the AFL and the CIO was the difference in their response to the changes the war imposed. CIO unions generally—although not always, and not without internal resistance—supported and worked for egalitarian employment policies, and were actively supported in this by the parent body. AFL unions varied considerably in their responses; some acted honorably and vigorously to open new opportunities for Negro workers, but others actively resisted any Negro inroads. Northrup has described the response of such unions as the International Association of Machinists, the International Brotherhood of Electrical Workers, the Boilermakers, the Shipbuilders, and the Plumbers. At the same time, in industries where both AFL and CIO unions were actively organizing, the CIO zeal for racial progress was often dampened by the presence of an AFL rival prepared to accommodate itself to local race prejudice; in these cases, quite often, CIO unions soft-pedaled their characteristic approach to race and accepted practices they would normally have criticized.[32]

Where the factor of competition was not present, CIO unions often showed themselves ready and willing to press actively for open hiring and promotion policies. The Marine and Shipbuilding Workers, a CIO union, frequently did this, though the results were not always those hoped for.[33] And it must also be said that the AFL unions frequently responded to the CIO challenge by recognizing the importance of opening their ranks to Negroes where Negro employment made a difference in organizing success. This response was part of the general loosening in the strict craft approach to organizing that was forced on AFL unions by the CIO challenge; it had its roots more in a strategy for survival and growth than in any moral or ethical change. Naturally, as some of the older bastions of racism such as the printing trades and the railroads began to decline in economic importance, the balance of strength inside the AFL shifted. Unions with a stake in the principle of industrial organization grew as they responded, under CIO

16

prodding, to these exigencies, and to a degree the pattern of practices inside the AFL as a whole was seen to alter. This change should not, however, be exaggerated. It would not be correct to say that the AFL leadership as a whole underwent any significant change of attitude on race questions during the CIO period. Such changes as have occurred have their origins to more recent events and forces.

General comments tend to understate the real range of response among international unions—and among local unions within a given international—to the rising tide of pressure for greater racial equality. The most blatant, persistent, and deliberate of union policies of Negro exclusion or segregation were to be found in AFL unions; the most determined and far-reaching efforts to combat racism were carried out by CIO unions. At the same time, CIO local unions did discriminate, especially in the South, while some AFL unions won and kept the loyalty of significant numbers of Negro members, even resisting CIO organizing efforts in certain instances. The racism of some Birmingham, Alabama, Steelworkers locals was well known before the merger.[34] Segregated locals have existed at one time or another in such CIO unions as the Amalgamated Clothing Workers, the Oil Chemical and Atomic Workers, and the Textile Workers.[35] (It should be added that the list of AFL unions in this category is far longer.) In such CIO unions as the United Rubber Workers and the United Paperworkers, *de facto* segregated locals were long accepted. In virtually every case these were an accommodation to prevailing patterns and customs. In these unions, and in many others, the leadership sought to counteract reactionary forces, with varying degrees of energy and commitment and with varying results. In many cases the instability of leadership—the dangers of losing strength to a rival bloc or candidate for top office—was an inhibiting factor. It was only when Walter Reuther had achieved unchallenged dominance in the UAW that he was able to move resolutely against Dallas, Atlanta, and Memphis locals. Because the UAW's great strength lies outside the South, Reuther could act without

204

17

serious risks. By contrast, the Textile Workers have never been able to deal with racism in Southern locals because any attempt to promote equality jeopardizes the union's chances of making inroads where the bulk of the industry now is found.

In some cases CIO unions took considerable risks for the principle of racial equality. The best-known of these situations involved the United Packinghouse Workers (UPWA), where the risks were significant in the North as well as in the South.[36] A large Negro membership from the outset and a strong ideological commitment to equality help to explain the union's position. The UPWA's opposition to racism has been militant, consistent, and thorough. The leadership never ducked the issue. In fact, its position placed in jeopardy its standing with other CIO leaders; protests forced the CIO to investigate charges of Communist influence in the union in 1953.[37] The United Electrical Workers and its CIO successor, the International Union of Electrical Workers (IUE), shared a commitment to racial equality, though they applied it less energetically than did the UPWA. IUE President James Carey was chairman of the CIO Civil Rights Committee, a position that tended to reinforce his role in his own union; at the same time, he had less freedom of action than did the UPWA leaders, because of his closeness to Reuther and because of organizing rivalries with other nations, particularly the International Brotherhood of Electrical Workers. Neither the IUE nor any other union has come close to the UPWA in a thoroughgoing commitment to full racial equality.

Marshall states that the CIO had considerable influence in causing the AFL to "abandon its discriminatory practices and to try to project a more favorable image."[38] Most of the effects of this influence, however, seem to have been felt at the top. They took the form of public utterances by AFL leaders, more determined organizing efforts among Negro workers, greater use of Negro organizers and staff, and convention resolutions on issues of racial justice. Once the postwar Southern organizing drive had lost momentum and

18

sputtered to a halt, there seems to be little evidence that the
AFL exerted any real pressure on its affiliates to abandon
formal or informal racial barriers. Since 1934 A. Philip Randolph had been making an annual impassioned plea at
AFL conventions for racial justice in the unions; throughout
the CIO period nothing significant occurred to mitigate the
urgency of that plea. In 1959—four years *after* the merger—
Randolph's charges of failure to act and his attempts to
block the readmission of the International Longshoremen's
Association and to secure the expulsion of two unions which
retained race bars sparked a bitter exchange with George
Meany. The issue was fought publicly in 1959, in contrast to
the 1934 refusal even to consider a report on the subject,
but the substantive result was much the same.[39]

The events that really altered union racial practices have
been of more recent date. For all its devotion to the principles of equality, the CIO did not decisively affect patterns
of employment, pay, promotion, or apprenticeship opportunity in the craft unions. It dramatized the issue and made it
highly visible, an important achievement. It brought the
benefits of union membership to millions of Negroes employed in mass-production industries. It forced the AFL to
drop, not its racist preferences, but many of the organizational principles that were required to buttress those preferences. In industry after industry its success stimulated AFL
unions to accept the necessity of industrial organization and
to expand their membership. This, in turn, weakened the
relative strength inside the AFL of the craft groups that had
always been centers of white privilege. The ultimate result
was bound to be a steady erosion of the historic barriers to
Negro equality. But it must be recognized that those whose
philosophies had long dominated the AFL resisted these
tendencies with great tenacity and endurance. There was no
substantial weakening of basic attitudes until the immediate
premerger period, when it became necessary to accept the
language of racial justice as the condition of reunification. As
we have seen, there were few sanctions to give the language
meaning, and little disposition in the CIO to fight to get

206

19

them. Only when the race revolution of our own time began, five long years after merger, did the forces that have now started to change the racial practices and policies of the American labor movement make themselves felt. These forces originate and have their strength outside the ranks of organized labor.

Conclusion

CIO influence in American life reached its peak in the war years. It helped to solidify the Democratic Party as the voice of domestic liberalism, the modern instrument through which the state has acted to protect men's rights and promote their welfare. It made organized labor a new force in economic life, and gave it a strong voice with which to support the new role of the state. CIO unions sparked the transformation of American labor from an aristocratic, ineffectual minority into the largest labor movement in the Western world. The CIO transformed industrial relations by breaking the resistance of the great mass-production industries to collective bargaining. It organized hundreds of thousands of Negroes and broke down the historic barriers between Negroes and trade unions. The new generation of leaders developed in the CIO included—for the first time—numbers of Negroes, some of them reaching high posts. All of this constitutes a significant achievement.

Yet the CIO could not—perhaps never wanted to—acquire the influence in political and economic life that many looked forward to in its period of greatest growth. An irony intrudes here. It was largely the full employment brought about by the Second World War that enabled the CIO to reach its maximum membership and influence. Yet the war imposed new priorities on the political systems, forcing the CIO—and most of America—to subordinate all other goals to that of victory. Thus, when Sidney Hillman sought to persuade President Roosevelt to adopt a Fair Employment Practices Commission, he was unsuccessful. It was only

207

20

the threat of the first modern March on Wahington by A. Philip Randolph that forced the President's hand.[40] The CIO and the Negro organizations gave the FEPC strong support; AFL members of FEPC did not. When the Commission faced its crisis of survival, CIO pressure alone could not save it. The story is instructive; the war and the victory of the New Deal had deprived the CIO of any real freedom of action. It could not consummate its symbolic triumph over the historic albatross of racism. Nor were other cherished hopes to be permanently realized. As the CIO faced internal dissension, stagnation, decline, and then absorption into the merged Federation, the mood of the nation changed and left unfulfilled a host of noble dreams, preserved as in amber in the records of CIO convention proceedings. Another era had to arrive before these tasks were again taken up.

The conclusion seems inescapable that the CIO did much to change the rhetoric of our society's response to social evils, but less to alter permanently the substance of this response. The AFL unions emerged from their prolonged confrontation with the CIO deeply affected in several important respects, but the leaders had not basically revised their approach to race questions. Perhaps more important is the fact that the economic position of Negro workers in the United States was changed by forces over which the CIO had little or no influence. What the CIO did demonstrate was the difference between actively welcoming the opportunities to better this economic situation and actively resisting them, between articulating a challenge and remaining silent. AFL resistance, however, did not seriously change the balance of power between the two groups. And when the war was over, the CIO did not find the levers of power that would have enabled it to continue the historic alteration in the Negro's position which the war had begun.

208

21

SECTION 7a AND THE BLACK WORKER

By RAYMOND WOLTERS

According to President Franklin D. Roosevelt, the purpose of the National Industrial Recovery Act was to put people back to work at wages that would provide more than a bare living. The crucial point in inducing recovery was thought to be the expansion of purchasing power, and the preamble of the legislation declared that the economy would be invigorated by "increas[ing] the consumption of industrial and agricultural products by increasing purchasing power."

The legislation authorized a wide range of governmental activity, and one of the most important aspects of the new program was its effort to encourage the development of trade unions. Several important New Deal advisers believed that without the countervailing power of well-organized unions the excess supply of labor would put workers at a serious disadvantage when bargaining with employers, with the result that the wage earners' real income would not be large enough to sustain the mass purchasing power that would stimulate recovery. It was felt that by encouraging collective bargaining the government would enable workers to wrest higher wages from management and that the resulting increase in consumer spending would benefit the entire economy. Accordingly, Section 7a of the National Industrial Recovery Act provided

> 1) that employees shall have the right to organize and bargain collectively through representatives of their own choosing, and shall be free from the interference, restraint or coercion of employers of labor, or their agents, in the designation of such representatives . . . .
> 2) that no employee and no one seeking employment shall be required as a condition of employment to join any company union or to refrain from

RAYMOND WOLTERS *is an Assistant Professor of History at the University of Delaware.*

joining, organizing, or assisting a labor organization of his own choosing. . . .[1]

Yet it soon became apparent that there was much disagreement as to the meaning of collective bargaining "through representatives of their own choosing." Labor leaders such as John L. Lewis insisted that President Roosevelt wanted workers to join independent unions, but many businessmen noted that the legislation had not specified the manner in which representatives were to be chosen, and they sought to comply with the terms of Section 7a by establishing company unions. Almost from the beginning of the NRA experiment, it was apparent that Section 7a did not ensure labor's right to organize independent unions. Determined employers were able to avoid meaningful negotiation with outside unions.[2]

Historians and economists often have assumed that all wage earners would have benefited if the NRA had supported collective bargaining more enthusiastically and had provided adequate legislative protection of the workers' right to organize in independent unions. Yet insofar as Negro workers are concerned, this assumption is questionable. The great majority of Negro wage earners were members of the working class, but during the early years of the New Deal Negroes were rarely found in the ranks of organized labor. Altogether in 1930 there were at least nineteen independent unions which excluded Negroes from membership, either by constitutional provision or by initiation ritual. An additional ten unions admitted Negroes to membership only in segregated auxiliary locals. Of course these were only the more blatant examples of union discrimination. Many unions prohibited Negro membership by tacit consent, while others permitted only token membership. Still others—perhaps a majority—discriminated against colored workers in more subtle ways. While admitting that it was impossible to determine exactly the number of Negro trade union members, the

---

[1] "Presidential Statement on NIRA," *The Public Papers and Addresses of Franklin D. Roosevelt,* (New York, 1938-1950) II, 251. *United States Statutes at Large,* XLVIII, 195. See the following for some representative examples of New Deal thinking with regard to collective bargaining: Hugh Johnson, *The Blue Eagle* (New York, 1935), 334-350; testimony of Donald Richberg, United States House of Representatives, *Hearings Before the House Committee on Ways and Means,* 73rd Congress, 1st Session, 68-69; testimony of Robert F. Wagner, *ibid.,* 105. Irving Bernstein has written perceptively on the formulation of *The New Deal Collective Bargaining Policy* (Berkeley and Los Angeles, 1950). *United States Statutes at Large,* XLVIII, 195.
[2] Arthur M. Schlesinger, Jr., *The Coming of the New Deal* (Boston, 1959) chapter 9. Irving Bernstein, *op. cit.,* chapters 3 and 4.

N.A.A.C.P. felt it was "safe to say that there were in 1930 no more than 50,000 colored members of national unions," and almost half of these were members of the Brotherhood of Sleeping Car Porters. These colored union members represented about 3 percent of the 1,500,000 Negroes engaged in transportation, extraction of minerals and manufacturing in 1930 (compared with a figure of about 10 percent for all non-agricultural American workers).[3]

From its inception the A.F.L. showed little enthusiasm for the task of organizing unskilled, industrial workers. Indeed, some writers have interpreted the emergence of the A.F.L. and the decline of the Knights of Labor in the late 1880s and early 1890s as the turning point which "marked the triumph of craft individualism over industrial brotherhood." Although the A.F.L. occasionally issued statements concerning the need to organize the mass-production industries, it had not made a major attempt in this direction since the abortive steel strike of 1919. During the 1920s membership in the Federation's largest industrial unions declined precipitously, and this reinforced the general impression that the Federation represented only those skilled workers who composed the "aristocracy of labor." During the early years of the Depression several federal labor unions were chartered for the express purpose of organizing mass-production industries, but these federal unions were largely unsuccessful, and they did not receive enthusiastic support from A.F.L. headquarters; Horace Cayton and George Mitchell expressed the skepticism of most Negroes when they noted that "the national office did nothing until its position became so paradoxical that some gesture was necessary to prevent a new union movement. . . ."[4]

---

[3] Herbert Northrup, *Organized Labor and the Negro* (New York, 1944) 2-4. Sterling D. Spero and Abram L. Harris, *The Black Worker* (New York, 1931) 58, 85-86. Irving Bernstein, *op. cit.*, 84. Herbert Hill, "Labor Unions and the Negro," *Commentary*, XXVIII (December, 1959) 482. N.A.A.C.P. Office Memorandum, "The Negro and Trade Unions," n.d. N.A.A.C.P. Files. National Urban League, *Negro Membership in American Labor Unions*, 1930 pamphlet in Urban League Files. Interdepartmental group concerned with the special problems of Negroes, "Report on Negro Labor," NA RG 48.

[4] Sterling Spero and Abram Harris, *op. cit.*, 53. Norman Ware, *The Labor Movement in the United States*, 1860-1895 (New York), *passim*. Irving Bernstein has written that union membership, which rose to slightly more than 5,000,000 in 1920, fell to less than 3,500,000 by 1930. By this later date union members constituted only 10.2 percent of the 30 million nonagricultural employeees counted in the census, compared with 19.4 percent in 1920. "A significant feature of labor's decline in the 1920's is that it struck especially hard at organizations that were either wholly or predominantly industrial in structure. . . . At the same time many craft unions either held their own or made gains." Membership in the largest industrial unions, the United Mine Workers, the International Ladies Garment Workers, and the Amalgamated Clothing Workers of America, declined from a total of about 670,000 in 1920 to 150,000 in

Since a disproportionately large number of Negroes were either semi-skilled or unskilled workers, it was inevitable that they would play a minor role in craft unions. Of the 825,000 Negroes employed in manufacturing industries in 1920, Spero and Harris calculated that only 16.6 percent were skilled workers; 67.9 percent were laborers, and 15.5 percent were semi-skilled. The percentages for white workers were 32.4 skilled, 19.1 semi-skilled, and 48.5 laborers. Thus, if skill was to be made the prerequisite for trade union membership, less than one-third of the Negro workers, and only slightly more than half of the whites, were eligible for organization. Statistics such as this convinced the National Urban League that there was "little hope for the black worker so long as [the A.F.L.] remains structurally a craft organization."[5]

The effects of race prejudice and the craft system of organization were compounded further by the large degree of independence which the A.F.L. gave its constituent members. The A.F.L.'s official declarations that all workers should be organized without regard to race, creed, or color were ineffectual, because authority in matters of membership and participation was left in the hands of the local union. Thus, while the A.F.L. itself barred racial discrimination in union membership, the policy was of little significance because admission standards were set by the independent unions.[6]

Yet Negro spokesmen believed that there was much that Federation officials could have done in the way of informal persuasion to break down the pattern of racial discrimination. Unfortunately, it seemed to Negro leaders that the Federation's constitutional difficulties were complicated by a fundamental unwillingness to actively persuade member unions to remove Negro exclusion clauses from their constitutions. Ira De A. Reid of the Urban League declared that "Through the American Federation of Labor has uttered pronouncement upon pronouncement

---

1930. Bernstein, *The Lean Years* (Boston, 1960), 85-86, 335. See also Schlesinger, *op. cit.*, 138. Horace Cayton and George Mitchell, *Black Workers, and the New Unions* (Chapel Hill, 1939) 125.

[5] "The AFL and the Negro," *Opportunity*, VII (November, 1929) 338. Sterling Spero and Abram Harris, *op. cit.*, 85-86.

[6] Herbert Northup has observed that "In a very real sense the government of labor unions can be compared to the American federal system. Unions have their national, state, and local organizations as does the government of our country. In the administration of programs of relief, housing, industrial training, etc., Negroes receive the most equitable treatment, as a rule, when the federal government administers the program directly. . . . The same results are observable in matters of union policy. Negroes almost invariably fare better when national officers assume charge than they do when such questions as admissions or promotions are left for the local leaders to handle." Northrup, *op. cit.*, 236-237.

favoring the admission of Negro workers, that body has failed to convince the masses of Negro workers that it is rendering other than lip service to such expressed principles." W. E. B. Du Bois of the N.A.A.C.P. was even more emphatic: "The A. F. of L. has from the beginning of its organization stood up and lied brazenly about its attitude toward Negro labor," he proclaimed. "They have affirmed and still affirm that they wish to organize Negro labor when this is a flat and proven falsehood." T. Arnold Hill, the Industrial Secretary of the Urban League, complained that the A.F.L. had never "campaigned among its members for its idea of fair play reiterated in frequent resolutions."[7]

William Green, the President of the A.F.L., admitted that the Federation's bi-racial ideals had not always been realized, but he reminded Negroes of the enormous problems faced by those who would change popular attitudes. He suggested that the A.F.L. as a whole was not to be condemned because some of its affiliates discriminated against black workers, any more than a church should be condemned because all church members were not leading perfect lives. This explanation failed to satisfy most Negroes; indeed, many agreed with Elmer Carter, the editor of the Urban League's journal, *Opportunity,* who maintained that Green's reference to the church was singularly unfortunate. "For the church," Carter observed, "does not pursue a laissez faire policy; it does not wait until its candidates are ready . . . as is the policy of the A.F.L. The church makes its candidates ready. It seeks them out, petitions, urges, pleads, cajoles, threatens; it goes into the far places where dwelleth the heathen and by every means of persuasion seeks to lure them under its enfolding mantle."[8]

The A.F.L.'s lack of enthusiasm for organizing mass-production workers and the fundamental inconsistency between the racial policies of the member unions and the affirmations of the parent body caused many Negroes to reject the assumption that all workers would benefit by increasing the power of organized labor. Roy Wilkins, the Assistant Secretary of the N.A.A.C.P., expressed views that were widely shared

---

[7] Ira De A. Reid, "Lilly White Labor," *Opportunity,* VIII (June, 1930) 170. W. E. B. Du Bois, "The A. F. of L.," *Crisis,* XL (December, 1933) 292. T. Arnold Hill, "Letter to William Green," *Opportunity,* VIII (February, 1930) 56.
[8] William Green to Elmer A. Carter, November 7, 1929. *Opportunity,* VII (December, 1929) 381-382. "The President of the AFL Replies," *Opportunity,* VII (December, 1929) 367.

in the Negro community when he observed that "while Section 7a was a powerful weapon for the workers if they would use it and fight for the correct interpretation of it, we came shortly to realize . . . that while the American Federation of Labor was seizing upon Section 7a to carry on the most stupendous drive for membership in its history, it was doing little or nothing to include Negroes in the organizing." Jesse O. Thomas, the Urban League's Southern Field Secretary, made the same point when he noted that "While Section 7a has greatly increased the security of labor in general, insofar as the different labor organizations thus benefited deny and exclude Negroes from their membership by constitutions or rituals, the position of Negro labor has been made less favorable." Thomas believed that in passing this legislation Congress had intended to benefit all workers; but because of the "unsportsman-like and anti-social attitude of the majority of the membership and heads of many of the unions and crafts, the position of Negroes has been made even more disadvantageous." W. E. B. Du Bois expressed a prevalent attitude most succinctly when he wrote that "The American Federation of Labor is not a labor movement. It is a monopoly of skilled laborers, who join the capitalists in exploiting the masses of labor, whenever and wherever they can. . . ." "The most sinister power that the NRA has reinforced is the American Federation of Labor."[9]

Negro leaders were apprehensive about the prospect of A.F.L. unions taking advantage of the encouragement and protection offered by Section 7a to organize workers and establish themselves as the sole representative of labor. In a special memorandum prepared for President Roosevelt, the Urban League warned of the dangers inherent in the new recovery legislation. The League pointed out that Section 7a did not explicitly accord protection "to minority groups of workers whom the union wishes, for racial or religious reasons, to exclude from employment." Consequently, there was the danger that after establishing itself as the sole collective bargaining agent, organized labor would demand that management discharge black employees. Such incidents had occurred in the past, and the League feared that the practice would become more serious in the immediate future when it was likely that union membership would become a necessary prerequisite for an increas-

---

[9] Roy Wilkins to Horace Cayton, October 30, 1934. Cayton and Mitchell, op. cit., 413-414. Jesse O. Thomas, "Negro Workers and Organized Labor," Opportunity, XII (September, 1934) 278. W. E. B. Du Bois to Martha Adamson, March 27, 1936. Du Bois Papers. Du Bois, "The A. F. of L.," Crisis, XL (December, 1933) 292.

ing number of jobs.[10]

During the 1930s several examples of trade unions' using their power to force the dismissal of colored workers came to the attention of Negro leaders, an experience which understandably served to confirm their original pessimistic suspicions. In Long Island City, New York, the Brotherhood of Electrical Workers, Local No. 3, organized several electrical supply shops, refused membership to the Negro workers already employed there, and used its newly won power to force the managements to discharge several dozen Negro employees. In Manhattan, some locals of the Building Service Employees' Union demanded that employers discharge Negro workers and fill the vacancies with white unionists. As a result, several hotels, restaurants, and office buildings were forced to discharge Negro elevator operators and restaurant workers and hire whites. In Milwaukee the Urban League reported that the A.F.L. affiliate had called a strike at the open shop Wehr Steel Foundry but had not informed the Negro workers in the plant. According to the League, "The blanket demand made by the union was that the A.F.L. be recognized. They did not strike for higher wages, shorter hours or better working conditions. . . . After the plant was closed entirely, the specific demand of the A.F.L. union was dismissal of Negroes from the plant." In St. Louis the depth of this anti-Negro sentiment was strikingly illustrated when all the A.F.L. men working on the Homer Phillips Hospital (a $2,000,000 colored hospital erected in the middle of a Negro neighborhood) walked off the job and halted construction for two months in protest against the General Tile Company's decision to employ a black man as a tile setter. Examples such as these naturally made other employers reluctant to hire black labor; they knew, as one independent contractor observed, that if they did so they would run the risk of having their white employees "suddenly become ill, or have to take care of personal business, or for any number of other fictitious reasons quit work." It was for this reason that the Building Committee of the St. Louis Board of Education would not allow black workers to do repair work on any of the city's seventeen colored schools. Other large contractors followed suit, and St. Louis' Negro mechanics were effectively barred from work on everything except small jobs.[11]

---

[10] Urban League Memorandum. "The Negro Working Population and National Recovery," January 4, 1937. Urban League Files.

[11] Urban League Memorandum, "The Negro Working Population and National Recovery," January 4, 1937. Urban League Files. Workers' Council Bulletin 17, "Labor Re-

Roy Wilkins stated the viewpoint of many Negro leaders when he declared that all too often the A.F.L.'s strategy was to take advantage of Section 7a "to organize a union for all the workers, and to either agree with the employers to push Negroes out of the industry or, having effected an agreement with the employer, to proceed to make the union lily-white." The editor of the *Baltimore Afro-American* concluded that "unless the A.F.L. is able to make its locals throughout the country open their doors to colored members in all crafts, it may be necessary for colored labor to organize and join in a country-wide fight on the union." And when Horace Cayton and George Mitchell interviewed Negro workers they discovered that resentment of the A.F.L. was widely shared. One Homestead, Pennsylvania, steel worker told them that outside unions wanted Negroes to go out on strike with white workers, but that after the battle was won the black worker would be made the victim and cast aside. Another steel worker in Cleveland told Cayton that the Negroes in his plant had "decided after studying that if labor organizations were to get a footing the colored would lose out. There are [a] few jobs that the colored hold which they [white union workers] would like to get; that is one reason why we have to fight against the labor organizations." According to the N.A.A.C.P., most Negroes believed "that labor unions usually oppose the economic interests of Negroes. This follows from the fact that every union seeks to establish a closed-shop or as near the closed-shop as possible. Since American unions have largely excluded Negroes, the closed-shop has meant an arrangement under which there are no job opportunities offered black workers."[11]

Throughout the country and in a variety of ways, Negroes protested against the practice of union discrimination. Walter White, the Executive Secretary of the N.A.A.C.P., urged the A.F.L. "not only to make unequivocal pronouncement of opposition to any discrimination based

lations and the Position of Negro Minorities," September 23, 1937. Copy in N.A.A.C.P. Files. Charles Lionel Franklin, *The Negro Labor Unionist of New York* (New York, 1936) 241. *Chicago Defender*, August 25, 1934. St. Louis Branch of the Urban League, "Report on Local Labor Conditions, 1934," typescript in N.A.A.C.P. Files. John T. Clark to Donald Richberg, *Chicago Defender*, March 31, 1934. Interdepartmental group concerned with the special problems of Negroes, "Report on Negro Labor," NA RG 48. Jesse O. Thomas, "Negro Workers and Organized Labor," *Opportunity*, XII (September, 1934) 277-278. Lester B. Granger, "Negro Workers and Recovery," *Opportunity*, XII (May, 1934) 153.
[11] Roy Wilkins to Horace Cayton, October 30, 1934. Cayton and Mitchell, *op. cit.*, 413-414, 175. *Baltimore Afro-American*, April 19, 1934. N.A.A.C.P. office memorandum, "The Negro and Trade Unions," n.d. N.A.A.C.P. Files.

on color but to take tangible steps to put the pronouncement into practice." The delegates to the N.A.A.C.P.'s 1934 annnual conference reminded the Federation of the essential solidarity of interests of all labor and suggested that "there can and will be no industrial peace for white labor as long as black labor can be excluded from union membership." When the annual convention of the A.F.L. met in San Francisco in 1934, local Negroes ringed the convention hall with pickets bearing signs proclaiming that "White Labor Cannot Be Free While Black Labor is Enslaved," and that "White Unions Make Black Scabs." On the floor of the convention, A. Philip Randolph, the Negro President of the Brotherhood of Sleeping Car Porters, proposed that the A.F.L. expel "any union maintaining the color bar." The resolutions committee rejected Randolph's motion on the ground that "The American Federation of Labor . . . cannot interfere with the autonomy of National and International Unions." However, the committee did accept an amendment authorizing the appointment of a five member committee "to investigate the conditions of the colored workers of this country and report to the next convention."[13]

The A.F.L.'s Committee of Five to Investigate Conditions of the Colored Workers met in Washington on July 12, 1935, and heard the testimony of a number of witnesses familiar with the problems of Negro workers. (The members of this all-white Committee of Five were: John Brophy of the United Mine Workers, Chairman; John E. Rooney of the Operative Plasters and Cement Finishers; John Garvey of the Hod Carriers and Common Laborers; Jerry L. Hanks of the Journeyman Bargers; and T. C. Carroll of the Maintenance of Way Employees.) Specific examples of union discrimination were described by Reginald Johnson of the Urban League, Charles Houston of the N.A.A.C.P., and A. Philip Randolph. In addition, several black workers appeared to tell of the difficulties they encountered when they tried to join union locals. In the course of his testimony, Houston informed the Committee that a number of N.A.A.C.P. branches were "assembling data on discrimination against Negro workers in their cities" and urged that additional hearings be held in other sections of the country. Believing that suffi-

---

[13] Walter White telegram to William Green, *The New York Times*, October 4, 1933, 4:3. Resolutions of the 25th Annual Conference of the N.A.A.C.P., 1934. N.A.A.C.P. Press Release, August 2, 1935. N.A.A.C.P. Files. *Pittsburgh Courier*, October 13, 1934. *Report of the Proceedings of the Fifty-fourth Annual Convention of the American Federation of Labor* (Washington, 1934) 330-332. Northrup, *op. cit.*, 11.

cient information had been uncovered at the first and only hearing in Washington, however, President Green informed the N.A.A.C.P. that the Federation had decided that additional regional hearings were not necessary. Ever suspicious, Walter White reminded Green that this refusal "to go further into this vitally important question will be construed as justification of the skepticism widely expressed of the sincerity of the American Federation of Labor's action."[14]

After concluding its hearings, the Committee of Five recommended a threefold plan: 1) that all international unions which discriminated against colored workers should take up the "Negro question at their next convention for the purpose of harmonizing constitution rules and practices to conform with the oft-repeated declarations of the A.F.L. conventions on equality of treatment of all races within the trade union movement"; 2) that the A.F.L. should issue no more charters to unions practicing discrimination; and 3) that the A.F.L. should begin an educational campaign "to get the white worker to see more completely the weaknesses of division and the necessity of unity between white and black workers to the end that all workers may be organized."[15]

The Committee had been specifically instructed to report to the next convention, and if its recommendations had been accepted and implemented significant internal reform of the A.F.L. might have been achieved. The Federation's Executive Council had grave reservations concerning the wisdom of the report, however, and President William Green arranged for it to be submitted to the Council rather than to the open convention. At the same time the Council also received a second report on the Negro question from one of its own members, George Harrison, the President of the exclusionist Railway Clerks. Harrison's report, advocating no action except "education," was considerably less forceful than the Committee's recommendations. But because of its innocuousness, it was more to the liking of President Green and the Council, who refused to release the Committee's report and instead arranged for Harrison's inoffensive document to be presented to the convention. Even so, Harrison delayed his presentation until about 10 p.m. on the eleventh and last day of the 1935 convention. By then

[14] N.A.A.C.P. Press Releases, July 12, 1935, July 19, 1935, July 26, 1935 and September 26, 1935. N.A.A.C.P. Files. "Reports of the Executive Secretary of the Joint Committee on National Recovery," June 19, 1935, and September 20, 1935. NA RG 183. Oxley File.
[15] *Report of the Proceedings of the Fifty-fifth Annual Convention of the American Federation of Labor* (Washington, 1935) 809. Northup, *op. cit.*, 11.

31

the delegates were exhausted and divided by the craft versus industrial union controversy (this was the convention which saw the final split in labor's ranks and the emergence of the C.I.O. as an independent body) and were ready to accept any report that speeded progress toward adjournment.[16]

This sabotage of the Committee's report by the A.F.L.'s Executive Council seemed to destroy the Negro's last hope for reform coming from within the Federation. Writing to John L. Lewis, Walter White observed that "the recent hypocritical attitude of the American Federation of Labor in suppressing the report of the Committee . . . has destroyed the last vestige of the confidence which Negro workers ever had in the A.F.L." The Committee's chairman, John Brophy of the United Mine Workers, was even more outspoken. In a sharply worded letter of resignation, Brophy charged that the "maneuvering on the part of the executive council plainly indicated that [they] wanted the Committee of Five . . . to be merely a face saving device for the American Federation of Labor, rather than an honest attempt to find a solution of the Negro problem in the American labor movement."[17]

Given the record of A.F.L. discrimination and the Negro's distrust of organized labor, it could be argued that colored workers were fortunate that Section 7a did not adequately safeguard labor's right to organize independent unions. Certainly many Negroes were convinced that their position would have been even more desperate if the Recovery Act had established effective machinery for enforcing its collective bargaining provisions. Moreover, while Negroes realized that company unions were not altogether satisfactory—that, especially during the NRA period, many employers had encouraged the organization of company unions as a defense against real collective bargaining—they understandably did not share the aversion which many white workers felt toward these management-controlled employee representation programs.[18]

Yet organized labor and large segments of the American liberal

---

[16] "Report of the Executive Secretary of the Joint Committee on National Recovery," November 23, 1935. NA RG 183. Northup, *op. cit.*, 12.

[17] Walter White to John L. Lewis, November 27, 1935. N.A.A.C.P. Press Release, November 15, 1935. N.A.A.C.P. Files.

[18] See Spero and Harris. *op. cit.*, chapter VII, and Cayton and Mitchell, *op. cit.*, 61-63 and 171-175. The attitudes of important Negro leaders in this regard are stated in the following letters: Trevor Bowen to Roy Wilkins, March 30, 1934; Wilkins to Walter White, March 21, 1934; White to Franklin D. Roosevelt, March 21, 1934. N.A.A.C.P. Files. Also see Lloyd N. Bailer, "Negro Labor in the Automobile Industry" (unpublished Ph.D. dissertation, University of Michigan, 1943) *passim*.

community believed that proliferation of company unions was under-mining the entire recovery program. Recalling the earlier argument that strong trade unions were needed to force management to increase mass purchasing power, the liberal-labor group maintained that NRA had failed to stimulate full recovery largely because ambiguities in the language of the recovery bill and the absence of enforcement powers had "enabled a minority of employers to deviate from the clear intent of the law and to threaten our entire program with destruction." Rally-ing behind the leadership of Senator Robert F. Wagner of New York, this group maintained that new legislation was needed to establish another labor board with the power to enforce its decisions and to clearly prohibit employers from dominating or supporting workers' organizations. Consequently, early in 1934 Senator Wagner and his assistants began to work on a new bill that would "clarify and fortify the provisions of Section 7a." As it finally emerged, the new legislation proposed to establish a strengthened National Labor Relations Board (N.L.R.B.) with the authority to investigate any disputes involving Section 7a, to order elections so that employees might choose their own representatives for collective bargaining *with membership in the union chosen by the majority a mandatory prerequisite for continued employ-ment,* and the power to prohibit certain "unfair" employer practices such as company domination of the workers' organization. The legisla-tion also provided that the N.L.R.B. was to be an independent admin-istrative agency with the power to enforce its decisions.[19]

---

[19] J. Joseph Huthmacher, *Senator Robert F. Wagner and the Rise of Urban Liberalism* (New York, 1968) chapters 5 through 10. National Labor Relations Board, "Article by Senator Robert F. Wagner on Labor Unions," *Legislative History of the National Labor Relations Act, 1935* (Washington: United States Government Printing Office, 1949) 22-26. Bernstein, *The New Deal Collective Bargaining Policy,* chapters 5 through 10.

The bill Senator Wagner introduced in February 1935 differed in some respects from the original 1934 version; most significantly, it emphasized the NLRB's position as a Supreme Court of labor relations by stressing the enforcement of labor's rights rather than the adjustment of differences and by providing that all members of the Board would represent the public (thus rejecting the earlier proposal to create a tripartite body with representation from management, labor, and the public). These changes were of considerable importance, but they did not affect black workers specifically and were not commented on by black leaders; indeed, Negro comment on the Wagner bill focussed almost wholly on the 1934 measure. At first I suspected that some of the N.A.A.C.P. and Urban League files for 1935 had been misplaced, but Negro newspapers also ignored the revised 1935 bill, and I have concluded that black people decided they had stated their case and done what they could in 1934 and that nothing further could be done in 1935. There is another interesting aspect to this, one that relates to the factional struggle within the N.A.A.C.P., but limitations of space prevent a full discussion here. Briefly, it is that the pro-labor forces within the Association—those who thought that the economic problems of black and white workers were inextricably intertwined and could be solved only by bi-racial working-

Negro leaders were not entirely out of sympathy with Senator Wagner's approach to collective bargaining. They approved of the requirement that certain conditions, among them free elections and majority choice, had to be fulfilled before a union could be certified as a legitimate bargaining agent. But Negro leaders also insisted that it was essential that the Wagner bill be amended so as to outlaw racial discrimination by unions. Without such an amendment, they reasoned, there was the very real danger that discriminatory unions would use their power to restrict the Negro's economic opportunities. With such an amendment Negroes would have, as Washington attorney William Hastie noted, "a strong weapon . . . for compelling unions to accept into membership all qualified employees."[20]

The demand for an anti-discrimination clause in the Wagner bill was widespread in the Negro community. T. Arnold Hill warned that "If the Wagner Bill passes in its present form, the power and influence of the labor movement will be greatly enhanced with the consequent danger of greater restrictions being practiced against Negro workers by organized labor." Dean Kelly Miller of Howard University insisted that "Every effort should be made to amend the Wagner Bill so as to safeguard the rights of the Negro. . . . Unless this is done it is easy to foretell the doom of the Negro in American industry." Roy Wilkins observed that the Wagner Bill "rigidly enforces and legalizes the closed shop," and he noted that "the act plainly empowers organized labor to exclude from employment in any industry those who do not belong to a union." He thought it was "needless to point out the fact that thousands of Negro workers are barred from membership in American labor unions and, therefore, that if the closed shop is legalized by this act Negro workers will be absolutely shut out of employment." Harry E. Davis, a member of the N.A.A.C.P.s' Board of Directors, summed up the sentiments of many Negroes when he observed that "it is not a 'closed' shop which is in the offing, but a 'white' shop."[21]

Negroes also pointed out that the Wagner legislation would require

class cooperation—had become so strong by 1935 that the national officers decided to forego further criticism of trade unions. I have discussed this matter in some detail in a forthcoming book, *Negroes and the Great Depression: The Problem of Economic Recovery.*

[20] William Hastie to Walter White, March 27, 1934. N.A.A.C.P. Files.

[21] T. Arnold Hill to Walter White, April 3, 1934. N.A.A.C.P. Files. Hill, "Labor Marches On," *Opportunity*, XII (April, 1934) 120-121. Kelly Miller, "Amend the Wagner Bill," *Norfolk Journal and Guide*, March 31, 1934. Roy Wilkins memorandum to N.A.A.C.P. Office Staff, March 23, 1934. Harry E. Davis to Walter White, March 20, 1934. N.A.A.C.P. Files.

employers to rehire all striking employees after a settlement had been reached. According to the N.A.A.C.P. and the Urban League, this would jeopardize the position of Negro strikebreakers who had been given employment while union men were off the job. While they "deplore[d] the necessity for strikebreaking," the Negro protest organizations maintained that "it is the one weapon left to the Negro worker whereby he may break the stranglehold that certain organized labor groups have utilized in preventing his complete absorption in the American labor market." The N.A.A.C.P. viewed the prospect of indirectly penalizing strikebreakers with particular alarm; it was convinced that "practically every important entry that the Negro has made into industries previously closed to him has been through his activity as a strikebreaker."[22]

While Congress was considering the Wagner bill, the N.A.A.C.P. and the Urban League urged the inclusion of an amendment which would have denied the benefits of the legislation to any union which discriminated on the basis of race. Elmer Carter was sent to Washington, where he acted as the League's chief lobbyist, and T. Arnold Hill and Lester B. Granger prepared for the Senate Committee on Labor and Education a "Statement of Opinion" which summarized the League's objections to the unamended Wagner legislation. William Hastie prepared a similar document for the N.A.A.C.P., and Walter White kept in close touch with Senator Wagner and his secretary, Leon Keyserling. From Keyserling, White learned that "The Act as originally drafted by Senator Wagner provided that the closed shop should be legal only when there were no restrictions upon members in the labor union to which the majority of workers belonged." But, according to Keyserling, "The American Federation of Labor fought bitterly to eliminate this clause and much against his will Senator Wagner had to consent to the elimination in order to prevent scuttling of the entire bill."[23]

---

[22] N.A.A.C.P. office memorandum, "The Negro and Trade Unions," n.d. Workers' Council Bulletin 17, "Labor Relations Legislation and the Position of the Negro Minorities," September 23, 1937. N.A.A.C.P. Files. National Urban League, "A Statement of Opinion on Senate Bill S 2926," Urban League Files. Interdepartmental group concerned with the special problems of Negroes, "Report on Negro Labor," NA RG 48.

[23] National Urban League, "A Statement of Opinion on Senate Bill S 2926," Urban League Files. The proposed N.A.A.C.P. amendment read as follows: "Provided, however, that the term labor organization shall not include any organization, labor union, association, corporation, or society of any kind, which by its organic law or by any rule or regulation, or any practice excludes any employee or employees from membership in the organization or from equal participation, with other employees by reason of race, creed or color." It should be noted that Senator Wagner supported

Negro spokesmen also presented their objections to the Wagner bill in correspondence to and informal conferences with labor leaders and government officials. Walter White, for example, wrote to William Green, specifically requesting Green's support for the proposed N.A.A.C.P.-Urban League amendment. Green, however, answered in an equivocal fashion that, in White's view, "boiled down, means precisely nothing." The N.A.A.C.P. leader forwarded a copy of Green's reply to Senator Wagner "so that you may see how he dodges answering our specific question as to whether or not he and the American Federation of Labor will support a provision to eliminate discrimination by labor unions." White also wrote to President Roosevelt, reminding him that unions ".with ill grace can ask benefits for white labor while these unions discriminate against black labor," and he demanded that "full safeguards . . . be given to prevent this." "We rely on you," he declared, "to prevent [the] sacrifice of [the] Negro to Jim Crow unionism." Within the Roosevelt administration, Clark Foreman, Secretary of Interior Harold Ickes' adviser on the special problems of Negroes, called attention to "the fact that the American Federation of Labor was being recognized more and more by government agencies as the spokesman of labor—although quite commonly Negroes are excluded from local unions belonging to the A.F.L." Foreman maintained that "if we could assume, as had been claimed, that Negro workers were better off under the company unions than under the A.F.L., the Administration should be advised before sponsoring any measures which would indirectly worsen the condition of the Negro." He suggested that "whether or not the A.F.L. or other labor organizations were involved, the government should not do anything against any element of the population or negotiate preferential agreements with any organization which discriminated against certain elements of the population."[34]

The opposition to the proposed N.A.A.C.P.-Urban League amendment was led by the American Federation of Labor (though it is significant that the leaders of the emerging industrial unions of the C.I.O.

the N.A.A.C.P.'s attempt to add this anti-discrimination clause to the Wagner bill. Robert F. Wagner telegram to Walter White, April 16, 1934. White to William Hastie, March 28, 1934 and April 17, 1934. N.A.A.C.P. Files.

[34] Walter White to William Green, April 17, 1934. Green to White, May 2, 1934. White to Robert Wagner, May 15, 1934. Also see William Hastie telegram to White, March 29, 1934 and White to Hastie, May 16, 1934. White telegram to Franklin D. Roosevelt, March 21, 1934. N.A.A.C.P. Files. Minutes of the second meeting of the interdepartmental group concerned with the special problems of Negroes, March 2, 1934. NA RG 48.

were not recorded in opposition). The A.F.L. maintained that recalcitrant employers would use this amendment as an excuse to involve even non-discriminatory unions in costly litigation and thus delay the recognition of the unions' right to bargain collectively with the employer. Employing the rhetoric of working-class solidarity, the A.F.L. warned Negroes that they should not support legislation which would impede the progress of trade unionism, "for in the progress of honest trade unionism lies the future security of all workers, of both minority and majority groups." Some Negro leaders admitted that the A.F.L.'s position in this regard was not entirely without merit. Nevertheless, most concluded, as the Urban League did, that while "it is a dangerous thing for Negroes to request governmental interference in the internal affairs of unions, the least that Negroes can demand is that [the] government shall not protect a union in its campaign to keep them out of present and future jobs."[25]

Despite the essential validity of their arguments, Negroes suffered a defeat in 1935 when Congress passed and President Roosevelt signed the National Labor Relations (Wagner) Act without the N.A.A.C.P.-Urban League amendment. The reason for this seems clear: the American Federation of Labor had more political power and influence than the two Negro protest organizations. Government officials candidly explained that "because there was no organization of Negroes, and therefore no one who could command the support of any considerable number of Negro workers, there was little likelihood of their gaining" special consideration. Negroes learned once again that insofar as labor was concerned the dominating forces in the government were, as Clark Foreman explained during the NRA's first year, "the industrialists and the A.F.L., both of whom are hostile to Negro labor, the former because they want to keep Negroes as a reserve of cheap labor, and the latter because they want to eliminate Negro competitive labor." Negro leaders had appealed for an amendment on grounds of equity and justice, but their request was not granted because it conflicted with the claims of better organized and more powerful white interests.[26]

---

[25] The AFL arguments were summarized by the Urban League, Workers' Council Bulletin 17, "Labor Relations Legislation and the Position of the Negro Minorities," September 23, 1937. N.A.A.C.P. Files. The quotation attributed to the League is from this document.

[26] Minutes of the second meeting of the interdepartmental group concerned with the special problems of Negroes, March 2, 1934. Clark Foreman to Harold Ickes, December 13, 1933. NA RG 48.

REBIRTH OF THE
UNITED AUTOMOBILE WORKERS:
The General Motors Tool and Diemakers'
Strike of 1939

by
John Barnard*

In the summer of 1939 the United Automobile Workers (UAW) conducted a five week strike of skilled tradesmen against the General Motors Corporation. Although this strike secured the UAW's position in GM, and therefore in the auto industry, it has drawn no more than fleeting attention from historians. The history of this strike throws light on several themes of significance in auto unionization and subsequent auto industrial relations. Among these are the role of skilled workmen in building and sustaining an industrial union, the divisions within the auto workforce that emerged as the union took root, the dogged reluctance of management to accept the union's presence except under the duress of economic injury, and the union's need for both a bold strategy and unerring execution of plans to overcome the weaknesses of its position.

The autoworkers' union, like many of the industrial unions that emerged in the labor upheaval of the 1930s, contained skilled workmen whose presence helped to shape its history. Automotive employees have usually been depicted as unskilled and semiskilled workers with simple, quickly learned tasks. In fact, a crucial element in the industry's work force consisted of highly skilled craftsmen whose mastery of the branches of the metal trades rested on lengthy apprenticeships. The contingent

*Earlier versions of this essay were read at the meeting of the Organization of American Historians, Los Angeles, April 6, 1984, and to The National Endowment for The Humanities Seminar on ''Business in the History of American Society,'' at the University of California, Berkeley, July 30, 1984. The author thanks the participants in both sessions for their comments and suggestions.

of skilled workmen fluctuated in size but averaged about 15% of the total number of autoworkers.[1]

Two kinds of auto factory work required skills. The first was the preparation of the tools and dies needed for manufacturing new models. The tools are mainly jigs, welding bucks, and other kinds of metal fixtures that hold and align auto parts during different stages of production. Dies are the mating forms installed in presses to produce stamped body and chassis parts. Tool and die work required proficiency in diverse and difficult metal working skills including the use of all kinds of metal shaping machines and the ability to produce objects to precise measurements in extremely hard metals from blueprints.[2] In 1939, 85% of automotive tool and die work was located in the Detroit area.[3]

Skilled workmen were also required for the set-up and maintenance of machinery and other kinds of factory equipment. Electricians, welders, machinists, carpenters, millwrights, pipe fitters, and other tradesmen installed and maintained the modern plant's machines, conveyors, and assembly lines. With a few exceptions, none of the skilled workmen in the auto industry had been successfully organized prior to the appearance of the United Automobile Workers.[4]

From July 5 until August 7, 1939, the UAW conducted a skilled tradesmen's strike against GM. While there had been a flood of wildcat job actions in the turbulent aftermath of the 1937 sitdown, the 1939 strike was the first sanctioned against GM since that earlier victory. The distinctive feature of the strike was that the union called out only a few thousand skilled tool and diemakers and maintenance men, not the nearly 200,000 GM production workers. The aim of this "strategy strike," as it was called by Walter P. Reuther, was to block the

---

[1]Robert M. MacDonald, *Collective Bargaining in the Automobile Industry* (New Haven and London, 1963), 111, 137.

[2]A detailed description of automotive tool and die work is in Orrin Peppler interview, Mar. 26, 1961, 1-25. This and other interviews cited hereinafter are located in the Archives of Labor and Urban Affairs, Wayne State Univ. This series of interviews with auto workers and union officials has proved an invaluable source for this essay.

[3]William H. McPherson, *Labor Relations in the Automobile Industry* (Washington, 1940), 7, n. 7.

[4]For early unionization efforts see Sidney Fine, "The Tool and Die Makers Strike of 1933," *Michigan History*, 42 (1958), 297-323, and Sidney Fine, *The Automobile Under the Blue Eagle* (Ann Arbor, 1963).

corporation's preparations for manufacturing its 1940 models scheduled to be introduced in the fall of 1939.[5] With improving sales forecast for 1940, GM, it was hoped, would settle quickly.

When the strike was called the UAW faced serious challenges both from the auto companies and within its own ranks. Success in the 1937 sitdown had not assured the union's future. Although General Motors and Chrysler had accorded the UAW a limited recognition in 1937, officials of both companies were opposed to the union's presence. The Ford Motor Company resisted even more stubbornly.[6]

In addition, the commitment of many rank-and-file workers to unionization was still in doubt. "The general body of GM employees," an observer noted, "was not yet union minded."[7] Both the union and the autoworkers were caught in a vicious circle in which weakness fed upon and reinforced weakness. Uncertain of the union's strength, especially of its ability to protect their jobs against retaliation by the employers, many ordinary workmen were reluctant to commit themselves to the union. But the union could neither lay claim on workers' loyalty nor demonstrate strength and staying power unless it had the workers' support. Possibly a successful strike by a cadre of committed unionists would break the circle and earn for the UAW the active support of the majority of workers.

The union's public and political position had deteriorated since 1937. Frank Murphy, Michigan's Democratic governor during the sitdown strike whose restrained use of the state's power was a key to its success, had been defeated in 1938 by a Republican challenger in an election dominated by Murphy's handling of the strike.[8] Furthermore, in February 1939 the

---

[5]Walter Reuther probably gave the strike this name when he announced that "the UAW-CIO fights with discipline, with intelligence, and with strategy." *G.M. Strike Bulletin*, No. 2, July 6, 1939.

[6]For management attitudes, see McPherson, 150-154; Howell J. Harris, *The Right to Manage* (Madison, 1982), 26-32, and Richard C. Widcock, "Industrial Managements' Policies Toward Unionism," in Milton Derber and Edwin Young, eds., *Labor and The New Deal* (reprint, New York, 1972), 275-315. The Ford Motor Company's decade-long battle against auto unions is detailed in Allan Nevins and Frank Ernest Hill, *Ford: Decline and Rebirth, 1933-1962* (New York, 1962), 28-54, 133-167.

[7]Carl Haessler interview, Nov. 27, 1959, Oct. 24, 1960, 53.

[8]Sidney Fine, *Frank Murphy: The New Deal Years* (Chicago and London, 1979), 502-515. For the sitdown strike, see Sidney Fine, *Sit-Down* (Ann Arbor, 1969).

Supreme Court denounced a sitdown strike as "a high-handed proceeding without shadow of legal right," crisply dispelling any doubts about the illegality of the union's most effective weapon.[9]

Economically, the industry had been on one of its roller coaster rides. Factory passenger car sales dropped by nearly 50% from 1937 to 1938, the steepest year to year decline in the industry's history before or since. Layoffs decimated the workers' ranks. By the spring of 1938 half the work force was idle and most of those still working were on reduced time. UAW dues paying membership fell by about 75%.[10] Although business and employment started to pick up in 1939, important items in the UAW's strike calculations, complete recovery did not come about until 1941.

Finally, and perhaps most seriously, the UAW's survival was jeopardized by internal power and ideological rivalries. A split developing since 1937 between its president, Homer Martin, and its other officers was now beyond repair. Both sides plunged into a no-holds-barred struggle in which the survival of an effective autoworkers' union was at stake. For months what one observer called "the long series of incidents which have practically been an earthquake in the auto union field," a ceaseless round of verbal attacks and counterattacks, suspensions and expulsions from office, appeals to the CIO for mediation, rival conventions, and even pitched battles in crucial locals, rocked the UAW.[11] The momentum and confidence generated by the successful strikes against General Motors and Chrysler in 1937 were being thrown away in bitter, internal warfare.

---

[9]N.L.R.B. v. Fansteel Metallurgical Corp., 306 U.S. 270 (1939).
[10]McPherson, 19, n. 3.
[11]Arthur G. McDowell to J. A. Mattson, Jan. 26, 1939, copy in Socialist Party of America Collection, National Correspondence, 1939, Box 171, Perkins Library, Duke Univ. Accounts of the split include: Clayton Fountain, *Union Guy* (New York, 1949), 95-106; Matthew B. Hammond interview, Mar. 6, 1961, 10; Norman Bully interview, Oct. 12, 1961, 11; Ken Morris interview, June 28, 1963, 32-34; Theodore LaDuke interview, Aug. 5, 1960, 31-34; Everett Francis interview, Oct. 13, 20, 27, 1961, 40-47; Ray Vess interview, Oct. 12, 1961, 9; *New York Times*, Jan.-June, 1939; *United Automobile Worker*, Jan.-June 1939 [weekly: came under control of the anti-Martin group with the issue of Jan. 14, 1939]; George D. Blackwood, "The United Automobile Workers of America, 1935-51 (unpublished PhD diss., Univ. of Chicago, 1952), 117-119; Jack Skeels, "The Background of UAW Factionalism," *Labor History*, 2 (1961), *158-81;* Walter Galenson, *The CIO Challenge to the AFL* (Cambridge, MA, 1960), 157-171; Irving Bernstein, *Turbulent Years* (Boston, 1970), 561-569.

The struggle between Martin and anti-Martin forces inevitably affected the union's relations with GM. Since the 1937 contract had no expiration date, the UAW sought to open talks on a new agreement, including a supplementary settlement for skilled workers whose particular interests had been hitherto ignored. General Motors, claiming that because of the factional rivalry it did not know who represented its workers, broke off the talks. Notifying the rival factions that it would negotiate with neither "until their position and authority have been clarified," GM argued that the dispute between the two UAW contenders should be settled either by the National Labor Relations Board or by the courts. The anti-Martin element claimed that neither government agency had jurisdiction over an intra-union contract ownership dispute. Furthermore, the delay required by an NLRB hearing and election, a process that could stretch out for many months, would make an immediate resolution of the tangled, unsatisfactory situation impossible.[12]

In addition to refusing to negotiate, GM, the UAW charged, exploited the union rivalry by stalling grievance settlements in plants where competing committees claimed representational rights. "Under GM's distorted interpretation of its contract," said the *United Automobile Worker*, "it can take three stooges in a plant of 10,000 workers and use the phony claims of these stooges to defeat bargaining for the entire 10,000."[13] Dual committees (Martin and anti-Martin) were present in 11 plants with more than 50,000 workers, while in 12 smaller plants there were only Martinite committees. The anti-Martin group had undisputed control of only three plants with less than 2,000

[12]*Detroit News*, June 9, 1939. Martin had negotiated a disadvantageous supplementary agreement in Mar. 1938, which had been forced on the GM workers without ratification. *Report of R.J. Thomas, President . . . Submitted . . . 1940 Convention*, 20. See also *New York Times*, Jan. 26, 31, Mar. 26, 1939; General Motors Department, UAW, press release, July, 1939, in Walter P. Reuther Collection, Box 5, Folder: "Tool and Die Strike, July 5-August 12, 1939," Archives of Labor and Urban Affairs, Wayne State Univ.; General Motors Department, UAW, press release, June 11, 1939, in Walter P. Reuther Collection, Pre-presidential papers, Box 26, Folder 19. For the debate over a possible role for the NLRB or the courts, see *New York Times*, July 2, 1939 and Federal Mediation and Conciliation Service, press release, July 1, 1939, copy in Federal Mediation and Conciliation Service, case 199/3975, National Archives; "Memorandum for the Record," June 29, 1939, Federal Mediation and Conciliation Service, case 199/3975; *Flint Journal*, July 3, 5, 9, 1939.
[13]*United Automobile Worker, West Side Conveyor Edition*, June 28, 1939; *New York Times*, Mar. 26, 1939; *Flint Journal*, June 26, 1939.

workers.[14] The anti-Martin element believed GM encouraged the formation of dual committees as a handy pretext to avoid bargaining and grievance settlement. Referring to grievance processing and protection against harmful shop conditions, a worker in a Flint Fisher Body plant recalled that the "employees . . . almost lost all that they had fought for in the earlier years." R. J. Thomas, the union's new president, conceded that UAW contracts had become no more than "scraps of paper."[15]

The result, as Thomas added, was "the almost complete destruction of our organization in GM." The city of Flint, where normally 32,000 GM blue collar workers were employed, had less than 500 UAW members in good standing.[16] In most General Motors plants a "deplorable situation" prevailed, with the union organization practically non-existent and what little membership there was "demoralized and disillusioned." By the union's estimate, only 12,000 out of a potential 200,000 General Motors employees were UAW members in the spring of 1939.[17]

Rebuilding the UAW's shattered organization began with the March 1939 convention in Cleveland. R. J. Thomas, acting president since the first of the year, was elected to that position to replace the ousted Homer Martin. A critical appointment was that of director of the General Motors Department, a post formerly held by Elmer Dowell, Homer Martin's brother-in-law. The two leading candidates were Ed Hall, aligned with the union's leftwing element, and Walter P. Reuther, whose close ties with the left had been unraveling for more than a year.

[14]*Report of R. J. Thomas President . . . Submitted . . . 1940 Convention*, 19-20. UAW press release, June 28, 1939, Walter P. Reuther Collection, Box 5, Folder: Tool and Die Strike, July 5-August 12, 1939.
[15]Everett Francis interview, Oct. 13, 20, 27, 1961, 41. For similar statements by UAW local leaders see Dick Coleman interview, June 23, 1960, 24; James M. Cleveland interview, Oct. 3, 1961, 11; and Theodore LaDuke interview, Aug. 5, 1960, 33. *Report of R. J. Thomas, President . . . Submitted . . . 1940 Convention*, 8.
[16]*Report of R. J. Thomas, President . . . Submitted . . . 1940 Convention*, 8, 19-20.
[17]History of General Motors Department [1941-42], typescript, Walter P. Reuther Collection, Pre-presidential papers, Box 20, Folder 4. A few GM locals began to recover membership even before the tool and die strike, presumably because of better times and rising employment. See Arthur L. Case, Region No. 1-C Report, p.1, copy in George Addes Collection, Box 3, Folder—Regional Report 1-C, August 8-12, 1939, Archives of Labor and Urban Affairs, Wayne State Univ.

Thomas appointed Reuther.[18] Although Reuther had been a member of the UAW's board since 1936, and president of Local 174, a rapidly growing and powerful amalgamated local on the west side of Detroit since 1937, the GM director's post was his first executive position in the international union. It was the platform from which he ultimately mounted a successful challenge for the UAW's presidency.[19]

Under Reuther's direction, the General Motors Department, which had been both ineffectual and a crude instrument for expressing rank-and-file sentiment, was reorganized and revitalized.[20] Constitutional amendments adopted at the Cleveland convention had partially decentralized power in order to block the emergence of another would-be autocrat, and all of the union's departments were restructured through setting up a two-level hierarchy of councils to coordinate organizational activities and negotiations.[21] An executive committee, chosen by the national council, would formulate policy and conduct negotiations.[22] Reuther moved quickly to implement these changes.[23]

----

[18]Several accounts have sought to explain Thomas' choice of Reuther over Hall. Thomas later said he simply considered Reuther "best qualified," and overrode the opposition of many board members to his appointment. R. J. Thomas interview, Mar. 26, 1963, 17-18. Another version is in Carl Haessler interview, Nov. 27, 1959, Oct. 24, 1960, 37-38. Thomas distrusted Hall and they were not on good terms prior to the convention. See Minutes of the International Executive Board Meeting of the United Automobile Workers of America . . . Mar. 13, 1939, 63, copy in George Addes Collection, Box 4, where a hot, profane exchange between Hall and Thomas occurred. Reuther later indicated that he "had [an] agreement with Thomas" that Reuther would be appointed if Thomas became president. Walter P. Reuther interview with Frank Cormier and William J. Eaton, July 1, 1968. Probably Reuther had promised support for Thomas' election, who was more acceptable to him than the other candidates in any case, and Thomas knew that Reuther would ably conduct the union's business with GM.

[19]For a brief account of Reuther see John Barnard, *Walter Reuther and The Rise of the Autoworkers* (Boston, 1983). More detail on certain episodes is available in Victor Reuther, *The Brothers Reuther and the UAW: A Memoir* (Boston, 1976).

[20]*United Automobile Worker*, Dec. 24, 1938.

[21]Legislative powers continued to be lodged in the convention and, in the interim between conventions, the executive board.

[22]History of General Motors Department [1941-1942], typescript, Walter P. Reuther Collection, Pre-presidential papers, Box 20, Folder 4. See also Blackwood, 126; *United Automobile Worker*, April 22, 1939; Minutes of International Executive Board, Meeting held in Toledo, Ohio, April 25-30, 1939, 17-19, 31, where Reuther presented the council reorganization plan which was approved by the board. Copy in George Addes Collection, Box 14. *Detroit Free Press*, May 9, 1939; *Detroit News*, May 8, 1939.

[23]Walter P. Reuther to General Motors Locals, May 18, 1939, in Walter P. Reuther Collection, Pre-presidential papers, Box 26, Folder 7; *United Automobile Worker*, May 13, 20, 1939. Because of the shift in control of the union, the Thomas-Reuther leadership had no record of grievances. Reuther had to ask the locals to resubmit their grievance documents. Walter P. Reuther to General Motors locals, May 16, 1939, in UAW-General

Although Reuther moved quickly, Homer Martin, whose UAW was now armed with an American Federation of Labor charter, moved first by calling a strike of his GM followers.[24] Not bothering with an authorization vote, Martin ordered all GM workers out. The strike, as Thomas said, was "a flop from the start."[25] About 300 pickets were reported at Fisher Body and Chevrolet plants in Flint, the center of Martin's strength, but non-striking UAW-CIO members entered the plants despite a few fist fights and pop bottle barrages. At a Chevrolet plant four workers started to walk out but sheepishly returned to their places when no one followed them.[26] Martin called off the strike after only three days.

Simultaneously Reuther prepared for a strike. The executive board, at his urging, "resolved to make a vigorous drive in localities where GM locals need strengthening and get in position to demand of the corporation an improved agreement that has been long overdue."[27] Although the decision to call a strike confined to the skilled workers has usually been attributed to Reuther, the evidence does not permit a conclusive statement.[28] A former diemaker at Ford Motor Company, Reuther had personal ties with the skilled workers and recognized their strong economic position at a time of peak demand for their services. However, William Stevenson, head of the large west side Detroit tool and die local, No. 157, recalled that "we happened to have an idea of striking the plants using the skilled workers. We had long talks with Walter about it, . . ."[29]

Motors Collection, Series I, Box 1, Folder-Letters to Locals, Jan. 7-Sept. 30, 1939, Archives of Labor and Urban Affairs, Wayne State Univ.

[24]*Detroit News*, June 22, 1939, for the AFL charter; *Flint Journal*, June 27, 1939.

[25]Thomas, radio address, station WJR, June 11, 1939, reported in *United Automobile Worker*, June 14, 1939.

[26]*United Automobile Worker*, June 14, 1939. See also, Report of George F. Addes, Secretary-Treasurer, UAW-CIO, Covering Activities and Progress of the Last Three Months, April-June, 1939, 7, copy in George F. Addes Collection, Box 3. Folder: Report, Board, G. F. Addes, Aug. 8-12, 1939; *New York Times*, June 11-14, 1939. In addition to the sources already cited, accounts by eye witnesses of the Martin strike are in *New York Times*, June 15, 18, 1939; *Detroit News*, June 11-15, 1939; *New York Herald-Tribune*, June 13, 1939; *United Automobile Worker*, June 21, 1939; Theodore LaDuke interview, August 5, 1960, 34; Everett Francis interview, Oct. 13, 20, 27, 1961, 43-44; Tom Klasey interview, Sept. 10, 1960, 48; William Genske interview, July 23, 1960, 16-17.

[27]*United Automobile Worker*, April 29, 1939.

[28]See, for example, Irving Howe and B.J. Widick, *The UAW and Walter Reuther* (reprint, New York, 1973) 78-79.

[29]William Stevenson interview, July 6, 1961, 20. See also interview of Frank Cormier and William J. Eaton with Frank Winn, Nov. 14, 1967.

Probably both Stevenson and Reuther drew upon an earlier, and in 1939 by no means remote, precedent. In the summer of 1933 a strike in GM and several parts manufacturers plants in Detroit, Flint, and Pontiac of Mechanics Educational Society of America skilled tradesmen, although failing to accomplish most of its objectives, had, as Sidney Fine noted, "definitely delayed the introduction of the 1934 models. . . . "[30]

The arguments in favor of the strategy were clear and compelling. In the first place, a strike of production workers, the only alternative, might well fail. Employment in the auto industry was too uncertain and the union's support among the mass of production workers too insecure to risk a general strike. A strike confined to skilled workmen, on the other hand, would allow the production workers to stay on the job, drawing pay for as long as the 1939 model run lasted. If production workers were laid off because of a skilled workers strike, they might qualify for unemployment compensation payments, providing virtually a form of strike pay when the union had no strike fund of its own. The eligibility of non-striking production workers for unemployment compensation was in question until the strike was nearly over when the union's position was affirmed. The rare skills of the tool and die men made their immediate replacement with scab labor impossible. Nor was there any reason to fear a pro-Martin division within their ranks since, as one tradesman recalled, "Homer Martin may have taken some production people along with him but very few if any of the skilled workers."[31]

The skilled workmen, especially the tool and die men, had a pride in and consciousness of both craft and class that set them apart from most production workers. They had had more experience with unions and were, for the most part, more committed to militant union action. "The boys" in the tool and die shops, said one of them, were "very receptive to unionism when the union came. So, when the union came around and asked the boys if they would like to join, there was no problem whatsoever."[32] It was common knowledge in the auto industry

[30]Fine, "The Tool and Die Makers Strike of 1933," 323.
[31]Orrin Peppler interview, Mar. 16, 1961, 11.
[32]Orrin Peppler interview, Mar. 16, 1961, 2. According to Stanley Aronowitz, skilled work-

that "the average tool and diemaker has a history of trade union
association either in this country or in the old country. . . . "[33]
A majority of automotive tool and die makers, 70% by one
close observer's estimate, came from England, Scotland, Germany and other European countries, bringing with them records
of union membership and, in some instances, of radical political convictions and activity.[34] The presidents of the two large
amalgamated Detroit tool and die locals, John Anderson and
William Stevenson, were both of Scottish birth and were experienced trade unionists. Anderson was, as well, a leading
figure in the union's Communist faction. Stevenson came from
Glasgow where he had served a machinist's apprenticeship and
been a member of the Amalgamated Society of Engineers. As a
young man on the Clydeside he participated in lunch time
classes, taught by shop stewards, "where we gradually began
to pick up the drift of the whole system of capitalism and its
economic impact on society." Among the native born in the
tool and die shops many were from the eastern states where
they similarly had served apprenticeships and joined trade
unions.[35]

Immediate economic interests also bound tool and die men
to the union. Three kinds of shops divided the work. First were
the "captive shops," as those operated by the car manufacturers were called. At General Motors most of these were in Fisher
Body plants. Second were the "job shops," established firms
that performed die work on contract; most of them were unionized. Third were the "alley shops," small non-union
operations.[36] Employment in all shops was irregular. When laid

---

ers at the turbulent GM plant in Lordstown, Ohio, in the 1970s generally supported the
union with more conviction and fervor than the production workers. Stanley Aronowitz,
False Promises, (New York, 1973), 46-48.

[33]*United Automobile Worker, Tool, Die and Engineering News Edition.* Feb. 14, 1940.
[34]William Stevenson interview, July 6, 1961, 1-4. For discussion of some British and Irish
UAW members, see Steve Babson, "Pointing the Way. The Role of British and Irish
Skilled Tradesmen in the Rise of the UAW," *Detroit in Perspective: A Journal of
Regional History*, 7 (1983), 75-96. For British skilled immigrants in an earlier era, see
Rowland T. Berthoff, *British Immigrants in Industrial America, 1790-1950* (Cambridge,
MA, 1953), 21, 23, 74, 88-106.
[35]William Stevenson interview, July 6, 1961, 1-4. A good account of the industry's skilled
tradesmen and their role in the early days of the union is in John W. Anderson interview,
Feb. 17, 1960, 187ff. For historical accounts of the industry's skilled workers before the
founding of the UAW-CIO, see Fine, "The Tool and Die Makers Strike of 1933,"
293-323, and Fine, *The Automobile Under the Blue Eagle.*
[36]Prior to unionization, it was not uncommon for tool and die makers in job shops to work on

off by a manufacturer, the union card gave the captive shop journeyman access to the job shops where work might still be available. "It was union membership," said one observer, "that gave them this mobility and relative security. So there was a much stronger core of union sentiment among the skilled than among the production workers."[37]

Skilled workers in the captive shops were not only more committed to the union, they also needed to demonstrate their power within it. When the UAW was organized, the captive shop skilled workers were thrown into locals with the production workers in their plants. The more numerous production workers dominated the locals when officers were elected and policies formulated. Captive shop tradesmen felt their interests were ignored. In 1938 the international agreed to set up a Tool and Die Council to give them a voice, but its authority was limited. It had no power to negotiate, which would have made it a dual union, but it could formulate statements in behalf of the tradesmen and act as a pressure group. A successful strike of captive shop tradesmen that rescued the sinking organization would strengthen their claim to consideration.[38]

Reuther depended on the support of two groups besides the GM tool and diemakers to make the strike successful. Most crucial were the tool and diemakers in the independent shops. If they agreed to work on GM jobs, the strike could be broken.[39] The strike also had to have at least a minimal level of support from GM's production workers. Since there were so few skilled workmen, effective picket lines could not be established without the participation of some production workers. Even more important, production workers, who stood to realize no immediate gains from the strike, might have to make a sacrifice. If the strike continued beyond the 1939 model run, production men would be laid off and lose paychecks, creating a direct

a competitive bid basis in which the workers bid against each other for available work. The worker estimated the time required to complete the job and put in his bid accordingly. If more time was needed, the diemaker in effect worked for a lower hourly wage. See Fine, "The Tool and Die Makers Strike of 1933," 297, n. 2.
[37]Carl Haessler interview, Nov. 27, 1959, Oct. 24, 1960, 52-3.
[38]Orrin Peppler interview, Mar. 16, 1961, 9-10.
[39]According to Orrin Peppler, everyone in the job shops had joined the union without question. They were a close knit group and evidently social pressures were strong. Interview, Mar. 16, 1961, 24-25.

conflict of interests within the union's ranks. Production workers disaffected with a strike by and for skilled workmen might
pressure the union's leaders to call it off.

On June 8 Reuther notified GM that the UAW-CIO wished
to negotiate a supplemental agreement covering skilled workmen. The corporation replied with a press release reiterating its
refusal to bargain until the question of conflicting claims between the two unions was settled.[40] A few days later he
presented the case for action to a mass meeting of 2,000
tradesmen, pointing out that tool and die operations in GM
were then at "fever pitch" with the demand for labor still
unsatisfied.[41] At the end of the meeting, "Brother Reuther
advised the group that now is the time to deal with their
problems but if it is the desire of the men not to deal with their
problems at this time then no action will be taken."[42] It was
unanimously decided by those present to take a strike authorization vote among the tool and diemakers.[43]

The demands included a minimum 10 cents per hour wage
increase, higher overtime pay, a 10% shift differential. more
inclusive seniority provisions, the rehiring of laid off workers
before increasing the hours of those still on the job, a standard
apprenticeship system for all plants, and a provision for affix-
ing a union label to all dies and tools produced in GM plants
with an agreement by the company to use only those labelled by
the UAW or another bona fide union.[44]

---

[40]*Detroit News*, July 7, 9, 23, 1939; Federal Mediation and Conciliation Service case, 199/
3975.
[41]*United Automobile Worker*, June 7, 14, 1939; *Detroit News*, June 9, 1939; press release,
June 11, 1939; in Walter P. Reuther Collection, Pre-presidential papers, Box 26, Folder
19. *United Automobile Worker, Tool and Die Edition*, June 14, 1939.
[42]"Minutes of the Tool and Die, Engineering and Maintenance Workers Held at 51 Sproat
Street, Detroit, Michigan," copy in Walter P. Reuther Collection, Pre-presidential papers, Box 26, Folder 18.
[43]*United Automobile Worker*, June 14, 1939; *New York Times*, June 26, 1939; undated press
release, General Motors Department, UAW, copy in Walter P. Reuther Collection, Box
5, Folder: Tool and Die Strike, July 5-Aug. 12, 1939.
[44]The demands are given in many sources. General Motors Department, UAW, press release,
June 25, 1939, in Walter P. Reuther Collection, Box 5, Folder: Tool and Die Strike, July
5-Aug. 12, 1939. The 10 cents increase would apply to 44 separate classifications in the
tool and die, drop forge, maintenance, and engineering (experimental) skilled trades. On
overtime, production workers, who received time and a half over 40 hours, were better
treated than skilled workers. *Report of R. J. Thomas, President . . . Submitted . . . to the
Special Convention, Cleveland, Ohio, March 27, 1939*, 29. A knottier problem was the
wage differential existing between different GM plants and even within a single plant for
the same work. Two UAW international representatives reported that in the tool room of

Although the fundamental purpose of the strike was recognition, if GM entered into and concluded negotiations it would acknowledge the UAW-CIO as party to a binding labor contract, the demands advanced on behalf of the skilled workers were aimed at real problems. During the 1930s the earnings of skilled workers in most car plants declined, certainly in relation to the wages of production workers and perhaps even absolutely. In 1930, tool and diemakers received 51% higher average hourly earnings than material handlers (a common unskilled classification). By 1940 they received 40% higher earnings.[45] Fewer hours of work for skilled workmen reduced pay differentials even further. Similar work in the job shops received approximately 20% higher pay.[46] Stricter provisions on scheduling overtime, the payment of overtime premiums, and changes in seniority rules would pressure the corporation to spread work throughout the year. The two-fold purpose behind the union label demand was to force non-union alley shops to organize and to return work to the captive shops.

Strike votes confirmed the readiness of the skilled workers to walk out. About 8,000 voted, with over 90% in favor.[47] The strike began on July 5 at Fisher Body 21 in Detroit where 800 men made welding tools and fixtures: "Soon as the 10 o'clock bell rang, the power went off and every machine in the plant stopped running. The men quietly put away their tools, washed

---

the Olds Motor Works in Lansing, "the many differences for one operation seems to be for the men who took the largest, rosiest apples for the boss every morning." Leroy Sherman and John S. Wilson to Ed Gieger, July 22, 1939, in Walter P. Reuther Collection, Pre-presidential papers, Box 28, Folder 22.

[45]MacDonald, 138. See also, *Detroit News*, Aug. 6, 1939. It was also the case that skilled tradesmen within the plants received less than their counterparts on the outside. GM electricians received $1.05 to $1.15 an hour, while building trades electricians were paid $1.65 to $2.00 an hour. *New York Times*, July 9, 1939. Erosion of skilled workmens' wages in relation to those of production workers had been going on for a long time. After Ford's introduction of the $5 a day wage in 1914, Ford skilled workers "complained bitterly" that a floor sweeper could now make almost as much as they. Joyce Shaw Peterson, "A Social History of Automobile Workers before Unionization, 1900-33" (unpublished PhD diss., Univ. of Wisconsin, 1976), 91. See also *United Automobile Worker, West Side Conveyor Edition*, April 8, June 28, 1939: *Report of R. J. Thomas, President . . . Submitted . . . to the Special Convention, Cleveland, Ohio, March 27, 1939*, 28-9.

[46]The wage differential between job shops and captive shops was traditional in the industry, justified on the grounds that job shops provided less steady employment and required more all around skill. Workmen in the captive shops had never found such arguments persuasive. See MacDonald, 163.

[47]*Detroit News*, June 30, July 3, 1939; *New York Times*, July 4, 1939. Detailed breakdowns are in *G.M. Strike Bulletin*, No. 1, July 3, 1939 and No. 2, July 6, 1939.

up, changed clothes, punched the clock, thumbed their noses at the manager, and walked out. By 10:25, not a man was left inside.''[48] The corporation's 1940 tool and die program was only two weeks away from completion, with production of some models scheduled to begin the following week.[49]

One tactic decided upon was to escalate gradually, starting out in one plant and then moving to others until, if necessary, all tool and die operations were shut down. By this strategem, momentum and impact would mount and the timid would be encouraged to follow the example of the bold. By July 24, twelve shops with 7,600 workers were closed, and GM conceded that preparations for its 1940 models were at a standstill. This tactic, which *Time* magazine called Reuther's ''new and shrewdly conceived'' technique, ''not unlike amputating one finger at a time to cripple a hand,'' caught the attention of reporters, brought pain to the corporation, excited the workers, and fostered the impression that an irresistible tide was flowing in the strikers' favor.[50]

Support for the strike built quickly as workers ''displayed enthusiasm such as [had] not been seen since the great fight of '36.''[51] Picket lines were set up at all the struck plants to deter entry of skilled workers. Production men and supervisory employees were allowed free access. Many production workers showed their support by joining the picket lines before and after their shifts with the ranks sometimes swelling to thousands.[52] In

---

[48]*G. M. Picket*, No. 1, July 8 [1939]; *G. M. Strike Bulletin*, No. 1, July 3, 1939; *New York Times*, July 6, 1939; *Detroit News*, July 5, 1939; Federal Mediation and Conciliation Service, case 199/3975.
[49]Federal Mediation and Conciliation Service, case 199/3975; *Flint Journal*, July 5, 1939.
[50]*Time*, 34 (July 17, 1939). Federal Mediation and Conciliation Service, case 199/3975.
[51]*United Automobile Worker*, July 12, 1939.
[52]According to one observer there were twenty production men on the picket lines in Flint for each skilled worker. Theodore LaDuke interview, Aug. 5, 1960, 34. A picket duty card entitled ''The Way to Win a Strike,'' listed these rules. ''1. Report daily to Picket Captains. 2. In case of emergency call headquarters. 3. Attend all Strike Meetings. 4. Carry out all directions of the Strike Committee. 5. Stay sober to avoid unnecessary trouble.'' Walter P. Reuther Collection, Box 5, Folder: Tool and Die Strike, July 5-Aug. 12, 1939. Pressure tactics were sometimes used. It was reported in the *Cadillac Steward*, a mimeographed strike bulletin, that the houses of some workers who had not yet appeared on the picket lines were being picketed and lists of ''rats'' that is, non-picketers, were published. Copies in Walter P. Reuther Collection, Box 5, Folder: Tool and Die Strike, July 5-Aug. 12, 1939. See also, Federal Mediation and Conciliation Service, case 199/3975; Fountain, 109-114; *Detroit News*, July 6, 1939; *United Automobile Worker*, July 12, 1939; *G.M. Picket*, No. 1, July 8, 1939; Arthur Case interview, Aug. 4, 1960, p. 21; *Flint Journal*, July 6, 1939.

appealing for production workers support, Reuther and other strike leaders stressed that a victory for the skilled workmen would lead to improvements for all, while a defeat would blight their common prospects.[53] General Motors sought to generate anti-strike pressure among production workers by suspending its program of providing interest free loans to workers idled in slack periods. Inaugurated only six months earlier as the corporation's solution to the problem of irregular earnings, the loans were withdrawn for production workers who, although not on strike themselves, were laid off as a consequence.[54]

Although no surplus skilled work force was available to break the strike, dozens of independent tool and die job shops in the Detroit area, employing approximately 1,500 tool and diemakers, provided an alternative labor source. While they could not replace GM's employees, they could, if put to work on GM materials, complete enough jobs to enable the corporation to produce a few new models for their scheduled introduction and display at the fall auto shows. Here a sense of common interests, shared status, and fraternal sentiments among skilled workmen had a decisive effect. Job shop employees realized they would ultimately gain from improvements in wages and conditions won in the captive shops. Furthermore, the tool and

---

[53]See, for example, his statements in *G.M. Strike Bulletin*, No. 2, July 6, 1939 and *G.M. Strike Bulletin*, No. 3, July 8, 1939. See also *United Automobile Worker*, July 12, 1939. Homer Martin tried to arouse production workers against the strike, charging that "it would victimize hundreds and thousands of workers without giving them an opportunity to vote democratically on the question," an ironic complaint in view of the source. *New York Times*, July 7, 1939. For a Reuther counterstatement, see *ibid.*, July 8, 1939. For picket line violence in Pontiac, Flint, Cleveland, and Detroit, and incidents of scabbing, see the following sources: *Flint Journal*, July 7, 12, 13, 18, 1939; John McGill interview, July 27, 1960, 11-12; *G.M. Picket*, No. 3, July 11, 1939, No. 15, July 31, 1939; *Detroit News*, July 10-13, 23, 1939; *New York Times*, July 11-14, 1939; Federal Mediation and Conciliation Service, case 199/3975; Bert Foster interview, July 26, 1961, 18-21. Foster estimated there were as many as 7,000 on the picket lines at Fisher Body in Cleveland, nearly all of them production workers and many from other plants. According to a UAW report, about 20 scabs entered the Cleveland Fisher plant. *G.M. Strike Bulletin*, No. 8, July 31, 1939. For the situation in Cleveland, where the most serious instances of violence occurred, see *Cleveland Plain Dealer*, July 15, 1939, August 1,1939; *Cleveland Press*, July 31, 1939; *New York Times*, Aug. 1-2, 1939; *Detroit News*, July 31-Aug. 2, 1939. A committee of non-strikers, probably Martin supporters, asked the Dies Committee to investigate the "Communistic tendencies . . ." of the Cleveland strike leaders, but the strike ended before the Committee could hold hearings. Bob Travis, one of the UAW's leading leftists, was in charge in Cleveland. *New York Times*, Aug. 3, 1939. William Stevenson said there was no scabbing at any of the key GM facilities in Detroit. William Stevenson interview, July 6, 1961, 21-22. *G.M. Strike Bulletin*, No. 8, July 31, 1939; *G.M. Picket*, No. 16, August 2, 1939.

[54]*Flint Journal*, July 8, 1939.

diemakers fraternity was relatively small with many opportunities for association. Although GM attempted to place work in the job shops during the strike, the workers refused to touch the "hot dies," a "severe jolt" to the corporation. One non-union employer attempted to discharge 29 of his employees who refused to work on GM dies, but the threat of a strike led to their reinstatement.[55] As Carl Haessler later said, the most effective picketing was done by the job shop employees within their own shops.[56]

Reuther, noting "the importance of solidarity in the home as a basis for solidarity on the picket line," nurtured support for the strike among the strikers' families.[57] The Women's Auxiliaries of UAW locals were especially active in some locations, as their members marched on picket lines, handed out leaflets, and, cast in a domestic role, prepared and served meals. The Auxiliaries formed committees to call upon those wives of strikers whose indifference or hostility to the strike was suspected, in order to explain to them the strike's aims and portray the benefits of standing together. The role of the Auxiliaries, although not given special prominence in written records and accounts, was highlighted in a film entitled "Union Action Means Victory." The first feature length documentary produced at the instance of an American labor union, it "brilliantly capture[d] the spirit of the industrial union crusade of the late 1930s."[58] Although the film, which contained both

[55]*G.M. Strike Bulletin*, No. 4, July 13, 1939; *G.M. Picket*, No. 4, July 12, 1939; *United Automobile Worker, Tool, Die and Engineering News Edition*, Feb. 20, 1940. Region No. 1-A Report, by Richard T. Leonard, Regional Director, to the Executive Board Members, UAW-CIO, 1. Copy in George F. Addes Collection, Box 3, Folder: Regional Report 1-A, Aug. 8-12, 1939. Walter P. Reuther to John Anderson, Aug. 11, 1939, and Reuther to William Stevenson, Aug. 11, 1939, in Walter P. Reuther Collection, Pre-presidential papers, Box 26, Folder 17.

[56]Carl Haessler interview, Nov. 27, 1959, Oct. 24, 1960, 54.

[57]Walter P. Reuther Collection, Pre-presidential papers, Box 26, Folder 17. One UAW leaflet headed "SOS WIVES MOTHERS SISTERS DAUGHTERS!" announced a meeting for women on the subject "The Union Way is the American Way to protect your home and family." Copy in Walter P. Reuther Collection, Pre-presidential papers, Box 26, Folder 15. See also *United Automobile Worker*, July 19, 1939.

[58]An analysis of the film and an account of its production is in Roy Rosenzweig, " 'United Action Means Victory': Militant Americanism on Film," *Labor History*, 24 (1983), 274-288. The quotation is from page 278. The film consistently downplayed, even verged on omission of, the role of Walter P. Reuther in the strike. Although at odds with other evidence, this is not surprising since the film was produced by Frontier Films, many of whose members "belonged to, or sympathized with, the Communist party. . . ." Rosenzweig, 282.

documentary footage and staged scenes dramatizing strike issues, was not completed until after the strike was over, it was eventually seen by several hundred thousand UAW members and was an important means of building support and morale prior to the National Labor Relations Board election in the GM plants in 1940.

In order to show production workers' support a giant demonstration and march around General Motors' Detroit headquarters, with 12,000 participants, by the union's estimate, took place on July 27. The marchers, ten abreast, completely surrounded the vast building.[59] Reuther scheduled a speech for delivery over station WJR on July 30 (owing to a brief illness, the speech was read by his brother Victor) in which he proposed to attack the DuPont interests as the real power in GM, accuse the company of stirring up class hatred, and dwell upon the salaries of executives Alfred P. Sloan and William S. Knudsen. The station censored those passages, but Reuther and other UAW spokesmen, no slouches at public relations, ensured that the press knew of the station's action. The incident probably generated more favorable publicity than would otherwise have been the case. As a union leaflet put it, the "industrial barons not only want to dominate their own plants, like kings of old, but, they want to rule God's free air."[60]

For a week a confident GM management refused to meet with union negotiators. Officially, the corporation and its defenders argued that there was nothing GM could do since, in their view, the dispute was solely between two union factions.[61] Behind the scene, some corporation executives, believing the union was fatally weakened by the factionalism within its ranks, were ready for the showdown they thought would rid them of the UAW.[62] As the strike spread, however, and preparations for the 1940 model stalled, the company's attitude softened. On July 12, Philip Murray, CIO vice-president, conferred with James E. Dewey, a federal mediator, and William

---

[59]*G.M. Strike Bulletin*, No. 6, July 20, 1939; *G.M. Strike Bulletin*, No. 8, July 31, 1939. The Detroit police put the number of marchers at about 3,000. Federal Mediation and Conciliation Service, case 199/3975.
[60]*Fisher Strike News*, Aug. 1, 1939.
[61]*Flint Journal*, July 12, 22, 1939.
[62]*New York Times*, Aug. 3, 1939; Blackwood, 131.

S. Knudsen, the corporation's president and spokesman.[63] During the next four weeks intermittent, often stormy, meetings were held, marked by "some exceedingly acrimonious disputes" involving these three, Thomas and Reuther for the UAW, and additional company personnel.[64] Reuther, still tagged as a far leftist, was the main target of GM's wrath. At one point Knudsen, shaking his finger, warned, "Now, see here, Reuther, we don't want any commissars in America," to which he provocatively retorted that the actions of the leaders of industry would determine the issue.[65]

Rejecting a binding arbitration proposal accepted by the UAW, GM refused to budge on three demands. It rejected an across the board wage increase, insisting instead on local adjustments to reduce pay differentials between plants. Also unacceptable was the demand for the union label which, the company charged, would give the UAW control over its suppliers, and GM refused to pay some of the overtime rates sought by the union for Sundays and holidays.[66]

By early August, with the strike holding firm after a month and around 150,000 production workers idled as work on the 1939 models ended, both sides were ready to settle. The pressure was beginning to be felt. Newspapers carried articles on the rosy sales prospects for the 1940 cars and noted that Packard was already producing its new models while Chrysler, then the second firm in the industry, expected to have them available in two weeks. Nor was GM's cause helped by its

---

[63]*New York Times*, July 3, 13, 1939; *Detroit News*, July 12, 1939; *United Automobile Worker*, July 19, 1939. The UAW noted: "CIO Vice President Philip Murray who's sitting in [on] negotiations is a Miner. But he feels at home among tool and die makers. He's Scotch—with a burr from here to Glasgow." *G.M. Picket*, No. 5, July 13, 1939. The negotiations may be followed in the records of Federal Mediation and Conciliation Service, case 199/3975.
[64]*New York Times*, Aug. 4, 1939.
[65]*Detroit News*, Sept. 3, 1948. According to Louis G. Seaton, a GM executive who sat in on one of the sessions, "C. E. (Wilson) was executive vice-president then and he liked to get into these things. We sat down there and he offered Reuther about eight different positions, all variations of the thing, and it got to be about midnight, and Walter pushed his chair back and laughed like hell and he says: 'I'm going to offer a recess until morning. I damned near took that last position of yours and it's not as good as the first one you offered.'" Louis G. Seaton interview with Frank Cormier and William J. Eaton, June 20, 1968. After the strike was over, Knudsen told a reporter, "We want to forget all the names we have called each other." *Flint Journal*, August 5, 1939.
[66]*New York Times*, July 23, 1939. Statement of R. J. Thomas, July 22, 1939, in Walter P. Reuther Collection, Pre-presidential papers, Box 26, Folder 19. Federal Mediation and Conciliation Service, case 199/3975.

announcement of net profits of $100,992,531 for the first six months of 1939, triple the $33,030,019 it earned for the comparable period in 1938.[67] Corporate hardliners were forced to back down, at least temporarily, from the "final show-down," in view of the "enormous expense of such a policy . . . at this time."[68]

A consideration that may have affected GM's decision to end the strike was the prospect of making unemployment compensation payments to the production workers who were being laid off in ever larger numbers as the strike continued. The State of Michigan had only recently implemented its payroll-tax supported compensation system as authorized by the Social Security Act. GM argued that employees idled as a result of a strike were not eligible but the Michigan Unemployment Compensation Commission ruled by a 3-1 vote on August 4 that unemployed production workers not themselves on strike could collect. Although benefits would be limited to $16 a week for only three weeks, this decision made it less likely that pressure generated from the ranks of production workers would end the strike. The decision immediately benefited 5,000 to 10,000 production workers who stood to collect as much as $320,000. Had the strike continued the number would have grown. With this the "last element of the union's strategy panned out. . . ."[69]

General Motors, the federal mediator now reported, was "willing to get matters properly and finally disposed of and get rid of Martin."[70] The final difference was over a nickel an hour for 100 electricians; by contrast it was estimated that GM was losing a million dollars a day in future sales.[71] A tentative

[67]*Detroit News*, July 27, 28, 1939.
[68]*New York Times*, Aug. 3, 1939.
[69]*United Automobile Worker*, Aug. 9, 1939. *Detroit News*, Aug. 4, 1939; *New York Times*, Aug. 5, 1939; *Flint Journal*, Aug. 4, 1939. For background see *United Automobile Worker*, July 12, 1939; *G.M. Picket*, No. 8, July 18, 1939; *Detroit News*, July 23, 1939; press release, Michigan Unemployment Compensation Commission, July 25, 1939, copy in Walter P. Reuther Collection, Pre-presidential papers, Box 26, Folder 19.
[70]Memorandum on telephone conversation between John A. Steelman and James Dewey, Aug. 2, 1939, Federal Mediation and Conciliation Service, case 199/3975.
[71]Memorandum for the Record, Aug. 3, 1939, Federal Mediation and Conciliation Service, case 199/3975. According to the *MESA Educator*, Aug. 1939, the organ of a rival union, the UAW was eager to settle "because of the weaknesses that had developed at the Fisher Body, Cleveland, and the Cadillac in Detroit with minor defections at Plant No. 37 in Detroit," a remark that severely distorts the situation and ignores the pressure that was building on GM.

agreement was reached at 12:30 a.m. on August 4. GM wanted the UAW officials to sign immediately, but they insisted on following constitutional procedures which required ratification by the strike committee, the executive board, and the tool and die locals. The vote was 5,500 in favor to 50 against.[72]

The material gains were modest but significant. Wages were adjusted upward to reduce the worst discrepancies between plants and the rates at Fisher 23, whose skilled workers were the best paid GM manual employees, would henceforth serve as a model for future adjustments. Average rates went up 5 cents an hour, only half of what the union had sought. In an important concession, the corporation agreed to pay double time for Sunday and holiday work and time and a half for Saturday. GM accepted union labels on its own dies and in unionized job shops (a concession of little importance), but refused to stop using non-union alley shop dies if a need for them arose. Seniority provisions and a uniform apprenticeship system were put off for future discussions. The UAW pledged, with some conditions, that there would be no strikes during the 1940 model run.[73]

The chief gains, neither included among the stated demands but always recognized as the most important goals, were, first, GM's agreement to deal exclusively with the UAW-CIO in 42 of its 59 plants. The key provision read: "In the plants of the corporation where UAW committees are now functioning, substitute committees established by either faction will not be recognized by the corporation under the UAW-General Motors Agreement."[74] This, as Reuther claimed, "repaired much of the damage done by the dual union and . . . restored to many thousands of GM workers the grievance machinery which has

---

[72]*Detroit News*, Aug. 4, 1939; *New York Times*, Aug. 6, 1939.

[73]The settlement, dated Aug. 3, 1939, is available in many sources. Copies are in Federal Mediation and Conciliation Service, case 199/3975 and Walter P. Reuther Collection, Box 5, Folder: Tool and Die Makers Strike, July-Aug. 12, 1939. See also the summaries in *New York Times*, Aug. 5, 1939, *Detroit News*, Aug. 5, 1939, and *Flint Journal*, Aug. 5, 1939. There were two brief, unauthorized strikes. Report of R. J. Thomas, President, UAW-CIO, to International Executive Board, Dec. 4, 1939, copy in George F. Addes Collection, Box 1, Folder: Departmental Reports, Board Meeting, Dec. 4-9, 1939.

[74]Press commentary in the *New York Times, New Republic, Newsweek, Time, Detroit News, New York Herald-Tribune*, the *Wall Street Journal*, and other publications recognized representation rights as the key gain. See roundup in *United Automobile Worker*, Aug. 16, 1939. *Time*, 24 (Aug. 14, 1939).

been denied them for some time.''[75] A closely related accomplishment was the UAW-CIO's signing of a new contract with GM. While this supplementary agreement covered only skilled workers, it was the first company-wide wage agreement signed by GM, since the 1937 contract had covered only those plants that had been on strike.[76] With its decision to settle, General Motors grudgingly acquiesced in a permanent autoworkers' union. Some bitter struggles between the company and the UAW lay in the future, but henceforth GM adopted a "realist" stance in its labor relations consisting of hard bargaining over issues and an unyielding opposition to union encroachment on its "management prerogatives" combined with acknowledgement and toleration of the UAW's role in representing the corporation's work force. It was the first of the major auto manufacturers to adopt this position.[77]

The consequences of success were quickly demonstrated. The UAW-CIO experienced a resurgence of morale and membership. Local unions conducted massive drives.[78] "Six months ago," trumpeted the union paper, "we were torn by the treachery of men whom we had trusted. Since then we have set our house in order and reached out with the strength of lions to tame one of the toughest and richest industrial corporations in the country.''[79]

Eager to put the union on as secure a foundation as possible, and now confident of the outcome, the UAW petitioned the

---

[75] Walter P. Reuther, press release, Aug. 6, 1939, Walter P. Reuther Collection, Pre-presidential papers, Box 26, Folder 19. The plants and UAW locals affected are listed in *United Automobile Worker*, Aug. 16, 1939. In eleven plants in which bargaining committees were maintained by both groups grievances would be handled through either committee with improved procedures. The remaining six were either non-union or solely UAW-AFL. Federal Mediation and Conciliation Service, case 199/3975. The 1937 settlement with GM had given the UAW-CIO exclusive bargaining rights for six months in the seventeen plants on strike, a limited recognition that was pledged in a letter to Governor Frank Murphy but which GM refused to put in the agreement with the union.

[76] *United Automobile Worker*, Aug. 9, 1939; *Detroit News*, Aug. 6, 1939. Contrasting ex parte summaries of the pact's meaning were given by Knudsen and Reuther in the *New York Times*, Aug. 6, 1939.

[77] Harris, 29.

[78] For Flint locals, see Report of Region No. 1-C, Presented by Arthur L. Case to International Executive Board, Dec. 4, 1939, 1-2; for Pontiac, Report of Region No. 1-B, Report by William McAulay, Regional Director, to the International Executive Board, Dec. 9, 1939; for Cleveland, Report of the Activities of Region 2A, Paul E. Miley, Regional Director, all in George F. Addes Collection, Box 1, Folder: Reports to the Executive Board, December, 1939.

[79] *United Automobile Worker*, Aug. 9, 1939.

National Labor Relations Board to conduct collective bargaining agent elections throughout the General Motors empire. On April 17, 1940, the elections were held in 55 plants. With over 134,000 votes cast, it was the largest election ever conducted by the NLRB.[80] The outcome was an emphatic victory for the UAW-CIO which received 68 percent of the vote, to 19 percent for AFL unions (nearly all for the Martinite UAW-AFL).[81] On the strength of this victory the UAW negotiated an improved contract in June for all GM workers, the first agreement obtained with the corporation without the need of a strike.

Skilled workers played a crucial role in establishing the UAW and in rebuilding it during its time of trouble. In later years participants testified to their conviction that the strke "was really a fight for the survival of the union," the "turning point in saving the CIO in the automobile industry. . . . "[82] The skilled tradesmen gained respect and a new sense of their power within the union. According to one analyst, this planted the seeds of a later disruption. "The skilled tradesmen were given almost sole credit for reestablishing bargaining rights for the UAW-CIO with General Motors. And as a result of this, they thought and began to feel that they required and should receive special treatment within the UAW. Here we see," he continued, "the beginning of a division within the UAW-CIO."[83] By the 1950s a significant portion of the skilled tradesmen,

---

[80]The figure includes those ballots cast on April 17 plus a few others from run off elections later in the year. With 146,821 GM workers eligible to vote, the turnout of 92% (134,474) was high for such elections. Data calculated from *Report of R. J. Thomas, President . . . 1940*, 9-10, 88-91. For a brief account of the UAW's campaign, see the same source, 23-24.

[81]The vote totals and percentages were as follows:
Eligible: 146,821
Total vote: 134,474 (92%)
CIO vote: 91,318 (68%)
AFL vote: 26,052 (19%)
Independent unions: 1,376 (1%)
Against: 1,010 (1%)
Neither: 14,111 (10%)
The remaining 1% are accounted for by spoiled ballots.
All of the large GM plants went CIO, although there were sizeable AFL minorities at Chevrolet and Fisher 1 in Flint, Lansing Oldsmobile, and Pontiac Motors. Of the medium sized GM facilities, the Martinites won only in Kansas City and Norwood, Ohio. *Report of R.J. Thomas, President . . . 1940*, 88-91.

[82]Leonard Woodcock interview, April 30, 1963, 14; George Merrelli interview, Feb. 21, 1963, 4. See also Everett Francis interview, Oct. 13, 20, 27, 1961, 44-45, and William Stevenson interview, July 6, 1961, 21.

[83]John W. Anderson interview, Feb. 17, 1960, 87.

convinced that the UAW had failed to meet its obligations to them, were prepared to break away in a dual union movement.[84]

As an education in tactics, the UAW learned valuable lessons. In a situation fraught with danger and uncertainty, the union discovered the means and took the initiatives that maximized the leverage it could exert while minimizing the effect of its weaknesses. By devising a strategy that took into account the corporation's vulnerability during model changeovers, the character of the work force, the nature and needs of the production process, and the existing and anticipated market demand for the product, the union reversed its downward course and assured its permanence. Henceforth the union bargained for and obtained contract expiration dates that coincided with the beginning of a new model year.

Preeminent among the strike's winners was Walter P. Reuther. Involved in the 1937 sitdown in only a minor way, the 1939 strike was Reuther's first major opportunity to demonstrate the skills in strike leadership and bargaining required for high union office. As a worker in a Flint Chevrolet plant recalled, Reuther as a result of the strike became a "hero" there, a man who both knew how and could be trusted to get the job done.[85]

---

[84]For an analysis see Seth Wigderson, "Reuther's Last Fight: The Skilled Trades Revolt of the 1950's," a paper read at the meeting of the Organization of American Historians, Los Angeles, April 6, 1984.
[85]F. R. "Jack" Palmer interview, July 23, 1960. See also *United Automobile Worker*, Aug. 9, 1939 for President R. J. Thomas's statement.

RITE OF PASSAGE:
The 1939 General Motors
Tool and Die Strike

by
Kevin Boyle*

In early 1939 the United Automobile Workers (UAW-CIO) stood at a crossroads. The dramatic success of its 1937 organizational drive, which brought General Motors, Chrysler, and a host of lesser auto producers to terms, had thrust the union into national prominence. In the intervening year-and-a-half, however, internal conflict had split the UAW in two, while the 1938 recession had caused massive industry layoffs that thinned union ranks. If the decline was not arrested quickly, experts contended, the UAW might suffer irreparable damage.[1]

The union's answer was a dramatic month-long strike against General Motors, orchestrated by the UAW's young, ambitious vice-president, Walter Reuther. Reuther hoped the strike would crush his union's rival, the UAW-AFL, by reaffirming his organization's strength and, not incidentally, place Reuther himself in a position of power.

The situation hardly fostered such high hopes. A year of infighting had resulted in January 1939, in the expulsion of the UAW-CIO's president, Homer Martin. A former Baptist preacher of electric personality but limited organizational skill, Martin quickly formed the UAW-AFL, composed of a substantial minority of the UAW-CIO's membership and

---

*I am deeply indebted to Sidney Fine, without whom this paper would not be possible.
[1]Sidney Fine, *Sit Down* (Ann Arbor, 1969), offers a detailed view of the strike. For information on the UAW-CIO from 1937 to 1959 see Walter Galenson, *The CIO Challenge to the AFL* (Cambridge, MA, 1960), 157-173; Irving Bernstein, *Turbulent Years* (Boston, 1970), 555-569; Frank Cormier and William J. Eaton, *Reuther* (Englewood Cliffs, NJ, 1970), 141-161; and John Barnard, *Walter Reuther and the Rise of the Auto Workers* (Boston, 1983), 36-69.

based in Flint, Michigan.[2]

Martin was replaced in the UAW-CIO's presidency by R. J. Thomas. It was generally agreed that Thomas was a figurehead; the struggle for real power was among his lieutenants. On one side stood Reuther, at 31, the president of the massive Detroit Local 174 and recently-appointed head of the union's powerful General Motors Department. The dynamic long-time unionist George Addes, Thomas' secretary-treasurer, stood in opposition. The Communists, still a potent political force within the UAW, promoted their favorite, Richard Frankensteen.[3] To this point, none of these men had emerged as dominant, but whoever solved the union's serious problems would clearly have the upper hand.

As head of the UAW-CIO's General Motors Department, the division that set policy concerning the giant auto maker, Reuther held an envious position. General Motors union members had long been dissatisfied with their existing contract, which, they claimed, did not give them sufficiently high wages. Skilled workers, who had a long history of militancy,[4] were most vocal in their criticisms — the corporation paid different wages for the same job in different plants, overtime work was not properly compensated, and the threat of layoff was constant. Faced with such rank-and-file pressure, Martin had attempted to reopen negotiations with GM in late 1938, but had been unsuccessful. If Reuther could deliver where Martin had failed, his political stock would skyrocket.[5]

That was no easy task. Both the UAW-AFL and the UAW-CIO claimed to represent the GM hourly workers. Until that dispute was settled, the corporation announced in January, 1939, it would negotiate with neither. Only a successful shutdown by the UAW-CIO would cast doubt on the UAW-AFL's

---

[2]Galenson, 168-173; Bernstein, 568-569. Estimates of UAW-AFL strength ranged from 60,000 to 200,000 workers.

[3]Cormier, 147. For details on the UAW-CIO infighting, see Oral History Interview of Ed Hall, 37-39, Bentley Historical Library, Univ. of Michigan, Ann Arbor, (all oral history interviews at Bentley Library): and Oral History Interview of R. J. Thomas, 17-18.

[4]Sidney Fine, *The Automobile Under the Blue Eagle* (Ann Arbor, 1963), 141-142; Harry Dahlheimer, *A History of the Mechanics Educational Society of America From Its Inception in 1933 Through 1937* (Detroit, 1951).

[5]Homer Martin to Charles Wilson, Oct. 21, 1938, UAW-GM Collection, Series I, Box 1, Archives of Labor History and Urban Affairs, Walter P. Reuther Library, Wayne State Univ., Detroit; Homer Martin to Officers and Members of All GM Locals, Dec. 20, 1938, Walter Reuther Collection, Box 1, Folder 25, Reuther Library.

legitimacy and force General Motors to the bargaining table, but the 1938 recession had depleted the UAW-CIO's treasury, making a long walkout unfeasible.

Reuther sidestepped the problem with a novel proposal put forth in May 1939: only the skilled workers would strike GM. In mid-summer, he pointed out, the corporation retooled its plants to prepare for model changeover, a process that could not be completed without skilled workers. If they struck, the corporation would have to shut down, forcing the layoff of other production workers, who would then be eligible for unemployment compensation. In effect, the state would pay the bulk of the strike fund. General Motors, on the other hand, could not weather a prolonged walkout since that would delay the introduction of the corporation's 1940 models beyond the time when Ford, Chrysler, and GM's other competitors introduced their new models.

Ignoring Thomas, Addes and Frankensteen, Reuther took his proposal directly to the CIO leadership, Philip Murray in Pittsburgh and Sidney Hillman in Washington, DC. The two had kept tight rein on the UAW-CIO since the factional fight,[6] and the UAW could take no dramatic action without their, and, tacitly, John L. Lewis's approval. Murray and Hillman both agreed to the Reuther plan.[7]

The skilled workers also liked the idea. Tool and die work was concentrated in Detroit plants, especially Fisher #23, the world's largest tool and die plant. At a tool and die makers' meeting in early June, Reuther announced that the UAW-CIO was seeking a supplementary contract for the GM craftsmen. The union demanded satisfaction of all the skilled workers' grievances, including, for the first time, the use of the union label. Consistent to its policy, General Motors refused to negotiate.[8]

Martin must have sensed that the UAW-CIO was on the move. At 2:30 pm, June 8, he issued strike orders for workers in Flint's Fisher #1 and Chevrolet Body #2 and Chevrolet

---

[6]Cormier and Eaton, 141-161; Bernstein, 563-568.
[7]Oral History Interview of William Stevenson, 20.
[8]*United Automobile Worker*, June 14, 1939; R. J. Thomas and Walter Reuther to Charles Wilson, June 8, 1939, UAW Research Department Records, Box 89, Reuther Library; *United Automobile Worker*, Aug. 9, 1939.

Grey Iron Foundry in Saginaw to take effect just two hours later. His lightning action took everyone by surprise, including the workers, who had taken no strike vote. The response was wholly unspectacular; only twelve workers walked off the job at the Grey Iron Foundry; and although Fisher #1 was shut down for the evening, all three plants were back in operation by the next morning. The UAW-CIO ordered its workers to cross picket lines, and they complied. Less than a week later, Martin was forced to call off the strike.[9]

Reuther claimed that Martin's failure clearly showed that the UAW-CIO was the rightful representative of GM workers. The corporation's repeated refusal to negotiate, however, left the union no choice but to request strike votes. "We must inform GM that we are prepared to speak the only language it understands," Reuther declared at a meeting of 3,000 skilled workers in Detroit on June 25. Within the next few days, critical Detroit plants such as Fisher #21, #23, and #37, Chevrolet Gear and Axle, Chevrolet Forge, and GM Research and Styling all voted to strike.[10]

General Motors still refused to negotiate, turning instead to the Federal government. In mid-June the National Labor Relations Board had announced that henceforth an employer could appeal to it when two or more unions claimed exclusive jurisdiction over a company's employees, an option previously reserved for workers and their representatives. On June 30 General Motors became the first corporation to use the new ruling, requesting the NLRB to intervene to prevent the threatened strike, which GM argued really would be a jurisdictional squabble. The UAW-CIO answerd that the NLRB's new rule did not apply since the strike would involve only CIO locals, not all UAW workers, and that the union was consequently making no claim for total jurisdiction.[11] The NLRB ruling was so new that no guidelines had been established to deal with the question. The board consequently announced that

---

[9]*Detroit News*, June 9-14, 1939, provided thorough coverage of the UAW-AFL Flint strike, Galenson, 172-173, tells the same story.
[10]*United Automobile Worker*, June 28, 1939; Minutes of Tool and Die Meeting, June 25, 1939, and press release of June 28, 1939, Reuther Collection, Box 26, Folders 18 and 19.
[11]*Wall Street Journal*, July 7-8, 1939.
[12]*Ibid.*, July 8, 1939.

it was giving the matter "routine attention."[12] GM was sty-mied.

The UAW-CIO executive board approved the strike on July 2, as had the skilled workers in the nine GM plants, each by at least 90% of the men. Reuther spent the Fourth of July holiday on last-minute preparations and then sprang another surprise: on July 5, he called out on strike only the 800 skilled workers in Detroit's Fisher #21. All other skilled workers remained on the job.

The next day, tool and die craftsmen walked out of Chevrolet Gear and Axle, Chevrolet Experimental, Fisher #23, and the Fisher Body Plant in Pontiac, raising the total number of strikers to 3,500. On July 7, three more Detroit plants — Fisher #47, Fleetwood, and Ternstedt — followed suit. Over a three-day span, Reuther had brought 6,300 people out.[13]

The concept of pulling out a few plants a day — "not unlike amputating one finger at a time to cripple a hand," according to *Time* — was designed for maximum effect. In a standard strike, the initial walkout attracts great attention, but press coverage is substantially reduced within days. The gradual shutdown, however, kept the strike on the front pages and gave the public a definite sense of movement.[14]

Reuther must also have realized that a full-scale strike might fail as badly as had the UAW-AFL's effort the month before. He consequently began the strike in plants where success was assured and momentum could be established; of the first eight plants struck, six were under the jurisdiction of Reuther's local or that of a trusted ally.[15]

Reuther was understandably concerned as to whether production workers would support a strike of skilled workers. During the first few days of the strike General Motors gambled that they would not. On July 10, GM President William Knudsen announced that any employee put out of work because of the strike would become ineligible for the corporation's "Income Security Plan," which provided loans of up to 60% of the pay of laid-off employees. The same day the Pontiac Fisher Plant management issued a back-to-work order for all night-

---

[13] *United Automobile Worker*, Aug. 9, 1939, has an invaluable strike chronology.
[14] *Time*, July 17, 1939, 15.
[15] *United Automobile Worker*, Aug. 9, 1939.

and day-shift workers. Pontiac city officials promised the workers police protection to enter the plant, while UAW-CIO flying
squadrons from various Detroit locals were sent to the site to
bolster the picket lines. The police attempted six times to
remove the strikers from plant entrances, but they were con-
tinually repulsed. They made one arrest, and no injuries were
reported.

The next day plant management arranged for 30 cars to
carry workers into the plant. 1,000 picketeers, however, resisted attempts to drive through the lines. They smashed car
windows, disconnected wires, and attempted to overturn vehicles. Only five cars entered the plant as Pontiac police, caught
off guard, did little to stop the melee beyond arresting seven
strikers. Incensed, Michigan's conservative governor, Luren
Dickinson, ordered state police to the scene. Twenty state
troopers arrived early in the morning on July 12 and ordered all
but a token 40 strikers from the picket line.[16]

The UAW-CIO countered the corporation's moves with a
propaganda campaign designed to keep the nonskilled workers
in line. Reuther lashed out at the cancellation of the Income
Plan as a "piece of petty vindictiveness," while Thomas
claimed that a successful tool and die strike would put the union
in a stronger bargaining position for every worker for the next
year. "A victory for one will be a victory for all," he
proclaimed.[17] For the most part, the rank-and-file agreed. Despite the troopers' presence, a maximum of 220 production
workers crossed the picket line in Pontiac, and none of the
striking plants was able to resume production.[18]

General Motors would have liked to take its tool and die
work to local independent jobbing shops, a move that the
UAW-CIO feared would destroy the strike. Detroit jobbing
shop workers, directed by one of the UAW-CIO's leading
leftists, John Anderson, voted on July 10, however, to refuse
work on GM dies.[19] The same day, the NLRB announced that

---

[16]*Detroit News*, July 6, 1939; *Time*, July 17, 1939, 16; *Detroit News*, July 10, 1939; *United
    Automobile Worker*, July 12, 1939.
[17]*Detroit News*, July 6, 1939; "Tool and Die Strike is Your Strike, Too," Henry Kraus
    Papers, Box 15, Reuther Library; *United Automobile Worker*, July 12, 1939.
[18]The estimate of 220 workers was made by General Motors.
[19]*Detroit News*, July 10-11, 1939; *United Automobile Worker*, Aug. 9, 1939.

its investigation of GM's appeal would take "two or three months."[20]

Reuther now felt sufficiently confident to raise the strike stakes in an effort to force General Motors to open negotiations. On July 10, Cleveland's Fisher and Saginaw's Steering Gear plants became the first GM plants outside the Detroit metropolitan area to be shut down. Detroit's Cadillac workers walked out the next day, bringing the total number of strikers to 6,500. The *Wall Street Journal* commented, "General Motors must, in view of the competitive situation, find some means in the very near future of breaking the deadlock."[21]

Behind the scenes, Knudsen was seeking a way to bring the sides together. He had told Federal Mediator James Dewey, who had arrived in Detroit on July 6, that the corporation would not confer with the UAW-CIO leadership, which Knudsen considered unreliable, but the GM president was willing to meet with Philip Murray or John L. Lewis. The CIO leaders were agreeable, but only if Knudsen promised an eventual agreement. Knudsen was unwilling to give that assurance, but he agreed on July 10 to begin talks with the UAW-CIO if he could first meet with Murray. Murray arrived in Detroit on July 12 for a morning-long session with Knudsen that Dewey described as "a rough one." That afternoon, GM officials and UAW-CIO representatives, led by Reuther, opened negotiations.[22]

Reuther's primary aim in the negotiations was to fashion an agreement that would eliminate the UAW-AFL. Secondarily, he needed to wring some shop-floor concessions from General Motors to satisfy the strikers. The corporation, on the other hand, wanted to concede as little as possible to the workers, but, like Reuther, was more than anxious to put an end to dual unionism. The UAW's instability, Knudsen complained, had caused 435 strikes since 1937; the time had come, he said "to

[20]*Wall Street Journal*, July 12, 1939.
[21]*Ibid.*, July 13, 1939.
[22]James F. Dewey to J. R. Steelman, July 7, 1939, Federal Mediation and Conciliation Service Collection (partially unprocessed collection), Reuther Library (henceforth Conciliation Service Collection will be referred to as CS); Dewey to Carl R. Schedler, July 10, 1939, CS.

settle the whole issue now and forever."[23]

Little progress was made in the first week of talks as both sides waited to see whether events outside the conference room would change the strike's status. Governor Dickinson, seemingly convinced that the threat of anarchy in Pontiac had abated, withdrew the state troopers on July 13. The same day workers in Flint Fisher #1 voted to strike, giving Reuther the ability to shut down another major production center at any time. Mounted police clashed with pickets on July 14 at the Cleveland Fisher Body Plant gates. Two strikers were injured in the five-minute skirmish.[24]

The big break in the strike came on July 18, when Detroit Packard Local 190, the UAW-AFL's largest local, switched to the CIO. It was a serious blow to the UAW-AFL's claim of legitimacy, one the *Wall Street Journal* claimed signaled the end of dual unionism in the auto industry.[25]

The next day General Motors offered to recognize the UAW-CIO as the exclusive bargaining for those plants, 41 in all, where only the UAW-CIO had established committees. The appropriate local was to have complete control of the substitution of committeemen, making it practically impossible for the UAW-AFL to replace the UAW-CIO in any of the 41 plants. In return for this concession, the UAW-CIO was not to call any strike, tolerate any wild-cat walkout, or demand any adjustment in the contract for its duration.[26]

The GM proposal placed Reuther in a dilemma. It promised the virtual elimination of the UAW-AFL by limiting it to the 11 plants where both unions had established committees, but Reuther, as the president of a local, had long opposed the centralization of power in the International that the no-strike pledge implied. He must have realized, however, that his own chances of ascending to the presidency of the UAW-CIO would be greatly enhanced if he showed the CIO leaders his willingness to control rank-and-file wildcatters. Led by Reuther, the

---

[23]Dewey to Steelman, July 13, 1939, CS.

[24]Dewey to AWS, July 15, 1939, CS; *Detroit News*, July 12-14, 1939.

[25]*Wall Street Journal*, July 19, 1939.

[26]General Motors and UAW notes, undated, Reuther Collection, Box 26, Folder 16; Dewey to Schendler, July 19, 1939, CS.

negotiators consequently accepted GM's proposal.[27]

The UAW-CIO next wanted to settle the representation issue in the 11 disputed plants. Having refused to recognize either union in the plants, the corporation at the time dealt with employee grievances in these plants on an individual basis but refused to enter into collective bargaining. GM now agreed to meet with representatives of the International for grievance cases but it still would not bargain. The change in GM's position was nevertheless significant since it amounted to an admission by the corporation that the UAW-CIO did represent at least some of the men in these plants.

Reuther was now anxious to find some means of determining whether the UAW-CIO or the UAW-AFL represented the workers in the disputed plants. GM continued to press its appeal to the NLRB, while the UAW-CIO proposed the creation of a three-man board to decide the matter, one member from both the UAW-CIO and the UAW-AFL, and the third appointed by the Department of Labor. GM opposed the idea and the issue remained unresolved until the NLRB concluded its investigation. Eventually, NLRB elections would be held, and the UAW-CIO would win a convincing victory.[28]

The union and the company had cooperated to emasculate the UAW-AFL, but they clashed over shop-floor concessions. From the opening of negotiations, General Motors had refused to negotiate on a company-wide basis. Accordingly, Reuther proposed on July 14 that the corporation give special concessions to the 1,600 skilled craftsmen of Fisher #23. "In the Fisher 23 Plant here last year," he argued, "men with upwards of five years seniority obtained only six weeks of work in the entire year." He proposed that skilled workers with seniority be guaranteed 1,250 hours of work or its equivalent in pay annually. Should work be moved to another plant, the craftsmen were to be transferred with their jobs.

General Motors was receptive to negotiations on a single-plant basis. The company's representatives promised to study

[27]General Motors and UAW notes, undated, Reuther Collection, Box 26, Folder 16.
[28]General Motors and UAW notes, undated, Reuther Collection, Box 26, Folder 17. The disputed plants were: Flint Fisher #1, Fisher-Tarrytown, Chevrolet-Flint, Chevrolet-Tarrytown, Chevrolet Gray Iron Foundry, Guide Lamp, Delco-Remy Anderson, Pontiac Motor, Cadillac Motor, Buick Motor, and Delco-Remy Kokomo.

ways to bring more work into the plant but stopped short of guaranteed hours. They did promise workers the chance to change plants, however, and extended the Income Security Plan to newly-hired skilled workers, who had not previously been covered. The union accepted the offer.[29]

GM hoped to use the Fisher #23 agreement as a model for further plant-by-plant negotiations, but when the *Wall Street Journal* reported that the UAW-CIO had backed away from its insistence on a company-wide agreement, the union issued a quick denial, claiming it would accept no "piecemeal peace."[30]

It appeared that General Motors had changed its position when company negotiators on July 16 proposed a $1,200 annual guaranteed wage. Corporation officials in New York, who firmly opposed any wage concessions, ordered the offer withdrawn that afternoon. The UAW-CIO was incensed,[31] and it became increasingly clear that the wage issue was to be the most difficult strike issue to resolve.

The negotiators turned instead to the question of overtime pay. The UAW-CIO requested the eight-hour day, the 40 hour week, and the doubletime pay for overtime. The union also asked for doubletime on Sunday and six holidays: New Year's, Memorial Day, the Fourth of July, Labor Day, Armistice Day, and Christmas. GM agreed to doubletime on holidays, but rejected double pay for overtime except in Fisher #23, where, "on account of special conditions," the corporation granted Sunday doubletime. GM added an important qualifier, however: since the union's primary purpose was to maintain Sunday as a day of rest, only those employees not normally required to work Sundays were to qualify for overtime, which would prevent many workers from receiving any extra pay. Trapped by its own rhetoric, the UAW-CIO accepted the qualifier but held out for Sunday doubletime in all plants and time-and-a-half for Saturday work in excess of 40 hours. The corporation agreed to the demand.[32]

---

[29]General Motors and UAW notes, undated, Reuther Collection, Box 26, Folder 16; Dewey to Steelman, July 14, 1939, CS.
[30]Wall Street Journal, July 15, 1939; *United Automobile Worker*, July 19, 1939.
[31]Dewey to Schendler, July 17, 1939, CS.
[32]General Motors and UAW notes, undated, Reuther Collection, Box 26, Folder 16; Dewey to Schendler, July 19, 1939, CS.

70

GM was unyielding on the union label issue. The UAW-CIO proposed that union representatives be given all the time necessary to afix a union label on all dies, tools, jigs, and fixtures in the plants. Of all the UAW-CIO demands, the label "irked General Motors most," *Time* claimed, because it would limit the corporation's choice of the union with which it had to deal. Although GM rejected the UAW-CIO's proposal, it promised to accept labeled parts made in the jobbing shops if the union would not discriminate against unlabeled parts brought into company plants.

Reuther must have had mixed feelings about the GM proposal. If he accepted the GM proposal, it meant that he had failed to introduce the label into GM plants, but he felt confident that the now inevitable collapse of the UAW-AFL would make the battle for the label easier in the years to come. GM's concession, furthermore, gave the UAW-CIO the chance to fulfill the long-held goal of introducing the union label into organized jobbing shops, a move shop owners had opposed because GM had refused to use labeled parts. Reuther consequently accepted the GM offer.[33]

By July 19, only the wage issue remained to be settled. The UAW-CIO negotiators called for at least a ten-cent an hour increase for all tool and die, engineering, and maintenance workers. They also sought to even out wage differentials by proposing company-wide rates for a detailed list of 44 skilled job classifications: 26 tool and die jobs, two drop forge, five maintenance, and 11 engineering positions. Each type of worker was to receive a beginning wage of at least $1.00 an hour, with the highest wage, $1.45 an hour, going to patternmakers, pattern checkers, and sheet metal power hammermen. The union proposed an average wage of $1.30 an hour.[34]

Despite previous indications to the contrary, General Motors was not prepared to negotiate on a company-wide basis and certainly was not willing to grant a ten-cent a hour wage boost. Mediator Dewey suggested that the matter be submitted

---

[33]General Motors and UAW notes, undated, Reuther Collection, Box 26, Folder 16; *Time*, July 17, 1939, p. 15.
[34]General Motors and UAW notes, undated, Reuther Collection, Box 26, Folder 16.

to arbitration, but GM resisted. As the strike entered its fourth week, the talks bogged down.[35]

Reuther hoped to break the deadlock by once again applying pressure on the corporation. On July 23, powerhouse men voted to join the strike should negotiations not conclude soon. The next day tool and die workers in Flint Fisher #1 struck, the first to walk out since negotiations had begun. Reuther had picked the plant carefully: Not only was it an important unit within the corporation, but it was also one of the 11 plants with both UAW-AFL and UAW-CIO committees and the site of the UAW-AFL's failed general strike the month before.[36]

The UAW-CIO next announced plans to bring the strike to the corporation's front door on July 25 with mass picketing at GM headquarters in Detroit. Knudsen threatened to break off talks in retaliation, but when Dewey got Reuther to agree to a two-day postponement of the action, the GM president backed down.

The Detroit police expected trouble, but Reuther was determined to prove that he could maintain the worker discipline that had characterized the strike to that point. Over 8,000 UAW-CIO pickets marched eleven abreast around the GM Building to the taunts of the office workers inside. The only violence during the hour-long demonstration was caused by two motorists who were distracted by the display and collided.[37]

As July came to a close, the UAW-CIO also began to feel the pressure to settle the strike. When union tool and die workers in Frederick Colman and Sons, Inc., a Detroit jobbing shop, blocked General Motors truckers from removing completed GM dies from the Colman Plant on July 26, the corporation secured a writ of replevin that was to be enforced on July 28. When GM truckers, accompanied by sheriff's deputies, arrived at the plant, however, they found that workers inside the shop had blocked the door with scrap metal. Union pickets then pushed the deputies out of the way and attacked the trucks with a barrage of rocks. Order was restored in a few minutes, but the police and the workers remained at a standoff throughout the afternoon until UAW-CIO Secretary-Treasurer Addes

---

[35]General Motors and UAW notes, undated, *Ibid.*, Box 26, Folder 17.
[36]*United Automobile Worker*, Aug. 9, 1939; *Wall Street Journal*, July 25, 1939.
[37]*Detroit News*, July 27, 1939.

arrived to counsel against violence and to explain to the men that GM had a legal right to the dies. The workers then permitted the trucks to proceed.[38]

Reuther's hopes for a peaceful strike collapsed in Cleveland, where he enjoyed less control than in Detroit. City Security Director Eliot Ness had ordered the pickets to keep the Fisher Plant gates clear following the brief July 14 scuffle. The Cleveland UAW-CIO challenged this edict on July 31, massing over 5,000 pickets at the plant to prevent the morning shift from entering. When a striker tossed a brick through the window of a car attempting to drive workers into the plant, the police sought to disperse the pickets by lobbing tear gas into the crowd from the factory windows 300 yards away. Fearing that the men, some of whom tossed the shells back at the windows, were going to rush the plant, the police turned high-power water hoses on the throng. Thirty-four strikers were injured, none seriously.[39]

The AFL, hoping that the violence would undermine the strike's effectiveness and that the walkout's duration would drain the UAW-CIO's treasury, launched a counter-offensive at the end of July. Meeting in Detroit on July 29 to plan an organized response to the strike, the presidents of 15 AFL building trades union ordered their workers not to honor UAW-CIO picket lines. UAW-AFL officials met the same day to begin reorganizing their Detroit GM locals. The Federation sent 35 of its most experienced organizers to aid in the rehabilitation of the UAW-AFL, while the union formally required NLRB elections in all GM plants.[40] It appeared that Martin's union, dormant for the preceeding month, was to be revived.

Reuther's fear of a resurgent UAW-AFL, coupled with General Motors' losses of a million dollars a day, forced the two sides to resume serious negotiations on wages. On July 28, the corporation seemed to back away from its opposition to a wage increase. Murray rejoined the negotiations the next day

---

[38]*Ibid.*, July 28, 1939.
[39]Kraus Papers, Box 15, contains a copy of the edict. For details on the riot, see *Detroit News*, July 31, 1939.
[40]*Wall Street Journal*, Aug. 2, 1939. Not every AFL union opposed the UAW-CIO strike. Reuther proudly displayed a letter from a local of the International Association of Machinists pledging its support.

while Dewey, pressing for a settlement, threatened to go public with a statement as to just how little separated the two sides.[41]

The negotiators finally reached an acceptable compromise on August 2 — wage rates were to be set for numerous classifications of tool and die and maintenance workers in Fisher #23, and these rates were to serve as a standard for wage rates in other plants. The plants involved were put into two groups. The first group, in which wages were to correspond to those in Fisher #23, was made up of Fisher #21 and #37, Ternstedt, and Fleetwood, all in Detroit, Pontiac Fisher, and Fisher #1 in Flint. The second group — Cadillac, Chevrolet Gear and Axle, Chevrolet Experimental, Pontiac Motor, Buick, Chevrolet Flint, Oldsmobile, Fisher-Lansing, and Fisher-Cleveland — was to receive wages no more than five cents below the Fisher #23 rates. Although General Motors, technically, did not submit to a company-wide agreement, as each plant was to set its own wage scale in negotiations between union committeemen and management, the required adherence to the Fisher #23 model virtually eliminated wage differentials.[42]

General Motors won a major victory on the wage issue, however. The agreement set minimum and maximum rates for 25 job classification. Only one position, die maker, received a maximum wage greater than the union proposed, while seven classifications received maximum wages equal to the proposal, and eight received maximums five, ten, *or* fifteen cents an hour less than the union had requested. For example, according to the union proposal, a pipefitter was to earn $1.25 an hour, whereas under the final agreement, he earned a maximum of $1.10 and a minumum of 95 cents, and then only if he worked in Fisher #23 or the other six plants of equal status. The maximum rate for every classification of maintenance worker was below that of the proposal, and engineering workers were not even included in the plan.[43]

Although Reuther and the union negotiators did not win a

[41]Dewey to Steelman, July 29, 31. Aug. 3, 1939, CS.
[42]Dewey to Steelman, Aug. 3, 1939, CS.
[43]Reuther Collection, Box 26, Folders 16-17, contain copies of the proposed supplement and the final agreement.

complete victory on the wage issue, they had negotiated an agreement that they found quite satisfactory. The UAW-CIO and General Motors signed the agreement on August 4, bringing the 29 day strike to an end. The rank-and-file ratified the contract the next day, an overwhelming 7,500 of 7,600 workers giving their approval. Production on the 1940 model cars resumed on August 7.[44]

The contract crushed the UAW-AFL's planned revival. As the *Wall Street Journal* pointed out, "Unquestionable domination of organized automotive labor by the CIO's United Workers' Union is clearly foreshadowed by terms of the settlement of the union's July 5-August 5 strike . . ." General Motors, which, according to Dewey, was anxious to "finally . . . get rid of Martin," still pushed for NLRB elections.[45] Agreeing, the UAW-CIO scored a resounding victory when the vote was finally held in GM plants on April 17, 1940: 84,024 workers backed the CIO, 25,911 supported the AFL, and 13,919 approved of neither.[46]

Reuther also made it clear that the rank-and-file agitation that had caused such instability in the early UAW-CIO would no longer be tolerated. "Members have been given notice," he declared, "that when they get out of line in the future, there will be no wildcat departmental strikes to back them up."[47] He had proved his ability to orchestrate a strike; now he set out to show his skill in managing a union.

The General Motors tool and die strike had been decisive for the UAW-CIO. Walter Reuther had set himself on the road to the union presidency by destroying the UAW-AFL while showing a flair for organization, negotiation, and the formulation of strategy. Though the UAW-CIO was not yet powerful enough to wring substantial shop-floor concessions from the corporation, it had put itself in a position to do so in the years to come. Reuther later called the strike the beginning of the union's "renaissance,"[48] but it was actually more a rite of

---

[44]*Detroit News*, Aug. 4, 1939.
[45]*Wall Street Journal*, Aug. 7, 1939; Dewey to Steelman, Aug. 2, 1939, CS.
[46]Bernstein, 569. Martin was ousted from the UAW-AFL presidency in late 1940.
[47]*Wall Street Journal*, Aug. 7, 1939.
[48]Cormier and Eaton, 156.

passage. Although the UAW was still to be plagued by factionalism, it no longer had to contend with a rival for leadership
of the auto workers.

THE LIMITS OF SHOP FLOOR STRUGGLE: WORKERS VS. THE BEDAUX SYSTEM AT WILLAPA HARBOR LUMBER MILLS, 1933–35

by

Jeremy R. Egolf*

In 1933 the Weyerhaeuser Timber Company (WTC), then the largest company in the milling of timber in the northwestern U. S., initiated the Bedaux system of bonus wages and speedup in its subsidiary Willapa Harbor Lumber Mills (WHLM). The millworkers objected strenuously from the first appearance of the stop-watch bearing time-studies men. The ensuing 17-month struggle at the shop floor and through the union the workers formed culminated in the spring of 1935 in the removal of the Bedaux system from the plant. Several leaders went on to active roles in the conflicts between pro-and anti-Communist factions in the International Woodworkers of America (IWA-CIO) in the late 1930s and early 1940s. The anti-Bedaux fight thus offers light on the question of whether or not antagonisms of this sort over the use of speedup and more direct controls by management over the workplace necessarily carry workers beyond pure-and-simple business industrial unionism into more explicitly anti-capitalist thinking and movements.[1]

Workers' struggles for dignity and control at the point of production have been a central concern of recent studies in labor history. The work of David Montgomery, for example, in-

---

* The author gratefully acknowledges the comments by Joseph Lawrence, Norbert MacDonald, Gordon F. Moir, William W. Wallace, Jerry Lee Lembcke, Marty Hart-Landsberg, and, especially, Virginia Brodine on earlier drafts of this article.
[1] For the IWA, see Vernon Jensen, *Lumber and Labor* (New York, 1945), and a view friendly to the left wing, William Tattam and Jerry Lembcke, *One Union in Wood* (New York, 1984).

dicates that machinists and other industrial craftsmen were at
the heart of both the socialist and anti-scientific management
movements during the first two decades of the 20th century, but
the relationship between the active members of the two movements remains unclear. Montgomery and others working in the
field have thus far not fully explored the responses of less
skilled workers to management imposition of new methods and
organization of work in the later decades of the twentieth century. And, as David Brody has pointed out, we lack analyses of
shop-floor conditions in mass production industries during the
1930s. We need to know the degree of workers' control of production and on-the-job independence. How did management's
alteration of such independence influence the early development
of the industrial unions which formed the core of the CIO?[2]

The struggle against the Bedaux system shaped the early history of the Federal Labor Union (FLU) which the WHLM workers established in 1934 under the AFL, but the WHLM experience suggests that there is no simple relationship between
anti-speed-up or other struggles at the point of production and
overtly anti-capitalist movements at a given locale. Opposition
to the Bedaux system was rooted ideologically not only in the
workers' control and direct action legacy of the IWW, but also
in liberal pluralist notions of the democratic rights of free,
white, male American workers. The aftermath of the struggle
indicates that rank-and-file unionists fighting to preserve or restore the comparative benefits they see in their accustomed way
of work do not necessarily support, and may even vigorously
fight, politics whose ultimate goal is to give working people the
balance of power in decisions regarding capital investment,

---

[2] David Montgomery, *Workers' Control in America* (Cambridge, 1979); David Brody, "The
Old Labor History and The New: In Search of an American Working Class," *Labor His-
tory*, 20 (1979), 111-126, "Radical Labor History and Rank and File Militancy," *Labor
History*, 16 (1975), 117-126; Hugh G. J. Aitkin, *Taylorism at Watertown Arsenal* (Cambridge, MA, 1960); Katherine Stone, "The Origins of Job Structures in the Steel Industry," *Radical America*, #7, 19-66; Harry Braverman, *Labor and Monopoly Capital* (New
York, 1974), 85-138; Daniel Nelson, *Managers and Workers* (Madison, 1975), *passim*,
"Scientific Management, Systematic Management and Labor, 1888-1915," *Business His-
tory Review*, 48 (1974), 479-500, "Taylorism and the Workers at Bethlehem Steel," *Penn-
sylvania Magazine of History and Biography*, 101 (1977), 479-500, "The New Factory
System and the Unions: The National Cash Register Company Dispute of 1901," *Labor
History*, 15 (1974), 163-178; Jeremy Brecher, "Uncovering the Hidden History of the
Workplace," *Review of Radical Political Economics*, (Winter, 1978), 1-23.

technological change, and the distribution of wealth, as well as the ability to determine their conditions of work.

The WHLM was created as a corporate entity May 6, 1931, when the Weyerhaeuser Co. financed the merger of a block of its own vast timberlands with the greater part of several nearly bankrupt companies' assets—especially mill facilities—in Southwest Washington's Pacific County. The WHLM held 190,000 of the county's 271,000 acres of privately owned timber, and locational factors favored the company's cutting most of the county's 115,200 acres of government forests. By 1933, the WHLM's three sawmills, located at Raymond and South Bend, were able to produce about 600,000 board feet of lumber per eight hour shift, the sixth largest plant capacity in the Douglas fir region. Although there were lesser saw and shingle mills, box factories, and an extensive oyster fishery and canning industry in the county, the WHLM immediately became the area's dominant employer. The WHLM's mill and logging camp work force of over 1000 men included nearly one-fifth of the county's male population over ten years old.[3]

One of the WHLM's predecessor companies had been affiliated with the Loyal Legion of Loggers and Lumbermen (4L), an industry-wide federation of client unions. Following the merger, J. W. Lewis, WHLM's first general manager, promptly enrolled the company's other mill units in the 4L.[4] The 4L had been formed late in 1917 by lumber operators and the U. S. Army,

---

[3] Ralph W. Hidy, et al, Timber and Men (New York, 1963), 401; "Plan of Merger of Willapa Lumber Company, Raymond Lumber Company, and Lewis Mills and Timber Company with Certain Properties of Weyerhaeuser Timber Company," Weyerhaeuser Timber Company Executive Committee Minutes, 22-27 (Weyerhaeuser Company Historical Archives); Weyerhaeuser Timber Company Executive Committee Minutes, Mar. 4-7, Nov. 3, Dec. 4 and 20, 1930; Willapa Harbor Lumber Mills Articles of Incorporation, in "Willapa Harbor Lumber Mills Corporate Meetings," (Weyerhaeuser Company Historical Archives); transcript of "Hearing in the Matter of Willapa Harbor Lumber Mills and Sawmill and Timber Workers No. 19446, Raymond, Washington, Feb. 15-16, 1935," Case File 333, Office of the Executive Secretary, Records of the National Labor Relations Board, 1933-1935, Record Group 25, National Archives, 259-260, 268-9, 313 (J. W. Lewis testimony), and 296, 301-2 (W. H. Turner) (This transcript will hereafter be cited as NLRB-Willapa Transcript); Timberman, June 1931, 142; Willapa Harbor Pilot, May 14, 1931; 4L Lumber News, June 1933, notes the total mill capacity at Raymond was 620,000 board feet per day, of which 400,000 was attributed to the WHLM.
[4] W. C. Ruegnitz to C. H. Ingram, April 20, 1931, W. C. Ruegnitz to C. L. Lewis, April 20 and 30, 1931, both in William C. Ruegnitz Papers/1/18, University of Washington (hereafter cited as WCR); Timberman, June 1931, 142-44; "NLRB-Willapa Transcript," 41, 258, 316 (Lewis).

apparently with the blessing of then AFL President Samuel
Gompers. Its purpose was to break the power of the IWW in
the Northwest woods, where a prolonged series of strikes, wildcats, and slowdowns was threatening the production of spruce
for war-planes. The result was a military occupation of logging
camps (two armed soldiers for every seven civilian workers), imposition of loyalty oaths, and similar forms of intimidation coupled with the concession of the eight hour day and marked
though temporary improvements in logging camp housing and
sanitation. Membership was mandatory for all mill and camp
operators and was generally forced on the workers. The membership contract forbade strikes. Government support was withdrawn at war's end, but the peacetime 4L's were retained at numerous mills and were revived during the National Recovery
Administration (NRA) period, 1933-35, as operators hastened
to comply with the collective bargaining provisions of the 1933
National Industrial Recovery Act.[5]

The 4L's ties with operators and trade associations and its
corporatist approach to uniting workers and management in a
single organization were themselves incorporated in the NRA
Code of Fair Competition for the Lumber and Timber Products
Industries. The Code designated the 4L as the agency to set
wage and hours regulations in the Douglas fir and western pine
districts. Operators attempted to use the Lumber Code administration to strengthen the 4L against the AFL but unionists
turned to representation elections supervised by the NRA's National and Regional Labor Boards. The 4Ls were broken in
western Washington and the lower Columbia basin by the 1935
northwest lumber strike, but their life elsewhere was terminated
only when the Supreme Court upheld the National Labor Relations Act outlawing company unions in 1937.[6]

WHLM manager J. W. Lewis served periodically on the 4L's

---

[5] For the 4L's origins, see Harold M. Hyman, *Soldiers and Spruce* (Los Angeles, 1963), and
Robert Fickens, "The Wobbly Horrors: Pacific Northwest Lumbermen and the Industrial Workers of the World, 1917-1918," in *Labor History*, 24 (1983), 325-341. For the
4L's in the 1930s, see Jensen, Chapts. 6 and 7, and Jeremy R. Egolf, "Labor Control in
Crisis: The 4L and the Bedaux System in the U. S. Northwest Lumber Industry, 1931-
1935," (unpublished MA Essay, Univ. of British Columbia, 1980), Chapts. 1-3.
[6] Jensen, Chapts. 8 and 9; Egolf, Chapt. 3.

Board of Directors between 1931 and 1935. During the summer of 1933 (NRA Code-writing period) he was a member of the West Coast Lumbermen's Association Logging Labor Committee. He also sat on the Joint Committee on Labor, established under the Lumber Code Authority by five Douglas fir trade associations to investigate alleged violations of Code wage and hours rules. Thus, the anti-Bedaux struggle meant fighting one of the Northwest's leading corporate paternalists, a man who was also associated with the New Deal's quasi-governmental administrative bodies.[7]

During the NRA period, Lewis used Pacific County's economic dependence on the WHLM to cow those who opposed his anti-union position and to justify his rationalization of shop management methods. Shortly after assuming management, Lewis had the combined output of the WHLM's two Raymond mills increased from 325,000 to 400,000 board feet (bf) per day, largely by speeding up the mill transport systems to their full capacity. A plant modernization program overhauled and speeded up power, transfer, and manufacturing equipment, improved transport between shops and brought better physical integration of sawmills, dry kilns, storage sheds, and planing mills. Average hourly capacity was thus expanded from 49,207 bf in 1931, to 61,000 bf during the first half of 1933.[8]

The combined costs of capital improvements, debt service to the WTC, and the general price decline and market collapse resulted in a $750,000 loss for the WHLM's first two years of operation. The company's financial problems, as well as a desire to take advantage of the rising market for lumber which developed in the first months of the New Deal, were ample moti-

---

[7] Minutes, 4L Board of Directors and 4L Washington Fir Districts Board, 1931-35, passim; Minutes of Logging and Lumber Labor Committees, June 21, 1933, in St. Paul and Tacoma Lumber Company Papers/35/4L, Univ. of Washington (hereafter cited as "SPT"); Minutes, Joint Committee on Labor, 1933-35, West Coast Lumbermen's Association Papers, Oregon State Historical Society; For Lewis and the 4 see also Egolf, Chapt. 4, footnotes 5 and 7.

[8] "NLRB-Willapa Transcript," J. W. Lewis to Our Employees, Sept. 12, 1934, (Respondent's Exhibit "A"); *ibid*, 259-60, 268 (Turner); Raymond *Advertiser* Jan. 17 and April 18, 1935; *West Coast Lumberman*, July, 1931, 58-59; unsigned affidavit, Sept. 1933, in J. P. Weyerhaeuser, Jr. Papers/3/Code Matters (hereafter cited as "JPW") (Weyerhaeuser Company Historical Archives).

81

vation for Lewis to consider use of the Bedaux system which
promised to use the WHLM's work force to its physical limits,
without entailing further expenditures for upgrading plant and
equipment. In the Autumn of 1933, Lewis, with the WTC general management's encouragement, invited the Bedaux Company to install its system at the WHLM's Raymond mills.[9]

The Charles E. Bedaux Co., established in 1916, utilized
work accounting and control methods generally derived from
the Taylorism of the 1900-1920 period.[10] Like Taylor, Bedaux'
stated goal was the increase of profits through cutting labor
costs and increasing productivity without reducing individual
workers' take-home pay. Taylor's methods often involved the
revision of the work process itself, transforming it into a series
of simple, repetitive motions, thereby undermining the power of
skilled workers (and the craft unions which defended them in
the market place). The Bedaux system, which might be characterized as the "Taylorism of the Depression," was principally a
method of speeding up the already mechanized, subdivided, and
simplified labor of unskilled and semiskilled industrial operatives, generally introducing only minor changes in the work process as such. At Raymond, at least, the Bedaux system had little
impact on the craftsmen ancillary to the main line of the production process. What it did do was alter the management of
production, the "direction, evaluation, and incentive" of work,
changing the relationship between workers and foremen, and
enabling upper management to see statistically how much was
produced by each and every worker on the shop floor.[11]

The heart of the Bedaux system was the standardization of
production quotas as "B units." For each task, the standard

9 J. W. Lewis to C. H. Ingram, Oct. 19, 25, and 30, 1933, in Charles H. Ingram Papers/1/
   Willapa Harbor (hereafter cited as "CHI"), Weyerhaeuser Company Historical Archives;
   "NLRB-Willapa Transcript," 269 and 285 (J. W. Lewis) and 185 (E. Younglove); J. W.
   Lewis to F. R. Titcomb, Feb. 13, 1934, and J. W. Lewis to C. H. Ingram, Feb. 12, 1934,
   both in F. R. Titcomb Papers/2/Willapa Harbor, Weyerhaeuser Company Historical
   Archives.
10 For the Bedaux system, see Geoffrey C. Brown, "The Bedaux System," *American Federa-
   tionist*, 45 (1938), 942-949; Janet Flanner, "Annals of Collaboration: Equivalism," *New
   Yorker*, Sept. 22, 1945, 28-47, Oct. 6, 1945, 32-45, and Oct. 13, 1945, 32-48; Charles
   Higham, *Trading With The Enemy* (New York, 1978), 165-66, 177, and Chapt. 10.
11 Richard Edwards, *Contested Terrain* (New York, 1978), *passim*; the author is indebted to
   David Montgomery for the concept of "Taylorism of the Depression."

minute of 60 seconds was translated into a B unit including work time and some vaguely determined fatigue or rest time. When a plant department was selected for initiating the system, time-study men charted the movements of a fast worker, timed each component motion, and adjusted the timing after guessing how hard the man or woman was actually laboring. Time in minutes was established for each task, and a standard rate of performance in B units was calculated. When the system was fully installed, workers were paid a bonus for completion of B units above those mandated for a day's work by the Bedaux engineers. Foremen received a premium which was deducted from the workers' bonuses; in effect, the workers paid the foremen for speeding them up.

Geoffrey Brown, an industrial engineer retained by the AFL in 1930 to analyze the Bedaux system, found numerous shortcomings. Although Brown accepted F. W. Taylor's changes in materials routing and factory supply, in careful studies of machine feeds and speeds, and in other aspects of factory work and organization as methods for increasing production and profits, he noted that under Bedaux improvements in work process had been "neglected or rendered secondary to speeding up of the work force." Bedaux engineers were brought into the shops without consulting the workers; the laborers' experience and intelligence were not utilized in devising methods for improving the production process. Nor could the engineers, who typically had little knowledge of or experience with the work they were observing, intelligently suggest improvements. The workers underwent unnecessary physical and mental stress while their standard rates were finally juggled to realistic levels. The B units were needlessly mystifying; specific quotas of things to be produced struck Brown as being more sensible. While some individuals' earnings might be increased with Bedaux incentives, the workers' wages per unit were invariably reduced. It was impossible to standardize highly skilled work; production was spoiled as quality was sacrificed for quantity. Brown concluded that the "Bedaux system, stripped of its pseudo-technical verbiage, is nothing more or less than a method of

83

forcing the last ounce of effort out of workers at the smallest possible cost in wages"; in short, "Work like hell."[12]

By the 1920s, the Bedaux Company had grown to a European-headquartered multi-national consulting firm with branch offices in such diverse cities as Paris, London, Milan, Berlin, Stockholm, Sydney, New York, Chicago, and Portland, Oregon. At its height, the Bedaux system was used to control the labor of 675,000 workers by 720 companies, including Fiat, Swift, Jantzen, Campbell Soup, DuPont, General Motors, General Electric, Eastman Kodak, Levi-Strauss, Crown Zellerbach, and B. F. Goodrich.[13]

In practice, foremen and production workers were noticeably less pleased with Bedaux's "happy relationship" than were the centralizers and accountants. An observer at one Oregon lumber mill noted that although Bedaux methods did reduce planing mill costs 15%, the workers' response ranged "all the way from uneasiness to mental 'bloody murder.'" In a regionally publicized strike in the autumn of 1934, the killing gangs of Swift's Portland, Oregon, meat packing plant demanded the removal of the "infamous speed up B system," declaring that "Chicago stockyard standards will not suffice for the people here." A spontaneous anti-Bedaux strike wave swept non-union southern textile mills during the spring of 1929, and repeated strikes, including wildcats, were waged against the system at Ohio rubber plants from 1934 to 1936.[14] Events at the WHLM fell within this current of opposition, and illuminate the relationship among established workplace practices and the relations of work, management innovations, and the ideological parameters of struggle at the point of production.

Raymond, located near the southwest coast of Washington and isolated from larger towns by long miles of virgin forests, had a regional reputation as a "wild timber town." Pacific

---

12 Brown.
13 C. W. English to E. G. Griggs II, Nov. 6, 1934, in SPT/51/E. G. Griggs; Flanner, *passim*; Daniel Bell, *Work and its Discontents* (Boston, 1956), 9; *Timberman*, Jan. 1931, 20, June, 1931, back cover, and July, 1931, back cover. See also Egolf, 68-72.
14 H. E. Vaness to 4L Headquarters, Nov. 25, 1936, in WCR/1/18; *Washington State Labor News*, Sept. 21, 1934, 1; Tacoma *Labor Advocate*, Oct. 12, 1934, 1; *Monthly Labor Review*, May, 1929, 171-72; Ruth McKenney, *Industrial Valley* (New York, 1935), 166-67, and 269.

County's 1930 population was 14,970, including 5420 male wage earners over ten years of age; 1024 of these worked at saw and planing mills while another 1078 worked in logging (i.e., about 14% of the entire county population was composed of males working in the timber industry). Raymond's 1930 population of 3828 included nearly equal numbers of married men and women over 15 years old, but there were 320 more single men than women in this age group, indicative of the overwhelmingly male and, in good measure, transient quality of loggers. In December 1934, 392 workers were employed at the WHLM's Raymond plant, 92 at the company's South Bend sawmill, and another 82 at the WHLM shingle mill.[15]

The small entreprenurial class was heavily dependent on the patronage of mill workers, loggers, and longshoremen. The four block long First Street skid road, livelier than the similar area in the larger timber cities on Grays Harbor, 30 miles to the north, boasted at least 16 taverns and pool halls, 13 brothels, and numerous hotels and boarding houses catering to the transients. Credit from grocers, restaurants, and taverns helped workers survive the Depression and aided the success of the 1934 longshore and 1935 lumber strikes. Although Seattle and timber towns including Bellingham, Mt. Vernon, Tacoma, Everett, and Aberdeen had flourishing unemployed movements by 1932, no such organization seems to have taken root in Pacific County during the early 1930s. Raymond's First Street social life and inter-occupational mobility among "stump farmers," dock and mill workers, loggers, and shingle weavers facilitated solidarity among workers.[16] This gave the broad working class familiarity with the saga of the IWW and its repression by the hated 4L's.

Weyerhaeuser's entry into the community to become the dominant employer magnified existing social divisions; the Louisiana origins of J. W. Lewis helped to characterize the new economic era in the minds of local inhabitants as potentially one of

[15] Gordon F. Moir interview, April 1, 1983; U. S. Bureau of the Census, Fifteenth Census, 1930, *Population Vol. I* (USGPO, 1930), 1150; *ibid.*, *Vol. III:2*, 1220, 1234; *Census of Manufactures, 1929, Vol. III*, 540; J. W. Lewis to C. H. Ingram, Dec. 8, 1934, in CHI/2b/Labor.
[16] Author's interviews with Clifford Kight, Jan. 9, 1981; C. W. Sowers, Nov. 15, 1980; Jack Spurrell, Jan. 9, 1981; and Edson Stallcop, May 4, 1980.

enslavement to the absentee-owned WHLM. As a local insurance agent described the situation to President Roosevelt, Lewis

> came here from Louisiana where he had nothing but niggers (sic) and
> poor kind of white men to deal with and he cannot, or will not, get used·
> to dealing with a white man . . . . He would not be dictated to by the
> government, by the state, or by the county. He was running the business.[17]

The racism exemplified by the statement—one which also summed
up unionists' typical characterization of Lewis as a "slavedriver"
—may have undermined class consciousness by casting the
struggle for unionism in terms of the rights of free white male
workers rather than the needs of all workers regardless of race
or gender. But it was also a reflection of industrial demograph-
ics. In Louisiana, 37.5% of all employed people in 1930 were
black, as were 45% of woods workers and 64.9% of saw and
planing mill operatives. In contrast, only 29 of Washington's
51,683 loggers and millworkers were black. Pacific County's entire reported black population that year consisted of two males
(occupation unrecorded) residing in the oceanside communities
of Ilwaco and Long Beach.[18]

Although there is no evidence that the WHLM employed
women in production jobs, 66 of the 860 Pacific County women
tallied as employed in 1930 worked in various wood working industries, predominantly box factories. Other major occupational categories included 92 women employed in agriculture (this
figure may have included seafood processing); 82 in wholesale
trade; 175 in professional or semiprofessional work; and 133 in
miscellaneous domestic and allied trades. Of particular significance for the organized labor movement were the 110 women
employed in hotel and restaurant work; many of these were
unionized in 1934, permitting workers to take their leisure in
"fair" premises and probably contributing to community-wide,
cross-gender union consciousness. Pearl Sowers, the Culinary
Workers, Cooks, and Bartenders business agent who organized

---

[17] M. N. Ryder to F. D. Roosevelt, July 21, 1935, in Federal Meditation and Conciliation
Service Records, File 182-362, Record Group 280, National Archives; for a Raymond
Democratic journalist's views on the Weyerhaeuser "timber octopus," see *Willapa
Harbor Pilot*, May 19, June 2 and 29, 1932, and July 13, 1933.
[18] U. S. Bureau of the Census, *op cit*, *Vol III:2*, 1220, 1246, 225, and 1706.

the First Street skid road, was especially closely tied to the loggers and millworkers union: her son, Wayne, served a term as the Sawmill and Timber Workers Union recording secretary in 1936.[19]

Efforts to organize the Raymond area timberworkers pre-dated the 1930s. The IWW had been very active in the area during the 1910s and 1920s. When the Wobblies struck Pacific County camps and mills during their first Washington timber strike (1912), 155 Finns and Greeks were rounded up from their First Street hotels and boarding houses and deported from Raymond on boats and boxcars. The area was also affected by the Wobblies' 1917 strikes and slowdowns which were crushed by the 4 IWW supporters were tried en masse for vagrancy at Raymond in 1918 when they refused to work 12 hour shifts; 100 uniformed soldiers were present in the court room as suitably intimidating spectators.[20]

Hundreds of women and men struck several plants spontaneously on May 1, 1924, when a woman at the Siler box factory was fired for talking union after the 4L minimum wage was cut 60¢ to $3.40 per day. Despite IWW intervention, including speeches by Elmer Smith (attorney for the 1919 Centralia incident defendants) and James Rowan (leader of the Lumber Workers Industrial Union), the strikers' prevailing sentiment was to remain aloof from any organization. Strikebreakers dispatched by the 4L's refused to cross picket lines; the end result was a partial roll back of the pay cut.[21]

As elsewhere, numerous Pacific County loggers, longshoremen, and lumberworkers who were active unionists in the 1930s had participated in or were otherwise aware of IWW direct actions such as the 1923 "bindle burning" strike (when itinerant loggers burned the bedrolls they had been required to pack from camp to camp and sawed apart the double and triple bunks the

---

[19] *Ibid*, 1234; Sowers interview.
[20] Philip Foner, *History of the Labor Movement,* Vol. IV (New York, 1965), 220-225; Mrs. Nels Olsen, ed., *Willapa Country: History Report* (Raymond, 1965), 70-72; Robert Tyler, *Rebels of the Woods* (Eugene, 1967), 57; Harvey O'Connor, *Revolution in Seattle* (New York, 1964), 171.
[21] *Industrial Worker*, May 10, 17, 21, and 31, and June 7, 1924; *Willapa Harbor Pilot*, May 2 and 23, 1924; 4L *Bulletin*, June 24, 1924, 12 and 18; for Rowan, see Foner, Chapt. 23, and Tyler, 213-14; for Smith, see O'Connor, Chapt. 8.

operators provided, converting them into single beds). Although the Communists' National Lumber Workers' Union struck the WHLM camps east of Raymond in February 1934, this action seems to have contributed less to the mill workers' anti-Bedaux fight than it did to the general mood of militancy in the district and especially to the solidification of left-wing sentiment among loggers who joined hands with the mill union a few weeks before the 1935 timber strike. The IWW's own division between pro-and anti-Soviet factions in the 1920s was paralleled by the IWA's similar faction fights in the 1930s, suggesting that the common heritage of opposition to the boss did not overcome differences regarding the proper ultimate form of worker-capital relations.[22]

The AFL Timber Workers' Union had been active in the Northwest during the 1910s, but, like the IWW, it largely succumbed to operator attacks and the ravages of the 1920-21 depression. With the coming of the NIRA's Section 7(a) paper guarantees of the right to organize, AFL Federal Labor Unions chartered directly by the AFL national office rather than by one of the constituent international unions were established in principal Washington and Oregon timber towns. The Raymond Federal Labor Union was not founded until April 1934, five months after the first Bedaux time studies were begun. The fight against the Bedaux system was initially the paramount

---

[22] Tyler, 203-15; Melvyn Dubofsky, *We Shall Be All* (Chicago, 1969), Chapt. 18; leaflet in SPT/150/Memos.
Several of Raymond's key unionists in the 1930s had significant exposure to the IWW. Clifford Kight first encountered them in 1920; in 1923, he had a contract to haul single bunks and other supplies into camps as a result of the Wobblies' bindle burning strike. A logger he aided with a ride to camp signed him into the IWW. Wayne Sower worked in camps with his father, an IWW logger, and help him saw apart bunk beds in 1923. Ed Stallcop joined the IWW in 1922 and was a leading left-wing logger and partisan in the IWA's faction fights of the 1930s and 1940s. Jack Price joined the IWW during World War I, was active in the 1924 Raymond strike, and, when blacklisted, went to work on the waterfront. He was the founding president of the Raymond longshore local in the early 1930s and worked briefly in the WHLM boiler room in 1935 while on loan to the wood workers as an organizer. Price served as an ILWU International Vice-President during the 1940s. Leslie Younglove, first president of the Raymond FLU had worked as a youth in a logging camp, cutting firewood and feeding it into a donkey engine. He was so proficient he put another man out of work. When he refused to heed the donkey engineer's admonition to slow down, the engineer, a Wobbly, hauled in wood so filled with pitch that Younglove could not cut it. Younglove quit the job. Kight, Sowers, and Stallcop interviews; author's interviews with Leslie Younglove, July 17, 1979, and Jack Price, June 22, 1980. See also Spurrell interview, and author's interview with Donald Shamley, Dec. 28, 1980.

issue in the minds of the local's founders. The Raymond local was formed in a period when the AFL had already been stalemated in lumber by the operators' opposition and stalling tactics. Very little serious aid was forthcoming from the AFL national office, whose authoritarianism and lack of understanding of workers in other mass production industries such as auto, rubber, and steel was infamous.[23] The AFL's dilatory actions and the inability of the NRA labor agencies to offer material aid left the Raymond lumberworkers and their local allies dependent on their own resources and ingenuity in confronting the WHLM and the Bedaux system. The development of resistance to the Bedaux speedup cannot be adequately understood without knowledge of the complex pre-Bedaux mix of work processes and social relations at the WHLM. Although integrated mass production and marketing methods characterized the lumber industry by the end of the 19th century, the subdivision and subordination of labor to machine pacing and central management control was prolonged and uneven.[24]

Lumber plants typically embodied elements of what Richard Edwards has identified as "simple control" (commands issued personally by the entrepreneur or intermediate layers of superintendants and foremen, backed up by the power to fire workers in the face of economic insecurity) as well as "technical controls" (controls over labor power embodied in the technique of production, especially in the development of machinery which brought materials to the worker for the performance of a few simple operations, and then carried the product away for further processing).[25] Lumber plants' diverse departments combined these control paradigms in varying measure.

The sawmills themselves, where logs were broken down into dimensions approximately those of the consumer product, were by 1900 essentially organized as a continuous flow disassembly

---

[23] Jeremy Egolf, "The 4L's, 1930-35: Anti-Union Arm of the Business Commonwealth in the Northwest Lumber Industry" (unpublished manuscript); Jensen, Chapt. 8 and 9; McKenney, *passim*; Roger Keeran, *The Communist Party and the Auto Workers' Union* (Bloomington, 1980); Irving Bernstein, *The Turbulent Years* (Boston, 1970), Chapts. 3, 5 & 8; Sidney Fine, *The Automobile Under The Blue Eagle* (Ann Arbor, 1963), *passim*.

[24] Alfred J. Van Tassell and David W. Bluestone, *Mechanization in the Lumber Industry* (Philadelphia, 1939), 10 and *passim*.

[25] Edwards, Chapts. 2 and 7.

line similar to that of the modern slaughterhouse, with many of the dozens of jobs dependent on the workers' judgement of how to maximize product value. The whole work force was paced by conveyor chains on transfer tables between machines and by the rate at which the head sawyer, at the beginning of the line (and usually as well paid as the foremen), cut whole logs into massive cants for further processing. The sawyer carved up the logs not only according to his knowledge of value maximization to meet inventory needs and orders at hand, but also so as to keep the workers following him in the sawmill production process continuously occupied. At the other end of the plant, lumber was hand-piled for air drying (if not dried in kilns) and rail cars were loaded manually, piece by piece, by pairs of workers paid by the thousand board feet handled. Small crews at dry kiln stackers and unstackers, planers, and other machines had tasks varying widely in the degree to which the workers set the pace or were themselves paced by the rate at which they received their material for handling. Lumber plants also typically bore a complement of metal workers and building tradesmen to do general repairs and construction, who had little direct involvement with the production process.[26]

Planing mills, vital departments of most large northwestern lumber plants, and, at the WHLM, the initial locus of both the Bedaux installation and union leadership, offer an extended example of the complex interrelations of tools, work processes, and worker autonomy.[27] Skill demands in a large planing mill varied widely, though most jobs required little technical knowledge or innovative judgement for effective performance.

---

[26] The departmental breakdown of workers in one of the northwest's largest lumber plants was: 26.7%, sawmills; 21.4%, planing mills; 8.8%, shingle mills; 4.2%, lath mills; 4.1%, dry kilns; 5.5%, maintenance; 5.2%, wood and waste; 4.2%, transportation; 4.2%, rail shipping; 4.2%, storage sheds and yards; 3.8%, power; 3.7%, log booms; 1.7%, wharves; 4.0%, miscellaneous. 27% of the workers were heavily subject to machine pacing; 67.9% essentially free of mechanical controls; 8.3%, skilled craftsmen; and 31.6% semiskilled or highly mill-specific skilled. (Sawmill Wage Scale, St. Paul and Tacoma Lumber Company, May 1, 1936, SPT/199/Wages).

[27] The discussion of planing mills, except where noted, is based on H. B. Oakleaf, *Lumber Manufacture in the Douglas fir Region* (Chicago, 1920); U. S. Bureau of Labor Statistics, *Job Descriptions for the Lumber and Timber Products Industries* (Washington, DL, 1939); author's interviews with Howard Knauf, Feb. 22 and 24, and May 17, 1979, and Jan. 5, 1980; and, for practices specific to the WHLM in the '30s, author's interviews with Frank C. Mason, Jan. 4, 1980, and with Leslie Younglove.

FLOW CHART: Processing of timber in lumber plants.

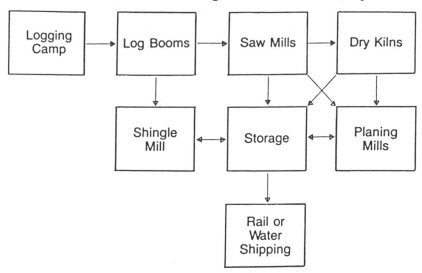

At the peak of the planing mill hierarchy was the foreman who was responsible for profitably processing stock according to inventory and current sales needs, ensuring both high quality and quantity of production, scheduling major repairs or equipment changes in cooperation with the plant superintendent and maintenance department, training and placing workers, and enforcing discipline (a task whose interpretation varied widely among foremen). Especially in those shops where the responsible autonomy mode of supervision was favored, the foreman's task was to maintain the mechanical and supply conditions permitting a full crew to produce, with minimal fatigue or safety hazards, the optimal quantity and quality of product his experience and the machinery speeds indicated was possible. In this model, foremen opposed "driving" the workers as unnecessary, undignified, and unsafe.[28] Several of the WHLM's first line supervisors were sufficiently offended by top management's assumption of their work evaluation role, overriding of custom-

---

[28] Author's interview with retired foreman, Longview, WA, May 9, 1981. This foreman, who prefers anonymity, was fired for refusing to speed up his crew under the Bedaux system at the Long-Bell Lumber Sales Company. J. D. Tennant, western general manager of Long-Bell and, from 1933-35, president of the NRA Lumber Code Authority, told a colleague that foremen's cooperation was absolutely essential if the Bedaux system was to be successfully installed. E. G. Griggs to Messrs. Young and Wagner, May 4, 1933, in SPT/149/Memos.

ary work pace, and disruption of industrial life that they allied with the local union activists to fight the Bedaux system.

As in other mass production workplaces, planing mills' most highly skilled and self-directed jobs were those of craftsmen such as the planer repairman (whose technical innovations might be embodied in machine redesign by capital goods firms) and the saw filer and knife grinder, who kept cutting tools in effective condition. The grinder prepared knives according to models and blue prints indicating width, depth, and pattern of cut for a variety of products including silo stock, siding, ceiling, flooring, bull-nose stepping, and a wide assortment of trim and wainscoting items as well as ordinary surfaced construction dimension and other stock. The filing and grinding rooms, analogous to the tool rooms of machine shops, were set apart from the main mill floor, reinforcing status distinctions while providing adequate work space for the craftsmen.

Depending on the size of the mill, setup men or the grinders themselves, changed and adjusted planer knives as necessary. A 1930 survey found only one northwestern mill which followed a pre-set schedule for knife changing and grinding.[29] Although the lack of rigid scheduling was partially attributable to technological and sales considerations such as the varied physical stresses associated with manufacturing a wide variety of products and the irregular quantity of material processed per order, the skilled craftsmen enjoyed considerable autonomy in organizing their irregularly paced tasks, although they were subject to the overriding controls of orders booked by the sales department and the progress of the production process.

What was the actual process of planing lumber at the WHLM? Loads of lumber appropriate to the order at hand, pre-sorted by size and grade, were carried by crane from the dry lumber storage shed and deposited upon descending dead rolls at one of the dry planing mill's three planers or the trim-cutting molder-matcher. A single feeder at each machine hand-placed the lumber, piece by piece, upon live rolls which swept the lumber into and through the machine, where whirling knives chipped off

---

[29] *Timberman*, May, 1930, 64.

flakes of wood to produce a smooth finish or cut the stock to pattern. An offbearer or divider, generally an older man or a teenage boy, stood behind each planer and, grasping the finished material as it was ejected into a trough, flipped alternate pieces onto one of two sloping tables, down which it slid to either of the two graders who stood behind each machine. The graders evaluated every piece according to quality and size, cut out flawed sections with an electric trim saw, and "pigeonholed" the material in the appropriate slot of a three-tiered bank of temporary storage compartments which stood behind each planer.

Graders bore greater decision-making responsibility than did the other direct planing mill operatives. They were essential to the industry's quality control and product standardization system and were regarded as one of the few classifications of workers who could "make or break" a mill. At large mills, a head grader trained learners and certified their thorough knowledge of established grades and their ability to discern at a touch or glance the widths and thicknesses of lumber. After the craftsmen, the head grader was typically the most highly paid planer worker; he cooperated with inspectors from regional grade supervising bureaus to ensure that orders were filled in conformity with the standards established by lumber trade associations to facilitate nationwide marketing. If lumber was not properly finished, graders brought this to the attention of setup men, or the grinders themselves, who corrected the problem. Lumber companies' national reputations for providing a standardized product clearly rested upon the daily judgements made by these men in the shops and on the shipping docks. At the WHLM, graders assumed an aggressive union leadership role out of proportion to their numbers, in good measure as a response to the Bedaux system's obvious attack on their autonomy and ability to do their work.

When four to six pieces of lumber from the planers accumulated in a given pigeonhole, pullout men placed them on sawhorses, tied the bundle, and handpiled the bundles on blocks to make up loads for a motorized lumber carrier to transport to dry storage and shipping sheds. At the WHLM George Cleveland, the dry planer foreman, modified this procedure in 1933 when he invented a device which compressed several pieces of random length material delivered from the sorting racks, trimmed the tied bundles square, and stamped each piece with the WHLM trademark before it was sent to storage.

Subjection to machine pacing varied greatly for workers at different stations in the planing mill. Offbearers, bundle ti-ers, and general laborers were the least paid workers, performing tasks with little interest or self-direction. One life-long planer-man recalls that, before his promotion after fourteen years of offbearing and pigeonholing,

> time used to drag . . . . They needed sombody to be a feeder on the planer so they asked me if I would like to do that. I says, "I sure would." That was a change from somebody pushing me until I got the chance to push somebody else. You work behind the planer and the guy over feeding the planer he had to push you, he had the control over you a little bit. So I liked [feeding] because I could push the guy on the other side . . . . Of course, it wasn't nasty or anything like that, but if there was something I had to do or if I wanted to slow up a bit I couldn't be-cause the stuff kept coming anyway. It was a wonder we did it at all but then . . . the 4L was there and they cracked the whip and said, "You do it or out."[30]

Strength, speed, and agility were essential attributes of offbear-ers and pullout men, because finished lumber, as large as 3' × 10' in cross section, would be scratched and dented (lowering its salability) if allowed to pile up behind the planer. The inability to do quality work while maintaining pace with the speeded up flood of lumber became a central grievance when the Bedaux system came to the WHLM.

For some workers shared working conditions, economic in-security, deference, friendship, and mutual admiration provided cohesion and discipline—balancing monotony, the division of la-bor, age, and other social differences. The workers were suffused with a sense of the norms associated with each job in the hierarchy and with cooperative values resistant to being "pushed" inappropriately by other men. The workers surely learned to expect that hard work to gain greater skill and respon-

---

[30] Knauf interview, Feb. 22, 1979.

sibility would bring more, not less, freedom from machine pacing and incessant human supervision. The sense of solidarity at the WHLM dry planer supported the collective resistance by the foremen and production workers to management's imposition of time studies, speedup, and interference with the work process.

Application of the Bedaux system was initiated at the WHLM on November 20, 1933. The project engineer, Edwin Hayward, promised workers that machinery would not be speeded up and that daily wages would not be reduced. Perhaps to reduce production costs by more rapidly finishing lumber from the already speeded up sawmills, time studies began at the dry stock planing mill. Piece counters and lineal foot meters were installed at each machine to precisely measure the lumber processed. Hayward immediately remarked upon the workers' "interest and curiosity" and intense "nervousness under observation." Earl Younglove, a dry planer grader and the WHLM Federal Labor Union's first recording secretary, recalled the workers' resentment:

> Everybody that was around there was very bitter against the idea of having somebody standing over them, looking down their necks, that never saw a sawmill in their life; as a matter of fact, they don't know a one by four from a one by six. They had to ask you. Still they asked you, and made a time study of your job.

Planer feeders were submitting daily production reports by mid-December. Lineal foot reports for each day, keyed to numbered boards hung over each machine, were first posted shortly after the New Year. Incentive wages were imposed at the planers by March 1934.[31]

Timing of even the most highly skilled jobs for full shifts was extended to all departments. Every saw, crane, lumber carrier, and transfer table bore a meter of some description. By January 1935 most WHLM mill workers were involved in the work accounting and bonus system.[32]

---

[31] Charles E. Bedaux Company of the Pacific States, Willapa Harbor Lumber Mills Report, E. J. Hayward, Engineer, Nov. 20, 27, and 29, 1933, Dec. 2, 5, 15, and 19, 1933, and Jan. 4, 19, 23, Feb. 16, and Mar. 14, 1934, all in CHI/2/Bedaux (these reports hereafter cited as "Bedaux-Willapa"); J. W. Lewis to Our Employees, Sep. 12, 1934, Respondent's Exhibit "A," "NLRB-Willapa Transcript"; "NLRB-Willapa Transcript," 58 (Paul Fowler), 109 (Leslie Younglove), 185 and 192 (Earl Younglove).

[32] "Bedaux-Willapa," Jan. 29, April 5, 9, and 14, and Nov. 23, 1934, in CHI/2/Bedaux; Jan. 14 and 21, 1935, in CHI/3/Bedaux; "NLRB-Willapa Transcript," 58 (W. H. Turner).

Hayward intervened directly in the production process. For example, work at the dry kiln lumber unstackers was normally organized by foremen, straw bosses, and the workers themselves within the limits imposed by the machinery. Hayward suggested methods for redistributing the work load and creating a more continuous flow of lumber and told the unstacker offbearers to allow graders and kiln operators to spot loaded kiln cars at the unstackers rather than assisting them with this work. Thus, the offbearers' work cycle was stripped of some of its irregular variety. Furthermore, the unstacker was speeded up and the offbearing crew reduced from eight to six. Because a principal problem was "getting the kiln crews [and others] to forget the old methods," Hayward conducted "educational programs" for the workers, and had the kiln and other departments placed under more intense supervision. The speedup was reinforced with rituals of humiliation; workers with years of industrial experience were required to "make up any overloading . . . by increased labor activities or be criticized for lack of efficiency." George Cleveland, the dry planer foreman who was highly regarded by the workers and on friendly terms with the unionists, was more interested in perfecting his bundle trimmer than assisting with the Bedaux installation so he was replaced with another man at Hayward's instigation.[33]

Raymond Federal Labor Union #19446 was chartered April 5, 1934, a few weeks after incentive wages were imposed at the dry planing mill. Membership was initially limited to the WHLM's Raymond operations; the company's South Bend mill and logging camps in the surrounding territory were added to the local the following spring. The Bedaux system's early disruption of work life in the WHLM's dry lumber sections led to the union's leadership being drawn primarily from the dry kilns and dry planing mill, as graders and others attempted to restore pre-Bedaux conditions. Local union leaders noted strong rank-and-file pressure for an early strike against the "unAmerican, de-

---

[33] "Bedaux-Willapa," Feb. 14 and 20, Mar. 6, April 10, 17, and 18, and Aug. 7, 14, 15, 17, and 20, 1934, all in CHI/2/Bedaux; Minutes of the Meeting, Sept. 6, 1934, in American Federation of Labor Papers/Strike Files/Federal Union #19446, Wisconsin State Historical Society (hereafter cited as "AFL"); Younglove interview and author's interview with D.C. King, Jan. 4, 1980.

moralizing, slave-driving" Bedaux system. Removal of the system was to be the union's first demand if they overturned the 4L's in the National Labor Board certification process.[34]

The early thrust of union activity and shop floor resistance to the Bedaux speed up undercut the 4L as an institution to ensure worker acquiescence at Raymond. Early in July 1934, F. C. Beckman, a popular planing mill setup man and, since the 1924 strike, perennial district employee representative to the 4L Board of Directors, complained to a visiting 4L officer that the "Bedaux system was burning the men up and they were told by outsiders [i.e., AFL activists] that if the 4L was any good they would stop it." Beckman complained that he got the "blunt of the blow," and insisted that although he was "still 4L and still believed in it . . . two years would be required to overcome the ill feeling caused by this Bedaux mess and I am not going to be active until there is a chance to do some good."[35]

The anti-Bedaux unionists were distressed that the new methods undermined amicable working relations. One observed that the Bedaux system "meant generally working against the other fellow and caused considerable strife." Chet King, who worked at the bundle trimmer, used an egalitarian, cooperative conception of efficiency, pointing out that "any man that is mad on the job, or mad at somebody else because he made more bonus, isn't at the best of his efficiency at work." Ray McAndrews, a rail car loader and vice-president of both the local and the Raymond Central Labor Council, contended that piece work was the "easiest and most logical way to reduce the real wages of the employee." Counterposing a "fair day's work" to Bedaux's demands for ever-increasing productivity, he charged that "an efficiency system weeds out the men who are not capable of doing a little more than a day's work." The system was erratic in its application: "one day you work real hard and you cannot get anything; the next day you have it

---

[34] Raymond *Advertiser*, Mar. 29, 1934; "RLB-Willapa Transcript," 19 (Paul Fowler), 35, 63, 195 (Rowland Watson), 61 (William T. Krause), 106 (L. Younglove), 136 (D. C. King), 157 and 162 (R. L. McAndrews), 180-81 and 194-95 (E. Younglove), 208 (Joseph C. Leonard), and 224 (Al Meek).

[35] Minutes, 4L Board of Directors, 1924-33, *passim*; F. S. Ford to 4L Headquarters, July 4-6, 1934, in WCR/4/12.

easy, have a lot of down time you don't have to do anything
and you make a good bonus." And the long arm of the speedup
disrupted family and social life off the job: "The men are extended beyond their ability when they go home at night. The
graders . . . sit down and they don't go anyplace."[36]

The planer graders' certifications were directly threatened as
their proportion of correctly graded lumber declined significantly in the face of the increased work loads and substandard
manufacture and sorting by undermanned, speeded up crews
earlier in the production process. Although the planer graders
received a good bonus—in good measure because they "cheated,"
repeatedly tapping their trim saw meters between loads of lumber and whenever the feeders paused to clear splintered lumber
from their overloaded machines—four of the six dry planer
graders opposed the system because it meant "too hard work."
Leslie Younglove, planer grader and founding president of the
Federal Labor Union, did not believe the speedup was "fair for
the workers for the whole." His brother Earl (mentioned earlier) also denounced Bedaux's irrationality and detrimental effect upon the "efficiency" of older workers. The WHLM, he
noted, was

> paying all the skilled men a good bonus and working the common labor
> to the point of disability, so that old men cannot really do their work
> well. I could name you several men down there that are working in that
> plant that are well along in age who can't do their work efficiently any
> more, and there are several fellows that have been put out down there
> because they couldn't move fast enough.

The union's drive for a non-disabling work pace was supported
by the notion that workers had an almost proprietary right to
their jobs, a matter of real concern—especially in the absence of
old age pensions and unemployment insurance—during the winter of 1934-35, when official unemployment figures for Washington timber cities such as Aberdeen, Everett, and Tacoma
ranged from 25% to 28%.[37]

---

[36] "NLRB-Willapa Transcript," 26 (Fowler), 140 (King), 155 and 157-8 (McAndrews), 185-6
and 188 (E. Younglove).

[37] "NLRB-Willapa Transcript," 185-7 (E. Younglove), 104 (L. Younglove); Washington Emergency Relief Administration, *Occupational Characteristics of Unemployed Persons in Cities
of 11,000 or more Population* (Olympia, 1935), 2. The Mason, King, and Younglove interviews all volunteered the point that graders "cheated."

The Raymond Central Labor Council, chartered August 31, 1934, was controlled by the mill workers and longshoremen, and generously offered to call a general strike in support of the lumberworkers' recognition and anti-Bedaux demands. Such action was restrained by several factors: hesitant local leadership, financial weakness, and pressure from the AFL hierarchy. As in other port towns, lumberworkers' grocery credit and meager savings (if any) were sorely strained by the 1934 longshore strike. The problem of mass unemployment remained unresolved. By mid-autumn, the WHLM was operating only three days per week. Under AFL rules, the FLU was ineligible for financial aid until April, 1935, and then only if approved by a majority of the AFL Executive Council—as AFL President William Green unfailingly reminded northwestern lumber FLUs contemplating strike action. Earl Younglove advised Green that

> Our local voted 100% against the Bedaux system but we are not strong enough [to fight it] ourselves as yet being a young organization. The men themselves even 4L's members have gotten together and plan a walkout in protest against the unfairness of the rotten Bedaux system . . . . The Bedaux system is just cause for a strike but I believe we should be prepared . . . we have in mind plans for next spring when the lumber market is most always on the upgrade.

Although Green did offer his moral support, he instructed a state AFL representative to "hold the boys down and don't do anything so there would be a strike" pending the Regional Labor Board election for which the FLU had petitioned in August.[38]

The Board, however, pointed to its full docket of cases and simply promised to conduct an election at the earliest possible date, leaving the Raymond local to its own devices until the spring of 1935.[39] In the absence of a walkout or government sanctioned negotiations, the fight against the Bedaux system proceeded through grievance meetings, attempts to bargain with management, and shop floor activity.

The workers held a mass meeting on September 5, 1934. Al-

[38] Raymond *Advertiser*, Mar. 29 and Sept. 6, 1934; "NLRB-Willapa Transcript," 11, 44, 77, and 95 (R. Watson), 23, 29, and 32 (Fowler), 191-4 (E. Younglove) 75-6 (Krause), 160-63 (McAndrews), and 227 (Meek); Earl Younglove to William Green, Sept. 1 and 9, 1934, and Green to Younglove, Sept. 7, 1939, and to Rowland Watson, Sept. 7, 1934, all in AFL/Strike Files/Federal Union #19446.

[39] "NLRB-Willapa Transcript," 162-3, (R. McAndrews), and 181-2 (E. Younglove).

though 189 WHLM employees attended the meeting, only 89 were then under Bedaux incentives. Thus, the majority were responding to time studies alone or were, as J. W. Lewis suggested, "dependent entirely upon hearsay and rumor for their judgement." The strong participation evidenced the vitality of the workers' social networks and their fear of further layoffs and work degradation. Contrary to expectations, no strike vote was taken. Instead, organizers obtained endorsement of a petition directed to the WTC head offices and various government agencies. Speakers argued that a moderate pace of work was the right of all workers; they declared that Bedaux had introduced speedup "on a par with the so-called sweatshops." Workers were "compelled to labor beyond reasonable physical endurance to keep their machines clear of accumulated lumber [and] to do additional work whenever there was a slack period in the regular work assigned." Finally, the mutually reinforcing speed up and layoffs were "not in keeping with the employment plan of President Roosevelt," but were "contrary to the National Recovery Act." The petition concluded with the demand that "normal reasonable working conditions be established, which will ensure the laborer a chance to render a reasonable service under reasonable conditions."[40] Thus, the activists justified their resistance by combining their interpretation of the New Deal's purpose with their sense of proper workplace ethics.

The conciliatory conclusion suggested the isolated and economically weak position of the mill workers, but also grew from the community support and liberal social and political alliances of the local union's leadership; the alliances encompassed supervisory personnel for the purpose of fighting the Bedaux system. Dr. Frederick Irwin, a chiropractor who treated local lumberworkers' and athletes' sprained backs and spoke frequently at Pacific County Democratic Party and Townsend Club functions, was unanimously elected "impartial chairman." Ex-foreman George Cleveland, Gordon King (a Raymond 4L activist, foreman of a WHLM sawmill, and, later, plant superintendant), and

---

[40] "NLRB-Willapa Transcript," J. W. Lewis to Our Employees, Sept. 12, 1934, Respondant's Exhibit "A"; *ibid.*, 71 (Kraus), 144 (King), and 193-94 (E. Younglove); Minutes of the Meeting, Sept. 6, 1934, in AFL/Strike Files/Federal Union #19446.

Leo Johnson (Leslie Younglove's neighbor, former planer foreman, and knife grinder at the green lumber planing mill) were selected as a "temporary committee to recognize all those who
wished to speak" and to tabulate votes. Leslie Younglove, Paul
Fowler (a planer and shipping dock grader), Ray McAndrews'
brother Tom (who fed a planer) and two men for whom occupational data is lacking, Douglas Rains and Joe Leonard, were
elected as a grievance committee. Persons making and second-
ing nominations to the committee were: Ralph Nelson and Vernon
Dunning (graders behind the kiln unstacker and friends of
the Younglove brothers; both Nelson and Dr. Irwin were Mor-
mons and were close friends, and Nelson was later appointed
Raymond's postmaster); Glen Fykerud (Leslie Younglove's
partner when grading flooring); Henry Orkney (who fed the
planer behind which Fykerud and Leslie Younglove graded during the Bedaux installation); Earl Younglove; and William
Stairs, Douglas Rains, and the McAndrews brothers. The local
union's president Leslie Younglove was unanimously elected
grievance committee chairman after his nomination was made
and seconded by graders Fykerud and Dunning.[41]

Several points about these proceedings are readily evident.
First, at least three present or former foremen lent open support
to the resistance movement (Leslie Younglove had also been a
foreman or straw boss at a local box factory in the 1920s). Their
presence helped define the struggle as a conservative one de-
fending the local, customary indirect production controls which
predated the expanding Weyerhaeuser group's introduction of
systematic speedup. This effort to combat the effects of the
Depression economic collapse (including unemployment) by re-
storing the accustomed way of work probably helped cement
the more conservative, "loyal" workers to the cause. The second point is that several men tied by family, work, political, religious, and leisure bonds, among whom graders were conspicuous, took key positions at this meeting. As has been noted,

---

[41] Minutes of the Meeting, Sept. 6, 1934, in AFL/Strike Files/Federal Union #19446; Younglove,
   Mason, King, Kight, and Spurrell interviews; *Willapa Harbor Pilot*, June 13, 1924; 4L
   Bulletin, April, 1924, 10; 4L *Lumber News*, July, 1924, 22, and April, 1926, 20; "NLRB-
   Willapa Transcript," 188 (E. Younglove); *West Coast Lumberman*, Aug. 1931, 24-25.

these graders were the most highly skilled workers directly tied to machine processes at the kiln unstackers and planing mills: the departments where the Bedaux system was first introduced and shop floor resistance was most remarked upon by Hayward. Finally, overt resistance to the Bedaux system was led by men with many years of local pre-Bedaux work experience. The Youngloves had lived in the Raymond area about 23 or 24 years. Their father had operated a confectionary store until he sold the business' assets early in the Depression and went to work as a fireman in a local shingle mill. Joe Leonard had also been a Raymond resident 23 or 24 years; Paul Fowler, 9 years; Chet King, 25 years; the McAndrews, 10 years. These men had all been employed by the WHLM's predecessor companies or had been hired shortly after the 1931 merger.[42]

When the grievance committee met with the WHLM management, it was clear that both parties regarded the locus of power to determine work pace as the central point of contention. To Joe Leonard's query of who was to determine when the men were overworked, Lewis replied "We will," meaning the management. Leonard pressed further, asking Lewis whether "in his opinion didn't he believe that a man was competent to judge after he had worked all day in a mill whether he was overworked or not," and Lewis stated he did not. Lewis invited the committeemen to quit if they didn't like their jobs; the unionists turned away convinced that the WHLM was uninterested in serious collective bargaining.[43]

The union did gain one insignificant concession. Hayward surveyed the mills for "unfair" applications of the bonus system and eventually posted a notice to the effect that the productivity ratings of three planer offbearers who had proven absolutely unable to reach the standard set by the time studies would thenceforth be posted in black rather than red figures. But neither the speedup nor the extension of the bonus system were halted.[44]

[42] Younglove interview; "NLRB-Willapa Transcript," 15 (Fowler), 134 (King), 150, 155-56, and 160-61 (McAndrews), 206 (Leonard), and 99 (E. Younglove).
[43] "NLRB-Willapa Transcript," 26 and 98 (Fowler), 111 and 112 (L. Younglove), and 213-14 and 218-19 (Leonard). Lewis reiterated his position at the RLB hearing; *ibid*, 283.
[44] Notice, Sept. 17, 1934, in CHI/2/Bedaux.

Resistance continued on the shop floor. The kiln men complained that their earnings per unit were reduced though they worked harder. Hayward in turn castigated their work habits, failure to make "progress," and alleged lack of coordination and "intelligent direction." He proposed that a supervisor be introduced at the kiln unstacker, that output standards for all work not directly paced by machinery be raised (cutting the piece rate), and that work be further "rebalanced." According to Hayward, nearly one-third of the kiln men's time was "lost," so he ignored the protests against speedup and promised Lewis that the increase in bonuses that would allegedly follow a mechanical speedup would "improve the morale in the department" as the monthly bonus rose.[45] Hayward's delusions regarding his subjects' motivations simply prolonged their agony.

The engineer observed that the men behind the planers "consider[ed] one machine to be their own, rather than working for the unit as a whole." They refused to run from planer to planer, "balancing" their work, as pileups developed. While bunkloaders cleared the sawhorses of accumulated lumber, the pullout men stood idle, rather than aiding other pullout men or the bunk loaders with their work. Hayward was mystified; in his eyes, the men were paid the same standard rates and premiums so there was, he concluded, "no logical reason for their attitude."[46] More plausibly, management's logic of the company union shop and the maximization of individual productivity and company profits was being countered by the workers' logic of full employment, a moderate work pace, and noncooperation with the speedup.

Hayward noted the behavior of the planer workers on December 29, the same day that J. W. Lewis reiterated his refusal to cooperate with a Labor Board election. On December 6, the Seattle Regional Labor Board had solicited Lewis' voluntary compliance with election preliminaries. After discussing the matter with WTC and 4L officials, Lewis determined to delay the issue. Although the Weyerhaeuser group had cooperated

---

[45] "Bedaux-Willapa," Dec. 12, 1934, in CHI/2/Bedaux; "Bedaux-Willapa," Jan. 5 and Feb. 1 and 4, 1935, in CHI/3/Bedaux.
[46] "Bedaux-Willapa," Dec. 29, 1934, in CHI/2/Bedaux.

with previous election orders, it appears that a stand was taken at the WHLM for several reasons. The NLRB's recent Houde decision had established the procedure of granting sole collective bargaining rights to the victor in representation elections, thus ending any grounds for the WHLM and other companies to continue relations with the 4L and similar company unions that lost elections. The Lumber Code minimum price structure had already been swept away, meaning a restoration of pre-NRA competitiveness. With cases challenging the legality of the entire NIRA progressing through the courts, there was no incentive for the WHLM to place itself in a position to pioneer written contracts with the Federal Labor Unions.[47]

Furthermore, Lewis remained personally opposed to union recognition. He argued that management's task was to retain stockholder control of the firm, aggressively seek to expand markets, ensure investment security, and "handle employees efficiently and humanely." Lewis contended that the WHLM's sponsorship of 4L representation, life insurance, relatively high wages, and good working conditions was already doing more for the workers than were the majority of operators; thus, he argued, AFL contracts were unnecessary. Finally, Lewis argued that the closed shop would raise production costs, even if wages were not increased. The manager would "wake up to find that his business was being run by walking delegates rather than his foremen." The pro-union, anti-Bedaux struggle was clearly a challenge to the paternalistic style of management Lewis was accustomed to exercising. One wonders if he was unwilling to admit that not only the unionists, but also his own foremen, questioned the management methods he had brought to Pacific County.[48]

On January 11, 1935, FLU#19446 once again requested recognition for bargaining purposes; once again, the company refused. The Seattle labor board conducted a hearing at Raymond in mid-February, to determine whether election compliance was

---

[47] W. E. Heidinger to J. P. Weyerhaeuser, Jr., Dec. 17, 1934, in JPW/2/Regional Labor Board; J. W. Lewis to Charles Hope, Dec. 27, 1934, and Charles W. Hope to J. W. Lewis, Dec. 24, 1934, both in CHI/2/Labor. Egolf, "Labor Control," 43-44.
[48] J. W. Lewis to C. H. Ingram, Dec. 31, 1934, in CHI/2/Labor.

legally enforceable. The bulk of the pro-election testimony centered on the workers' desire to negotiate removal of the Bedaux system through their recognized union. More significant legally were the facts that 255 of 415 persons employed at the Raymond plant had petitioned for an election, and that Leslie Younglove's promotion to head grader following the 1934 mass grievance meeting was revoked because he refused to change his affiliation from AFL to 4L. On the basis of the available evidence, the board ordered that an election be held.[49]

To avoid antagonizing the unions and the Federal labor boards, the WHLM played a quiet waiting game during the early months of 1935. Local secretary Earl Younglove compared J. W. Lewis to Franklin Roosevelt: "he is a good diplomat, but as far as any material realization, any special interest on the workers' part, well, they would never get it."[50]

A year after the local union's founding, the Federal labor agencies had proved impotent to help the union secure bargaining recognition. The workers' patience in dealing with management's intransigence and the Bedaux system was finally exhausted. Clifford Kight recalled his role in the late winter 1935 action that led to the removal of the Bedaux system:

> I had joined the IWW in 1923, when I was still a teenager. During the 1930s they called me a Communist. What a Communist was I didn't know then and I don't know now and it don't bother me. But I believed in good honest trade unionism. Early in 1935, I was working at the South Bend sawmill on the green chain, where we sorted lumber fresh out of the sawmill. J. W. Lewis' brother-in-law came with him from the South and was superintendant of the mill. He'd worked with colored people his whole life and started driving us the same way. We started with 17 men on the green chain and they took two off. They weren't satisfied with that so they took away two more. That broke the camel's back. The fifteen of us talked it over. I said, "There's just one way to stop this. We'll walk off the job and shut the whole mill down." The boys thought this was a good idea so we set the day. We hoped nobody would take our place and nobody did. We was out setting in the office and we asked the timekeeper for our pay. About half or three-quarters of an hour later this guy dashed madly over and say, "Boys, I

[49] National Labor Relations Board, *Decisions and Orders, Vol II* (Washington, 1935), 406; W. E. Heidinger to A. W. Clapp, Feb. 20, 1935, in JPW/3/Labor; "NLRB-Willapa Transcript," passim.
[50] "NLRB-Willapa Transcript," 206 (E. Younglove).

wish you wouldn't take this version of it. Why didn't you take it up with the 4L's?" The boys had asked me to be the spokesman. I said, "F___ you and your 4L's. We don't want anything to do with them. You're going to talk to all of us here and not to the 4L's." "I wish something could happen." "You want to run the mill?" "Oh, yes." "All right, but put all fifteen of us back on. We'll go back to work, but don't take any more of us off." We went back to work. That's what really started the organization at the South Bend mill. In about a month's time all but three or four were signed up in the union.[51]

The direct action by Kight and his fellow workers against the speed up was reminiscent of the similar tactics used by the IWW to deal with speedup and other problems during the 1910s and early 1920s, with which Kight was familiar. The informal strike spurred the WTC, sensitive to public relations and probably anxious to avoid a full strike at Raymond, to cancel the Bedaux contract, claiming that promised savings in labor costs had not been attained.[52] Although machinery remained speeded up, the stop watch, incentive bonuses, and Hayward's obnoxious meddling disappeared from the mills, and layoffs were halted. The South Bend action may have helped to prevent the use of Bedaux methods at other Weyerhaeuser group plants.

Despite the workers' victory over the Bedaux system, management was still not ready to recognize the union. Lewis urged the WTC general management to ignore the NLRB's April 23 decision upholding the regional board's election order and to refuse to bargain with any local of the Lumber and Sawmill Workers' Union (LSWU), the name given the logging and lumber unions when the AFL Executive Board granted jurisdiction over them to the United Brotherhood of Carpenters and Joiners (UBCJA) in mid-March 1935. The WHLM was granted an extension of the compliance deadline to June 15, and prepared to petition the courts for an injunction against the NLRB.[53]

51 Kight Interview.
52 C. W. English to Willapa Harbor Lumber Mills, Mar. 8, 1935, in CHI/3/Bedaux.
53 J. W. Lewis to C. H. Ingram, April 8, 1935, in CHI/3/Willapa Harbor; J. P. Weyerhaeuser, Jr., to F. E. Weyerhaeuser, May 2 and 4, 1935, in JPW/3/F. E. Weyerhaeuser. On May 15, 1935, the WTC again refused to allow an election to be held at the WHLM, charging that the NLRB was violating Amendments 4, 5, and 6 of the U. S. Constitution, that the NLRB had no jurisdiction in the case, and that all employees as of April, 1935, had since discontinued their employment (i. e., were on strike), and were, therefore, ineligible to vote. W. E. Heidinger to National Labor Relations Board, May 15, 1935, in JPW/3/Labor.

While the company continued its delaying tactics, the Raymond mill workers heeded the Carpenters' call for a regional strike and surged onto the picket lines May 6th. Within days, over 30,000 timber workers were on strike. The strike lasted 14 weeks; the WHLM was very nearly the last company to resume operating under a standard agreement granting a 5-10¢ raise and recognition of the LSWU locals as bargaining agents for their own members, effectively destroying what power the 4L had still exerted in Western Washington and the lower Columbia basin.[54]

The anti-Bedaux struggle had forged community solidarity and militant unionism against large capital at Raymond. The Raymond local also was united against the rule of Abe Muir, who had been appointed by the Carpenters' to command the lumber strike. Anti-Bedaux activists held key positions in the anti-Muir Northwest Joint Strike Committee, an insurgent, cross-local body formed with Communist support and evidently modelled after the similar committee the West Coast longshoremen had used to coordinate their 1934 strike. Ray McAndrews was elected the committee's vice-president. The Raymond local's 1100 members voted almost unanimously to affiliate with the anti-Muir coalition; Leslie Younglove, Paul Fowler, and Joe Leonard served on the Raymond insurgents' liaison committee.[55]

Ideological as well as leadership continuity tied the anti-Bedaux fight and the 1935 strike's appeals to the democratic rights of the rank-and-file. The union communique announcing the Raymond LSWU's affiliation with the Joint Strike Committee declared that

> local Sawmill and Timber unions throughout the northwest have united in an attack against the dictatorship of Abe Muir. The general belief is that Mr. Muir has disregarded the rights of American citizens to have a rank and file vote in an American organization.

The union responded to a WHLM-engineered back-to-work movement by declaring that its members were "not Communists or Anarchists but American citizens"; the strike was "the only weapon we have to force the financiers to recognize us as a

---

[54] Jensen, Chapt. 9; Egolf, "Labor Control," 97.
[55] South Bend *Journal*, June 21, 1935; Tacoma *Daily Ledger*, June 7, 1935.

group of men with an American right of independence." They
noted that the Carpenters' oath, in use since the 1880s, was
made "at Independence Hall, Pennsylvania, and [was] nothing
to be ashamed of." Earl Younglove's denunciation of the "un-
American, slave-driving" Bedaux system, and unionists' and
their allies' references to the slave heritage of J. W. Lewis' native South, were cut from the same ideological cloth.[56]

This working class Americanism defended the union as advocate of the shop work group's integrity, democratic pluralist
institutions, values of skill, solidarity, and competent workman-
ship, as well as the ability of members of the workers' community to make a living wage for their families under decent working conditions. While the crystallization of an ethic of working
class solidarity against the negative aspects of the changing economic order was not the same as developing a perspective consciously opposing capitalist ownership of industry, working
class Americanism was certainly populistic.[57]

The Carpenters' tutelage proved a frustrating hindrance for
loggers and lumberworkers. Though they had been promised
full rights, benefits, voice and vote in the organization, they
were treated as mere fraternal delegates at the 1936 UBCJA
Convention. They did not receive full guarantees of an industrial form of union, without which they feared they would lose
their power against the operators. John L. Lewis' punch that
knocked Carpenters' President Bill Hutcheson to the floor at
the October 1935 AFL convention certainly struck an encouraging note for lumberworkers. It gave hope to the woodworkers'
delegates who complained to the CIO's John Brophy that the
Carpenters were making only half-hearted efforts to organize
the industry, "didn't know our language," and were ignorant
of the work actually performed in sawmills and logging camps.[58]

By 1936, the Raymond timber local leadership, including the
anti-Bedaux activists, unanimously favored "going CIO."

---

[56] South Bend *Journal*, June 4 and 28, 1935.
[57] A useful discussion of 1930s working-class Americanism is Roy Rosenzweig, "'United Action
Means Victory': Militant Americanism on Film," *Labor History*, 24 (1983), 274-288.
[58] Notes of meeting of woodworkers' delegates with John Brophy, Dec. 17, 1936, in Katherine P.
Ellickson Papers, Reuther Archives, Wayne State Univ.; Robert Christie, *Empire in Wood*,
(Ithaca, 1956), 291-298; Jensen, Chapt. 11; Bernstein, 627.

Recognized pro-CIO leftists were elected officers of both the Raymond local and the LSWU's Grays-Willapa Harbor District Council, which spearheaded the drive to break away from the Carpenters, resulting in the founding of the IWA in July 1937. The Raymond local's executive was "red," save for Chet King, who became the union's business agent. Communists and their allies were elected to fill the IWA's international offices. Operator attacks and the ravages of the 1938 recession were compounded by a sharp internal struggle as a business industrial unionist element sought to wrest control of the IWA from its left-wing leadership. CIO Assistant Director of Organizations Michael Widman found when he investigated the IWA in May, 1940, that "Anybody that is anti-administration is considered an opposition bloc of phonies, stooges, etc. Everybody who is pro-administration are considered Communists, fellow travellers, etc." The self-described "white-bloc's" final overthrow of the administration forces came in 1940-41, under the guidance of Adolf Germer, who was personally delegated to the IWA as Director of Organization by John L. Lewis. The IWA's Southwest Washington District Council was torn by the factional struggle's most furious intra-local fights, and the Raymond local split in two for a brief period in early 1941, when the "white" victory was nearly complete.[59]

The anti-Bedaux activists' careers during the red-white faction fights demonstrated that their opposition to the extension of managerial controls was not in itself a certain predictor of their attitudes toward left-wing unionism and the competence of capitalists to operate industry in the interests of working people. Chet King emerged as a key district leader on the anti-Communist bloc, and served (1945-65) in the state legislature as a conservative Democrat. The Younglove brothers were promoted to head graderships at the WHLM and at the Weyerhaeuser group plant

---

[59] *Timberworker*, Sept. 7, 1935, Feb. 14 and Labor Day, 1936, and Oct. 30, Nov. 20, and Nov. 27, 1937; *Willapa Harbor Pilot*, June 18, 1936, and June 17 and Nov. 11, 1937; Harold Slater to Russell Trace, Dec. 29, 1941, in Harold Slater Papers/III A 51/1, Washington State Historical Society; Jensen, Chapt. 12; Lembcke and Tattam, IWA International Executive Board Minutes, May 12-15, 1940; Bruce Berrey to B. J. McCarty, Mar. 8, 1941, R. Francis to H. C. Fremming, Mar. 12, 1941, Donald L. Shamley to Adolph Germer, April 7, 1941, and Adolph Germer to Allan S. Haywood, Mar. 9, 1941, all in Adolph Germer Papers, Mar.-April, 1941, Wisconsin State Historical Society.

at Enumclaw, Washington. They dropped away from union office but sided with the white bloc. Leslie Younglove has, however, recently expressed misgivings at the vigor of the suppression of the left-wing. Ray McAndrews joined the Communist Party, was blacklisted because of his role in the Northwest Joint Strike Committee, and worked variously as a dockworker, paid IWA organizer, and for WPA, until he joined Harry Bridges' Longshoremen permanently around 1939. Paul Fowler was fired during the 1938 recession for cutting firewood on WHLM land; as chairman of the Pacific County Workers Alliance, he continued working closely with left-wing unionists. Clifford Kight, who led the anti-speed up walkout at South Bend, was allied with the left wing of the IWA while he served as Secretary of the Willapa Harbor Industrial Union Council in the latter 1930s.[60]

For the Raymond IWA local, there remained a strong commitment to dignified working conditions, although this did not necessarily include working-class control of industry. In the IWA's faction fights, the concept of American liberal pluralist unionism which had been used to legitimize opposition to the Bedaux system was used to rally opposition to those elements, including Communists, who were pragmatic in their legislative and negotiating tactics but looked forward to the ultimate socialization of industry. As Chet King recently stated:

> The first thing we talked about . . . was Stalin and his gang over in Russia and we didn't want our country run by a dictator over here and that included the companies. The companies was wanting to dictate.[61]

For the IWA as a whole, it is difficult to estimate how much of the red bloc's early support was the result of the left wing's organizational competence and militant leadership for industrial unionism and improvements in wages, hours, and conditions, and how much represented the existence of a more developed class consciousness among wood workers. The protracted struggle between the "reds" and "whites" was effected by many things including personality conflicts, the changing policies of the CIO, and the nation's gradual economic improvement. It

---

60 Younglove, King, Kight, and Spurrell interviews.
61 King Interview.

is certainly clear, however, that, after the "white" victory, debate in the IWA came to be cast not in terms of long-range strategies for eliminating capitalism from the United States, but, rather, one or another tactic for improving wages, hours, and working conditions within the context of industrial capitalism.

The Bedaux system was imposed at the WHLM in a period of economic collapse, creating a sharp dissonance between the ideals of experienced industrial workers and their altered working lives. The anti-Bedaux struggle was cast in the framework of conserving jobs and an accustomed way of work. The conservative aspect of this localized struggle helped to draw in men whose class position and thinking were ambiguous.[62] Although building a union in opposition to the Bedaux system and in favor of the CIO enjoyed a broad base of support, this solidarity foundered on the harder questions of the CIO's role in determining the economic future of the United States. While many of the anti-Bedaux activists had or developed an anti-capitalist perspective, others justified their struggle for the restoration of their accustomed way of work in terms of American rights, free labor standards, the New Deal, cooperative working relationships, and dignified, secure work. While the anti-Bedaux activists shared a principled opposition to speedup and dictatorship by the boss, only a few considered opposition to capitalism itself as a logical conclusion to draw from their experience.

---

[62] The events at Raymond in the early 1930s are markedly similar to the small town resistance to changes brought by "outside" industrialist innovators in the latter 1800s (Herbert Gutman, "The Workers' Search for Power: Labor in the Gilded Age," in H. Wayne Morgan, ed., *The Gilded Age* [Syracuse, 1963], 38-68).

111

The Emergence of Mass-Production Unionism

DAVID BRODY

AT THE coming of the New Deal, American organized labor was an arrested movement. Membership was slightly under three million in 1933. The unionized portion of the non-agricultural labor force—one-tenth—remained unchanged after thirty years. It was not only a matter of numbers. Labor strength was limited to the needle trades, public utilities (excluding communications), coal-mining, building construction, and the railroads. A vacuum existed in manufacturing, above all, in the mass-production sector. Organized labor had not breached the industries characterized by the giant firm; by multiplant operation for a national market; by an advanced technology involving mechanization and division of labor; and by a work force composed primarily of unskilled and semi-skilled men. The mass-production core—iron and steel, non-ferrous metals, rubber, electrical products, chemicals and petroleum, and food-processing—seemed impervious to trade unionism.

The great breakthrough occurred after 1935. A decade later, most of the mass-production industries had experienced thorough unionization. The consequences were, of

112

course, profound. It was, as Walter Galenson said, "a fundamental, almost revolutionary change in the power relationships of American society." [1] The accomplishment had its origin in the 1930's. But the favoring climate of that decade failed to carry the new unionism to its conclusion. Ultimately, permanent success came from the very events that ended the Great Depression and the New Deal.

The unionization of the mass-production industries still requires explanation; that is the purpose of this preliminary essay. [2]

The achievement began within the changing labor movement. The central fact, obviously, was the creation of the Congress of Industrial Organizations (initially, the Committee for Industrial Organization) as the unionizing agency for the basic industries. Several related questions claim our attention here. What was the necessity that split organized labor? What did the CIO bring to bear that had been lacking in the American Federation of Labor approach to the unionizing of mass production? And, finally, was the union effort decisive in accounting for the organization of the mass-production sector?

The irreconcilable issue seemingly was a matter of structure: industrial versus craft unionism. Industrial organization—the inclusion of all workers in an industry within one union—was a choice closed to the AF of L for several reasons. Foremost was the numerical dominance of the craft unionists: since theirs were the interests to be injured, industrial-union resolutions had never mustered a majority

1. Walter Galenson, *The CIO Challenge to the AFL* (Cambridge, 1960), p. xvii, and for growth of union membership, pp. 583–93.

2. Important recent research based on new sources has added much information on this subject. The documentation will reveal my debts. But no satisfying analysis has emerged from this scholarship. It was this conclusion which led to the undertaking of the present essay.

in AF of L conventions. The Federation was also in a constitutional bind. Jurisdiction was exclusive: only one union could hold rights to a given category of workers. And it was absolute: a union did not have to organize its jurisdiction in order to maintain its right. The craft unions had a kind of property interest within the basic industries. Beyond that was the immovable fact of trade autonomy; the locus of power rested with the national unions. The AF of L was a voluntary institution, William Green observed, and therefore had "no power to compel any union or person to do anything." [3] Even the passage of an industrial-union resolution, Philip Taft has pointed out, "would not have forced any craft union to surrender its jurisdiction, nor compelled unions to amalgamate with each other." [4] There was, finally, the subtle role of *machtpolitik* within the labor movement. Themselves lacking power, Federation officers respected it in other hands. The power realities ordinarily favored the craft interests, and so, therefore, did the inclination of the AF of L leadership. (William Green, agreeing as he did with the viewpoint of the Lewis group, surely displayed that practical quality when the chips came down in 1935 and after.)

These considerations remained binding during the historic debate over structure that took place in the mid-1930's. At the AF of L convention of 1934 in San Francisco the issue was joined over the question of chartering national unions in the automobile, cement, aluminum, and other unspecified mass-production fields. Industrial-union sentiment, stimulated by recent events, forced the convention to recognize that "a new condition exists requiring organization upon a different basis to be most effective." But the conven-

3. James O. Morris, *Conflict within the AFL: A Study of Craft Versus Industrial Unionism, 1901–1938* (Ithaca, N. Y., 1958), p. 8.
4. Philip Taft, *The A.F. of L. in the Time of Gompers* (New York, 1957), p. 200.

tion also wanted to "fully protect the jurisdictional rights of all trade unions organized upon craft lines. . . ." [5] This second statement carried more weight. The Executive Council, to which the actual choice was left, excluded tool-, die-, and machine-making workers and parts plants from the jurisdiction of the new United Automobile Workers and maintenance and machine-installing men from the United Rubber Workers. The fateful Atlantic City convention of 1935 ratified the decision against industrial unionism.

It was a choice that John L. Lewis and his supporters could not accept. They insisted, as Charles Howard of the Typographical Union said, that "in the great mass-production industries industrial organization is the only solution." The aftermath of the 1935 convention was independent action that turned rapidly into dual unionism.

It has been hard to hold the momentous events of 1934-35 in perspective. The debate then was couched in the terminology of industrial unionism, and the outcome was the creation of a group of strong industrial unions. So it seemed to follow that the conflict over structure was the key to the formation of the CIO. That conclusion misplaces the emphasis.

The AF of L did not lack an alternative arrangement. No less than his critics, Samuel Gompers had seen the inappropriateness of the original craft structure for emerging American industrialism. Over the years, there had developed a response to mass production. Gompers had early accepted the need "to organize our fellow workers in unskilled labor."

> With the invention of new machines and the application of new forces, the division and subdivision of labor, many workers who had been employed at skilled trades find themselves with their

5. AF of L, *Proceedings* (1934), pp. 586–7.

occupations gone. . . . Thus we see the artisan of yesterday the unskilled laborer of today.

The essential device was the federal labor union. Gathered first into these mixed local bodies, the unorganized would be drawn off by occupation into the appropriate national unions or into local trade unions affiliated, as were the federal unions, directly with the AF of L. The federal labor unions, said Gompers, were "the recruiting ground for the trade union movement." [6]

Besides organizing non-craft workers, the Federation tried to alter the existing structure to make room for them. Charters were granted to national unions covering the unskilled and semi-skilled within single industries; for instance, the Hod Carriers in construction and the Tin Plate Workers in tin plate manufacture. But Gompers' preference was for the less skilled to find a place within the "primary unions," that is, national unions covering the occupations specific to an industry.[7] To that end, the AF of L urged unions to amalgamate or to accept broader jurisdictions. The optimum result was a national union covering all occupations specific to an industry, irrespective of the skills involved, plus common labor. Such residual jurisdictions in fact were operative at some time in practically every mass-production industry before the 1930's. The craft unions were not victimized thereby. Defining its position in the Scranton Declaration of 1901, the AF of L adhered as closely to the "fundamental principle" of craft organization "as the recent great changes in methods of production and

6. *Ibid.* (1897), pp. 6, 15.
7. For lack of an apt term in the literature, I have coined the phrase "primary union" to describe organizations with residual jurisdiction in mass-production fields. It should be noted that the local unions of these nationals tended to be organized around trades or departments rather than plants, as would be the case with industrial unions.

employment make possible." [8] Primary jurisdictions would not normally encompass such inter-industry occupations as teamsters, carpenters, machinists, and similar trades.

Co-ordination, finally, was encouraged. The primary and craft unions had to act together in the basic industries. As early as the Scranton Declaration, the suggestion had been made of "closely allying the sub-divided crafts" through "the organization of district and national trade councils. . . ." Much of the subsequent co-operation, particularly in joint organizing drives, was on an informal and sporadic basis. During and after World War I, national unions in meat-packing joined together only when faced with the need for common decisions. In steel, on the other hand, twenty-four national unions acted in 1918-20 through the permanent National Committee for Organizing Iron and Steel Workers. At the district level, local unions had formal bodies in the Schenectady plant of General Electric for over a decade after 1911, in meat-packing centers from 1901 to 1904 and again in Chicago from 1917 to 1920, and in steel during the union upsurge of the war period. The departments of the AF of L also promoted joint union activity. The Metal Trades Department chartered local councils and mounted co-operative organizing drives, for instance, in the automobile industry in 1914 and 1927. Inadequate though most of these ventures were, they did not show that organizational unity was unattainable under the primary-craft structural arrangement for the mass-production fields.

The AF of L was adhering to this established plan in 1935. Its advocates insisted that the formula was workable.

8. AF of L, *Proceedings* (1901), p. 240. AF of L organizing assistance, for instance, required prior agreement, as the Butcher Workmen were informed in 1915, "that when the employees of the meat trust are organized, [they] shall be assigned to their respective organizations" (AF of L Executive Council Minutes, February 21–26, 1916, p. 5).

The separation of craft workers would not, after all, be numerically important in mass production. The rubber industry was a case in point. Its labor force, according to a breakdown in the census of 1930, was composed of the following:

     559 carpenters
     395 compositors, linotypers, and typesetters
     915 electricians
  1,206 mechanics
  1,148 stationary engineers
     482 millwrights
  4,665 machinists
     805 plumbers
     300 toolmakers
  1,267 truck drivers
     456 painters and glaziers
80,835 operatives
29,123 laborers[9]

Jurisdiction over the last two categories would give a rubber workers' union nearly 90 per cent of the labor force in the industry. William Hutcheson of the Carpenters could not see why organization would be impeded by separating "a comparatively small number as compared to the total number employed in the rubber industry." And coordination could surely be made to work. John Frey was convinced that "joint negotiations and joint agreement reached through the [Metal Trades] Department forms the most effective answer to . . . the so-called industrial form of trade union organization . . . enabling an employer to negotiate but one agreement which will cover all his em-

9. Harold S. Roberts, *The Rubber Workers: Labor Organization and Collective Bargaining in the Rubber Industry* (New York, 1944), p. 98.

ployees. . . ."[10] In September, 1934, this policy had been adopted for the metal and building trades. Both AF of L departments entered negotiations on this basis with the Anaconda Copper Company.

If not the optimum solution, the AF of L alternative nevertheless seemed adequate and reasonable. The primary-craft formula could not be ruled out as unworkable on the basis of past experience. While deprecated by Lewis adherents, it could not by itself drive the breach in the labor movement.

Nor, for that matter, could the appeal of industrial unionism. "Much has been said about principles in the war between the C.I.O. and the A.F. of L.," commented the informed labor consultant Chester M. Wright in 1939. "As I see it, the whole dispute is one involving tactics and practices. I fail to find any principles involved at any point." [11] Earlier, industrial unionism had involved fundamental differences. Its advocates had been mainly Socialists and others seeking to make the labor movement a vehicle for political action and/or basic social change. That was not the case in the 1930's. Industrial unionism then was directed only at the mass-production industries, not, as in the amalgamation movement of the early 1920's, at the entire economy. The ideological groundwork was mostly gone. John L. Lewis himself had opposed the amalgamationists of the postwar period. His emergence as industrial-union leader in the early New Deal period presumed that the debate over structure did not reflect basic differences about the role of the trade-union movement.

The antagonists were not doctrinaire even on the narrow structural issue. Bitter opponents of Lewis as they were, the Carpenters, Machinists, and Electrical Workers were

10. Philip Taft, *The A.F. of L. from the Death of Gompers to the Merger* (New York, 1959), pp. 86, 91.
11. Chester M. Wright, *Here Comes Labor* (New York, 1939), p. 47.

themselves asserting industrial jurisdiction over limited areas between 1934 and 1936.[12] For his part, Lewis was not rigid on industrial unionism. When the AF of L Executive Council was considering in February, 1935, what craft groups to exclude from an auto workers' union, Lewis pleaded that the "cavilling be deferred until in the light of what accomplishment is made in the objective we can take up the question of dividing the members, that contention over the fruits of victory be deferred until we have some of the fruits in our possession." While he retained hope in the AF of L, Lewis did not commit himself to industrial unionism.[13]

It was not in itself of importance. Lewis was a pragmatist in the dominant tradition of American trade unionism. Labor leaders responded, as William Green said, to "the fact, not a theory but a situation actually existing. . . ."[14] The formation of the CIO was a drastic measure which, from Lewis' standpoint, had to yield a commensurate return. The structural reform of industrial unionism was not such a return. Nor, in fact, was it absolutely precluded from the pragmatic labor movement. Industrial unions could find a place—as did the United Mine Workers of America itself—within the AF of L. The Butcher Workmen had put the fact neatly back in 1922 when the issue over requesting industrial jurisdiction in meat-packing arose. It would be better, the convention decided, first to unionize the industry "and then by reason of the strength that would accompany such an organization, take and retain control over all men of whatever craft

12. Morris, *Conflict Within the AFL*, p. 177; Robert A. Christie, *Empire in Wood: A History of the Carpenters' Union* (Ithaca, N.Y., 1956), chap. ix; Mark Perlman, *The Machinists: A New Study in American Trade Unionism* (Cambridge, 1961), pp. 90–91.
13. Taft, *A. F. of L. from the Death of Gompers*, pp. 105, 107; AF of L, *Proceedings* (1934), p. 588.
14. Taft, *A. F. of L. from the Death of Gompers*, p. 106.

employed in the industry." [15]   The obstacles to that first point—not the second—were the operative ones in 1935.

What excited Lewis and his adherents was a concrete objective: the organization of the mass-production industries.   That accomplished, the structural issue would resolve itself and would, in any case, not be of great moment.   "The fundamental obligation is to organize these people," Lewis insisted. The resulting problems should be considered "after we had accomplished organization and not before, after the fact of organization has been accomplished [,] not tie on reservations that will in themselves deter an effective campaign." [16] This revealed the heart of the crisis: would the AF of L take the measures necessary for the organization of mass-production workers?

Industrial unionism fitted into this larger context. The immense influence of the idea sprang from the contemporary assessment of the psychology of industrial workers. "I know their state of mind," William Green asserted, speaking of the automobile workers. ". . . If you tell them to go here, you here and you there, you will never get anywhere. They are so closely related and inextricably interwoven they are mass minded." [17] In her perceptive *Industrial Valley*, Ruth McKenney described the problem as she saw it in Akron rubber plants.

> . . . The machinists and the electricians kept coming to the Federal local meetings. [The AFL organizer] could never make them understand they were supposed to stay away, supposed to belong to a separate union. He could never teach them that their interests were different from the common ordinary rubberworker. Stubbornly and stupidly they clung to the Federal locals.[18]

15. Amalgamated Meat Cutters and Butcher Workmen of North America, *Proceedings* (1922), pp. 18, 35, 81–82.

16. Taft, *A. F. of L. from the Death of Gompers*, p. 107.

17. *Ibid.*; AF of L, *Proceedings* (1934), p. 592.

18. Ruth McKenney, *Industrial Valley* (New York, 1939), p. 109.

Industrial unionists had here an explanation for the failure
to hold the thousands of industrial workers who had flocked
into the AF of L federal unions in 1933. Sidney Hillman
noted, for example, that during the NRA period over 40,000
rubber workers had been organized. Then the AF of L
"started to divide those workers among the different unions
claiming jurisdiction over them. As a result of that procedure, the membership of the rubber workers union fell as
low as 3,000." [19]

The problem was *tactical*. Since industrial labor was
"mass minded," the first stage of organization had to be on
a mass basis. "Vice President Lewis said there is a psychology there among the men . . . ," read the minutes of
the February, 1935, meeting of the AF of L Executive
Council. "What he has in mind [is that] the time to quarrel
over jurisdiction is after we organize the men rather than
before." [20] William Green shared Lewis' view. The mass-
production industries should be organized "as best we can,
then after they are organized if the question [arises] on the
jurisdiction of an international union, perhaps by education
we can bring about respect among these workers of the
jurisdiction of the national and international unions." [21]

That reasoning explained the hopefulness following the
San Francisco convention of 1934. The objectives then
enunciated seemed irreconcilable: to protect craft jurisdictions and to organize mass-production fields on "a different basis." But an apparent accommodation had emerged
from the many hours of talks off the floor of the convention.
The Executive Council was "directed to issue charters for

19. Mathew Josephson, *Sidney Hillman: Statesman of American
Labor* (New York, 1952), p. 385.
20. AF of L Executive Council Minutes, January 29–February 14,
1935, p. 213. I have utilized the Council minutes in this account. I
have, however, thought it more helpful to give references to Taft or
Galenson except in instances in which selections from the minutes do
not appear in those secondary sources.
21. Taft, *A. F. of L. from the Death of Gompers*, p. 91.

National or International Unions"—the instructions did not specify precise jurisdictions. Second, "for a provisional period" the chartered unions should be under AF of L direction "in order to protect and safeguard the members of such National and International Unions as are chartered. . . ." Both these points—temporary AF of L control and an undefined jurisdiction—were included in John L. Lewis' seven-point program for an automobile union which was presented to the Executive Council in February, 1935. And there was a final point:

> That all questions of overlapping jurisdiction on the automobile parts and special crafts organizations encountered in the administration policy be referred to the Executive Council for consideration at such time as the Council may elect to give these questions consideration.[22]

"This proposal is in strict conformity with the action of the A. F. of L. convention of 1934," Lewis explained, "and in proposing it I intend that if this policy does an injury to any international union that the union thus affected will have the right to take up these questions with the Executive Council of the American Federation of Labor and I assume that judgment will be rendered in conformity with . . . the record of the previous actions of the Council." [23]

Confronting the proposal, the craft leaders could not accept it. Dan Tobin of the Teamsters saw "some merit"

22. *Ibid.*, p. 105; AF of L, *Proceedings* (1935), pp. 94–96, 538. At the San Francisco convention of 1934, Lewis' explanation of the industrials union resolution was thoroughly unrevealing, no doubt for good tactical reasons. The most he would say, when pressed, was that the jurisdictional decisions rested with the Executive Council (to which he and his supporter David Dubinsky were being added). But see the speech of Mathew Woll, AF of L, *Proceedings* (1934), pp. 593–94; also, the editorial in the *American Federationist*, XLI (November, 1934), 1177.

23. AF of L Executive Council Minutes, January 29–February 14, 1935, pp. 68–69, 218–19.

in Lewis' view and was willing to permit a "dispensation for six months or so in the hope we will unscramble them later on. . . ." [24] But others, above all Wharton of the Machinists, had higher stakes in the automobile field. They were responding to the realities of the American labor movement: could they successfully exert their jurisdictional rights *after* organization had occurred on an industrial basis? In fact, they had grown critical even of the standard AF of L practice of placing skilled recruits in federal unions because these recruits then became reluctant to transfer to the appropriate craft unions.[25] William Hutcheson of the Carpenters thought the jurisdictional question "should be straightened out now to avoid trouble." [26] The Executive Council so decided: specific groups were excluded from the jurisdiction of the Auto Workers and, at the next Council meeting, of the Rubber Workers. In essence, the craft unions were refusing to gamble—at long odds—their vested rights in order to unionize mass-production workers. Tobin put the fact bluntly: "We are not going to desert the fundamental principles on which these organizations have lived and are living to help you organize men who have never been organized." [27]

The jurisdictional problem was only the most visible of the obstacles to effective action. National unions with old-line leadership had primary jurisdiction in a number of basic industries—most importantly, the Amalgamated Association of Iron, Steel and Tin Workers. The industrial bloc agreed with Green's view that "the officers of the

24. *Ibid.*, pp. 214–15.

25. See Morris, *Conflict within the AFL*, pp. 152–58; Sidney Fine, "The Origins of the United Automobile Workers, 1933–35," *Journal of Economic History*, XVIII (September, 1958), 254–55.

26. AF of L Executive Council Minutes, January 29–February 14, 1935, p. 213.

27. AF of L Executive Council Minutes, April 30–May 7, 1935, p. 124.

Amalgamated cannot organize these workers with their own resources or with the set-up as is. . . . The change has been taking place but the Amalgamated has been standing committed to its old tradition policy." Lewis urged the chartering of another national union with jurisdiction over steel. The craft unionists refused to abrogate the sacred rights of an autonomous union, as William Hutcheson said, "even if it was in bad straits." [28] They were willing to permit others to mount a steel campaign, but the bulk of the steelworkers would have to go into an organization which had amply proved its incapacity. Exclusive jurisdiction and trade autonomy seemed to be immutable principles.

Finally, the necessary resources were not being directed to the organization of the basic industries. The income of the labor movement accumulated in the national unions, not in the Federation. President Green was able to augment his organizing staff by only fifteen in the critical year 1933. The affiliated unions were unwilling either to raise the per capita going to the AF of L or to expend adequate funds directly in the organizing effort. (The response to Green's appeal in March, 1936, for funds for a steel drive totaled $8,625 from five unions.) The flabbiness of the financial support could be gauged by the later reaction to the CIO threat: AF of L organizing expenses during 1937–39 were triple those of 1933–35. [29] Nor were the unions with jurisdiction in the basic industries roused to a common effort. No joint drives were mounted in 1933–34 that would compare to those of earlier years in steel, autos, textiles, and meat-packing. The AF of L convention of 1934 instructed the Executive Council not only to charter national unions in mass-production industries but to inaugurate a union

28. Taft, *A. F. of L. from the Death of Gompers*, p. 116.
29. Morris, *Conflict within the AFL*, p. 162.

drive in steel. The Council had done nothing beyond passing a resolution by the time of the fateful convention of 1935.

At bottom, the AF of L was experiencing a crisis of will. Lewis bitterly commented in May, 1935, "that some six months have gone by since we adopted that resolution in San Francisco and there still remains the fact that there has been no administration of that policy, no execution of the promissory note that this Federation held out to the millions of workers in the mass-production industry. . . . Neither do I understand there is any immediate desire to carry out that policy. . . . "[30] The choice rested with the controlling craft unionists. And they were not really committed to organizing the mass-production workers. Dan Tobin of the Teamsters, for instance, spoke contemptuously of "the rubbish that have lately come into other organizations." A widespread feeling was, as Mathew Woll said in 1934, that the industrial workers were "perhaps unorganizable." Tobin was saying in February, 1936, that "there isn't a chance in the world at this time to organize the steelworkers." [31]

To John L. Lewis, the basic obstacle was the indifference of the craft leaders. They were the object of his plea at the 1935 convention:

> Why not make a contribution to the well-being of those who are not fortunate enough to be members of your organizations? . . . The labor movement is organized upon a principle that the strong shall help the weak. . . . Is it right, after all, that because some of us are capable of forging great and powerful organizations of

30. AF of L Executive Council Minutes, April 30–May 7, 1935, p. 115.

31. *Ibid.*, p. 174; Taft, *A. F. of L. from the Death of Gompers*, p. 118; Edward Levinson, *Labor on the March* (New York. 1938). p. 84; also, the speech of A. O. Wharton, AF of L, *Proceedings* (1935), pp. 569–72.

skilled craftsmen in this country that we should lock ourselves
up in our own domain and say, "I am merely working for those
who pay me"?

The AF of L had to choose between becoming "an instru-
mentality that will render service to all of the workers" and
resting "content in that comfortable situation that has prevailed through the years. . . ." Convinced at last that the
craft bloc preferred the second path, Lewis saw independent
action as the only remedy to "twenty-five years of constant, unbroken failure." [32]

Mass-production unionization merged with industrial unionism only when hope was lost in the AF of L. Actually,
this began to happen months before the Atlantic City convention of 1935. Lewis started to shift his ground after the
defeat of his program for an auto union at the February
meeting of the Executive Council. At the May meeting, he
did not try to apply his compromise formula to the Rubber
Workers. Rather, he wanted "the jurisdiction granted to
the organization to cover all workers employed throughout
the rubber industry." Nothing was said at the subsequent
convention either in Lewis' arguments or in the Minority
Report about the postponement of jurisdictional questions
until after the achievement of mass-production organization
(although there were such intimations in the speeches of
Lewis' supporters Charles Howard and Sidney Hillman).[33]
The full commitment to industrial unionism became evident

32. AF of L, *Proceedings* (1935), pp. 534, 536, 541.
33. *Ibid.*, pp. 526, 746; AF of L Executive Council Minutes, April
13–May 7, 1935, pp. 113–16. At the May meeting of the Council a
resolution was offered to postpone the jurisdictional decision on the
Rubber Workers until after they had formed an international and
drawn up a constitution with a proposed jurisdiction. This compromise came not from Lewis but, significantly, from AF of L Secretary
Morison, probably with Green's backing. The craft majority refused
this alternative, as well as Lewis' offer to exclude "those engaged in
new construction work." (*Ibid.*, pp. 135–39.)

in Lewis' offer of $500,000 toward an AF of L steel-organizing fund on February 22, 1936. One condition was that "all steel workers organized will be granted the *permanent* right to remain united in one international union." [34]

Having opted for independent action, Lewis had every reason to espouse industrial unionism: it was a desirable structural reform; it would draw in unions such as the Oil Workers and the Mine, Mill and Smelter Workers that were having jurisdictional troubles within the AF of L;[35] and, above all, it would serve as a rallying cry in the union rivalry and in the organizing field. But industrial unionism remained a subordinate consideration. When the occasion demanded, it was sacrificed to the necessities of the organizing task and to the inevitable ambitions for the CIO as an institution.[36] Nor did industrial unionism fulfill the expectations of earlier advocates. No real transformation was worked in the objectives of the labor movement. Differing in some ways, the rival federations were, as Chester Wright insisted, "brothers under the skin," and the passage of twenty years was time enough to permit them to join in a merger.

The CIO had been created with the fixed purpose of organizing the mass-production industries. Liberated from past practice and vested interest, the effort could be made with optimum effectiveness. Starting fresh, the CIO thoroughly exploited its opportunity.

34. Galenson, *CIO Challenge to AFL*, p. 79 (my italics).

35. See, for example, Vernon H. Jensen, *Nonferrous Metals Industry Unionism, 1932–1954: A Story of Leadership Controversy* (Ithaca, N.Y., 1954), chap. iii; Lowell E. Gallaway, "The Origin and Early Years of the Federation of Flat Glass Workers of America," *Labor History*, II (Winter, 1962), 100–102.

36. In some instances, for example, CIO unions attempted to keep groups out of bargaining units if a close election was forthcoming or in order to avoid trouble with the strategic Teamsters. (11 NLRB 950 [1939], 14 NLRB 287 [1939], 16 NLRB 334 [1939], 21 NLRB 1189 [1940].)

The previous restrictions were immediately thrown off. The separation of skilled men no longer, of course, constituted an impediment to organization. Funds in massive amounts were now injected in some areas. The Steel Workers Organizing Committee received in six years $1,619,613 from outside sources, as well as the services of many organizers who remained on the payrolls of other unions.[37] In part, the money came as direct contributions from affluent CIO affiliates. The Mine Workers and the Clothing Workers, frankly anxious for the organization of industries related to them, directed most of their assistance to steel and textiles, respectively. The rest of the CIO income came from a high per capita tax of five cents a month. Proportionately, the investment far surpassed what had been possible within the AF of L (although, it should be noted, the latter in response was doing likewise). Finally, the CIO was able to build the new industrial unions, particularly those which first took the form of organizing committees, free from the restricting hand of the past. There were instances, notably in steel and textiles, where AF of L unions with old-line leaders came over to the CIO, but they were held to subordinate roles. Able officials were recruited from men rising from the ranks or, as in the case of steel, from experienced unionists elsewhere in the CIO.

The job of organizing was meanwhile changing radically. First, mass-production workers were bursting with militancy. The upsurge of NRA-inspired unionism, for instance, was very largely spontaneous. At the time, it seemed to William Green "a sight that even old, tried veterans of our movement never saw before." Another official believed it would surpass in "numbers, intensity, and duration" the union experience of World War I.[38] Even before the CIO, popular militancy was expressing itself in internal resist-

37. Galenson, *CIO Challenge to AFL*, p. 110.
38. Morris, *Conflict within AFL*, p. 147.

ance to AF of L policies and/or in independent unionism, and in rank-and-file strikes such as that at the Toledo Chevrolet plant in April, 1935.[39] The second change followed from the Wagner Act. For the first time, workmen had the legal right to express through majority rule their desires on the question of union representation. On the counts of both rank-and-file sentiment and federal law, success came to depend on the union appeal, hitherto of secondary importance, to the workingmen. To this requirement, the CIO responded brilliantly.

The ingredients of success were unremitting effort and a mastery of the techniques suited to the special conditions of the mass-production industries. A pool of effective organizers for this work could be drawn from CIO affiliates, above all, the Mine Workers; from left-wing groups; and from militants within the industrial ranks. In addition to using the standard methods, CIO organizers emphasized rank-and-file participation. These were the instructions to a group of adherents in Fort Worth on how to organize their Armour plant:

> It takes Organizers inside the plant to Organize the plant.
>
> The Committee that organized the Oklahoma City plant was a voluntary committee established inside the plant.
>
> You cannot wait for the National Organizer to do all the work. . . . You people here can have a Union, but you will have to work to build it.

Typically, an intricate network of unpaid posts was established in CIO plants, so that "more men are given responsibility, and our organization becomes more powerful and

39. On the experience in automobiles, see Fine, "Origins of the United Automobile Workers," *passim,* and Sidney Fine, "The Toledo Chevrolet Strike of 1935," *Ohio Historical Quarterly,* LXVII (1958), 326–56.

more closely knit." The aim was to avoid "bureaucratic" rule by putting the leadership, as one organizer said, not in a few hands, but in "the whole body, in one, acting as one." [40]

Another significant CIO tactic arose out of sensitivity to the deep-seated resentments of the workers. At the plant level, grievances characteristically received aggressive support. When the men saw "how the CIO was fighting to protect workers' rights . . . ," a Packinghouse Workers' official explained, they flocked into the organization. Direct action was another expression of CIO militancy. Sudden strikes and slowdowns, although often against official policy, were frequently encouraged by local officers. For, as one functionary observed of the stoppages at the Armour Chicago plant, they "demonstrated to all, union members and non-union members, that the CIO had plenty of stuff on the ball and that there was no such thing as waiting for something to happen." [41]

The effectiveness of the CIO had another dimension. The basic industries had drawn the newcomers and underprivileged of American society. Eastern Europeans and then, when the flow of immigrants was stopped by World War I, migrants from the South filled the bottom ranks of mass-production labor. The colored workers had unquestionably been among the chief obstacles to earlier union efforts. William Z. Foster, who had taken a leading part in the AF of L drives of World War I, admitted that "we could not win their support. It could not be done. They were constitutionally opposed to unions, and all our forces could

40. Joint Executive Board Minutes, Oklahoma City and Ft. Worth Locals, Packinghouse Workers Organizing Committee, August 9, 1942; District 2 Conference Minutes, PWOC, January 14, 1940, Files of United Packinghouse Workers of America; *People's Press*, July 23, 1938.

41. Arthur Kampfert, "History of Unionism in Meat Packing," MSS in UPWA Files; *CIO News. Packinghouse Edition*, November 5, 1938, p. 8.

not break down that opposition." [42] The problem was of diminishing magnitude in the 1930's. Negro workers, mostly new arrivals from the South fifteen years before, had gone through a lengthy adjustment. In addition, racial tensions had largely abated. There would be no counterpart to the Chicago race riot of 1919 which had disrupted the union drive in the stockyards. Yet the Negro workers still required special treatment.

Here again the CIO capitalized fully on the opportunity. It became an aggressive defender of Negro rights. After a foothold had been gained in the Armour Chicago plant, for example, one of the first union victories was to end the company practice of "tagging" the time cards of colored employees: "the Stars will no longer offend the Negro workers of Armour & Co." The initial informal agreement at the Swift plant included a company pledge to hire Negroes in proportion to their numbers in the Chicago population.[43] The AF of L could not match these zealous efforts. From the start, Gompers had insisted on the necessity of organizing the colored workers, not out of concern for "social or even any other kind of equality," but to insure that they would not "frustrate our every effort for economic, social and political improvement." [44] This view prevailed, before as well as during the New Deal, wherever the membership of Negroes was essential to the success of a union. But many craft affiliates could afford to exclude or segregate such workers, and the Federation reluctantly accepted what it could not prevent. Besides being tainted by discrimination, the AF of L failed to crusade even where it favored racial equality. Doing so, the CIO swept the Negroes in mass

42. Chicago Commission on Race Relations, *The Negro in Chicago* (Chicago, 1922), p. 429.
43. *CIO News. Packinghouse Edition*, January 2, 1939, p. 2; Kampfert, "History of Unionism in Meat Packing."
44. Gerald N. Grob, "Organized Labor and the Negro Worker, 1865–1900," *Labor History*, I (Spring, 1961), 168.

production into its ranks. The same sensitivity to non-economic factors marked the CIO approach to immigrant and female labor and to the fostering of public support through political work and such communal activities as the "back of the yards" movement in the Chicago packing-house district.

The labor movement thus generated an effective response in the basic industries. A further question remains: Was this the decisive change? It does not seem so. More than the incapacity of organized labor had prevented earlier success. Had everything else remained constant, the CIO effort alone would not have resulted in permanent unionization of the mass-production sector—nor, for that matter, would it even have been attempted.

The sense of urgency was significant. At his last AF of L convention, John L. Lewis told Powers Hapgood that a union drive in the basic industries in the past "would have been suicide for organized labor and would have resulted in complete failure. But now, the time is ripe; and now the time to do those things is here. Let us do them."[45] The American system of industrial relations was being profoundly shaken during the mid-1930's. "Conditions as they exist now," Charles Howard told the Atlantic City convention, "make it more necessary, in my opinion, for effective organization activity than at any time during the life of the American Federation of Labor." [46]

In retrospect, employer resistance looms largest in accounting for the long years of union failure in mass production. The sources of that hostility need not be explored here. Suffice it to say that American industrialists found compelling reasons and, more important, adequate means for resisting labor organization. Lewis noted the "great

45. Hapgood quoting Lewis in Saul Alinsky, *John L. Lewis: An Unauthorized Biography* (New York, 1949), p. 80.

46. *Ibid.*, p. 70; AF of L, *Proceedings* (1935), p. 525.

concentration of opposition to the extension and logical expansion of the trade union movement."

> Great combinations of capital have assembled great industrial plants, and they are strong across the borders of our several states from the north to the south and from the west in such a manner that they have assembled to themselves tremendous power and influence. . . .

"There is no corporation in America more powerful than these corporations—General Motors and Ford," William Green said respectfully. "Everybody knows their financial strength. . . . It is a fact we have always recognized." [47] No real possibility of countering the resources and advantages available to industry had earlier existed; the power balance had been overwhelmingly against labor.

In the 1930's, a new legal framework for industrial relations emerged. In the past, the right to organize had fallen outside the law; unionization, like collective bargaining, had been a private affair. Within normal legal limits, employers had freely fought the organization of their employees. Now that liberty was being withdrawn. World War I had first raised the point. The National War Labor Board had protected workers from discrimination for joining unions and thus contributed substantially to the temporary union expansion of the war period. The lesson was inescapable. Unionization in the mass-production industries depended on public protection of the right to organize. The drift of opinion in this direction was discernible in the Railway Labor Act of 1926 and the Norris-LaGuardia Act of 1932. But the real opportunity came with the advent of the New Deal. Then key union spokesmen, notably Green and Lewis, pressed for the insertion of the famous section 7a in

47. AF of L, *Proceedings* (1935), p. 535; AF of L Executive Council Minutes, January 29–February 14, 1935, p. 64, also, for example, p. 213.

the National Industrial Recovery Act. After an exhilarating start, section 7a foundered; loopholes developed and enforcement broke down long before the invalidation of the NRA. But the intent of section 7a was clear, and it soon received effective implementation.

"If the Wagner bill is enacted," John L. Lewis told the AF of L Executive Council in May, 1935, "there is going to be increasing organization. . . ." [48] The measure, enacted on July 5, 1935, heavily influenced Lewis' decision to take the initiative that led to the CIO. For the Wagner Act did adequately protect the right to organize through a National Labor Relations Board clothed with powers of investigation and enforcement. Employer opposition was at long last neutralized.

The Act made it an unfair labor practice for an employer "to interfere with, restrain, or coerce employees in the exercise" of "the right of self-organization." This protection unquestionably freed workers from fear of employer discrimination. Stipulation cases required the posting of such notices as the following at a Sioux City plant:

> The Cudahy Packing Company wants it definitely understood that . . . no one will be discharged, demoted, transferred, put on less desirable jobs, or laid off because he joins Local No. 70 or any other labor organization. . . . If the company, its officers, or supervisors have in the past made any statements or taken any action to indicate that its employees were not free to join Local No. 70 or any other labor organization, these statements are now repudiated.[49]

Even more persuasive was the reinstatement with back pay of men discharged for union activities. The United Auto Workers' cause at Ford was immensely bolstered in

48. Taft, *A. F. of L. from the Death of Gompers*, pp. 89-90.
49. 31 NLRB 967–68 (1941).

1941 by the rehiring of twenty-two discharged men as the result of an NLRB decision which the company had fought up to the Supreme Court. By June 30, 1941, nearly twenty-four thousand charges of unfair labor practices—the majority involving discrimination—had been lodged with the NLRB.[50] More important in the long run, vigorous enforcement encouraged obedience of the law among employers. Assured of their safety, workers flocked into the unions.

The law also resolved the knotty problems of determining union representation. During the NRA period, company unions had been widely utilized to combat the efforts of outside organizations. The Wagner Act now prohibited employers from dominating or supporting a labor union. Legal counsel at first held that "inside" unions could be made to conform with the law by changing their structure, that is, by eliminating management participation from the joint representation plans. The NLRB, however, required the complete absence of company interference or assistance. Few company unions could meet this high standard, and large numbers were disestablished by NLRB order or by stipulation. In meat-packing, for instance, the Big Four companies had to withdraw recognition from over fifteen company unions. Only in the case of some Swift plants did such bodies prevail over outside unions in representation elections and become legal bargaining agents.[51] Besides eliminating employer-dominated unions, the law put the selection of bargaining representatives on the basis of majority rule. By mid-1941, the NLRB had held nearly six thousand elections and cross-checks involving nearly two million workers. Given a free choice, they overwhelmingly preferred a union to no union (the latter choice resulting in

50. Harry A. Millis and Emily Clark Brown, *From the Wagner Act to Taft-Hartley* (Chicago, 1950), p. 77.
51. James R. Holcomb, "Union Policies of Meat Packers, 1929–1943" (Master's thesis, University of Illinois, 1957), pp. 101–2, 124, 139, 161–62.

only 6 per cent of elections in 1937 and, on the average, in less than 20 per cent up to the passage of the Taft-Hartley Act). Having proved its majority in an "appropriate" unit, a union became the certified bargaining agent for all employees in the unit.

An unexpected dividend for union organization flowed from the Wagner Act. In the past, the crisis of mass-production unions had occurred in their first stage. Rank-and-file pressure normally built up for quick action. Union leaders faced the choice of bowing to this sentiment and leading their organizations into suicidal strikes—as happened on the railroads in 1894, in the stockyards in 1904, and in steel in 1919—or of resisting the pressure and seeing the membership melt away or break up in factional conflict —as occurred in meat-packing after World War I. The Wagner Act, while it did not eliminate rank-and-file pressures, eased the problem. A union received NLRB certification on proving its majority in a plant. Certification gave it legal status and rights which could be withdrawn only by formal evidence that it lacked majority support. Defeat in a strike did not in any way affect the status of a bargaining agent. Restraint, on the other hand, became a feasible policy. The CIO unions as a whole were remarkably successful in resisting workers' demands for national strikes in the early years, although not in preventing local trouble. The resulting dissidence could be absorbed. The Packinghouse Workers Organizing Committee, for instance, was in continual turmoil from 1939 to 1941 because of the conservative course of Chairman Van A. Bittner; but internal strife did not lead to organizational collapse there or elsewhere. NLRB certification permitted labor leaders to steer between the twin dangers—external and internal—that earlier had smashed vigorous mass-production unionism.

Years later, the efficacy of the Wagner Act was acknowledged by an officer of the most hostile of the major packing firms: ". . . The unions would not have organized Wilson [and Company] if it had not been for the Act." [52] That judgment was certainly general in open-shop circles.

Yet the Wagner Act was not the whole story. For nearly two years while its constitutionality was uncertain, the law was virtually ignored by antiunion employers. And after the Jones and Laughlin decision in April, 1937, the effect was part of a larger favoring situation. John L. Lewis was not reacting to a single piece of legislation. He saw developing in the mid-1930's a general shift toward unionization.

The change was partly in the workers themselves. Their accommodation to the industrial system had broken down under the long stretch of depression. The resulting resentment was evident in the sitdown strikes of 1936-37, which involved almost half a million men. These acts were generally not a calculated tactic of the union leadership; in fact, President Sherman Dalrymple of the Rubber Workers at first opposed the sitdowns. Spontaneous sitdowns within the plants accounted for the initial victories in auto and rubber.[53] Much of Lewis' sense of urgency in 1935 sprang from his awareness of the pressure mounting in the industrial ranks. A local auto-union leader told Lewis in May, 1935, of talk about craft unions' taking skilled men from the federal unions. "We say like h—— they will and if it is ever ordered and enforced there will be one more independent union." [54] Threats of this kind, Lewis knew, would surely become actions under existing AF of L policy,

52. James D. Cooney, in Holcomb, "Union Policies of Meat Packers," p. 173.

53. Galenson, *CIO Challenge to AFL*, pp. 135 ff., 269 ff.; Roberts, *Rubber Workers*, pp. 144 ff.; McKenney, *Industrial Valley*, Part III. On the spontaneous character of the decisive shutdown of the Ford River Rouge complex, see Irving Howe and B. J. Widick, *The UAW and Walter Reuther* (New York, 1949), pp. 100–101.

54. Fine, "Origins of the United Automobile Workers," p. 280.

and, as he warned the Executive Council, then "we are
facing the merging of these independent unions in some
form of national organization." [55] That prophecy, Lewis
was determined, should come to pass under his control. The
CIO succeeded in large measure because it became the vehicle for channeling the militancy released by the Great
Depression.

The second factor that favored union organization was
the impact of the depression on the major employers. They
had operated on a policy of welfare capitalism: company
paternalism and industrial-relations methods were expected
to render employees impervious to the blandishments of
trade unionism.[56] The depression forced the abandonment
of much of this expense and, beyond that, destroyed the
workers' faith in the company's omnipotence on which
their loyalty rested. Among themselves, as an official of
Swift and Company said, industrialists had to admit that
grounds existed for "the instances of open dissatisfaction
which we see about us, and perhaps with us. . . ." [57]

The depression also tended to undermine the will to fight
unionization. Anti-union measures were costly, the La
Follette investigation revealed. The resulting labor troubles,
in addition, cut deeply into income. The Little Steel companies, Republic in particular, operated significantly less
profitably in 1937 than did competitors who were free of
strikes. Economic considerations seemed most compelling,
not when business was bad, but when it was getting better.
Employers then became very reluctant to jeopardize the
anticipated return of profitable operations. This apparently influenced the unexpected decision of U. S. Steel to

55. Taft, *A. F. of L. from the Death of Gompers,* pp. 89–90. See
also, for example, Howard's speech, AF of L, *Proceedings* (1935), p.
525.

56. See, for example, Irving Bernstein, *The Lean Years: A History
of the American Worker, 1920–1933* (Boston, 1960), chap. iii.

57. F. I. Badgeley, *National Provisioner,* October 28, 1933, pp. 82–84.

recognize the Steel Workers Organizing Committee. In 1937 the Steel Corporation was earning substantial profits for the first time during the depression; net income before taxes that year ultimately ran to 130 million dollars. And the first British purchases for defense were just then in the offing. During the upswing, moreover, the competitive factor assumed increasing importance. Union firms had the advantage of avoiding the disruptions incident to conflict over unionization. Certainly a decline of 15 per cent in its share of the automobile market from 1939 to 1940 contributed to the Ford Company's retreat of the following year.[58]

Finally, the political situation—the Wagner Act aside—was heavily weighted on the side of labor. Management could no longer assume governmental neutrality or, under stress, assistance in the labor arena. The benefits accruing to organized labor took a variety of forms. The Norris-LaGuardia Act limited the use of injunctions that had in the past hindered union tactics. A federal law prohibited the transportation of strikebreakers across state lines. The *Thornhill* decision (1940) declared that antipicketing laws curbed the constitutional right of free speech. Detrimental governmental action, standard in earlier times of labor trouble, was largely precluded now by the emergence of sympathetic officeholders on all levels, from the municipal to the national. Indeed, the inclination was in the opposite direction. The response to the sitdown strike illustrated the change. "Well, it is illegal," Roosevelt commented. "But shooting it out and killing a lot of people because they have violated the law of trespass . . . [is not] the answer. . . . There must be another way. Why can't those fellows in General Motors meet with the committee of workers?"[59]

58. Galenson, *CIO Challenge to AFL*, pp. 93–94, 108–9, 182.
59. Frances Perkins, *The Roosevelt I Knew* (New York, 1946), p. 322.

This tolerance of unlawful labor acts, as sitdowns were generally acknowledged to be, could not have happened at any earlier period of American history. These were negative means of forwarding the labor cause.

But political power was also applied in positive ways. The La Follette investigation undermined antiunion tactics by exposure and, among other ways, by feeding information on spies to the unions.[60] At critical junctures, there was intercession by public officials ranging from President Roosevelt and Labor Secretary Perkins down to Mayor Kelly of Chicago. Governor Frank Murphy's role in the General Motors controversy is only the best known of a number of such mediating contributions to the union cause.[61] At the start of the CIO steel drive Pennsylvania's Lieutenant-Governor Thomas Kennedy, a Mine Workers' officer, announced that organizers were free to move into steel towns and that state relief funds would be available in the event of a steel strike. The re-election of Roosevelt in 1936 no doubt cast out lingering hopes; many employers bowed to the inevitable after F.D.R.'s smashing victory with labor support.

These broader circumstances—rank-and-file enthusiasm, economic pressures on management, and the political condition—substantially augmented the specific benefits flowing from the Wagner Act. In fact, the great breakthroughs at U. S. Steel and General Motors in early 1937 did not result from the law. The question of constitutionality was resolved only some weeks later. And the agreements them-

60. Robert R. R. Brooks, *When Labor Organizes* (New Haven, 1937), p. 72.

61. J. Woodford Howard, "Frank Murphy and the Sit-Down Strikes of 1937," *Labor History*, I (Spring, 1960), 103–40; Barbara W. Newell, *Chicago and the Labor Movement: Metropolitan Unionism in the 1930's* (Urbana, Ill., 1961), pp. 178–79; George Mayer, *Floyd B. Olson* (Minneapolis, 1951), pp. 159-60. For a summary of New Deal "sensitivity" to labor, see Milton Derber and Edwin Young (eds.), *Labor and the New Deal* (Madison, Wis., 1957), chap. v.

selves did not accord with the provisions of the Wagner
Act. The unions dared not utilize procedures for achieving
certification as bargaining agents in the auto and steel
plants. Lee Pressman, counsel for the SWOC, later admitted
that recognition could not then have been won "without
Lewis' brilliant move" in his secret talks with U. S. Steel's
Myron C. Taylor.

> There is no question that [the SWOC] could not have filed a peti-
> tion through the National Labor Relations Board . . . for an
> election. We could not have won an election for collective bar-
> gaining on the basis of our own membership or the results of the
> organizing campaign to date. This certainly applied not only to
> Little Steel but also to Big Steel.[62]

Similarly, the *New York Times* reported on April 4, 1937:
"Since the General Motors settlement, the union has been
spreading its organization rapidly in General Motors plants,
which were weakly organized at the time of the strike."
The NLRB could not require either U. S. Steel or General
Motors to make agreements with unions under those circumstances. Nor did the companies grant the form of recognition contemplated in the Wagner Act, that is, as *exclusive* bargaining agents. (This would have been illegal under
the circumstances.) Only employees who were union members were covered by the two agreements. These initial
CIO victories, opening the path as they did for the general
advance of mass-production unionism, stemmed primarily
from the wider pressures favorable to organized labor.

The Wagner Act proved indecisive for one whole stage
of unionization. More than the enrollment of workers and
the attainment of certification as bargaining agent was
needed in unionization. The process was completed only

62. Alinsky, *Lewis*, p. 149.

when employers and unions entered bona fide collective bargaining. But this could not be enforced by law. Meaningful collective bargaining was achievable ultimately only through the interplay of non-legislative forces.

The tactics of major employers had shifted significantly by the 1920's. Their open-shop doctrine had as its declared purpose the protection of workingmen's liberties. "We do not believe it to be the wish of the people of this country," a U. S. Steel official had said, "that a man's right to work shall be made dependent upon his membership in any organization." [63] Since the closed shop was assumed to follow inevitably from collective bargaining, the refusal to recognize unions was the fixed corollary of the open shop. The argument, of course, cut both ways. Open-shop employers insisted that their employees were free to join unions (whether or not this was so). The important fact, however, was that the resistance to unionism was drawn tight at the line of recognition and collective bargaining. That position had frustrated the attempt of the President's Industrial Conference of October, 1919, to formulate principles for "genuine and lasting cooperation between capital and labor." The union spokesmen had withdrawn in protest against the insistence of the employer group that the obligation to engage in collective bargaining referred only to shop committees, not to trade unions.[64] In effect, the strategy was to fight organized labor by withholding its primary function.

Federal regulation of labor relations gradually came to grips with the question of recognition and collective bargaining. During World War I, the NWLB only required employers to deal with shop committees. Going further, the NRA granted employees the right to "bargain collectively

63. David Brody, *Steelworkers in America: The Non-Union Era* (Cambridge, 1960), p. 176.
64. Lewis L. Lorwin and Arthur Wubnig, *Labor Relations Boards: The Regulation of Collective Bargaining under the National Industrial Recovery Act* (Washington, D.C., 1935), pp. 13–18.

through representatives of their own choosing. . . ." This was interpreted to imply an obligation of employers to deal with such representatives. The major failing of section 7a was that the NRA did not implement the interpretation. In practice, determined employers were able, as earlier, to escape meaningful negotiation with trade unions.[65] It seems significant that the permanent union gains of the NRA period came in those areas—the coal and garment industries—where collective bargaining did not constitute a line of employer resistance. Profiting by the NRA experience, the Wagner Act established the procedure for determining bargaining agents and the policy of exclusive representation and, by the device of certification, withdrew recognition from the option of an employer.

But recognition did not mean collective bargaining. Section 8 (5) did require employers to bargain with unions chosen in accordance with the law. Compliance, however, was another matter. In the first years, hostile employers attempted to withhold the normal attributes of collective bargaining. When a strike ended at the Goodyear Akron plant in November, 1937, for example, the company insisted that the agreement take the form of a "memorandum" signed by the mediating NLRB regional director, not by company and union, and added that "in no event could the company predict or discuss the situation beyond the first of the year." [66] (Although the Rubber Workers' local had already received certification, it would not secure a contract for another four years.) Westinghouse took the position that collective bargaining "was simply an opportunity for representatives of the employees to bring up and discuss problems affecting the working force, with the final decision

65. On the difficulties over this question in the automobile industry, see Irving Fine, "Proportional Representation of Workers in the Automobile Industry," *Industrial and Labor Relations Review*, XIII (January 1959), 182–205.

66. Roberts, *Rubber Workers*, p. 223.

reserved to the company. It rejected the notion of a signed agreement because business conditions were too uncertain. . . ." [67] Some companies—for instance, Armour in April, 1941—unilaterally raised wages while in union negotiations. The contractual forms were resisted: agreements had to be verbal, or take the form of a "statement of policy," or, if in contractual terms, certainly with no signatures. These blatant evasions of the intent of section 8 (5) were gradually eliminated: a series of NLRB and court rulings prohibited the refusal to negotiate or make counteroffers, the unilateral alteration of the terms of employment, and opposition to incorporating agreements into written and signed contracts.

The substance proved more elusive than the externals of collective bargaining. "We have no trouble negotiating with Goodyear," a local union president observed, "but we can never bargain. The company stands firmly against anything which does not give them the absolute final decision on any question." [68] The law, as it was interpreted, required employers to bargain "in good faith." How was lack of good faith to be proved? The NLRB tried to consider the specific circumstances and acts, rather than the words, of the employer in each case. That cumbersome procedure was almost useless from the union standpoint. Delay was easy during the case, and further evasion possible afterward. Barring contempt proceedings after a final court order, moreover, the employer suffered no penalties for his obstruction; there was no counterpart here for the back-pay provisions in dismissal cases. The union weakness was illustrated at Wilson & Co. The Cedar Rapids packing plant had been well organized since the NRA period, but

67. Twentieth Century Fund, *How Collective Bargaining Works: A Survey of Experience in Leading American Industries* (New York, 1945), pp. 763–64.
68. Roberts, *Rubber Workers*, p. 247.

no agreement was forthcoming from the hostile management. In 1938 the union filed charges with the NLRB. Its
decision came in January, 1940, and another year was consumed by the company's unsuccessful appeal to the Circuit
Court. The negotiations that followed (interrupted by a
strike which the union lost) led nowhere because, a union
official reported, Wilson "as always . . . tried to force the
Union to accept the Company's agreement or none at all." [69]
The contract which was finally consummated in 1943 resulted neither from an NLRB ruling nor from the free
collective bargaining that was the aim of the Wagner Act.
Clearly, "good faith" was not to be extracted from recalcitrant employers by government fiat.

The collective-bargaining problem had a deeper dimension. The bitter-enders themselves constituted a minority
group in American industry. For every Westinghouse,
Goodyear, Ford, and Republic Steel there were several
major competitors prepared to abide by the intent of the
law and enter "sincere negotiations with the representatives
of employees." But, from the union standpoint, collective
bargaining was important for the results it could yield.
Here the Wagner Act stopped. As the Supreme Court noted
in the Sands case, "from the duty of the employer to bargain collectively . . . there does not flow any duty . . . to
accede to the demands of the employees." [70] No legal force
sustained the objectives of unions either in improving
wages, hours, and conditions or in strengthening their position through the union shop, master contracts, and arbitration of grievances.

The small utility of the law in collective bargaining was
quickly perceived by labor leaders. The CIO packing-house

69. National Wilson Conference Minutes, PWOC, February 14, 1942,
UPWA Files. See also, 19 NLRB 990 (1940).

70. Quoted in Joseph Rosenfarb, *The National Labor Policy and
How It Works* (New York, 1940), p. 197.

union, for instance, did not invoke the Wagner Act at all
in its three-year struggle with Armour. The company, in
fact, objected to the intercession of Secretary of Labor
Perkins in 1939 on the ground that the union had not
exhausted, or even utilized, the remedies available through
the NLRB.[71] The dispute actually did involve issues which
fell within the scope of the Wagner Act. But the union
clearly was seeking more effective ways—federal pressure
in this case—of countering Armour's reluctance to negotiate and sign contracts. For the prime union objective
was a master contract covering all the plants of the company organized by the union, a concession which could only
be granted voluntarily by the company. Collective bargaining, both the process itself and the fruits, depended on the
working of the other advantages open to the unions in the
New Deal era.

Where negotiation was undertaken in "good faith," there
were modest initial gains. The year 1937, marking the
general beginning of collective bargaining in mass production, saw substantial wage increases as the result of negotiations and/or union pressure. In steel, the advances of
November, 1936, and March, 1937, moved the unskilled
hourly rate from 47 cents to 62½ cents. In rubber, average
hourly earnings rose from 69.8 cents to 76.8 cents; in
automobiles, from 80 to 93 cents. Other gains tended to be
slender. The U. S. Steel agreement, for instance, provided
the two major benefits of time-and-a-half after eight hours
and a grievance procedure with arbitration. The vacation
provision, on the other hand, merely continued an existing
arrangement, and silence prevailed on many other questions. The contracts were, in contrast to later ones, very
thin documents.[72] Still, the first fruits of collective bargaining were encouraging to labor.

71. *New York Times*, September 12, 1939.
72. For an analysis of the U. S. Steel agreement, see Robert R. R.
Brooks, *As Steel Goes . . .: Unionism in a Basic Industry* (New
Haven, 1940), chap. viii.

Then the economy faltered again. In 1938 industrial unions had to fight to stave off wage cuts. They succeeded in most, but not all, cases. Rates were reduced 15 per cent at Philco after a four months' strike. Less visible concessions had to be granted in some cases. For example, the SWOC and UAW accepted changes which weakened the grievance procedure at U. S. Steel and General Motors.[73] The mass-production unions were, in addition, hard hit by the recession. Employment fell sharply. The UAW estimated that at the end of January, 1938, 320,000 auto production workers were totally unemployed and most of the remainder of the normal complement of 517,000 were on short time. The union's membership was soon down to 90,000. It was the same story elsewhere. In the Chicago district of the SWOC, dues payments fell by two-thirds in the twelve months after July, 1937 (that is, after absorbing the setback in Little Steel).[74] Declining membership and, in some cases, internal dissension rendered uncertain the organizational viability of the industrial unions. And their weakness in turn further undermined their effectiveness in collective bargaining. They faced a fearful choice. If they became quiescent, they would sacrifice the support of the membership. If they pressed for further concessions, they would unavoidably become involved in strikes. By so doing, they would expose their weakened ranks in the one area in which labor legislation permitted the full expression of employer hostility—and in this period few even of the law-abiding employers were fully reconciled to trade unionism.

Collective bargaining was proving a severe obstacle to the new mass-production unions. The Wagner Act had little value here; and the other favoring circumstances had declining effectiveness after mid-1937. Hostile employers were

73. *Ibid.*, p. 211; Galenson, *CIO Challenge to AFL*, p. 158.
74. Galenson, *CIO Challenge to AFL*, p. 157; Newell, *Chicago and the Labor Movement*, p. 144.

evading the requirement of negotiating in good faith. For
the larger part, the industrial unions achieved the first
approximation of collective bargaining. But from 1937 to
1940 very little more was forthcoming. The vital function
of collective bargaining seemed stalled. The situation was,
in sum, still precarious five years after the formation of
the CIO.

John L. Lewis had made something of a miscalculation.
The promise of the New Deal era left mass-production
unionism short of permanent success. Ultimately, two fortuitous circumstances rescued the industrial unions.

The outbreak of World War II finally ended the American
depression. By 1941, the economy was becoming fully engaged in defense production. Corporate profits before taxes
leaped from 6½ billion dollars in 1939 to 17 billion in
1941. The number of unemployed fell from 8½ million
in June, 1940, to under 4 million in December, 1941. It was
this eighteen-month period that marked the turning point
for the CIO. Industry's desire to capitalize on a business upswing, noted earlier, was particularly acute now; and rising
job opportunities and prices created a new militancy in the
laboring ranks. The open-shop strongholds began to crum-
ble. Organization came to the four Little Steel companies, to
Ford, and to their lesser counterparts. The resistance to collective bargaining, where it had been the line of conflict,
was also breaking down. First contracts were finally being
signed by such companies as Goodyear, Armour, Cudahy,
Westinghouse, Union Switch and Signal. Above all, collective bargaining after a three-year gap began to produce
positive results. On April 14, 1941, U. S. Steel set the pattern for its industry with an increase of ten cents an hour.
For manufacturing generally, average hourly earnings from
1940 to 1941 increased over 10 per cent and weekly earnings 17 per cent; living costs rose only 5 per cent. More

149

than wages was involved. Generally, initial contracts were
thoroughly renegotiated for the first time, and this produced
a wide range of improvements in vacation, holiday, and
seniority provisions and in grievance procedure.   Mass-
production workers could now see the tangible benefits
flowing from their union membership.   These results of
the defense prosperity were reflected in union growth: CIO
membership jumped from 1,350,000 in 1940 to 2,850,000 in
1941.[75]

The industrial unions were arriving at a solid basis. That
achievement was insured by the second fortuitous change.
American entry in the war necessitated a major expansion
of the federal role in labor-management relations.   To prevent strikes and inflation, the federal government had to
enter the hitherto private sphere of collective bargaining.
The National War Labor Board largely determined the
wartime terms of employment in American industry. This
emergency circumstance, temporary although it was, had
permanent consequences for mass-production unionism.
The wartime experience disposed of the last barriers to
viable collective bargaining.

For one thing, the remaining vestiges of anti-unionism
were largely eliminated. The hard core of resistance could
now be handled summarily. In meat-packing, for instance,
Wilson & Co. had not followed Armour, Swift, and Cudahy
in accepting collective bargaining.   In 1942 the NWLB
ordered the recalcitrant firm to negotiate a master contract
(Wilson was holding to the earlier Big Four resistance to
company-wide bargaining). Years later in 1955, a company
official was still insisting that Wilson would not have accepted "a master agreement if it had not been for the war.

75. Joel Seidman, *American Labor from Defense to Reconversion*
(Chicago, 1953), pp. 27, 31, 32; Galenson, *CIO Challenge to AFL*,
p. 587; on contract terms, Twentieth Century Fund, *How Collective
Bargaining Works, passim*.

Such an agreement is an unsatisfactory arrangement; today or yesterday." [76] Subsequent negotiations having yielded no results, a Board panel itself actually wrote the first Wilson contract.[77]

Beyond such flagrant cases, the NWLB set to rest an issue deeply troubling to the labor-management relationship in mass production. With few exceptions, the open shop remained dogma even after the acceptance of unionism. "John, it's just as wrong to make a man join a union," Benjamin Fairless of U. S. Steel insisted to Lewis, ". . . as it is to dictate what church he should belong to." [78] The union shop had been granted in auto by Ford only; in rubber, by the employers of a tenth of the men under contract;[79] in steel, by none of the major producers (although they had succumbed under pressure in the "captive mines"). The issue was profoundly important to the new unions. The union shop meant membership stability and, equally significant, the full acceptance of trade unionism by employers. The NWLB compromised the charged issue on the basis of a precedent set by the prewar National Defense Mediation Board. Maintenance-of-membership prevented members from withdrawing from a union during the life of a contract. Adding an escape period and often the dues checkoff, the NWLB had granted this form of union security in 271 of 291 cases by February, 1944. The CIO regarded maintenance-of-membership as a substantial triumph. And, conversely, some employers took the measure, as Bethlehem and Republic Steel asserted, to be a "camouflaged closed shop." Among the expressions of resentment was the indication in contracts, following the example of Montgomery

76. Holcomb, "Union Policies of Meat Packers," p. 172.

77. 6 War Labor Reports 436–41 (1943).

78. Benjamin F. Fairless, *It Could Only Happen in the United States* (New York, 1957), p. 38.

79. Roberts, *Rubber Workers*, p. 310.

Ward, that maintenance-of-membership was being granted "over protest." [80] This resistance, however, was losing its force by the end of the war. The union shop then generally grew from maintenance-of-membership.

The war experience also served a vital educational function. A measure of collective bargaining remained under wartime government regulation. Both before and after submission of cases to the NWLB, the parties involved were obliged to negotiate, and their representatives had to participate in the lengthy hearings. From this limited kind of confrontation, there grew the consensus and experience essential to the labor-management relationship. Wartime education had another aspect. The wage-stabilization policy, implemented through the Little Steel formula by the NWLB, tended to extend the issues open to negotiation. Abnormal restraint on wages convinced labor, as one CIO man said, that "full advantage must be taken of what leeway is afforded" to achieve "the greatest possible gains. . . ." [81] As a result the unions began to include in their demands a variety of new kinds of issues (some merely disguised wage increases) such as premium pay, geographical differentials, wage-rate inequalities, piece-rate computation, and a host of "fringe" payments. Thus were guidelines as to what was negotiable fixed for use after the war and a precedent set that would help further to expand the scope of collective bargaining. The collapse of economic stabilization then also would encourage the successive wage increases of the postwar rounds of negotiation. However illusory these gains were in terms of real income, they endowed the industrial unions with a reputation for effectiveness.

80. Seidman, *American Labor from Defense to Reconversion,* chap. vi.
81. Officers' Report, 2nd Wage and Policy Conference, July 8–10, 1943, PWOC, UPWA Files.

Finally, the wartime restrictions permitted the groping advance toward stable relations to take place in safety. The danger of strikes that might have pushed the parties back to an earlier stage of hostilities was eliminated. Strikes there were in abundance in the postwar period, but these could then be held to the objective of the terms of employment, not the issue of unionism itself. Nothing revealed more of the new state of affairs than the first major defeat of an industrial union. The packing-house strike of 1948 was a thorough union disaster in an industry traditionally opposed to trade unionism. Yet the United Packinghouse Workers of America recovered and prospered. As one of its officials noted with relief, it was the first time in the history of the industry that a " 'lost' strike did not mean a lost union." [82]

Unionization thus ran its full course in mass production. The way had been opened by the New Deal and the Great Depression. The legal right to organize was granted, and its utilization was favored by contemporary circumstances. John L. Lewis seized the unequalled opportunity. Breaking from the bounds of the labor establishment, he created in the CIO an optimum instrument for organizing the mass-production workers. These developments did not carry unionization to completion. There was, in particular, a failure in collective bargaining. In the end, the vital progress here sprang fortuitously from the defense prosperity and then the wartime impact on labor relations. From the half-decade of war, the industrial unions advanced to their central place in the American economy.

82. *Packinghouse Worker*, August 20, 1948, p. 7.

FROM THE "NEW UNIONISM" TO THE NEW DEAL

by
Steve Fraser*

From the onset of the Great Depression, and continuing throughout the lifetime of the New Deal, re-casting the nation's political economy became the overriding preoccupation of American politics. The economic crisis inevitably called into question the prevailing relationship between the government, the economy, and society. In particular, the power of dominant industrial, commercial, and financial institutions was severely tested. Political alternatives proliferated, but tended to gather around one of two possible general approaches. On the one hand, numerous proposals, some more conservative than others, suggested deploying the moral authority of the Federal government to sanction a system of industrial self-regulation. On the other hand, this corporatist politics was opposed by those who envisioned a more autonomous and active role for the state in regulating and encouraging the growth of the national economy, and prescribed policies, some more liberal than others, subsequently characterized as Keynesian.

Generally speaking, the organized labor movement, during the first years of the depression and formative period of the National Recovery Administration, was so weak and isolated that it could exercise little leverage over the outcome of the strategic contest between corporatist and Keynesian alternatives. The union leader Sidney Hillman, almost alone among his peers,

* I owe a great debt to the as yet unpublished work of Peter Friedlander on the economic and political development of the Keynesian elite. In addition, for their criticisms and suggestions I would like to thank: Jill Andresky, Melvyn Dubofsky, Stanley Engerman, Eric Foner, and Ronald Schatz.

0023-656x/84/2503-405

was deeply involved in this protracted struggle to determine the contours of public policy.

Previous assessments of labor politics, and in particular of Hillman's approach to reform and recovery in this period, have claimed a neat fit between the specific policies pursued by Hillman and the program of "corporate liberalism." "Corporate liberalism," in this view, sought to deliberately incorporate industrial unionism into its design for the new industrial state and represented the dominant outlook of American big business. And it has been additionally argued that the basic working arrangements between corporate liberals and industrial unionists like Hillman were established decades earlier in the first collaborations between reform-minded corporate leaderships, represented particularly in the National Civic Federation, and AFL executives. Thus, a more or less unbroken line of coherent policy supposedly connects the activities of Samuel Gompers in the pre and post-war eras with those of Sidney Hillman during the depression.

An examination of Hillman's behavior in the formative period of the New Deal, however, undermines this argument of historic continuity. More importantly, this examination suggests that the "corporate liberal" view has over-simplified the relationship between organized labor, industry, and the state. That relationship can be reinterpreted.

It is true that the precarious conditions facing a number of industries in the 1920s, coal and textile particularly, predisposed corporate managements and union bureaucrats toward corporatist ideas and practices. The decade witnessed the proliferation of trade associations and other forms of business self-regulation with which the AFL cooperated.

However, even among long-established business elites there was never an enduring consensus on the organizational and political implications of corporatism. There were those elements, represented by the United States Chamber of Commerce and the National Association of Manufacturers, who were reluctant to invite the state to undertake a more substantial role in the conduct of business. Moreover, they adopted an extremely narrow view of which groups, outside of the restricted circles of industrial leadership, might be permitted inside the inner councils of policy formulation. "Corporate liberals," on the other hand, were prepared to accept an enlarged role for the government and to share power with other organized interest groups as a way of insuring economic stability and the long-term political hegemony of business. The NRA was the first comprehensive effort at this kind of state-supported corporatism. It represented a compromise between those interests still committed to strictly voluntarist arrangements and those for whom some government intervention had come to seem inevitable.

The corporatist viewpoint, especially its more privatist versions, by and large represented the interests of an older grouping of business elites concentrated in railroads, public utilities, primary commodities, and raw materials. They were frequently linked to those older investment banking houses which first emerged after the Civil War and had continued ever since to dominate the Republican Party. Plagued by over-production, older technologies, foreign competition, and an enormous burden of debt and inflated capital values, they sought cartel-like arrangements to control and limit production and technical innovation while sharing out the existing market among dominant producers.

Corporatism, however, whether of the private or statist variety, did not circumscribe the horizon of business politics. Standing apart from this traditional business elite was a milieu of emerging, diversified, mass-consumption oriented industries. They were often technologically advanced, and linked to a network of mass retailing interests and to a newer generation of investment and savings bank institutions. Together with other technocratic, managerial, and political elites, this segment of business sought to eliminate the obstacles to economic development and expansion presented by the inefficiencies, restrictions on mass purchasing power, and over-capitalization of corporatist industry and finance.

This newer Keynesian milieu was particularly concerned with expanding the mass market, and was thereby led to promote the power of the state to regulate the market, to engage in macro-economic planning and unorthodox fiscal policy, and to preserve and enhance "human capital." This concern with "human capital"—the welfare dimension of the "welfare state"—entailed support for a cluster of measures including legislation covering wages, hours, working conditions, the rights of unions, unemployment insurance, and social security. Keynesian strategy also envisioned a more prominent role for trade unions in the industrial, political, and administrative process. For these reasons, Hillman was most closely associated with this Keynesian elite rather than its various corporatist opponents.

A closer analysis of Hillman's activities may thus help clarify the inner dynamics of labor politics at a critical moment. It may also illuminate those structural and political conflicts that would later culminate in the creation of the corporate-bureacratic and administrative welfare state.[1]

* * * * *

Shortly before the stock market collapsed, Hillman observed that "a high standard of living is no more a question of mere

---

[1] Keynesianism is not used here to refer to a formal theoretical system as of course in the period under discussion such theory was neither fully elaborated nor generally known outside of professional circles. It is instead a convenient way of referring to a set of practices and policies, and in particular the role of the state in manipulating monetary and fiscal policy in order to maintain aggregate demand at a level necessary to fuel economic growth and employment. Although during the early 1930s very few if any of the persons or institutions examined here would have identified their outlook and policy reccomendations as Keynesian (with the possible exception of Frankfurter), they were all committed to partial or more comprehensive public policies that targeted demand and mass consumption as the key to economic recovery. In that sense, its use here is not anachronistic.

Ronald Radosh, "The Corporate Ideology of American Labor Leaders from Gompers to Hillman," in James Weinstein and David W. Eakins, eds., *For a New America* (New York, 1970) systematically interprets the labor movement, and in particular the activities of Hillman from the standpoint of corporate liberalism. See also Radosh's "Myth of the New Deal" in Ronald Radosh and Murray N. Rothbard, eds., *A New History of Leviathan: Essays on the Rise of the American Corporate State* (New York, 1972) and Barton Bernstein, "The New Deal: The Conservative Achievement of Liberal Reform," in Barton J. Bernstein, ed., *Towards a New Past: Dissenting Essays in American History* (New York, 1968). The best discussion of corporatist tendencies in the 1920's occurs in Ellis W. Hawley, *The Great War and the Search for a Modern Order: A History of the American People and Their Institutions, 1917-1933* (New York, 1979). Useful also are the appropriate sections of Jordan Schwartz, *The Speculator: Bernard M. Baruch in Washington, 1917-65* (Chapel Hill, 1981). Robert F. Himmelberg, *The Origins of the NRA: Business, Government, and the Trade Association Issue, 1921-33* (New York, 1976) provides a detailed analysis of the explicit connection between trade association practice and ideology in the 1920s and the NRA. Ellis W. Hawley, *The New Deal and the Problem of Monopoly: A Study in Economic Ambivalence* (Princeton, 1966) examines the struggle between corporatist and alternative strategies during and after the NRA. Kim McQuaid, "The Frustration of Corporate Revival During the Early New Deal," *The Historian,* Aug. 1979, also argues against the notion that corporate liberals comprised a cohesive group with a consistent strategy of reform.

justice . . . It is essential to our system of mass production to create a consumers' demand for almost unlimited output." He went on to assert that "to meet these problems, only the labor movement holds out a constructive program," and suggested that the historic experience of the Amalgamated Clothing Workers ought to be exemplary: "From almost the beginning the organization has been alive to the importance of sound economic policy and efficient administrative procedure . . . . It has learned from contact with the problems of industry that in order to serve its members effectively, it must achieve the capacity and willingness to share in the responsibilities of management and to participate in the administration of industry." And indeed, through an active collaboration with pro-union elements of the industry, mass retailers, and members of the Taylor Society, the union had, by the late 1920s, assumed a large share of the technical and supervisory functions of management.[2]

The ACW was exemplary of the era's "new unionism." What was new about it was precisely this sense of itself as an institution responsible not only for the material well-being of its members, but for the efficient and equitable functioning of the industrial order as a whole. The Hillman leadership was thus firmly committed to the practices of scientific management under union supervision. It was widely known as a leading exponent of social welfare liberalism and favored extensive government regulation of business, as well as the redistribution of national income. By the eve of the depression, the "new unionism" had already helped to invent a new vocabulary of reform whose "key words" were economic rationalization, social security, income redistribution, national planning, co-management, and industrial democracy in the interests of mass production and mass consumption.[3]

These historic commitments developed over the two formative decades of the union's life. A system of "industrial democracy" was perhaps the most noted outgrowth of this period. It

[2] *St. Louis Post-Dispatch* (50th. Anniversary Edition), Dec. 9, 1928; *Documentary History of the Amalgamated Clothing Workers of America* (hereafter *Doc. Hist*) 1926-28.
[3] Steve Fraser, "Dress Rehearsal for the New Deal", in Michael Frisch and Daniel J. Walkowitz, eds. *Working Class America: New Essays on the History of Labor, Community, and American Society* (Urbana, 1983).

was based on a close collaboration between the union leadership and pro-union wing of the scientific management movement. Together they recognized that independent labor organizations were the only vehicles through which voluntarily internalized work discipline could be maintained to insure stability on the shopfloor. By the end of World War I, the accommodation with scientific management had become a wide-ranging political alliance, thanks especially to the remarkable relationship that grew up between Hillman and the post-war leader of the Taylor Society (and future New Dealer) Morris Cooke.

Although first of all concerned with the internal mechanisms of the clothing industry, this collaboration expanded to cover broader issues, including unemployment insurance as well as the re-casting of the nation's political economy. For his part, Cooke was convinced that the co-management and workers' participation schemes operating in the clothing industry were generally applicable to the economy at large. The apparatus and ideology of the "new unionism" seemed to represent the best available strategy for dealing with the problems of legitimacy and efficiency that accompanied the badly eroded authority of management on the shopfloor. Moreover, he and Hillman agreed that it would help re-orient the attention of workers to matters of consumption and purchasing power and to instill a sense of *individual* rights and obligations, psychological transformations which lay at the root of the "new capitalism."[4]

As early as 1920 their discussions envisioned an enormously enlarged role for organized labor in the management and administration of business: in a new order devoted to expanded production the labor movement would

> stand out before the country as not only back of a program of production, but energetically claiming . . . a responsible part of scheming out and executing such a program. If . . . labor is to ultimately have a radically different part to play in industry, these new constraints and duties will provide the best possible training for the larger responsibilities which would come to labor under any re-vamping of the present order.[5]

---

[4] Fraser, *passim*; Morris Cooke to Sidney Hillman, 6/18/19, 10/10/22, 6/7/19, 9/10/19, 4/15/20, Morris L. Cooke Papers, Box 9, Files 73-90, FDR Library, Hyde Park; Cooke to Harlow Person, *et al*, 6/18/20, 6/22/20, Box 9, Files 73-90, Cooke Papers; Meyer Jacobstein to Cooke, 3/13/20, 2/10/20, Box 21, File 211, Cooke Papers.
[5] Cooke to Hillman, 12/29/19, 4/15/20, Box 9, "Jacobstein File," Cooke Papers.

The "industrial democracy" for which Hillman and Cooke expected so much developed alongside and as a part of the ACW's historic commitment to social democracy. From its inception, the union maintained an organic relationship with the worlds of ethnic, particularly Jewish and Italian, socialism, and with a wider milieu of Progressive social reformers, including Jane Addams, Louis Brandeis, Walter Lippmann, Felix Frankfurter, Robert LaFollette, and Florence Kelley. During the 1920s the union undertook a series of successful ventures in cooperative housing and labor banking as well as a pioneering program of employer-employee funded unemployment insurance it hoped would be emulated in other industries. So too, the ACW was invariably associated with an array of reforms, some the fragile remains of Progressivism, including the nationalization of the railroads, state ownership and/or operation of public utilities, and cooperative manufacturing.[6]

For the Hillman leadership the prospect for industrial and social democracy was in the end a political question, a matter of state policy. Depending on the prevailing balance of power, however, the union was prepared, if necessary, to pursue these objectives privately as was evidenced by its cooperative manufacturing, retailing, and financial ventures. But the erratic nature of the clothing industry together with the cyclical oscillations of the economy at large, had, ever since World War I, impressed upon the union leadership the need for government intervention and regulation. Domestic wartime economic mobilization had convinced Hillman not only of the advantages of government intervention, but also acquainted him with the interior of a state apparatus just then undergoing a vast functional and organizational expansion.[7]

Political relationships established during and immediately after the war with Progressives in both parties, which were sub-

---

[6] Fraser, *passim*; Sidney Hillman, "A Successful Experiment in Unemployment Insurance", *Annals of the American Academy of Political and Social Science*, Philadelphia, March, 1931; Steve Fraser, "The New Unionism and the New Economic Policy" in James Cronin and Carmen Sirianni, eds., *Labor Insurgency and Workers' Control, 1900-1925* (Philadelphia, 1983); Matthew Josephson, *Sidney Hillman: Statesman of American Labor* (New York, 1952), *passim*.

[7] Cooke to Hillman, 12/29/19, 4/15/20, Box 9, "Jacobstein File", Cooke Papers; Fraser, "The New Unionism . . ."; Fraser, "Dress Rehearsal . . .".

stantially responsible for the growth and consolidation of the union, endured throughout the 1920s. However, the political quiescence and deceptive economic and industrial well-being of that decade as well as the influence momentarily exerted by the ideology and practice of welfare capitalism relegated programmatic political initiatives to the periphery of national politics. There was a growth of trade associations and corporate bodies designed to regulate and police economic activity privately. But in the public realm there was little more than a mooting about of ideas for a functionally organized national economic council, modest proposals for counter-cyclical public works, and quasi-public undertakings like Owen Young's Business Cycle Committee, which searched for private ways to shore up aggregate consumer demand. The only serious effort to realign politics in favor of reform died with the disappointments of the 1924 LaFollette campaign with which the ACW was directly associated.[8]

The Depression of course generated a crisis of confidence in the old order. By upsetting most prevailing political institutions and coalitions, it became the occasion to renew old Progressive alliances as part of a strategic regroupment and redistribution of power. From Hillman's standpoint the collapse of the economy presented at one and the same time a specific and desperate emergency for the life of the ACW, and a broader imperative to fashion a new set of national political and administrative institutions. He was furthermore convinced that these two goals were inseparable, that rescuing the union entirely depended on the realignment and re-orientation of national politics and the systematic creation of an enlarged state apparatus with the authority to regulate and direct the whole economy.

The crisis facing the ACW was acute. By 1932, the industry was functioning at 30% of capacity, 50% of the workforce was unemployed, and unemployment reserves were exhausted. Wages

---

[8] Hillman to Cooke, 7/9/32; Cooke to Hillman, 7/11/32, 4/19/33, Box 128, Cooke Papers; Fraser, "Dress Rehearsal . . ."; Josephson, *passim*. Circles organized by Felix Frankfurter and Louis Brandeis participated in what amounted to a series of legislative and propaganda exercises on behalf of progressive reform in which Hillman was sometimes involved —see Bruce Allen Murphy, *The Brandeis-Frankfurter Connection: The Secret Political Activities of Two Supreme Court Justices* (New York, 1982), 91-95.

had fallen between 40 and 50%, bankruptcies had become epidemic, and the union could barely support itself. All the worst abuses of the pre-union era reappeared including fratricidal competition, sweatshop labor and homework, sub-contracting, and the spread of runaway shops. Hillman used every piece of tactical ingenuity developed over the previous 20 years to prevent the industry from devouring itself and the ACW. Mass organizing campaigns, self-sacrificing concessions by the rank and file in the interests of reduced costs, and institutional retrenchments were skillfully orchestrated with joint initiatives by grateful retailers and manufacturers to maintain minimal labor standards and to police transgressors.[9]

But the forces against which he contended were simply overwhelming. Early in 1933, Hillman wrote, deeply deeply depressed, to his long-time friend, legal adviser, and political confidante, Felix Frankfurter, to say, "what seems so very sad to me is the fact that whatever constructive work was accomplished in the last two decades in industry is being broken down and our drifting toward chaos is being accelerated almost from day to day." The period was, in his view, "the darkest since the Depression began," and he was "fearful that before Mr. Roosevelt will

---

[9] Hillman to William Leiserson, 8/13/30, Box 1, William Leiserson Papers, Wisconsin State Historical Society; ACWA General Executive Board Minutes (hereafter GEB Min), Nov. 1930, ACWA Papers, Labor-Management Documentation Center, Martin P. Catherwood Library, New York State School of Industrial and Labor Relations, Cornell Univ.; GEB Min., 8/25-28/31; Josephson, chapt. 15; Joseph Branders, "From Sweatshop to Stability: Jewish Labor Between Two World Wars," *YIVO Annual of Jewish Social Science*, 16 (1976), 49, 60-70; Hillman testimony before the sub-committee of the Senate committee on Manufactures, 72nd. Congress, 1/8/32; Jacob Potofsky Memoir, Oral History Collection of Columbia University (hereafter OHCCU), 208-11; Hillman testimony before Men's Clothing Code Authority of the National Recovery Administration as reported in the *Daily News Record* (hereafter *DNR*), 1/28/33; Harry A. Corbin, *The Men's Clothing Industry: Colonial Times Through Modern Times* (New York, 1970) 163, 166-70; Morris Greenberg to Mark Cresap, 5/8/35, ACWA Papers; Testimony at NRA hearings on Code of Fair Practices and Competition: Men's Ready-to-Wear Clothing Industry, 7/26-27/33, NRA Collection, Box 7112, National Archives; H.K. Herwitz to Hillman, 10/12/34, ACWA Papers; *Doc. Hist., 1930-34*; Joel Seidman, *The Needle Trades* (New York, 1942), 187; "Report on Industrial Homework in the Men's Clothing Industry," 3/16/49, ACWA Papers; Robert P. Ingalls, *Herbert H. Lehman and New York State's Little New Deal* (New York, 1975), 102-06; "Report on Child Labor", Box 129, Felix Frankfurter Papers, Library of Congress; Hillman to Louis Kirstein, 8/13/32, 12/19/32, and Hillman to Lessing Rosenwald, 12/19/32, and Hillman to General Wood, 10/20/32, Sidney Hillman Papers, Labor-Management Documentation Center, Cornell University; Potofsky Memoir (OHCCU), 234-36; Mark Cresap to Moritz Rosenthal, 12/1/31, and Rosenthal to Alexander Levy, 11/18/31, and Cresap to Rosenthal, 12/6/32, and Rosenthal to Cresap, 12/5/32, 11/28/32, ACWA Papers; GEB Min., 2/1-3/32, ACWA "Diaries", 1/30/30, ACWA Papers.

do anything along constructive lines a great deal of disaster will overtake us."[10]

Hillman's conviction that the future of the clothing industry and the ACW were hostage to developments in the arena of national politics was no sudden revelation brought on by three long years of Depression. It had informed his behavior from the earliest days of the collapse. In a report prepared by Hillman's chief economic adviser, Leo Wolman, concluded that despite the record of great success established in the clothing industry, for planning to succeed in any one industry required a measure of control and forecasting by a majority of the country's basic industrial and financial institutions. At the same time, Hillman was arguing that, ". . . No one industry can stabilize itself entirely by its own efforts. Regularity in production and employment depends on the general state of industry and agriculture, in short, on the economic health of the country as a whole and that means national planning." Moreover, he was familiar with the ideas of economists like Waddell Catchings and William T. Foster who emphasized the importance of mass purchasing power for the revival of any specific industrial sector and the role of government fiscal policy in achieving a balance between savings and investment. He was also aware of the range of specific programs for national planning and was involved in the on-going political efforts on behalf of national relief, unemployment insurance, and counter-cyclical public works.[11]

As the union's own unemployment reserves proved wholly inadequate, Hillman quickly became active, in 1931, in the campaign by the Socialist Party to organize an Emergency Conference on Unemployment, and in the lobbying efforts of long-time Progressive associates like Paul Kellogg organized through the National Unemployment League. He worked as well with

---

10 Hillman to Frankfurter, 1/16/33, Hillman Papers.
11 Leo Wolman, "Economic and Social Planning—Planning in the Clothing Industry," for the Bureau of Personnel Administration in private collection of Delia Gottlieb now housed at the Labor-Documentation Center, Cornell Univ.; Sidney Hillman, "Labor Leads Toward Planning", *Survey Graphic*, (Mar., 1932) *passim*; William T. Foster and Waddill Catchings, *Profits* (New York, 1925), vi; Lewis Lansky, "Isador Lubin: The Ideas and Career of a New Deal Labor Economist," (unpublished PhD diss., Case Western Reserve Univ., 1976), 90-95; Hillman testimony before sub-committee of Senate Committee on Manufactures, 72nd. Congress, 1st. Session on Senate Bill 6215, 1932; Josephson, chapt. 15.

John B. Andrews of the American Association for Labor Legislation, and testified in support of the Association's legislative plan at hearings in Albany on the Mastick-Steingut Unemployment Insurance Reserve Fund Bill.[12]

In addition to emergency relief and some system of Federal unemployment insurance, Hillman began advocating the shorter work week, public works, and a national standard of hours and wages. At a New York State conference of social workers late in 1930, he reiterated earlier demands for the government to legislate the five-day week and a shorter working day along with a 5% unemployment reserve fund to be collected from industry. He proposed as well a system of joint labor-management planning modelled after the more successful efforts of this kind during World War I. Since industry lacked the foresight to inaugurate such steps voluntarily, "the government should step in and use its power to compel reluctant or unenlightened industrial leaders to accept this program as a national policy."[13]

In formulating proposals for relief and recovery, including the most ambitious schemes for planning and regulatory councils, Hillman drew on the path-breaking experiences of the "new unionism." For example, the principle of equal division and sharing of work during slack periods had long ago been instituted in the clothing industry. Similarly, in a speech endorsing Senator Wagner's Federal Unemployment Insurance bill, Hillman suggested the government might do well to emulate the accomplishments of the ACW in this area as well. He emphasized the broader perspective, shared by many promoting unemployment insurance legislation in the twenties, which viewed

---

[12] Morris Hilquit to Hillman, 12/31/31, Hillman Papers; Hillman testimony on Mastick-Steingut Unemployment Reserve Fund bill, 3/18/31, Hillman Papers; Hillman testimony before sub-committee of Senate Committee on Manufactures, 1/8/32; National Unemployment League to Hillman, 1/31/31, Hillman Papers; Irving Bernstein, *The Lean Years: A History of the American Worker, 1920-33* (Boston, 1972), 491; John B. Andrews to Hillman, 9/19/30, Hillman Papers; Alfred B. Rollins Jr., *Roosevelt and Howe* (New York, 1962), 300; Hillman was also part of a group including Frances Perkins, Paul Douglas, Broadus Mitchell, and Irving Fisher that petitioned in support of Senator Wagner's employment exchange bill see: Jordan A. Schwartz, *The Interregnum of Despair: Hoover, Congress, and the Depression* (Urbana, 1970), 38.

[13] Josephson, chapt. 15; Hillman speech to International Ladies Garment Workers convention, 5/10/32, and speech to Federation of Jewish Charities, 12/4/130, Hillman Papers; Sidney Hillman and Paul Kellog, "How to Meet the Problems Arising Out of Unemployment", address in *Quarterly Bulletin: New York State Conference on Social Work*, Jan., 1931, ACWA Papers.

such insurance as a counter-cyclical device providing industry with positive incentives to stabilize employment.[14]

Each specific proposition submitted by Hillman was offered both as a remedy for a particular problem and as part of a wider proto-Keynesian, under-consumptionist outlook. Even after the depression was well underway, at a time when the immediate problem was to somehow meet the elementary needs of the population, Hillman continued to emphasize the peculiar dynamic upon which the revival, expansion, and stability of the "new capitalism" depended: "Greater needs and desires must be created to take care of the rapidly developing technological improvement and efficiencies in the management of industry." He further asserted that such a process could no longer be entrusted to the self-interested leadership of business, but "implies planning on a national scale."[15]

It was one thing to propose, quite another to dispose, and Hillman was, above all, mindful of the question of power. Thus, he argued for the extension of government authority to "plan a more equitable distribution of our national income," and proposed to accomplish it, against the opposition of the Chamber of Commerce through the considerable expansion of executive branch powers.[16]

As for the power of the labor movement itself, in the period immediately preceding the creation of the NRA it was practically at its nadir. Notwithstanding the most drastic threats to its own

[14] Josephson, chapt. 15; Hillman speech to Conference on Unemployment Insurance Legislation, 4/8/31, Hillman Papers; Hillman and Kellogg, "How to Meet . . ."; John A. Garraty, *Unemployment in History: Economic Thought and Public Policy* (New York, 1978), chapts. 8 & 9; *The Advance*, 8/26/27 as quoted in Daniel Nelson, "Waiting for the Government: The Needle Trades Unemployment Insurance Plans, 1919-28," *Labor History* 11 (1970), *passim*; Hillman, "A Successful Experiment . . ."; Hillman, "Labor Leads Toward . . ." In the 1920s, the ACW's unemployment insurance program reflected the more general "preventive approach" to social welfare developed by John Commons and others, which in devising ways of inducing the private economy to shoulder such responsibilities in its own self-interest, deliberately sought to accommodate the period's ethos of "welfare capitalism".

[15] Hillman testimony before sub-committee of Senate Committee on Manufactures, 72nd. Congress, 1st. Session, 1932; Hillman, "Labor Leads Toward . . ."; Address by Frances Perkins to the ACWA Convention, *Proceedings of the 10th. Biennial Convention of the ACWA* (hereafter Conv. Proc.), May, 1934; Hillman speech to New York Conference for Unemployment Legislation, 4/8/31, Hillman Papers; Jacob Potofsky, "Personal Notes —Interest in Politics", Potofsky Papers, Labor-Management Documentation Center, Cornell University.

[16] Potofsky, "Personal Notes . . . ," Potofsky Papers; Hillman testimony before sub-committee of Senate Committee on Manufactures, 72nd. Congress, 1st. Session, 1932.

continued existence, the AFL leadership could not extend its social imagination beyond the voluntarism, craft autonomy, and
political agnosticism that together comprised its tradition and
sense of the possible. Apart from Hillman, only John L. Lewis,
albeit from a more parochial standpoint, forthrightly supported
direct government participation on behalf of industrial stabilization. Meanwhile, the rest of the official labor movement still
opposed, even as late as 1932, Federal unemployment insurance. The AFL leadership feared the creation of a social welfare
bureaucracy that might compete with the trade union movement's own insurance functions and programs. Furthermore,
they feared, and not without reason, the moral imperialism of
such middle class bureaucrats, especially given their association
with a tradition of progressive reform, including charitable
"uplift" and "good government," that frequently attacked
those urban political machines with which trade union leaders
cooperated. Thus the AFL did little more than add its vote of
confidence to Senator Hugo Black's 30 Hour bill, legislation
also endorsed by elements of the business community as part of
a more comprehensive program of restricted production.

Not one to forego even the most limited palliatives, Hillman
later testified in favor of the Black bill, along with leading
clothing and textile manufacturers, as a way of preventing the
spread of sweatshop conditions and ruinous competition. Briefly, the legislation enjoyed widespread support because it was
vague precisely on those issues, for example the re-distribution
of national income and wealth, likely to generate the most political heat. Although Hillman continued to support the bill, he
urged the inclusion of a national minimum wage provision, a
position opposed by the AFL.[17]

The organizational weakness and political timidity of the
labor movement led Hillman to seek help by re-opening and
widening channels of communication into the multiple circles of
Progressive reform, both in and outside of government. Thus,

---

[17] Irving Bernstein, *The Lean Years, passim*.; Melvyn Dubofsky and Warren Van Tine, *John
L. Lewis: A Biography* (New York, 1977), 139; Garraty, 214; Hearings on the 30 Hour
Week Bill, House Committee on Labor, April-May, 1933; Solomon Barkin, "NRA Poli-
cies, Standards, and Code Provisions on Basic Weekly Hours of Work", Office of the
NRA, Division of Review, Box 7054, NRA Collection; Schwartz, *Interregnum*, 42.

he maintained his connections on the left by allowing his election to the National Committee of the League for Independent Political Action. The League was organized by John Dewey and Paul Douglas and committed to some amorphous form of independent electoral politics roughly modelled after the British Labour Party. Meanwhile, Bruce Bliven, editor of *The New Republic*, brought Hillman together with Gifford Pinchot, an early proponent of state planning, to discuss the future of progressive politics in Pennsylvania.[18]

The efforts at Progressive regroupment culminated in a "bi-partisan" conference in March 1931 called by Senators LaFollette, Norris, Costigan, Cutting, and Wheeler. Hillman appeared, advocating the creation of national unemployment reserves and the five-day week. The conference officially endorsed, as did the ACW, LaFollette's proposal for a general economic council and some system of industrial stabilization. Hillman urged that the council include labor representation and that it be endowed with executive as well as advisory powers, suggesting that the War Industries Board might serve as appropriate models.[19]

At about the same time as the "bi-partisan" conference, Hillman suggested to LaFollette that the senator, as chairman of the Committee on Manufactures, hold hearings to investigate the causes of the Depression. The hearings were carefully planned in small gatherings that included George Soule, Hillman, LaFollette, Harlow Person of the Taylor Society, and Isador

---

[18] John Dewey to Hillman, 9/27/32, and Hillman to Dewey, 9/30/32, Hillman Papers; Minutes of the United Conference for Progressive Political Action, 9/2-3/33, J.B.S. Hardman Papers, Box 38, Tamiment Library; Karel Denis Bicha, "Liberalism Frustrated: The League for Independent Political Action, 1928-33"; Bruce Bliven to Hillman, 12/17/30, Hillman Papers.

[19] *New York Times*, 3/13/31; Minutes and Proceedings of a Conference of Progressives", 3/11-12/31, and Hillman remarks at Roundtable on Unemployment and Industrial Stabilization at "Conference of Progressives", 3/12/31, Hillman Papers; *Doc Hist., 1930-34*; Fraser, "Dress Rehearsal . . ."; The WLB, and more specifically the Bureau of Labor Standards established under its authority had been critical to the growth and consolidation of the ACW during the war. Although the WLB had functioned mainly on the basis of eliciting, with positive material incentives, the voluntary cooperation of particular industries and trade associations, its tendencies in the direction of state capitalism, including its occasional commandeering and seizure of productive facilities, its coercive priorities system, its active intervention into the labor market, and its willingness to entertain state ownership, appealed to Hillman as equally applicable to the peacetime emergency (see Schwartz, *The Speculator*). The organizers of the conference had hoped to formulate a legislative agenda covering industrial stabilization, agriculture, public utilities, and tariffs, but it was too diffuse a coalition for that to happen—see: Thomas E. Vadney, *The Wayward Liberal: A Political Biography of Donald Richberg* (Lexington, 1970), 95-96.

Lubin, then with the Brookings Institute and an advocate of counter-cyclical public works and unemployment insurance. The group discussed who was to testify and what questions were to be asked. They designed the sequence of testimony so as to first display the ideological and programmatic exhaustion of the business community, and then to follow with "expert" analysis by friendly economists and industrial engineers so as to provide the "scientific" basis for the Committee's ultimate political recommendations. The principal recommendation was to establish a national economic council or planning agency. The "council" was to be composed of 15 representatives of industry, finance, agriculture, transportation, and labor.

The hearings proceeded according to plan. LaFollette questioned Hillman about the recently released report by Henry Harriman, president of the Chamber of Commerce, which had come out in opposition to a representative council on the grounds that such a body would be paralyzed by the contradictory interests comprising it. Hillman responded that the Depression had gone on long enough to compel even the most myopic of interest groups to adopt a national view of the economy, if only from the standpoint of enlightened self-interest. A closely related set of questions allowed the union president to launch his first attack on the Swope Plan for industrial self-regulation, then generating considerable public attention. As an alternative, he suggested emergency legislation to put the whole country on the six hour day, to relieve the distress of the unemployed, to undertake a major program of public works, and to guarantee labor standards through the creation of a tri-partite council representing labor, management, and the public. He warned that other less democratic organizational formulas, including by implication the Swope Plan, could conceivably lead to fascism.[20]

The Swope Plan was genealogically connected to the trade association movement of the previous decade. However, the

[20] George Soule, *Sidney Hillman: Labor Statesman* (New York, 1939), 158-62; Josephson, chapt. 15; Lansky, "Isador Lubin . . ."; Garraty, 152; Catherine Williams to Robert LaFollette, 11/23/51, and LaFollette to Williams, 12/12/51, Hillman Papers; Catherine Williams to Charles Ervin, 4/30/51, Hillman Papers; Hillman testimony at hearings to establish a National Economic Council, sub-committee of Senate Committee on Manufactures, 72nd. Congress, 1st. Session, 10/22/31 to 12/19/31; Schwartz, *Interregnum*, 148.

Depression proved undeniably that movement's vision of a vol-
untaristic self-regulation of business to be little more than a chimera. Gerard Swope was not the first to be converted to the
belief that under conditions of shrinking markets and declining
profits sterner political and legal sanctions were essential to prevent the self-destruction of American industry. The "Plan" was
little more than the logical extention of trade association theory
reinforced by the authority of the state, and never pretended to
a more systematic view either of the economic crisis itself or its
solution.

While both Swope and Hillman favored government intervention into the economy, the differences separating them were
by no means trivial. To begin with, trade unions played no significant role in Swope's calculations. Corporatist groups in the
U.S. were simply not prepared to accomodate a substantial role
in the policy-making process for a labor movement excluded
from much of basic industry and severely weakened by unemployment, labor surplus, and low wages. Even from the nar-
rowest standpoint of institutional survival, Hillman could not
abide an arrangement that so totally dismissed the legitimate
interests of trade unionism. The broader circles of reform with
which he identified were furthermore concerned with preventing
those administrative, executive, and private solutions which
sought to de-politicize economic issues. Corporatist approaches
often sought to suspend temporarily or permanently the risky
business of interest group, parliamentary, and mass politics. As
an entrenched industrial and financial elite, they had little to
gain and much to lose, especially during an acute crisis that
challenged their ability to run the economy in the national interest. On the other hand, for those seeking the power to accomplish a more fundamental transformation of the role of the
state in the economy, the institutions of democratic politics remained critical for mobilizing broad-based support.

It is true that, ultimately, Federal labor policy would include
tripartite arrangements akin to those proposed by Hillman and
based on a body of administrative law and practice relatively
immune to political influence. However, if the labor movement
were not to be victimized by such new administrative organs, it

had to exercise some influence over their formation. That first required penetrating the more formal arena of political competition and establishing access to levers of power in party, Congressional, and executive institutions. Moreover, even under the far more favorable circumstances of the mid-1930s, Hillman and a newer generation of labor leaders still pursued legislative, judicial, and fiscal measures to redistribute economic power and wealth. They remained wary of the more private and informal arrangements envisioned by a corporate dominated system of "crisis management."[21]

Thus, by late 1931, Hillman was publicly decrying the Swope Plan as well as the similar, if somewhat less legally coercive arrangements sponsored by the Chamber of Commerce and the NAM. All such corporatist schemes continued to focus on price competition, and on the arguably fraudulent problem of overproduction rather than on questions of aggregate demand. The Swope proposal was, Hillman asserted, critically flawed as it contained no provision for wage and hour standards, deliberately neglected to afford a place for labor representation in the regulatory mechanism, was niggardly in its proposal for unemployment reserves, depended essentially on a process of voluntary compliance, and was intrinsically inefficient. At best, it would permit price-fixing and the restriction of production in those industrial sectors subject to monopolistic or oligopolistic domination.[22]

Hillman was not without important allies, however, in the worlds of industry and commerce. For years he had carried on close working relations with a network of manufacturing, retailing, and financial interests more directly tied to mass consumption than were those industrial lobbies most closely associated with corporatism. These interests were, if only by virtue of their structural and functional position, more amenable to Keynesian approaches to shoring up aggregate demand throughout the economy.

---

[21] Gabriel Kolko, *Main Currents in Modern American History* (New York, 1976), 111, 116-17, 119; Schwartz, *The Speculator*, 223.

[22] Kolko, chapt. 4; Hillman testimony at hearings to establish a National Economic Council; Hillman radio speech transcript on national economic planning, 3/22/32, ACWA Papers.

It was not a homogenous group but a dynamic coalition with multiple sources of political, economic, and regional power. Nevertheless, it comprised a coherent milieu with discernable connections between technologically advanced and vertically integrated enterprises (combining mass marketing and manufacturing) and major national and regional distribution and financial institutions. It included, for example, important segments of the housing industry, both construction and housing supply manufacturing, and the network of credit institutions that integrated the mass market for housing and house furnishings. As a whole, this milieu depended on the regular expansion of mass distribution and consumption. It was linked financially to those newer investment houses, commercial banks, and real estate interests, (including Goldman, Sachs and Lehman Brothers as well as the Gianinni banking empire and Bowery Savings Bank) which had begun to migrate into the orbit of the Democratic Party's progressive wing during the Wilson campaign of 1912. This business grouping relied on the advice of pre-Keynesian economists like Wadell Catchings, and adopted a decidedly less authoritarian approach to labor relations, often encouraging the development of independent unionism. They also cultivated relations with the liberal segments of the Taylor Society and the Democratic Party. Thus, for example, Harry Hopkins maintained close ties with Lehman Brothers; Frances Perkins had for some time worked with Henry Bruere of the Bowery; Rexford Tugwell consulted regularly with Robert Strauss of Macy's.[23]

Edward and Lincoln Filene, founders of the Federated Department Stores retailing complex, were representatives of this Keynesian-Progressive elite. They were staunch supporters of the New Deal, including most of the legislative initiatives that

---

[23] Peter Friedlander, "Hollow Victory: The Rise of the Corporate Welfare State in America, 1905-54," unpublished ms., establishes the broader historical and theoretical critique of corporatist and corporate liberal interpretations of this period as well as the empirical analysis of sectoral conflict and the emergence of the Keynesian business and political elite sketched here; Michel Aglietta, *A Theory of Capitalist Regulation: The U.S. Experience* (London, 1979); Michael Burroway, "Terrain of Contest: Factory and State under Capitalism and Socialism," *Socialist Review*, July-August, 1981; Schwartz, *The Speculator*, 35; Frances Perkins, *The Roosevelt I Knew* (New York, 1946), 102, 320; Philip H. Burch, *Elites in American History: The New Deal to the Carter Administration* (New York, 1980), 18, 22-23, 27, 30-35, 38; Lessing Rosenthal to Mark Cresap, 12/5/32, ACWA Papers; Elliot Rosen, *Hoover, Roosevelt, and the Brains' Trust: From Depression to New Deal* (New York, 1977) *passim*.

otherwise alienated corporatist business circles during the "second New Deal". Thus, in 1930, Edward Filene, with the cooperation of Leo Wolman, and along with like-minded businessmen such as Henry Dennison, Morris Leeds, and Henry Kendall, and pro-union Taylorites like Harlow Person, assembled a conference to promote the idea of the "new capitalism." They envisioned an expanding system based on high wages, low prices, and scientifically and nationally planned production and distribution. Of this group, Dennison particularly exemplified the organizational connections and strategic outlook of this Keynesian business milieu. Committed to scientific management, he had served as president of the Taylor Society from 1919 to 1921, during which period he became a leading exponent of managerial capitalism and works councils. In the 1930s, he became an advocate of counter-cyclical government planning and of the legislative program to enhance "human capital." He shared that position with those more liberal members of the Business Advisory Council who were often affiliated with high technology and mass consumption enterprises. Dennison had worked for years with Hillman and Filene. Moreover, all three men conferred regularly with Felix Frankfurter who made their views known within the inner councils of the group gathering around Roosevelt in the summer of 1932.[24]

Frankfurter, together with the active, if concealed collaboration of Louis Brandeis, presided over this emerging reform group as it sought to dislodge older industrial and financial interests from the centers of political power. The Depression helped. It exacerbated sectoral and regional tensions endemic to the economy even under the best of circumstances. In turn that created a more fluid field of power relations which increased the options available to the Brandeis-Frankfurter group. This process of in-

---

[24] Fraser, "Dress Rehearsal . . ."; Edward Filene, "Summary Report—Project #8—American Academy of Political and Social Science," 9/1/31, "American Academy of Political and Social Science" file, Edward A. Filene Papers, Bergengren Memorial Library, Madison, Wisconsin; Edward A. Filene, "Remedies for Business Crises and Unemployment", 12/2/31, "Unemployment" file, Filene Papers; Edward A. Filene, "Report on a Study Tour of Business Conditions in Fourteen Large Cities in the U.S. Affected by the President's Recovery Program," to FDR, 3/1/34, President's Personal File, 2116, FDR Papers; Kim McQuaid, "The Frustration . . ."; Kim McQuaid, "Henry S. Dennison and the 'Science' of Industrial Reform, 1900-1950," *American Journal of Economics and Sociology*, 36 (1977), 79-98.

ternal differentiation and division among business and political elites is slighted, however, by those who perceive only a ubiquitous and unified "big business" concerned with protecting entrenched positions of power and wealth and opposed, if at all, by an equally opaque mass of small business. Instead, there were fundamental programatic and strategic alternatives represented by corporatist and Keynesian groups as they contended for influence within the policy-making apparatus of the new regime.

Corporatist policy was sometimes presented publicly as an attack on low wages, long hours, unemployment, and child labor. In fact, the operative core of this program of guild-like cartelization was a system of production controls, the regulation of new entry into industry, price-fixing, and the cooperative sharing out of the remaining market provisions soon incorporated into the NRA codes. Strategically, its outlook was intrinsically parochial, consisting essentially of the arithmetic summation of individual corporate and trade association self-interests.[25]

Keynesian progressives resisted such policies as technically regressive and based on an economy of stagnation and scarcity. Those in the Brandeis-Frankfurter circle placed emphasis on a series of regulatory, political, and fiscal reforms. During the formative period of the Roosevelt administration especially, they promoted re-distributive tax policies, social insurance, labor legislation, and a vast expansion of public works. Strategically, they were concerned with macro-economic aggregates, and an enlarged role for the state. Almost invariably, those leading circles associated with anti-monopoly politics were at the same time committed to national planning for expanded production and productivity, and for government control of monopoly or "administered" prices in the interests of mass consumption. Even Brandeis' celebrated opposition to "bigness" had as much to do with his belief in its inherent inefficiency, a standpoint adopted during his work with the scientific management movement, as it

---

[25] Hillman testimony at hearings on Federal unemployment relief, sub-committee of Senate Committee on Manufactures, 72nd. Congress, 1/8/32; Radosh, "The Corporate Ideology . . ."; Louis Galambos, *Competition and Cooperation: The Emergence of a National Trade Association* (Baltimore, 1966), 178-79, 190-95; Himmelberg, 63, 76, 83, 162; Murphy, *passim*.

did with a populist antipathy to the "interests." Thus, the purported antagonism between the Brandeis-Frankfurter group and members of the original Brains' Trust over the question of state intervention and planning has been exaggerated. Indeed, Raymond Moley functioned as the principal conduit for Brandeis-Frankfurter proposals on tax reform and deficit financed public works.[26]

It is only within this broader context of competing strategic outlooks that Hillman's own behavior can be assessed. On the one hand, he was willing to grant the usefulness of cartelization under government auspices in special cases of emergency, in particular for those industries that even in the 1920s were generally recognized as "sick"—textile and mining for example. But these exceptional cases never led Hillman to adopt a more global corporatist orientation. He was rather attuned to the general ideological and programmatic position of the Keynesian elite, and was bound by numerous personal, professional, and political ties to the Brandeis-Frankfurter circle.

For example, throughout 1931 and 1932, Frankfurter and Brandeis drew on the legal advice of Max Lowenthal and the political assistance of Senators LaFollette and Wagner and Congressman LaGuardia on behalf of their proposals for public works and tax reform. Lowenthal had performed innumerable legal services for the ACW, and LaGuardia, Wagner, and LaFollette were Hillman's long-time political allies. Similarly, Brandeis, who before the war had been intimately involved in attempts to reform and unionize the New York garment industry, pursued his interest in unemployment insurance through the offices of men like Robert Bruere, Paul Kellogg, and Lincoln Filene, all of whom had worked with Hillman since the war.[27]

Indeed, it was the old-line AFL leaders like Matthew Woll who supported the cartel-like stabilization schemes developed

---

[26] Himmelberg, 83, 112, 135, 157, 162, 192; Galambos, 198, 221-22, 236; Murphy, 104, 123-25, 126, 128-29, 131-38, 144, 108-11; Theodore Rosenof, *Dogma, Depression, and the New Deal: The Debate of Political Leaders over Economic Recovery* (New York, 1975), 81, 92-94, 101-04; Friedlander, "Hollow Victory . . ."; Arthur Schlesinger Jr., *The Coming of the New Deal* (Boston, 1958), *passim*.

[27] Hillman testimony before Senate Finance Committee, 3/20/35; Minutes of the United Conference for Progressive Political Action, 9/2-3/33, Box 38, Hardman Papers; Murphy, 93-96; Schwartz, *Interregnum*, 144-46, 210-11.

by Bernard Baruch and others. AFL officials, with few exceptions, subscribed to a voluntarist ideology which mirrored the traditional wariness of state intrusion into industrial affairs characteristic of those corporate executives with whom men like Woll had been dealing for some time. Furthermore, any radical departure by the Federation's leadership from accustomed practice represented a threat to that network of industrial, managerial, and political associations into which the AFL had been assimilated, albeit in a distinctly subordinate capacity.

Yet it remains true that Hillman was directly involved in the whole political process leading up to the creation of the NRA, immediately accepted appointment to its Labor Advisory Board, and later to the more administratively powerful National Industrial Recovery Board. And he did so despite the fact that the final draft of the bill clearly represented a triumph, if not a total one, for corporatism. This is perhaps a comment on Hillman's single-minded pursuit of power. But in the tactical maneuvering leading up to the creation of the NRA, Hillman also made clear his enduring political perspective and attachments.

Late in 1932, Hillman drafted a memo for the President-elect. He was encouraged to do so by Frankfurter and Frances Perkins with whom Hillman had conferred regularly about unemployment insurance during Roosevelt's second term as governor. The memo addressed the overriding issue of economic recovery, and prescribed industrial regulation, national planning, and a Federal labor board to enforce wage and hour legislation. It suggested that Roosevelt convene a small group to work out specific plans for "protecting the purchasing power of our industrial communities . . . ." Roosevelt discussed the substance of the memo with Frankfurter and seemed to react favorably to Hillman's policy recommendations while noting his specific suggestions for personnel to administer the proposed Federal labor board. On his own initiative, Frankfurter urged Hillman to put together a working group, including Wolman and Henry Bruere, for the purpose of formulating a concrete set of legislative proposals for an imminent Senate inquiry into the question of recovery and economic planning.[28]

---

[28] Barton Bernstein, "The New Deal . . ."; *10th. Biennial Conv. Proc.*; Sidney Hillman to

During this same period Hillman, together with Donald Richberg, and in consultation with Frankfurter, prepared a series of amendments to the Black bill, worked out with Brandeis and later identified with Perkins. They were designed to create an adequate enforcement mechanism consisting of regionally centered tripartite labor boards, to provide greater flexibility with respect to hours of work, and to establish a minimum level of wages. Hillman testified before the Senate Finance Committee in early 1933, reproducing the essentials of his earlier memorandum to Roosevelt in supporting these amendments.

The temporary collaboration with Richberg this episode involved was based on the latter's plan for an industrial council to oversee economic re-organization which explicitly included labor representatives and endorsed independent labor organization. It also called for planning to expand consumption through higher wages, lower prices, and a limit on profits. In fact, Richberg had been selected, on the basis of Frankfurter's recommendation to Raymond Moley, to draft the labor provisions of the NIRA (and subsequently as chief counsel of the NIRA). It would be some time before his commitment to corporatism became clear.[29]

Hillman was soon invited to consult directly with one of the working groups drafting recovery legislation for Roosevelt. The group was headed by Wagner and included Lubin, Harold Moulton of the Brookings Institute, Fred Kent of Bankers Trust, progressive businessmen Malcolm Rorty and James Rand, Senator LaFollette, and Jett Lauck—Taylor Society member and eco-

William Leiserson, 12/31/30, Box 1, William Leiserson Papers, Wisconsin State Historical Society; Murphy, 113-15, 126, 136, 167-68, 170; Potofsky Memoir, (OHCCU), 230-34; Hillman to Frances Perkins, 12/21/32, Frances Perkins Special Manuscript Collection, Part I, Columbia Univ.; Hillman to Frankfurter, 12/20/32, Box 125, Frankfurter Papers; Frankfurter to Hillman, 1/5/33, Potofsky Papers.

[29] Frankfurter to Hillman, 1/5/33, Potofsky Papers; Larry Gerber, "The Limits of Liberalism: A study of the Careers and Ideological Development of Josephus Daniels, Henry Stimson, Bernard Baruch, Donald Richberg, and Felix Frankfurter", unpublished PhD diss., 1978, 233, 355, 379, 445; Himmelberg, 192; The Advance, Mar., 1933; Frankfurter to Frances Perkins, Richberg, and Wagner, 5/30/33, Box 159, Frankfurter Papers; LaFollette to Frankfurter, 2/4/33, Box 153, Frankfurter Papers; Max Freedman, Roosevelt and Frankfurter: Their Correspondence, 1928-45 (Boston, 1967), Sidney Hillman, passim "A Proposal for Labor Boards as an Essential in the Emergency," 3/31/33, Hillman Papers; Schlesinger, 89-91; Murphy, 125-26; Perkins, The Roosevelt I Knew, 194; Hawley, 21-23; Gerber, "The Limits of Liberalism", 355-60, 445; Vadney, 115-16; Grace Abbott, "Memorandum for Felix Frankfurter—re: the Labor Department and the administration of the Industrial Recovery Bill," 5/25/33, and Frankfurter to Abbott, 5/30/33, Box 62, Frankfurter Papers.

nomic adviser to John L. Lewis. Present also was Meyer Jacobstein, Rochester banker, Congressman, member of the Taylor
Society, and former labor manager for Hickey-Freeman, and a
colleague of Hillman's since the earliest days of the ACW in
Rochester. The group favored a moderate form of Keynesian
economic management emphasizing the interim usefulness of
counter-cyclical fiscal policy. But they were reluctant to install
government manipulation of fiscal aggregates as a permanent
feature of public policy. This group in turn conferred with
another including Perkins, Jerome Frank, and Tugwell, similarly inclined in favor of public works, government loans, and
the guaranteed right to collective bargaining.[30]

The process of policy formulation leading up to the NIRA
was thus occurring simultaneously in several allied circles of reform and in competing groups convened by corporatists centered around Bernard Baruch and Swope. In the event, the
Brandeis-Frankfurter circle lacked sufficient political weight to
determine the shape of the NIRA. Only the labor provisions of
the act, which they viewed as genuine devices for re-employment
and recovery, commanded their whole-hearted support. The
command centers of the Democratic Party were still densely
populated with proponents and practitioners of corporatism
and fiscal conservatism. Some, like Baruch, were at least prepared to support minimum labor standards and to resist the efforts of other corporatists to simply turn over the operation of
the NIRA to the U.S. Chamber of Commerce. At the same
time, business opposition to any Federal law regulating working
hours was strong enough to assure that the NRA would allow
prospective industrial codes to vary depending on the "needs"
of particular industries and to exclude any manifest connection
between hours of work and the problem of re-employment.[31]

Although he publicly supported the act, especially its separate
public works section, Hillman was franker, if still cautiously optimistic in discussions with his own General Executive Board. He

---

[30] Lansky, "Isador Lubin . . . ," 156-57; Perkins, *The Roosevelt I Knew*, 198-99; Memoir of
    Frances Perkins (OHCCU), 302-21; Josephson, chapt. 16; Freedman, *Roosevelt and
    Frankfurter*, 289; Schlesinger, 96-98; Vadney, *The Wayward Liberal*, 114-17; Hawley,
    The New Deal . . ., 23-25.
[31] Schwartz, *The Speculator*, 292-93; Schlesinger, *The Coming . . . , passim.*

told them that the bill was not intended to help labor and had been essentially drafted by the major banking and manufacturing interests. While noting that he, along with Richberg and Wagner, had managed to incorporate a collective bargaining clause, he acknowledged their failure to have it made mandatory. He recognized Hugh Johnson's open shop sentiments, but felt he might be flexible, especially as Wolman and Richberg were to work closely with the General. Although Hillman accepted appointment to the NRA's Labor Advisory Board, he doubted it could have much effect on the codes that were clearly, in most cases, to be designed by industrial trade associations. Most importantly, he speculated that the ACW could count on its "extraordinary contacts within the Administration," that Wolman would be of great assistance, and that the bill's rhetorical support for collective bargaining could be used to mount a mass organizing campaign.[32]

To a degree far more limited than Hillman hoped, the NRA became a useable instrument of labor organization. Between 1933 and 1934, ACW membership increased by 50,000, and the International Ladies Garment Workers, a practically moribund organization in 1932, was healthy again by 1934. In both cases, the influence of labor leaders in the code-making machinery was partly responsible. There were similar results elsewhere, as for example in the growth of the UMW. But, in general, the NRA, so far as the labor movement was concerned, amounted to the "national run-around." It might fairly be said, therefore, that Hillman was overly sanguine, if not naive, that he miscalculated. But it would be a mistake to also assume that he was committed to corporatist politics simply by virtue of his association with an institution dominated by corporatist thinking.[33]

---

[32] Solomon Barkin, "NRA Policies, Standards . . . ;" Raymond S. Rubinow, "Section 7a: Its History, Interpretation, and Administration", Box 7055, NRA Collection; Soule, *Sidney Hillman*, 162-64; Hillman was generally less willing to compromise than the AFL leadership with the Industrial Advisory Board over the position and power of labor in the recovery administration—see: "History of the Industrial Advisory Board," Record Group 9, Series 37, NRA Records, Miscellaneous Reports and Documents Section, Box 8336, NRA Collection; Hillman radio speech, WEVD, 6/9/33, Hillman Papers (transcript); GEB Min., June 5, 1933.

[33] Brandes, 70-71; Schlesinger, 140-42; Hawley, *The New Deal . . .* , *passim*; Kolko, *passim*; Robert Maurice Collins, "Business Responses to Keynesian Economics, 1929-64: an Analysis of the process by which the Modern American Political Economy was Defined" (unpublished PhD diss. Johns Hopkins, Univ. 1975), 60-67.

The Depression had undermined traditional forms of social and political integration. Even before it began, however, a protracted search was underway for new institutional arrangements appropriate to an economy and society based on mass consumption and a complex, interdependent national system of production. One variant of that search pursued the strategy of "enlightened," private, functional orders collaborating with public agencies presumably in the service of the nation. As a practical matter, what this entailed was mortgaging the moral and political authority of the state to established centers of concentrated industrial and financial power whose needs could not be adequately accommodated within an unpredictable party and Congressional political system too susceptible to the pressures of mass politics.

It is true that the NRA embodied such an institutional innovation, albeit imperfectly. And it is furthermore true that both corporatists on the one hand, and men like Hillman on the other, often talked about creating a community of interests out of a fractious industrial, capitalist society. But differences over the basis upon which that community was to be constituted and over the distribution of power within it were not so amenable to negotiation. While it is also true that Hillman would continue to defend the NRA through to its demise in 1935, he did so because the agency had been the main available arena in which to carry on the struggle for social democratic and Keynesian objectives not shared by the architects of the corporatist order.[34]

---

[34] Hawley, *The Great War . . .* , 100-03; Collins, 50-59.

THE COMMUNISTS AND THE DRIVE TO ORGANIZE STEEL, 1936

By MAX GORDON

When in 1936 John L. Lewis, as head of the recently organized Committee for Industrial Organization (CIO), initiated the drive to organize the nation's steel workers by setting up the Steel Workers Organizing Committee (SWOC), he turned to erstwhile bitter foes, the Communists, for assistance. The Communist Party's national chairman, William Z. Foster, later maintained that of the approximately 200 full-time SWOC staff organizers, 60 were Communists. According to John Williamson, then the CP's Ohio State chairman, in that state's steel areas, entire staffs of the Party and Young Communist League were incorporated into the steel drive. He specifically referred to John Steuben, the Youngstown area party organizer who was placed in charge of the SWOC drive in that steel center, and Gus Hall in the Warren-Niles Area. Foster observed, however, that Lewis made certain to keep all key positions in SWOC in the hands of his own mine worker associates whom he had assigned to the steel drive and whom he could control. As a result, an "authentic" steel workers' union leadership never developed. [1]

The flavor of the relationship between Party staff members and the SWOC miners union organizers in the drive's early stages is suggested in a detailed report by Steuben to Jack Stachel, then the CP's national trade union secretary. This report (reproduced below) was found in the Nelson Frank papers in the Tamiment Ben Josephson Library at New York University. The

---

[1] William Z. Foster, *History of the Communist Party of the United States* (New York, 1952), 349-50; John Williamson, *Dangerous Scot* (New York, 1969), 125-26.

late Nelson Frank was for many years a crusading anti-Communist labor reporter.

Why did Lewis turn to the Communists for assistance? (As a Communist Party organizer in upstate New York at the time, I can testify that some of my fellow organizers were placed on the staff of the Textile Workers Organizing Committee, which was the responsibility of Sidney Hillman, Amalgamated Clothing Workers Union president, a top CIO figure who similarly placed heavy reliance on Communists to get the textile drive rolling.) Saul Alinsky, a Lewis biographer, has written that while "the fearfully rigid, unwilling, unbelievably inept, bureaucratic AFL" nearly wrecked the "surging drive" for unionism among indusetrial workers that followed the 1933 of the National Industrial Recovery Act with its section 7A giving government blessing to unionism, the "left-wingers" zealously picked up the pieces. The Communists, according to Alinsky, were working "indefatigably" to build unions among the unorganized. Lewis noted that in the rapidly growing United Auto Workers, Communists were prominent, tireless builders. He concluded that he could utilize, and believed he could control, them.[2]

Labor historian Bert Cochran observes that *The Nation* was "voicing a widespread opinion of the time" when it wrote that the Communists, despite past mistakes in the unions, "were indispensable for providing the labor movement with 'much-needed vigor,' something they were given the opportunity to display with the formation of the CIO." James B. Carey, an anti-Communist who was secretary-treasurer of the CIO after his ouster in 1941 as United Electrical Workers Union president on the Communist issue, has written that "Lewis desperately needed trained organizers in the early days of the CIO—and your seasoned Stalinist, to give the devil his due, is often a hot-shot labor salesman . . ."[3]

Lewis also counted on the Communists to provide a link to the great mass of foreign-born, largely East Europeans, as well as blacks, in steel. Boleslaw (Bill) Gebert, a top Communist and

---

[2] Saul D. Alinsky, *John L. Lewis: An Unauthorized Biography* (New York, 1970), 152-55.
[3] Bert Cochran, *Labor and Communism: The Conflict That Shaped American Unions* (Princeton, NJ, 1977), 95; Carey is cited in Cochran, 98.

head of the Party's Polish bureau, was placed in charge of the SWOC's foreign language organizing. A conference in Pittsburgh in late 1936 involving some 500 officers of national and district organizations of Poles, Croatians, Lithuanians, Serbs, Slovenes, Ukrainians, and Russians was chaired by Gebert, and addressed by Phil Murray, SWOC Chairman, and Clinton Golden, Pittsburgh Regional Director. A "large number" of foreign-language newspapers were enlisted in the drive.[4] A Communist-led fraternal order, the International Workers Order, with 15 separate language societies supporting some two dozen dailies and weeklies, was a major force in this mobilization of the foreign-born. Many of its East European members had been blacklisted as coal miners fighting Lewis and the operators, and Lewis was well aware of their union dedication and militancy.[5] A national conference of black groups in support of the steel drive was set up in February, 1937, by Ben Carreathers, a leading Pennsylvania black Communist who was also on the SWOC staff; this conference drew representation from 110 organizations.[6]

The Communists from their founding in 1919 had as a primary goal the organization of workers in mass industries into industrial unions. In 1921 William Z. Foster, who had led the unsuccessful steel strike of 1919, had joined the party and brought with him his Trade Union Educational League (TUEL), a group of radical unionists dedicated to working within the AFL and reshaping it as a militant force. Major planks in his program included organization of the unorganized, particularly in the mass industries, and amalgamation of existing craft unions into industrial unions.[7] An amalgamation resolution, introduced at the TUEL's instigation and circulated by it throughout the AFL in 1922, was endorsed by 16 state federations, 14 national unions, scores of city central bodies, and hundreds of local unions.[8]

4 Cochran, 96; Bill Gebert, "The Steel Drive and the Tasks of the Communists in Mass Organizations," *Party Organizer*, Sept., 1936, 14; Foster, *History*, 350.
5 Interview with Jerry Trauber, then an organizer of the International Workers Order, New York, Feb. 27, 1980.
6 Cochran, 96; Foster, *History*, 349-50.
7 Foster, *History*, 185, 203-06; Theodore Draper, *American Communism and Soviet Russia* (New York, 1960), 69-70.
8 Foster, *From Bryan to Stalin* (New York, 1937), 172-173; Draper, 71; David J. Saposs, *Left-Wing Unionism* (New York, 1926), 48; Earl Browder, "Reminiscences" (Columbia Univ. Oral History Research Project, Oct., 1965), 120.

The Communists were an especially strong opposition force during the 1920s in the United Mineworkers, led by Lewis. They cooperated with progressive elements led by John Brophy, who bitterly contested Lewis' leadership and policies as autocratic and "sell-out." But when Lewis assumed leadership of the CIO, Brophy became a chief lieutenant as CIO executive director and was influential in recruiting Communists for the CIO drive. Earl Browder, then the CP's general secretary, recalled many years later that prior to the steel drive, he met with Brophy to offer full party cooperation and received from Brophy a pledge of non-discrimination against Communists.[9]

In 1923, the AFL retaliated against the TUEL's opposition to its bureaucratic leadership with an expulsion drive. This and the CP's sectarian practices isolated the Party during the next few years and sapped TUEL influence in all but a few unions. The expulsions of militants and the AFL's deterioration through the 1920s led to a shift in the Party's emphasis from work within the AFL to an effort to organize the unorganized into independent revolutionary unions, as urged by Solomon Lozofsky, head of the Red International of Labor Unions; continued activity within the AFL, where possible, was still formally urged. There had always been tension in the international Communist movement between the two aspects of the dual tactic of working within existing non-revolutionary unions (boring from within) and building revolutionary unions. In 1928 the American CP shifted to independent unions both because of domestic considerations and because of an increasing Stalinist expectation of Communist-led revolutionary outbreaks arising out of the predicted world crisis. In 1929, the TUEL was transformed into the Trade Union Unity League (TUUL), a federation of independent unions eventually amounting to some two dozen. As put many years later by James P. Cannon, then a top party leader, the initiative for the shift to independent unions came from Lozofsky, but the Americans readily adopted it because it was becoming increasingly clear that organization of the unorganized required independent unionism in certain fields.[10]

<hr>

[9] Browder, Interview with William Goldsmith (Daniel Bell Papers, Box 8, Tamiment Institute, Bobst Library, New York Univ.), Feb. 1, 1956.

[10] Draper, 76; Browder, "The American CP Under Attack" (Bell Papers, Box 8); Foster, *Bryan to Stalin*, 210-17; Foster, "The Decline of the American Federa-

One of the TUUL affiliates was the Steel and Metal Workers Industrial Union, which tried to organize in the steel plants. It led a strike of 1500 at Republic Steel in 1932 but generally made little headway until the spontaneous union upsurge that followed Roosevelt's inauguration and the promulgation of the NIRA's Section 7A in 1933. This revitalization of the labor movement led the party to a gradual abandonment of its isolationist position and a reintegration of its union forces with rapidly developing CIO and AFL unions. In 1934 the steel members of the Steel and Metal Workers Union went into the AFL's Amalgamated Association of Iron, Steel and Tin Workers, until 1933 a rather moribund organization of 5,000 skilled craftsmen.[11] By early 1934 the A.A. had jumped tenfold as a result of spontaneous growth. By the time of the steel organizing drive, Communists were entrenched in various AA locals in Ohio and Western Pennsylvania.[12]

The Communists had also gained some positions of influence among steel workers as a result of party tactics adopted early in 1934 of penetrating company unions, which were also multiplying as a consequence of Section 7A. These company unions, known as company representation plans, consisted of councils composed of elected department representatives, presumably company stooges. But Communists ran for, or encouraged other genuine unionists to run for, these positions and often won. *Bonafide* unionists were thus able to capture many a company union. As the Steuben report below indicates, this tactic was a bone of contention between the Communists and Mineworkers' SWOC staff members, who wanted to steer clear of the company unions.[13]

The SWOC was strikingly successful with the giant of the industry, US Steel, whose chief affiliate in the Pittsburgh-Youngstown area was the Carnegie-Illinois Company. Following the defeat of General Motors by the auto workers in the historic Flint

tion of Labor," *The Communist*, Jan./Feb., 1929, 47-58; James P. Cannon, *The First Ten Years of American Communism* (New York, 1962), 199.

[11] Foster, *Bryan to Stalin*, 240; Cochran, 75.

[12] Cochran, 84; interview with John Gates—a party leader in the Youngstown area until 1937 when he and Joe Dallett, Steuben's associate as party organizer, joined the International Brigades in the Spanish Civil War—June 19, 1979. Dallett was killed in Spain.

[13] Browder, *The People's Front* (New York, 1938), 40; Gates interview.

sit-down strike in early 1937, many corporations came to terms with the unions. US Steel's capitulation without a struggle startled the country and laid the basis for the steelworkers union.[14]

Following the agreement, workers streamed into the union in great numbers, but "Little Steel," consisting of five large corporations including Youngstown Sheet and Tube, while forced to bargain with the union as it won bargaining rights, refused to sign written agreements. There were long, violent struggles and not until 1942, after the war began, were written contracts obtained from the "Little Steel" corporations.[15]

After SWOC established itself in the industry, its leaders had little trouble in dismissing CP staff members since it, and the United Steel Workers union that grew out of it, were administered in authoritarian, highly centralized fashion. The SWOC held no conventions or elections, and functioned with little local autonomy.[16] Steuben and Hall were given the option of remaining with the union if they gave up their Party membership; they chose to remain with the Party and were fired.[17] Steuben, after military service in World War II, became secretary-treasurer of Local 144 of the Building Service Employes Union in New York. Following the Khrushchev revelations of Stalin's crimes at the Soviet party's 20th Congress in February 1956, and the Soviet invasion of Hungary in November, Steuben, then quite ill, publicly announced his break with the Party. He died in May, 1957.[18]

In his Communist Party history, Foster maintained that the Communists in steel paid too little attention to the development of a progressive union leadership. He argued that they could have insisted upon "representative steel workers" being brought into top leadership but failed to do so. Foster, then in sharp behind-the-scenes rivalry with Browder, who ran the party, had his own factional reasons for the critique. But "New Left" radicals widely share the view that the prewar communists were too subservient to both CIO and New Deal officialdom. Cochran, however,

[14] Alinsky, 148-49; Gates interview.
[15] Alinsky, 149, 155, 281; Cochran, 162. See also David Brody's review of Alice and Staughton Lynd's *Rank-and-File, Labor History,* 16 (1975), 125.
[16] Cochran, 100-01.
[17] Gates interview.
[18] *The New York Times,* Jan. 19, 1957, 1; *The New York Times,* obituary, May 10, 1957.

is highly skeptical of this view. The Communists could have exercised independence, he argues, only if they "wanted to break the entente cordiale with Lewis and Murray and be prepared to lose their vested position in the CIO." [19]

While Cochran is undoubtedly right in his reaction to Foster's critique, the CP generally could probably have exercised more independence even within the narrow framework of the coalition with the CIO and New Deal leadership, a coalition that was instrumental in building a labor movement in America's mass industries and that enabled the Communists to break through the crippling sectarianism of radical organization in America, to become the only significant socialist force between the two world wars.

*   *   *   *   *

Youngstown, Ohio
August 31, 1936

Dear Comrade Stachel:

Because of the strenuous daily work and the long hours involved, I am not writing as often as I used to. I will make this letter as detailed as possible so that it will give you an all around view on the status of the drive and the problems we are confronted with.

STATUS OF DRIVE:

The drive in the Youngstown steel district like throughout the country has not yet assumed a mass character. However, this does not express the real sentiment of the steel workers, meeting hundreds of them every week, both American and foreign-born, I have yet to find one case of real hostility towards the union. On the contrary, I am met with open arms and the steel workers are keenly interested in the drive and are anxiously hoping to see the drive go over big. I am absolutely convinced that the greatest majority of the steel workers will join the union in the next few months to come.

Why then is there this great discrepancy between the favorable sentiment and the actual growth of the union? The way I see it, these are some of the reasons:

1. The open warning of the companies to fire the men who join the union, still constitute the greatest obstacle. Although we can already observe a definite break down of this fear.

2. Many old foreign-born workers are still bitter against the American steel workers who didn't back them in the 1919 strike and want to see the Americans come in first.

---

[19] Foster, *History*, 351; Cochran, 101n.

3. The self-satisfaction of the SWOC on the top with the progress of the drive. This results in a failure to press the field organizers to produce better results. Very poor instructions from the top. Lack of flexibility and does not call for initiative on the part of the many organizers. These people on the top (SWOC) also picture the steel drive as a mere series of mass meetings and a mechanical signing up of members without developing any partial struggles and obtain certain initial victories for the workers, without necessarily calling local strikes. Also the desire of the SWOC to "go slow," has a lot to do with the drive.

4. The work of the organizers, especially the UMWA organizers, is perhaps one of the weakest links in the whole drive. When you read Comrade Foster's pamphlet on the 1919 experiences and the work of the organizers then and you compare it with the work of the UMWA organizers today . . . you find a vast difference, reaching almost to a dangerous point.

ORGANIZERS AND METHODS OF WORK:

This is so important a question that I therefore must deal with it in detail. The organizers staff in Youngstown can be divided into two categories: The UMWA organizers and the Party forces. There is a vast difference between the two. It is amazing how people can be so long in the labor movement and know so little! Not only are they political babies, they are not even good union organizers. To give you an example, a UMWA official from the anthracite (Gwyn) was in Youngstown five weeks and recruited three men. Another from the soft coal (Buhaley) was here six weeks and recruited five men and these were supposed to be well trained organizers. Then take the man who is in charge here (Frank Shiffka) completely incompetent and if not for our forces he would have left the field long ago. Then there is the well-known Cappelini, who is of the same type, but a little more slick and shrewder. We have succeeded in convincing Shiffka to remove Buhaley and Gwyn and in their places we have assigned workers from the mills as part-time organizers. On the other hand our forces that are on the staff are the best organizers and produce more results than any of them. I, personally, have established myself as the best recruiter and on the average I recruit close to fifty percent of the total recruits. Our youth organizer and the other comrades are also doing fine.

In face of such a vast difference between our and the UMWA forces, it was necessary to establish a proper relationship. Having in mind that these people don't know what criticism and self-criticism means, we have to avoid any head-on-collision with them. Instead we pursued a policy of winning their confidence. This was fully accomplished with the result that our suggestions and our policies are unquestionably accepted. We have also from the very start, decided that the Party comrades must be the best organizers and by our example bring up the rest of the crew. This is just what is happening now.

187

A few remarks about the methods of organization. We have pursued somewhat different methods than in other places. If you receive accurate reports from the field you then know that as yet in no place are the mass meetings a real success and in many places these "mass" meetings only expose the weaknesses of the union and sometimes make it look even worse than it really is. For example, I think it is crazy to now call mass meetings in towns like Alliquippa. On the basis of the experiences in other places and on the basis of Foster's lessons in Youngstown (1919), we have decided not to call any mass meeting until we have at least two thousand men signed up. Then when we have such a number of workers signed up and these are involved in preparation for a mass meeting, we are sure that at least five thousand steel workers will attend the meetings. The workers like this policy very much, as they would be afraid (and with full justification) to attend open meetings. However, we have engaged a radio station in Akron and we broadcast from there twice a week, this will go on till after Labor Day and then we will fight for a further allowance for the radio. The radio and STEEL LABOR are the medium through which we are reaching thousands of workers with the voice of the union. The first two speeches were prepared in Pittsburgh, but since then I was assigned to write these speeches. By the way, the speech last week contained most of Budenz' introduction to Foster's pamphlet and a couple of pages from the pamphlet.

A few words on the method of recruiting. Of course we are using Comrade Foster's three point theory of organization as our starting point. On the basis of this theory, I have developed a method which has been proven and tested to be the best and the whole crew in Youngstown is now practicing it. I call it the "chain form of recruiting." In brief, it works like this—when I sign up a worker, I ask him to recommend three or five other men from his department. Then I ask him to talk to these workers in the mill and prepare the ground for me. Then two days later I visit these workers, most of them already expect me and when I come to their house and present my credential, they already know who I am and I find no difficulty in signing them up. These men in turn recommend other and the chain is endless. Right now, for example, over a hundred workers are expecting me at their homes. This week, every house that I went to, as soon as I present my credential, the reply was, "Come in, I have been waiting for you." My list is already so big that another organizer will be attached to me so that the workers will not be kept waiting too long. Those organizers that begun to practice this chain form of organizing are also meeting with similar success.

Another method that I am using is not to spread out too much. Instead, I am concentrating on certain departments. For example, I have already signed up the majority of the men in the Condroit Department of the Ygstn Sheet and Tube (over 40 men). From there I began to move into the 40 inch mill. The experience is that once you establish a base in one department it is much easier to spread out into the other departments.

188

To summarize this point: the tempo in recruiting depends entirely on the organizers, the methods they use, the hours they put in, the ability to convince the worker not to fear signing up and even enthusing them for active participation in the drive.

PARTIAL STRUGGLES:

While it is absolutely correct to discourage local strike at this stage of the game and even be on guard against any strikes that may be contemplated by the steel companies, yet, the union must already begin to develop certain partial struggles that will result in some immediate victories for the workers. These can be developed through progressive company union representatives, through committees and petitions. The companies are terribly nervous and it is possible to obtain all kinds of concessions that in turn will help to build the union. It is unfortunate that the SWOC don't realize the importance of such actions. Then, there is another aspect to the same problem: when a worker joins the union he expects some kind of help and if this is not forthcoming he will fall for the company propaganda of "Why pay dues"? I think that our forces on the staff should raise this question everywhere and bring it to the attention of the CIO.

COMPANY UNION DEVELOPMENTS:

You of course know the developments in Carnegie-Illinois, in the Pittsburgh-Youngstown District. Comrade Tom Moore from here is leading the whole works. We also have other very important developments in Ygstn Sheet and Tube and Sharon Steel Hoop. I recruited two company union representatives from Sharon Steel Hoop and two from Ygstn Sheet and Tube. I am now also negotiating with both chairmen of these two company unions. Many of these representatives will play a leading role in the drive, some of them already assumed such a role.

However, I think we have very serious differences with the SWOC over this question and sooner or later we may come to a head on this question. They are absolutely against the company unions presenting demands, fearing that if these are granted it will strengthen the prestige of the company unions. They don't seem to realize that the company unions will crack and eventually be won over only in the process of struggle. At the same time they adopt the most "leftist" policies toward the company unions. Take for example this sudden brain storm of a meeting of the Central Committee of the Carnegie-Illinois representatives from Pittsburgh-Youngstown district. This Central Committee is elected on the basis of two delegates from each Carnegie mill. Comrade Moore was elected from the Ygstn territory. Last week Harold Ruthenberg and Mullins dashed to Ygstn, grab Moore to Pittsburgh to canvass the members of the Central Committee to call a special meeting to endorse the CIO, etc. No preparations were made, it became quite open that the meeting was called by the CIO and that they are paying for it, etc. The result was that the resolution was defeated, Moore was forced to resign as a delegate and it only sharpened the situation between certain forces inside the company union that could have been won over. I knew in advance that this would happen. It could have been prevented. I called Golden and told him what will happen, but he thought it would be too late to call it off, and of course, it happened just as I have predicted.

I told Moore that in the future not to take any steps until I have been consulted. Ruthenburg will be in Ygstn this week and I will discuss with him the whole situation.

On this whole question of tactics in the company unions I would like to hear from you. Personally, I am convinced that if this becomes the policy of the CIO we are heading towards disastrous mistakes and this policy will become an obstacle in the whole drive.

PRESENT POLICIES OF STEEL CORPORATIONS:

Our secret method of recruiting and organization created a very difficult situation for the companies. They are really not aware of the degree of progress we have made so far. The decentralized form of organization is an additional obstacle to them. However, we know that they are careful in firing union men. Sixteen of our people were uncovered (I will tell you how later) including many of our comrades. But so far only the YCL organizer was fired out of the Sheet & Tube. All the others were called in, warned but not yet fired.

Through a friendly federal man we have also learned that the companies have brought in a lot of ammunition inside the mills. Sheet & Tube has deputized 151 men, Republic 50 men. We have also learned that when the first public meeting is held, they will provoke a fight and open a barrage of tear gas.

Meanwhile, they are publishing every Sunday a full page ad. I will send you a sample of this Sunday ad. They are also circulating a petition among wives of steel workers against the CIO. The spies continue to shadow the organizers and all our wires are tapped. Recently I moved to a new house hoping to keep it secret, several days later two cars with the stool pigeons were in front early in the morning. I figure it is no use to move again, I have arranged for another sleeping place in case of emergencies. I have also learned from the same source that they are especially out to get us and to link us up with the CIO and then make a big splash in the papers. We are now expecting it to break soon and we are prepared for it.

One of the organizers, Harold Tetlow, the son of Percy Tetlow from the UMWA turned traitor and worked for a detective agency for $500.00 a week. The first sixteen men who joined were turned in by him. Fortunately, we have discovered him in time and got him out of town. It was a whole scandal, this man was appointed by Lewis himself and for two days the wires were burning between Ygstn, Pittsburgh and Washington. When I see you in person I will tell you the details. Please keep it to yourself as I was strictly instructed to keep it confidential and the only one I have reported it to was Bill Gebert.

ON THE PARTY:

The letter is already too long so I will conclude with a few remarks on the Party. The functioning of the Party is very unsatisfactory. It has been that way since the Section Convention and we didn't yet get out of the rut. At present I devote all my time to the drive. However, as soon as I personally recruit 500 into the union (I have already reached the 200 mark) and the other comrades recruit another 500 steel workers, it will no longer be necessary for me to devote my time on individual recruiting and I will have more time for direct Party work. However, I have already established dozens of splendid contacts for the Party. I look forward that within six months from now the bulk of the Party will be composed of powerful nuclei inside the mills. We have already made a start by recruiting one of the organizers into the Party. He was the legislative representative for the Railway union for a long time, he is a local man and former Director of the Ygstn YMCA, a few years ago he ran for the Board of Education and got 12,000 votes. I am now working on several other leading people in the drive and I am sure we will soon have them in the Party.

The Party comrades inside the mills are doing splendid work and they are coming forward very nicely. Up to now the active comrades were busy with putting the Party on the ballot, now we're through with this work, we will get busy on stabilizing the units and involve our Party forces in the steel drive.

We are planning a real reception for Browder and good mass meeting. We have also paid $50 for a half hour radio speech when Browder will be here. Because of the expense for the radio and putting our local candidates on the ballot we have not taken out yet the steel leaflet and didn't order the Foster pamphlet, it will be done this week.

Dallet is working real hard taking care of the daily tasks of the Party. However, with him being the leading Party candidate, with myself deeply involved in the steel drive and with the org. sec'ty leaving our section, thus created a shortage of forces. The district seems to be itself in a hell of a shape and very little can be expected from them. If we could get some org. instructor for a couple of weeks it would help us a lot.

Now a few suggestions.—

1. The work of the Party forces in the steel drive must be more centralized. More frequent meetings to exchange experiences is highly important.
2. What has happened to our language buros and the steel drive?
3. Lately the D.W. doesn't carry as much material on steel.
4. I realize how busy you are, but it would be well to arrange either in Pittsburg or Ygstn a national Party conference of our forces in steel.

Excuse the length of the letter.

                    Comradely yours,

                              Steuben

191

ORIGINS OF THE SIT-DOWN ERA:
WORKER MILITANCY AND INNOVATION
IN THE RUBBER INDUSTRY, 1934-38

By DANIEL NELSON*

On June 8, 1937, Byron H. Larabee, former assistant city law director of Akron, Ohio and executive secretary of the Greater Akron Association, a business organization recently investigated by the LaFollette Committee, spoke knowingly to the local Rotary. In a nation convulsed by worker unrest, labor management confrontation, and that novel, often frightening phenomenon, the sit-down strike, Akron, he said, "has a civic and industrial stability that many Akron citizens would have considered . . . impossible twelve months ago." He believed that Akron had passed through a cycle . . . which practically all industrial sections of the United States are destined to pass through before the present . . . unrest has reached a stopping point."[1] Larabee's analysis was overly optimistic, particularly in proclaiming the return of "industrial stability," but it contained a valuable insight. For reasons distinctive to the rubber industry and its employees, Akron played a key role in the labor upheaval of the mid-1930s. Rubber workers pioneered the sit-down strike and helped ignite the wave of unrest that engulfed American industry between 1936 and 1938. Most important, their experiences anticipated the complex process of initiative and reaction that characterized industry generally in the late 1930s and made the

* An earlier version of this paper was read at the 1979 meeting of the Organization of American Historians. I am indebted to David Brody, Sidney Fine, and Maureen Greenwald for their comments and suggestions.
[1] *Akron Beacon Journal*, June 8, 1937.

0023-656x|82|2302–198 $01.00

sit-down era the decisive phase in the turbulent years of labor dynamism and innovation inaugurated by the Great Depression.

The decade after 1933 was a critical period in American labor history. Spurred on by Section 7A of the National Industrial Recovery Act, hundreds of thousands of hitherto unorganized industrial workers formed local and national organizations in 1933-34 and became a force in and out of the plant. Initially, however, their external impact exceeded their effect on the factory or mine. Worker militancy was a major force in the rise and decline of the NRA, the breakup of the early New Deal coalition, and the fragmentation of the AFL, but it had only a fleeting effect on the operation of most industries.[2] Between 1936 and 1938 workers and unions once again seized the initiative, with far more profound and permanent results. Together with the NLRB they inaugurated the modern era of industrial relations and labor politics. Public hostility and the recession of 1937-38 curbed the workers' activities but did not restore the pre-1936 status quo. The sit-down movement, the most prominent symbol of the resurgent militancy of the mid-1930s, was thus the critical link between New Deal labor initiatives and the wartime period of consolidation, the final phase of the turbulent years.

The dynamics of reemergent worker militancy were first apparent in the rubber industry and the city where it was peculiarly concentrated—Akron, Ohio. In 1936-37 sit-down strikes overshadowed more familiar contemporary events—the lingering depression, the New Deal, even the union organizing campaigns and the AFL-CIO split—and brought far reaching, even revolutionary changes to industry and community alike. First, they accelerated the process of industrial evolution that was a major effect of the labor unrest of the 1930s. More than in any previous period, production workers became the principal agents of change. Their actions profoundly, irreversibly influenced the operation of the factory. Second, worker militancy had an ambiguous impact on the labor movement, alternately stimulating and retarding it. To union officials, particularly those at the

---

[2] See William E. Leuchtenburg, *Franklin D. Roosevelt and The New Deal* (New York, 1963), Ch. 5; Irving Bernstein, *Turbulent Years* (Boston, 1970), Chs. 4-6; Sidney Fine, *The Automobile Under the Blue Eagle: Labor, Management, and the Automobile Manufacturing Code* (Ann Arbor, 1963), *passim*.

higher levels, the effect was highly unsatisfactory. Long before the sit-down had spread from Akron to Detroit, Flint, and the nation, the leadership had resolved to curb rank and file activism. Finally, labor militancy had a disruptive effect outside the factory and union hall. It polarized the local community, unleashed virulent anti-union forces, and persuaded manufacturers to flee. Militancy and "decentralization"—the movement of the industry to other, usually non-union towns, were two sides of a common coin.

*   *   *   *

Since the turn of the century the rubber industry had consisted of two contrasting elements. The first, embracing a majority of firms, produced traditional industrial and consumer products— mechanical goods, footwear, and rubber sundries. Most of these firms were small, family-owned operations; the exception was the DuPonts' United States Rubber Company, a late 19th century trust that had combined the largest and most efficient companies of that era.[3] In this sector of the industry technology was simple and labor intensive. Working conditions were disagreeable, often dangerous, and wages were among the lowest in all northern manufacturing. Nearly half the employees were women.[4] Clustered in Boston, central Connecticut, New Jersey, and scattered midwestern towns, these manufacturers and their employees left little mark on the industry or the United Rubber Workers before World War II. The plants were relatively easy to organize, but the tangible benefits of union membership were slight. The very marginality of the firms acted as a deterrent to militancy and innovation.

The other sector of the industry, the manufacture of automobile tires, could not have been more dissimilar. With few exceptions the tire companies were products of the auto era. Survivors of a harsh winnowing process, they were large and efficient; by the 1920s and 1930s tire manufacturing was probably the most

---

[3] Glenn D. Babcock, *History of the United States Rubber Company: A Case Study in Corporate Management* (Bloomington, 1966), Ch. 2.

[4] See US Dept. of Commerce. Bureau of the Census, *Biennial Census of Manufactures, 1935* (Washington, DC, 1938), 757, 764. Low wages and women workers were also the rule in the non-tire divisions of the tire plants in Akron and other cities. For a similar situation in another industry see Robert H. Zieger, "The Limits of Militancy: Organizing Paper Workers, 1933-35," *Journal of American History*, 63 (1976), 638-57.

highly concentrated major industry in the United States.[5] Good-year Tire & Rubber, the industry leader with a market share of more than 30 percent, Firestone, B. F. Goodrich, General Tire, and the tire division of U.S. Rubber accounted for 96 percent of US production.[6] Geographical concentration was almost as great. In 1935 two thirds of the tires manufactured in the US were made in Akron.[7] Mechanized, conveyorized, meticulously organized, the Akron tire factories were tributes to the ingenuity of the engineer and the transforming influence of the automobile.

The aura of centralization, power, and modernity that impressed visitors to the factories was nevertheless misleading. The extension of the automobile market led to the establishment of regional manufacturing facilities in Los Angeles, Gadsden, Alabama, and other sites in the 1920s. In the factory itself, the development of the Banbury mixer drastically altered the economics of tire production.[8] A capital and labor saving invention, the Banbury eliminated the slower roller method of "milling" the rubber, the first major step in the production process. But it also affected the entire manufacturing process. Because of the Banbury, optimum plant size fell to as little as 1000 casings per day, approximately 2 percent of the capacity of the giant Goodyear or Firestone plants.[9] By the mid-1930s the competitive edge of the large Akron plants had disappeared. Manufacturers faced new challenges and opportunities. In time the Banbury became an important anti-union weapon.

The work of the tire plants revolved around a few key tasks. In essence chemical reactions transformed a natural material into a complex consumer good. Machines guided these processes and men supplemented the machines, overseeing their operation and performing tasks that resisted mechanization. In a large tire plant nearly 20 percent of the employees were tire builders—assemblers—and 15 percent were vulcanizers or "pit" workers.[10] Most

[5] See Alfred D. Chandler, Jr., "The Structure of American Industry in the Twentieth Century: A Historical Overview," *Business History Review*, 43 (1969), 258-59.
[6] "The Rolling Tire," *Fortune*, 14 (Nov., 1936), 99.
[7] *Census of Manufactures, 1935*, 757.
[8] Ralph William Frank, "The Rubber Industry of the Akron-Barberton Area: A Study of the Factors Related to Its Development, Distribution and Localization (unpublished PhD Diss., Northwestern Univ., 1952), 27; D. H. Killeffer, *Banbury the Master Mixer* (New York, 1952).
[9] Frank, 27; Lloyd G. Reynolds, "Competition in the Rubber-Tire Industry," *American Economic Review*, 28 (1938), 466.
[10] See "Statements of Enrollment," NLRB Files, RG 25, Box 2116, File 1832, National Archives.

tire workers facilitated machine operations; tire builders performed manual tasks with the aid of machines. Yet unlike assembly line workers in the mechanical industries they made the
entire product. The essential attributes of a tire builder were
agility and quickness. Any reduction in his pace immediately
affected work in the pit and eventually in other departments.
To maintain production schedules, foremen "drove" the tire
builders, who responded with informal production limits.[11] The
pit or curing room worker was also a select employee. Because
of the heavy work and debilitating heat of the pit, he had to be
strong and durable. The rule of thumb was that pit workers had
to weigh at least two hundred pounds. Like the tire builders,
they were aggressive, self-confident individuals, proud of their
abilities and awesome duties.

Tire employees in general were an elite element of the industrial labor force. Their work was not skilled in the usual sense;
manufacturers classified only 10-15 percent of their employees,
principally machine repairmen, as skilled operatives.[12] But tire
manufacturing was responsible work. The slightest dereliction
could destroy the casing or tire. Competence and diligence if not
manual dexterity, experience, and creativity were essential. This
characteristic of tire production coupled with rapid technological
change accounted for the industry's high wage rates. In the 1920s
and 1930s tire workers were among the best paid mass production workers.[13] Despite the trials of the following years, they
maintained that distinction; at the time of the sit-downs they
earned on the average 10 percent more than the typical auto
worker.[14]

These features of the industry made Akron a mecca for ambitious young men in the pre-Depression years. During the World
War I boom, manufacturers had turned to the South for their
workers. Perhaps to their surprise, the employers liked what
they found. By 1920 they had a clear conception of the ideal
worker. He was a product of Appalachia, had the rudiments of
a formal education, and took hard physical labor for granted.[15]

[11] Interview with John D. House, April 5, 1972.
[12] Frank, 83-101.
[13] John Dean Gaffey, *The Productivity of Labor in the Rubber Tire Manufacturing Industry* (New York, 1940), 138-39.
[14] *Akron Beacon Journal*, July 13, 1937.
[15] Howard and Ralph Wolf, *Rubber A Story of Glory and Greed* (New York, 1936),

The fact that he was willing to undertake an uncertain trek to a distant city testified to his ambition. Eschewing elaborate interview procedures. IQ tests, and other accoutrements of wartime personnel management, personnel officials at Goodyear and Firestone asked to see the prospective employees' hands. The uncalloused applicant had little future in the tire shops.[16] Though Akron, like most cities, had immigrant enclaves, the rubber plants were known for their strapping young "Snakes"—the local pejorative for West Virginians.[17]

To retain their employees, manufacturers introduced extensive welfare plans during and after the war. They emphasized insurance and athletic programs, the types of benefits that supposedly appealed to a predominantly male labor force. Goodyear supplemented its efforts with an Industrial Assembly, an elaborate "congressional-style company union.[18] Although the Industrial Assembly had limited powers, it performed useful services and commanded the sympathies of a substantial group of workers. Moreover, it was a symbol of the advanced state of tire company management. By 1930 Goodyear and Firestone were notable examples of firms that had stripped the foreman of most of his traditional powers in production and personnel management, and had created a direct link between the corporation and the worker.[19]

The Depression had a devastating impact on the social system of the tire plants. Production and employment declined precipitously; short hours became the rule for those who remained. To preserve the labor force, manufacturers went to four six-hour shifts in 1931, but this move only partially offset the downward spiral. By 1933 the surviving workers were veteran employees, individuals with five or more years service. Of this group the men most sensitive to their plight were the instigators of the

---

435-37; Hugh Allen, *The House of Goodyear* (Akron, 1949), 167, 175, 178.
[16] This is a frequent observation of retired workers. See references to oral history interviews.
[17] Alfred Winslow Jones, *Life, Liberty and Property* (Philadelphia, 1941), 59, 64-5.
[18] Paul W. Litchfield, *Industrial Voyage* (New York, 1954), 183-86; Paul W. Litchfield, *The Industrial Republic* (Akron, 1919).
[19] See Allen, *The House of Goodyear*, 181-191; Alfred Lief, *The Firestone Story* (New York, 1951), Ch. 5. For welfare capitalism in the 1920s see David Brody, "The Rise and Decline of Welfare Capitalism" in John Braeman, Robert H. Bremner, and David Brody, eds., *Change and Continuity in Twentieth Century America: the 1920s* (Columbus, 1968), and Stuart D. Brandes, *American Welfare Capitalism* (Chicago, 1976).

union movement. At Goodyear, where a systematic survey was made in the late 1930s, United Rubber Workers officers had been the upwardly mobile young men of the 1920s. Nearly every union official had been a delegate to the Industrial Assembly or a member of the "flying squadron," an elite corps of versatile workers that supplied a large proportion of Goodyear supervisors.[20] In the other locals a similar pattern was evident. Rarely did such men have trade union experience; even more rarely were they committed agitators or ideologues. They were, on the contrary, men closely identified with the pre-1929 status quo.[21]

The early history of the Rubber Workers reflected the industry dichotomy and the larger trends of the NRA period. Spontaneous organization occurred in rubber factories throughout the country during the summer and fall of 1933. In the eastern plants local leadership was the decisive factor. Where a strong individual or group appeared, organization was rapid and successful; the employer's position was usually too precarious for an extended contest. However, where union leadership was weak or divided, the organization languished and died. The net result was a handful of enclaves and several thousand dedicated members. The eastern plants had little or no impact on the early development of the union.[22]

In Akron organization closely followed the pattern of the auto and other "mass production" industries.[23] With the passage of the NIRA tire workers rushed to join the AFL federal union locals, creating unprecedented challenges for the manufacturers and the AFL. By late 1933, 85 percent of Akron area rubber workers were union members.[24] Led by the tire builders and pit employees, the locals negotiated grievances and pressed for the recognition of seniority in layoffs and transfers. Their fates depended

---

20 "List of Officers, U.R.W.A. Local 2 from 1937 to Date," NLRB Files, G 25, Box 1873, #1578. For a similar pattern in the electrical industry see Ronald Schatz, "American Electrical Workers: Work, Struggles, Aspiration, 1930-1950" (unpublished PhD diss., Univ. of Pittsburgh, 1977), 88.

21 Radical writers have greatly exaggerated the role of Communists in the early URW. See Ruth McKenney, *Industrial Valley* (New York, 1939) and John Williamson, *Dangerous Scot* (New York, 1969), Ch. 9.

22 See Harold S. Roberts, *The Rubber Workers* (New York, 1944), 100-104.

23 See Roberts, Ch. 5; Irving Bernstein, Chs. 2-4; Sidney Fine, *Sit-Down: The General Motors Strike of 1936-37* (Ann Arbor, 1969) Chs. 2-3; Walter Galenson, *The CIO Challenge to the AFL* (Cambridge, 1960), Ch. 6.

24 W. W. Thompson, "History of the Labor Movement in Akron, Ohio," CIO Papers, National and International (Catholic University)..

less on local leadership than on AFL policy—a policy that soon proved deficient. AFL organizers emphasized craft organization and the negotiation of collective bargaining contracts, neither of which was feasible in 1933-35. When the locals urged strikes to break the manufacturers' resistance, AFL officials counseled patience. With considerable difficulty local leaders restrained their charges. Finally, the General Tire local, the strongest of the federal unions, rebelled. Rejecting AFL leadership, the local officers waged a successful strike, including the nation's first important sit-down, in June and July 1934. The settlement provided for an informal bargaining arrangement with the General Tire management. Meanwhile, the other Akron locals declined rapidly.[25] By late 1935, when they rebelled and formed an international only nominally tied to the AFL, the locals retained only a fraction of their former strength.

The revival of the Rubber Workers did not await favorable political developments, outside leadership, or elaborate organizing campaigns.[26] For the tire workers the business revival of late 1935 and 1936 had an effect similar to the boom of the 1920s and the passage of Section 7A. The increase in hours, income, and employment opportunities that swelled the factory throngs revived the sense of opportunity that had been missing in the early 1930s and again in 1934-35. However, there was no parallel resurgence of faith in the industry or its employers. Energies that in earlier years had been devoted to personal advancement now were devoted to the reconstruction of the union, the improvement of the workers' status in the plant, and acts of defiance. Prosperity reignited the forces of worker militancy that made the industry a model for unionization in American manufacturing in 1936.

*   *   *   *

The strike "started when I walked through the plant and gave the signal to shut it down."[27] In this fashion Rex Murray, pres-

---

[25] "Report of General President Sherman H. Dalrymple, September 14, 1936," *Report of Executive Officers and Research Director to the First Convention, URWA, September 14, 1936* (Akron, 1936), 4.

[26] Compare this situation with the union resurgence in the auto, steel and other mass production industries. See for example, Bernstein, Chs. 10-12.

[27] Daniel Nelson, "The Beginning of the Sit-Down Era: The Reminiscences of Rex Murray," *Labor History*, 15 (1974), 94; *Akron Beacon Journal*, Mar. 29, 1937. Larry Englemann exposes the myth of the 1934 sitdown at Hormel Co. in " 'We were the Poor People' The Hormel Strike of 1933," *Labor History*, 15 (1974),

ident of the General Tire local, inaugurated the sit-down era
in June 1934. The next sit-downs occurred in November 1935
as conditions improved. Between early 1936 and late 1937 at
least sixty-two sit-downs, including forty in the critical months
before the great General Motors strike, in December 1936, provided a focus for the expanding influence of the workers and
the URW in the industry. There were three distinct phases to
the Akron sit-down movement. The first covered the period from
June 1934 to February 18, 1936, and culminated in the five
week Goodyear strike of February-March, the "first CIO strike."
The second extended from March to December 1936, when the
sit-down emerged as a popular protest technique in other industries. The third stage lasted from December 1936 to June 1938;
during this period worker militancy took other forms and the
sit-downs declined, casualties of the reactions they had set in
motion and the return of depression conditions.

The 1934 General Tire sit-down was a model for the sit-down
movement of 1936-37. It was a planned, possibly rehearsed move
by local union leaders. It lasted approximately eighteen hours,
was non-violent, and ended when union officials decided to evacuate the plant and conduct a conventional strike.[28] In later years
no union president or executive board ever called a sit-down
(though critics frequently charged that they acquiesced in the
actions of unruly followers). Otherwise, the General Tire strike
serves as a useful guide to the Akron sit-downs.[29] Just as it reflected the militancy of the NRA period, so the sit-downs were
expressions of the resurgent activism of the mid-1930s. The sit-
downs of 1936-37 were diverse, embracing four of the five categories of sit-downs the Bureau of Labor Statistics identified in
1937.[30] They lasted anywhere from a few minutes to nearly three
days, and they involved anywhere from a single individual to
several thousand employees. They were generally non-violent.
Although strikers made no formal arrangements to avoid the destruction of machines or tires, property damage was negligible.

.   497-99, 507-08.
[28] Nelson, 93-7.
[29] The following analysis of the Akron sit-downs is based on newspaper accounts,
    oral history interviews, and government documents. I have only footnoted quo-
    tations and references to sources of special importance.
[30] "Sit-Down Strikes During 1936," Monthly Labor Review, 44 (1937), 1233-34. URW
    strikers did not use the "third" technique, sitting for the length of a shift only.

Pit workers, who might have destroyed tires simply by not tending their machines, scrupulously synchronized their work with their protests. Personal injuries were somewhat more frequent, particularly at Goodyear, where a large anti-union group added special turbulence to the sit-downs. But with one possible exception, the injuries were not serious. Violence was a common feature of conventional URW strikes and organizing campaigns, but not the sit-downs.

There was another similarity with the General Tire strike. Whatever the causes of the sit-downs, they did not result in efforts to control factory operations. There were few explicit challenges to the foreman's realm, no reports of shared power, no efforts to redefine the managerial role except in the personnel area. Tire builders had traditionally attempted to limit production; their sit-downs against renegade workers in 1936-37 were simply a new phase of an old contest. The one exception was the workers' efforts to control the labor force. But even this activity was confined to discrimination against non-union workers. Once a man became a URW member in good standing, he became immune from attack. In this area, as in others, the sit-down was an act of censure rather than a step toward a new type of industrial management.[31] As a result the sit-downs had a greater impact on the distribution of power and authority among managers than they did on the duties of workers.

The General Tire strike also foreshadowed the employer's role in the sit-downs. No manager ever attempted to expel strikers. Even after August 1936, when city police were available for strikebreaking duty, there was no effort to forcibly remove the workers, presumably because of danger to the plant. Nor was there any attempt to invoke the law against participants in sit-downs. The only instance when workers were prosecuted was an unusual case; the charge was not that they sat down, but that they held their supervisors hostage. In general manufacturers were remarkably accommodating. They kept cafeteria and janitorial employees on the job and maintained heat and light in occupied departments. By the summer of 1936 they concluded

---

[31] In this respect the rubber workers were apparently like other CIO militants. See David Brody, "Radical Labor History and Rank and File Militancy," *Labor History*, 16 (1975), 123.

that the most effective response to the sit-downs was simply to close the plant until the dispute ended. By this tactic they insured that non-striking workers and townspeople, frightened by the specter of a silent factory, would pressure union leaders and strikers for a settlement.

The five sit-downs that occurred at Firestone, Goodyear, and Goodrich between January 28 and February 18, 1936, built on the pioneering General Tire strike.[32] They reflected the improving economic environment, the managers' determination to return to "normal" operations, the workers' familiarity with the sit-down tactic, the decline of URW effectiveness, and the impotence of the company unions. In every case tire builders were the leaders. By trade union standards the sit-downs accomplished little. By the historian's gauge, however, they were a social innovation of the greatest significance. At a time when New Deal initiatives in the labor area had stalled and manufacturers were recapturing their customary prerogatives, successful acts of defiance were more meaningful than the settlement of any grievance.

The Firestone sit-down of January 28-30 was probably the single most important event in the history of the sit-down movement. In late January the company cut piece work rates in the tire room. When the tire builders, all URW Local 7 members, slowed their pace in protest, the company assigned a non-union man named Godfrey to the tire room, presumably to act as a "pacemaker." Godfrey proceeded to disregard the disapproving looks of his fellow workers and traded insults with Clay Dicks, the Local 7 committeeman. At one point Godfrey suggested that Dicks would be more circumspect without a "gang" to back him and Dicks accepted the challenge. The two men met at the plant gate after work and exchanged blows; Godfrey was knocked unconscious. He promptly complained to his supervisor who suspended Dicks for a week. When Local 7 officials objected, W. R. Murphy, Firestone's personnel manager, agreed to meet them.

---

[32] There was also a sitdown on November 8 by Goodyear first shift tire builders. It lasted less than an hour and resulted in a delay in a wage cut. Its most interesting feature, however, was the fact that first shift workers instigated it. In the following months first shift tire builders, the oldest, most secure employees, led the anti-URW, anti-sit-down effort at Goodyear. The November 8 incident was quickly forgotten, perhaps because the memory of the first Goodyear sit-down embarrassed first shift workers and URW militants alike. *Akron Beacon Journal*, Nov. 8, 1935.

However, before the local officials had an opportunity to plead Dicks' case, the tire builders stopped work and refused to resume their duties until Dicks was reinstated. Their action was spontaneous, as surprising to union officials as it was to the management. The protest spread to the auto tire room and other departments. "In place of feverish work a carnival spirit pervaded the shop." The workers "clustered in groups and talked. Some played cards. Others played checkers with the tops of pop bottles."[33] After a day of fruitless negotiations the local leaders turned to the International union for assistance. Sherman H. Dalrymple, the International president, henceforth led the union negotiators. "Our main effort," he explained on January 30, "is to get all those men back to work as soon as possible."[34]

The key incident in the dispute occurred later that evening. Murphy offered to pay the workers half their customary wages for the time they had lost if the union would drop the Dicks' case. Dalrymple and the Local 7 negotiators rejected this offer, insisting that Dicks be reinstated. As the meeting broke up a superintendent suggested to a Local 7 executive committee member that Murphy might pay Dicks too. Dalrymple immediately reconvened the conference and settled the strike on that basis.[35] The reason for this remarkable concession—paying the suspended man for his lost time—is unclear. Whatever Murphy's motive, "union men were unanimous in their declarations that the outcome of the protest was a 'victory.'" Dicks called the settlement "the finest thing in the world."[36] In his official statement Dalrymple asserted that the incident would "teach the men what an organization can do to settle their grievances."[37] In fact, the sit-down taught the men what they could do for themselves. The Firestone "victory" rekindled the optimism of 1933-34 and confirmed the lesson of the General Tire experience. Progress did not have to await a formal contract.

The sit-downs of the next two weeks bore the imprint of the Firestone strike. On Friday January 31 non-union Goodyear Plant 1 pit and tire workers sat down to demand the restoration

[33] *Akron Times Press*, Jan. 30, 1936.
[34] *Akron Beacon Journal*, Jan. 30, 1936.
[35] *Akron Times Press*, Jan. 31, 1936; *Akron Beacon Journal*, Jan. 31, 1936.
[36] *Akron Beacon Journal*, Jan. 31, 1936.
[37] *Akron Times Press*, Jan. 31, 1936.

of a piece rate cut. The head of the company union dismissed the sit-down as a reaction to the Firestone incident and maintained a "hands off attitude." [38] URW Local 2 officers were equally unenthusiastic at first. Secretary E. E. White told the press that "It isn't our baby and we're paying no attention to it." [39] Over the weekend, however, they did pay attention to a sudden resurgence of interest in the union. Men who had left in disgust paid back dues and others joined for the first time. On Sunday the union endorsed the protest and on Monday union members gathered at the gates to urge workers to continue the sit-down. First shift employees sat down briefly at 6 am and second shift workers sat down from noon to 2 pm, until the personnel manager threatened to discharge them. Work resumed but negotiations, with Local 2 representing the workers, continued through the week. In the meantime Goodrich tire builders sat down on February 7 to protest wage losses due to minor changes in the piece rate system. Negotiations followed and the company, as one committeeman reported, gave "more than had been asked for." But when the settlement was announced, the men sat down again demanding half pay—à la Firestone—for the time they had been on strike. Only when Dalrymple explained in the strongest possible terms that "they could not expect the company to pay them 'strike defense funds'" did they agree to leave the plant. On the following Sunday the International held a mass meeting for tire workers. Dalrymple led a parade of union officials, including Adolph Germer of the CIO, in condemning the sit-downs. "Such cessation of work does not demonstrate efficiency," he declared. "On the other hand it does demonstrate a dual movement. The proper way to handle grievances is through your union officers...." [40]

Five days later another major sit-down occurred at Goodyear Plant 2. At 3 am on February 14 the fourth shift truck tire department foreman began to notify between fifty-five and seventy non-union tire builders that they were to be furloughed as the company returned to the eight-hour day. As he went from machine to machine the men stopped their work to watch. Soon

[38] *Ibid.*, Feb. 5, 1936.
[39] *ibid.*, Feb. 1, 1936.
[40] *Akron Beacon Journal*, Feb. 10, 1936.

they gathered around him. The news was disheartening; fourth shift workers were low seniority employees who had been recalled in late 1935. Pleading that he was simply the bearer of bad news, the foreman suggested that the tire builders choose a committee to talk to the shift foreman.[41] This move proved to be a turning point in the history of the sit-down. The committee members—notably C. D. "Chuck" Lesley, George Boyer, and James W. "Jimmy" Jones—became leading figures in the sit-downs of the following transitional months. If the Firestone strike provided the spark that ignited the movement, Lesley—a large, tough National Guardsman and former anti-union militant who "spoke well," Boyer—a spare family man who had weathered the worst of the Depression on a hard scrabble southern Ohio farm, and Jones—a small "dapper" Georgian and union zealot, provided the fuel that sustained it.

From that point the Goodyear dispute escalated rapidly. The Lesley committee received no satisfaction from the shift foreman and returned to the tire department at 5 am. When asked to leave the plant Lesley supposedly challenged his coworkers: "What are we, mice or men? If we're going to be men, let's stick with it." The men responded: "We're going to be men!"[42] They sat down for the rest of their shift and half of the morning shift. When they left at 9 am, having been promised a meeting with the plant manager and personnel manager later that day, John D. House, Local 2 president, was waiting at the gate. He offered support and the use of the union hall. Local 2 thus became a factor in the protest. Sit-downs on the afternoon and evening shifts closed the plant—as it turned out, for more than a month. On the evening of February 17, Local 2 held a rally for tire workers. After several hours of increasingly strident speeches, a union officer, without prior warning, seized a flag from the podium and led a motley army to the plant gates. The great Goodyear strike had begun.[43]

The Goodyear conflict, famous for reviving the URW and inaugurating the CIO, was also important as a gauge of public

---

[41] Interview with George Boyer, July 1, 1976.
[42] Ibid.
[43] For various accounts of the strike, none of which is entirely satisfactory, see Edward Levinson, *Labor on the March* (New York, 1938), 143-46; Jones, 99-103; McKenney, 277-370; Roberts, 147-51; and Bernstein, 593-97.

attitudes toward the union and its tactics. Local 2 was hardly a formidable contestant; it had a paid-up membership of less than six hundred, perhaps 5 percent of the Goodyear labor force, when the strike began.[44] It succeeded because it commanded a much larger informal following, both in Goodyear and in the community at large. This support reflected widespread disillusionment with the corporation and a feeling that the strikers were merely demanding what they deserved. Many local residents, non-union workers and others, undoubtedly saw the sit-downs as appropriate responses to the company's intransigent approach to New Deal labor initiatives, including the union. As a result local businessmen contributed more than $25,000 to the strike relief fund.[45] The two local newspapers maintained a careful neutrality, and most important, the city administration of Republican Lee D. Schroy refused to allow the police to be suborned into a strike breaking force. The concessions the union ultimately won seemed just rewards for what had been a broad-based public undertaking.

The settlement of the Goodyear strike on March 21 marked the beginning of the second, more innovative and disruptive phase of the sit-down movement. In January and February worker militancy revived the union; between April and the Fall it had a far more profound impact on factory operations and public attitudes toward the union and labor issues. By the time of the General Motors strike, the process of innovation and adjustment was largely complete. The subsequent history of the sit-down movement in the industry and the nation was largely an extension of the experiences of the turbulent spring and summer of 1936.

Between April and November periodic waves of sit-downs convulsed the rubber factories. Typically a sit-down in one plant would spark a rash of sit-downs in other plants. There was no apparent pattern to the waves nor any indication of coordinated activity. Even the workers' most vocal critics never detected a conspiracy of militants.[46] Indeed, they agonized over the opposite tendency, the "chaotic," "anarchistic," and "syndicalistic"

---

[44] Local 2 Membership Record.
[45] *United Rubber Worker*, 1 (May, 1936), 1. For public opinion, see Jones.
[46] The Goodyear management suggested that "communistic" or "radical" influences were behind the sit-downs on several occasions, but with little effect.

character of the sit-downs.[47] In January and February workers sat down in response to managerial initiatives, wage cuts and layoffs; after April they sat down for varied, occasionally frivolous reasons. The most common substantive grievance, a reflection of the Goodyear role and the growth of the URW in 1936, was the presence of non-union workers in a department. This complaint accounted for approximately one-third of the sit-downs. Other grievances included wage adjustments, layoffs and transfers, and the refusal of a worker or group of workers, often non-union employees, to adhere to production limitations. However, external concerns—the beating of Dalrymple by local toughs in Gadsden, Alabama, a cross-burning near the Goodyear plant, and the supposed abduction of a Goodyear committeeman—also prompted sit-downs. Others were responses to rumors; still others seem to have had no reason at all. A common management complaint was that it was impossible to negotiate because no grievances had been presented. Charles L. Skinner, Local 2 vice president, recalled that "sometimes it was laughable. I've been so damn mad I could have killed them all."[48] Clearly, the workers' new outlook rather than any shop problem or group of problems provided the principal stimulus for the sit-down movement.[49]

If there was a central theme to the sit-downs of mid-1936, it was their association with night work. Of the 35 sit-downs that occurred during this period (and the Goodyear management claimed a dozen more), at least twenty-two started between 6 pm and 6 am. At first this tendency surprised observers who assumed that the low seniority night employees, the principal beneficiaries of the economic boom and the men most vulnerable to layoff, would be least troublesome of all the workers. But two factors appear to have offset their insecurity. First, night shifts workers were younger and freer. Though industry veterans, they

---

[47] See for example *Akron Times Press*, Feb. 9, 1936; *Akron Beacon Journal*, May 8, May 20, May 23, 1936.
[48] Interview with Charles L. Skinner, April 23, 1976.
[49] A similar perspective fueled Detroit area sit-downs after the General Motors strike. Carlos A. Schwantes writes that Michigan sit-downs "cannot be linked solely to the mode of production, but must also be considered a psychological phenomenon. . . ." Carlos A. Schwantes, " 'We've Got 'em on the Run, Brothers;' The 1937 Non-Automotive Sit Down Strikes in Detroit," *Michigan History*, 56 (1972), 190.

were less likely to have mortgages and other inhibiting commitments. Second and possibly more important, the euphoria of the sit-down era militated against a long-term outlook or a rational calculation of costs and benefits. To many workers the possibilities of the moment were all that counted. "We didn't care" is a common recollection of the sit-down veterans.[50]

Of the night shift employees, the Goodyear Plant 2 tire builders were by far the most belligerent and irrepressible. Between May and July, the period during which more than half the sit-downs occurred, the Lesley group was the major irritant in the industry. They struck at least 10 times, set off three waves of sit-downs, and insured that the sit-down strike remained a major topic of discussion in and out of the plant.

The group's most controversial acts occurred in late May. During a sit-down in the Plant 2 tire department on May 6, the shop supervisors had remained in one of the plant offices. The reason for their action is unclear, but Lesley and his followers observed the supervisors' behavior, possibly encouraged it, and certainly learned from it. On May 20, Plant 2 third and fourth shift tire builders and pit men sat down to protest the transfer of a non-union man to the fourth shift pit crew. Lesley and Jones took control of the tire room and herded supervisors into a "bullpen," an area of the room they set off by arranging tire racks in a rectangular shape. A crude poster identified the men as "red apples"—friends of the management. The strikers kept the supervisors in the bullpen for the duration of the strike.

A foreman recalled his experience:

> I had been in the office not more than five minutes when I was informed by — — — that I was to go with a number of other supervisors. I asked where we were to go and — — — replied, 'Come on, get out of here, don't ask questions.'
>
> We were marched to the south end of building 73 and told to stay in the location of the repair section. The section was guarded by quite a large number of men varying from 15 to 50 at various times. . . .
>
> I walked to the windows once to look out and was told by — — — to get back in my place. He was armed with an iron pipe about two feet long in one hand and home-made black jack in the other hand.

---

[50] Interview with George Boyer, July 1, 1976.

Practically all the guards were armed with clubs, tomahawks, shears and one man carried a rubber mallet.

When the prisoners wanted to go to the lunch room, the guards would permit only three to go at one time. — — — would pick the three prisoners and appoint three or four guards to accompany them.

The same condition existed when one of us wanted to go to the toilet or get a drink of water.

During the morning, the group of tire builders, assisted by some men from the pit, would bring in more prisoners. A pit man, who I later learned was Steve Friday [the non-union man] was brought back and told in very unpleasant words to stay with the rest of the 'red apple' bunch.

— — — told the group at this time not to bother Friday if he stayed in his place but if he got out of place to give him the works—that he didn't give a damn.

Later on another pit man was brought in who showed evidence of having been handled rather roughly. His forehead was cut and he also looked bruised about his face, head and shoulders.

Some of the gang said 'Stand this — — — against a post and don't let him sit down.' He stood for 10 minutes and then two guards were appointed to take him to the hospital.[51]

The sit-down ended at noon on May 21 when the management agreed to transfer the non-union man to another shift.

The next morning at the 6 am shift change, Jones and other fourth shift tire builders confronted Lyle Carruthers, a first shift worker who was a leader of the anti-union group. Blandishing "tomahawks," heavy knife like tools, they attacked Carruthers, chased him through the plant, surrounded him, and beat him unmercifully. When another worker came to his aid, he too, felt the militants' wrath.[52]

The bullpen and tomahawk episode impressed many observers as revolutionary acts, efforts to use the sit-down to control the plant rather than to "veto" company policies. To John N. Knight, local newspaper editor, the bullpen incident was "guerilla warfare,—undeclared, ruthless, uncontrollable."[53] Company officials, who pressed riot charges against the men, and the local prosecutor apparently took a similar view. In retrospect, however, these accusations seem unduly melodramatic. If the strikers had a larger objective, they never mentioned it, either during the

---

[51] *Akron Beacon Journal*, May 25, 1936.
[52] *Ibid.*, May 22, 1936; *Akron Times Press*, May 22, 1936.
[53] *Ibid.*, May 21, 1936.

sit-down or afterward.[54] During the bullpen episode Jones, Lesley, and Boyer assigned the participants to various tasks but made no effort to lecture the supervisors, bargain with them, or suggest that the workers would not tolerate certain activities. At his trial in June, Jones described the incident as an attempt to protect supervisors from marauding workers and, more credibly, as a lark. Despite considerable bitterness at their treatment, the foremen subscribed to the latter view. As a result Jones' jury deadlocked and the other tire builders were never tried.[55] Local 2 officials, on the other hand, were less tolerant. They viewed the bullpen episode as an irresponsible act of terrorism, directed as much against the union as the company. Publicly they defended the exuberant tire builders; privately they resolved to put an end to the antics of Lesley and his followers.

Spurred by the tire builders, the Lesley group in particular, workers in the non-tire divisions of the Akron factories and in other local industries also began to sit down in the spring of 1936.[56] During a strike by Goodyear Plant 2 tire and pit workers on May 7, footware employees stopped work for fifteen minutes. Two weeks later Goodrich mechanical goods employees sat down for more than five hours to protest the layoff of three co-workers. This was the first sit-down conducted independently of the tire workers. And on August 18 Firestone mechanical goods employees sat down for twelve hours over a wage dispute. This was the first sit-down involving large numbers of women workers. Although tire builders and pit workers remained at the forefront of the movement, they no longer monopolized it. After May, a sit-down could occur in any department in any plant.

The Akron sit-downs greatly accelerated the process of industrial change that the advent of unions had inaugurated. In the short term, at least, they speeded the organization of the plant, as non-union workers were forced to commit themselves. At Goodyear, where the largest company union group remained, Local 2 grew rapidly. The third and fourth shifts were soon one

---

[54] Goodyear attorneys questioned the defendants after they had been arrested, very likely to obtain such admissions. Although the men spoke freely their statements were of little value to the prosecution. *Akron Beacon Journal*, May 25, 1936.

[55] *Ibid.*, July 2, 1936.

[56] The first local sit-down outside the rubber industry occurred on Feb. 18, 1936, at the Pittsburgh Plate Glass plant in Barberton.

hundred percent URW. "We put everybody in," Boyer recalled, "of course, some of them joined the union just out of fear." [57] At the other companies the process was less dramatic but the results were similar. By late 1936 the Goodrich and General factories were almost completely organized; even the appearance of a "red apple" would shut down many departments.

The sit-downs also had a profound effect on the day-to-day operation of the plants. Most important, apart from the greater number of workers who looked to the union as well as to the management for direction, were the appearance of large numbers of worker litigants and the steady erosion of the supervisors' already tenuous position. Before 1936 union officers and committeemen had negotiated disputes with company officials. But these sessions had been infrequent due to the uncertain membership of the locals and the presence of company unions. And they had little if any impact on the roles of the foreman and other shop officials. [58] In 1936 this situation changed rapidly. Negotiations became a way of life. [59] The surviving documents do not permit an accurate comparison of the pre and post-Goodyear strike periods, but the number of hours and individuals involved must have risen dramatically. At Goodyear, formal negotiating sessions were nearly daily occurrences. [60] They often began in the affected departments and focused on the foreman's role and behavior. Whatever their cause, the sit-downs raised doubts about the supervisor's competence if not the powers he should exercise. The "bullpen" incident was an isolated event, but it symbolized the degradation of the foremen that may have been the most important long-term effect of the sit-downs. Supervisory morale plummeted in 1936-37. At Goodyear foremen complained bitterly of "insubordination," a "peace at any price policy," "giving undeserving men too many chances," and the "inability to get rid of men that are no good." [61]

As the foremen's confidence and self-esteem declined, the de facto role of the personnel department and its managers grew.

[57] Interview with George Boyer, July 1, 1976.
[58] This conclusion is based on the statements of various union officials.
[59] Interview with A. A. Wilson, May 17, 1973.
[60] Local 2 Plant Legislative Committee records, 1936-37.
[61] "Supervisory Conference, 1937-38," Goodyear Tire & Rubber Co., NLRB Files, RG 25, Box 1873, File 157B. John D. House recalls foremen who welcomed the sit-downs (interview, April 5, 1972).

Foremen and committeemen seldom were able to end sit-downs. If nothing else, the strikers demanded the attention of higher-level managers and union officials. The supervisor necessarily called in the personnel manager and union officers. After that point he had little part in the negotiations. When foremen complained of a "peace at any price policy," they referred to the staff specialists whose paramount objectives were to end disputes and maintain reasonable harmony with the union officials. The personnel experts, the foremen objected, did not have to live with the results of their agreements. Historians have often noted the managerial response to New Deal labor legislation and bureaucratized collective bargaining.[62] In Akron, at least, these adjustments preceded the advent of union contracts and formal negotiating procedures. Earlier stages of the factory revolution, so apparent in the rubber plants, had circumscribed the foreman's role in the personnel area; the sit-downs introduced a second, more decisive phase of that process.

The waves of sit-downs between April and December were sporadic and unpredictable, but the public response to the sit-downs, particularly as measured by newspaper statements and the actions of community officials, the "public" most critical to the welfare of the union movement, followed a clearer course. In April Goodyear, Goodrich, and General made their first "decentralization" announcements. By implication the sit-downs and the Goodyear strike were the cause, or at least one major cause. The exact reasons are impossible to ascertain—the Banbury mixer and marketing considerations made the establishment of additional branch plants inevitable. But labor militancy, by creating uncertainty among the executives and their customers, was also a factor. Most likely it encouraged manufacturers to confront the challenges of technological change, automobile marketing, and low wage competition in non-tire product markets by moving at least part of their operations elsewhere. Public officials sensed the executives' wariness.[63] With each wave of sit-

---

[62] See e.g., Thomas C. Cochran, *Business in American Life: A History* (New York, 1972), Chs. 16-17.
[63] Though manufacturers were ambitious about the effects of labor unrest on their plans, city fathers perceived it as one factor they could influence and therefore accorded it great, perhaps undue, significance. See *Akron Beacon Journal*, July 22, Aug. 19, 1936.

downs their concern grew. Regardless of the cause of the sit-down, the number of workers idled, or the immediate consequences, the officials antipathy toward the sit-down and the URW, which they believed had the power to halt the sit-downs, increased. By the Fall the process of polarization was complete. The newspapers, the business community, and the city administration, neutral as late as March, became bulwarks of the anti-union camp. The Greater Akron Association, formed in July to combat decentralization, signified this transformation.

URW International and local union leaders resisted these trends to little avail. Pragmatic politicians, they fought to enhance the union and their authority. This dictated a policy of opposing both the sit-downs and the managers' efforts to deal decisively with men like Lesley. Union news releases at the conclusion of a sit-down typically celebrated the workers' "victory" and condemned their lack of discipline. Dalrymple was the most direct and forthright of the URW officials. As early as May he threatened to expel sit-down leaders.[64] He continued to urge local leaders to take a firmer stand and was probably responsible for the 1936 URW convention resolution authorizing the expulsion of members who caused "a stoppage of work . . . without having the consent of the local union or its executive board."[65] By virtue of his position, moreover, he had another resource that proved more valuable. As the head of one of the early CIO organizations, he had a substantial claim on the Committee. Dalrymple soon turned to John L. Lewis and his United Mine Workers assistants for help in combatting the sit-downs.

In early July Thomas Burns, the URW vice president, met Lewis and other CIO leaders to plan organizing strategies.[66] As a result of these discussions URW leaders pledged a more vigorous effort to recruit members in the East and in other non-union centers. Lewis, on the other hand, agreed to pay the salaries of three rubber industry organizers, two of whom were to be

---

[64] *Ibid.*, May 9, 1936.
[65] *Proceedings of the First Convention of the URW of A, Sept. 13-21, 1936*, 429-31.
[66] Dalrymple had been severely beaten by anti-union workers in Gadsden, Alabama several weeks before. For the CIO action see "Report of Director to CIO Meeting on July 2, 1936," Minutes of CIO Meeting, July 2, 1936. Katherine Pollak Ellickson Papers (Franklin D. Roosevelt Library, Hyde Park), Reel 1; *Akron Times Press*, July 8, 1936; Melvyn Dubofsky and Warren Van Tine, *John L. Lewis: A Biography* (New York, 1977), Ch. 11.

URW men. The latter included William Carney, a Goodyear Plant 1 militant, who·was dispatched to Detroit to devote his abundant energies to organizing the U.S. Rubber Company. (Lesley, who was sent to Gadsden on an organizing mission in June, joined the ranks of URW organizers in September.[67]) The other organizer, Allen Haywood of the UMW, arrived in Akron in late July and spent nine months taming the sit-down monster. Described in the local press as the CIO "disciplinarian," Haywood had a marked effect.[68] In speeches, negotiations, and informal discussions with workers he preached the virtues of routinized grievance procedures, union rules, and group responsibility. In December he became a full-time advisor to House at Local 2, still the source of most of the turmoil.

Local union officials were necessarily more circumspect. The sit-downs had helped revive their organizations and had attracted considerable rank and file support. Nevertheless, the stoppages reflected adversely on their leadership and threatened to discredit their organizations. L. S. Buckmaster, of the Firestone local, often considered the most conservative of the local presidents, was the first of the Akron leaders to attack the sit-downs. Speaking to striking tire builders on May 8, he ordered an end to "unsanctioned stoppages of work."[69] Thus chastened, the men returned to work. Firestone experienced only three other sit-downs and Local 7 soon became the least militant of the major locals. House was the next to act. As a result of a July 14 sit-down, during which a "roving squadron" of fourth shift tire builders closed other departments and drove non-union men out of the plant, House called a mass meeting. After heated discussion, he and other executive board members pushed through a resolution threatening the expulsion of sit-down leaders.[70] In early August L. L. Callahan, the fiery president of the giant Goodrich local, won acceptance of a similar resolution. When workers in the braided hose department sat down in September, local officers, spurred

[67] URW General Executive Board Minutes, Sept. 21, 1936.
[68] Akron Times Press, July 22, 1936; Lorin Lee Cary, "Institutionalized Conservatism in the Early CIO; Adolph Germer, A Case Study," Labor History, 13 (1972), 483-84, 487-92.
[69] Akron Times Press, May 9, 1936. As early as March 29, Adolph Germer had received a sympathetic response from Local 7 leaders when he condemned the sit-downs. Germer Diary, Mar. 29, 1936, Adolph Germer Papers (State Historical Society of Wisconsin).
[70] Akron Times Press, July 20, 1936.

by Dalrymple, urged the management to close the plant and discussed sanctions against the men.[71]

Union efforts against the sit-down did little to restore the URW's public standing, however. The city's newspapers occasionally praised Dalrymple, Haywood, and the local presidents for their courage, but more frequently condemned them for weak leadership and "chaotic" labor relations. Resolutions, statements of policy, and threats obviously were not enough to reassure community leaders. Only an end to the sit-downs and evidence that union discipline would end the "decentralization" threat would redeem the union's reputation.

The most serious external effect of the sit-downs was the alienation of the Schroy administration. Faced with decentralization and a restive business community on the one hand and a militant union movement on the other, the mayor found it increasingly difficult to maintain his impartial stance. In late May he called for union-management conferences to deal with the sit-downs, but retreated when Goodyear and Local 2 indicated little enthusiasm for the proposal. He renewed his call at the time of the July 13-14 sit-down. However, when Lesley and the fourth shift tire builders drove non-union men out of the plant, the mayor exploded:

> The city is absolutely through with sit-downs.
>
> I issued orders to the police department to muster every available member . . . to go in and clean out the plants as soon as Goodyear officials saw fit to call us.
>
> We are going to keep the factories running at all costs.[72]

Possibly to his chagrin, the sit-down had ended by the time the police arrived at the plant and the crisis passed without further incident.

The final break between Schroy and the URW occurred three weeks later when municipal employees struck the water department and URW members from Goodyear and General Tire joined the picket line. Though House and Rex Murray, the General local president, rushed to the scene to keep order and the police reported no incidents, the mayor insisted that the police disperse the pickets. A journalist noted: "At one point Schroy

---

[71] *Akron Beacon Journal*, Aug. 3, Sept. 23, Sept. 24, 1936.
[72] *Ibid.*, July 14, 1936.

said that if the police department would admit to him it could not clear the grounds 'a group of citizens will go out and show those people they cannot tie up the city.' The mayor called the strikers and strike sympathizers communists."[73] Schroy was more candid in a conference with the president of the central labor union. "You know . . . how far I stuck my neck out for the unions last winter [during the Goodyear strike]," he raged, "and now I'm getting it cut off in nice fashion."[74] The riot that followed the mayor's order also eliminated the last vestiges of impartiality in other quarters. Henceforth Akron consisted of pro and anti-union factions.[75]

By the fall of 1936 an astute observer of the Akron rubber workers could have forecast the effects of the nationwide labor upheavals of 1937 with reasonable success. Months before Roosevelt's reelection, the General Motors strike, the national sit-down movement, the Little Steel strike, and other events associated with militant unionism, Akron residents had had abundant opportunity to examine the new labor activism. In January 1937 the *Akron Beacon Journal* sent its veteran labor reporter James S. Jackson to Flint to cover the General Motors conflict. He found a "stage setting almost identical, a plot that is similar and many leading characters who are the same"—the last a reference to the URW militants who made a similar trek. "The chief difference," he added, "was that events which took a year to transpire in the rubber capital have here been telescoped into a few brief weeks. . . ."[76] Largely as a result of that "telescoping" process, labor activism and the sit-down emerged as national phenomena. Workers, organized and unorganized, instigated far reaching changes in industrial relations. Union leaders labored often frantically, to contain and direct the new activism and the public divided into pro and anti-union factions.[77] Labor militancy became an innovative force in factory and society alike.

*　*　*　*

[73] *Ibid.*, Aug. 7, 1936.
[74] *Ibid.*
[75] See Jones, Part II.
[76] *Akron Beacon Journal*, Jan. 4, 1937.
[77] See "Sit Down Strikes During 1936," *Monthly Labor Review*, 44 (May 1937); Joel Seidman, *"Sit Down"* (New York, 1937). For the critical Michigan situation see Fine, *Sit Down*; Fine, *Frank Murphy: The New Deal Years* (Chicago, 1979), Chs. 8-9; Schwantes; and Roy Boryczka, "Militancy and Factionalism in The

After December 1936 militancy in the rubber industry became inseparable from larger trends in labor and union affairs. Though the local situation remained as turbulent as before, the roles of managers and workers became more conventional. Manufacturers made important concessions in principle—formal collective bargaining contracts at Firestone in 1937 and Goodrich in 1938 for example—but they also regained the initiative in the industry. Their enlarged personnel and legal staffs, the continued "decentralization" of production, and the anti-union sentiment of business and government leaders in Akron were important, perhaps decisive, factors in the new equilibrium. On the other hand, URW leaders diverted rank and file militancy to more "positive" ends and increasingly relied on the NLRB to preserve their position in the plants. URW legions supported CIO strikers in the auto and steel industries and in numerous local disputes. In the fall of 1937 the URW and other CIO organizations waged an aggressive but unsuccessful effort to capture the city government. These activities were highly controversial, occasionally as controversial as the sit-downs.[78] In addition, union leaders mounted vigorous organizing efforts in the eastern plants. On the eve of the recession they were preparing similar campaigns for new "decentralized" plants in Michigan, Indiana, Pennsylvania, Vermont, and Tennessee.

In this new atmosphere the sit-downs declined in number and consequence. There were 17 in the Akron rubber factories in 1937 and five in 1938, approximately one-half the total that occurred in the city during that period. At Goodrich, Firestone, and General they were shorter and more peaceful than they had been in 1936. A January 1937 strike at Goodrich, called "the most friendly sit-down ever conducted in American industry," ended with the protesters singing "Happy Birthday" to the plant manager who, because of the disturbance, had missed the party his family had planned.[79] Even at Goodyear there were important changes. As a result of a February 1937 sit-down, Local 2 and the management formed a joint council—"supreme court" was

---

United Auto Workers Union, 1937-1941," *The Maryland Historian*, 8 (Fall 1977), 13-25.
[78] URW confrontations with Youngstown deputies during the Little Steel strike and with Akron Police during the Enterprise Manufacturing Company strike in July, 1937, are excellent examples.
[79] *Akron Times Press*, Jan. 31, 1937.

the workers' euphemism—to arbitrate grievances that might lead to sit-downs. In the following months the council resolved numerous disputes, and personal relations between plant officials and union leaders improved.[80] Conceivably a permanent relationship might have evolved. Yet a variety of factors in the summer and fall, periodic sit-downs, NLRB litigation, the company's refusal to sign a collective bargaining contract, and the onset of recession, underminded the atmosphere of early 1937. A mass layoff in November provoked an extended sit-down that embittered relations between the union and the company. The last Goodyear sit-down, in May 1938, sparked a three-hour battle between police and militants, the most violent incident in the history of the industry.[81]

With these exceptions the sit-downs of 1937-38 did not have the kinds of effects they had had in 1936. The Goodyear joint council was the only sit-down induced managerial innovation of the period. The protests may have contributed to the growth of anti-union sentiment and ultimately to the URW's difficulties in 1937-38, but other factors, national and local, likely would have had the same effects, given the precedents of 1936. In most respects the creative phases of the sit-down movement in the rubber industry had ended, well before the collapse of the economic "boom" and the revived opportunities that accompanied it.

The legacy of the era was nevertheless substantial. Between mid-1934 and late 1936 the rubber workers inaugurated a new stage in the development of American industry and the public perception of the union and industrial relations. Spurred by economic fluctuations and the signal victories at General in 1934 and Firestone in early 1936 they briefly held the initiative in the industry. Managers, union leaders and public officials recaptured their customary powers in 1937, but the sit-down experience left a permanent imprint on the industry. The workers' actions radically altered the duties of shop managers, the executives' conception of personnel management, and the role of union officials in the day-to-day operation of the plant. They likewise redefined the relationship between components of the union; a loosely organized coalition of locals embarked on the path to centralized

---

80 Minutes of Joint Council, NLRB Files, RG 25, Box 350, Folder 8.
81 Roberts, 169-72.

leadership and bureaucratic structure. Worker initiatives similarly disabused many local citizens of the notion, popular during the NRA years, that union expansion and local economic growth could occur simultaneously. Similar trends were apparent in other industries in the late 1930s. The extent, timing, and specific circumstances of the militant upsurge varied but it was a factor, often the decisive factor, in most of the union initiatives of 1937. The reactions of employers and union leaders also paralleled those of the rubber manufacturers and URW officers. As Byron H. Larabee told the Akron Rotary, "virtually all industrial sections" of the United States were "destined to pass through" the "cycle" that Akron had experienced. The rubber workers, particularly that responsible elite that created and assembled the nation's tires, ignited the labor revolution of the mid-1930s; it remained for others to carry it to fruition.

NEW DEAL WORK RELIEF AND ORGANIZED LABOR: THE CWA AND THE AFL BUILDING TRADES

By BONNIE FOX SCHWARTZ

"We are going to have to find some way to secure the approval of organized labor," warned Aubrey Williams, as he and Harry Hopkins began planning a work relief program in October, 1933. As the New Deal struggled to meet the winter's unemployment crisis, the two social workers knew they had to placate the American Federation of Labor, which had historically opposed government "made jobs." The AFL did favor tax-supported public works, undertaken by private contractors and covered by collective bargaining agreements. But "work for relief" schemes smacked of charity, and Federation unions feared relief standards would undercut prevailing wages and hours and threaten gains negotiated with management. Before Hopkins presented his proposal for the Civil Works Administration (CWA) to President Roosevelt, he sent Williams to Madison, Wisconsin, to discuss the idea with Dr. John R. Commons. "If there is any one person in this country who can tell us how to make this thing palatable to organized labor, he is the man," said Williams. Commons dug up an old statement of Samuel Gompers in which the AFL leader had outlined a "Day Labor Plan" similar to Williams' suggestions. When Hopkins learned of this precedent, he believed he had the means to overcome the unions' initial objections to CWA.[1]

---

[1] Searle Charles states that Hopkins used the Gompers' precedent to win over President Roosevelt's support for the CWA. See *Minister of Relief: Harry Hopkins and the Depression* (Syracuse, 1963), 47. Williams' own memoirs, however, reveal an immediate concern to mollify organized labor, with no mention of the President in this context. See "The New Deal: A Dead Battery," 78-80, Aubrey Williams Papers, Box 44, Franklin D. Roosevelt Library, Hyde Park. See also "Employment Ideas Started by Labor Men," *Federation News*, XXXIII (November 25, 1933), 8; Louis Stark, "Labor on Relief and Insurance, *Survey*, LXVIII (November 15, 1931), 186–187.

As the nation's largest single employer during the winter of 1933-34, the Civil Works Administration created jobs for four million Americans on "economically and socially desirable" public projects. Conceived as a temporary stop-gap measure to "tide the country over the winter" until Harold Ickes could get his Public Works program underway, the CWA became the first federal experiment in work relief. Instead of dispensing surplus food or subsistence checks, Hopkins and Williams offered real work at real wages. Although half the applicants would come from relief rolls, the remainder would be among the self-sustaining unemployed, who could avoid a demeaning investigation and simply register at the local United States Employment Office. By reaching out to skilled artisans and even white collar workers and professionals, many out of work for the first time and too proud to accept charity, Hopkins intended to preserve skills and boost morale. For enlightened social workers, the CWA represented the most significant reform in relief giving.

Four lean years had changed organized labor's hostility toward "made work" into a determination to carve out a new role in civil works. By November, 1933, when AFL membership dropped to under three million and the Building Trades unions reported 65 per cent of their membership unemployed, the Federation came to view the CWA as a public works boon which promised "recovery" for rank and file wage earners as well as the union structure. Even though carpentry, masonry, and similar trades amounted to just 10 per cent of all CWA jobs, craft unions sought an inordinate amount of influence within the agency. Desperate for members and dues, the AFL demanded priorities in hiring and suggested projects that required more skills. Locals insisted on union rates for skilled jobs, realizing the impact of CWA practices. When Washington later ordered state and county boards to determine pay scales and redress grievances with worker participation, the AFL moved to insure that its officers sit as labor representatives. Characterized by one historian as the "sleepy headquarters of the American labor movement," the Federation as of 1933, proved wide awake, when its leaders demonstrated their ability to lobby for union interests on federal work relief.[2]

As a result, the CWA administrators faced the delicate task of blending labor practices in private industry with public welfare goals. While extending "uplift" to "down and outers," who were the traditional wards

---

[2] Philip Taft, *The AF of L from the Death of Gompers to the Merger* (New York, 1959), 46-47; Walter Galenson, *The CIO Challenge to the AF of L: A History of the American Labor Movement 1935-1941* (Cambridge, 1960), 514; Arthur M. Schlesinger, Jr., *The Coming of the New Deal* (Cambridge, 1965), 385.

of social workers, Hopkins had to reckon with unemployed union men who wound up on the federal payroll and still insisted on their prerogatives as skilled mechanics. To accede to the AFL's demands would clearly look like favoritism, since the Federation barely claimed 6 per cent of the entire work force. Yet, at the same time, Hopkins did not want the CWA to have the image of a union-busting agency, jeopardizing gains previously won in collective bargaining agreements. Although he and Williams had shown greater solicitude than many early New Dealers for organized labor, as social workers, they had little experience in negotiating with trade unions. When they sought out Dr. Commons instead of William Green or another AFL leader, they demonstrated how little "professional altruists" knew about the world of the "walking delegate." But Hopkins keenly sensed the inadequacy of his approach, and he quickly entrusted all labor policy decisions to his chief engineer, John M. Carmody.[3]

With a long record in management and union relations, Carmody brought to the CWA a new dimension. A Cleveland business executive during World War I, he differed from associates in the Chamber of Commerce and supported the War Labor Board. "They were afraid of trade unions," he recalled; "I dealt directly and frankly with every employee." In 1922, he surveyed the bituminous fields of western Pennsylvania and Ohio for the U.S. Coal Commission and supported stronger unionization for the miners. He then worked as vice president of merchandising for Davis Coal and Coke Company until 1927, when he became editor of *Coal Age* and later *Factory and Industrial Management* for McGraw Hill. As a technocrat, Carmody appreciated how more responsible labor organization could dovetail with the efficiency movement. The next call to Washington came from Senator Robert F. Wagner to serve as a mediator for the National Labor Board of NRA. Carmody

---

[3] The attitude of early New Dealers toward organized labor was, at best, "paternal." James MacGregor Burns wrote of President Roosevelt that "he looked on labor from the viewpoint of a patron and benefactor, not as a political leader building up the labor flank of future political armies," in *Roosevelt: the Lion and the Fox* (New York, 1956), 218. Both Hugh Johnson and David Richberg of the NRA rejected the right of a union with majority support to speak for all the workers. Neither man favored the use of governmental power to compel businesss to accept collective bargaining, and they resented usurpation of their authority by the National Labor Board. See William E. Leuchtenburg, *Franklin D. Roosevelt and the New Deal* (New York, 1963), 108. Secretary of Labor Frances Perkins claimed from her experience that "unions never had any ideas of their own; most labor and welfare legislation in her time had been brought about by middle-class reformers in face of labor indifference." Frances Perkins, *The Roosevelt I Knew* (New York, 1946), 303–304, 307–310; Civil Works Administration Meeting, Minutes, November 27, 1933, Harry L. Hopkins Papers, Box 45, Franklin D. Roosevelt Library (hereafter cited as Hopkins Papers).

traveled throughout the Northeast and Midwest settling strikes and setting up regional boards, until Wagner consented to his going over to CWA as chief engineer. Carmody went reluctantly, for he preferred "labor work." But he soon discovered that his new position included the responsibility for ironing out crucial labor decisions, which had eluded the good intentions of welfare administrators.[4]

In the rush to place four million at work within thirty days, social workers on the CWA could not stop to take account of union prerogatives. Regulations announced on November 15, 1933, authorized state and local authorities to transfer persons from Federal Emergency Relief rolls to civil works. Those on relief lists, previously certified for aid by a case-work investigation, made up the first half of the quota. After December 1, however, agencies designated by the United States Employment Service would make some attempt to classify applicants according to skill and training. But state and county officers, anxious to fill their quota by December 15, lest they lose it to other areas, did not trouble to assign workers along strict craft lines. The wholesale transfer of relief recipients flooded the rosters with the unskilled and unclassified. A California supervisor noted:

> The 40,000 men assigned by the welfare organization were not classified as to occupation and on work relief projects taken over by the CWA they were carried as laborers at laborers rates regardless of the class of work they were doing.

Both job seekers and interviewers were influenced by openings immediately available on specific projects, and state executives readily admitted that few positions called for special skills. "Having a quota to keep within we soon saw we were filling it with unskilled labor," confessed the DeKalb County, Illinois, head; "to make it possible to have mechanics available when they would be needed on the projects we sent mechanics out as laborers." Some skilled workers, desperate for any kind of job, went on the CWA in the unskilled category, while others without proper training slipped into skilled positions and even wound up as foremen or supervisors.[5]

[4] John M. Carmody, Oral History Memoir, Vol. 1, 140-144, 146, Columbia University Library; statement of John M. Carmody, U. S., Congress, Senate, Committee on Education and Labor, *Hearings, To Create A National Labor Board*, on S. 2926, 73rd Cong., 2nd sess., 1934, 307-312; CWA Reminiscences, April 24, 1958, John M. Carmody Papers, Box 73, Franklin D. Roosevelt Library (hereafter cited as Carmody Papers); Carmody to Thomas Baker, November 28, 1933, Carmody Papers, Box 50.

[5] Civil Works Administration, *Rules and Regulations, Number 1* (November 15, 1933), Civil Works Administration Papers, Record Group 69, National Archives (hereafter cited as CWA Papers); Henry E. Walker to Harold English, January 18, 1934, United States Employment

This haphazard hiring provoked AFL leaders to lash out in rhetoric that revealed their adherence to the work ethic and insistence on traditional craft union prerogatives. *Federation News* called the ratio of half relief clients a "deliberate penalization of self-independence and the fostering of a spirit of dependence." Emphasizing the dignity of labor, union brothers had frowned on direct cash relief. "Very few of our men have applied [for] or been on the relief," said a Chicago machinist officer, "as we have been trying to take care of them for the past three years and for that reason we are finding it hard to get men jobs under relief." "Most members of our association have done everything humanely possible to keep off the relief rolls," added a plumber; "now when an opportunity is presented . . . they are deprived of the opportunity of maintaining a livelihood because we have not enrolled for relief." Resenting the preference given FERA recipients, the Galesburg, Illinois, Trades Assembly summed up:

> The rules governing the expenditure of funds in taking men off the relief rolls do not make any provision for a type of people we have in Galesburg who have refrained from asking for charity but who were really more entitled to it than many who are now on the rolls. The people I have reference to are mainly members of the building trades unions who have been unemployed for the past three years, have been too proud to beg, but have borrowed from their friends and neighbors in the hope that work would pick up.[6]

The CWA's failure to place aplicants according to craft angered many old-line AFL affiliates. Locals not only claimed the exclusive right to do certain kinds of work in their territory, but also tried to regulate the number of persons entering apprenticeships in an effort to maintain a closed shop. Each local also asserted its right to classify workers, which in effect meant that their officers customarily did the hiring. CWA executives therefore encountered objections when they offered employment on relief work in any craft over which a union had assumed prior control.[7]

The carpenters, already embroiled in a jurisdictional feud with the Building Trades Department, carried their objections over to the CWA.

Service Papers, Box 233, Record Group 183, National Archives; Edward Macauley to Harry Hopkins, January 12, 1934, CWA Papers, Box 4; Anna O'Berry to John Carmody, December 29, 1933, CWA Papers, Box 33; quoted in Illinois Civil Works Administration, *Final Report*, (March, 1934), 46–47; John Charnow, *Work Relief Experience in the United States* (Washington, 1943), 32–33.
[6] *Federation News*, XXXIII (November 25, 1933), 4; D. M. Burrows to Victor Olander, November 21, 1933, Victor A. Olander Papers, Box 73, Chicago Historical Society (hereafter cited as Olander Papers); Frank Murphy to the Civil Works Administration, January 4, 1934, CWA Papers, Box 93; Thomas Downie to Victor Olander, November 19, 1933, Olander Papers, Box 73.
[7] Nels Anderson, *The Right to Work* (New York, 1938), 113–114.

"No attempt is being made to ascertain an individual's qualifications," wrote the California Brotherhood to Senator William G. McAdoo. The secretary of the Brotherhood claimed that laborers were sent out as carpenters while first-class carpenters fell into the unskilled category. North Carolina Local #1460 reported to William Green that the Guilford County Civil Works Administrator had assumed "arbitrary powers" in assigning jobs. Foremen were chosen regardless of previous knowledge or experience, while thoroughly competent people received a rating of "carpenters' helper." President William Hutcheson insisted that "with union skilled mechanics as foremen and supervisors to whom it rightfully belongs, then and only then will the intended results be obtained." [8]

Organized labor's desire to dominate CWA hiring was expressed in working-class resentment toward various professionals who interviewed the applicants. *Federation News* condemned social workers who "pry into personal and private lives." An editorial demanded that "American citizens shall no longer be compelled to live under the auspices of charitable agencies." The AFL also disliked USES personnel, whom the union charged with a "white collar complex against skilled labor in the building trades." "The organized labor movement will oppose in every possible way," stated William Green, "any proposal to classify skilled mechanics, men who have devoted all of their years to working at their particular trade, by tests laid down by so-called engineers." [9]

In response to union pressure, as well as out of a desire for more skilled workers on the payroll, CWA officials changed the federal rules. "If an artisan is acceptable to the union after the tests required by the union—the most practical test that can be applied," stated Carmody, "then there should be no question as to his status." On December 13, Hopkins qualified the hiring procedures. All persons given employment on CWA projects other than those on relief rolls were to be assigned through the United States Employment Service *except* members of labor unions who were cleared through their trade councils. This provision meant that organized labor, skilled and unskilled, did not have to register at designated agencies but would be referred in "customary ways" through

---

[8] Galenson, 515; George D. Hammond to William G. McAdoo, January 3, 1934, William G. McAdoo Papers, Box 390, Library of Congress; J. M. Purgason to William Green, January 1, 1934, CWA Papers, Box 34; quoted in Maxwell C. Raddock, *Portrait of an American Labor Leader: William L. Hutcheson* (New York, 1955), 188.
[9] *Federation News*, XXXIII (November 18, 1933), 4; William Green to John Carmody, January 9, 1934, CWA Papers, Box 54.

recognized union locals. Only if the locals did not furnish qualified workers within forty-eight hours could the USES then select applicants.[10]

Although the new ruling provided for greater union participation in hiring, its implementation varied at the grass roots. In many Southern states, for example, county CWA's disregarded national regulations, and some employment offices discriminated against union members. "The superintendent in charge of this particular job," grumbled a Greensboro, North Carolina, carpenter, "had firmly maintained his right to judge the qualifications of those under his direction." Carmody received numerous complaints from Alabama that "affiliation with organized labor is tantamount to elimination." Other locals were afraid to challenge county administrators when they flouted federal rules and classified applicants as they chose. North Carolina's *Final Report* explained its few placements through union locals because "only a few such organizations exist in the state outside specialized manufacturing trades." About thirty men were employed through the builders council at Fayetteville and about the same in Wilmington.[11]

Violations angered Pennsylvania labor leaders, and they ultimately achieved redress. Building trades councils and central labor union CWA committees notified state administrator Eric Biddle, Governor Gifford Pinchot, William Green, and federal officials that few unemployed craftsmen were selected from lists of union mechanics furnished by their locals. They charged outright discrimination in some counties and offered statistics to substantiate their claims. When these efforts failed, building trades agents secured an appointment with Carmody in Washington. "Your complaint seems to be a just one and must be remedied immediately," replied the chief engineer, after hearing their cases. Carmody readily admitted,

> Pennsylvania has been one of the worst offenders ... in not carrying out the work relief set up. I personally wrote paragraph seven in Bulletin 10 [which specified union hiring] and it means just what it says and I mean to see to it that it is carried out.

[10] Green to Carmody, January 9, 1934, CWA Papers, Box 54; Civil Works Administration, *Rules and Regulations Number 10* (December 13, 1933), CWA Papers. The CWA defined a skilled worker as "one who has gone through a number of years apprenticeship required to make him a competent skilled workman under standards usually recognized by organized labor." "Labor Definitions," December 28, 1933, Hopkins Papers, Box 49.

[11] J. M. Purgason to William Green, January 1, 1934, CWA Papers, Box 34; L. M. Cooper, United Brotherhood of Carpenters and Joiners, Local 87, to Harry Hopkins, January 1, 1934; and John Carmody to Thad Holt, December 27, 1933, CWA Papers, Box 1; J. J. Pettyjohn, Winston Salem Central Labor Union, to Harry Hopkins, March 18, 1934, CWA Papers, Box 34; North Carolina Civil Works Administration, *Final Report* (March, 1934), 25.

He immediately telephoned Harrisburg, and the delegation returned to iron out a settlement with state and county executives.[12]

In New York State, because of their established position and forceful leadership, unions eventually exercised priority in filling CWA jobs. But skilled labor was not hired through the locals until February, 1934, after several weeks of negotiation by George Meany, vice president of the state federation, James Quinn, secretary of the Central Trade and Labor Council, Hopkins, and Alfred Schoellkopf of the CWA. The group agreed that the selection of skilled workers be left to unions in the vicinity of the project. "It is only just that we help the CWA in picking out the men," commented the president of the Central Trades and Labor Council; "in that way we can be sure they will get honest, capable men." [13]

Differences were hammered out in New York City after the municipal administrator appointed a committee, which included Meany, the chairman of the Building Trades Employers Association, a state employment service "expert," and a Columbia University professor of labor economics. The group drew up elaborate instructions to insure proper procedures. Each union local appointed an "authorized representative" to transact all business for the CWA. This person obtained "referral cards" and gave the CWA office a specimen of his signature. When a project needed workers, the representative received a requisition stating the number of men and other specifications. He then selected the candidates and gave each a referral card to present at the CWA office. If any union member believed someone unqualified, he filed a complaint to the representative who reported to central union headquarters, which in turn presented to the CWA a written statement. A "rerating board," established by the local CWA, investigated the fitness of any particular man.[14]

In Illinois, organized labor gained a head start by having its own officers on state and local branches of the Emergency Relief Commission, which initially ran the CWA. Victor Olander, secretary-treasurer of the state federation and once a staunch advocate of voluntarism, sat on the IERC, while many county committees also had a labor representative. When the

[12] Reading *Labor Advocate*, January 19, 1934, 1, 5; W. C. Roberts to Bruce McClure, January 10, 1934, CWA Papers, Box 40; Reading Building Trades to John Carmody, February 12, 1934, CWA Papers, Box 40; Reading *Labor Advocate*, January 26, 1934, 1; February 16, 1934, 2; quote from February 23, 1934, 3; R. H. Rothrauff to Frank Conner, February 15, 1934, CWA Papers, Box 40.

[13] Central Trades and Labor Council of Greater New York and Vicinity, *The Union Chronicle*, XV (March, 1934), 4; The New York *Times*, February 4, 1934, 24; New York *Herald Tribune*, February 6, 1934, 36.

[14] The New York *Times*, February 6, 1934, ˀ; statement of James A. Emery, Senate, *Hearings, To Create A National Labor Board*, 386.

CWA began, Olander suggested a list of state union leaders as an advisory board to the Illinois Free Employment Service. He sent copies of all rules and regulation changes to the central labor bodies to insure they had accurate information at all times. When IERC Chairman Robert Dunham appointed him to handle registration of the non-relief unemployed, within a week, Olander set up a central placement bureau in Chicago of fifty-one offices with twelve hundred clerks! Twenty additional locations outside Cook County went up during the second week, along with arrangements to expand downstate facilities. Governor Henry Horner congratulated Olander on his "splendid work." Nonetheless, the Seamen's leader expressed disappointment over the limited positions opened to skilled trades; and, with staunch support from the labor community, he lobbied effectively for changes in hiring. Olander visited Hopkins in Washington, having arranged at the same time for county leaders to deluge the office with telegrams of complaint during his stay. He notified locals in advance of the office guidelines on union participation in hiring, which enabled them to take better advantage before the December 15 deadline. While Pennsylvania craftsmen submitted lists of members to the county employment offices, Cook County unions had their own special recruiting system set up with the aid of the Chicago Building Trades president. Olander assured the state federation that "organized labor has a very definite place in the present reemployment drive," but he cautioned them to sign up at the USES to afford themselves of all available channels. Illinois later boasted of the "primary value" of its CWA to the building and structural trades.[15]

As unions achieved greater participation in CWA hiring, however, questions arose regarding initiation fees and dues. Organized labor reasoned that members in good standing had the right to expect a CWA job first, since they paid dues to insure this priority. But because of the

[15] IERC rules provided for a labor representative on all work relief committees and that trade unions be consulted, but downstate counties did not always comply. Victor Olander to Paul Huston, Aurora Building Trades, November 21, 1933, Olander Papers, Box 73; Olander, as secretary of the resolutions committee at the 1931 AF of L convention, had bitterly opposed unemployment insurance. Irving Bernstein, *The Lean Years: A History of the American Worker 1920-1933* (Baltimore, 1966), 347; Victor Olander to Martin Durkin, November 17, 1933, and Victor Olander to Officers of Central Bodies of Organized Labor in Illinois, November 18, 1933, Olander Papers, Box 73; Illinois State Federation of Labor, *Proceedings of Fifty-Second Annual Convention, September 10-15, 1934*, 45; Henry Horner to Victor Olander, November 24, 1933, Olander Papers, Box 73; Victor Olander to Miss Hibbard (his secretary), December 15, 1933, Olander Papers, Box 74; Victor Olander to Secretaries, Central Bodies of Organized Labor in Illinois, December 9, 1933, "Procedure with reference to Union Cards," December 10, 1933, Olander Papers, Box 73; *Federation News*, XXXIII (December 16, 1933), 1; Illinois CWA, *Final Report*, 193-194.

depression, many had been unemployed for a long time, had fallen behind in dues, and had lost their union standing. When CWA jobs opened, leaders argued that non-paid members could not step ahead of those who had maintained the union during hard times. "Others would have to pay half their earnings until they squared arrearages and restored their membership," insisted the Pittsburgh Carpenters' District Council president.[16]

In a few areas, either the county CWA or the local union took the initiative to set down provisions to prevent abuses. In New York City, official directives emphasized "the privilege of supplying men to the CWA shall in no case be used to force payment of dues by men delinquent" and forbade discrimination with respect to the status of anyone regarding dues. The municipal administrator reserved the right to withdraw this privilege if improprieties occurred. On the other side, the executive council of the Internation Hod Carriers, Building, and Common Laborers of Chicago scaled down financial obligations of members who got onto CWA payrolls and reduced the initiation fee and dues for those previously unaffiliated.[17]

In the absence of any national policy, either from union headquarters or the CWA, some locals took the occasion to increase membership and enhance depleted treasuries under the CWA's auspices. "We men of . . . labor sympathies must take advantage of the situation and get as many of our number as possible into positions where we can build up an organization," wrote a Chicago union attorney. Chapters of the Brotherhood of Painters, Decorators, and Paperhangers of America frankly described the benefits. "CWA [is] now employing a large number of painters and we will be able to take in quite a number of members," predicted one secretary. Another officer reported, "We are making a drive for members and are taking advantage of a large amount of work being done on civil works." [18]

The drive to build up local organizations led to abuses where labor leaders were more confident of their influence. In Chicago, after a carpenter showed his credentials with five years in arrears, a union officer replied he had hundreds of such requests and could square him for $125. A certain percentage of wages was required as part payment of back dues by local

---

[16] Anderson, 114; Pittsburgh *Post Gazette,* January 14, 1934.
[17] Statement of James A. Emery, Senate, *Hearings, To Create A National Labor Board,* 386; International Hod Carriers, Building, and Common Laborers Executive Council of Chicago and Vicinity to Robert Dunham, December 11, 1933, Olander Papers, Box 73.
[18] From August, 1933, to August, 1934, the Federation's organizational expenses tripled, as locals enlarged their staffs in response to the NRA. Edwin Young, "The Split in the Labor Movement," in Milton Derber and Edwin Young, eds., *Labor and the New Deal* (Madison, 1957),51; Wm. H. Seed to Victor Olander, November 27, 1933, Olander Papers, Box 73; "Works Administration Boosts Organization," *Painter and Decorator* (February, 1934), 24–25.

229

secretaries in California before they would detail men for CWA jobs through their offices. "Most of the men cannot afford to give much," sympathized state CWA administrator Captain Edward Macauley, "and in some cases the demand seems excessive." Macauley noted that discretion was left to the local secretary whose salary depended on these dues. The Pittsburgh *Post Gazette* charged that the Cathedral of Learning Project was a closed shop and wired Hopkins that it had documentary evidence of union officers' deducting "terrific sums" for dues from members on CWA jobs.[19]

Weighing such evidence, along with complaints from the National Association of Manufacturers and local chambers of commerce, CWA administrators in Washington decided to eliminate the worst abuses, while maintaining the policy of union hiring. "It is commonly understood that CWA employees have a right to organize," said Carmody, "but this kind of organization work and dues collected should not be carried on." Various federal agencies helped to clear up violations through their field offices. In Illinois, many workers refused jobs because of non-membership could appeal to the regional conciliator for the Department of Labor. Also the state director of the National Emergency Council acted as a "watchdog" against possible "union racketeering." Hopkins dispatched field representative Robert Kelso to Pittsburgh to look at employment files and interview complainants. In a majority of instances, Kelso noted only ten to twenty dollars owed in back dues, and he smoothed over differences at a conference with trade union representatives and CWA officers.[20]

Despite the furor, organized labor actually enjoyed more hiring power on paper than in reality. By the time the ruling to select employees through union locals had filtered down to most counties and labor representatives had negotiated with CWA offices, the December 15 deadline to fill all quotas had passed. Although new projects approved after that date afforded greater opportunities for skilled craftsmen, a large proportion of the more specialized plans failed to get underway since quotas were

---

[19] Henry S. Kariel notes, "As unions find fewer reasons to protest against specific employer injustices, they become less concerned with promoting the expressed interests of the workers and more concerned with making organizational demands," in *The Decline of American Pluralism* (Stanford, 1961), 56; Charles, 57; Chicago *Tribune*, December 9, 1933; Edward Macauley to Harry Hopkins, March 7, 1934, CWA Papers, Box 13; telephone conversation, Eric Biddle and Aubrey Williams, January 13, 1934, CWA Papers, Box 39; Pittsburgh *Post Gazette*, January 13, 1934.

[20] John Carmody to Jacob Baker, January 26, 1934, CWA Papers, Box 13; Chicago *Tribune*, January 26, 1934, National Emergency Council Papers, Box 403, Record Group 44, Federal Records Center, Suitland, Maryland; Pittsburgh *Post Gazette*, January 14, and February 1, 1934.

already completed. In addition, federal regulations had specified that a "working crew" should have continuous employment. Men assigned from relief lists prior to December 1 were considered "permanent employees," and civil works administrators recognized their first obligation to outline new jobs to absorb these people when they finished their original assignments. Washington did grant some additional allotments in January, 1934, and unions proposed projects that required more skills. But only a few unemployed members could benefit, since CWA officials prepared for demobilization and reduced their payrolls on February 15.[21]

Yet the gains on paper had their significance. Even though the AFL could claim no more than 10 per cent of the CWA jobs, union spokesmen appeared satisfied. "The government has left the door as wide open as possible for our members to secure work," wrote *Bricklayer, Mason and Plasterer*. Because of the recognition of their "customary ways" of selecting job applicants, the Building Trades president expressed his "highest admiration and confidence in the policies and fair dealing pursued by Harry L. Hopkins and the staff of the CWA." [22]

The good faith between Hopkins and AFL leaders, however, stemmed more from CWA wage policies than union recognition in hiring. Labor had traditionally feared that work relief payments would undercut existing scales in private industry. But because CWA appropriations initially came from the Public Works Administration, rates spelled out for that agency applied to the CWA as well. The PWA set hourly minimums of $1.00, $1.10, and $1.20 for skilled labor in southern, central, and northern zones respectively, with the unskilled receiving $.40, $.45, and $.50 per hour. Each person could put in up to thirty hours a week with an eight-hour day maximum. These rates followed suggested "floors" established by the blanket code of the NRA, which stipulated minimums of $.30 or $.40 an hour. The CWA further protected union gains by ordering that where either prevailing rates or union rates exceeded the zone minimum, the higher one should be paid, but with fewer hours. Union rates were defined as those which resulted from a collective bargaining agreement in the community before April 30, 1933, for the particular kind of work involved. This clarification gave CWA labor the added benefit of higher rates, which were set before locals in many areas had agreed to lower them in May and

---

[21] Edward Macauley to Harry Hopkins, January 12, 1934, CWA Papers, Box 4; Illinois CWA, *Final Report*, 38; telegram, Jacob Baker to all state administrators, December 4, 1933, CWA Papers, Box 73; William Green to Victor Olander, Dec. 27, 1933, Olander Papers, Box 74.

[22] *Bricklayer, Mason and Plasterer*, XXXVII (January, 1934), 4; M. J. McDonough to Franklin D. Roosevelt, December 27, 1933, CWA Papers, Box 65.

August, 1933.[23]

Though CWA pay scales pleased the unions, management sharply objected to rates that exceeded levels in private industry. Hopkins had assured unions that wages would provide a "standard of living in decency and comfort," and CWA benefits, in fact, marked an abrupt change from previous local work relief, which paid in "kind" or subsistence checks. But CWA wage levels set off an explosion of complaints from private employers. General Hugh Johnson, too, termed it "a perfectly absurd situation" that CWA paid above the NRA code minimums. Though Hopkins publicly defended his program, for he was determined to keep his pledge to organized labor, he privately confessed to his staff:

> I personally thought some of these wage rates were too high, but people approved those rates who were far more conservative than I am, and put their names on those wage rates. I am inclined to think no matter what public relations will say to us, we have got to use those rates.[24]

Unions knew full well that the CWA wage scales set an example for private industry, and locals sought to ensure that all administrators complied. The Building Trades commended Hopkins on "the great work" that enabled millions of "worthy" citizens to earn a "decent living wage." "Success of the NRA is dependent upon the establishment of a living wage for workers through the CWA," commented another labor spokesman. Union chiefs feared that state and county executives might not carry out the civil works rates and urged local affiliates to report violations. *Painter and Decorator* published the names and addresses of all state administrators and exhorted members to deal directly with them. "Every official of every subordinate local union should be on the job to secure and maintain fair conditions on CWA," echoed *Bricklayer, Mason and Plasterer;* "if a private

---

23 Within the skilled category, wages were graded in accordance with the union scales. After a protest by the Washington Building Trades Council, Carmody ordered the following hourly rates: bricklayers, $1.75; carpenters, $1.00; cement finishers, $1.25; electrical workers, $1.65; structural iron workers, $1.65; painters and decorators, $1.37; plasterers, $1.75; plumbers, $1.50; steamfitters, $1.29. "Union Wage Rates Won on Civil Works Jobs," *The Garment Worker*, XXXIII (December 22, 1933), "Union Wage Rates Won on Civil Works Jobs," *The Paving Cutters Journal*, XXVIII (January, 1934), 1; CWA, *Rules and Regulations Number 1* (November 15, 1933), CWA Papers; Charnow, 51, 54, 58; Arthur Edward Burns and Peyton Kerr, "Survey of Work Relief Wage Policies," *American Economic Review*, XXVII (December, 1937), 714–715; Civil Works Administration, *Rules and Regulations Number 6* (November 27, 1933), CWA Papers; Jacob Baker to all state administrators, November 27, 1933, CWA Papers, Box 92.

24 Richard A Lester, "Emergency Employment in Theory and Practice," *Journal of Political Economy*, XLII (August, 1934), 483–484; M. J. McDonough to Franklin D. Roosevelt, December 27, 1933, CWA Papers, Box 65; Harry Hopkins, *Spending to Save: The Complete Story of Relief* (New York, 1936), 117; The New York *Times*, December 23, 1933, 6, December 27, 1933, 6; Minutes, December 6, 1933, Hopkins Papers, Box 45.

employer were engaged in such tremendous operations, all subordinate unions would be awake day and night, looking after wages and conditions."[25]

Some local CWA executives and union representatives ironed out complaints through friendly negotiation. In Madison County, Illinois, for example, M.D. Cox led a group of labor officials to the CWA office. When the local director explained that low rates were necessary to spread jobs among a larger number of people, the union countered that the prevailing rate simply meant the same number of employees would work for a shorter time. "Instead of working out people say for a three months period at a low wage scale they could just as easily work the same number of people for two months at the union level," reasoned Cox. The county CWA agreed and sent copies of the settlement to Springfield as well as union locals.[26]

Other administrators, however, did not prove as amenable. Carmody later recalled:

> Many of the local administrators and other officials that had gotten into the program were anti-union. None of them were accustomed to dealing with a union in the fashion that some of us were. They shied away from meeting with union officials. They were fearful of going into negotiation. They were even, some of them, concerned about the wage scale. They thought that the wage scale that was adopted was too high.

Pennsylvania's Eric Biddle declared, "The perpetuation of the present PWA wage rates and other union exceptions have no place in the civil works program." Illinois Relief Chairman Dunham expressed open hostility toward union "privileges" on the CWA and permitted rates below those prescribed for the zone in several downstate counties.[27]

Carmody first attempted to deal with state executives through personal contact. As a mediator for the National Labor Board he had negotiated directly with both management and unions, and he continued this approach with Pennsylvania's CWA. Carmody learned that Eric Biddle had rewritten the wage bulletin in his own language, "leaving out some things essential to a correct understanding" of federal regulations. Biddle's version gave counties the impression that local prevailing rates, which were

[25] William C. O'Neill, Secretary-Treasurer, Building Trades Department, to Harry Hopkins, December 28, 1933, and telegram, Leo P. Burke, Trades and Labor Assembly, to Harry Hopkins, December 22, 1933, CWA Papers, Box 65; "CWA to Receive All Complaints Directly," *Painter and Decorator*, XLVIII (January, 1934), 30-31; *Bricklayer, Mason and Plasterer*, XXXVII (January, 1934), 3.

[26] R. G. Soderstrom to Victor Olander, December 7, 1933, Olander Papers, Box 73.

[27] Carmody, Oral History, Vol. 2, 308-309; Eric Biddle to Harry Hopkins, February 1, 1934, CWA Papers, Box 39; Victor Olander to William Green, December 13, 1933, Olander Papers, Box 73; Chicago *Tribune*, December 24, 1933, 6.

lower than the PWA scales, could be paid instead of the zone minimum. When this action triggered complaints of local violations, Carmody stepped in. "We can't have him interpret our official rulings," said Carmody, as he ordered the return of all directives sent out to the counties and had his own office forward correct ones. He also received several delegations of Pennsylvania trade union representatives and wrote Biddle:

> Irrespective of our personal opinions about these various wage scales, we are required to advise you that Bulletin 10 . . . was intended to guide all administrators, state and local, in the application of wage rates to CWA projects. It is of course an official CWA bulletin and represents your authority to apply these rates.

Carmody expected the complaints to diminish with new instructions. Nevertheless, grievances kept coming from the Keystone State, leading Washington to suggest "more drastic measures . . . to accomplish an adjustment which will really adjust." [28]

Carmody resorted to other means to enforce wage rates in Illinois, when labor protests broke out in several areas. On December 9, union leaders called a strike on twenty-seven projects in DuPage County and ordered a thousand men to stop work because the hourly rate fell below prevailing levels. Hod Carriers in St. Clair County threatened a stoppage and charged, "this set up will break down wage standards as well as conditions of employment which the labor movement has consciously and honestly fought for these many years." The Tri-City Trade Council wired Olander that unless an immediate adjustment came, "strike, riot, and general disorder will prevail." In response, Carmody asked Benjamin Marshman, regional commissioner for the Department of Labor Conciliation Service, to visit these "trouble spots" and determine if rates were properly applied.[29]

---

[28] Carmody, Oral History, Vol. 2, 317; Joseph Guffey to Harry Hopkins, December 15, 1933, CWA Papers, Box 41; telephone conversation, John Carmody and Aubrey Williams, January 10, 1934, CWA Papers, Box 41; John Carmody to Eric Biddle, December 21, 1933, Federal Emergency Relief Administration Papers, Box 249, Record Group 69, National Archives (hereafter cited as FERA Papers); John Carmody to Eric Biddle, February 2, 1934, CWA Papers, Box 92; Myron Jones (for John Carmody) to W. C. Roberts, Chairman Legislative Committee, American Federation of Labor, January 26, 1934, CWA Papers, Box 39.

[29] DuPage Building Trades Council and DuPage Teamsters and Chauffeurs International, Local 673, to Frances Perkins, December 13, 1933, Olander Papers, Box 73; Earl H. Rieck, DuPage Building Trades Council, to Frances Perkins, December 12, 1933, CWA Papers, Box 13; International Hod Carriers, Building and Common Laborers to John Carmody, December 11, 1933, CWA Papers, Box 13; telegram H. Pinkerton to Victor Olander, December 8, 1933, Olander Papers, Box 73; John Carmody to Wilfred Reynolds, December 13, 1933, CWA Papers, Box 103, CWA *Rules and Regulations, Number 10,* provided, "In the event that any question be raised as to what wage rates prevail in any district under agreements and understandings between organized labor and CWA administrators, the U.S. Department of Labor shall determine such rates if and when requested."

After conferring with the field representative, IERC Chairman Dunham, and chief engineer Frank Chase, Marshman "arrived at an understanding" that he handle all CWA wage disputes in Illinois and that his recommendations be accepted for the localities affected. Labor could now appeal grievances directly to Marshman's Chicago office and negotiate CWA rates on a higher scale if they had resulted from a collective bargaining agreement that existed prior to April 30, 1933. They had to furnish sworn affidavits from at least three reputable employers that had actually paid the higher rate to the type of skilled workers requesting the adjustment. The contract as well as all statements together with affidavits were investigated by the Conciliation Department staff, who filed a detailed report, from which Marshman made his decision.[30]

Marshman heard 111 cases in Illinois but was disappointed with the limited results: "CWA cases are not matters in which mediation can be used as we do in controversies between contractors and unions." In a majority of disputes, local administrators either "willfully ignored" the zone rate or were simply uninformed of the rules. Marshman cited an example where his recommendation just sat on the desk. After he had decided for two other counties, IERC Chairman Dunham overruled him. The vice president of the state federation and member of the St. Clair County CWA reported that Marshman's order had been disregarded in his area. The Illinois' federation president concluded, "Federal intervention . . . will accomplish nothing unless recommendations made by them are adhered to."[31]

The inability of the CWA in Washington to enforce PWA wage standards forced Hopkins to adjust national policy to conform with local practices. Conscious of organized labor's desire to maintain hourly rates, he decided to lower total wages by cutting the work week. He accommodated unions in the cities, however, by only reducing the maximum hours from thirty to twenty-four per week. For rural areas and towns under 2500, where union strength was negligible, he set maximum hours at fifteen. In March, 1934, when the CWA was no longer financed by PWA money, Hopkins discarded the zones altogether and returned to the FERA approach. He ordered state and county administrators to pay the prevailing rate in the locality for the type of job performed, but in no instance less

[30] Benjamin Marshman to Hugh Kerwin, December 23, 1933, CWA Papers, Box 40; Howard Hunter to Benjamin Marshman, December 20, 1933, CWA Papers, Box 13; Illinois CWA, *Final Report*, 149-150.

[31] Benjamin Marshman to Hugh Kerwin, January 17, 1934, Olander Papers, Box 74; Illinois CWA, *Final Report*, 148-149; Al Towers to Victor Olander, January 20, 1934, Olander Papers, Box 74; R. G. Soderstrom to Hugh Kerwin, no date, CWA Papers, Box 14.

than $.30 an hour minimum.[32]

In setting these prevailing rates, however, Civil Works administrators remained concerned about organized labor. "We cannot afford to be placed in the position anywhere of pulling down wages," wrote Carmody's assistant Nels Anderson; "we have to be fair in these matters, and one way to do that is to arrive at our rates through the aid of the workers involved, or their elected representatives." Following the model of regional labor boards under the NRA, Carmody ordered that county committees be established composed of one representative from organized labor, one from the local relief administration, and one from business or the professions selected by the first two. Carmody further recommended that local boards consider union rates and public construction project agreements between unions and employer associations with each county unit. Their task was to discover rates already in effect as of 1934 rather than set new ones. Findings had to be unanimous; if not, a new body was appointed.[33]

Although appreciating these steps to safeguard wage standards, some leaders feared drastic cuts in rates as well as total wages would follow. Plasterer head Michael Colleran warned his locals that state administrators would immediately set up scales "according to their own ideas." With greater urgency, Bricklayer secretary John Gleason suggested "if possible, a member of this International Union as the labor member, and where that is not possible to secure the selection of a member of some other building trades organization." Gleason cautioned his brothers to be on the job" otherwise these new regulations "will be seized upon by private employers as a means of further attacking our standards and beating down our conditions."[34]

Labor's apprehensions proved justified in North Carolina, when the state administrator Anna O'Berry adopted a state-wide schedule of $.75 an

---

[32] Harry Hopkins to Franklin Roosevelt, February 15, 1934, Franklin D. Roosevelt Papers, Official File, Box 444, Franklin D. Roosevelt Library; Charnow, 59; Burns and Kerr, "Survey of Work Relief Wage Policies," 715; Arthur E. Burns and Edward A. Williams, *A Survey of Relief and Security Programs* (Washington, 1934), 26.

[33] Nels Anderson to Edward Macauley, March 21, 1934, CWA Papers, Box 4. Carmody personally set up four regional labor boards for the NLB in 1933. Patterned after the national one, they were composed of an employer chosen from the business leaders of the community, a leader from the local AF of L unions, and an "impartial chairman" from among outstanding citizens of the locality, known for their interest in public welfare. Reminiscences, Carmody Papers, Box 50; Lewis L. Lorwin and Arthur Wubnig, *Labor Relations Boards: The Regulation of Collective Bargaining under the National Industrial Recovery Act* (Washington, 1935), 119; Night letter, John Carmody to all State Civil Works Administrators, March 6, 1934, CWA Papers, Box 73; Burns and Kerr, "Survey of Work Relief Wages," 716–717; Charnow, 62–63.

[34] "Changes in Wages and Hours," Illinois State Federation of Labor, *Weekly News Letter*, XIX (March 24, 1934), 2; *The Plasterer*, XXVIII (March, 1934), 1; *Bricklayer, Mason and Plasterer*, XXVIII (March, 1934), 39.

hour for skilled labor and $.30 for unskilled, which she considered "slightly in excess" of the prevailing rate. "How can a fair competitive wage be maintained as is declared for in the NIRA ... with the CWA paying almost any price a bunch of state contractors and administrators wish?" asked the *Union Record and Carolina Farmer.* Craftsmen went out on strike in Wilmington and Salisbury, and the Winston Salem Central Labor Union appealed to Washington. Their resolution charged Mrs. O'Berry had failed to set up wage boards or consult labor, and had disregarded regional income variations. "This would set a standard for all types of construction which would tend to pauperize a large and respectable part of the population," wrote the local secretary.[35]

Other states apparently sought to comply with Carmody's orders, but union locals quickly protested violations. The Los Angeles Central Labor Council claimed a lack of proper representation on its county committee; the Pennsylvania federation accused some counties of "hand-picking labor representatives notoriously anti-union." Although upstate New York generally managed to settle on prevailing rates, county CWA's forced limits on weekly hours, thereby cutting wages below the agreement.[36]

In addition to raising procedural questions, unions also protested against any committees' attempts to lower wages below the PWA zone standard. "Boards set up with an eye to fairness have been turned into agencies for the perpetuation of low wages," cried *Bricklayer, Mason and Plasterer.* During March and April, upstate New York witnessed demonstrations, marches, and strikes over "arbitrary" pay cuts by county CWA heads. "The general situation in Pennsylvania has become even more aggravated since the sending out of new rules," reported Bricklayer secretary John J. Gleason to Hopkins. Craftsmen walked off in Reading and Harrisburg, while a thousand laid down their tools in Lancaster. The business agent for the Keystone Building Trades Council called the reductions an "injustice and contrary to the spirit of President Roosevelt's decision to increase purchase power." [37]

---

[35] Anna O'Berry to Harry Hopkins, March 8, 1934, CWA Papers, Box 34; *Union Record and Carolina Farmer,* XXV (March 9, 1934), 4; Raleigh *News and Observer,* March 7 and 8, 1934; J. A. Pinkston, Resolution of Salisbury Labor Union, April 9, 1934, and Winston Salem Central Labor Union to Harry Hopkins, March 27, 1934, CWA Papers, Box 34.

[36] John Carmody to Edward Macauley, March 31, 1934, CWA Papers, Box 3; Philadelphia *Union Labor Record,* May 4, 1934; telegram, Joseph P. Ryan to Harry Hopkins, March 22, 1934, CWA Papers, Box 32.

[37] Memo, John Carmody to Bruce McClure, March 13, 1934, CWA Papers, Box 62; *Bricklayer, Mason and Plasterer,* XXXVII (April 1934), 55; telegram, M. W. Collins, Schenectady Painters Union, Local 62, to Frances Perkins, April 2, 1934, CWA Papers, Box 32; Alexander

CWA officials both in Washington and in the states attempted to resolve the disputes to the satisfaction of all parties. In North Carolina, field representative Alan Johnstone held a conference with union delegates, the governor, and Mrs. O'Berry to arrange for wage boards. He circulated a letter to all county executives directing them to disregard Mrs. O'Berry's niggardly rates, call committees to meet, and establish new scales for each locality. Eric Biddle appeased union protests in Pennsylvania by creating a Technical Advisory Board to investigate and mediate complaints. Composed of registered architects (recommended by chapters of the American Institute of Architects) and union representatives chosen by the state federation president, the board had its members travel in pairs to assigned territories to handle grievances. County CWA's in New York worked out settlements with strikers, and employees returned to their jobs. In all cases reported, decisions restored the PWA scale.[38]

Although wage disputes made up the majority of complaints brought by organized labor, cases also resulted from charges of arbitrary dismissals. Again, Carmody favored decentralized handling of grievances to make adjustments more speedy and effective. At the same time, he sought to "regularize the machinery" and began by mailing a questionnaire to all state offices on January 2, 1934, asking how they had conducted labor relations. While his aides sorted the replies, Carmody ordered all states to outline at least some steps for the right of appeal in case of discharge. On January 17, preliminary instructions emphasized that every dismissed worker had the right to a hearing before the local CWA and have representation by a person of his own choosing. State and federal offices were to be informed of all final decisions.[39]

Illinois announced the creation of appeal boards on January 26, 1934, and notified every employee of his right to use this facility. In downstate counties, IERC committees frequently acted as the agency, but Chicago set up a separate body, consisting of a chairman, two members, and an

Leopold Radowski, *Work Relief in New York State, 1931-1935* (New York, 1947), 308; John J. Gleason to Harry Hopkins, March 19, 1934, CWA Papers, Box 40; Philadelphia *Public Ledger*. March 21, 1934, 8; Reading *Labor Advocate*, March 23, 1934, 1.

[38] John Carmody to C. P. Barringer, April 5, 1934; Alan Johnstone to John Carmody, April 7, 1934; and William L. Nunn to William O'Neill, Secretary of the Building Trades Council, April 18, 1934, all in CWA Papers, Box 34; Eric Biddle to Corrington Gill, June 26, 1934, FERA Papers, Box 248; Pennsylvania CWA, *Final Report*, 64; New York *Herald Tribune*. March 17, 1934, 9.

[39] Myron Jones (for John Carmody) to Howard Hunter, March 5, 1934, CWA Papers, Box 81; John Carmody to Corrington Gill, March 20, 1934, CWA Papers, Box 62; Harry Hopkins to all state administrators, January 2, 1934, CWA Papers, Box 64; Doris Carothers, *Chronology of the Federal Emergency Relief Administration, May 12, 1933, to December 31, 1935* (Washington, 1937), 17.

attorney. Each petitioner had a private interview with a member, who had the authority to render a decision immediately. If the member decided on a general hearing or if the complainant insisted, the case was docketed for the worker to appear with supporting affidavits and witnesses. Foremen, timekeepers, and other CWA officials also testified. Wherever further investigation proved necessary, the legal department assisted. Orders for demobilization of the CWA brought an onslaught of petitioners, charging discrimination in layoffs. When the investigation showed that orders were not properly complied with, the board adjudicated the case to prevent injustice. Illinois also created a State Board to consider appeals after the county hearing.[40]

By early April, 1934, state and county CWA's across the nation had wage committees and grievance boards as evidence of Carmody's achievements in bringing management and labor together at the local level. "It's a big country and sometimes when a man is on the job, he is in closer contact with the situation than a man who is behind a desk 3,000 miles away," he recalled; "That applied to me too." He tangled with conservative local administrators and forced them to recognize unions and accept their participation in hiring, the determination of wages and hours, and on grievance bodies. "We must not be placed in the position of denying our citizens rights that are normally given them in our courts, nor ought we to make this machinery difficult or complex," wrote the chief engineer in the spirit which would shape the Wagner Act. Through the establishment of these institutions in the CWA, unions began to take on a new presence with the local business and professional leaders who served as civil works officials, many of whom had not previously had such close contact with labor leaders. At a time when "union recognition was basic to everything else" and the Federation was not as yet welcomed as a participant in the New Deal, the CWA provided a first forum.[41]

---

[40] Colonel Daniel Sultan, Report on Cook County, no date, 20-21, Illinois State Library, Springfield; Chicago *Tribune*, February 8, 1934, p. 3; Illinois CWA, *Final Report*, 153–154. Only one man appeared before the State Board, and the decision upheld the local action. Illinois CWA, *Final Report*, 155. Other states followed through with slight variations. On February 2, Pennsylvania organized its county grievance committee, made up of one building tradesman, one architect, and one "non-political property owner." New York had boards of four members—two from the business community and two from the workers, with at least one of the latter from organized labor. Philadelphia *Record*, February 2, 1934, 5; Pennsylvania CWA, *Final Report*, 63–64; Fred Daniels to William Nunn, April 30, 1934, CWA Papers, Box 32; Radomski, 129.

[41] Carmody, Oral History, Vol. 2, 317, John Carmody to all state administrators, January 16, 1934, Carmody Papers, Box 73; Schlesinger, 385.

THE GREAT DEPRESSION AND THE ACTIVITIES OF THE CATHOLIC WORKER MOVEMENT

By NEIL BETTEN

European Catholicism always had its communitarian perfectionist followers, but these did not develop among American Catholics until the 1930s. Utopian sentiments, in the United States, were shaped by the societal dislocation of the Depression and by disenchantment with the capitalist system on the part of educated laymen and clerics. With the Depression many young Catholic intellectuals questioned the capitalist system, and the Catholic Worker Movement attempted to provide an alternative.

The Movement itself was founded by Peter Maurin and Dorothy Day. Maurin, a French itinerant philosopher, borrowed from thinkers such as Hillaire Belloc, Eric Gill, and Peter Kropotkin, in order to work out the Catholic Worker Movement's anti-capitalist utopian ideology. Dorothy Day, the Movement's administrator, kept Maurin's ideology relevant to contemporary America by superimposing her sometimes conflicting point of view. The result was a dualism consisting of Maurin's agrarian communitarianism and Miss Day's more pragmatic ideas oriented to the urban industrial worker. Though equally committed to an alternative economic order, her willingness to work within the capitalist system sowed the intellectual seeds of social reformism; Maurin's philosophy, on the other hand, was more uncompromising.

Maurin considered capitalism a completely corrupting way of life, a system that trained man to prey on his fellows through economic competition.[1] Personal destruction by competing individuals and, supplementing it, the impersonal psychological destruction by machines,

---

[1] Peter Maurin, *The Green Revolution, Easy Essays on Catholic Radicalism* (Fresno, California, 1961) 57, 102. This work is a compilation of Maurin's essays over the years and goes back prior to the establishment of the Catholic Worker Movement.

NEIL BETTEN *is an Assistant Professor of History at Florida State University in Tallahassee. He acknowledges the financial assistance of the Indiana University Foundation and the Council on Research in Economic History.*

destroyed the potential creativity in life and work. Man thus faced, in Maurin's view, continuous assault by economic competition and psychological assault by the inhuman machine.[2]

Maurin argued that a compromise must not be made with the immoral system; a new way of life had to replace the old. He considered the 1930s a propitious time to construct it since capitalism was in disfavor and the social mood favored change. The New Deal, Maurin argued, did not go far enough in its attempts to reform the system. It merely reinforced the rotten beams of a corrupt structure. A complete change, Maurin felt, was needed; he called for a peaceful revolution through the establishment of agrarian communes across the country.[3]

This utopia was the center of Maurin's ideological program: a decentralized back-to-the-land movement based on independent, primarily agricultural, communes, in which neither agriculture nor industry would be mechanized.

Maurin, however, did not set policy at the actual Catholic Worker communes which the members established; nor did he want to. He felt each commune should be truly independent and respond to the needs of its own community. When asked for a specific communal plan, he responded: "I don't give blueprints."[4] Each commune was owned, administered, and financed independently. Local communal leadership often solicited advice from Maurin and Dorothy Day, but the founders gave only philosophical direction and extended no controls.

By the end of the 1930s, several Catholic Worker communes were functioning, and approximately a dozen more arose independently but worked closely with the Movement.[5] Martin Paul, the director of the Catholic Worker group in Minneapolis, helped start the Holy Family Farm at Rhineland, Missouri.[6] The founders of the Philadelphia Catholic Worker house rented a large farm in Oxford, Pennsylvania, and used it for many years. The Burlington urban Catholic Worker unit operated in conjunction with a commune in Colchester, Vermont.[7] The Boston group established St. Benedict's farm in Upton, Massachusetts.[8] At Cape

[2] Maurin, op. cit., 98; Dorothy Day, The Long Loneliness. The Autobiography of Dorothy Day (New York, 1952) 280, 184, 202; Ade De Bethune, Work (Newport, 1939) 7, 30, 4.
[3] Maurin, op. cit., 70, 7, 60, 62, 70; Day, op. cit., 179, 222; Dorothy Day, House of Hospitality (New York, 1932) 71.
[4] Quoted in Arthur Sheehan, Peter Maurin: Gay Believer (Garden City, L. I., 1959) 186.
[5] Day, Loneliness, 228; Catholic Worker, June, 1939, 3.
[6] Sheehan, op. cit., 174.
[7] Ibid., 187.
[8] Ibid., 186.

May, New Jersey, Akron, Ohio, and South Lyon, Michigan, small independent communes sprang up trying to restore the idea of community.[9]

The New Yorkers' commune set the institutional pattern—even to the point where the others also seemed to emulate its uncertain beginnings. Its first attempt at agriculture began as a vegetable garden on Staten Island. This venture was superseded by a twenty-eight-acre farm situated about seventy miles from New York City near Easton, Pennsylvania.[10] In 1936, its first year, the farm had less than five acres plowed, mostly by a neighbor who was paid ten dollars to do the work. Catholic Worker settlers worked the remainder with a two-horse plow pulled by an old truck. While the settlement had some cows, chickens and pigs, the main produce consisted of vegetables. Expanding in the following summer, the commune rented an adjoining forty-four acre farm.

James Montague and Joseph Karella managed the New York commune during its early years, and much of the agricultural work was directed by Paul Toner, a Catholic Worker from Philadelphia.[11] Actual legal title of the property rested in the hands of what Dorothy Day called "the leaders of the movement" as trustees for the *Catholic Worker*, the movements' newspaper.[12] The original capital as well as operating expenses came mainly from donations.

The settlers worked the farm both communally and privately. Each member of the commune cultivated land that was held by all as well as a plot granted for his "exclusive and permanent use." The Community, however, had final control over all sales of property and title reverted back to it if a member left permanently.[13]

Staff members, permanent residents, and people who visited for short stays—from a weekend to several weeks—did the actual daily labor. Each contributed according to his own conscience. Slackers were officially accepted along with the others. The group's extreme toleration may be seen in the case of an asocial resident who lived alone on the commune but still caused continuous friction. Besides being an alcoholic who seldom worked, he apparently periodically stole the meager tools of the commune to finance a binge. Nothing in the way of personal, legal, or communal action was undertaken to exclude him from the commune. He lived there, taking what he felt he needed from the common storehouse

---

[9] Day, *Long Loneliness*, 228.
[10] Dorothy Day, *Loaves and Fishes* (New York, 1963) 43; Sheehan, *op. cit.*, 131.
[11] *Catholic Worker*, May 1939, 2; Sheehan, *op.cit.*, 133.
[12] *Catholic Worker*, February 1936, 2; Day, *The Long Loneliness*, 234.
[13] *Catholic Worker*, February 1936, 8.

of goods, until he died as an old man.[14]

While the New York commune was permissive, it still had problems concerning work distribution. Some of the permanent residents claimed that others were slackers, and they disapproved of the policy of providing hospitality to the many visitors, often students, who stopped at the farm. These guests often consumed communal produce and did only token work. The commune, nevertheless, continued its open policy. Maurin encouraged young intellectuals to visit the commune, hoping such visits would serve as an avenue for ultimate involvement. He stressed the role of the scholar on the land who, he felt, would become a whole person and better scholar through physical and craft labor. Like Kropotkin, he emphasized the regenerative power of the land; on it the scholar would be manually educated and the worker would become a scholar.[15] Scholars, however, are hardly the most productive of agricultural laborers, and it was predictable that the commune would be economically unsound.

Given the sources available, it is difficult to measure the prosperity of Catholic Worker communal life. Compounding this difficulty, the commune was also used as a recuperative center for the sick who sought help at the New York City Catholic Worker center. Certainly the commune operated efficiently enough so that residents ate well, at least by Depression standards. It also gave unconsumed produce to the New York house which distributed it to the unemployed. Consequently, unlike most communal movements, the Catholic Worker settlement did not attempt to reach any grand material heights. Idealizing the voluntary poverty of St. Francis, Maurin himself had few material possessions. He believed that in being poor, though not destitute, one could be truly free. Following his point of view, the commune never stressed material ends; still, it had adequate food and living space.

Visitors and workers alike lived in communal buildings and ate together in a large dining room. Maurin did not plan it this way. He preferred each family to own its individual private house. But a single family did not long occupy any new separate structure built by the commune. Lack of capital and, perhaps, the very experience of joint living at the New York settlement house resulted in the more communal course being adopted. Evidently, there was little dissatisfaction with the arrangement, since the commune is still in operation. Other com-

[14] Day, *Loaves and Fishes*, 53-57.
[15] e.g. Maurin, *op. cit.*, 93.

munes emerged and died. Yet the members recall them with fondness. William Gauchat, for example, one of the founders of the Cleveland commune, typically felt that life there was "never uncomfortable . . . we felt poor and we were very happy there."[16]

Given the objectives of the Movement, however, the communal system failed. The New York commune never attracted many people. Nor did a large back-to-the-land movement come along to emulate it. The communes became, as Joseph Zarella of the New York commune said, "Second houses of Hospitality"[17] (that is, urban settlement houses, which are discussed directly below). Those attracted to the Movement liked the idea of a return to the land but the communes remained, as Zarella had pointed out, "mostly theoretical propositions since the great majority were more concerned with the immediate problems of daily living than with such grandiose philosophical schemes."[18]

The Movement's goal nevertheless remained a society based on a communal way of life. Maurin and Dorothy Day began a propaganda drive to spread news about the Movement and its objectives. They also established urban settlement houses, both to deal with the problem of the unemployed and to win converts to the Movement. While they organized these activities in order to foster the primary goal of agricultural communitarianism, the secondary activities in time came to dominate the history of the Movement.

Dorothy Day, administrator and journalist, lived at the New York settlement house. She helped direct its work and inspired most of it. Maurin, to be sure, was highly respected by the staff, as the ideological leader of the Movement, but Miss Day's personality was the more formidable. Nina Poleyn, one of the founders of the Milwaukee commune, and with the New Yorkers for a time, described Maurin as "an intellectual with a non-stop mind" who was "harder to be with" than the warmer Miss Day.[19] Zarella felt that her vibrant personality helped explain the movement: "There was nothing I wouldn't do for her,"[20] he admitted. That Maurin failed to emphasize the labor movement, a panacea for many intellectuals in the 1930s, heightened her influence since, as a result, many Catholic Workers looked to her for direction. Also Miss Day's experience as a journalist led to her editorship of the

[16] Interview with William Gauchat, December 13, 1968.
[17] Interview with Joseph Zarella, December 13, 1968.
[18] *Ibid.*
[19] Interview with Nina Poleyn, December 13, 1968.
[20] Interview with Joseph Zarella, December 13, 1968.

Movement's house organ, the *Catholic Worker*. The administrative leverage it provided, combined with her personality, leadership qualities, and urban-labor orientation, led to an emphasis upon a more pragmatic approach to social problems in *Worker* columns. The newspaper regularly published Maurin's "Easy Essays," which consisted of melodic free verse, but he had little else to do with the publication.

The *Catholic Worker* covered all aspects of what Dorothy Day (not Maurin) considered the workers' main concerns: the labor movement, racial problems, politics, the Church and encyclicals, war, and general Catholic labor activities. It had a homespun quality which attempted to achieve an intimacy with its readers. Articles on the commune tended to be personal and gossipy. Miss Day's columns often discussed her family and her friends within the Movement, and seemed to be directed toward an ingroup of readers.

Circulation nonetheless increased considerably during the 1930s. By the end of 1933 *Worker* readers numbered about 20,000. There were only about 700 subscribers, though many of these, local priests particularly, placed large orders and distributed the paper themselves. The balance were sold on the streets.[21] By 1938, circulation had risen from the previous year's 115,000 to 125,000.[22]

In addition to its newspaper, the Movement had other propaganda techniques. One was the street-corner meeting. Soon after the Movement began, two Catholic college students spoke on a Manhattan street corner for the Movement and distributed its newspaper.[23] Eventually street meetings of the New York group were held on a regular basis three times a week.[24] Sometimes Maurin spoke on a corner or in Union Square, New York's popular gathering place for radicals. Frequently he made arrangements for hecklers to attack his opinions, thereby giving him the attention needed to draw a crowd.[25]

Maurin's statements often drew heated responses (which were legitimate), but Catholic Worker outdoor activities seldom led to physical violence. Conflicts with the followers of Father Charles Coughlin, the radio priest of the 1930s, were the only exceptions. William Gauchat

[21] John Gillard Bruni, "Catholic Paper Versus Communism," *Commonweal*, November 24, 1933, 97.
[22] "For Christ the Worker," *Time*, April 18, 1938, 46. Following the Depression, circulation decreased considerably: see "Dorothy Day's Diary," *Newsweek*, January 21, 1952, 85; "Fools for Christ," *Time*, May 24, 1948, 56.
[23] *Catholic Worker*, July-August, 1933, 2.
[24] Sheehan, *op. cit.*, 111.
[25] Maurin would then put down the heckler with a cogent argument which was meant to appear spontaneous.

reported that Coughlin's supporters harassed and threatened Catholic Worker activists in Cleveland. Comparing Coughlin's followers with another opposition group, the Communists, Gauchat depicted the Communists as "much more polite," almost sympathetic. "They would say here's a dollar; I'll take a half a dozen of the *Catholic Worker*."[26] While the Coughlinites harassed Gauchat's group, violence did not erupt in Cleveland; it did in New York and Pittsburgh, however. Father Charles Owen Rice, head of the Pittsburgh group admitted (to Catholic theologian John A. Ryan) that Coughlinites disrupted local meetings by heckling and violence. Joseph Zarella reported similar confrontations as Coughlinites occasionally disrupted New York Catholic Worker picketing and outdoor demonstrations.[27]

Another aspect of Maurin's propaganda program, organized public discussions, caused fewer problems. The Manhattan Lyceum, at that time primarily a Communist and Socialist meeting place, hosted Catholic Worker meetings on a regular monthly basis.[28] In conjunction with these gatherings, the Movement attempted to establish a labor school, a common adjunct of worker-oriented organizations in the 1930s. At first, classes were held almost daily. They consisted of a talk or two generally preceded and followed by a discussion. Professors at local universities lectured without payment and sometimes writers or clerics spoke.[29] By the middle of the decade, the labor school held more formal sessions but only on one evening a month.[30] Maurin found that the popularity and spontaneity that he desired for the schools could not be sustained. His idea, however, did not die in the 1930s, since other units of the Movement had their own schools, and some ran summer schools for college students.

Maurin also advocated urban refuges for the poor. These Houses of Hospitality, or hospices, as he called them, would serve as an immediate response to the Depression. At these urban settlements the unemployed could live along with Catholic Worker staff and everyone, ideally, would take what they needed from the common storehouse of goods

---

[26] Interview with Wiliam Gauchat. December 13, 1968.
[27] Interview with Joseph Zarella, December 13, 1968. Letter from Rev. Charles Owen Rice and John Ryan, February 10, 1938, Catholic University archives, Ryan Correspondence, 1938 E-R.
[28] John Gilliam Bruni, *op. cit.,* 97.
[29] John Sheery, "The Catholic Worker School," *Commonweal,* August 3, 1934, 349; *Catholic Worker* February 1, 1934, 1, 4; *Ibid.,* March 1, 1934, 1; Joseph Brieg, "Apostle on the Bum," *Commonweal,* April 1938, 12.
[30] Eleanor Carroll, *The Catholic Worker,* M. A. Thesis, Catholic U., 1935, 20.

while giving what they could of their time and abilities to society.[31] The establishment of hospices would, Maurin believed, lessen the need for impersonal bureaucratic unemployment measures. The destitute could be fed and housed with the expenses coming from charity. Once established, however, the houses went beyond being urban refuges and avenues for rural communalization. They became centers for Catholic dissidents, intellectuals, and radicals, gathering places where they could read, argue, and test their views in informal debate. Major American Catholic social thinkers of the period—Virgil Michel, John A Ryan, and Paul Hanley Furfey, among others—visited frequently, and thereby made contact with the resident radicals of these houses.[32] These youthful residents eventually stimulated considerable activity of their own; and Dorothy Day guided a number of programs, many alien to Maurin's main thrust.

At the same time, Miss Day and her followers still created the House image Maurin desired and carried out many functions among the poor which he had visualized. The Catholic Worker staff procured food by begging at neighboring markets. The farming communes provided all its excesses over subsistence.[33] Unemployed were fed and housed at autonomous Catholic Worker hospices in numerous cities.

Each local unit operated and financed itself independently, for Miss Day did not extend her administration beyond the New York group. Nina Poleyn described the communes as autonomous but "similar in spirit."[34] William Gauchat also could so testify. When his group wrote to the New York center for help in solving a problem, he was consistently told that "we can't give you any advice—you will have to work it out yourself."[35]

Thus each hospice concentrated on a program particularly needed in its area or suited to its staff. The Boston group ran a bread line for men, feeding over two hundred daily.[36] In St. Louis, Timothy Dempsey, a priest, established a house where thousands were aided over the years.[37] The average daily meals for the month of April 1935, the only figures that appear in *Catholic Worker* for this hospice, indi-

[31] *Ibid.*, 92, 93, 125.
[32] David O'Brien, "American Catholic Thought in the 1930s," Rochester University, Ph.D., 1965, 99.
[33] Maurin, *op. cit.*, 1, 11.
[34] Interview with Nina Poleyn, December 13, 1968.
[35] Interview with William Gauchat, December 13, 1968.
[36] *Catholic Worker*, April, 1938, 2.
[37] Sheehan, *op. cit.*, 144.

cate that the St. Louis hospice fed over 2,700 daily and distributed 700 baskets of food a week.[38]

In Washington, D. C., there were several houses. One established to aid black unemployed included among its founders Father Paul Hanley Furfey, the personalist theologian.[39] Another Washington house, St. Christophers Inn, served as a sleeping quarter for transients and, though closed for most of the day, provided meals to the destitute.[40] The Blessed Martin Home in Washington was virtually a one-man operation. Dorothy Day described it as dilapidated with paper hanging from the wall, plaster falling off, and slats protruding. The floor sloped and the house was unheated; yet Llewellyn Scott, its manager, housed forty-five men a night during the winter of 1938-39.[41]

In Harrisburg, Pennsylvania, the house of hospitality sheltered evicted women until the Catholic Worker staff could find them new homes.[42] In Akron and Chicago the main efforts went into feeding hungry children. The Detroit group, in addition to feeding six hundred daily and participating in demonstrations, established a workers' school.[43]

The degree of autonomy that existed for Catholic Worker units may be seen at the hospice established in Pittsburgh. Considering itself a Catholic Worker unit, as its correspondence to the *Catholic Worker* indicated, the hospice also visualized its role as an umbrella for various other Catholic radical causes.[44] In addition to organizing the largest hospice in the Movement, the Pittsburgh unit held lectures, classes, distributed the *Catholic Worker*, and even sponsored a radio program. "Your Pittsburgh branch," its founder Father Charles Owen Rice reported, "has been prospering." Housed in a three-story building that belonged to the diocese, it completely supported forty staff members, fed 800 on its food lines, slept 300 nightly, and was the only Catholic Worker branch at the time to have a clinic.[45] In the spring of 1938, the Pittsburgh group began working a farming commune.[46]

Significant differences, however, arose between the Catholic Worker Movement and its Pittsburgh affiliate as the latter enlarged the scope

[38] *Catholic Worker*, June 1935, 1.
[39] Sheehan, *op. cit.*, 145.
[40] *Catholic Worker*, February 1, 1934, 1.
[41] Dorothy Day, "Tale of Two Capitals," *Commonweal*, July 14, 1939, 280-83.
[42] Day, *House of Hospitality*, 271.
[43] *Catholic Worker*, May 1938, 1.
[44] Father Charles Owen Rice, *Catholic Worker*, February 1938, 6.
[45] *Ibid.*
[46] *Catholic Worker*, April 1938, 6.

of its activities. Some of the Pittsburgh unit's subsidiary agencies, such as Pax, which was an organization of Catholic conscientious objectors, and a local branch of the Association of Catholic Trade Unionists, severed their institutional ties with the New York Catholic Worker Movement. In addition the Pittsburgh unit's strong anti-communist position combined with a strong trade-union orientation led eventually to a merger with the national Association of Catholic Trade Unionists. It next dissolved its relations with the Catholic Worker Movement altogether.[47]

Each Catholic Worker group thus went its own direction without being hampered, controlled, or administered by the parent group in New York. Lists of Catholic Worker institutions appeared in the *Catholic Worker* for 1938 and 1939. In 1938, twenty-two houses existed in the United States; nineteen cells, *i.e.*, families, that provided room for the overflow from local hospices; and three commnues. In 1939 three houses were added, increasing the total to twenty-five; the number of cells fluctuated between thirteen and sixteen; and there were four farms.[48]

The New York group was the most important. Here once again patterns developed that were followed by other houses. It first developed an open informality emulated by many later units. Miss Day stated that they did not want the house to have the aspect of a mission: no one preached to men who had to listen on empty stomachs.[49] She also emphasized the necessity of smallness so that bureaucratic machinery would not impersonalize relations with the hospices.[50]

The first house of hospitality in New York City began as a co-operative apartment in a condemned tenement. It housed three men of the Catholic Worker group.[51] A cooperative apartment for unemployed women followed a short time later.[52] A store, office, dining room, and kitchen housed several more; Dorothy Day's own apartment, which she and her daughter shared with several women, became another Movement residence.[53] Donations from laymen, revenue from canvassing, and contributions from either individual priests or from their collections

[47] *Ibid.*, May 1931, 7.
[48] *Ibid.*, September 1938, 7; March 1939, 4; June 1939, 3. To the list of houses established in June, the New York house added two more founded after the list was compiled.
[49] Day, *Long Loneliness*, 249.
[50] Day, *House of Hospitality*, 236.
[51] *Catholic Worker*, May 1939, 1.
[52] *Ibid.*, December 15, 1933, 1.
[53] *Ibid.*, May 1939, 1.

paid the rent.[54] Since these resources were unable to keep so many places running at one time, the Movement replaced the various apartments with one small old house, the Charles Street house. Residents— clients and staff—lived on the upper floors while the newspaper and pamphlets were published on the first floor as well as in the basement.[55]

In the spring of 1936, the Catholic Worker Movement was permitted to use a building, the Mott Street house, one block from New York's China Town. It had twenty rooms plus several other apartments in an adjoining building that the Movement could utilize. Two stores on the ground floor served as a dining room for the unemployed, and as reading room, editorial offices, print shop as well as kitchen. The main building provided one floor for men and two for women. Sometimes the stores and offices also served as bedrooms. In addition, several Catholic Worker staff members had their own apartments or rooms elsewhere and spent their days working at Mott Street.[56]

The Catholic Worker house remained at Mott Street through the 1930s. This unlikely headquarters, full of neighborhood children, lines strung with laundry, radios blasting, and countless discussions going on, managed to feed breakfast to 1,000 a day in addition to its regular resident and staff members.[57]

The New York house, in serving as a center for various types of Catholic dissidents, provided an atmosphere that encouraged the emergence of other Catholic social action groups. It also acted as a catalyst for various tangents of the Catholic Worker Movement that disturbed Maurin but were supported by Miss Day.

In contrast with Maurin, Dorothy Day visualized the labor movement and the strike as a temporary means for dealing with immediate material problems. "When we were invited to help during a strike," she felt "we went to perform works of mercy, which include not only feeding the hungry, . . . but enlightening the ignorant and rebuking the unjust."[58] She also believed that when participating in strikes "we are reaching the workers when they are massed together for action. We are taking advantage of a situation."[59] Miss Day argued

[54] *Ibid.*, December 15, 1933, 5.
[55] *Ibid.*, May 1939, 1.
[56] *Ibid.*, May 1939, 1.
[57] "House of Hospitality," *Commonweal* (April 15, 1938), 683; "For Christ the Worker," *Time* April 18, 1936, 46; Marieli G. Benziger, "Caitas Christ," *Catholic World* February 1938, 6.
[58] Day, *Long Loneliness*, 181.
[59] Day, *House of Hospitality*, 148.

that when men are striking, "they are fighting for a share in management, for the right to be considered partners. . . . They are fighting against the idea of their labor as a commodity, to be bought and sold."[60]

The *Catholic Worker,* advancing Miss Day's point of view, strongly supported organized labor and regularly reported labor news. The readers were told not to buy specific products or patronize particular concerns.[61] Catholics were urged to organize within the union, to fight for social justice.[62] A 1936 editorial clearly illustrated the Movement's point of view: "The *Catholic Worker* does not believe that unions as they exist today in the United States, are an ideal solution for social problems. . . . We do believe that they are the only efficient weapon which workers have to defend their rights as individuals."[63]

In 1934 and 1935 the Catholic Worker group participated in its first major strike as Manhattan department-store employees walked off the job. The strike affected only two large establishments, S. Klein and Ohrbach's, with the issues at the former being quickly resolved. The Catholic Worker Movement picketed with the workers and carried signs quoting papal support of unions. Police regularly arrested the picketers not belonging to the Catholic Worker group.[64] Enjoined by the courts from picketing, the Catholic Workers engaged in civil disobedience by violating the injunction. In addition the Movement's staff attended strike meetings and informed the workers of Catholic thought regarding strikes, picketing, and nonviolent techniques.[65] Meanwhile, the *Catholic Worker* told its readers not to patronize the department store. "You are not upholding social justice if you disregard the plea of these workers."[66] Catholic Workers, during this strike, worked closely with local Communists, a repeated situation which inevitably led to criticism within the Church. Miss Day, however, defended these working arrangements. She found that the issues raised by the Communists were just: " 'The truth is the truth,' writes St. Thomas, 'and proceeds from the Holy Ghost, no matter from whose lips it comes.' "[67]

---

[60] *Ibid.*, 142.
[61] *Catholic Worker* July-August, 1933, 1.
[62] *Ibid.*, 5.
[63] Editorial, *Catholic Worker* February 1936, 4. For differences between Miss Day who supported the New Deal and Maurin who did not, see Day, *Long Loneliness,* 174; *House of Hospitality,* 71; Maurin, *op. cit.,* 57, 70. The *Catholic Worker* followed her point of view, see *Catholic Worker* September 1933, 6; October 1933, 3; November 1933, 2; February 1934, 71.
[64] Day, *Long Loneliness,* 206.
[65] *Catholic Worker,* March 1935, 1.
[66] *Ibid.*, February 1935, 1.
[67] Day, *Long Loneliness,* 206.

The Catholic Workers' greatest involvement with strike action emerged out of their support of Joseph Curran's leftist leadership in the organization of the National Maritime Union, at the time of the maritime strike of May 1936. The young union appealed to the *Catholic Worker* to help in housing and feeding some of the strikers; about fifty men were immediately accepted into the Mott Street house.[68] Before the strike was over the Catholic Workers had rented a store in the strike area, using it as a reading room and kitchen.[69] They also performed the usual service of picketing with Catholic-oriented signs.[70]

During the New York seamen's strike of 1937, the Catholic Worker Movement again participated on the docks. Once more a waterfront branch became a resting place for idle seamen. Conveniently located around the corner from strike headqaurters, it attracted many strikers. The seamen filled the store to capacity from early morning until midnight. Picketers could relax and read Catholic newspapers and magazines.[71] More important, the Movement fed thousands of strikers, which resulted in a $3,000 debt; yet the store remained open, even after the strike had ended, feeding over 1,000 a day until the men again went back to their ships.[72]

The Catholic Worker group in Pittsburgh particularly aided the labor movement, especially the C.I.O.'s Steel Workers Organizing Committee (S.W.O.C.). Father Charles Owen Rice, the local Catholic Worker leader, spoke to overflow crowds at the immigrant meeting houses where large numbers of Catholic laborers gathered. Concurrently, his supporters distributed the *Catholic Worker* at ethnic social halls.[73] Father Rice and his associate, Father Carl Hensler, led their staff members on steel worker picket lines, and encouraged workers over S.W.O.C. loud speakers.[74]

Sometimes the Catholic Worker Movement negotiated with management over a labor dispute. A major New York City department store chain, for example, laid off a number of non-unionized saleswomen without severance pay. They had been employed there from twelve to twenty years. Catholic Workers offered to join the women in picketing company stores, and then met with company officials, threatening them

[68] *Ibid.*, 208.
[69] *Ibid.*, 208-9.
[70] *Catholic Worker*, June 1936, 4.
[71] Day, *House of Hospitality*, 180-181.
[72] Day, *House of Hospitality*, 188.
[73] *Catholic Worker*, May 1937, 7; June 1937, 1.
[74] Day, *House of Hospitality*, 263.

with public attacks both in the *Catholic Worker* and from the lecture platform. The firm then agreed to provide severance pay for some and to take back the rest.[75]

These instances were typical of the labor activities of the Catholic Worker Movement. The Movement harassed numerous companies it considered unjust: the National Biscuit Company, Borden Milk, Heinz Corporation, Loose-Wiler, and American Stores of Philadelphia were some of the more well-known.[76] Vermont marble workers, Boston fishermen, Arkansas sharecroppers, Michigan autoworkers, Massachusetts textile workers, New York brewery workers, printers, librarians, meatpackers, were just some of the striking workers that sought and received moral support, publicity in *Worker* columns, and countless thousands of meals from Catholic Worker groups throughout the country.[77] At least one company placed paid advertisements in the *Catholic News* and *Brooklyn Tablet,* a major Catholic newspaper, attacking the Movement.[78]

To judge by the space accorded organized labor in the *Worker's* front page its role was, for the Movement at least, equal to that of the hospice during the 1930s. Yet Dorothy Day's effort did not end here. Catholic Workers also founded a Catholic Union of Unemployed headed by Timothy O'Brien,[79] an ex-communist. They also spent considerable effort in moving evicted families. They transported furniture, found new apartments and, when a family was settled, provided it with clothing and additional furniture.[80] To coordinate these kinds of activities, they organized a number of neighborhood councils, patterning them after the Communist Party's unemployed councils.[81]

The Catholic Worker Movement, in this manner, attempted to influence the lives of the worker and the effectiveness of the labor movement. It is difficult to measure its success, especially when such activities as art classes for culturally-deprived slum children or resettlement of the homeless and the evicted are involved. Obviously, however, considering the totality of problems in depression America, the Move-

---

[75] *Catholic Worker,* February 1935, 3.
[76] *Catholic Worker,* July 1937, 6; June 1936, 1; April 1935, 1; May 1935, 1; March 1935, 1; Day, *Long Loneliness,* 207-8; *Catholic Worker,* April 1938, 1.
[77] *Catholic Worker,* June 1936, 1; March 1935, 1; April 1935, 1; May 1935, 1; March 1935, 1; April 1936, 1; February 1936, 1; Day, *Long Loneliness,* 207-9.
[78] *Catholic Worker,* April 1936, 1; Day, *Long Loneliness,* 208.
[79] "For Christ the Worker," 47.
[80] Day, *Long Loneliness,* 203, 183; *Catholic Worker,* November 1933, 3.
[81] *Catholic Worker,* September 1933, 4.

ment's influence was meager. It did, to be sure, feed thousands, provide shelter and clothing for a significant number, aid in many strikes, and at times contribute to a settlement favorable to the workers. Nonetheless, the total accomplishment could not have been great. The Movement also supported the C.I.O. by aiding in organization, and providing it with propaganda in its conflict with the A.F.L. But C.I.O. growth was unrelated to the Movement itself.

Catholic Workers made no concentrated attempt to affect Catholic social reform; yet, ironically, they had their greatest influence in this area. By stressing the disparity between the practices of American life and the social ideals of the Church, the Movement attracted young Catholic radicals who otherwise might have filtered into the secular left. The Catholic Worker Movement, therefore, provided a source of direction for social Catholicism and an early avenue of involvement for Catholic radicals who later moved in other, though still liberal, directions. Numerous Catholic social institutions were directly stimulated by the Catholic Worker Movement. William Callahan organized the first American branch of Pax at Mott Street. It eventually became the Association of Catholic Conscientious Objectors, and ran forestry as well as hospital camps in New Hampshire, Illinois, and Maryland during World War II.[82] Sitting around the kitchen table of the Mott Street house, John Cort and other Movement members organized the Association of Catholic Trades Unionists.[83] Moreover, many independent labor schools and Interreligious Friendship Houses were outgrowths of the Movement.[84]

A number of liberal Catholic journalists and publishers received their first impetus from the Catholic Worker Movement during the '30s. In addition to the New York City newspaper, Movement newspapers were published in Chicago, England, and Australia. The Canadian *Social Forum*, the first *Christian Front*, and *The Source* also emerged out of the Movement.[85] Individuals such as John Cogley, editor of *Commonweal*, began their activities in social action causes by leading Catholic Worker units. Cogley ran the Movement's hospice in Chicago and edited the Chicago *Catholic Worker*.[86] Edward Willock, co-founder of *Integrity*, and Edward Marcinak, founder of *Work*, came out of the

---

[82] *Ibid.*, 127-8.
[83] *Labor Leader*, March 28, 1947, 1.
[84] "Peter Maurin," *Commonweal*, August 27, 1949, 165.
[85] Day, *House of Hospitality*, xxxi; *Catholic Worker*, October 1938, 4.
[86] Day, *Long Loneliness*, 226; Sheehan, *op. cit.*, 149.

Movement. John Cort, a prolific writer on social Catholicism, and social critic Michael Harrington were members of the New York group. The *Catholic Student's Digest* was specifically launched by the New York house.[87]

The Catholic Worker Movement may have done little to affect the labor movement directly, but its contribution to the development of Social Catholicism in America supported a climate of opinion favorable to organized labor. More important, it rekindled Catholic social reform activities, relatively dormant for over a decade, and began a tradition of anti-establishment American Catholic activism which exists today in the vanguard of anti-draft activities. These results of the Catholic Worker Movement are to a degree ironic, for neither the labor movement nor the social reformism of groups and individuals that grew out of the Catholic Worker Movement represented Peter Maurin's goal of a communitarian society.

[87] *Ibid.*

"UNITED WE EAT":
THE CREATION AND ORGANIZATION OF
THE UNEMPLOYED COUNCILS IN 1930

By DANIEL J. LEAB

"Fight!—Don't Starve." Utilizing this slogan the American Communists, even before widespread unemployment began late in 1929, had attempted to organize the jobless. The party, while still in its underground stage, had called an "Unemployment Conference for Greater New York" in March of 1921. Thirty-four A.F. of L. and independent unions as well as the I.W.W. had sent representatives to the conference, which established the Unemployed Council of Greater New York with Israel Amter, a communist leader, as Secretary.[1] Among its "immediate demands," the Council listed public works, unemployment insurance, low-cost housing, and resumption of trade with Russia (which according to the American Communists would, because of the Soviet Union's many needs, re-employ great numbers of men).[2] To publicize and support these demands, and to give substance to the Council, Amter tried to form local neighborhood groups to be known as Councils of Action.[3] At sparsely attended "mass" meetings, to which the party attemped to lure the out-of-work with false promises of free soup and sandwiches, Amter would declare "the unemployed must organize and take action."[4] Hoping to capitalize on the hard times, the party expected to attract an army of jobless, though at best it enlisted a corporal's guard. Attempts to develop the group nationally as the Worker's Unemployed Council

---

[1] Theodore Draper, *American Communism and Soviet Russia* (New York, 1960), 175-176. Draper calls the Unemployed Council of Greater New York "one of the first real membership fronts."

[2] *The Toiler*, December 31, 1921; *The New York Times*, November 27, 1921, 16.

[3] *The Toiler*, April 9, 1921.

[4] *The New York Times*, February 5, 1922, 21. The action demanded by Amter could mean many things. In this instance it meant admission by the unemployed to the empty homes (on Fifth Avenue and Riverside Drive) of the rich who had gone away for the winter.

DANIEL LEAB *is Instructor in history at Columbia University.*

of America came to naught. In New York, where fear of communism and a fairly harsh winter had enabled the Council to achieve some local notoriety, the group faded rapidly into oblivion once economic conditions improved.[5]

Despite this initial failure, the Communists continued trying to organize the jobless during the 1920s, especially in those chronically depressed areas which did not share in the prosperity of the times. Periodically, the party would announce new organizational drives among the unemployed. It again declared in 1923 that one of its major tasks in the American labor movement would be "the organization of groups of unemployed . . . to force resolute action for the improvement of their position."[6] A few years later the party's Central Executive Committee issued a "Program on Unemployment" which concluded with instructions for the party "to set up Councils of Unemployed everywhere. . . ."[7] Communists efforts during this period, however, had almost no success, and invariably their organizational drives among the unemployed resulted in nothing but paper groups.[8] In 1929 the newly organized Trade Union Unity League (T.U.U.L.)—the Communist Party labor group—determined to try once again to organize the jobless.[9]

The first T.U.U.L. convention took place on August 31-September 1 —about the time the collapse of the American economy began. During the winter of 1929-30, the first large numbers of previously employed persons were idled, and began to discover the scarcity of jobs and the inadequacies of relief.[10] From the Communists' point of view, it is hard to imagine how the unemployment situation initially could have developed along lines more favorable to them. Most people had become

---

[5] Louis Eisman, "The First Decade of the Communist Party" (Unpublished Master's Thesis, Department of Political Science, University of California, 1935), 100. During February 1922, *The New York Times,* which had previously ignored the group, devoted a number of reports to the movement, one (February 14, 1922) even appearing on the front page. However, most New York newspapers continued to ignore the group.

[6] Quoted in *Resolutions and Decisions of the Second World Congress of the Red International of Labor Unions* (Chicago: Trade Union Educational League, 1923), 8; Eisman quotes a Communist at this time asserting that groups of unemployed should be formed to "ask for legislation compelling the capitalists to pay wages to the workers to whom they cannot give employment." (Eisman, *op. cit.,* 101-102.)

[7] Quoted in Eisman, *op. cit.,* 221-222.

[8] Eleanor Kahn, "Organizations of the Unemployed as a Factor in the American Labor Movement," (unpublished Master's thesis, Department of History, University of Wisconsin, 1934), 103.

[9] The new union, in fact, specifically declared in its statement of purpose that "the Trade Union Unity League organizes the unemployed." (As quoted in David Carpenter, "The Communist Party: Leader in the Struggle of the Unemployed," *Political Affairs,* XXIX (September, 1949), 83).

[10] By the end of 1929 close to 3,000,000 fewer persons held jobs than in September.

accustomed to the prosperity of the boom years of the 1920s. The sudden economic collapse in 1929 came as a shock; but it did not leave the jobless disspirited. The dull apathy which characterized so many of the unemployed as the Depression dragged on had not yet set in. Under Communist leadership people expressed their anger at the turn of economic events, and their frustration at being unable to help themselves. As Howe and Coser have pointed out "the Communist Party [in the winter of 1929-30] managed to seize upon a highly explosive issue and to rally a considerable number of non-Communist workers under its banners."[11] The party, once again utilizing the slogan "Fight—Don't Starve," set out to take organizational advantage of the increasing distress caused by decreasing means of support.[12] Working through the T.U.U.L., the Communist Party intensified its efforts to organize the jobless into groups that ultimately became known as Unemployed Councils.

These Councils, like the earlier "front" instruments used by the Party in its attempts to win over the jobless, were patterned in structure and philosophy on the Saint Petersburg Councils of the Unemployed, which during the 1905 uprising in Czarist Russia had been revolutionary units formed by the displaced factory workers.[13] The Communists had intended that these American counterparts should also be "revolutionary centers," in which "the unemployed by participation in the class struggle on a mass action basis would gain political insight into the historical destiny of the proletariat and join the Party."[14] The Communist Party,"

[11] Irving Howe and Lewis Coser, The American Communist Party (Boston, 1957), 192. An example of this would be the activities of John Pace, who at one time led the Communist veterans' group. Testifying before the Dies Committee in 1938, after he had abjured his earlier Communist position, Pace recalled that "when the crash came in 1929, I lost my business and what money I had in a bank that closed. I lost that and the money that I had gone into business with which I had figured pretty hard to earn. Well, I just got sore, that is all. I got sore at myself and everybody else, and got connected with an unemployed group." (U. S. Congress, House of Representatives, Special Committee on Un-American Activities, Hearings, Investigation of Un-American Propaganda Activities in the United States, 75th Congress, 3d session, 1938, 2267, hereafter referred to as House Un-American Activities Committee, 1938.)

[12] Fight! Don't Starve, Organize—Demands for Unemployment Insurance Made Upon the United States Congress (New York: Trade Union Unity League, 1931), 1. This was but the first of a long line of belligerently defiant slogans which the Councils hurled at society. Perhaps the crassest of the lot was the one which Council members shouted at Mayor La Guardia during a public hearing in 1934 concerning relief in New York City, namely, "Feed us or shoot us." (New York Post, June 22, 1934, 1.)

[13] Helen Seymour, "Organization of the Unemployed" (unpublished Master's Thesis, Department of Sociology, Columbia University, 1940), 10; at this time the party press published a short history of the St. Petersburg Unemployed Councils, presumably so that it might serve as an example to the American jobless. See Sergei Malyshev, Unemployed Councils in St. Petersburg in 1906 (New York: Workers' Library Publishers, 1930).

as Irving Bernstein points out, "had as one of its main goals the organization of the unemployed into a cadre of revolution."[15] In the radical changes of American social and economic conditions, the Communists thought they saw the beginnings of the objective revolutionary situation predicted by "third period" ideology. The United States, it was declared, abounded with "revolutionary potentialities" which the Councils might help to exploit.[16]

Under T.U.U.L. aegis, the Communist organizers—"hatless young men in simulated leather jackets," as Arthur Schlesinger Jr., described them[17]—sought out the jobless wherever the involuntary idle queued up. Council organizers hung out in parks, on breadlines, outside soup kitchens and flop-houses, among the groups of men loitering at factory gates or waiting in crowded relief offices. Using the rapidly spreading unemployment as a comon denominator, the organizers created and expanded Unemployed Councils all over the country. In city after city, Party-led groups of jobless men organized demonstrations, led marches, and created committees of protest—all demanding that something be done.[18]

At this early stage in their development, the Councils (also known as the Councils of the Unemployed) conducted their campaigns on a local basis. In each particular locality the Communist Party organizers would importune the out-of-work to elect or form a Committee of Action.[19] Usually some of the more dissatisfied or more militant among the listeners would give heed, and around this small core the local Council would form.[20] Steve Nelson, describing "How Unemployed Councils Were Built in Lackawanna County," recalled that he and his fellow organizers made contact with a few jobless they had heard complaining and induced them to come to a series of meetings, out of which eventually emerged one local group.[21] Joe Brandt reported to the *Party*

---

[14] Kahn, *op. cit.,* 102.
[15] Irving Bernstein, *The Lean Years* (Boston, 1960), 426.
[16] M. J. Olgin, "From March 6 to May 1," *Communist,* IX (May, 1930), 417-422.
[17] Arthur Schlesinger, Jr., *Crisis of the Old Order* (Boston, 1951), 219.
[18] Harold Lasswell and Dorothy Blumenstock, *World Revolutionary Propaganda* (New York, 1939), 192-193; Seymour, *op. cit.,* 11; Bernard Karsh and Phillips Garman, "The Political Left," in *Labor and the New Deal,* edited by Milton Derber and Edwin Young (Madison, 1957), 88-89.
[19] Herbert Benjamin, *A Manual for Hunger Fighters: How to Organize and Conduct United Action for the Right to Live* ("Unemployment Series No. 3," New York: Workers' Library Publishers, 1933), 4.
[20] Seymour, *op. cit.,* 9.
[21] Steve Nelson, "How Unemployed Councils Were Built in Lackawanna County," *Party Organizer,* VII (March, 1934), 7-9.

Organizer that he had been able to create a Council local by bringing housewives together to hold "empty pot and pan demonstrations."[22] Mrs. Mildred Olsen, a Council member from San Francisco, told the California State Unemployment Commission how she had been recruited by a housewife who had canvassed her apartment building.[23] In large cities and thickly populated areas, the organizers attempted to form committes or councils based on the neighborhood, the block, or even on one or two large apartment houses. In smaller towns and in sections where one-, or two-family dwellings prevailed, the organizers attempted to group together those locals which were in a larger area, such as the ward or the county.[24] In some areas the organizers attemped, with more success, to form groups built along language or ethnic lines, such as the all Yiddish-speaking locals in New York City.[25]

During this embryonic period the Councils existed on an extremely unstable basis. No real interaction existed between the separate components. Rarely did one Council act in unison with another. Indeed, the only points they had in common were their demands for more relief and more public works, their emphasis on the philosophy of class struggle, and their over-all Communist sponsorship. Despite Party urging that local Committees of Action "register all workers . . . willing to record themselves as supporters . . .," most Committees proved reluctant or unable to do so and remained loose entities without membership meetings or an integrated framework.[26] After a demonstration had ended, only the hard core of militants and Communists remained to continue the life of the local group until the next mass gathering.[27] But because of the temper of the times, this hard core managed to bring out ever-increasing numbers of people for the various protest demonstrations.

The early developments of these Unemployed Councils reached its apex in the country-wide demonstrations of March 6, 1930, while they

---

[22] Joe Brandt, "How Our Block Committee Works," *Party Organizer* V (May-June, 1932), 38-41.

[23] *Abstract of Hearings on Unemployment before the California State Unemployment Commission,* April and May 1932 (Sacramento: California State Printing Office, 1933), 161-162.

[24] "Self Help Among the Unemployed," *Information Service* XII (January 28, 1933), 4.

[25] Kahn, *op. cit.,* 106. Evictions helped in the formation of these Council locals. Miss Kahn reports how people who had come in contact with the Council would be evicted and in the new neighborhood, to which they often had moved by virtue of their ethnic or lingual relations, they would spread the news about the Councils.

[26] Benjamin, *op. cit.,* 12.

[27] Clarence Hathaway, "Our Failure to Organize the Unemployed," *Communist,* IX (September, 1930), 786-788.

were still linked directly to the Trade Union Unity League. March 6 had been designated "International Day for Struggle Against World-Wide Unemployment" by the Comintern, and marked the first successful Communist attempt to coordinate their activities among the unemployed on a national scale.[28] Originally scheduled for February 27, "the Day" had been postponed for a week because the Comintern, sensing from the initial response the possibility of a great international propaganda success, delayed the event in order "to enable all [Communist] Parties to thoroughly prepare . . . and carry on a broader campaign."[29]

On March 6, "International Unemployment Day" took place as planned. Throughout much of the world demonstrations duly protested "the exploitation of the unemployed," demanded an "end to hunger," and prophesied the imminent "failure of the capitalistic system."[30] In those countries such as the United States where no provisions for any form of employment insurance had been enacted, the demonstrators also clamored for "work or wages."[31]

The American Communist Party went to great lengths to insure the participation of large numbers of unemployed in its demonstrations. Not relying solely on the Councils organized through the T.U.U.L. it had marshalled all its forces. For example, a few days prior to March 6, the Agit-Prop Department of the Party's Chicago branch informed all Party members in the Chicago area that it had printed 50,000 stickers, 50,000 shop papers, and 200,000 leaflets which must be distributed. Agit-Prop also counted upon every Party member to hold meetings in his neighborhood, to recruit participants for the "International Unemployment Day" demonstrations under the Councils' banner, and whether employed or jobless, to take an active part in "the Day's" activities.[32] Similar instructions had been sent out by the local Agit-Prop Departments and Party groups across the country, so that in one way or another such instructions reached all Party members.[33]

While few in number (the Party had only about 10,000 dues-paying

---

[28] *Daily Worker*, March 6, 1930.
[29] Cable from the Executive Committee of the Communist International to the Executive Committee of the Communist Party of the United States, quoted in Lasswell and Blumenstock, *op. cit.*, 191-192.
[30] *The Times*, March 7, 1930, 12. In Germany, where the demonstration played a part in the bloody political war the Nazis and the Communists fought over who should inherit the Weimar Republic, "the Day's" activities resulted in a number of deaths.
[31] *The New York Times*, March 7, 1930, 1, 2, 5.
[32] Lasswell and Blumenstock, *op. cit.*, 192-193.
[33] *Ibid.*, 192.

members at the end of 1929), they did their job thoroughly and well.[34] Demonstrations took place in almost every important American industrial and commercial center on March 6. Although the *Daily Worker*, the press organ of the American Communist Party, exaggerated when it claimed that millions had participated in the demonstrations, large numbers did take part, many of them ostensibly at the instigation of the local Unemployed Councils under T.U.U.L. aegis.[35]

Many of the demonstrations were orderly, uneventful affairs. In San Francisco, some 2,000, joined en route by the chief of police, marched to the municipal office building, where Mayor James Rolph, Jr. listened to their petitions and addressed them.[36] In Chicago, despite anticipated police violence (which did not materialize), nearly 5,000 paraded through the streets while a committtee of fifteen—headed by Nels Kjar, a prominent Communist leader and Chairman of the Chicago Unemployed Council—presented a petition at Mayor William Thompson's office.[37] The Baltimore Police Department treated the whole affair as a joke. Upon the Party's refusal to ask for a permit to march, a Negro named "Alexander Turnipseed" received one for them at his request, and on March 6, the acting Mayor met the demonstrators wearing a red tie and a red carnation.[38] In Trenton, where about a thousand marchers paraded to the State House, the Director of Public Safety asked the speakers at the unemployment rally to "speak up louder."[39]

But serious clashes between police and demonstrators took place in other localities. The Washington, D.C. police used tear-gas bombs to

---

[34] Statistical figures as to exact membership are one of the most obscured aspects of the Communist movement in America. After a thorough study, Theodore Draper has come to the following conclusions: there were about 7,000 members in October 1925, and the membership slowly rose from that point to about 9,500 in 1927 and hovered around that figure until the end of the decade. Not until 1932 did the C. P. have more than 15,000 members. (Draper, *op. cit*, 186-187.) Howe and Coser, relying on party records, quote the following figures for C. P. membership: 1930, 7,500; 1931, 9,527; 1932, 14,475; 1933, 19,165 (Howe and Coser, *op cit.*, 225).

[35] *Daily Worker*, March 7, 1930. This newspaper claimed that 110,000 people had marched in New York City, 100,000 in Detroit, 50,000 in Chicago, 20,000 in Pittsburgh, and appreciably large numbers elsewhere. The doubtfulness of these estimates is displayed by the *Daily Worker*'s assertions that 20,000 police attacked the marchers in New York. Had this actually happened, it would have meant that more policemen would have been present at the rally than were on the force at that time.

[36] *San Francisco Chronicle*, March 7, 1930, 1.

[37] *The New York Times*, March 7, 1930, 3. This is one of the relatively few peaceful demonstrations of the unemployed which took place in Chicago. Sandwiched in between were serious riots where police and unemployed had battled viciously. Violence was anticipated because of a rumor that thirteen men had been imported from New York City to kill John Stege, Deputy Police Commissioner, and Make Mills, Captain of the Red Squad.

[38] *New York World*, March 8, 1930, 3.

[39] *New York World*, March 8, 1930, 3.

disperse crowds which had gathered before the White House.[40] The
Seattle police also had to use tear gas to break up the demonstrations.[41]
The Boston Common became a battleground between police and demonstrators as the Communists attemped to hold their protest meeting
there.[42] Serious conflict also occurred in Detroit when the marchers
resisted atempts to disperse them.[43] But the most violent clash, and the
one which gained the most notoriety, took place in New York. Some
35,000 persons had attended the "International Unemployment Day"
rally in Union Square.[44] The police had permitted the meeting, but had
expressly prohibited the Communist organizers from leading any protest marches away from the Square. The outburst came at the end of
the rally when, despite police orders, the Communist leaders urged the
crowd to march to City Hall and present their demands for work and
relief to Mayor James Walker. When one of the speakers shouted
"Let's go," the police charged and in the ensuing confusion, lashed
out at demonstrators and spectators alike.[45] "Thousands of terrified
people scattered," *The New York Times* reported, "rushing for safety
from the flailing police, shouting, stumbling, stepping over one another
in their fear and haste to get away."[46] Scores of citizens and two policemen sustained serious injuries.[47]

---

[40] *The Washington Evening Star* (March 7, 1930, 1) claimed that the Communists apparently were successful in holding off the police, and almost succeeded in driving
them back until the police used tear gas. The *New York World* also reported that the
fight had been apparently going against the patrolmen until they had used tear gas
(*New York World*, March 7, 1930, 2).

[41] Walter O'Dale of the Detective Bureau of the Seattle Police Department testified that the
March 6 demonstration had been "the largest single Communist meeting" until that
time, and one of the "most difficult" to handle. (U. S. Congress, House of Representatives, Special Committee to Investigate Communist Activities in the United States,
Hearings, Investigation of Communist Propaganda, 71st Congress, 2nd session, 1930,
hereafter referred to as House Committee to investigate Communist Activity in the
U. S., 1930).

[42] *Christian Science Monitor*, March 7, 1930, 1.

[43] *New York Times*, March 7, 1930, 2.

[44] Many of them may have been just passers-by. The rally had been called in an industrial
district during the lunch hour. By the time the riot broke out the crowd had been
reduced since many people had returned to their jobs. But one newspaper estimated
that many thousands were still in the Square. (*New York World*, March 7, 1930, 1-2.)

[45] Israel Amter, "William Z. Foster: Leader of the Unemployed," *Political Affairs*, XXX
(March, 1951) 82.

[46] *The New York Times*, March 7, 1930, 1.

[47] There are complexities to the rally which space precludes discussing. But it is difficult to
understand the actions of the Communist leaders. There is no doubt that they provoked
the police and caused the riot. Then they left by taxi for the Mayor's office, thus
escaping entirely the violence which they had incited. There is, to be sure, no excuse
for the police actions. "Hundreds of policemen and detectives, swinging nightsticks,
blackjacks, and bare fists, rushed into the crowd, hitting out all with whom they came
in contact, chasing many across the street and adjacent thoroughfares. . . . A score of
men with bloody heads and faces sprawled over the Square with policemen pummeling
them. The pounding continued as the men, and some women, sought refuge in flight."

News of the March 6 clashes, especially in New York, screamed out
in the headlines of the nation's press the next day. Any form of mass
demonstration, such as the Communists had envisaged, would have been
newsworthy. But the riots brought them much added publicity which,
while not of the most favorable sort, did serve their cause and that of
the Unemployed Councils.[48] The March 6 demonstrations had been the
first concerted, large-scale protest in this country against the downward
economic trend. They had broken through the generally optimistic,
cheerful tone of a press which had talked of little but quick recovery
and happy days.[49] Many people had been persuaded by the events of
March 6 that the Communists and their adjuncts, such as the Unemployed Councils, could help people face the deteriorating economic
situation.

The Party, still working through the Councils organized under
T.U.U.L. aegis, tried quickly to capitalize on the success of the demonstrations. A conference was called to meet in New York City on March
29-30, 1930. Known as "the First Preliminary National Conference on
Unemployment," this gathering, according to Communist sources, supposedly brought together "215 delegates from 13 states representing
19 industries . . . speaking for millions of unemployed workers."[50] In
reality, it assembled most of the Party's leaders in unemployed work.[51]
Under banners which bore such slogans as "Down with [William]
Green-[Herbert] Hoover-[Norman] Thomas—the Holy Trinity of Capitalism," John Schimes, assistant National Secretary of the T.U.U.L.,
called the meeting to order to discuss the unemployment situation.[52]

This matter-of-fact report of police brutality comes not from some portion of the
Left-wing press, but from The New York Times (March 7, 1930, 1) which, while
not openly condoning the police action, did not condemn it. The New York World
carried a report about a policeman who kicked an inspector who was trying to pull
him off a youth he was pummeling (New York World, March 7, 1930, 2). Both
papers prominently displayed front-page pictures showing a dapper Grover Whalen,
then Police Commissioner of New York, attended by an equally dapper Deputy
Commissioner, and a bodyguard, in the midst of the riot, looking on as the police
attacked the crowd.

[48] Bernstein, op. cit., 430. Louis Adamic believed that "these demonstrations became sensa-
tional front-page news all over the country—not because they were demonstrations of
the unemployed, or because the Communists had organized them, but because they
produced bleeding heads." Louis Adamic, Dynamite (New York, 1935), revised
edition, 458.
[49] Almost immediately after the riots of March 6 President Hoover predicted "the worst
effects . . . of the Crash . . . will have passed during the next sixty days." (The New
York Times, March 8, 1930).
[50] Daily Worker, March 31, 1960; Labor Unity, March 24, 1930.
[51] Howe and Coser, op. cit., 192.
[52] House Committee to Investigate Communist Activity in the U. S., 1930, op cit., 232-236.

The speakers who followed him, including William Z. Foster (the 1928 Party presidential candidate), Israel Amter (New York District Organizer for the Party), and Robert Minor (editor of the *Daily Worker*), declared that the Councils could now stand independently of the T.U.U.L., and should do so. They urged the formation of an autonomous national unemployed organization.[53] Accepting this view, the conference delegates laid plans for another meeting, to be held in Chicago during July, which would bring such an organization to life.[54]

The conference also adopted a preliminary program which, though it underwent revisions, became the general platform of the Unemployed Councils, and remained so for some years. Its demands included federal unemployment insurance; federal appropriations for relief; no discrimination against rehiring workers because of race, religion, or sex; exemption from taxes and mortgage payments for the jobless; and a fair distribution of all available employment.[55] This last differed sharply from the "share-the-work" proposals of industry in that it called for a curtailment of the working day without any reduction in wages.[56] To this program the various local organizations added their own immediate demands: such as free hot school lunches in New York City,[57] or free milk for babies in Detroit.[58] Before adjourning, the conference also selected Pat Devine, a Pittsburgh party functionary, to serve as interim National Secretary.[59]

Three months later, on July 4-5, 1930, 1,320 delegates attended the Chicago meeting which, acting as a convention, transformed the old T.U.U.L.-sponsored groups, and established a new national organization —"the Unemployed Councils of the U.S.A."[60] The new group adopted as its main task, to use words of Nels Kjar, chairman of the convention, "immediate organization of all unemployed."[61] To coordinate the activities of the various local Councils, the convention elected Bill Mathieson,

[53] *Ibid.* That not all the speakers limited their remarks to the matter at hand is evidenced by the chairman's repeated cautions to confine themselves more to the unemployed and less to extraneous matters such as racial discrimination.
[54] *Ibid; Labor Unity*, April 8, 1930.
[55] *Daily Worker*, March 31, 1930.
[56] *Labor Unity*, April 8, 1930.
[57] *New York Hunger Fighter*, March 4, 1932.
[58] A. Gerlach, "How Unemployment Formed Block Committees and Organized in Detroit," *Daily Worker*, August 13, 1932, 3.
[59] House Committee to Investigate Communist Propaganda Activity in the U. S., 1930, *op. cit.*, 236.
[60] *Labor Unity*, July 16, 1930; *Daily Worker*, July 7, 1930; much of the impressiveness of the delegate figure is lost when it is noted that at least 500 of the delegates came from Chicago. (Howe and Coser, *op. cit.*, 193.)
[61] *Daily Worker*, July 7, 1930.

a Party leader, National Secretary, and chose a National Committe of thirty-eight. Elected as honorary members were Minor, Foster, and Amter—at that time all serving prison sentences for their part in the New York riot of March 6.[61]

The convention in Chicago, while adopting the preliminary program prepared by the New York conference, also added a number of refinements. It demanded, among other things, that all relief be administered by representatives of the unemployed. Again calling for immediate action by Congress, the convention also insisted that federal expenditures for relief should be allocated "now" from funds already appropriated for military purposes. At the same time, the new organization declared that the United States ought to recognize the Soviet Union.[63] One proposed plank for the Council's platform had even gone so far as to call for "Defense of the Chinese Soviets."[64] The statement of purpose resulting from the convention's deliberations has been described, according to Howe and Coser, as one wherein "immediate demands pertaining to the needs of the unemployed jostled political slogans reflecting Communist ideology."[65]

Whatever else the Unemployed Councils achieved for the jobless, the Communist Party hoped they would serve as "transmission belts" to bring in new members.[66] It looked upon the day-to-day economic action of the Councils as "meaty bait" to attract the workers.[67]

As its organizational structure for "the Unemployed Councils of the U.S.A.," the convention adopted that which T.U.U.L. Councils used in their attempts to mobilize the unemployed. The new group claimed only

---

[61] These three (plus Harry Raymond who claimed to represent unemployed maritime workers) had been charged by the City of New York, because of their actions on March 6, with urging "unlawful assembly" and "creating a public nuisance." Found guilty, they served six months before being released. At the time of the Chicago meeting, Foster, Amter, and Minor were all on Blackwell's Island, the New York City prison. Upon their release, at the end of October 1930, all four were welcomed by a rally in Madison Square Garden (*Daily Worker*, October 22, 1930).

[63] *Labor Unity*, July 16, 1930.

[64] U. S. Congress, House of Representatives, Committee on Un-American Activities, *Hearings, Communist Metthods of Infiltration*, 83rd Congress, 2d session, 1954, 4527.

[65] Howe and Coser, *op. cit.*, 193.

[66] Clarence Hathaway, "On the Use of 'Transmission Belts' in Our Struggle for the Masses," *Communist*, X (May, 1931), 409-413. "Through these organizations . . . the Party must necessarily find its best training and recruiting ground" (p. 413) is how Hathaway described the Party's aims; Max Kampelman (*Communist Party versus the C.I.O.* (New York, 1957), 109), quotes a union official as saying "these organizations were created to capitalize on the misery and grief of the unemployed . . . merely to use these organizations as a transmission belt to the Party. . . ."

[67] Karsh and Garman, *op. cit.*, 90.

to have expanded the framework and supposedly used it with but few changes (except in name) until a merger of unemployed organizations in 1936 ended the Councils' separate identity.

Ideally, as in the Councils formed by the T.U.U.L., the basic unit remained the local—the Committee of Action—as Party organizers called it. The Unemployed Councils were to be made up of delegates selected by the Committees of Action. In the larger cities, the locals were expected to combine first on a ward, precinct, or borough basis, and then these lesser Councils would form a City Unemployed Council. In the smaller towns, where the organizers anticipated less success and a limited turnout, the locals were expected to form a County Council. Theoretically, these City and County Councils together, through their appointed delegates, formed the basis for the state and national organization.

As outlined by the Chicago convention, the local was expected to be the active force through which the Councils would demonstrate their militancy and effectiveness. It would create "listening posts" where its leaders could be found at fixed times by those unemployed who had grievances or other problems. It would set up committees—a food commitee, a housing commitee, an emergency relief commitee, and whatever other committees might be necessary to deal with the problems of the jobless. If "direct action" had to be undertaken, these measures would be carried out by the local. The Committee of Action also served "to popularize . . . [the Party] point of view through meetings, discussions, lectures, etc. . . ."[68] But primarily the local served as an instrument to bring the unemployed into the revolutionary ranks of the Party. No requirements for the number of persons needed to form a local existed until 1934, when the remnants of the organization adopted a written constitution which set the minimum membership in a single unit at twenty-five.[69]

The supreme governing body of the Councils was announced to be the National Convention. Between meetings the ultimate authority over

---

[68] Benjamin, op. cit., 20.
[69] Constitution and Regulations of the National Unemployment Council of the U. S. A. with a foreword by Herbert Benjamin (Unemployment Series No. 10) (New York: Workers Library Publishers, 1934), 8. (hereafter referred to as Unemployed Council Constitution.) The hey-day of the Councils had long since past by the time the constitution had been adopted. This absence of any requirement during their most flourishing period, coupled with an almost complete lack of registration records for those involved in Council activity, makes it very difficult to judge Communist estimates of membership. A claim of 100 locals in an area could mean only 100 interested people, or it could mean 100 locals with fifty members each.

the locals would rest with a national executive body. Throughout the Councils' existence the form and name taken by this body varied; only its supposed function remained the same—to coordinate the activities of the different Councils, and to speak for them nationally. Decisions in each local would be achieved by majority vote in an Assembly that met periodically and that would be composed of those who had registered as supporters of the group. So, too, the delegates to the various city, state, and national Councils should express the views of the locals.[70] Presumably, it should be added, the governing procedures of these Councils had been established according to democratic principles. But, as in most Communist fronts, behind the fiction of rank-and-file democracy, the Party caucus in each local held control. Joe Brandt mentions how Party members at local meetings should "inject very subtly certain suggestions."[71] Clyde Morrow told the House Un-American Activities Committee that for some locals the Party would choose "innocents" as its leaders, knowing that Communist members would have no difficulty keeping them in line.[72] Testifying before the same committee, John Pace recalled how the Party fraction in his group "would come together before a meeting. . . ."[73]

Initially, neither the national nor the local groups levied any dues. Finances were to be handled in a number of ways. The creators of the Councils had planned that the jobless adherents of Committees of Action should be registered every three months, and that upon registration each would pay a five cents fee. Another source of revenue was expected to come from the sale of "Penny Contribution" tickets. The locals, which would buy these tickets in bulk at reduced rates from the state or national organization, were to sell them at Council functions, unemployed gatherings, etc. The income of "the Unemployed Councils of the U.S.A." supposedly would come from the tickets and other items it might sell to the local groups.[74]

---

[70] Benjamin, *op. cit., passim;* organizational set-up outlined by Carl Winters, New York Unemployed Council leader, in the *New York Hunger Fighter,* March 7, 1932; "For Clarity in the Forms of Organization of the Unemployed," *Party Organizer,* IV (November, 1930) 1-5, *passim;* Seymour, *op. cit.,* 11-12; Brandt, *op. cit.,* 38-41; "Resolution on Work Among the Unemployed," *Communist,* X (October, 1931), 838-850, *passim.;* Unemployed Council Constitution, *op. cit., passim.*

[71] Brandt, *op. cit.,* 39.

[72] House Un-American Activities Committee, 1938, *op. cit.,* 1489.

[73] *Ibid.,* 2269.

[74] Other items the national organization sold included printed petition lists, Council buttons and stickers.

Between March 6 and July 5, 1930, the Unemployed Council movement had mushroomed. Previously, the American laborer had been adverse to the Councils because of their revolutionary bent; in 1930, however, the worsening times favored their formation. By mid-summer, the Councils had twelve locals in Chicago alone with over 1,000 people registered. Both Milwaukee and Indianapolis had active Councils which also were growing rapidly.[75] Seven flourishing locals existed in Philadelphia. A Council in Minneapolis had 375 jobless workers listed on its rolls; and Duluth's was vigorous and expanding.[76]

Yet the Councils proved unable to exploit these gains. For the most part, this failure resulted from their avowal of policies dictated by "third period" doctrine. The economic situation had not yet deteriorated so badly during the summer and fall of 1930 that the American working class, traditionally non-revolutionary, would accept a policy of gratuitous violence against society predicated on the belief that a dying capitalism must be dealt the death blow.[77] The jobless could not comprehend the Councils' attempts, as part of this policy, to assail other groups offering help to the unemployed, as in New York when a Council rally in August 1930 ended in a march on a free employment agency maintained by Tammany Hall.[78] Further dissatisfaction by the jobless with Councils' policies came from the continued call for demonstrations which often had nothing to do with issues arising out of unemployment. In Detroit, for example, a fairly serious riot ensued after an Unemployed Council protest march against the British bombing of Indian frontier rebels.[79] Louis Adamic believed that the average workingman,

---

[75] "Weekly Organizational Letter of District No. 8," cited in his exhibit by Captain Make Mills, Chief of the Red Squad of the Chicago Police Department. House Committee to Investigate Communist Activity in the U. S., 1930, *op. cit.,* 550.

[76] John Schmiess and Carl Miller, Council organizers, quoted in a report by Jacob Spolansky. House Committee to Investigate Communist Activities in the U. S., 1930, *op. cit.,* 234-235.

[77] "Self Help Among the Unemployed," 4. The general Communist attitude during these years (until the advent of the Popular Front) is made clear by this exchange at a Congressional hearing between Senator Hugo Black and an official of the T.U.U.L. who had helped in the formation of the first Unemployed Councils in 1929-30. The Senator asked William F. Dunne if it was true that "the Party does say the only way to accomplish anything is by force. . . ."

MR. DUNNE: Our Party believes that no ruling class . . . ever . . . has surrendered voluntarily or peaceably its powers . . . and . . . is going to. . . .

SEN. BLACK: Does your organization set that out as its objective?

MR. DUNNE: It says that the capitalist system will only be overturned by a forcible struggle.

(U. S. Congress, Senate, Subcommittee of the Committee on the Judiciary, *Hearings, Thirty Hour Week,* 72d Congress, 2d session, 1933, 115-116.)

[78] *Daily Worker,* August 22, 1930.

[79] *Daily Worker,* October 25, 1930.

even the jobless one, considered the policies practiced by the Councils
at this time to be "too radical, too violent."[80] Many of those who, after
March 6, had enlisted in the Councils abandoned them when they found
that instead of a larger relief ticket or a settlement of their grievances,
all their "radical militancy" got them was a crack on the skull from a
police club.[81]

As long as it had seemed that the Unemployed Councils would help
the out-of-work, and as long as they had no competition, the Councils
retained many of their members, and even gained new adherents. But
the continued call for demonstrations during the summer of 1930, many
of them on abstract issues which the jobless did not understand—such as
support of revolutionary action abroad—exhausted much of the popular
support that the Councils had gained after March 6. The Councils came
to be "politically branded," and less radical organizations began to
appear, competing with them for the support of the unemployed.[82] The
new groups attracted both those moved to action by the economic failure
of society, and those disillusioned by the crude violence so often per-
petrated by the Councils.

Only two months after the Chicago convention, some of the Communist leadership recognized the existence of trends away from the
Councils. Clarence Hathaway, a Chicago Party leader active among the
unemployed, complained in September 1930 about "organizational
weaknesses," and "the failure to organize the unemployed."[83] One Communist official described these months as "an initial period of adventur-
ism and confusion";[84] another, looking back to these early days, asserted
that the Party and the Councils had brought large numbers to "action,"
but had failed to retain them in "permanent" organization.[85]

In November 1930, shortly after the appearance of Hathaway's article, the Party's Central Committee, in a sharply self-critical evaluation
of its activities among the unemployed, took note of the shortcomings
of its unemployed policy.[86] Although reaffirming its faith in the prin-

[80] Louis Adamic, *Dynamite* (New York, 1930), 422.
[81] Kahn, *op. cit.*, 103.
[82] Seldon Rodman, "Lasser and the Workers' Alliance," *Nation*, CXLVII (September 10, 1938), 242.
[83] Clarence Hathaway, "Our Failure to Organize the Unemployed," *Communist*, IX (September, 1930), 788-795.
[84] Howe and Coser, *op. cit.*, 184.
[85] Herbert Benjamin, "Unity in the Unemployment Field," *Communist*, XV (April, 1936), 332.
[86] "Communication from the Central Committee of the Communist Party of the United States of America," published in the *Daily Worker*, November 8, 1930. The com-

ciples of the "third period," the Commitee determined to reorient the activities of the Unemployed Councils toward more direct work among the jobless; the Councils, in other words, would not abandon their revolutionary aspects, only de-emphasize them. It had also been decided that the Councils would operate on two levels: nationally, they would campaign for direct federal aid to the out-of-work, which in effect meant that the national organization was comatose except when revived by the Party for a supposed national demonstration, such as the Hunger Marches to Washington, D.C., in 1931 and 1932; locally, they would adopt as their main task "the protection of the unemployed," representing the jobless in their relations with relief authorities. The Committees of Action were to serve as representative agencies of the out-of-work, publicizing and settling their grievances.[87] However, the subsequent history of the Unemployed Councils is not that of a unified organization. Nor did they fulfill the expectations of their Party organizers. Notwithstanding their later notoriety, the Unemployed Councils never again duplicated for the Communists their success of March 6.

---

munication is entitled "From November to January," and after referring to the July convention, and what should have occurred thereafter, went on to describe what the Councils should do in the next few months. The "Communication" did not deal only in generalities. For example, it specifically suggested that the Councils take jobless persons into courtrooms so that they might view eviction cases and see how these were decided, the implication being that exposure to "the capitalistic law" would turn them toward the Councils.
[87] Ossip Piatnitsky, secretary of the Commintern, wrote a pamphlet at this time that indicates the line for the Councils. Piatnitsky, addressing himself to all the Communist unemployed organizations, those in Europe as well as the Councils in America, wrote that the Councils must be "centers both in the sphere of strugle—the organization of processions, hunger marchers, demonstrations, etc.; and also in . . . ideological and political activities." At the same time, he also referred to such specific tasks as fighting "against incivility on the part of . . . officials. . . ." (Ossip Piatnitsky, *Unemployment and the Tasks of the Communists* (New York: Workers' Library Publishers, 1931), *passim*.)

LABOR'S MEN: A COLLECTIVE BIOGRAPHY OF UNION OFFICIALDOM DURING THE NEW DEAL YEARS

By WALTER LICHT and HAL SETH BARRON*

In the mid-1940s, after a decade of unprecedented union activity, the American Federation of Labor and the Congress of Industrial Organizations jointly sponsored a project to compile a biographical dictionary of men and women then occupying leadership positions in the American labor movement. The project had the endorsement of Franklin Delano Roosevelt and resulted in the 1946 publication of *Who's Who in Labor*.[1] More than 3500 officials both from the two federations and from their constituent organizations are included. The information contained in this volume is a valuable source for historians interested in questions concerning labor leadership during the New Deal years. Who held positions of authority in the union movement during this era? Were there significant differences between AFL and CIO leaders? Who rose to the upper echelons of command, and did promotion practices differ in the two federations?

Historians of the American labor movement have generally

---

* This study began when the authors were participants in a workshop on quantitative methods taught by Professor Richard Jensen. The authors would like to thank Professor Jensen of the Univ. of Illinois at Chicago Circle and Professor James Banner of Princeton Univ. for their encouragement and assistance.

[1] Ruth Taylor and Marion Dickerman, eds., *Who's Who in Labor* (New York: Dryden Press, 1946). The data presented in *Who's Who in Labor* was compiled by Ruth Taylor, a syndicated columnist for several labor newspapers, and Marion Dickerman, an expert in union-management arbitration and a professor of industrial relations. A statement of the project's purpose and background information on the two editors can be found on pps. vii, 349, and 403. A reproduction of the original questionnaire used to gather information for the volume can be found in *Who's Who in Labor*, p. vi. Respondents were asked to list their addresses, birth places, birth dates, fathers' names, fathers' occupations, mothers' maiden names, wives' maiden names, dates of marriage, names of children, union affiliations, present labor posts, past labor posts, labor connected civic or government activities, public and community activities, political affiliations, church affiliations, club and fraternal organizations, writings, schooling, special interests and hobbies, and favorite sports.

followed the traditional methodological path of individual biography to study leadership patterns. Attention, as a result, has focused primarily on national figures of prominence to the exclusion of the mass of union officials below the top levels.[2] We know little of the socio-economic background of the "rank and file" union leadership. Did these men and women reflect the characteristics of the general population—the American working people whom they represented? Or were they cut from a different cloth, exhibiting characteristics typical of other leadership or elite groups?

A systematic sample of 400 officials from *Who's Who in Labor* indicates that labor leaders during the New Deal years were predominantly male, white, and middle-aged.[3] Though one-fourth of the labor force in 1940 was comprised of women, only 8.2 percent of union officials sampled were female.[4] Similarly, blacks represented only 4 percent of the group—a figure well below their proportion of the working population. The mean age was 46.3 years and three-fourths of the leaders were between thirty-five and sixty.

Union leaders were born in all parts of the country. When compared to the national profile reported in the 1940 Census, it

---

[2] For an example of the limited case history approach to studying American labor leadership see Charles A. Madison, *American Labor Leaders: Personalities and Forces in the Labor Movement*, 2nd enlarged ed., (New York: Frederick Ungar Publishing Co., 1950). After this study was completed, two works dealing with American labor leadership came to our attention. Both books are historical in nature and utilize a collective approach. They are: Gary Fink, *et al*, eds., *Biographical Dictionary of American Labor Leaders* (Westport, CT: Greenwood Press, 1974), and Warren Van Tine, *Making of the Labor Bureaucrat: Union Leadership in the United States, 1870-1920* (Amherst, MA: Univ. of Massachusetts Press, 1973). Both studies are concerned primarily with national figures of prominence, however, and do not focus on the New Deal era. The sociologist C. Wright Mills conducted a collective study of New Deal labor leaders in *The New Men of Power: America's Labor Leaders* (New York: Oxford Univ. Press, 1948). For his data, Mills used survey questionnaires from 410 national, state, and local officers of the AFL and CIO, but did not survey the leadership of the member unions affiliated with these two umbrella organizations. His study is thus best understood as an analysis of the AFL and CIO hierarchies and not as a study of the entire labor movement.

[3] The sample was constructed by selecting the first American labor leader on each page. To round the sample size to 400, a small number were chosen using random numbers. For further discussion of systematic sampling see Hubert M. Blalock, *Social Statistics* (New York: McGraw-Hill, 1972), 514-516. The entries were coded into fifty-eight variables and key-punched on IBM cards. SPSS (Statistical Package for the Social Sciences) programs were used to collate and cross tabulate the results.

[4] Ann R. Miller and Carol P. Brainerd, "Labor Force Estimates," in Everett S. Lee, *et al*, *Population Redistribution and Economic Growth, United States 1870-1950* (Philadelphia: American Philosophical Society, 1957), 364-631.

273

appears that their regional origins were fairly typical of the
American population (see Table I). Though they tended to be
less southern and more foreign born, the differences are not
marked. In fact, the relatively low percentage of immigrants
contradicts the popularly held view that New Deal labor leaders
were mostly "foreign born agitators." [5] Union officials, however,

TABLE I
Regional Origins of Labor's Men[6]

Region of Birth	Sample Number	Sample Percentage	U.S. Population Percentage (1940 Census)
New England	25	6	5
Middle Atlantic	89	22	19
Midwest	113	29	29
South	86	22	32
West	25	6	6
Foreign Born	59	15	9
	397	100	100

TABLE II
Types of Communities in which Labor's Men Were Born[7]

Type of Community	Population Base	Sample Number	Sample Percentage	U.S. Population Percentage 1900 Census	1910 Census
Rural-Small Town	Less than 5,000	144	40	64	58
Large Town	5,000– 24,999	65	18	10	11
Small City	25,000– 99,999	42	12	7	9
Large City	More than 100,000	110	30	19	22
		361	100	100	100

---

[5] For a discussion of popular attitudes toward labor leaders during the New Deal
  years, see Mills, 84-88.
[6] Census statistics from U.S. Department of Commerce, Bureau of the Census,
  Statistical Abstract of the United States, 1944-1945 (Washington, D.C., 1945), 7,
  31. Unless otherwise indicated, all percentage figures in this study have been
  rounded off to the nearest integer.
[7] Unfortunately the 1940 Census provides no means of comparing the types of com-

were slightly more urban and less rural in origins than the general population (See Table II).

Three hundred and thirty-five officials, or 83.8 percent of the sample, reported their father's occupations. Excluding missing cases, the figures on fathers' occupational status presented below reveal that labor leaders largely came from families on the lower rungs of the socio-economic ladder. Nearly three-fourths of the sample, in fact, were the sons and daughters of manual workers. When, however, one compares their occupational status backgrounds with the statistics for all adults reported as working in the 1910 Census (who, for purposes of analysis we will assume to be the fathers of the population at large in 1945) it appears that union officials were slightly above average in their socio-economic origins.

TABLE III
Occupational Status of Fathers of Labor's Men[8]

Fathers' Occupational Status	Sample Number	Sample Percentage	U.S. Population Percentage (1910 Census)
Professional	41	12	5
Businessman-Manager	29	9	7
Small Proprietor-White Collar Worker	31	9	9
Skilled Worker	75	23	12
Semiskilled-Unskilled Worker	91	27	50
Farmer	68	20	17
	335	100	100

Seventy-one percent of the sample (N=284) reported a church affiliation. Of these, thirty-eight percent were Roman Catholic, fifty-nine percent Protestant and three percent Jewish. This breakdown mirrors the Catholic-Protestant division measured by

munities in which labor leaders were born with the population at large. To overcome this difficulty a decision was made to use information on community of residence from the 1900 and 1910 Census, since the majority of officials were born within the first decade of the century. It was assumed for purposes of analysis that if census enumerators had gathered data in 1940 on "type of community born in," their figures would generally conform to the "type of community residing in" statistics reported by census takers in 1900 and 1910. Census statistics from U.S. Department of Commerce, Bureau of the Census, *Statistical Abstract of the United States, 1938* (Washington, DC, 1939), 6.
[8] Census statistics from *Statistical Abstract of the United States, 1944-45*, 144.

census takers in 1940 for the nation as a whole.[9] Almost half of the Protestant union officials were either Baptist or Methodist. Of the remaining half, fifty-five percent were members of other fundamentalist sects. Protestant labor leaders therefore were drawn primarily from the more pietistic and "low" church branches of American Protestantism.

The information compiled in *Who's Who in Labor* provides the means to determine the ethnicity of 338 officials, or approximately eighty-four percent of the sample.[10] Table IV shows that labor officials were drawn from a wide variety of ethnic groups. Unlike other American leadership groups which have been studied, their ethnic composition reflects the diversity of the nation as a whole. Unfortunately, the 1940 Census provides no means

TABLE IV
Ethnic Backgrounds of Labor's Men

Ethnic Group	Sample Number	Sample Percentage
Old Stock American	131	39
Irish-American	54	16
German-American	44	13
Jewish	34	10
Slavic-American	17	5
Italian-American	16	5
Negro	13	4
British-American	11	3
French-Canadian	10	3
Other	8	2
	338	100

[9] *Ibid.*, 68. The questionnaire used to gather information compiled in *Who's Who in Labor* asked respondents to list only their "Church Affiliation." As a result, religious information on non "Church" members was for the most part missing. This was particularly true of Jewish labor leaders.

[10] The format of *Who's Who in Labor* presented some difficulties in building a precise ethnic profile of union officials. A specific entry on "ethnic background" was not included in the questionnaire. To determine ethnicity a variety of factors were taken into consideration including religion, name, place of birth, union affiliation, father's occupation, club membership, interests and even writing. A few examples will illustrate: a union official with an obvious Italian name who belonged to several Italian-American fraternal organizations was coded as "Italian-American"; a union official not listing his religion but whose father was a rabbi was coded as "Jewish"; a state official of the Brotherhood of Sleeping Car Porters, who listed his religion as Baptist and who was active in the NAACP was coded as "Negro." In no case was only one factor, like a name, considered sufficient information to categorize an ethnic type. Where the slightest doubt existed, the individual's ethnic background was coded as "undetermined."

for a precise comparison of the profile of labor's men with the ethnic make-up of the general population.

Three hundred and seventy-seven labor leaders, or ninety-four percent of the sample, listed information on schooling. Though they reported a wide variety of educational experiences, most had not gone beyond high school. Close to one third, in fact, were only grade school graduates. In comparison to the general population, however, union officials tended to be above average in their educational backgrounds (See Table V).

TABLE V
Educational Backgrounds of Labor's Men[11]

Educational Level	Sample Number	Sample Percentage	U.S. Population Percentage (1940 Census)
Grade School	109	29	60
Some High School	25	7	
High School Graduate	115	30	30
Technical-Business School	37	10	
Some College	32	8	
College Graduate	30	8	10
Professional School Graduate	29	8	
	377	100	100

Of the sixty-nine percent of the sample who reported their political affiliations, more than sixty percent were Democrats, eight percent were Republicans, and the rest listed third party choices. Among the third party choices were parties and organizations closely allied to the national Democratic Party (the American Labor and Liberal parties of New York State and the CIO Political Action Committee). Only four leaders listed the Socialist and Communist parties. While this may not be an accurate poll of the actual political sentiments of those involved, it is clear that the great majority of labor leaders in 1945 cast their political support with the Democratic Party.

Labor leaders living and active during the Roosevelt years can be characterized by their age, sex, and race as well as their political affiliation. Union officials during this period were primarily male, white, middle-aged, and Democrats. In terms of

[11] Census statistics from *Statistical Abstract of the United States, 1944-45*, 230.

their geographical, socio-economic, religious, ethnic, and educational backgrounds, however, no one stereotype fits. Labor leaders were as diverse a group as the American population at large. Though they tended to be more urban in origins and slightly above average in their educational and socio-economic backgrounds, union officials comprised a more representative cross section of the American people than other elite or leadership groups which have been studied.[12]

The collective portrait so far presented does not deal with structural distinctions within the labor movement. For the New Deal years, the AFL-CIO split is an obvious division which demands examination. The open split began as an internal debate within the American Federation of Labor in 1934 over the interrelated issues of industrial unionism and the organization of unskilled and semiskilled workers in the nation's mass production industries. It further intensified in 1935 with the formation of a rebel AFL faction, the Committee for Industrial Organization, and became an open battle in 1936 with the expulsion of these militants from the Federation. In 1938 the rupture became formalized with the creation of a rival trade union association, the Congress of Industrial Organizations. Labor's house remained divided until the mid-1950s when the AFL and CIO finally reconciled their differences and merged into one organization.[13]

During the late Thirties and throughout much of the Forties, the AFL and the CIO engaged in a bitter internecine struggle for the control of the trade union movement and for the loyalty of American workingmen and women. During this period both

---

[12] Studies of American civic, business, military, political and educational leaders reveal socio-economic backgrounds very distinct from the population as a whole. These leadership groups tend to be disproportionately urban, well-educated, upper class, high-church Protestant, and native American. For two examples see: Richard Jensen, "Quantitative Collective Biography," in Robert Swierenga, ed., *Quantification in American History* (New York: Antheneum, 1970), and William Miller, "The Recruitment of the American Business Elite," in William Miller, ed., *Men in Business* (New York: Harper & Row, 1962).

[13] For excellent discussions of the AFL-CIO split see Walter Galenson, *The CIO Challenge to the AFL: A History of the American Labor Movement, 1935-1941* (Cambridge, MA: Harvard Univ. Press, 1960); Irving Bernstein, *Turbulent Years: A History of the American Worker, 1933-1941* (Boston: Houghton Mifflin, Co., 1971); and David Brody, "The Emergence of Mass-Production Unionism," in Robert Braemen and Everett Walters, eds., *Change and Continuity in Twentieth Century America* (Columbus, OH: Ohio State Univ. Press, 1964), 221-232.

organizations posed as the true representatives of labor; both organizations also offered significantly different programs for the future course of the American trade union movement. In contrast to the skilled labor, craft union orientation of the AFL, the CIO championed the principle of industrial unionism and actively sought to unionize unorganized workers. In contrast to the pure and simple trade union approach of the AFL, the CIO also advocated a more politically active role for labor. Finally, in contrast to their more conservative AFL counterparts, CIO leaders tended to be more militant in style and more class conscious in their rhetorical emphasis.

Beyond differences in style and trade union and political ideologies, the question arises as to how deeply split the American labor movement was during the New Deal years. Was this rupture, for instance, something more or something other than an ideological split? More specifically, were the two federations comprised of union officials who were from significantly different socio-economic or geographical backgrounds? Writing in 1948, for example, the sociologist C. Wright Mills concluded on the basis of his analysis that AFL and CIO leaders were decidedly different social types and that the "split ran deep." [14]

To measure differences between CIO and AFL union leaders, the federation affiliations of the officials sampled in this study were cross-tabulated with a number of key socio-economic background variables. The results of this analysis are presented below in Table VI. The table includes percentage breakdowns for AFL and CIO officials by age, father's occupation, ethnicity, religion, region of birth, type of community born in, and education. Below each breakdown appears a correlation coefficient to indicate the strength of association between these independent variables and the dependent factor of AFL or CIO affiliation. Levels of significance are also noted. Finally, the independent variables are listed in descending order of importance as measured by their respective strengths of correlation.

The figures in Table VI reveal that none of the independent variables correlate very strongly with either AFL or CIO affiliation. Knowing a particular leader's socio-economic background provides little clue to which federation he belonged. Only two

[14] Mills, Chap. 4, *passim.*

TABLE VI
Correlates of AFL and CIO Affiliation[15]

Age

	Sample Number	Under 45	Over 45
AFL	191	35%	65
CIO	187	65	35

Contingency Coefficient C=.28
Significance=.00

Father's Occupation

	Sample Number	White Collar	Skilled Worker	Semi or Unskilled Worker	Farmer
AFL	167	29%	28	19	24
CIO	159	31	16	37	16

Contingency Coefficient C=.23
Significance=.00

Ethnicity[16]

	Sample Number	Old Stock American	Old Immigrant Stock	New Immigrant Stock
AFL	160	43%	38	19
CIO	167	33	37	30

Contingency Coefficient C=.14
Significance=.03

Religion

	Sample Number	Protestant	Roman Catholic	Not Given
AFL	197	47%	23	30
CIO	193	35	31	34

Contingency Coefficient C=.12
Significance =.06

---

[15] Contingency Coefficient C was used as a measurement of association for these tables since the dependent variable was unordered categorically and independent variables were either ordered or unordered categorically. Contingency Coefficient C ranges in value from 0 to 1 (from 0 to .707 in the case of 2 x 2 tables); high values indicate strong relationship between independent variables and either CIO or AFL affiliation. Percentage breakdowns reveal which affiliation is associated with the independent variables. The level of significance is the probability that no pattern exists among all 3500 people in *Who's Who in Labor*.

[16] Ethnic categories were regrouped to create a more manageable 2 x 3 table. Old Immigrant Stock category includes Irish-American, British-American, German-American, Scandinavian-American and French-American. New Immigrant Stock includes Jewish, Slavic-American, Italian-American, Negro and Spanish-American.

TABLE VI (continued)

Region of Birth[17]

	Sample Number	New England	Middle Atlantic	Midwest	South	West	Foreign Born
AFL	197	7%	19	29	23	7	15
CIO	190	5	27	27	21	5	15

Significance=.47
Contingency Coefficient C=.11

Type of Community Born In

	Sample Number	Rural-Small Town	Large Town	Small City	Large City
AFL	179	43%	19	10	28
CIO	172	36	17	13	34

Contingency Coefficient C=.09
Significance=.37

Education

	Sample Number	Elementary	High School	Advanced
AFL	184	38%	29	33
CIO	184	34	31	35

Contingency Coefficient C=.04
Significance=.74

factors, age and father's occupation, show moderately strong correlations and noticeably different distributions between the two organizations. From the percentage breakdowns, it is clear that CIO officials were younger than their AFL counterparts. The statistics on father's occupation are less straightforward. While the proportions of leaders having white collar fathers are equivalent among those from blue collar backgrounds, AFL men had more skilled fathers while CIO fathers tended to be semi or unskilled workers. The ill-defined occupational category of "farmer" further complicates these results.

In terms of ethnicity, religion, education, types of communities born in, and region of birth, there seems to be little to distinguish AFL leaders from CIO leaders. The results of this analysis then suggest that except for age and possibly socio-economic origins

---

[17] The correlations for union affiliation with region of birth, type of community born in and education definitely fail to pass significance tests at the acceptable .05 level. This means that for all three correlations the chances are great that the null hypothesis would hold for the larger population of labor leaders from which our sample was drawn. The failure to pass significance tests here represents a positive result confirming the argument that the differences between CIO and AFL leaders in terms of their socio-economic backgrounds were not great.

as measured by father's occupation, CIO and AFL leaders were not dissimilar social types. It would be difficult to concur with C. Wright Mills' judgment that the AFL-CIO split "ran deep." If this split is to be understood as something more or something other than an ideological struggle, then the CIO-AFL age differential can be considered significant. In this vein the CIO challenge to the AFL represented not only an ideological challenge but a generational one as well.

The foregoing analysis has aimed at evaluating AFL and CIO union officials as social types. The conclusion that these leaders were men and women of basically similar social backgrounds does not deny the fact that they might have been different in temperament and personality. Information contained in *Who's Who in Labor* does provide a limited means for assessing behavorial distinctions. Cross-tabulating a number of additional variables in this study with union affiliation reveals that AFL leaders tended to be more conservative than their CIO counterparts in their political preferences, club orientation, amount and type of public activity, and even on the question of ethnic intermarriage.

CIO leaders, for instance, were more active in third party politics. They were apt to be involved in labor related public activities. AFL leaders, on the other hand, participated in civic and charity work to a greater extent and joined social clubs, especially fraternal lodges like the Elks and Moose. Finally, CIO leaders married outside of their particular ethnic group with greater frequency. It must be emphasized, though, that aside from political preference, none of these variables were above the C=.18 level of correlation. The results of this analysis then lend support to the generally accepted notion of historians and journalists that AFL leaders during the New Deal years were more conservative in orientation than their CIO analogues, yet the actual figures indicate that the phrase "slightly more conservative" would be a more accurate description.

The growth of the AFL and the formation of the CIO during the New Deal years created many new positions of leadership within the union movement. While AFL and CIO officials comprised a fairly representative cross section of the American population and were basically similar social and behavioral types, the question arises as to whether labor's men divided along leadership lines. Were national officers, for instance, different from local officials, perhaps better educated or more upper class in origins? The question is an important one for the answer will reveal how "open" the union movement was during the Roosevelt years, and whether promotion for an individual within the labor hierarchy was determined by ascriptive priorities.

To examine this question in detail, an index of level of leadership was created. This index separated local and state labor officials from their national counterparts and was cross-tabulated with a number of key variables for the sample as a whole. The process was then repeated controlling for AFL and CIO affiliation to see whether the two federations differed in their promotion practices. The results of this analysis are presented below in an encapsulated form without the lengthy percentage breakdowns. Table VII lists the independent variables in descending order of importance for labor's men as a whole. The separate correlations for AFL and CIO officials are also included, and levels of statistical significance are given in parentheses.

TABLE VII
Correlates of Levels of Leadership[18]

Variable	Labor's Men	AFL	CIO
Place of Birth	.12 (.30)	.13 (.63)	.14 (.55)
Type of Community Born In	.12 (.16)	.09 (.67)	.20 (.05)
Political Affiliation	.11 (.20)	.19 (.10)	.04 (.88)
Religion	.11 (.10)	.17 (.04)	.14 (.13)
Age	.08 (.14)	.05 (.63)	.13 (.09)
Father's Occupation	.07 (.67)	.07 (.82)	.12 (.50)
Ethnicity	.06 (.49)	.11 (.36)	.13 (.25)
Education	.06 (.48)	.09 (.51)	.15 (.10)

The measurements of association and levels of significance reported in Table VII indicate that *no* variable correlates strongly with levels of leadership. For labor's men as a whole, none of the correlation coefficients are above $C=.12$. Similarly, all correlations fail to attain the acceptable .05 level of statistical significance. Put in simple terms, this means that knowing an official's

---

[18] The measurement of association used in Table IX is Contingency Coefficient C. See footnote 15 for explanation.

age, political affiliation, or religious, ethnic, educational, geographical or socio-economic background is a poor predictor of what position that individual occupied in the union hierarchy. College educated men, for instance, were as likely to be local officials as they were to hold national offices. Similarly, children of semiskilled and unskilled workers were as likely to be in high echelon positions as in low leadership posts.

When AFL and CIO officials are analyzed separately, only the type of community born in proved to be a moderately strong and statistically significant predictor of level of leadership. CIO union officials born in large cities were more likely to become national level leaders. Conversely, local leaders were typically born in rural areas or small towns. This variable was not a distinguishing factor in the AFL. The pattern found here undoubtedly reflects the predominantly urban roots and orientation of the CIO.[19]

The foregoing analysis indicates that there were only slight differences between national labor leaders and their local and state counterparts, both within the AFL and the CIO. This finding, then, suggests that the American trade union movement during the New Deal years was remarkably open and pluralistic in its promotion practices. Whether American trade unions and trade union federations were as open and democratic in their decision-making processes is, of course, another question which does not concern us here. With respect to promotion, the record of the American labor movement during the Roosevelt years is impressive. It would be difficult to cite another institution in American society during this period in which leadership status was so unrelated to ascriptive priorities.

The New Deal years witnessed the emergence of organized labor as a powerful force in American society. With growth came the recruitment and promotion of thousands of men and women

---

[19] The results reported in Table VII permit us the opportunity to qualify two hypotheses advanced by C. Wright Mills. In *New Men of Power* (72-73), Mills argued that the power structure of the AFL rested on an age hirarchy. In contrast, he characterized the CIO as an educational hierarchy with the more educated occupying the upper ranks of authority. The very low correlation between age and levels of leadership in the AFL as well as the almost random nature of that measurement strongly suggest that age was not a salient determinant of power in AFL unions. Similarly, the correlation of education and level of leadership for CIO officials is weak and not statistically significant.

to fill new leadership posts. The finding that labor officials active during the Roosevelt years were a diverse group and representative of the American people suggests that recruitment into leadership positions was open and pluralistic. The low correlation between levels of leadership and socio-economic background further indicates that promotion practices were equally democratic. Finally, the fact that AFL and CIO leaders were basically similar social and behavioral types calls for an emphasis on ideological factors in gaining an understanding of the union movement during this period. These findings should prove of use to both historians and sociologists interested in the structural dynamics of the labor movement during its most crucial period of development.

Not So "Turbulent Years": Another Look at the American 1930's

Melvyn Dubofsky

ABSTRACT

In sharp contrast to most descriptions and analyses of American workers and their labor movement during the 1930's, which stress the turbulence and conflict of the depression decade, this essay explores the passivity beneath the turbulent surface of violent events as well as the persistence of many depression era beliefs and behavioral patterns among American workers. In order to understand why industrial conflicts of the 1930's in the United States and the labor upheaval which created the CIO failed to produce a durable mass radical, or socialist, working-class movement, it is necessary to understand that the vast majority of American workers were never themselves involved directly in labor conflict or violent events. It is equally important to comprehend precisely how underlying values and modes of behavior diluted working-class radicalism. Moreover, one must be aware of how Franklin D. Roosevelt's New Deal defused radical politics in the United States and also served as the American equivalent of North European social democracy. Finally, the essay suggests that a distinction must be drawn between class struggle as an historical reality and workers as a class subjectively aware of their historical role as agents of revolution or radical change.

Our conventional view of the 1930's was aptly caught in the title of Irving Bernstein's history of American labor during that decade, *Turbulent Years,* a title that the author borrowed from Myron Taylor's annual report to the Board of Directors of the United States Steel Corporation in 1938. That liberal historians and corporate executives perceive the 1930's as a "turbulent" decade should today occasion no surprise. For the American business elite especially, their social, economic, and political world had turned upside down during the Great Depression and New Deal. After nearly a full decade of corporate hegemony, class collaboration, and trade union retreat, the United States during the 1930's seemed chronically beset with class conflict, violence, and ubiquitous labor radicalism. In the words of one of the decade's radicals, Len DeCaux, a "new consciousness" awakened workers from lethargy. "There was light after the darkness in the youth of the movement," exulted DeCaux. "Youth that was direct and bold in action, not sluggish and sly from long compromise with the old and the rotten. There was light in the hopeful future seen by the red and the rebellious, now playing their full part in what they held to be a great working-class advance against the capitalist class. There was light, and a heady, happy feeling in the solidarity of common struggle in a splendid common cause."[1]

The picture one has of the 1930's, then, whether painted by a liberal scholar such as Bernstein, an activist like DeCaux, or a tycoon like Taylor, is of conflict and struggle. The foreground is filled with militant and radical workers, the masses in motion, a rank and file vigorously, sometimes violently, reaching out to grasp control over its own labor and existence.

Given the conventional portrait of the American 1930's, conventional questions arise, the most obvious of which are the following: 1) Why did labor militancy decline? 2) Why did militant, radical rank-and-file struggles produce old-fashioned, autocratically controlled trade unions in many cases? 3) Why did the turbulence create no lasting, mass radical political movement?

[1] Len DeCaux, *Labor Radical* (Boston, 1970), p. 230.

Before seeking to answer such questions, even assuming they are the best ones to ask about the thirties, I am reminded of a lesson contained in an American cartoon strip. A caveman reporter informs his stone-age editor that he has both good news and bad news. "Let's have the bad news first,"says the editor. "There's only good news," responds the reporter. Need I add that American journalists had a field day during the 1930's and that their editors rejoiced in an abundance of "bad news;" frontpage headlines shrieked class war and wire photos depicted strikers in armed conflict with police and troops.

But were class war and violent pitched battles the reality of the 1930's? And, if they were, how do we explain the absence of a mass radical political movement?

Frankly, all of us realize how difficult it is to create or grasp historical reality. As historians, we work with the available evidence, always, to be sure, seeking to discover more about the past, but always aware that the *total* record of what happened is beyond our recall or recreation. Ultimately, then, just as man through his thoughts and actions makes history, historians, in the process of research and writing, create their own history.

In examining the 1930's, how should we go about creating the history of that era? Two convenient models are at hand. In one we can seek lessons for the present in an instrumental view of the past. That approach suggests the might-have-beens of history. If only Communists had behaved differently; if nonsectarian radicals had pursued the proper policies; if the militant rank and file had been aware of its true interests (as distinguished from the false consciousness inculcated by trade-union bureaucrats and New Deal Democrats); then the history of the 1930's would have been different and *better*.[2] The second approach to our turbulent decade has been suggested by David Brody. "The interesting questions," writes Brody, "are not in the realm of what might have been, but in a closer examination of what did happen."[3] Brody's approach, I believe, promises greater rewards for scholars and may even be more useful for those who desire to use the past to improve the present and shape the future. As Karl Marx noted in *The Eighteenth Brumaire,* man indeed makes his own history, but only "under circumstances directly encountered, given and transmitted from the past. The tradition of all the dead generations weighs like a nightmare on the brain of the living."[4]

One more preliminary observation must be made about recreating the past in general and the American 1930's in particular. We must be zealously on guard against falling victim to what Edward Thompson has characterized as the "Pilgrim's Progress" orthodoxy, an approach that, in his words, "reads history in the light of subsequent preoccupations, and not in fact as it occurred. Only the successful [. . .] are remembered. The blind alleys, the lost causes, and the losers themselves are forgotten."[5] In light of what I intend to say below and also what such theorists of "corporate liberalism" as Ronald Radosh and James Weinstein have written about the history of the American labor movement, it is well to bear in mind

---

[2] Staughton Lynd, "The Possibility of Radicalism in the Early 1930's: The case of Steel," *Radical America,* VI (Nov.-Dec. 1972), 37–64; *idem.,* "Guerilla History in Gary," LIBERATION, XIV (Oct. 1969), 17–20; for a revised version of Lynd's views of the 1930's, one more in consonance with what actually happened, not what might have been, see "The United Front in America: A Note," *Radical America,* VIII (July–Aug. 1974), 29–37.

[3] David Brody, "Labor and the Great Depression: The Interpretive Prospects," *Labor History,* XIII (Spring 1972), 231–244; *idem.,* "Radical Labor History and Rank-and-File Militancy," *ibid.,* XVI (Winter 1975), 122.

[4] Karl Marx and Frederick Engels, *Selected Works* (London, 1968), p. 97.

[5] E. P. Thompson, *The Making of the English Working Class* (London, 1965), p. 12.

Thompson's comment that history written as the record of victors and survivors is not necessarily synonomous with the past as experienced by all of those who lived it and created it.[6]

I

Let us now see if we can uncover or glimpse the reality of the American 1930's. Certainly, the turbulence, militancy, and radicalism of the decade existed. From 1929 through 1939, the American economic and social system remained in crisis. Despite two substantial recoveries from the depths of depression, unemployment during the decade never fell below 14 per cent of the civilian labor force or 21 per cent of the nonagricultural work force.[7] Those workers who once believed in the American myth of success, who dreamed of inching up the occupational ladder, acquiring property of their own, and watching their children do even better occupationally and materially, had their hopes blasted by the Great Depression. As Stephan Thernstrom's research shows for Boston, the Great Depression thwarted occupational and material advancement for an entire generation of workers.[8] And what was true in Boston most likely prevailed elsewhere in the nation. If, in the past, American workers had experienced marginal upward social and economic mobility, during the 1930's they could expect to fall rather more often than to climb.

The thwarted aspirations of millions of workers combined with persistent mass unemployment produced a decade of social unrest that encompassed every form of collective and individual action from mass marches to food looting. One historian has pointed out that between February 1930 and July 1932, at least seventeen separate incidents of violent protest occurred. In Chicago in 1931, after three persons were killed during an anti-eviction struggle, 60,000 citizens marched on City Hall to protest police brutality. Indeed in nearly every city in which the unemployed organized and protested, violent confrontations with the police erupted.[9]

More important and more threatening to the established order than protests by the unemployed and hungry, which punctuated the early depression years, were the more conventional forms of class struggle which erupted with greater incidence after the election of Franklin Roosevelt and the coming of the New Deal. In 1934, after twelve years of relative quiet on the labor front, industrial conflict broke out with a militancy and violence not seen

[6] Ronald Radosh, "The Corporate Ideology of American Labor Leaders from Gompers to Hillman," In James Weinstein and David W. Eakins, eds., *For a New America* (New York, 1970), pp. 125–152; R. Radosh, *American Labor and United States Foreign Policy* (New York, 1969), pp. 18–29; James Weinstein, *The Corporate Ideal in the Liberal State* (Boston, 1968).

[7] Stanley Lebergott, *Manpower in American Economic Growth* (New York, 1964), p. 512.

[8] Stephan Thernstrom, *The Other Bostonians* (Cambridge, Mass., 1973), pp. 56, 59, 90, 203, 207, 233, 240, 249.

[9] Bernard Sternsher, *Hitting Home: The Great Depression in Town and Country* (Chicago, 1970), p. 10; John A. Garraty, "Radicalism in the Great Depression," in *Essays on Radicalism in Contemporary America,* ed., Leon B. Blair (Austin, 1972), p. 89; Roy Rosenzweig, "Radicals and the Jobless: The Musteites and the Unemployed Leagues, 1932–1936," *Labor History,* XVI (Winter 1975), 52–77; Daniel J. Leab, "United We Eat: The Creation and Organization of the Unemployed Councils in 1930," *Labor History,* VIII (Fall 1967), 300–315.

Melvyn Dubofsky

ince 1919. In Toledo, Ohio, National Guardsmen tear-gassed and drove from the city's
treets Auto-Lite Company strikers who had the support not only of the radical A. J. Muste's
American Workers party and Unemployed League, but also of the citywide central labor
ouncil, an A. F. of L. affiliate. And the following month, July 1934, witnessed still more
violent struggles. A strike by maritime workers in the San Francisco Bay area brought battles
between police and longshoremen, several dead strikers, and the dispatch of state troops. In
protest, the San Francisco central labor council declared a citywide general strike for July 16.
Here, too, a labor radical, Harry Bridges, an Australian immigrant and a Marxist, led a strike
unsanctioned by the A. F. of L. Only a day after the San Francisco general strike ended,
Americans read in their newspapers of July 21 that on the previous day in Minneapolis,
Minnesota, fifty men had been shot in the back as police fired on strikers. Within a week of
the bloody July 20 battle between police and teamsters in the city's main square, Minnesota
Governor Floyd Olson placed the Twin Cities under martial law. Once again, in Minneapolis,
as earlier in Toledo and San Francisco, left-wing radicals led the strike, in this instance the
Trotskyists, Farrell Dobbs and the brothers Vincent, Miles, Grant, and Ray Dunne. And only
a week after the shootings in Minneapolis, on July 28, 1934, deputy sheriffs in the company
town of Kohler, Wisconsin killed one person and injured twenty in what the New York *Times*
characterized as a "strike riot."[10]

Few areas of the nation seemed untouched by labor militancy in 1934. In the spring a
national textile strike called by the United Textile Workers of America brought out 350,000
workers from Maine to Alabama, and violent repression of the strikers proved the rule in the
south's Piedmont mill towns. Throughout the spring auto and steel workers flocked into
trade unions, like coal miners the previous year, seeming almost to organize themselves. And
when auto manufacturers and steel barons refused to bargain with labor, national strikes
threatened both industries. Only direct presidential intervention and the equivocal actions of
A. F. of L. leaders averted walkouts in autos and steel.[11]

If 1934, in Irving Bernstein's chapter title amounted to an "Eruption," 1937 experienced
an epidemic of strikes. The year began with the famous Flint sit-down strike in which the
United Auto Workers conquered General Motors; saw United States Steel surrender to the
Steel Workers Organizing Committee (SWOC)-CIO without a struggle less than three weeks
after the General Motors strike ended; and culminated in the late spring with perhaps the
most violent and bloodiest national strike of the decade: the Little Steel conflict that led to the
Memorial Day "massacre" outside Republic Steel's South Chicago plant. In between Flint
and Little Steel, more than 400,000 workers participated in 477 sit-down strikes. Twenty-five
sit-downs erupted in January 1937, forty-seven in February, and 170 in March. "Sitting
down has replaced baseball as a national passtime," quipped *Time* Magazine.[12]

The labor militancy and strikes of 1934 and 1937 created a solidarity that hitherto eluded
American workers. During the 1930's, it seemed, the United States had developed a true
proletariat, more united by its similarities than divided by its differences. Mass immigration
had ended in 1921, and hence the last immigrant generation had had more than a decade to

Irving Bernstein, *Turbulent Years* (Boston, 1969), Ch. 6 remains the best description of the 1934
"Eruption." New York *Times*, July 17, 20, 21, 27, 28, 1934.
S. Lynd, "The Possibility of Radicalism," pp. 38–40, 49–51; Sidney Fine, *The Automobile under the Blue Eagle* (Ann Arbor, 1963), pp. 298–315.
Sidney Fine, *Sit-Down: The General Motors Strike of 1936–1937* (Ann Arbor, 1969), p. 331.

integrate itself into the social system and for its children to have been "Americanized" by the public schools and other intermediate social agencies. Male-female role conflicts appeared notable by their absence, and strikers' wives provided their husbands with substantial assistance as members of women's auxiliaries. "I found a common understanding and unselfishness I'd never known in my life," wrote the wife of one Flint sit-downer. "I'm living for the first time with a definite goal. [. . .] Just being a woman isn't enough any more. I want to be a human being with the right to think for myself."[13] "A new type of woman was born in the strike," noted an observer of the struggle in Flint. "Women who only yesterday were horrified at unionism, who felt inferior to the task of speaking, leading, have, as if overnight, become the spearhead in the battle for unionism."[14]

Even racial tensions among workers seemed to diminish during the 1930's, especially after the emergence of the CIO whose "new unionists" often crusaded for civil rights as vigorously as for trade unionism. The changes wrought by CIO led two students of black labor to conclude in 1939 "that it is easier to incorporate Negroes into a new movement [. . .] than to find a secure place in an older one." Surveying the impact of depression, New Deal, and CIO on black workers, Horace Cayton and George S. Mitchell suggested that

in the readjustment of social patterns and ideologies, we find reflected a profound transition in Negro life as well as in the economic outlook of American workers generally. What has been for generations a racial stratification in occupations is, under present-day conditions, in process of transformation. Class tensions and class solidarity have measureably relaxed racial tensions and, by so doing, have mitigated the divisive effects of racial antagonism.[15]

One must not, however, romanticize working-class solidarity and thus lose sight of the tensions that continued to pit American workers during the 1930's against each other rather than a common enemy. In New Haven, Connecticut, American-born workers still denigrated Italians as "wops," and "it's dog eat dog all right," retorted an Italian-American machinist "but it's also Mick feeds Mick!"[16] A Hollywood film of the late 1930's, *Black Legion*, starring Humphrey Bogart as a frustrated white American-born Protestant machinist, captured the still lingering resentment harbored by the American-born against the foreign-born (and even their children), and depicted the sort of worker more likely to listen to Father Coughlin than to John L. Lewis, Franklin D. Roosevelt, or perhaps William Z. Foster. Or, listen to an official of an A. F. of L. union with jurisdiction in an industry that employed many Afro-Americans. "I consider the Negroes poor union men. You know as well as I do that they are shiftless, easily intimidated and generally of poor caliber. [. . .] What should have happened is what is being done in Calhoun County, Illinois, where Negroes are not allowed to stay overnight. As a result there are no Negroes there and no Negro problem."[17]

But it was the CIO, not the A. F. of L., that symbolized the labor upheaval of the 1930's. And in 1937 when CIO organized autos, steel, rubber, and other former bastions of the open shop, between three and a half and four million workers joined the labor movement, a larger number than the entire A. F. of L. claimed as of January 1, 1937. Now, for the first time in its

[13] *Ibid.*, p. 201.

[14] *Ibid.*

[15] Horace R. Cayton and George S. Mitchell, *Black Workers and the New Unions* (Chapel Hill, 1939), vi, viii.

[16] E. Wight Bakke, *The Unemployed Worker* (New Haven, 1940), p. 87.

[17] Cayton and Mitchell, *Black Workers*, p. 268.

history, organized labor in America wielded power in the strategic core of mass-production industry, and it did so under the aegis of a labor federation (CIO) whose leaders consciously repudiated the A. F. of L. tradition of class accomodation and collaboration. The CIO during the late 1930's exemplified solidarity rather than exclusiveness, political action in place of nonpartisanship, biracialism and bisexualism instead of racial and sexual chauvinism, and militancy rather than opportunism. "CIO started as a new kind of labor movement," recalled Len DeCaux in his autobiography. "A challenge to the old AFL and the status quo it complacently guarded. It was new in its youth and fervor, new in the broad sector of the working class it brought into action, new in the way it accepted and integrated its radicals, new in its relative independence of corporate and government control, new in its many social and political attitudes."[18]

DeCaux was not alone among radicals in looking to CIO as the instrument through which to build a new America. Powers Hapgood, the Harvard-educated son of a wealthy Midwestern family, who worked as a coal miner in order to share the worker's plight, felt compelled in 1935 to seek an accomodation with his ancient enemy John L. Lewis, who was then organizing the CIO. "It's surprising how many radicals think I ought to see Lewis," Hapgood informed his wife, "saying it's much less of a compromise to make peace with him and stay in the labor movement than it is to get a government job and cease to be active in the class struggle." To reject a reconciliation with Lewis in 1935, concluded Hapgood, would let the leftwing down.[19] After the CIO's first national conference in Atlantic City in October 1937, Adolph Germer, a former ally of Hapgood and then a Social Democrat evolving into a New Deal Democrat, wrote to an ex-associate in the Socialist Party of America: "I attended the Atlantic City conference and I assure you it was an educational treat. There was as much difference between that meeting and the A. F. of L. conventions I have attended as there is between night and day."[20] And Lee Pressman and Gardner Jackson, the former an ex-Communist and the latter a left-wing, socialist-inclined reformer, both of whom worked closely with Lewis from 1936 through 1940, observed that Lewis seemed a changed man in 1937, that the CIO experience had transformed him from "a labor boss of the most conventional kind, and a discredited one at that" into an eager, dedicated leader of a movement encompassing blue- and white-collar workers, farmers, small professionals and all sorts of "little people." Lewis, Pressman and Jackson believed in 1937, might well lead an independent populist or farmer-labor political movement in the event Roosevelt and the Democrats failed to implement full-employment policies and a welfare state.[21]

Had Lewis decided to lead such an independent political movement, the time never seemed riper. The Great Depression and the New Deal had wrought a veritable political revolution among American workers. Masses of hitherto politically apathetic workers, especially among first-generation immigrants and their spouses, went to the polls in greater numbers. And Roosevelt broke the last links that bound millions of workers across the

---

[18] L. DeCaux, *Labor Radical*, p. 303.

[19] Powers Hapgood to Sweetheart, July 24, 1935, Powers Hapgood Papers, Lilly Library, Indiana University, Bloomington, Indiana.

[20] Adolph Germer to Harry Hauser, Oct. 29, 1937, Adolph Germer Papers, Box 4, State Historical Society of Wisconsin, Madison.

[21] Gardner Jackson, *Columbia Oral History Collection*, pp. 727–728; Lee Pressman, COHC, pp. 96–97.

industrial heartland from Pittsburgh to Chicago to the Republican party.[22] Lewis exulted at the results of the 1936 election in which for the first time since the depression of the 1890's, Democrats swept into power in the steel and coal towns of Pennsylvania and Ohio, winning office on tickets financed by CIO money and headed by CIO members. A new consciousness appeared to be stirring among the nation's industrial workers. A social scientist sampling attitudes and beliefs among Akron rubber workers at the end of the 1930's discovered that the vast majority of CIO members valued human rights above property rights and showed little respect or deference for the prerogatives and privileges of corporate property. Akron's workers, and also many residents characterized as middle class, apparently distinguished between purely personal use-property and property as capital, which afforded its possessors power over the lives and labor of the propertyless.[24] Such an altered consciousness fed the dreams of Popular Fronters and third-party activists.

All this ferment, militancy, radicalism, violence, and perhaps even an altered working-class consciousness were part of American reality during the 1930's. Yet, as we know, American socialism expired during the depression decade, communism advanced only marginally, Roosevelt seduced the farmer-laborites and populists, the CIO came to resemble the A. F. of L., and John L. Lewis once again reverted to behaving like a "labor boss of the most conventional kind." Why? To answer that question we have to examine other aspects of social, economic, and political reality during the 1930's.

III

Just as one can claim that the 1930's represented a crisis for American capitalism that expressed itself most overtly in the eagerness and militancy with which workers challenged their corporate masters, one might just as easily assert that for most Americans, workers included, events during the decade reinforced their faith in the "justness" of the American system and the prospects for improvement without fundamental restructuring. For many workers capitalism never collapsed; indeed, for those employed steadily, always a substantial proportion of the work force, real wages actually rose as prices fell. For other workers, the tentative economic recovery of 1933–34 and the more substantial growth of 1937 rekindled faith in the American system. The two great strike waves of the decade, 1934 and 1937, erupted not in moments of crisis, but when hope, profits, employment, and wages all revived. Crisis, in other words, induced apathy or lethargy; economic recovery, a sign that the system worked, stimulated action. And when the recovery of 1936–37 was followed by the "Roosevelt depression," a more rapid and deeper decline than the Great Crash of 1929–33, the number of strikes diminished markedly and the more militant CIO affiliates concentrated in the massproduction industries suffered severe membership and financial losses.[25] Perhaps

---

[22] See Paul Kleppner, *The Cross of Culture: A Social Analysis of Midwestern Politics* (New York, 1970), Chs. 5 and 7, and Richard J. Jensen, *The Winning of the Midwest* (Chicago, 1971), Chs. 9–10.

[23] "Notes on CIO Meeting, November 7–8, 1938," Katherine Pollack Ellickson Papers, microfilm, Franklin D. Roosevelt Library, Hyde Park.

[24] Alfred Winslow Jones, *Life, Liberty, and Property* (Philadelphia, 1941), pp. 250–279, 350–351, 354.

[25] Walter Galenson, *The CIO Challenge to the AFL* (Cambridge, Mass., 1960), p. 585; Philip Taft, *The A. F. of L. from the Death of Gompers to the Merger*, (New York, 1959), pp. 199–200; W. Jett Lauck Diary, Dec. 13, 1937, W. Jett Lauck Papers, University of Virginia Library; John Frey to W. A. Appleton, Apr. 13 and Aug. 1, 1938, John Frey Papers, Box 1, File 8, Library of Congress.

this final crisis of the depression decade left unresolved might have snapped whatever bonds still tied workers to the American system. That, however, remains a problematic historical might-have-been, as the coming of World War II resolved the contradictions in American capitalism and substituted patriotic unity for class conflict.

An analysis of the statistics of working-class militancy during the 1930's – the incidence of strikes, the number of workers affected, the man – days lost – also leads to divergent interpretations. One can stress the high level of strike activity, the fact that only 840 strikes were recorded in 1932 but 1700 erupted in 1933, 1856 in 1934, 2200 in 1936, and in the peak strike year, 1937, 4740 broke out.[26] One can argue that no area of the nation and, more importantly, no major industry escaped industrial conflict. For the first time in United States history strikes affected every major mass-production industry and paralyzed the towering heights of the economy: steel, auto, rubber, coal, electrical goods; the list goes on and on. For the nation and its workers, the 1930's were indeed "turbulent years."

But the statistics of industrial conflict reveal another story, an equally interesting one. When the 1934 strike wave erupted, President Roosevelt sought to understand its origins and implications. He asked the Commissioner of Labor Statistics, Isidore Lubin, to analyze and interpret the 1934 outbreak. Lubin prepared a report that he transmitted to the President in late August 1934. Seeking to place the 1934 strikes in historical perspective, Lubin acted logically. He compared what had happened in the first half of 1934 to the last previous year in which the United States had experienced such massive labor militancy, 1919. And he concluded that the 1934 strike wave could not match 1919 in intensity, duration, or number of workers involved. More than twice as many strikes began each month in the first half of 1919, reported Lubin, than in the same period in 1934; moreover, more than two and a half times as many workers were involved in the 1919 strikes. He then proceeded to assure the President that July 1934, the month of the San Francisco and Minneapolis general strikes, witnessed no mass working-class upheaval. Only seventenths of one percent, or seven out of every thousand wage earners, participated in strikes. Only four-tenths of one per cent of man-days of employment were lost as a result of strikes. "In other words," Lubin reassured the President, "for every thousand man-days worked four were lost because of strikes." Selecting ten major industries for analysis, Lubin observed that only one-half of one per cent of the total number employed struck in July 1934. "Comparing the number employed with the number actually involved in strikes, one reaches the conclusion that for every thousand workers employed in those industries only five were affected by strikes. In terms of the number of man-days lost [. . .] it is estimated that for every thousand man-days worked [. . .] seven days of employment were lost because of strikes." And, in a final note of reassurance for the President, Lubin observed that the "recent strikes have been relatively short lived," less than half as long as the average duration during 1927 (24 compared to 51 days), a time of labor peace.[27]

But what of 1937, the decade's premier strike year, when more than twice as many workers struck as in 1934? Well, according to official statistics, only 7.2 per cent of employed

---

[6] See, for Example, James R. Green, "Working Class Militancy in the Depression," *Radical America*, VI (Nov.–Dec. 1972), 2–3.

[7] Isidore Lubin, Memorandum to the President, August 29, 1934, Franklin D. Roosevelt Papers, OF407B, Box 10, Roosevelt Library.

workers were involved in walkouts (practically the same percentage as in 1934) and their absence from work represented only 0.043 per cent of all time worked.[28]

Questions immediately arise from a reading of such strike statistics. What was the other 93 per cent of the labor force doing during the great strike waves of 1934 and 1937? More important, how were they affected by the upsurge of industrial conflicts which did not involve or affect them directly?

Such questions are especially important when one bears in mind the continental size of the United States. Geography could, and did, easily dilute the impact of industrial conflict nationally. The United States lacked a London, Paris, Berlin, or Rome, where massive, militant strikes affected the national state directly as well as private employers. Few of the major strikes of the 1930's occurred even in state capitals, most of which were isolated from industrial strife. When teamsters tied up Minneapolis and longshoremen closed down San Francisco in July 1934, truckers continued to deliver goods in Chicago and Los Angeles, and waterfront workers remained on the job in New York, Baltimore, and San Pedro. For trade unionists and radicals it was exceedingly difficult, as Roy Rosenzweig has shown for A. J. Muste's Unemployed League, to transform well-structured local and regional organizations into equally effective national bodies.[29] Just as the millions of unemployed during the 1930's did not experience the shock of joblessness simultaneously, so, too, different workers experienced industrial conflict at different times and in different places. As we will see below, what workers most often experienced in common – participation in the American political system – was precisely what most effectively diluted militancy and radicalism.

Despite the continental size and diversity of the American nation, it is possible to glimpse aspects of working-class reality in local settings that disclose uniformities in belief and behavior which do much to explain the dearth of durable radicalism in the United States. We are fortunate that two truly excellent, perceptive sociological field studies were completed during the 1930's that dissect the social structure and culture of two characteristic smaller American industrial cities. We are even more fortunate that the two cities investigated – Muncie, Indiana, and New Haven, Connecticut – proved so unlike in their economic structures, population mixes, and regional and cultural milieus. Muncie was dominated by two industries – Ball Glass and General Motors – characterized by an almost totally American-born, white Protestant population, and situated in the heartland of American agriculture, individualism, and evangelical Protestantism. Hew Haven, by contrast, claimed no dominant employers, encompassed a population differentiated by nationality, race, and religion as well as class, and was set in a region traditionally urban (also urbane) and non-evangelical in culture. Yet after one finishes reading Robert and Helen Lynd on Muncie and E. Wight Bakke on New Haven, one is more impressed by the similarities rather than the differences in working-class attitudes and behavior.[30]

Let us examine Muncie first. The Lynds had initially gone to Muncie in the mid-1920's in order to discover how urbanization and industrialization had affected American culture, how the city and the factory had altered beliefs and behavioral patterns developed in the country

---

[28] Calculated from *Historical Statistics of the United States, Colonial Times to 1957* (Washington, 1960), Series D 764–778, p. 99.

[29] R. Rosenzweig, "Radicals and the Jobless," p. 60.

[30] E. Wight Bakke, *The Unemployed Worker,* and *Citizens Without Work* (New Haven, 1940); Robert S. and Helen M. Lynd, *Middletown in Transition* (New York, 1937).

and on the farm.[31] They returned a decade later in order to see what impact, if any, the "Great Depression" had had on local culture and behavior. Surprisingly, for them at least, they found labor organization weaker in 1935 than it had been in 1925, yet the Muncie business class seemed more united and more determined than ever to keep its city open shop (nonunion). The Lynds discovered objectively greater class, stratification in 1935 than in 1925 and even less prospect for the individual worker to climb up the ladder of success (see Thernstrom on Boston's depression generation workers for similar findings), yet they characterized Muncie's workers as being influenced by "drives [. . .] largely those of the business class: both are caught up in the tradition of a rising standard of living and lured by the enticements of salesmanship." As one Middletown woman informed the sociologists: "Most of the families that I know are after the same things today that they were after before the depression, and they'll get them the same way – on credit."[32]

Union officials told the Lynds a similar tale of woe. Union members preferred buying gas for their cars to paying dues, and going for a drive to attending a union meeting. Local workers were willing to beg, borrow, or steal to maintain possession of their cars and keep them running. Despite seven years of depression, Muncie's workers, according to the Lynds, still worshipped the automobile as the symbol of the American dream, and, as long as they owned one, considered themselves content.[33]

"Fear, resentment, insecurity and disillusionment has been to Middletown's workers largely an *individual* experience for each worker," concluded the Lynds,

> and not a thing generalized by him into a 'class' experience.
> Such militancy as it generates tends to be sporadic, personal, and flaccid; an expression primarily of personal resentment rather than an act of self-identification with the continuities of a movement or of a rebellion against an economic status regarded as permanently fixed. The militancy of Middletown labor tends, therefore, to be easily manipulated, and to be diverted into all manner of incidental issues.[34]

So much for Muncie – what of New Haven with its more heterogeneous and less individualistic (culturally) working class, a working class that, in some cases, the investigator could interview and probe after the CIO upheaval of 1936–37? Again we see in E. W. Bakke's two published examinations of the unemployed worker in New Haven an absence of mass organization, collective militancy, or radicalism, despite an apparent hardening of class lines. New Haven's workers, unlike Muncie's, apparently did not share the drives of the business class and they did in fact develop a collective sense of class. "Hell, brother," a machinist told Bakke, "you don't have to – look to know there's a workin' class. We may not say so – But look at what we do. Work. Look at where we live. Nothing there but workers. Look at how we get along. Just like every other damned worker. Hell's bells, of course, there's a workin' class, and its gettin' more so every day."[35] Yet New Haven, like Muncie, lacked a militant and radical working class. Why?

Bakke tried to provide answers. He cited the usual barriers to collective action and working-class radicalism: – ethnic heterogeneity; fear of the alien; fear of repression; and

[31] R. and H. Lynd, *Middletown* (New York, 1929), pp. 3–6.
[32] R. and H. Lynd, *Middletown in Transition*, pp. 42–43, 73, 203, 447–448.
[33] *Ibid.*, pp. 26–28; cf., *Middletown*, p. 254.
[34] *Middletown in Transition*, pp. 41–44.
[35] E. W. Bakke, *Citizens without Work*, p. 102; cf. pp. 89–99.

capitalist hegemony that was cultural as well as economic and political.[36] Yet he also discovered that answers to the absence of militancy and radicalism lay embedded deep within the culture of New Haven's workers. In most cases, their lives had disproved the American Dream; rather than experiencing steady upward mobility and constantly rising material standards of living, Bakke's interviewees had lived lives of insecurity and poverty. They regularly had had to adjust their goals to actual possibilities, which almost always fell far below their aspirations. As one worker after another informed Bakke, life involved putting up with it, grinning and bearing it, and using common sense to survive. Explaining how the unemployed managed in a period of general economic crisis, a brass worker noted in a matter of fact fashion, "The poor are used to being poor."[37]

As Eugene Genovese has remarked in a different context, an attempt to explain the relative absence of slave rebellions in North America,

> Only those who romanticize – and therefore do not respect – the laboring classes would fail to understand their deep commitment to "law and order." Life is difficult enough without added uncertainty and "confusion." Even an oppressive and unjust system is better than none. People with such rich experience as that of the meanest slaves quickly learn to distrust Utopian nostrums. As Machiavelli so brilliantly revealed, most people refuse to believe in anything they have not experienced. Such negativity must be understood as a challenge to demonstrate that a better, firmer, more just social order can replace the one to be torn down.[38]

Just so with New Haven's workers. For the majority of them, alternatives to the existing system seemed most notable for their absence. The only alternatives the city's workers cited, German Nazism, Italian Fascism, and Soviet Communism, none of which to be sure they had experienced, held no allurement, promised them "no better, more just social order." Workers repeatedly referred to Soviet Russia to explain both Socialism's and Communism's lack of appeal.[39]

Lacking an alternative to the existing system, New Haven workers grabbed what few joys they could in an otherwise perilous existence. One worker explained his own resistance to Socialism in the following manner. He had fought enough losing battles in his life. But he knew one place where he could celebrate as a winner. As a Democrat or a Republican, at least once in a while he could get drunk on election night and act the part of a winner. But Socialists, he sneered, "when do you think they're goin' to have a chance to get drunk?"[40]

Ah, one might say, Muncie and New Haven were atypical and their working class more so. Look at Flint and Youngstown, Akron and Gary, Minneapolis and San Francisco. In those cities workers acted collectively and militantly. But a closer look at even such *foci* of labor struggle reveals a much more complex reality than suggested by conventional romanticizations of working-class solidarity and rank-and-file militancy.

Without militants, to be sure, there would have been no Flint sitdown strike, no San Francisco general strike, no walkout by Akron's rubber workers. Without rank-and-file participation, that is collective struggle, there would have been no union victories. Yet, in reality, solidarity rarely produced collective action; rather, more often than not, action by

---

[36] *Ibid.*, pp. 59–66.
[37] *Ibid.*, p. 69.
[38] Eugene D. Genovese, *Roll, Jordan, Roll: The World the Slaves Made* (New York, 1974), p. 115.
[39] E. W. Bakke, *Citizens without Work*, pp. 57–59.
[40] *Ibid.*, p. 64.

militant minorities (what some scholars have characterized as "sparkplug Unionism"[41]) pre-cipitated a subsequent collective response. And rank and filers frequently resisted the radicalism of the militant cadres who sparked industrial confrontations. In Flint, as Sidney Fine has shown, only a small minority of the local workers belonged to the UAW and paid dues on the eve of the strike, and the sit-down technique ,was chosen consciously to compensate for the union's lack of a mass membership base.[42] The story was the same in Akron. When that city's rubber workers gained CIO's first major victory in March 1936 after a strike against the Goodyear Tire and Rubber Company, Powers Hapgood disclosed the following to John L. Lewis: "Confidentially, I can tell you that it was a minority strike, starting with only a hand full of members and gradually building a membership in that Local Union to a little over 5000 out of 14,000 workers."[43] Lee Pressman, general counsel to the Steel Workers Organizing Committee, recalls that as late as the spring of 1937, after the UAW's success at Flint and United States Steel's surrender to SWOC, labor organizers had still failed to enrol in SWOC more than a substantial minority of the steelworkers employed by firms other than United States Steel.[44] For most rank and filers, then, militancy consisted of refusing to cross a picket line, no more. As one observer noted of the Flint sit-downers, a group more militant than the majority of auto workers, "Those strikers have no more idea of 'revolution' than pussy-cats."[45]

Even the most strike-torn cities and regions had a significantly internally differentiated working class. At the top were the local cadres, the sparkplug unionists, the men and women fully conscious of their roles in a marketplace society that extolled individualism and rewarded collective strength. These individuals, ranging the political spectrum from Social Democrats to Communists, provided the leadership, militancy, and ideology that fostered industrial conflict and the emergence of mass-production unionism. Beneath them lay a substantial proportion of workers who could be transformed, by example, into militant strikers and unionists, and, in turn, themselves act as militant minorities. Below them were many first- and second-generation immigrant workers, as well as recent migrants from the American countryside, who remained embedded in a culture defined by traditional ties of family, kinship, church, and neighborhood club or tavern. Accustomed to following the rituals of the past, heeding the advice of community leaders, and slow to act, such men and women rarely joined unions prior to a successful strike, once moved to act behaved with singular solidarity, yet rarely served as union or political activists and radicals. And below this mass were the teenage workers caught halfway between liberation from their parental families and formation of their own new households, more attracted to the life and rituals of street gangs and candy-store cronies than to the customs and culture of persistent trade unionists and political activists.[46]

A word must now be added concerning those scholars who have argued that during the

[41] Edward Shorter and Charles Tilly, *Strikes in France, 1830–1968* (London, 1974), *passim.*

[42] S. Fine, *Sit-Down*, p. 117. The UAW had signed up 1500 out of more than 12,000 auto workers. Cf. Adolph Germer to John Brophy, Dec. 8, 1935, Germer Papers, Box 2.

[43] Hapgood to Lewis, Mar. 29, 1936, Hapgood Papers.

[44] Lee Pressman, COHC, pp. 193–194; David J. MacDonald, Oral History Transcript, p. 11, Pennsylvania State University Labor Archives.

[45] S. Fine, *Sit-Down*, p. 331.

[46] Peter Friedlander, *The Emergence of a UAW Local, 1936–1939: A Study in Class and Culture* (Pittsburgh, 1975), xiii–xx, pp. 27–28, 119–131, and *passim.*

1930's a spontaneously militant and increasingly radical rank and file was either handcuffed or betrayed by bureaucratic and autocratic labor leaders. For those who accept the Leninist thesis that trade unions are, by definition, economist and hence nonrevolutionary, there is no problem in comprehending the behavior of American trade unions and their members during the 1930's. But for those who seek to understand why the militant beginnings of the CIO terminated in an ideological and institutional deadend, why, in David Brody's words, "the character of American trade unionism [. . .] made it an exploiter of radicalism rather than vice versa" – questions remain.[47] And it may seem easiest to answer, as Art Preis, Ronald Radosh, James Weinstein, and Staughton Lynd have done, that the blame for the failure of radicalism rests with such labor leaders as John L. Lewis and Sidney Hillman who sold out to the New Deal, collaborated with employers, and restrained rank-and-file militancy through the instrument of the non-strike union contract. That hypothesis, commonly subsumed under the rubric "corporate liberalism", contains a grain of truth.[48] But the small truth tends to obscure a greater reality. As J. B. S. Hardman observed a half century ago, labor leaders are primarily accumulators of power; and, need it be said, no man was more eager to accumulate power than John L. Lewis.[49] A businessman's power flowed from his control of capital; a politician's from influence over voters and possession of the instruments of government; and a labor leader's power derived from his union membership, the more massive and militant the rank and file the more influential the labor leader. Bereft of a mass membership or saddled with a lethargic rank and file, the labor leader lost influence, and power. All labor leaders, then, necessarily played a devious and sometimes duplicitous game. Sometimes they rushed in to lead a rebellious rank and file; other times, they agitated the rank and file into action; whether they seized leadership of a movement already in motion or themselves breathed life into the rank and file, labor leaders obtained whatever power they exercised with employers and public officials as a consequence of their followers' behavior. Yet, while they encouraged militancy, labor leaders also restrained their troops, in John L. Lewis's phrase, "put a lid on the strikers." They did so for several reasons. First, not all rank-and-file upheavals promised success; and nothing destroyed a trade union as quickly or diluted a labor leader's power as thoroughly as a lost strike. Second, leaders had to judge at what point rank-and-file militancy would produce government repression, an ever present reality even in Franklin D. Roosevelt's America. Third, and more selfishly, rank-and-file upheavals could career out of control and threaten a labor leader's tenure in office as well as strengthen his external power. Throughout the 1930's such labor leaders as John L. Lewis alternately encouraged the release of working-class rebelliousness and "put the lid back on." The labor leader was truly the man in the middle, his influence rendered simultaneously greater and also more perilous as a result of working-class militancy.[50]

[47] D. Brody, "Labor and the Great Depression," p. 241.

[48] See n. 6 above, and also S. Lynd, "The Possibility of Radicalism", pp. 50–51; idem., Guerilla History in Gary," pp. 17–20; idem., "Personal Histories of the Early CIO," Radical America, V (May–June 1971), 50; Alice and Staughton Lynd, Rank and File (Boston, 1973), pp. 4–5, 89–90; cf., Mark Naison, "The Southern Tenant Farmers Union and the CIO," Radical America, II (Sept.–Oct. 1968), 36–54; and Art Preis, Labor's Giant Step (New York, 1964), passim.

[49] J. B. S. Hardman, "Union Objectives and Social Power," in J. B. S. Hardman, ed., American Labor Dynamics (New York, 1928), p. 104.

[50] Melvyn Dubofsky and Warren Van Tine, John L. Lewis: A Biography (New York, 1977), is a study of precisely that process and the dilemma of trade-union leadership. Cf. P. Friedlander, The Emergence of a UAW Local, pp. 119–131, passim.

A final word must also be said about the union contract, the instrument that allegedly bound workers to their employers by denying them the right to strike. With historical hindsight, such seems to be the end result of the union-management contract under which the union promises to discipline its members of behalf of management. But one must remember that during the 1930's ordinary workers, the romanticized rank and file, risked their jobs, their bodies, and their lives to win the contract. And when they won it, as in Flint in February 1937, a sit-down striker rejoiced that it "was the most wonderful thing that we could think of that could possibly happen to people."[51]

IV

Paradoxically, the one experience during the 1930's that united workers across ethnic, racial, and organizational lines – New Deal politics – served to vitiate radicalism. By the end of the 1930's, Roosevelt's Democratic party had become, in effect, the political expression of America's working class. Old-line Socialists, farmer-labor party types, and even Communists enlisted in a Roosevelt-led "Popular Front." Blacks and whites, Irish and Italian Catholics, Slavic- and Jewish-Americans, uprooted rural Protestants and stable skilled workers joined the Democratic coalition, solidifying the working-class vote as never before in American history. Roosevelt encouraged workers to identify themselves as a common class politically as well as economically. As with David Lloyd George in Britain's pre-World War I Edwardian crisis, Franklin D. Roosevelt in the American crisis of the 1930's found revolutionary class rhetoric indispensable. It panicked the powerful into concessions and attracted working-class voters to the Democratic party. Just as Lloyd George intensified the earlier British crisis in order to ease its solution, Roosevelt acted similarly in New Deal America. By frightening the ruling class into conceding reforms and appealing to workers to vote as a solid bloc, Roosevelt simultaneously intensified class consciousness and stripped it of its radical potential.[52]

The dilemma of John L. Lewis showed just how well Roosevelt succeeded in his strategy. During the 1930's, no matter how much Lewis preferred to think of himself as an executive rather than a labor leader, however little he associated personally with the working class, he functioned as the leader of a militant working-class movement. Whereas Roosevelt sought to contain working-class militancy through reforms, militant workers pressured Lewis to demand more than the President would or could deliver. The more evident became the New Deal's economic failures, the more heatedly labor militants demanded a fundamental reordering of the economy and society, demands that Lewis, as leader of CIO, came to express more forcefully than any other trade unionist. "No matter how much Roosevelt did for the workers," recalls Len DeCaux, "Lewis demanded more. He showed no gratitude, nor did he bid his followers be grateful – just put the squeeze on all the harder."[53] But Lewis, unlike the British

---

[51] S. Fine, *Sit-Down*, p. 307; D. Brody, "Radical Labor History," p. 125.

[52] For the Edwardian British analogy, see Paul Thompson, *The Edwardians* (Bloomington, Ind., 1975), pp. 260–262. On the working-class core of the Democratic party, see Samuel Lubell, *The Future of American Politics* (New York, 1965 ed.), pp. 179–182 and *passim*; A. W. Jones, *Life, Liberty, and Property*, pp. 314–317; and P. Friedlander, *The Emergence of a UAW Local*, pp. 112–114.

[53] L. DeCaux, *Labor Radical*, p. 295; L. Pressman, COHC, pp. 91, 96–97, 188, 191, 352.

labor leaders of Lloyd George's generation who found in the Labour Party an alternative to the Prime Minister's "New Liberalism," had no substitute for Roosevelt's New Deal. In the United States, the President easily mastered the labor leader.

Lewis's lack of a political alternative to the New Deal flowed from two sources. First was the refusal of most American leftists to countenance a third-party challenge to the Democrats and the intense loyalty most workers felt to Roosevelt. Between the winter of 1937–38 and the summer of 1940, however much Lewis threatened to lead a new third party, his public speeches and private maneuvers failed to create among workers a third-party constituency. It was Lewis's radical speeches that made his eventual endorsement in 1940 of Wendell Willkie so shocking to many of the labor leader's admirers. Had those Lewis sycophants known that in June 1940, the CIO president plotted to win the Republican nomination for Herbert Hoover, they might have been even more startled.[54] And it was his support first of Hoover and then of Willkie that exposed the second source for Lewis's lack of a radical alternative to the New Deal. That was the extent to which Lewis, other labor leaders, and perhaps most workers had assimilated the values of a business civilization. This union, Lewis told members of the United Mine Workers at their 1938 convention, "stands for the proposition that the heads of families shall have a sufficient income to educate [. . .] these sons and daughters of our people, and they go forth when given that opportunity [. . .] they become scientists, great clergymen [. . .] great lawyers, great statesmen [. . .] Many of our former members are successful in great business enterprises." And two years later in 1940, he told the same audience: "You know, after all there are two great material tasks in life that affect the individual and affect great bodies of men. The first is to achieve or acquire something of value or something that is desireable, and then the second is to prevent some scoundrel from taking it away from you."[55] Notice the substance of Lewis's remarks to a trade-union crowd, the combination of urging the children of the working class to rise above it, not with it, and the materialistic stress on possessive individualism. Lewis, the most militant and prominent of the depression decade's labor leaders, remained too much the opportunist, too much the personification of vulgar pragmatism and business values to lead a third-party political crusade.

V

What, then, follows logically from the above description of the 1930's and the implied line of analysis? First, and perhaps obviously, however turbulent were the American 1930's, the depression decade never produced a revolutionary situation. Second, one observes the essential inertia of the working-class masses. Once in motion, the mass of workers can move with great acceleration and enormous militancy – but such movement remains hard to get started.

[54] L. Pressman, COHC, p. 380; Statement, Herbert Hoover Papers, June, 1940, Post-Presidential Files, John L. Lewis, Box 98, Herbert Hoover Library, West Branch, Iowa.
[55] United Mine Workers of America, *Convention Proceedings, 1938*, p. 172; *1940*, p. 14; A. W. Jones observes of Akron's workers in 1939, even the highly politicized ones, "Our measurements of opinion and the comments of workers indicate clearly that most of them do not want to feel that they have isolated themselves from the general run of 'middle class opinion.' The general climate of opinion bears in upon them and would make it impossible for them to turn decisively away into a workers' world, even if such a thing existed." *Life, Liberty, and Property*, p. 297.

Such social inertia combined with the inability of most workers and their leaders to conceive of an alternative to the values of marketplace capitalism, that is to create a working-class culture autonomous from that of the ruling class, was more important than trade-union opportunism, corporate co-optation, or New Deal liberalism (though the last factor was clearly the most potent) in thwarting the emergence of durable working-class radicalism. Third, and finally, it suggests that a distinction must be drawn between class struggle as an historical reality and workers as a class fully aware of their role, power, and ability to replace the existing system with "a better, firmer, more just social order [than] [. . .] the one to be torn down."

The CIO at Bay: Labor Militancy and Politics in Akron, 1936–1938

Daniel Nelson

CIO buttons "sprouted on overalls, shirtwaists, and workers' hats and caps . . . badges of a new independence. Labor was on the march as it had never been before in the history of the Republic." Thus did Edward Levinson capture the excitement and potential of the union upsurge of the mid-1930s. Between 1936 and 1938 industrial unionism and the Congress of Industrial Organizations (CIO) became important innovative forces in American society. They transformed the labor movement and industrial relations, influenced the American political life, and raised hopes and fears of a unified working class. Yet Levinson emphasized only one side of the events of 1936–1938. At its height the industrial union movement revealed unexpected weaknesses. It lost organizing campaigns and strikes, suffered rebuffs, and failed to consolidate its power. By 1939–1940 Levinson's imagery was outdated if not inaccurate. Although the reasons for the reversal are as numerous and as imprecise as the membership of the CIO in the late 1930s, one conclusion seems inescapable: CIO men and women were neither so united nor so determined as Levinson's language suggested. The workers themselves bore much of the responsibility for the relative fall of the CIO.[1]

The limits of labor power were nowhere more evident than in the 1937 CIO campaigns to extend the workers' influence from the union hall to city hall. In cities of all sizes, CIO leaders attempted to flex blue-collar muscles at the ballot box by electing local government officials. Their efforts, built on union

Daniel Nelson is professor of history at the University of Akron.

[1] Edward Levinson, *Labor on the March* (New York, 1937), 236; Walter Galenson, *The CIO Challenge to the AFL: A History of the American Labor Movement, 1935-1941* (Cambridge, Mass., 1960), 583–85; David Brody, "Reinterpreting the Labor History of the 1930s," in David Brody, *Workers in Industrial America: Essays on the Twentieth Century Struggle* (New York, 1980), 120–72; Staughton Lynd, "The Possibility of Radicalism in the Early 1930's: The Case of Steel," *Radical America*, 6 (Nov.-Dec. 1972), 37–64; James R. Green, "Working Class Militancy in the Depression," *ibid.*, 1–35; Robert H. Zieger, "The Limits of Militancy: Organizing Paper Workers, 1933-1935," *Journal of American History*, 63 (Dec. 1976), 638–57; Melvyn Dubofsky, "Not So 'Turbulent Years': Another Look at the American 1930's," *Amerikastudien*, 24 (no. 1, 1979), 5–20.

triumphs in industry and in politics in 1936–1937, were important steps in a concerted, though ill-defined, attempt to expand the CIO role outside industry. The significance of their actions was unmistakable. Victory in 1937 would encourage a more aggressive and identifiable union stance in politics and in society; defeat would dictate a more cautious and subdued role. In fact, union candidates won few victories and produced little evidence that labor's march to the polling booth would win many victories in the future. Directly or indirectly, the 1937 results encouraged unionists to remain within the New Deal coalition and to ally themselves with Democratic candidates.[2]

Of the CIO efforts of 1937, the most meaningful may well have been the union contest for control of Akron, Ohio, considered by contemporaries the most unionized city in the United States. By 1937 industrial unions had become the dominant influence in the city's economic life. They had recruited thousands of members, demonstrated their might in confrontations with employers, and transformed the practice of industrial relations. A move into the political arena would complete their rise to power. By most measures they ought to have had little difficulty capturing the city government. They had capable leaders, substantial resources, and more committed participants than did either political party. The 1937 election proved the error of such calculations. CIO failure in Akron exposed the unionists' misconceptions about their potential and, more important, about their ability to gauge their constituents. They assumed a unity of purpose and outlook that did not exist and overlooked forces that restricted the workers' willingness to act in concert. The Akron campaign was a measure of the limits of CIO power and of the tangled grass roots of the industrial union movement at the most critical phase of its development.[3]

The behavior of Akron unions and workers in 1937 was an outgrowth of the particular environment in which they worked and lived. In the 1910s the city had been the nation's preeminent boomtown, a sprawling tribute to the automobile age. Encouraged by advertisements and recruiters, men from hardscrabble farms in Ohio, Pennsylvania, West Virginia, and points south had arrived in large numbers to earn wages that, for the toughest and most resilient, far exceeded Henry Ford's five-dollar day. The boom ended with the recession of 1920–1921, and the slower expansion of the 1920s blurred many of its features. Gradually, Akron came to resemble other industrial cities. By the late 1920s it might have been "Middletown."[4] Yet the boom left a legacy that

[2] James Caldwell Foster, *The Union Politic: The CIO Political Action Committee* (Columbia, Mo., 1975), 6–9; David Brody, "The Uses of Power II: Political Action," in David Brody, *Workers in Industrial America*, 215–57; J. David Greenstone, *Labor in American Politics* (New York, 1969), 3–80.

[3] Levinson, *Labor on the March*, 265; Ruth McKenney, *Industrial Valley* (New York, 1939), 373–79.

[4] Federal Housing Administration, Division of Economics and Statistics, *Akron, Ohio: Housing Market Analysis* (Washington, 1938), 39–44; Robert S. Lynd and Helen Merrell Lynd, *Middletown: A Study in Contemporary American Culture* (New York, 1929), 7–9. Of the nine criteria Robert S. Lynd and Helen Merrell Lynd cite, Akron qualified in seven categories. It was too large (255,000 inhabitants in 1930) and too much an industrial city to meet their specifications.

accounted for several of the city's distinctive features. Though the overall distribution of occupations in 1930 and in 1940 did not differ from the national averages for cities, the manufacturing sector was highly concentrated. The rubber industry employed 79 percent of the city's industrial workers in 1929 and 69 percent a decade later. Rubber production in turn was concentrated in a handful of massive plants. Three companies, Goodyear Tire and Rubber Company, Firestone Tire and Rubber Company, and the B. F. Goodrich Company, together employed more than 30,000 Akron workers in the 1930s, at least 90 percent of all local rubber industry employees. Severe competition in the 1920s had eliminated many smaller factories; the depression completed the winnowing process. Only General Tire and Rubber Company, with more than 1,500 workers, approached the size of the "Big Three."[5]

Other homogenizing factors created a basis for united action. Wage rates in rubber manufacturing, on average, exceeded those of any other industry; before the depression production workers in the rubber industry enjoyed high, though often erratic, earnings because of the growth of the auto industry and because of rapid changes in the technology of tire production. As a result, they had more to lose than did most other industrial employees. After 1929 the rubber industry, dependent on auto production and use, became severely depressed. Unemployment was high, and underemployment, even higher. The affluence of earlier years became a bitter memory. Outside the plants workers confronted other difficulties. Akron was almost evenly divided between home-owners and renters, with younger rubber workers constituting the bulk of the latter. Housing in areas adjacent to the rubber plants was generally of poor quality, a legacy of the speculative boom of the 1910s. By the 1930s much of it had deteriorated badly. In 1937 Akron may have been the most dilapidated major city in the country. Unimaginative city administrators and severe municipal financial problems seemingly foreclosed any possibility of relief.[6]

The passage of the National Industrial Recovery Act (NIRA) in June 1933 was a powerful catalyst for Akron workers. It gave an aura of legitimacy to their

[5] U.S. Department of Commerce, Bureau of the Census, *Fifteenth Census of the United States: Manufacturers, 1929* (3 vols., Washington, 1933), III, 411; U.S. Department of Commerce, Bureau of the Census, *Sixteenth Census of the United States, 1940: Manufacturers, 1939* (3 vols., Washington, 1942), III, 795. The Goodyear Tire and Rubber Company averaged 14,304 hourly employees in 1936 and 12,767 in 1937. The Firestone Tire and Rubber Company had 10,368 workers in early 1936 and approximately 8,000 in late 1937. The B. F. Goodrich Company had 13,500 to 14,000 in early 1937. Employment records, 1920–1945, Goodyear Archives (Goodyear Tire and Rubber Company, Akron, Ohio); Alfred Lief, *The Firestone Story: A History of the Firestone Tire and Rubber Company* (New York, 1951), 225, 230; Federal Housing Administration, *Akron, Ohio*, 76; "Summary of Enrollment," [B. F. Goodrich Company] file 1832, box 2116, National Labor Relations Board Records, RG 25 (National Archives).

[6] *Akron Beacon Journal*, July 13, 1937, p. 23; Bureau of Labor Statistics, *Bulletin No. 737: Wages in Rubber Manufacturing Industry, August 1942* (Washington, 1943), 10–22; Federal Housing Administration, *Akron, Ohio*, 109–10, 132–38. The 1930 census reported 8.8 percent of the Akron labor force and 7.4 percent of rubber industry employees in Akron unemployed. Monthly employment fluctuations were reported for the 1930s. In November 1937, 11.7 percent of Akron workers were totally unemployed. Nearly as many were employed at government relief projects or partially employed. *Ibid.*, 94, 218–25, 228; U.S. Department of Commerce, Bureau of the Census, *Fifteenth Census of the United States, 1930: Unemployment* (2 vols., Washington, 1931), I, 775, 787.

grievances, provided a solution in collective bargaining, and neutralized traditional employer resistance to union organization. Rubber workers swamped the American Federation of Labor (AFL) federal labor unions that appeared in the wake of the NIRA. By the spring of 1934, 85 percent of Akron rubber workers were union members.[7] Depression conditions gave them a sense of shared distress, and the New Deal provided a blueprint for collective action. Henceforth, union membership would fluctuate with union fortunes, but a return to the status quo ante was no more likely than the reelection of Herbert Hoover.

In the following years the gulf between Akron employers and workers seemed to grow. Employer opposition to union demands strained whatever vestiges of company loyalty remained. Union leaders, unable to obtain positive results, became more vociferous in attacking the manufacturers, and workers became more aggressive. The first sit-down strike occurred at General Tire in June 1934. In late 1935, shortly after the federal locals had combined to form an international union, the United Rubber Workers (URW), a series of spontaneous sit-downs occurred at the Big Three plants, inaugurating the sit-down era in American industry. By that time depression conditions and the frustrations of the National Recovery Administration period had created the preconditions for a brief, though remarkable, period of worker-induced innovation.[8]

Those developments, which paralleled similar tendencies in the auto, steel, electrical, and other "mass production" industries and which form the core of traditional accounts of the rise of industrial unionism, were, however, only one side of the depression experience. Economic decline and New Deal policies had varied, even contradictory effects. They fragmented the working class at the same time they seemed to unite it, and they encouraged identification with a particular employer as well as hostility to employers generally. Labor may have been on the march, but it marched to a variety of drummers. In the rubber industry two factors were particularly divisive. The first was the enduring effects of earlier personnel innovations. All of the major rubber companies had had reasonably advanced personnel programs in the 1920s, but Goodyear, the unquestioned leader, had the only company union that predated the NIRA. This was a critical distinction. The Goodyear Industrial Assembly operated with considerable success in the 1920s and continued to hold the loyalties of many workers in the 1930s.[9] Company unions formed in response

[7] W. W. Thompson, "History of the Labor Movement in Akron, Ohio," [ca. 1936], United Rubber Workers file, Congress of Industrial Organizations Papers (Catholic University Library, Washington).
[8] Harold S. Roberts, The Rubber Workers: Labor Organization and Collective Bargaining in the Rubber Industry (New York, 1944), 124–47; Alfred Winslow Jones, Life, Liberty, and Property: A Story of Conflict and a Measurement of Conflicting Rights (Philadelphia, 1941), 88–96; Daniel Nelson, ed., "The Beginning of the Sit-Down Era: The Reminiscences of Rex Murray," Labor History, 15 (Winter 1974), 91–96; Levinson, Labor on the March, 171; McKenney, Industrial Valley, 251–73. For the movement generally, see Sidney Fine, Sit-Down: The General Motors Strike of 1936–1937 (Ann Arbor, 1969); and Joel Seidman, "Sit Down" (New York, 1937).
[9] Hugh Allen, The House of Goodyear: Fifty Years of Men and Industry (Akron, 1949), 183–84; Paul W. Litchfield, The Industrial Republic: A Study in Industrial Economics (Akron, 1919),

to Section 7A of the NIRA at the other plants were moribund by 1935; the Goodyear Industrial Assembly competed successfully with the URW local until 1936 and persisted, in the form of several "independent" unions, for years thereafter. To many veteran Goodyear employees, the company union provided a safe, respectable mechanism for adjusting grievances and obtaining additional benefits. It offered most of the advantages of URW membership without the necessity of dues payments or the dangers of an adversarial relationship. Above all, it ensured that the company would not waver from its commitments, formal and informal, to consider seniority in making layoffs.[10]

The second factor, little recognized, was equally important. By reducing employment opportunities, the depression curbed interplant mobility and created a more or less permanent labor force at each company. In the 1910s and 1920s, the city had had a single labor market characterized by high rates of turnover and mobility. Men and women changed employers at will; it was not uncommon for a veteran employee to have worked in all the city's major plants within the span of a few years. The World War I era probably marked the apogee of that trend. Goodyear had a net turnover rate (resignations and discharges exclusive of layoffs) of 197 percent in 1920. In the 1920s that rate declined as industry growth slowed and as the Goodyear management worked to retain proficient employees. Yet net turnover typically ranged from 45 percent to 55 percent of the labor force. Goodyear hired nearly 66,000 workers between 1924 and 1929 and lost or fired 53,000, while average employment ranged from 14,500 to 17,000. The depression abruptly altered that pattern. Net turnover fell to 10 percent in 1930 and declined steadily to 4.6 percent in 1935. Layoffs kept total turnover at about half the level of the 1920s from 1930 to 1933, but thereafter it, too, dropped. Altogether, Goodyear hired 17,000 employees and lost 17,000 to resignation or discharge between 1930 and 1935.[11] The pattern at the other plants must have been similar. By the mid-

41–59; Paul W. Litchfield, *Industrial Voyage: My Life as an Industrial Lieutenant* (New York, 1954), 183–87. For the company union movement, see Stuart D. Brandes, *American Welfare Capitalism, 1880–1940* (Chicago, 1976), 119–34; David Brody, "The Rise and Decline of Welfare Capitalism," in Brody, *Workers in Industrial America*, 55–56; C. Ray Gullett and Edmund R. Gray, "The Impact of Employee Representation Plans upon the Development of Management-Worker Relationships in the United States," *Marquette Business Review*, 20 (Fall 1976), 95–101; and Daniel Nelson, "The Company Union Movement, 1900–1937: A Reexamination," *Business History Review*, 56 (Autumn 1982), 335–57. For industrial unionism generally in this period, see Fine, *Sit-Down*, 54–99; Irving Bernstein, *Turbulent Years: A History of the American Worker 1933–41* (Boston, 1970), 92–125, 432–634; and Galenson, *CIO Challenge*, 75–459.

[10] "Annual Reports" of the Goodyear Industrial Assembly, cases 8-R-184 and 8-C-378, box 1878, National Labor Relations Board Records; "Constitution of the Employee Conference Plan," Oct. 14, 1933, Firestone Archives (Firestone Tire and Rubber Company, Akron, Ohio); H. S. Firestone to L. K. Firestone, Feb. 12, 1934, *ibid.*

[11] Goodyear Tire and Rubber Company, "Statement Submitted to the Fact-Finding Board," Nov. 30, 1935, file 195/336, Federal Mediation and Conciliation Service Papers, RG 280 (National Archives); John D. House interview by Daniel Nelson, April 18, 1972, tape recording (American History Research Center, Bierce Library, University of Akron, Akron, Ohio); Harley Anthony interview by Nelson, May 15, 1972, tape recording, *ibid.*; Rex Murray interview by Nelson, Sept. 20, 1972, tape recording, *ibid.*; Ralph Turner interview by Nelson, May 10, 1972, tape recording, *ibid.*; John Kumpel interview by Nelson, Oct. 25, 1972, tape recording, *ibid.*; A. A. Wilson interview by Nelson, May 17, 1973, tape recording, *ibid.*

1930s a large majority of workers at each company were veteran employees whose years at other plants were a dim memory and who necessarily equated their lot with a particular setting and group of individuals. Though working and living within a few city blocks of one another, they became Goodyear and Firestone workers more than rubber workers.

Union leaders reflected those trends. They were determined, often vociferous critics of the industry. With few exceptions they were also seasoned employees, American natives of southern origins who, after a period of transiency in the 1910s or early 1920s, had settled into permanent positions. Their demographic and occupational profiles are indistinguishable from those of Goodyear company union officials. A combination of background and personal qualities accounted for their rise. Southerners had long formed an important and widely recognized subculture in the plants and were thought of as "typical" rubber workers. In 1933 they looked to their own kind for leadership, boosting men known for sincerity, honesty, and assertiveness. Within that group individuals with leadership experience and visibility usually won the top positions. At Goodyear former company union officers were disproportionately represented in the union hierarchy. At the other plants trade union experience may have played a similar role. Men who had once been members of the United Mine Workers (UMW) or of the railway unions won many URW leadership posts.[12]

The sudden desperate need for competent leaders created similar disparities in other industries and unions after 1933. In Pittsburgh, Detroit, Woonsocket (Rhode Island), Covington (Virginia), and other industrial centers, workers turned naturally to men and women with leadership skills and other appropriate qualifications, such as education and prior union experience. The result was a new generation of union bureaucrats, who were younger, ethnically more diverse, and generally more favorable to political activism than were their counterparts in the established trade union movement. These individuals, together with a disparate mixture of AFL veterans, created and built the CIO.[13]

Until 1936 the URW, for all its organizing successes, was an untested, unproved organization. It had stumbled badly in efforts to win contracts in 1934 and 1935. In early 1936, however, a series of unforeseen events transformed it and the nascent industrial union movement. A series of spontaneous sit-downs at the Akron plants led to a full-scale strike at Goodyear in mid-

---

[12] Daniel Nelson, "The Leadership of the United Rubber Workers, 1933-1942," *Detroit in Perspective*, 5 (Spring 1981), 21-30; "The Rolling Tire," *Fortune*, 14 (Nov. 1936), 100; Exhibit 30, cases 8-R-184 and 8-C-378, box 1878, National Labor Relations Board Records.

[13] Ronald Schatz, "Union Pioneers: The Founders of Local Unions at General Electric and Westinghouse, 1933-1937," *Journal of American History*, 66 (Dec. 1979), 586-602; Peter Friedlander, *The Emergence of a UAW Local, 1936-1939: A Study in Class and Culture* (Pittsburgh, 1975), 10-21; Gary Gerstle, "The Mobilization of the Working Class Community: The Independent Textile Workers Union in Woonsocket, 1931-1946," *Radical History Review*, 17 (Spring 1978), 161-72; Robert H. Zieger, "The Union Comes to Covington: Virginia Paperworkers Organize, 1933-1952," *Proceedings of the American Philosophical Society*, 126 (no. 1, 1982), 51-89; Walter Licht and Hal Seth Barron, "Labor's Men: A Collective Biography of Union Officialdom during the New Deal Years," *Labor History*, 19 (Fall 1978), 538-39.

February. The strike, which idled 14,000 workers for five weeks and which resulted in a partial union triumph, was a turning point in the labor history of the 1930s. It destroyed the Goodyear Industrial Assembly and enhanced the reputation of the URW, enabling Akron locals to attract thousands of new members. Coming shortly after the founding of the CIO, it also provided John L. Lewis and his lieutenants with an opportunity to demonstrate the might of industrial unionism. The Goodyear strike was the first of a series of widely publicized confrontations that created an image of CIO militancy and invincibility—of "labor on the march."[14]

In the Akron plants waves of sit-down strikes followed the Goodyear strike. Between March and December 1936, when the sit-down technique spread to the auto and other industries, more than sixty sit-downs convulsed the rubber factories. Union officials, fearing a complete breakdown of worker discipline, opposed the sit-downs with increasing vigor. Local leaders at Firestone, and to a lesser degree at Goodrich, were most outspoken and successful in containing unrest. The sit-down movement gradually faded at those plants. Labor activists, especially those at Goodyear, the scene of more or less continuous upheaval, began to worry about the "conservatism" of the Firestone and Goodrich workers. Had union leaders undermined the organizations' vitality? In any event, the Goodyear strike and the sit-downs amply demonstrated the disruptive potential of the URW. Community alliances began to reform on pro-union and anti-union lines. By the fall of 1936, Akron probably had more union members per capita than any other city in the United States and had emerged as a "test tube" for industrial-relations innovations.[15]

In the following months Akron unionists made a concerted move into local politics, a step that was to serve as an augury of CIO influence in the political realm. Like other militants, they had been aware of their political potential and the deficiencies of conventional politicians and parties. They had taken no concerted action, however, until 1936. During the Goodyear strike the sheriff, the prosecuting attorney, and common pleas judges had sided with the antistrike forces, removing any lingering doubts about the role of politics in industrial relations. In the meantime a URW sympathizer, Wilmer Tate of the International Association of Machinists, had successfully challenged an AFL traditionalist for the presidency of the Akron Central Labor Union. A colorful, outspoken champion of industrial unionism, Tate was a proponent of working-class political action who maintained clandestine ties with the small, but vociferous, local Communist party. His rise pushed the unions toward an

[14] Daniel Nelson, "The Great Goodyear Strike of 1936," *Ohio History*, 92 (1983), 6–36; Bernstein, *Turbulent Years*, 352–431, 592–600; Roberts, *Rubber Workers*, 147–51; Levinson, *Labor on the March*, 143–46; Jones, *Life, Liberty, and Property*, 99–108; Melvyn Dubofsky and Warren Van Tyne, *John L. Lewis: A Biography* (New York, 1977), 226–28, 234; Galenson, *CIO Challenge*, 271–72.
[15] Daniel Nelson, "Origins of the Sit-Down Era: Worker Militancy and Innovation in the Rubber Industry, 1934–1938," *Labor History*, 23 (Spring 1982), 198–255; Harley Anthony interview by Nelson, April 5, 1972, Dec. 2, 1976, tape recording (American History Research Center); House interview; Kumpel interview; Robert Morehead, "The Test Tube City Rejects the Union," *Nation's Business*, 26 (Feb. 1938), 55–58, 91–93.

activist role. By the spring of 1936, "the boys were ready to go somewhere. They wanted some action on the political front."[16]

Tate took the lead in the following months. His aim was to make the rubber workers the nucleus of an Ohio Farmer-Labor party that would be affiliated with the Minnesota Farmer-Labor party, the Wisconsin Progressive party, and others.[17] With a platform emphasizing various pro-union legislative measures, Tate and other dissidents hoped to create a national movement for 1940. In June 1936 five hundred delegates, most of them union representatives, met in Akron to inaugurate the local movement. They soon encountered major, ultimately insurmountable obstacles. The national and state Farmer-Labor parties were stillborn, leaving them with no prospect of wider affiliation or influence. Local politicians undercut the Farmer-Laborites at every opportunity; the Democrats in particular pressured union sympathizers to abandon a movement that threatened to defeat President Franklin D. Roosevelt's local allies. Tate's flirtation with the radicals was the last straw. He tried to recruit unionists of all ideological persuasions, but his efforts merely provided a forum for Communists and Trotskyists from the teachers and Works Progress Administration (WPA) unions. To most unionists, including virtually all the URW leaders, that was too much. By the time election officials ruled the Farmer-Labor ticket off the Ohio ballot in October, the local effort, started with such zeal and fanfare in June, was a dim memory to most Akron voters.[18]

A second, less conspicuous, but ultimately more substantial, effort to extend URW power paralleled the rise and fall of the Farmer-Labor party. Lewis and other CIO leaders organized Labor's Non-Partisan League in the spring of 1936 to mobilize labor support for Roosevelt's reelection. Except in New York the league operated as an adjunct to the UMW. In Ohio, a UMW stronghold, it sponsored numerous rallies and radio addresses for Roosevelt. Those efforts presumably contributed to the Roosevelt landslide in Ohio and to the

[16] Richard W. Shrake II, "Working Class Politics in Akron, Ohio, 1936: The Rubber Workers and the Failure of the Farmer-Labor Party" (M.A. thesis, University of Akron, 1974), 31-33; McKenney, *Industrial Valley*, 94-95; Wilson interview; Ray C. Sutliff interview by Nelson, April 18, 1979 (in Nelson's possession). A union partisan, a Congress of Industrial Organizations (CIO) member, and, covertly, a Garnet L. Patterson speech writer, Ray C. Sutliff followed the campaign closely as a political reporter for the *Akron Times Press*. *Ibid.* For unions' political activism in other industries, see David J. Pivar, "The Hosiery Workers and the Philadelphia Third Party Impulse, 1929-1935," *Labor History*, 5 (Winter 1964), 18-28; and Eric Leif Davin and Staughton Lynd, "Picket Line and Ballot Box: The Forgotten Legacy of the Local Labor Party Movement, 1932-1936," *Radical History Review*, 22 (Winter 1979-80), 43-63.

[17] Hugh T. Lovin, "The Ohio 'Farmer-Labor' Movement in the 1930s," *Ohio History*, 87 (Autumn 1978), 419-37; Shrake, "Working Class Politics," 33-55. See also Hugh T. Lovin, "The Persistence of Third Party Dreams in the American Labor Movement, 1930-1938," *Mid-America*, 58 (Oct. 1976), 141-57; and Hugh T. Lovin, "The Fall of the Farmer-Labor Parties, 1936-38," *Pacific Northwest Quarterly*, 62 (Jan. 1971), 17.

[18] *Akron Beacon Journal*, June 8, 1936, p. 1; *ibid.*, Oct. 7, 1936, p. 21; Lovin, "Ohio 'Farmer-Labor' Movement," 429-30, 433-36; Shrake, "Working Class Politics," 51-52. Only one international union official, organizational director N. H. Eagle, and a handful of local union officials, chiefly Eagle's colleagues in the miniscule Mohawk Rubber Company local union, were sympathetic to left-wing causes. John Williamson, "Akron: A New Chapter in American Labor History," *Communist*, 15 (May 1936), 424. See also Kenneth Waltzer, "The Party and the Polling Place: American Communism and an American Labor Party in the 1930's," *Radical History Review*, 23 (Spring 1980), 108-12.

victories, by smaller margins, of Democratic Governor Martin L. Davey and nearly all other state and local Democratic candidates. In Akron the league embraced craft and industrial unionists and resuscitated a weak Democratic organization that had enjoyed little success outside several inner-city slum wards. Neither organized labor generally nor the URW had hitherto played a major role in local politics. The 1936 victories raised the inevitable question: Was the league a Democratic auxiliary, or vice versa? Though local league chairman M. S. Crouch, an officer of the Brotherhood of Painters, Decorators and Paperhangers and of the Central Labor Union, worked amicably with the Democrats during the campaign, he left little doubt that the CIO was the dominant partner. For the unionists a labor-Democratic coalition promised the benefits without the handicaps of an independent effort such as the Farmer-Labor party. Shortly after the elections, when a municipal judgeship became vacant, the league demonstrated its power by securing Davey's appointment of a prolabor candidate without consulting Democratic officials. The appointee, Garnet L. Patterson, was a former URW attorney who had joined the National Labor Relations Board in 1935. A New Dealer more than a Democrat, he acknowledged his ambition for elective office.[19]

Labor's Non-Partisan League officials, reflecting CIO policy and rank-and-file sentiment, pressed their advantage in the spring of 1937. They cast their net as widely as possible among unionists. To counter charges of Lewis and CIO domination, they promoted craft leaders for league offices. Crouch hoped to elect AFL loyalists to every position, but industrial unionists forced him to include members of the Akron Newspaper Guild and the WPA union. Only when the league formed a separate policy-making executive council did URW leaders appear. Crouch and his allies were less successful in attracting candidates for the Democratic and Republican primaries, though they did not abandon their hope for a Republican primary ticket until May. In the meantime, the Democratic county chairman was "making a strenuous effort" to find a candidate "on whom both the party and labor interests can agree." He and Crouch met on several occasions and agreed in principle to a joint effort to unseat Republican Mayor Lee D. Schroy and the Republican majority on the city council in 1937. Unionists made no secret of their determination to be the dominant partner in the alliance. They spoke publicly of taking over the local Democratic organization and in late April began to recruit candidates without consulting party leaders. League officials chose Judge Patterson, whose ties to the party organization were at best tenuous, to head the CIO ticket. To complete their coup they entered union officials in every ward as Democratic candidates for the city council. Long-suffering Democratic regulars countered by entering several opposition candidates, including a mayoral prospect with an anti-union background.[20]

[19] Thomas T. Spencer, "Auxiliary and Non-Party Politics: The 1936 Democratic Presidential Campaign in Ohio," *Ohio History*, 90 (Spring 1981), 117–18; Dubofsky and Van Tyne, *John L. Lewis*, 249–52; Lovin, "Ohio 'Farmer-Labor' Movement," 435–36; Philip Taft, "Labor's Changing Political Line," *Journal of Political Economy*, 45 (Oct. 1937), 641–42; *Akron Beacon Journal*, Nov. 5, 1936, pp. 1, 16; *ibid.*, Nov. 9, 1936, p. 17; *ibid.*, Jan. 1, 1937, pp. 1, 6.

[20] *Akron Beacon Journal*, April 5, 1937, p. 19; *ibid.*, May 3, 1937, p. 17; *Akron Times Press*, May

During the primary campaign Patterson emphasized his New Deal ties. Pledging repeatedly to put "Roosevelt democracy" and "New Deal democracy" into city hall, he called for improved housing and expanded recreational facilities. He was particularly critical of Schroy's failure to embrace the New Deal housing program. Coupled with that appeal were attacks—à la Roosevelt —on the supposed alliance between big business and the Schroy administration. An able public speaker, Patterson impressed many observers with his stage presence and Rooseveltian oratory. By mid-summer Labor's Non-Partisan league leaders and Democratic officials alike conceded that the only remaining issue, barring an anti-CIO backlash, was the size of Patterson's victory.[21]

Two other developments during the same period ensured that the mayoral election would be more than a local contest. In March the Firestone URW local struck, demanding recognition as the employees' bargaining agent. The eight-week conflict that followed was far less dramatic and colorful than the Goodyear strike of 1936 but hardly less important. The settlement, concluded in late April, was an exact replica of the landmark Chrysler Corporation contract that the United Automobile Workers (UAW) had won in Detroit a few weeks before. It provided for union recognition and formal collective bargaining procedures. Together with the General Motors Corporation and the United States Steel Corporation contracts signed in February and March 1937, the Chrysler and Firestone settlements marked the high tide of CIO power in the 1930s. Militant unionists appeared capable of sweeping all of American industry before them.[22]

The second development of the spring of 1937, the "Little Steel" strike of May-July, provided the first intimations of CIO vulnerability. Akron residents, like observers elsewhere, came to associate the Steel Workers Organizing Committee and, by extension, other CIO groups with violence. The turmoil associated with the conflict seriously compromised the efforts of union leaders to create an image of prudence and responsibility. The strike's collapse also demonstrated that the union upsurge could be halted. Contrary to earlier impressions, CIO unions apparently remained subject to the same divisive forces that had traditionally thwarted efforts to organize the mass production industries. No less important, the steel strike converted Governor Davey from a prolabor to an anti-CIO stance. Davey's shift ensured the failure of the Little

23, 1937, p. 1; *Summit County Labor News*, April 9, 1937, p. 1; *ibid.*, May 7, 1937, pp. 1, 5. Labor's Non-Partisan League endorsed the Republican incumbent mayor for reelection in nearby Barberton, Ohio—evidence, it declared, of its determination "to support its friends, regardless of party alliance." *Ibid.*, Sept. 24, 1937, p. 1.

[21] *Akron Beacon Journal*, July 23, 1937, p. 34; *ibid.*, Aug. 11, 1937, p. 1; *ibid.*, Oct. 5, 1937, pp. 1, 20; *ibid.*, Oct. 13, 1937, pp. 1, 6.

[22] *Ibid.*, April 29, 1937, p. 1; *ibid.*, April 30, 1937, pp. 1, 6; P. W. Chappell to H. L. Kerwin, April 6, April 14, April 18, April 19, 1937, file 182/2448, Federal Mediation and Conciliation Service Papers; memoranda on the strike, March 26, April 10, April 16, 1937, Firestone Archives; Carl Haessler, "Union Whips Firestone," *United Rubber Worker*, 2 (May 1937), 1, 4, 5; Roberts, *Rubber Workers*, 158-60; Bernstein, *Turbulent Years*, 466-72.

Steel strike in Ohio; it also signaled the emergence of an anti-CIO, increasingly anti–New Deal faction within the Democratic party.[23]

On August 8 Labor's Non-Partisan League candidates won sweeping primary victories in Akron. Patterson overwhelmed his opponent by 17,600 to 6,500 votes. His total was nearly 50 percent higher than that of any primary candidate in the city's history, confirming the new political might of the CIO. His appeal, moreover, was broad-based. He had gotten at least 20 percent of Roosevelt's 1936 total in each of the city's ten wards and had finished far ahead of the league-endorsed council candidates, who in turn had handily defeated their opponents, including two incumbents. Local gamblers made Patterson and the union city council candidates heavy favorites to win the general election.[24]

The ensuing campaign marked the beginning of a concerted CIO effort to build on the example of 1936 and to create a union presence in American politics. In New York, Pittsburgh, Detroit, Akron, and a handful of smaller communities with large concentrations of union members, CIO leaders attempted to extend their power to city hall. It was a prelude to a more ambitious effort, possibly an independent campaign, in the congressional elections of 1938 and in the presidential election of 1940. Politics, however, proved to be as challenging as the most complex negotiations, and CIO goals, as elusive as a Ford Motor Company or a Republic Steel Corporation contract. In New York the CIO was merely one member of the Fiorello La Guardia coalition. In Pittsburgh the CIO candidate failed to survive the primary. In Detroit UAW leaders running on an avowedly prolabor slate for the city council won places on the general election ballot but by margins so narrow that there was little prospect of a CIO-controlled government. Only in Akron did an attractive candidate offer a large group of voters an unambiguous choice. There the "CIO issue [was] more closely joined than in any other city."[25]

Patterson accordingly adopted a cautious campaign strategy. With few contacts outside the labor movement and with little money, he feared a blunder that would be impossible to overcome. Instead, he relied increasingly on the assurance of URW leaders that the unions would elect him. After August he seldom spoke about specific problems or plans. His substantive proposals for slum clearance, improved housing, and expanded public services gave way to attacks on the "closed," "undemocratic," and big-business-controlled Republican administration. Union leaders became more and more

---

[23] James L. Baughman, "Classes and Company Towns: Legends of the 1937 Little Steel Strike," *Ohio History*, 87 (Spring 1978), esp. 190–91; Bernstein, *Turbulent Years*, 478–97; Robert R. R. Brooks, *As Steel Goes. . . . : Unionism in a Basic Industry* (New Haven, 1940), 130–52. Forty United Rubber Workers (URW) members were arrested on June 22 while en route to picket in Youngstown, Ohio. *Akron Beacon Journal*, June 23, 1937, p. 1; *ibid.*, June 26, 1937, p. 13; *ibid.*, July 7, 1937, p. 13. For adverse public reaction to that incident, see *ibid.*, June 30, 1937, p. 13.
[24] *Akron Times Press*, Oct. 31, 1937, sec. D, p. 3; *Akron Beacon Journal*, Nov. 1, 1937, p. 6.
[25] Morehead, "Test Tube City," 55; *New York Times*, Nov. 2, 1937, pp. 1, 6; *ibid.*, Nov. 3, 1937, pp. 1, 12; Bruce Stave, *The New Deal and the Last Hurrah: Pittsburgh Machine Politics* (Pittsburgh, 1970), 154; Hugh T. Lovin, "CIO Innovators, Labor Party Ideologues, and Organized Labor's Muddles in the 1937 Detroit Elections," *Old Northwest*, 8 (Fall 1982), 234.

prominent in his campaign. Tate and URW officials regularly appeared at Democratic rallies and frequently upstaged him. The change of emphasis altered the character of the campaign. Despite his attractive qualities Patterson's approach emphasized his labor ties and conveyed a sense that union power, rather than the incumbent, was the principal issue. The Democratic council candidates reinforced that impression. They were union veterans who devoted most of their time to soliciting the support of fellow unionists. By November voters who followed the Democratic campaign had good reason to conclude that Patterson was first and foremost a union representative.[26]

Patterson's CIO ties also dictated the Republican strategy. After the primary the mayor's advisers decided on an aggressive campaign designed to highlight Patterson's union connection. The architects of that effort were Loren L. Poe, a public relations expert with big-business clients and close ties to Governor Davey, and Ray C. Bliss, an insurance executive who had recently embarked on a political career that would make him a fixture in state and national Republican affairs for nearly a half-century. In early September Poe arranged a secret meeting between Davey and Bliss at the statehouse in Columbus. The governor, reveling in the publicity that had accompanied his handling of the Little Steel strike, offered to throw the resources of his administration behind the Republican effort. Bliss eagerly accepted. Henceforth, state employees and interest-group representatives allied with Davey worked directly or indirectly for the Republicans. In late September the governor himself appeared before an Akron business group. His address was officially nonpolitical, but his attacks on Lewis and the CIO were tantamount to a Schroy endorsement.[27]

Poe and Bliss devised other ways to focus attention on the unions. The mayor's speeches, written by Poe, emphasized the sinister character of the opposition. Patterson was a "carpetbagger" who represented "outsiders," "radicals," and "communistic" elements that would ruin the city. Union victory would be synonymous with a "radical" takeover. Business would flee and the city would decline. When Bliss learned that Earl Browder, head of the Communist party, would endorse the Patterson effort in an Akron speech, he arranged to have Browder's remarks broadcast over a local radio station. The Republicans thus financed the local Communists' most important publicity coup of the decade. Later, when union zealots defaced Schroy billboards, Bliss left them as visible symbols of the unions' destructive potential. Poe and Bliss were equally shrewd in wooing nonunion Democrats and independents. With abundant funds contributed by local industrialists, they ran daily newspaper advertisements devoted to the "carpetbagger" and the "radical" themes. By

[26] Sutliff interview; Turner interview; *Akron Beacon Journal*, Oct. 5, 1937, pp. 1, 20; *ibid.*, Oct. 9, 1937, p. 6; *ibid.*, Oct. 23, 1937, pp. 1, 6. Despite the CIO's reputation for campaign spending, Labor's Non-Partisan League raised only $15,000 for the Patterson campaign. The league's national organization contributed $3,000; the Akron URW locals, more than $8,000. The Democratic party listed no campaign expenditures. The Lee D. Schroy campaign spent at least $38,000. *Ibid.*, Nov. 13, 1937, p. 1.

[27] *Akron Beacon Journal*, Sept. 20, 1937, pp. 1, 28; *ibid.*, Sept. 24, 1937, pp. 1, 6; Ray C. Bliss interview by Nelson, June 18, 1981 (in Nelson's possession).

the end of October, local observers predicted a closer race than had seemed possible in August. The outcome would likely depend on the unity of the union vote.[28]

Recognizing that likelihood, the Davey forces worked to widen the AFL-CIO rift. In September William Green, president of the AFL, ordered CIO unions expelled from central labor unions. Tate complied, but he and URW leaders immediately formed an AFL-CIO labor council to continue the craft-industrial union partnership that had been an important feature of Central Labor Union activity. Most AFL unions enthusiastically participated. A minority, led by building-trades business agents who had consistently opposed Tate, objected. When Tate indiscreetly criticized AFL national leaders at a URW gathering, they moved to oust him. Charging disloyalty, they obtained an order from Green dissolving the Central Labor Union, expelling Tate, and creating a new anti-CIO central body. Tate's AFL backers protested and boycotted the new organization. Davey's men, including several local AFL officials, attempted to exploit the situation. There were rumors of payoffs for union officers who would help "divert a small part of the labor vote into the . . . Schroy camp."[29] Labor's Non-Partisan League officials insisted that the dissidents would attract no more than 5 percent of AFL members, but they could ill-afford defections of any magnitude.

On November 2 Schroy defeated Patterson by 44,212 to 36,100 votes in a record turnout. Republicans also swept nine of thirteen council seats. Considering the city's large union membership and Patterson's appeal, it was a humiliating setback. If the CIO could not mount a successful campaign in Akron, where could it win? Republicans took heart and politicians generally took heed. Contemporary analysts from both camps attributed the debacle to the breakdown of the labor-Democratic coalition. Nonunion Democrats, troubled by union excesses during the previous year and by the Poe-Bliss strategy, supposedly rejected Patterson for the less attractive, but safer, Schroy. The unionists lost because they allowed themselves to be isolated. Even in Akron they could not win without allies.[30]

The election statistics provide some support for that interpretation. In 1936, 28.6 percent of the Akron electorate cast ballots for Alfred M. Landon, the Republican presidential candidate. Two years later 26.4 percent of Akron citizens identified themselves as Republicans in an opinon poll. Yet Schroy

[28] *Akron Beacon Journal*, Sept, 24, 1937, pp. 1, 6; *ibid.*, Sept. 27, 1937, p. 19; *ibid.*, Oct. 16, 1937, pp. 1, 7; *ibid.*, Oct. 22, 1937, p. 1; *Akron Times Press*, Oct. 31, 1937, sec. D, p. 3; Morehead, "Test Tube City," 55-56; Bliss interview; Nelson, "Origins of the Sit-Down Era," 200. The Republican charges were not just campaign rhetoric. The "flight" of rubber manufacturing to other, usually nonunion localities had begun in 1936; by 1937 it was a major local issue, and by 1938 the manufacturers' decision to "decentralize" was apparently irrevocable. *Ibid.*, 218-19; Charles B. Coates, "Labor Boomerang in Akron," *Factory Management and Maintenance*, 96 (July 1938), 38-39.

[29] *Summit County Labor News*, Oct. 1, 1937, p. 1; *Akron Beacon Journal*, Sept. 21, 1937, p. 29; *ibid.*, Oct. 2, 1937, p. 12; James O. Morris, *Conflict within the AFL: A Study of Craft versus Industrial Unionism, 1901-1938* (Ithaca, 1958), 247.

[30] *Akron Beacon Journal*, Nov. 2, 1937, p. 24; *ibid.*, Nov. 3, 1937, pp. 1, 6; *Akron Times Press*, Nov. 3, 1937, pp. 1, 4.

received 16,600 more votes than Landon and 7,800 more than the Republican gubernatorial candidate in 1938. In 73 percent of the precincts, Schroy's total was higher than a Republican could reasonably expect. Clearly Schroy did not win with Republican votes alone. An estimate of voting behavior in 1936–1937 suggests that in addition to virtually all the Landon supporters, Schroy attracted a quarter of the Roosevelt partisans and persuaded another quarter not to vote at all. It was the combination of Democrats and independents, people who continued to think of themselves as Democrats and independents after 1937, that made the difference.[31]

An analysis of the variables that best explain the outcome, in the order of their contribution, provides clues to the identities of the wayward Roosevelt partisans. (See table 1.) The level of rent paid by residents of a given neighborhood was the best predictor of the voters' mayoral choice. Low-rent neighborhoods were pro-Patterson; high-rent neighborhoods were anti-Patterson. Somewhat less important was the presence of middle-aged voters, men

[31] Jones, *Life, Liberty, and Property*, 316; Summit County manuscript election returns, Nov. 1934, Nov. 1936, Nov. 1937 (Board of Elections, Akron, Ohio); H. O. DeGraff, computations from 1930 population census, 1936 (in the possession of Akron, Ohio, Planning Department); Federal Housing Administration, *Akron, Ohio*, 129, 157; Burch Directory Company, *Akron, Barberton and Cuyahoga Falls Official City Directory, 1937* (Akron, 1936). The "reasonable" total for the Republican and Democratic candidates in each precinct was calculated by adding the party vote for prosecuting attorney and for state treasurer in 1934 and 1936 and dividing by four. The estimate of voting behavior is based on a comparison of 1936 and 1937 vote totals. Since no registration figures have survived, it is necessary to assume that the total for Franklin D. Roosevelt and Alfred M. Landon included all potential 1937 voters. The difference between the Roosevelt-Landon total and the Schroy-Patterson total in each precinct is therefore defined as the number of 1937 nonvoters. Based on this assumption, regression analysis ought to provide estimates of the distribution of the Roosevelt and Landon supporters in 1937. However, because of the method of calculating the nonvoters, the size of the Roosevelt majority, and other factors, the results were unsatisfactory. Despite this problem, it seems reasonable to assume that the Landon voters were highly motivated and extremely hostile to Patterson. If indeed they voted and cast their ballots overwhelmingly for Schroy, the Roosevelt vote must have gone approximately one-quarter to Schroy and one-half to Patterson, with the other quarter not voting. Working with data on population, sex, race, nationality, and age by decades, H. O. DeGraff showed population shifts between 1929 and 1936 and converted the data from political wards to census tracts. The tracts were more numerous than the wards, embracing 2–5 precincts rather than 15–25, and were organized by homogenous neighborhoods. After a house-by-house survey, the Federal Housing Administration listed values and rents by census tracts using a five-category classification. In this study values and rents are ranked from 1 (high) to 5 (low). A sample of 50 Akron precincts supplemented this information. The author selected 50 precincts (18 randomly chosen from the 65 that gave Schroy a 60 percent or greater majority, 10 randomly chosen from the 34 that gave Patterson a 60 percent or greater majority, and 23 randomly chosen from the 83 that gave either candidate a 50–60 percent majority). All individuals who lived in the area of each of the 50 precincts were listed and 100 names were drawn randomly from each list. The city directory supplied information on marital status, home ownership, and occupation for the 5,000 household heads. Altogether data was obtained on 34 variables: percent female, percent male, percent white, percent black, percent white native, percent white foreign born, percent immigrant, value of houses, level of rents, percent under age 20, percent age 21–24, percent age 25–34, percent age 35–44, percent age 45–64, percent age 65 and over, percent homeowners, percent married, percent professional, percent small business, percent clerical—total, percent clerical—rubber industry, percent factory—total, percent factory—rubber industry, percent craft—total, percent craft—rubber industry, percent supervisors, percent Goodyear wage earner, percent Firestone wage earner, percent Goodrich wage earner, percent General Tire wage earner, percent other rubber industry wage earner, percent unskilled, percent unemployed, percent unemployed—widows.

TABLE 1
Multiple Regression Coefficients for Democratic
Mayoral Vote on Selected Variables

INDEPENDENT VARIABLE	DEPENDENT VARIABLE: PATTERSON PERCENTAGE OF TOTAL VOTE BY PRECINCTS ($N = 50$)	
	'B' Coefficient (Standard Error)	Beta
Rent	.049 (.015)	.398
Age 35–44	−3.051 (.996)	−.311
Housing	.037 (.015)	.224
Firestone	.366 (.154)	.157
$R^2 = .831$		

SOURCES: Federal Housing Administration, Division of Economics and Statistics, *Akron, Ohio: Housing Market Analysis* (Washington, 1938), 129, 157; H. O. DeGraff, computations from 1930 population census, 1936 (in the possesison of Akron, Ohio, Planning Department); Summit County manuscript election returns, Nov. 1936, Nov. 1937 (Board of Elections, Akron, Ohio); Burch Directory Company, *Akron, Barberton and Cuyahoga Falls Official City Directory, 1937* (Akron, 1936).
NOTE: All coefficients are significant at the .01 level, except Firestone employment (.02). Computer programs of the Statistical Package for the Social Sciences were used for this and all other statistical operations.

and women in their late thirties and early forties, who strongly opposed Patterson. Housing values reveal the same distinction as rental levels. Poor neighborhoods supported Patterson; richer ones opposed him. Finally, employment at Firestone, the only variable that indicates union influence, helps explain the voters' preferences. All other variables are comparatively insignificant and in combination account for less than one-fifth of the differences between precincts.[32]

Despite the preoccupation of both camps with union membership and with interest-group politics, Akron citizens appear to have voted their pocketbooks in 1937. Economic station far overshadowed employment relationships and other factors that might have influenced the election outcome. Yet the disparity between rich and poor (see table 1) is potentially misleading. Few Akron voters had large incomes or sumptuous homes. The vast majority owned or rented dwellings that were only marginally habitable. If the contest had truly pitted haves against have-nots, the Democrats would have won by a

[32] Federal Housing Administration, *Akron, Ohio*, 129, 158; H. O. DeGraff, computations from 1930 population census, 1936; Burch Directory Company, *Akron, Barberton and Cuyahoga Falls Official City Directory, 1937*; Summit County manuscript election returns, Nov. 1934, Nov. 1936, Nov. 1937.

landslide. The problem for the Democrats was that a large portion of the middle range of voters, people of modest means and modest dwellings who had supported the New Deal in 1936, favored Schroy in 1937. Class distinctions may have been decisive, but they did not conform to the usual stereotypes. In Akron the "middle" class of Schroy supporters extended virtually to the slums.[33]

An examination of specific occupational groups, their voting patterns in 1937, and the attitudes of their members toward corporate property rights shortly thereafter helps clarify that division. (See table 2.) There was a strong negative association between white-collar occupations and the Democratic vote and a generally positive association between blue-collar work and support for Patterson. There was also a positive correlation between voting behavior and attitudes toward corporate property, as contemporary analysts of the campaign would have predicted. Blue-collar workers and the unemployed identified with Patterson and anticorporate sentiments while many white-collar workers took the opposite position.[34] But there were also exceptions to this pattern. When forced to choose between a union-dominated candidate and a seemingly anti-union candidate, many small-business operators, including auto service station owners and others whose incomes were no higher than the wages of factory workers, whose views of corporate rights did not differ markedly from those of many blue-collar workers, and who had generally backed Roosevelt, apparently rejected Patterson. Clerical and service workers, whose ranks also included many poorly paid employees, were even less enthusiastic, subscribing presumably to the Republican argument that a Patterson victory would be bad for business and consequently for unorganized individuals whose fates depended largely on the state of the local economy. Many white-collar employees seemingly placed their immediate prospects ahead of any sense of class identity. Like most American white-collar workers, they were pragmatists, flirting with organized labor when it promised to enhance their prospects, rejecting it when, as in 1937, it seemed to endanger those prospects.[35]

The data also suggest Democratic defections among certain blue-collar groups (see table 2). The high negative coefficient of the nonunion rubber

[33] Burch Directory Company, *Akron, Barberton and Cuyahoga Falls Official City Directory, 1937*; Summit County manuscript election returns, Nov. 1936, Nov. 1937; Federal Housing Administration, *Akron, Ohio*, 129, 157.

[34] Summit County manuscript election returns, Nov. 1936, Nov. 1937; Jones, *Life, Liberty, and Property*, 379. For Jones's method, see *ibid.*, 357–77. The correlation coefficients indicate strength of association between variables. A more direct estimate of behavior, the ecological regression, was unsuitable for most of the occupational groups because of dispersed housing patterns. For example, only 7 precincts had more than 15 percent professionals, only 11 had more than 15 percent small business proprietors and only 7 had more than 15 percent craft workers. Only clerical and factory employees were highly concentrated. See also J. Morgan Kousser, "Ecological Regression and the Analysis of Past Politics," *Journal of Interdisciplinary History*, 4 (Autumn 1973), 237–62.

[35] Jones, *Life, Liberty, and Property*, 196–207, 225–35. CIO unions had some success in organizing clerical and service workers. For the nation, see Jürgen Kocka, *White Collar Workers in America, 1890–1940: A Social-Political History in International Perspective* (London, 1980), 193–250.

TABLE 2
Akron Occupational Groups

OCCUPATIONS	PEARSON CORRELATION COEFFICIENTS OF SUPPORT FOR PATTERSON CANDIDACY, 1937	PERCENTAGE OPPOSED TO CORPORATE PROPERTY RIGHTS, 1938–1939
Professionals	−.747	36.0
Big-Business Executives	N.A.	00.0
Small-Business Operators	−.284	52.0
Clerical/Service Workers	−.598	27.0
Craft Workers	−.113	76.0ᶜ
Factory Workers	.700	69.0
CIO	.518*	84.0
Firestone	.449	N.A.
Goodrich	.422	N.A.
Goodyear	.219	N.A.
Nonunion	−.626ᵇ	40.0
Unskilled (Laborers, etc.)	.451	74.0ᵈ
Unemployed	.411	64.0
r = .783		

SOURCES: Summit County manuscript election returns, Nov. 1937 (Board of Elections, Akron, Ohio); Burch Directory Company, *Akron, Barberton and Cuyahoga Falls Official City Directory, 1937* (Akron, 1936); Alfred Winslow Jones, *Life, Liberty, and Property: A Story of Conflict and a Measurement of Conflicting Rights* (Philadelphia, 1941), 379.
NOTE: Occupational data was correlated with precinct-level returns for 1937, based on a fifty-precinct sample. All coefficients are significant at the .05 level except Craft Workers (.21) and Goodyear (.07). The Nonunion coefficient applies to all Goodyear workers who lived in Goodyear Heights, a measure that overstates the number of non-CIO workers but probably understates their support for Lee D. Schroy. The correlation coefficient for Goodyear rises from .219 to .319 when the Goodyear Heights precincts are omitted. The percentages reflect the proportion of respondents whose scores ranged from 0 to 11. Professionals are defined as Alfred Winslow Jones's Technicians, Teachers, and Ministers; Factory Workers as Employees Association, Non-CIO, and CIO; Nonunion as Employees Association and Non-CIO; Unskilled as Works Progress Administration, Manual; Unemployed as all Works Progress Administration. Because Jones's numbers are ordinal, percentages are indicated rather than means, which Jones used.
  ᵃ Firestone and Goodrich workers.
  ᵇ Goodyear workers living in Goodyear Heights.
  ᶜ Members of the AFL.
  ᵈ WPA manual workers.

workers, Goodyear employees who were former Goodyear Industrial Assembly activists, is hardly surprising.[36] The intense, often violent conflict between URW and anti-URW militants in the Goodyear plant had long since foreclosed any possibility of cooperation between them. The suggestion that many craft

[36] Non-CIO rubber workers were concentrated in the Goodyear Heights area, a company-sponsored residential development of the World War I era. Their number is uncertain, but 3,193 Goodyear workers voted against the CIO in a National Labor Relations Board election on August 24, 1937. *Akron Beacon Journal*, Aug. 25, 1937, p. 1.

workers, including AFL members, supported Schroy emphasizes both the disruptive character of the AFL-CIO conflict and Davey's ability to wean construction workers and possibly others from the Patterson camp. The figures indicate that their alienation did not extend to fundamentals, but even modest defections could jeopardize the success of a political campaign dependent on the labor vote.[37]

The Patterson campaign thus lost the support of many individuals who had voted for Roosevelt in 1936. That decline was due in part to developments beyond Patterson's control. Despite his platform manner he was not Roosevelt and could not exploit the aura of the presidency. Like many Democratic candidates after 1936, he also suffered from public disillusionment with the New Deal. The strikes, sit-downs, and labor upheavals, the onset of recession, and the president's effort to "pack" the United States Supreme Court created a different and more difficult atmosphere for New Deal candidates after 1936. But Patterson was hardly a victim of circumstances. By eschewing appeals to white-collar workers and others who had supported Roosevelt, he and his advisers made their success dependent on a unified labor vote. This tie exposed a second miscalculation, their assumption that the union vote could be mobilized en masse for union candidates. The AFL-CIO conflict ought to have alerted them to the dangers of that course. Yet the fundamental problem was not at the federation or international union level. The margin of Patterson's defeat is almost unimaginable in the face of a united CIO. In the end the rubber workers were the key to the outcome of the election, but their role spelled defeat and frustration for the unions and the CIO strategy.[38]

A closer examination of the CIO vote illuminates the flaw in the Patterson campaign. Factory workers, including employees at other manufacturing firms organized by CIO unions, are strongly associated with support for Patterson (see table 2). It is precisely the relationship that union leaders expected. But the impression of union cohesiveness begins to fade when the plant, or the local union, is the unit of analysis. In particular, there appears to have been a difference between Goodrich and Firestone workers on the one hand and Goodyear workers on the other, a difference that even the most generous definitions of the anti-CIO element at Goodyear does not eradicate. A more direct estimate of voting behavior, based on the precincts with the largest concentrations of Firestone and Goodyear employees, confirms the distinction. Goodyear factionalism, it appears, offset Firestone and Goodrich cohesiveness, leaving Democrats in command of the labor vote but far short of victory.[39]

[37] Jones, Life, Liberty, and Property, 379.

[38] Gavin Wright, "The Political Economy of New Deal Spending: An Econometric Analysis," Review of Economics and Statistics, 56 (Dec. 1974), 34–37; Richard Jensen, "The Last Party System: Decay of Consensus, 1932–1978," typescript, 1981 (in Nelson's possession).

[39] Summit County Labor News, Nov. 5, 1937, pp. 1, 4; Summit County manuscript election returns, Nov. 1937. Ecological regression estimates, based on the 15 precincts with the highest concentrations of Goodyear and Firestone workers suggest that 41 percent of Goodyear workers and 95 percent of Firestone workers voted for Patterson. Compared to local Democratic candidates in 1934 and 1936, Patterson received 81 percent of the "normal" Democratic vote in the Goodyear

Why would Firestone workers behave differently from Goodyear workers? The power and presumed unity of the CIO forces was, after all, the central issue of the campaign, the preoccupation of both camps. Neither union records and newspaper reports nor the reminiscences of union veterans provide answers to this question. Indeed, they suggest a misleading pattern. Goodyear unionists were the most visible of the URW activists. They sparked the sit-down movement and were responsible for most of the work stoppages. Levinson had them in mind when he wrote of "labor on the march." Goodyear union leaders were active in the Patterson campaign, and two Goodyear union officers were elected to the city council, the only two CIO members among the Democratic candidates to survive the Patterson debacle. It would not be unreasonable to assume that the Goodyear unionists went to the polls united in their determination to elect a labor mayor. The Firestone local, on the other hand, received little public notice, was responsible for few sit-downs, and despite its contract victory was viewed by militant unionists as the most "conservative" of the Big Three locals. A careful reading of the documents might reasonably suggest that the Firestone workers would be less enthusiastic toward Patterson's candidacy than would Goodyear unionists. If there were serious defections, they could likely be in the Firestone precincts.[40]

In fact, the election returns suggest a contrary pattern. The Goodyear workers seem to have been little more united than Akron Democrats generally, whereas Firestone workers conformed to the anticipated Goodyear model. This pattern in turn suggests a different reading of the documents. In 1936–1937 Goodyear militancy was a sign of union dissension and weakness; Firestone quiescence, an indication of union strength. Militancy and union power were inversely correlated. The experiences of these two groups, so near and yet so far apart, reflected the fragmenting as well as the unifying impact of the depression. By curbing interplant mobility, economic conditions increased the importance of specific working conditions and labor-management relationships. In the 1910s and 1920s, the peculiarities of a particular plant had relatively little effect on the workers' outlook; in the 1930s they had a substantial, in some instances a decisive, impact. At Goodyear the company's ambitious personnel program had created and the depression had preserved a corps of loyalists who sustained the Goodyear Industrial Assembly and who were responsible for the upheavals of the 1930s. Goodyear militancy was as much a reaction to them as it was an expression of union sentiment. The

precincts but 164 percent of the Democratic vote in the Firestone precincts. The anti-CIO Goodyear Heights militants helped account for the unusually low Goodyear estimates. Goodrich workers and other CIO members were much more widely dispersed, making direct estimates of their voting behavior less reliable. *Ibid.*, Nov. 1934, Nov. 1936, Nov. 1937.

[40] Minutes of Executive Board, Minutes of Membership Meetings, 1933–1937, Local 2 Records (United Rubber Workers Local 2 Offices, Akron, Ohio); House interview; Turner interview; Charles Skinner interview by Nelson, April 23, 1976, tape recording (American History Research Center); O. H. Bosley interview by Nelson, Oct. 23, 1973, tape recording, *ibid.*; Walter Kriebel interview by Nelson, Sept. 19, 1972, tape recording, *ibid.*; John D. House, "History of the United Rubber Workers of America," microfilm, 1981 (Ohio Historical Society, Columbus, Ohio); Levinson, *Labor on the March*, 143–46; Nelson, "Origins of the Sit-Down Era," 212–22.

Firestone personnel program, which was equally advanced except for the omission of a company union (until 1933), had the opposite effect in the 1930s. Depression conditions made Firestone workers union zealots but zealots with a single antagonist. And their antagonist, the Firestone management, was known for its liberal policies. The 1937 strike marked the apogee of both Firestone solidarity and Firestone "conservatism." In November 1937 Firestone unionists boosted Patterson's candidacy with greater élan than did any other CIO group.[41]

This pattern also helps explain the behavior of workers at Goodrich and possibly at the smaller plants. The Goodrich local occupied an intermediate niche between the extremes represented by Goodyear and Firestone. It was vocal and active on the one hand, united and relatively free of dissent on the other. It enjoyed a generally harmonious relationship with the Goodrich management at the time of the election and was beginning to bargain seriously for a contract, an objective that it realized in 1938. Goodrich workers seem to have backed Patterson with little dissent.[42]

Although the evidence is suggestive rather than conclusive, the behavior of CIO members in Akron lends support to several important hypotheses about the 1930s. First, it buttresses the arguments of historians who have found a negative or at best a neutral relationship between militancy and organization. In Akron rank-and-file militancy was a particularistic response to specific circumstances. In its most virulent forms, it was anti-union as well as anti-management, an indication of the absence of a shared outlook rather than an expression of worker unity in opposition to a common opponent. It played a major role in altering the industrial and the political environments, but Levinson's metaphor notwithstanding, it was not a synonym for union power. Second, the Akron experience confirms the critical role of the local union in the evolution of the labor movement. The URW was probably more decentralized than most CIO unions, but even URW leaders did not appreciate the extent to which their organization diverged at the local level. Employees who worked and lived in proximity to one another and under nearly identical circumstances viewed the union and its claims differently. The social milieus of the plant and the local union were the keys to their perspective. The character of the labor force, employer-employee relations, local union leadership, and small-group dynamics overshadowed most or all external forces, including the efforts of URW International and CIO leaders.[43]

[41] Firestone unity declined in 1938, in part because the major goals of the workers seemed to have been achieved and in part because recession layoffs broke up the close-knit group that had guided the union in earlier years. Donald Anthony, "Rubber Products," in *How Collective Bargaining Works: A Survey of Experience in Leading American Industries*, ed. Harry A. Millis (New York, 1942), 653–54.

[42] Roberts, *Rubber Workers*, 161–69; T. G. Graham to J. S. Knight, March 16, 1938, and accompanying documents, file 199/1326, Federal Mediation and Conciliation Service Papers; "Meetings with Management, 1938," Local 5 Records (United Rubber Workers Local 5 Offices, Akron, Ohio).

[43] See especially Zieger, "Limits of Militancy," 638–57; Friedlander, *Emergence of a UAW Local*, 93–131; and Robert H. Zieger, *Madison's Battery Workers, 1934–1952: A History of Federal Labor Union 19587* (Ithaca, 1977), 49–57.

   The election returns also suggest the enthusiasm of the unemployed for Patterson (see table 2).[44] On the basis of public statements and campaign issues, it would not be unreasonable to assume that the jobless might have supported Schroy, who promised a healthier local economy and more jobs. Like the small-business operators and clerical workers, the poor might have bet on economic growth. But powerful forces militated against that course. The Democratic machine had been based in the center-city slum wards, and patronage and tradition may have created bonds that transcended campaign appeals. There were also good reasons to discount Schroy's statements. His previous term coincided with a revival of the local economy that had led to the reemployment of factory workers but to no increase in local spending for public works or relief. One of the mayor's more accurate claims was that he had alleviated the city's financial plight by carefully husbanding public funds. That appealed to property owners, including many rubber workers, but was unlikely to endear him to the unemployed. In 1937 the city's frugality precipitated a series of public-relief crises that severely restricted payments to unemployables who did not qualify for federal aid. Cutbacks in WPA projects after the 1936 election exacerbated the problem. Despite a rapidly spiraling unemployment rate in 1937, Schroy was unable to secure more WPA jobs. Finally, prodded by the unions, the mayor endorsed a property tax increase to finance relief expenses. The proposal appeared on the 1937 ballot and was overwhelmingly defeated. In the meantime the plight of the poor worsened. It is hardly surprising that Patterson's early calls for expanded public services, slum clearance, and housing relief struck a responsive chord among them. Despite the Democrats' reticence during the general election campaign, the Poe-Bliss strategy sustained the impression that Patterson would be a big spender. In November the unemployed opted for public services rather than for economic growth.[45]

   The behavior of the poor further underlines the lost opportunities of the Patterson campaign. As already noted, economic status strongly influenced voting behavior (see table 1). Patterson could have mobilized victims of the depression—the small-business operators, clerical workers, craft workers, factory workers, laborers, and unemployed workers of all types. By devoting more attention to public services and less to union power, he might have sustained the New Deal coalition of 1936. His approach, however, encouraged

---

[44] It is impossible to determine from the city directory whether unemployed persons were temporarily jobless due to layoffs (and eligible or even employed on WPA projects) or unemployable. My estimate is that most of the unemployed in the sample were unemployable and therefore dependent on municipal relief. Burch Directory Company, *Akron, Barberton and Cuyahoga Falls Official City Directory, 1937.* For a valuable overview of the unemployment and relief problem in the 1930s, see James T. Patterson, *America's Struggle against Poverty, 1900-1980* (Cambridge, Mass., 1981), 37-77.

[45] *Akron Beacon Journal,* Feb. 23, 1937, pp. 1, 6; *ibid.,* May 25, 1937, p. 21; *ibid.,* June 29, 1937, p. 27; *ibid.,* July 1, 1937, p. 1; *ibid.,* July 2, 1937, p. 48; *ibid.,* July 26, 1937, p. 13; *ibid.,* July 27, 1937, p. 1; *ibid.,* Aug. 18, 1937, p. 17; *ibid.,* Aug. 21, 1937, p. 2; *ibid.,* Oct. 23, 1937, p. 4; *ibid.,* Oct. 29, 1937, p. 29; *ibid.,* Nov. 3, 1937, pp. 1, 8; *ibid.,* Nov. 27, 1937, pp. 1, 10. By 1937 Akron's financial condition was excellent. U.S. Department of Commerce, Bureau of the Census, *Financial Statistics of Cities Having a Population of Over 100,000, 1936* (Washington, 1938), 53, 72, 173.

middle-class voters, including many union members, to support the incumbent. Much the same pattern was evident elsewhere. In New York, where La Guardia transcended his labor base, the union forces won a landslide victory. In Detroit, where the CIO candidates behaved more like Patterson, they lost.[46] Although it is impossible to generalize about the behavior of specific groups, campaigns that had depended largely or solely on the union vote fared poorly.

Thus the 1937 Akron mayoralty contest confirmed the city's "test tube" reputation. Coming at the height of CIO power and expectations, it reflected the euphoria of the industrial union movement in the critical months between Roosevelt's reelection and the onset of the recession of 1937. To union leaders all things seemed possible; union power was sufficient to achieve union ends. In industry labor would speak with new confidence and authority; in politics it could eschew alliances and disregard potential supporters. The unionists' sense of omnipotence undoubtedly helped account for the ambitious, even reckless strategy of the CIO partisans in the Akron contest. Whether a shrewder assessment would have altered the outcome in 1937 cannot be known. What is clear is that Patterson's defeat had a sobering effect. The Akron results, coupled with other indicators of the isolation of the CIO and the disunity of the industrial unions, dashed the hopes of CIO leaders for a separate, possibly independent CIO presence in American politics and introduced a new realism into labor circles. In subsequent years the CIO was politically active but primarily as part of a coalition that supported Democratic candidates.[47] The prospect of a union government in a union city had proved to be a chimera. Union power, possibly decisive in the operation of industry, could be effective outside the plant only if carefully and wisely applied.

But the lessons of the Akron election were not confined to politics. The Patterson campaign provided a rare view of the grass-roots thrust behind the industrial union movement at its peak and of the reasons why that thrust would fail to confirm the hopes and the fears of contemporary observers. The illusion of extending labor power from the union hall to city hall was based in turn on the illusion of a monolithic CIO. Akron unionists, who more than most industrial workers might have been expected to conform to that image, nevertheless defied it. Despite their enthusiasm for the URW, they remained complex and unpredictable individuals. The CIO buttons that "sprouted on overalls, shirtwaists, and workers' hats and caps" may have signified a "new independence" from managerial authoritarianism, but they implied no decline in the traditional independence from dictation or manipulation that had been a hallmark of denizens of American industry. CIO members, like other workers, continued to defy precise categorization. In the late 1930s that meant that the CIO's reach often exceeded its grasp and that the industrial union potential substantially exceeded the unions' performance. Labor marched between 1936 and 1938 but seldom in the neat rows and columns that the John L. Lewises and Garnet Pattersons of that era would have preferred.

[46] *New York Times*, Nov. 3, 1937, p. 1; Lovin, "CIO Innovators," 238.
[47] Dubofsky and Van Tyne, *John L. Lewis*, 327–29; Lovin, "Persistence of Third Party Dreams," 153–56; Foster, *Union Politic*, 6–9; Brody, "Uses of Power II," 215–55.

The General Motors Sit-Down Strike: A Re-examination

Sidney Fine*

ALTHOUGH the General Motors sit-down strike of 1937 has been correctly described as "the most critical labor conflict of the nineteen thirties" and as of crucial significance to the subsequent growth of automobile unionism in particular and industrial unionism in general,[1] a great many questions regarding the strike and the role of its principal participants remain unanswered. It is still not possible to resolve all the doubts concerning this greatest of all automotive strikes, but the relevant manuscript collections now available, and especially the recently opened Frank Murphy Papers, do permit one to speak about at least some aspects of the strike with a greater degree of certainty than was heretofore possible.[2]

The general outlines of the GM sit-down strike are familiar enough. Following the outbreak of sit-down strikes at the Atlanta Fisher Body plant on November 18, 1936, and the Kansas City Fisher Body plant on December 16, 1936, Homer Martin, president of the United Automobile Workers, sought an "immediate general conference" with the top management of GM. The corporation, however, insisted that the union should discuss its grievances at the local plant level, in accordance with GM's established procedure for collective bargaining. The union responded that the principal issues that it wished to discuss with the company—recognition for collective bargaining, seniority rights, minimum wages, and the speed of the production line—were national in scope and must consequently be dealt with by union and management representatives for GM as a whole. Affairs were thus deadlocked when on December 28 the Cleveland Fisher Body plant

---

* A professor at the University of Michigan whose major field of interest is twentieth-century United States history, Mr. Fine is the author of *The Automobile under the Blue Eagle: Labor, Management, and the Automobile Manufacturing Code* (Ann Arbor, Mich., 1963).

[1] Walter Galenson, *The CIO Challenge to the AFL: A History of the American Labor Movement, 1935–1941* (Cambridge, Mass., 1960), 134, 141; Edward Levinson, *Labor on the March* (New York, 1938, 1956), 168; Saul Alinsky, *John L. Lewis, an Unauthorized Biography* (New York, 1949), 96.

[2] The principal manuscript collections on which this article is based are the Frank Murphy Papers, Michigan Historical Collections; Records of the Michigan Military Establishment Relating to the Flint Sit-Down Strike, 1937 [hereafter cited as National Guard Records], microfilm copy in Michigan Historical Collections; the relevant files in the Franklin D. Roosevelt Library; General Motors, Labor Relations Diary and Appendix Documents, GM Building, Detroit, Michigan; the John Brophy Papers, Catholic University; and the Joe Brown Collection, Wayne State University Archives.

was tied up by a sit-down strike, and two days later the same strike tactic closed down the two Fisher Body plants in Flint. The strike eventually spread throughout the GM empire, affecting approximately 140,000 of the corporation's automotive employees and more than 50 of its plants, but the center of the conflict from the end of December was Flint, whose Fisher Body plants, along with Cleveland Fisher Body, produced bodies and parts on which perhaps three-fourths of GM's automotive production depended.[3]

The most significant of the union's official demands, which were submitted to GM on January 4, 1937, was the request that the UAW be recognized as the exclusive bargaining agency for all GM employees.[4] The issue of exclusive representation had been in contention between automobile labor and automobile management ever since Section 7(a) of the National Industrial Recovery Act had stimulated the growth of unionism in the industry. The National Labor Relations Act of 1935 had endorsed the union position on this question, but since the constitutionality of the statute had not yet been determined at the time the strike began, GM, like many other large employers, continued to adhere to the policy with regard to representation that it had evolved while the NIRA was in effect: union representatives would be permitted to bargain with the corporation only for union members.[5]

General Motors made its position clear with regard to the sit-down tactic on the last day of 1936. William S. Knudsen, the executive vice-president of the corporation, stated for GM that the sit-downers were "clearly trespassers and violators of the law of the land" and that there would be no bargaining with the UAW while the strikers remained in "illegal possession" of GM's plants.[6] On January 2, 1937, GM received from Judge Edward Black of the Genesee County Circuit Court in Flint an injunction ordering the strikers to evacuate the two Flint plants, to cease picketing, and not to interfere with those who wanted to enter the plants to work. The strikers ignored the injunction, but both Black and his writ were discredited a few days later when it was revealed that the Flint judge held $219,900 of GM stock. General Motors, caught unawares, transferred its injunction to Judge Paul Gadola's court, but it did not, for the moment, press the issue.[7]

---

[3] GM, Labor Relations Diary, Sec. 1, 68–72; Martin to William S. Knudsen, Dec. 21, 1936, to Alfred P. Sloan, Jr., and to Knudsen, Dec. 24, 1936, Knudsen to Martin, Dec. 31, 1936, ibid., Appendix Documents to Accompany Sec. 1; Henry Kraus, *The Many and the Few: A Chronicle of the Dynamic Auto Workers* (Los Angeles, 1947), 78–79; New York *Times*, Feb. 12, 1937.

[4] Martin to Sloan and Knudsen, Jan. 4, 1937, Murphy Papers.

[5] The issue of representation in the automobile industry before the sit-down strikes is treated in Sidney Fine, *The Automobile under the Blue Eagle: Labor, Management, and the Automobile Manufacturing Code* (Ann Arbor, Mich., 1963), *passim.*

[6] Knudsen to Martin, Dec. 31, 1936, GM Appendix Documents, Sec. 1.

[7] Galenson, *CIO Challenge to AFL,* 136–37; Kraus, *Many and the Few,* 107–13; Detroit *News,* Jan. 3, 7, 25, 29, 1937.

On January 11, GM attempted to dislodge the strikers from the Fisher Body No. 2 plant, the smaller and the more weakly held of the two Flint Fisher Body factories. The heat in the plant was shut off, and company police tried to prevent food from being taken in to the strikers, but the sit-downers, who had held only the second floor of the factory, captured the plant gates from the company police to assure their supply of food. When Flint police sought to recapture the gates, the strikers drove them off with such improvised weapons as automobile door hinges and thus emerged the victors in what came to be known as "The Battle of the Running Bulls."[8]

The violence of January 11 prompted Michigan's newly elected governor, Frank Murphy, to send units of the National Guard[9] into Flint to maintain order, and at the same time the governor invited union and management representatives to Lansing to bring an end to the strike. A truce was arranged on January 15. The union, rejecting the advice of John Brophy, director of the CIO, that it was conceding too much, agreed to evacuate all GM plants held by the sit-down strikers, and GM consented to meet with UAW representatives on January 18 to bargain collectively on the proposals submitted to it by the union on January 4. Negotiations were to continue for at least fifteen days, unless a settlement had been effected earlier, and the corporation stated that it would not try to resume operations in any of the struck plants during this period nor would it remove from them any dies, tools, material (except for export), machinery, or equipment.[10]

Before the scheduled departure of the Flint workers from the two Fisher Body plants, the UAW learned that GM had agreed to meet with the Flint Alliance, a recently formed organization that had been sponsoring a back-to-work movement and that was viewed by the UAW as a company union. Charging the violation of the truce agreement, the UAW refused to evacuate the Flint plants, and a deadlock once again ensued. The scene of negotiations thereupon shifted to Washington, where Secretary of Labor Frances Perkins sought in vain to arrange a conference between GM's president, Alfred P. Sloan, Jr., and John L. Lewis, the CIO chieftain who was representing the UAW.[11]

In an effort to strengthen its position and gain the initiative in the strike, the UAW on February 1, after first drawing off the company police to the

---

[8] Kraus, *Many and the Few*, 125–41; Levinson, *Labor on the March*, 155–57; Detroit *News*, Jan. 12, 1937.
[9] The number of Guardsmen in Flint eventually reached 3,454. (G-1 Periodic Reports, Feb. 7, 1937, National Guard Records.)
[10] Detroit *News*, Jan. 12–15, 1937; Knudsen *et al.* to Murphy, Jan. 15, 1937, Murphy Papers; John Brophy, *A Miner's Life: An Autobiography*, ed. and suppl. John O. P. Hall (Madison, Wis., 1964), 269.
[11] Detroit *News*, Jan. 18–31, 1937; Kraus, *Many and the Few*, 157–65.

Chevrolet No. 9 plant by staging a decoy sit-down strike there, seized and occupied the Chevrolet No. 4 plant, which produced the engines for Chevrolet cars and was "the most important single unit" in the GM complex. The National Guard, on instructions from Governor Murphy, responded to this action by cordoning off the Chevrolet No. 4 plant and the nearby Fisher Body No. 2 plant.[12]

The day after the union captured the strategic Chevrolet No. 4 plant, Judge Gadola issued an injunction that ordered the union to evacuate the two Fisher Body plants and to cease picketing outside them. The injunction was again defied, but Murphy did not choose to use state troops to enforce the court order. In the meantime, GM agreed to confer with John L. Lewis, and a long series of talks began in Detroit on February 3. As Murphy later saw it, the crucial factor in breaking the strike deadlock was a letter that he read to Lewis on February 9 in which the Michigan governor stated that it was his duty to see to it that the laws were enforced.[13]

Agreement between union and management was reached on February 11, the corporation consenting to recognize the UAW as the bargaining agency for those of its employees who were union members and to commence negotiations with the UAW on the issues specified in its letter of January 4. The agreement was supplemented by a letter from Knudsen to Murphy in which GM agreed for a period of six months after work was resumed not to bargain or enter into agreements with any other employee organization with regard to such matters as were referred to in the union's January 4 letter unless this procedure was first sanctioned by Governor Murphy.[14] In effect, the UAW was given exclusive bargaining rights for a period of six months.

It seems clear from published accounts and from the transcripts of interviews with participants that have recently become available that the Flint sit-down occurred prematurely, and it would appear that the decision to conduct a sit-down rather than a conventional outside strike was made locally rather than by the UAW or CIO leadership. The UAW and the CIO regarded GM as "job number one" in the automobile industry, and there was at least talk among the leadership in the latter part of 1936 about striking the corporation as a whole by tying up the Cleveland and

[12] *Ibid.*, 189–219; Louis G. Seaton to H. W. Anderson, Feb. 2, 1937, GM Appendix Documents, Sec. 1; Executive Order, Feb. 1, 1937, Murphy Papers; Detroit *News,* Feb. 2, 3, 1937; *United Automobile Worker,* Feb. 25, 1937.

[13] Galenson, *CIO Challenge to AFL,* 139–40; Levinson, *Labor on the March,* 163–67; Kraus, *Many and the Few,* 229–34, 263–78; Detroit *News,* Feb. 3–11, 1937.

[14] There are copies in the Murphy Papers of the February 11 agreement and of Knudsen's letter to Murphy of February 11.

the Fisher Body No. 1 plants, but this was not to occur until after January 1, 1937. The holiday period between Christmas and New Year's, when the sit-down actually occurred, was regarded as "a very poor time psychologically to pull a strike" if only because the workers would be especially short of funds then and would be reluctant to lose any pay that they might otherwise earn. Also, Murphy was not scheduled to succeed Frank Fitzgerald as governor of Michigan until January 1, 1937, and the UAW expected Murphy to be more friendly to its position than Fitzgerald was likely to be.[15]

The conventional story as to why the strike began in Flint on December 30 is that Robert Travis, the director of organization for the UAW in Flint, learned that evening that GM, concerned about what might be impending because of the strikes in some of its plants, was planning to move some giant dies out of the Fisher Body No. 1 plant to Grand Rapids and Pontiac. Travis, according to the usual story, thereupon called the shop stewards together, and the decision was made to strike. Bud Simons, however, chairman of the Fisher Body No. 1 shop stewards, has recently challenged this version of the origins of the strike. As he recalls it, a strike at the time of the flat-glass workers was causing a glass shortage that might in itself have forced the closing of the Flint plants in a few days without a strike. Travis, anxious for the union to seize the initiative rather than be the passive victim of a plant shutdown, came to Simons and declared: "We have got to find something to start a strike about around here." The story about the shipment of the dies was then fabricated and spread throughout the plant, and Travis and the shop stewards called for the sit-down.[16]

It was alleged before the Dies Committee in the fall of 1938 that the Communists inspired and organized the sit-down strikes, and Larry S. Davidow, who served as one of the attorneys for the UAW during the Flint sit-down, also voiced this opinion in a recent interview. "The major fact to keep in mind," he has charged, "is that the whole strategy of the

[15] Oral History Interview of Wyndham Mortimer, June 20, 1960, 27, 34–35, Michigan Historical Collections (there are copies of all the UAW oral history interviews in both the Michigan Historical Collections and the Wayne State University Archives); Oral History Interview of George F. Addes, June 25, 1960, 15–16; Statement of Mr. Martin. . . , Sept. 11, 1936, Brown Collection; *Time*, XXIX (Jan. 11, 1937), 16; John Brophy, "The Struggle for an Auto Union," 1–3, MS for chapter of book, Brophy Papers; Levinson, *Labor on the March*, 149; Kraus, *Many and the Few*, 78–81.

[16] Levinson, *Labor on the March*, 152; Kraus, *Many and the Few*, 86–88; Flint *Auto Worker*, Jan. 5, 1937; Mortimer Interview, 35–36; Oral History Interview of Bud Simons, Sept. 6, 1960, 28–30. The union claimed that it sat down in the Fisher Body No. 2 plant because GM had transferred three inspectors when they had refused to quit the union. (Detroit *News*, Jan. 3, 1937); see William Weinstone, *The Great Sit-Down Strike* (New York, 1937), 21, for a Communist account of the strike that seems to support the Simons version of its origin.

sit-down strike was communist inspired, communist directed and communist controlled."[17]

That the Flint sit-down strike was part of a Communist plot would be difficult, if not impossible, to demonstrate, but that Communists and fellow travelers played crucial roles in the strike story is beyond dispute. It was Wyndham Mortimer, described by Benjamin Stolberg as "a Stalinist from the very beginning," who had begun the serious organization of automobile workers in Flint in July 1936 at a time when UAW strength in the city was at low ebb. When Mortimer was recalled from Flint in the fall of 1936, he was replaced by Travis, whom Max M. Kampelman has characterized as "a man with a long pedigree of Communist activity." Travis continued the work of organization begun by Mortimer, played the decisive part in calling the sit-down strike in the Fisher Body No. 1 plant, and has been accurately described as "The leading personality . . . in the strike." Inside the Fisher Body No. 1 plant, leadership was exercised by Simons, who had joined the Communist controlled Auto Workers Union in the late 1920's while working in Grand Rapids and had participated in at least one of the meetings arranged by Communists and "progressives" in 1934 to promote the establishment of an international, industrial union in the automobile industry.[18]

Communists or near Communists were also present at the UAW and CIO leadership levels during the strike. Maurice Sugar, characterized by Benjamin Gitlow as "top man for the Communist party in Detroit," served as a UAW counsel during the strike, and Lee Pressman, who later admitted his Communist connections, was one of John L. Lewis' closest advisers throughout the dispute, and his name, as well as Mortimer's, appears on the agreement that ended the strike.[19] It does not·follow, though, that these men or any of the Communists and fellow travelers who played prominent roles in the GM strike pursued policies that conflicted with the organizational interests of the UAW or that they succeeded to any extent

[17] House Special Committee on Un-American Activities, *Investigation of the Un-American Propaganda Activities in the United States*, 75 Cong., 3 sess. (Washington, D.C., 1938), II, 1454, 1494–96, 1551, 1554, 1649, 1689; August Raymond Ogden, *The Dies Committee: A Study of the Special House Committee for the Investigation of Un-American Activities, 1938– 1943* (Washington, D.C., 1943), 82, 106; Oral History Interview of Larry S. Davidow, July 14, 1960, 12–14, 22–23.

[18] Benjamin Stolberg, *The Story of the CIO* (New York, 1938), 164; Mortimer Interview, 28–33; UAW, Second Annual Convention, *Report of Wyndham Mortimer* (Aug. 23, 1937), 4–6, Joseph A. Labadie Collection, University of Michigan; Max M. Kampelman, *The Communist Party vs. the CIO: A Study in Power Politics* (New York, 1957), 64; Oral History Interview of Carl Haessler, Nov. 27, 1959–Oct. 24, 1960, 14; Simons Interview, 3–4, 11–13.

[19] Benjamin Gitlow, *The Whole of Their Lives: Communism in America—A Personal History and Intimate Portrayal of Its Leaders* (New York, 1948), 278–79; Oral History Interview of Len DeCaux, Mar. 11, 18, 1961, 29–30; Brophy, "Struggle for an Auto Union," 21, Brophy Papers.

in reaping advantages from the strike for the Communist as distinct from the union cause. It is perfectly clear, moreover, that Murphy knew nothing about the Communist role in the strike and that the workers were striking because of their grievances against management rather than from any desire to promote Communist objectives.

As was suspected at the time and as recently made available evidence, including undercover reports, has substantiated, the Flint auto plants that were struck were held by a minority of the workers in these plants, on some days by a very small minority. The Fisher Body No. 1 plant, which employed as many as 6,500–7,500 workers, had as few as 90 men in the plant at one point during the strike, according to Simons, and the much smaller Fisher Body No. 2 plant, which had a normal complement of about 1,100 workers, was held by 17 strikers on January 26, according to the National Guard. Nor were all the workers inside the plants employees of these plants. Flint GM workers who were not on strike and automobile unionists from Detroit, Toledo, Cleveland, and elsewhere found their way into and out of the plants. Thus the morning after the UAW had seized the Chevrolet No. 4 plant, Colonel Joseph H. Lewis, the commanding officer of the National Guard in Flint, reported to Governor Murphy that of 850 workers in the plant, only 150 were employees of that plant.[20] Of course, if only because of the food problem, it was in the interests of the union to hold the plants with as few persons as possible, but the small numbers within the plants also reflect the very limited membership and strength of the UAW in Flint when the strike began.

The major criticism leveled against Murphy with regard to his policy during the course of the sit-down strike in Flint was that he violated his oath of office by failing to eject the sit-downers who were illegally in possession of GM property and by refusing to enforce a court order requiring the evacuation of two of the corporation's plants. It must be recalled, however, that although the sit-down strikes were held by most, but not all, authorities to constitute an illegal trespass upon private property, the United States Supreme Court had not yet spoken on the matter, and the status of the tactic under the criminal laws was not altogether self-evident. As Murphy later wrote to a columnist, "Apart from private civil action, and owing to the novelty of the practice, it was not very certain what legal action was

[20] Simons Interview, 47; G-2 Journal, Jan. 26, 1937, National Guard Records; Strike Chronology [Feb. 1–8, 1937], Feb. 2, 1937, Murphy Papers; see also Norman Hill Memoranda to Murphy, Jan. 12, 15, 1937, *ibid.;* and Oral History Interviews of Arthur Case, Aug. 4, 1960, 6, Norman Bully, Oct. 12, 1961, 4–5, Joseph Ditzel, Sept. 25, 1960, 12, and Clayton Johnson, June 1, 1961, 9.

available or appropriate to deal with a body of men peacefully occupying their place of employment."[21]

Murphy informed the union negotiators more than once that the strikers were in illegal possession of the GM plants, and he referred publicly to "the unlawful seizure of private property."[22] He was not, however, prepared to push this point to its logical conclusion and thus impair the chances for a peaceful settlement. He saw the union as using the means at its disposal to safeguard its rights and as fighting back against employer violation of the Wagner Act and is thus understood to have told the GM negotiators that the occupation of their factories went "deeper into social and economic questions" than did the ordinary violation of property rights. Under the circumstances, he was content to follow the counsel of his legal advisers that the matter of legality was a problem at least initially for the local authorities to resolve; his own responsibility would not have to be considered until local officials called for his assistance in enforcing the law.[23]

As a matter of fact, Murphy has been less criticized for his failure to initiate action to dislodge the strikers than for his alleged refusal to act when the strikers were found in contempt of court. What is often ignored by Murphy's critics, however, is that only a few days actually elapsed between the time Murphy was requested by the sheriff to aid him in enforcing the court order and the settlement of the strike. From the start also, as is now evident, Murphy was painfully aware of his obligations with regard to the enforcement of the law.

Following the revelation of Judge Black's stockholdings, GM did not file an amended bill of complaint and a motion for injunction until January 28, and it was not until February 2 that Judge Gadola issued his injunction, which was to take effect in twenty-four hours. Speaking to Perkins by phone on the evening of February 2, Murphy observed that consideration had to be given to the fact that "tomorrow afternoon I have got to say that I will be obedient to the law or not."[24] When the workers in the two Fisher Body plants defied the injunction and informed Murphy that the use of

---

[21] Edward G. Kemp, "Frank Murphy as Government Administrator," 1951, Edward G. Kemp Papers, Michigan Historical Collections; Murphy to Mark Sullivan, Jan. 4, 1939, Murphy Papers; for the argument that the sit-down strike was not illegal, see Leon Green, "The Case for the Sit-Down Strike," *New Republic*, XC (Mar. 24, 1937), 199–201.

[22] Murphy statement, Jan. 14, 1937, Murphy to Lewis and Martin, Feb. 9, 1937, to Albert H. Dale, Feb. 25, 1937, to Paul Block, Dec. 9, 1938, Murphy Papers; Kraus, *Many and the Few*, 268; Detroit *News*, Jan. 12, 1937; cf. Murphy to Octave P. Beauvais, July 7, 1937, Murphy Papers.

[23] Murphy to Dale, Feb. 25, 1937, Murphy speech, Oct. 21, 1938, Kemp Memorandum to Murphy, Jan. 27, 1937, *ibid.*; New York *Times*, Jan. 14, 1937.

[24] Strike Chronology, Feb. 2, 1937, Murphy Papers. This document, covering the period February 1–8, contains a detailed, although incomplete, record of events relating to the strike as seen through Murphy's eyes. It was almost certainly prepared at the time of the strike.

force would mean "a blood bath of unarmed workers" for which he would be responsible, Murphy had drawn up but did not issue a statement declaring that he had no "honorable alternative but to see that the laws of the state are faithfully executed and the lawful orders of its courts promptly and effectively enforced."[25]

Informed by affidavit that the injunction was being violated, Judge Gadola on February 5 issued a writ of attachment commanding the sheriff "to attach the bodies" of all occupants of the two Fisher Body plants, their "confederates" who were picketing the No. 1 plant, and local officers of the UAW for refusal to comply with the February 2 injunction. Thomas Wolcott, the Genesee County sheriff, thereupon sent Murphy a telegram asking for the assistance of the National Guard in the execution of the writ and inquiring whether, as an alternative, it would be necessary for the sheriff to swear in deputies to enforce the court order. It was only at this point, six days before the final settlement, that Murphy incurred any clear-cut obligation to ensure that a court order be obeyed. Murphy, who had authorized Maurice Sugar to inform Judge Gadola that a settlement was near, was perturbed that the judge had not delayed the issuance of the writ. He told Perkins, as notes made of their conversation indicate, that GM had made "a rather serious mistake" and was trying to "embarrass" him and put him in a "bad position. I am not a representative for the G.M. or for the labor group but for the people," he said, ". . . and the public interest requires peace."[26]

Intent upon preserving the peace and at the same time aware that the enforcement of the court order could not long be delayed, Murphy, we now know, took a series of steps to avoid disruption of the negotiations but, at the same time, to clarify to the union negotiators his position regarding law and order. He decided on Friday, February 5, the day the writ of attachment was issued, that the time had come to draft a letter to Lewis explaining that the order of a court was "the law of the land" and would have to be obeyed, but he also instructed the National Guard, if it deemed the action necessary, to cordon off the Fisher Body No. 1 plant as it had already surrounded the Fisher Body No. 2 and Chevrolet No. 4 plants and thus to make it impossible for the sheriff or "a mob of deputies" to get into the plants. Most important of all, he requested the sheriff to delay over the weekend any effort to enforce the writ since a settlement seemed imminent.[27]

[25] Fisher No. 1 Sit-In Employes to Murphy, Feb. 3, 1937, Stay In Strikers of the Fisher Body Plant No. 2 to Murphy, Feb. 3, 1937, Murphy statement, Feb. 3, 1937, *ibid.*

[26] Affidavit by E. J. Parker, Feb. 4, 1937, Writ of Attachment, Feb. 5, 1937, National Guard Records; Sugar to Murphy, Oct. 25, 1938, Murphy to Sugar, Nov. 2, 1938, Strike Chronology, Feb. 5, 1937, Murphy Papers.

[27] Strike Chronology, Feb. 5, 1937, Murphy to the Rev. George H. Smith, July 22, 1937,

Actually, Sheriff Wolcott, a Democrat who "thoroughly hated his assignment," had no intention of taking any aggressive action without the approval of the governor.[28]

Murphy's decision to delay the enforcement of the writ of attachment was fully in accord with the wishes of the National Guard. As evidence recently made available indicates, Judge Advocate General Samuel D. Pepper, who disliked the idea of using the Guard at any time to make arrests under contempt orders, and Colonel Lewis and his staff were impressed with the difficulty under existing circumstances of apprehending and taking to court the several thousand persons against whom the writ of attachment was directed, and they advised the governor to delay an order to the Guard to aid the sheriff in executing the writ.[29]

On February 7, with a settlement not yet achieved, Murphy told President Roosevelt on the phone that he (Murphy) would have to make clear to Lewis the governor's responsibility as chief executive of the state to uphold the law, and on February 8 the famous letter to Lewis was drafted. The letter was read by Murphy to the CIO head at 9:15 p.m. the next day, with Conciliator James F. Dewey the only other person present. In the document, the original of which is preserved in the Murphy Papers,[30] Murphy informed Lewis that he wished to indicate in writing, as he had "already done verbally on several occasions," his position as chief executive of Michigan. It had been and still was his hope that the strike could be settled by negotiation, but since the parties had thus far been unable to come to an agreement, "the time has come for all concerned to comply fully with the decision and order of the Court and take necessary steps to restore possession of the occupied plants to their rightful owners." It was his duty "to demand and require" obedience to the laws and court orders, and he would be faithful to that obligation.[31] After further prolonged negotiating sessions, the governor was able to announce the settlement of the strike early in the morning of February 11. The writ had not been enforced, but

<hr>

ibid.; Detroit *News*, Feb. 6, 1937; Subcommittee of the Senate Committee on the Judiciary, *Nomination of Frank Murphy*, 76 Cong., 1 sess. (Washington, D.C., 1939), 3-4.

[28] Kraus, *Many and the Few*, 108; Wolcott to Murphy, Aug. 17, 1938, Statement by Wolcott, Oct. 21, 1938, Murphy Papers.

[29] Pepper to Raymond W. Starr, Mar. 22, 1937, Pepper to Kemp, Jan. 12, 1939, *ibid.*

[30] The original of the letter and the several carbon copies of it in the Murphy Papers bear the date February 9 rather than February 8. When the letter was typed, probably on February 8, the space for the day of the month was left blank, and the "9" was later added, presumably to make the date of the letter conform to the date of its presentation to Lewis. When a copy of the letter was first publicly revealed on January 13, 1939 (it was submitted by Murphy to a subcommittee of the Senate Committee on the Judiciary that was considering his nomination to be Attorney General), it bore the date February 8 and the notation that it had been read and delivered at 9:15 p.m. on February 9.

[31] Strike Chronology, Feb. 7, 1937, Murphy to Lewis and Martin, Feb. 9, 1937, Murphy Papers.

neither had a single life been lost in one of the most volatile strikes in all of American history.

As a matter of fact, Murphy's delay in enforcing the writ of attachment was not without precedent, and even Judge Gadola conceded at the time that the sheriff "had the authority to wait indefinitely before serving it." Commenting in 1938 on the delay, Wolcott agreed that there was "no hurry about it especially when such great issues were at stake." Sheriffs in Michigan and elsewhere, after all, regularly delayed the execution of writs of attachment issued after property had been foreclosed and writs of attachment requiring them to take action to satisfy judgments against merchants. "If the Governor is to be accused of obstructing justice," a member of the Michigan Parole Board wrote Murphy's brother George, "then every sheriff and public officer might be accused of the same thing."[32]

Among the factors that persuaded Frank Murphy to delay enforcement of a court order, none was more compelling than his great reluctance to take any step that might lead to violence and the loss of life. A man with a "deep reverence for human life," Murphy told his friend Mrs. Fielding H. Yost during the course of the strike, "I am not going to do it. I'm not going down in history as 'Bloody Murphy!' If I sent those soldiers right in on the men there'd be no telling how many would be killed. It would be inconsistent with everything I have ever stood for in my whole political life." In his first statement on the strike, the newly inaugurated governor declared on January 4 that he would see to it that "no force is used," and a few days later he wrote in a private letter to a Flint clergyman, "I abhor violence and you may be sure that the State of Michigan will do everything honorably within its power to prevent it." Throughout the strike, as the record indicates, Murphy did everything that could reasonably have been expected of him to remain faithful to the assurances with regard to violence that he had given.[33]

When he was compelled by the Battle of the Running Bulls and the likelihood of further violence to send the National Guard into Flint, Murphy gave the command of the troops to Colonel Joseph H. Lewis, commander of the 119th Field Artillery and a seasoned soldier, rather than to the ranking officer of the Michigan Guard, General Heinrich Pickert, the police commissioner of Detroit. Pickert was passed over by the governor not only because the Detroit official had other duties but because his "militaristic

---

[32] Detroit *News*, Feb. 8, 1937; Statement by Wolcott, Oct. 21, 1938, John H. Eliasohn to George Murphy, Oct. 24, 1938, Murphy Papers.
[33] Kemp, "Murphy as Government Administrator"; transcript of interview with Mrs. Fielding H. Yost, Oct. 28, 1963, 6, in my possession; Strike Chronology, Feb. 8, 1937, Murphy Papers; Detroit *News*, Jan. 4, 1937; Murphy to the Rev. R. M. Atkins, Jan. 9, 1937, Murphy Papers.

policies" as police commissioner had antagonized labor and civil rights groups, and Murphy was afraid to rely on Pickert's discretion in an emergency.[34] Murphy also let it be known that "The state authorities will not take sides. They are here only to protect public peace . . . and for no other reason at all." John S. Bersey, Michigan's adjutant general, advised the area commander at the outset, as the records of the National Guard reveal, that Murphy was particularly concerned that "everything be done by the troops to avoid bringing on a conflict. He does not desire that anyone be shot or seriously injured." By maintaining "a calm and peaceful attitude," the troops, the governor hoped, would provide the opportunity for the disputants to reach an amicable settlement.[35]

Murphy's reluctance to use force was put to a severe test on February 1, when the union staged its attack on Chevrolet No. 9 to cover its seizure of Chevrolet No. 4. In his headquarters in a Detroit hotel, the governor received an almost blow-by-blow account of the unfolding developments in Flint. When Colonel Lewis suggested that the National Guard might be used to "scatter the crowd in a quiet manner," Murphy refused permission and declared, "I don't like the militia in it unless it is necessary but if it . . . [is] we have to go in strong." A short time later Sheriff Wolcott recommended that martial law be declared, but Murphy resisted taking such drastic action. In the evening Murphy made his decision and directed the National Guard "to take immediate and effective steps to bring the situation under the control of the public authorities, suppress and prevent any breach of the peace, and ensure that the laws of the state are faithfully executed." The "immediate and effective steps" taken by the Guard, at the instruction of the governor, were to establish a cordon guard around Chevrolet No. 4 and Fisher Body No. 2—"Importance #1" in the parlance of the Guard, to prevent anyone from entering this area, and to deny supplies of any kind, including food, to the occupants of the two plants. Murphy made the decision to cut off the entry of food into the plants on the basis of early reports that the majority of the occupants of Chevrolet No. 4, which had been seized with the aid of outsiders, were not employees of the plant.[36]

[34] Frank Martel to Murphy, Apr. 28, 1936, *ibid.;* Detroit *News,* Jan. 28, 1937; Conference for Protection of Civil Rights, *Civil Rights Guardian* (1937), Brown Collection; Winston Wessels, "Importance #1: The Michigan National Guard and the 1937 Flint Sit-Down Strike," seminar paper, 1963, 10, MS in my possession.

[35] (Lansing) *State Journal,* Jan. 12, 1937; Bersey to Commanding Officer, Jan. 12, 1937, National Guard Records.

[36] Strike Chronology, Feb. 1, 2, 1937, Executive Order, Feb. 1, 1937, Murphy Papers; G-2 Journal, Feb. 1, 1937, G-3 Periodic Reports, Feb. 1, 1937, 63rd Brigade S-3 Periodic Reports, Feb. 2, 1937, Pepper to Lewis, Feb. 20, 1937, National Guard Records; Kraus, *Many and the Few,* 219–22; Detroit *News,* Feb. 2, 1937.

When John Brophy learned that food was being denied the occupants of the two plants, he phoned Murphy and, according to Brophy's manuscript account of the event, "berated" the governor for his action and asked him whether he wanted to " 'starve to death poor workers who are only asking for their lawful rights.' " When Murphy explained the reason for his decision, Brophy asked for and received permission to enter the plant. By the time he visited the factory most of the outsiders had departed; Brophy found only four persons in the plant, including Walter and Roy Reuther, who were not employees, and all of them left the plant with him.

The National Guard conducted its own investigation of the personnel in Chevrolet No. 4, and when Colonel Lewis reported to Murphy on the evening of February 2 that he was "confident" that "practically all" the men in the plant were "regular employees," Murphy instructed the area commander to allow food to pass through the National Guard lines. Murphy spoke to Brophy on the phone that night and gave him a categorical and perhaps an unwise promise that "The military will never be used against you. I'd leave my office first."[37]

Writing to a clergyman a few months after peace terms had been arranged, Murphy observed that the Flint strike had been "loaded with dynamite that might have been touched off by a single injudicious act."[38] Whatever else might be said about Murphy's strike policy, he did avoid the "injudicious act" that could have led to the loss of life.

Some writers on the strike have pictured the National Guard as spoiling for a fight and as having been thwarted in its desire for action by a governor who was unwilling to use force.[39] Actually, the leadership of the Guard and the judge advocate general of the state were as anxious as Murphy to avoid provocative acts in Flint and were as reluctant as he to use the Guardsmen in a frontal assault on the plants to evict the strikers. At least some of the credit for the peaceful outcome of the Flint strike must go to the Michigan National Guard.

From the start, the troops in Flint were closely restricted to their billets and were "kept well in hand." Colonel Lewis left no doubt in the minds of the Guardsmen regarding the nature of their task in Flint.

---

[37] Brophy, "Struggle for an Auto Union," 18–19, and Brophy Diary, Feb. 2, 1937, Brophy Papers; G-3 Periodic Reports, Feb. 2, 1937, National Guard Records; Strike Chronology, Feb. 2, 1937, Murphy Papers; Official Strike Bulletin No. 10, Strike Bulletin, Feb. 2, 1937, Brown Collection; Kraus, *Many and the Few*, 222–26.

[38] Murphy to Smith, July 22, 1937, Murphy Papers.

[39] Levinson, *Labor on the March*, 163; Irving Howe and B. J. Widick, *The UAW and Walter Reuther* (New York, 1949), 61.

Our mission here in Flint [he informed them in the first bulletin issued to the men] is to protect life and property should the situation develop to a point where civil law enforcement agencies cannot do so. Unless and until such a situation develops, our task is that of mere watchful waiting. During this period of waiting, let me again emphasize the fact that officers and men must not, under any circumstances, enter into discussions or arguments with civilians regarding the strike. We must not take sides. We must lean backwards so as to avoid the semblance of seeming to take sides. Our troops include men of all walks of life and many of us are naturally sympathetic to one side or other. However, as long as we are in uniform, our personal leanings must be made secondary.

Guard leaders, as a matter of fact, tried not only to restrain their own men, but, in the words of Lieutenant Colonel John H. Steck, assistant chief of staff, to make all parties in Flint realize that "personal and group differences of opinion should be subordinated in an attempt to prevent any untoward act that might jeopardize the success of the conference being conducted by the Governor."[40]

On February 1, Colonel Lewis, Judge Advocate General Pepper, and Adjutant General Bersey conferred with Governor Murphy, and "certain studies were directed to be immediately made and decisions arrived at."[41] The records available do not tell us any more than this about the February 1 conference, but almost certainly it was decided at that time that the National Guard should devise some plan for the possible eviction of the sit-in strikers. Responsibility for formulating the plan was assigned to Steck, and he was ready with his recommendations on February 5.

Steck considered three possible lines of action for the Guard to follow: the first involved the actual eviction of the strikers from both "Importance #1" (Chevrolet No. 4 and Fisher Body No. 2) and "Importance #2" (Fisher Body No. 1); the second called for containing "Importance #1" and the ejection of the occupants of "Importance #2"; and the third provided for containing "Importance #1" and isolating "Importance #2" by a cordon guard and then securing the ouster of the strikers, if desired, by denying them the necessities of life. Steck recommended the third option rather than a direct assault on either or both of the plants because he believed that it was likely to result in considerably fewer casualties. Steck must also have realized that if the strikers attacked to break the cordon around "Importance #2," the responsibility for violence would rest on them rather than on the Guard. Apparently agreeing with Steck's reasoning, Colonel Lewis endorsed his subordinate's recommendation.[42]

---

[40] Steck to Lewis, Feb. 20, 1937, Michigan National Guard Bulletin No. 1, Jan. 19, 1937, National Guard Records.
[41] Pepper to Lewis, Feb. 20, 1937, *ibid.*
[42] Steck to Lewis, Feb. 5, 1937, *ibid.* There is an "O.K.L." written on the plan recommended by Steck.

According to Pepper, the military staff also believed that the execution of its mission required a formal declaration of martial law, and the governor was so advised on February 8. Murphy, however, vetoed this proposal. On the afternoon of the next day Bersey called the governor and advised him that the "Investment [of "Importance #2"] can be made without weakening our position" and that it might strengthen the position of the Guard "in the event of orders to be enforced."[43]

When Murphy read his letter to John L. Lewis that evening, he spoke only of his obligation to enforce the law, but he carefully avoided any mention of the means he might employ to secure that end. It has been assumed that Murphy was delivering a veiled threat to use troops to eject the strikers forcibly from the plants,[44] and Lewis himself has given this interpretation currency by an account of his confrontation with Murphy which he delivered to the 1940 convention of the UAW. " 'I do not doubt your ability to call out your soldiers and shoot the members of our union out of those plants,' " Lewis told the delegates he had said to Murphy, " 'but let me say that when you issue that order I shall leave this conference and I shall enter one of those plants with my own people (Applause.) ... And the militia will have the pleasure of shooting me out of the plants with you [them?].' "[45] Whether Lewis actually spoke these words to Murphy or was simply indulging in retrospective fiction we do not know, but at all events Murphy was not planning at that time to use the Guard to shoot anyone. The probability is that, following the advice of his military staff, he intended merely to place a cordon guard around "Importance #2" and then, if the negotiations broke down and if the isolation of the strikers from very much contact with the outside world failed to discourage them,[46] to deny the necessities of life to them and thus to compel their surrender.

As he surveyed the record of the National Guard in Flint some weeks after the troops had been demobilized, Colonel Lewis concluded that the experience had "demonstrated that effective use can be made of troops at

[43] Pepper to Kemp, Jan. 12, 1939, Strike Chronology, Feb. 5, 8, 1937, Murphy Papers; Record of Phone Conversation with Murphy, Feb. 9, 1937, National Guard Records.
[44] Kraus, *Many and the Few*, 275–76; Alinsky, *Lewis*, 144; Detroit *News*, Jan. 14, 1939; Richard D. Lunt, "The High Ministry of Government: The Political Career of Frank Murphy," doctoral dissertation, University of New Mexico, 1962, 229. Russell B. Porter reported in the New York *Times* of February 8, 1937, that if the strike talks failed, Murphy was likely to order the investment of the Fisher Body No. 1 plant rather than the forcible eviction of the strikers, but on February 10 Porter was reporting that the talk was that Murphy would declare a "state of insurrection" and that Colonel Lewis would then order the Guard to aid in evicting the strikers.
[45] UAW, *Proceedings of the Fifth Annual Convention, 1940* (n.p., n.d.), 105; there is a more embellished version of the Lewis story in Alinsky, *Lewis*, 144–46.
[46] Contact between the sit-in strikers in the plants that had been cordoned off and the outside world was being curtailed in the final days of the strike. (Regulations Nos. 1 and 2, Feb. 10, 1937, National Guard Records.)

such times without loss of life or distruction [*sic*] to property. . . ."[47] That violence had been avoided was pleasing not only to the colonel and the governor but also to the executives of GM, for it would be a mistake to assume that Knudsen and other officials were anxious to see the injunction they had sought enforced if it meant bloodshed. The loss of life was deplorable not only in itself, but it might have damaged the corporation's reputation and weakened its position in the race for sales with its two major competitors. Lawrence P. Fisher, of GM, a close friend of Murphy's, told the governor during the strike, as Norman H. Hill, Murphy's executive secretary, later remembered the governor's account of the conversation: "Frank, for God's sake if the Fisher . . . brothers never make another nickel, don't have any bloodshed in that plant. We don't want to have blood on our hands. . . . just keep things going and . . . it'll work out." There is every reason to believe that Knudsen fully shared these views.

When violence broke out in Flint on February 1, it was Fisher, we now know, who at first advised delay when Murphy asked if the GM executive thought it necessary "to put militia in there." On February 10, Arnold Lenz, the Flint Chevrolet plant manager, called Detroit for permission to use company police to eject the strikers in the No. 4 plant, but Lenz's superiors, the National Guard records reveal, vetoed the plan because they did not want to take responsibility for breaking up the negotiations.[48]

It is possible as the result of the manuscript resources now available to trace with greater accuracy than was previously possible the course of the negotiations that led to the settlement of the strike. The documents reveal that Murphy leaned toward the union, but, contrary to the popular image of him, was not an invariable supporter of the union point of view, that President Roosevelt involved himself in the negotiations to a greater extent than we have previously been led to believe, and that the importance of the Murphy-Lewis confrontation has been greatly exaggerated. The evidence also indicates that Murphy at the outbreak of the strike in all probability held 1,650 shares of GM stock, with a market value of more than $100,000 as of December 31, 1936.[49] One wonders if the UAW would have

---

[47] Lewis to Murphy, June 18, 1937, *ibid.*

[48] Speech by John Lovett, Apr. 1937, 6, Joseph H. Creighton Memorandum to Murphy, May 11, 1938, Speech by Murphy, Oct. 21, 1938, 12, Strike Chronology, Feb. 1, 1937, Murphy Papers; transcript of interview with Hill, Aug. 21, 1963, 22–23, in my possession; Lunt, "Career of Murphy," 247; New York *Times*, Jan. 29, 30, Feb. 3, 9, 1937; Norman Beasley, *Knudsen: A Biography* (New York, 1947), 168–69; G-2 Journal, Feb. 10, 1937, G-2 Periodic Reports, Feb. 10, 11, 1937, National Guard Records. There are several extant versions of Fisher's statement to Murphy regarding bloodshed.

[49] Murphy transferred 1,650 shares of GM stock from his Manila to his New York broker on October 3, 1936. He received the GM dividend of $1.50 per share on this same number of shares on December 12, 1936. The market value of GM stock as of December 31, 1936, was $63.50 per share. The stock subsequently seems to have been transferred to Murphy's sister,

sought to discredit Murphy, as it had succeeded in discrediting Judge Black, had it known that the Michigan governor was at the time of the strike, or at least very recently had been, the holder of a sizable block of GM stock.

Murphy, aided throughout by Conciliator James F. Dewey, involved himself in the strike as a mediator even before the Battle of the Running Bulls, but his efforts as a peacemaker came to naught since GM refused to negotiate while the strikers held its plants and the union was unwilling to withdraw from the plants unless GM first recognized it, agreed to keep the struck plants closed and not to remove any equipment from them until a national agreement was concluded, and promised not to coerce its employees.[50]

At the insistence of the governor, negotiations were resumed after the violence of January 11 had resulted in the dispatch of Guardsmen to Flint. When Murphy brought the negotiators face-to-face on January 14, he informed them that the strike would have to be settled in accordance with the principles of law and order. "No one," he declared, "should wish or attempt to place the Governor of this state in the position of suspending the law of the land. This is not right and he is not going to do it."

If Murphy followed the notes that he seems to have taken with him to this conference, he suggested that GM meet the union demand for exclusive bargaining rights by accepting the UAW as the representative of "a *large* if not the largest organized group of employees." The union, he apparently said, should withdraw from the plants since there could be "no serious dispute" that it was in "unlawful possession" of GM property. Similarly, the union could not insist that the corporation make a definite commitment regarding the removal of its equipment during the period of the truce lest this qualify GM's lawful control over its own property, but GM might nevertheless state its intentions in this regard. The next day, largely as the result of Murphy's efforts, a truce was concluded, with GM declaring its intention not to reopen its plants or remove equipment from them during the scheduled period of negotiations.[51]

Mrs. William Teahan, and was sold by her on January 18, 1937, at an estimated profit of over $50,000. (Hayden, Stone and Co. to Murphy, Oct. 3, 5, 1936, Eleanor Bumgardner to Kemp [Dec. 31, 1936?], copy of Murphy's 1936 income tax return, J. E. Swan to Mrs. Margaret [Marguerite] Teahan, Dec. 29, 1937, Murphy Papers; GM, *Twenty-Eighth Annual Report, Year Ended Dec. 31, 1936* (n. p., 1937), 56; New York *Times*, Jan. 1, 1937.

[50] Draft of agreement, Jan. 7, 1937, Knudsen to Murphy, Jan. 8, 1937, Knudsen statements, Jan. 9, 1937, Martin to Murphy, Jan. 9, 1937, Murphy Papers; Detroit *News*, Jan. 10, 1937; Kraus, *Many and the Few*, 122.

[51] Murphy statement, Jan. 14, 1937, "Notes," Jan. 14, 1937, Knudsen *et al.* to Murphy, Jan. 15, 1937, Murphy Papers; Brophy, "Struggle for an Auto Union," 11–12, Brophy Papers. The "Notes" of January 14 and the law-and-order statement of February 3, noted above, were almost certainly prepared by Murphy's close friend and legal adviser, Edward G. Kemp, who had a more conventional view of law and order than Murphy did.

Following the collapse of the January 15 truce agreement, Perkins took charge of the negotiations in Washington, but she was unable to bring Sloan and Lewis together. During the Washington talks, Murphy offered to surround the struck plants with the National Guard while negotiations were in progress if the strikers were evacuated. Lewis accepted a similar proposal during the Chrysler sit-down strike in March 1937, but he rejected Murphy's proposition in January. Although the proposal would appear to have been agreeable to many of the strikers, Lewis was unwilling to accept any plan for the evacuation of the plants that did not grant the union exclusive bargaining rights.[52]

When the UAW's seizure of the Chevrolet No. 4 plant markedly heightened strike tensions, Perkins asked Murphy to resume control of the negotiations in Michigan. She informed him on February 2 that Lewis would arrive in Detroit the next day, and she requested Murphy to summon Knudsen into conference with the CIO chief. Knudsen and Lawrence Fisher, however, advised Murphy that GM would not retreat from its position of refusing to negotiate with the union until the corporation's plants were evacuated unless ordered to do so by the President himself. Murphy very much opposed presidential intervention in this form since he believed that the intent was to embarrass Roosevelt, but the Secretary of Labor advised him that Roosevelt wanted him to tell the GM negotiators that it was the President's wish that they confer with the union representatives. Murphy transmitted this information to the management representatives, but still obviously unhappy with the idea, the governor tried to persuade Knudsen to omit any reference to the President from his letter agreeing to confer. General Motors, however, believing it necessary to explain to the public why it was now consenting to negotiate while the sit-down remained in effect, stated in its letter to Murphy of February 2 that it was agreeing to a conference because the governor had indicated that this was "In accordance with the wish of the President," and "The wish of the President of the United States leaves no alternative except compliance."[53]

Perkins makes it appear in her memoirs that President Roosevelt, after helping to arrange for the resumption of strike talks, played no significant part in the ensuing negotiations.[54] As we shall see, however, Roosevelt involved himself directly and indirectly in the strike talks that began on

[52] Perkins Memorandum to the President, Jan. 19, 1937, President's Secretary's File [hereafter cited as PSF], Roosevelt Library; G-2 Periodic Reports, Jan. 23, 1937, National Guard Records.

[53] Strike Chronology, Feb. 2, 1937, Murphy to Knudsen, Feb. 2, 1937, Knudsen to Murphy, Feb. 2, 1937, Murphy Papers; Donaldson Brown to Sidney Fine, Aug. 18, 1964.

[54] Frances Perkins, *The Roosevelt I Knew* (New York, 1946), 322, 323–24; Perkins to Fine, Apr. 30, 1964. It is possible that the former Secretary of Labor confuses two different events in her account of Roosevelt's intervention in the strike.

February 3 and almost certainly used his influence to help secure acceptance of the agreement that finally brought the strike to a close.

Mainly, Roosevelt worked behind the scenes, urging Murphy on and expressing a willingness to speak to the union and management representatives in support of one or another peace plan. At no time, however, did he evidence any desire to take charge of the negotiations personally. Possibly his caution was accounted for by his recollection of the prolonged criticism that organized labor had directed at the settlement that he had arranged for the automobile industry on March 25, 1934;[55] possibly he simply wanted to avoid becoming involved in the conflict between the AFL and the CIO that was being exacerbated by the UAW's quest for exclusive representation.[56] Had Murphy been a poor negotiator, the President might have been compelled to involve himself more openly in the efforts to settle the strike. As it was, he was delighted with the manner in which the Michigan governor was handling the negotiations, and he was as reluctant as Murphy to have the National Guard used to evict the strikers.[57]

The President called Murphy on February 4 and asked him to tell the negotiators that the public welfare demanded that they settle the strike. Roosevelt offered to convey this message personally to Knudsen or Lewis if Murphy thought this necessary. On that same day the union retreated a bit from its original position by proposing that GM recognize it as the bargaining agency only for the employees of the twenty plants then on strike rather than for all the corporation's employees. General Motors also took a step toward a settlement on the same day by declaring that it would not "sponsor, aid or abet" any organization in opposition to or paralleling the UAW. It stated that it recognized and would not interfere with the right of its employees to join the union and that it would not discriminate against or coerce any employees because of their union membership. It was also willing by this time to declare that it would not conclude an agreement with any other organization that contained more favorable terms than it granted the UAW.[58] But GM would not yield on the crucial issue of exclusive representation: it would recognize the union as the collective bargaining agency only for those employees in the struck plants who were

[55] The President's settlement provided for proportional representation in the choice of employee representatives rather than majority rule and exclusive representation.

[56] The AFL, from the start of the strike, opposed the grant of exclusive bargaining rights to the UAW. (See Galenson, *CIO Challenge to AFL*, 142–43; William Green *et al.* to Murphy, Feb. 6, 1937, Murphy Papers; and Kraus, *Many and the Few*, 269.)

[57] Detroit *News*, Jan. 31, 1937; Strike Chronology, Feb. 4, 5, 1937, Creighton Memorandum to Murphy, May 11, 1938, Murphy Papers; Roosevelt to Samuel I. Rosenman, Nov. 13, 1940, President's Personal File 64, Roosevelt Library.

[58] Strike Chronology, Feb. 4, 1937, Proposals of UAW, Feb. 4, 1937, "Recognition," Feb. 4, 1937, Murphy Papers; Proposal for General Motors-Lewis Agreement [Feb. 5, 1937?], PSF.

members of the union. It would be necessary to resolve the difference between the company and the union on this point if the strike were to be terminated.

The next day, February 5, GM supplemented its statement on recognition of the previous day by agreeing to the conduct of a poll among the employees of the struck plants to determine the extent to which the UAW represented these workers. The election was to be conducted under the auspices of Murphy not less than sixty days after the resumption of work. General Motors did not say that it would accept the UAW as the representative of all the workers in these plants should it win a majority in this poll, and its plan could readily have served as a basis for some form of proportional representation. The UAW was not, however, interested in any kind of poll of membership at this point since it was far from confident that it could make an impressive showing. Neither it nor GM, thus, for different reasons, was anxious to invoke the election procedure for which the National Labor Relations Act provided.[59]

It appears from the evidence in the Murphy Papers that the governor concluded on February 5 that the hope for a settlement lay in a formula that would afford the union the degree of recognition and the status in the struck plants that GM had already indicated it was willing to concede but that deferred any decision on the troublesome question of exclusive representation for several months, at which time it would be resolved by collective bargaining, the examination of union membership cards, a poll, or the appointment of a board by the President. Since Roosevelt had advised Murphy once again earlier in the day that he would be willing to talk to Knudsen and Lewis and to help reconcile what he thought was the small difference between them, the governor asked Perkins that afternoon to request the President to express to the two men his approval of the peace formula. Roosevelt might tell Lewis, Murphy advised, that the proposed plan would gain him exclusive representation and that he would therefore be yielding nothing in accepting it. Murphy did not indicate how he had arrived at this conclusion.[60]

On the basis of her conversation with Murphy, the Secretary of Labor prepared a memorandum for the President to use in speaking to Knudsen and Lewis, and, as Murphy had suggested, she advised the President to tell Lewis that the plan would, in effect, grant him the exclusive representation that he was seeking for the UAW.[61] The next day, February 6, Roosevelt

[59] GM to Murphy, Feb. 5, 1937, Murphy Papers; Alinsky, *Lewis,* 138; Detroit *News,* Jan. 13, Feb. 9, 1937; New York *Times,* Jan. 26, 1937.
[60] Strike Chronology, Feb. 5, 1937, Murphy Papers.
[61] Memorandum for the President, Feb. 5, 1937, Proposal for GM-Lewis Agreement [Feb. 5, 1937?], Memorandum for the President's conversation with John Lewis and with Knudsen and Brown [Feb. 5, 1937?], PSF. Whereas Murphy talked of a truce period of six to nine

spoke to Lewis and Knudsen on the phone, presumably following the memorandum that the Secretary of Labor had prepared for him.[62]

On the same day, but we do not know whether it was before or after the President spoke to Knudsen, GM handed Murphy a confidential letter setting forth its own alternative to the union's demand for exclusive representation. The UAW, GM declared, insisted that it must have exclusive representation because GM would otherwise proceed to bargain with other groups in order to undermine the UAW's position. The company had said that it had no intention of doing this, and, as evidence of its good faith, it would now agree with the governor for a period of ninety days after the basic agreement went into effect not to bargain with any other organization in the struck plants regarding matters of general corporation policy without first submitting the facts to Murphy and gaining his sanction for this procedure. This arrangement would leave the UAW, for all practical purposes, as the sole bargaining agency for a period of three months, but would permit GM to avoid any statement to that effect in the proposed agreement and did not commit it to accept any particular plan of representation once the truce period had expired.[63]

Lewis was willing to accept a ninety-day truce only if the truce agreement specifically granted exclusive bargaining rights and thus at least recognized the principle for whose recognition the UAW was striving. Murphy supported Lewis on this issue, but, as the governor informed the Secretary of Labor, GM would "not under any circumstances agree to it." Murphy, sometime during the day on February 8, therefore suggested to Perkins that the President might ask Lewis to accept the GM proposal of February 6,[64] but the governor abandoned this approach that evening after he had had "a grand talk" with Lewis in which Lewis had agreed that if GM would extend the truce period from three months to six months, he would accept the February 6 proposal even though it did not, in so many words, concede the principle of exclusive representation.[65]

All that now remained to achieve a settlement was to secure GM's approval for the extension of the truce period. Since Knudsen and Fisher in Detroit were apparently unwilling to make this concession on their own,

---

months, the memorandum Perkins prepared for the President limited the period to four months. The Perkins memorandum said nothing about how the issue of representation was to be resolved at the end of the truce period.

[62] Strike Chronology, Feb. 6, 1937, Murphy Papers.

[63] GM to Murphy, Feb. 6, 1937, Strike Chronology, Feb. 6, 1937, *ibid*.

[64] Strike Chronology, Feb. 7, 1937, *ibid*.; Memorandum for the President, Feb. 8, 1937, Official File [hereafter cited as OF] 407-B, Roosevelt Library; GM Statement, Feb. 8, 1937, Brown Collection. Alinsky claims that Roosevelt tried to persuade Lewis to accept a truce period of three months or less. (Alinsky, *Lewis*, 133–34.)

[65] Strike Chronology, Feb. 8, 1937, Murphy Papers. Unlike the confrontation of the next day, the Murphy-Lewis meeting of February 8 seems to have been devoted to a discussion of the terms for settling the strike rather than to the issue of law and order.

Murphy asked Perkins to speak to Sloan or, better still, to have the President do so.[66] It is possible that Murphy said at this time that if Roosevelt did not want to involve himself, Marvin McIntyre, the President's secretary, should "insist on it at the request of the president" since Knudsen had said, "if the president told them they would do it."[67] McIntyre called Knudsen that day, but the GM official was either unwilling or unable to agree to a longer truce period; for when McIntyre called Murphy a few minutes after he had spoken to Knudsen, the governor said: "The Boss has to get in touch with Sloane [*sic*] or the Duponts [*sic*]—tell them this is okay."[68]

The next night, as GM continued to hold out for a ninety-day truce, Murphy confronted Lewis with his law-and-order letter and warned him that if a settlement were not immediately negotiated, the governor would read the statement to the other conferees the next morning and would also make it public. Carl Muller, a Detroit newspaperman and a close friend of Murphy, claims that Murphy on this occasion "grabbed Lewis by the coat collar, and in no uncertain terms told him the men would get out of the plants 'or else.'" George Murphy, the governor's brother, declared in an interview that Lewis told Murphy after the letter had been read, "Governor you win," and Murphy himself has described the event as "the turning point" in the strike.[69] The fact of the matter is, though, that Lewis did not alter his position in the slightest as the result of the February 9 confrontation with Murphy. The union leader had insisted on a six-month truce before the letter was read to him, and he continued to insist on a six-month truce after the letter had been read. It was GM that now had to be persuaded to yield.

Murphy had asked for the assistance of Washington in securing GM's consent to a truce period of six months, and that assistance was forthcoming. Not only had McIntyre spoken to Knudsen on February 8, but the next day Secretary of Commerce Daniel Roper talked to Donaldson Brown, a GM vice-president who represented Sloan in the negotiations with the union, and that same day or the next day S. Clay Williams, at Roper's request and in response to Perkins' desire that the aid of an "outstanding" business leader should also be enlisted, talked with Sloan and Brown. Brown explained to Roper that GM was less interested in the length of the "experiment" than in "the phraseology relating to a definition of the words 'exclusive bargaining agents' in such an experiment."[70] Brown was seemingly unaware that

[66] *Ibid.*

[67] Pencil notes attached to copy of Strike Chronology [Feb. 8, 1937?], *ibid.*

[68] Strike Chronology, Feb. 8, 1937, *ibid.*; Beasley, *Knudsen*, 169.

[69] Subcommittee of Senate Committee on Judiciary, *Nomination of Frank Murphy*, 10; Carl Muller, "Frank Murphy, Ornament of the Bar," *Detroit Lawyer*, XVII (Sept. 1949), 183; Interview of George Murphy, Mar. 28, 1957, 4, Michigan Historical Collections; pencil notes by Murphy (Aug. 1938, undated folder), Murphy Papers. For Lewis' account of how he "frightened" Murphy into not executing the order, see Alinsky, *Lewis*, 144–46.

[70] Roper Memorandum for McIntyre, Feb. 10, 1937, OF 407-B; Donaldson Brown, *Some*

Lewis by this time had decided that the substance of the GM concession was more important that its form and no longer was insisting on an outright grant of exclusive bargaining rights.

It was probably more than the inclusion of satisfactory "phraseology" in the final agreement, however, that caused GM to retreat on the question of the length of the period during which the UAW would enjoy a favored position in its plants. The corporation's automotive production had dwindled to the vanishing point, and it must have appeared to GM negotiators, who were unaware of Murphy's law-and-order letter to Lewis,[71] that the sit-downers were simply not going to be dislodged from its plants in the near future and that the company's automotive production would not be resumed until an agreement with the UAW was reached. General Motors was also undoubtedly responding to the informal pressure being exerted from the White House through McIntyre and Roper. When Knudsen later reported that "the Government practically ordered" the settlement of the strike, it may well have been the President to whom he was referring. The corporation, after all, had been warned by one of its officials at the very outset of the strike that the temper of the times required it to adopt a reasonable posture toward unionism in its plants and not to forget that "there has been an election."[72]

The negotiations continued until 2:35 a.m. on February 11, when a weary Murphy was finally able to announce that peace terms had been arranged. The news that the strike had been ended made Murphy the hero of the hour, and praise was lavished upon him by government officials from the President on down, business and labor leaders, the press, and the general public. Murphy had "succeeded," as Josephus Daniels put it, "in what most people thought was an impossible achievement." *Time* reported that it was "apparent that the first vehicle to roll off General Motors' revived assembly lines will be a bandwagon labeled 'Frank Murphy for President in 1940.' "[73] Murphy's "star" seemed "in the ascendant"[74] on February 11, and had not the GM strike been followed by a rash of sit-downs across the land and especially in Michigan, it is unlikely that Murphy would have been subjected to the severe criticism that was soon to be directed at him and that was to plague him for the remainder of his days.

Reminiscences of an Industrialist (n.p. [1957]), 96. Williams was given substantially the same information as was conveyed to Roper.

[71] Kemp, "Murphy as Government Administrator."

[72] Detroit *News*, Oct. 29, 1937; SMD [DuBrul], "The Problem of Union Agreements," Dec. 31, 1936, GM Appendix Documents, Sec. 1.

[73] Daniels to Murphy, Feb. 12, 1937, Murphy Papers; *Time*, XXIX (Feb. 22, 1937), 14; for praise of Murphy as a peacemaker, see the Murphy Papers for Feb. 12, 1937 ff., Murphy Scrapbook #12, and New York *Times*, Feb. 12, 1937.

[74] "Governor Murphy's Star Is in the Ascendant" is the title of an article by Russell B. Porter in the New York *Times Magazine*, Feb. 21, 1937.

THE JOURNAL OF ECONOMIC HISTORY

VOL. XVIII   SEPTEMBER 1958   NO. 3

The Origins of the United Automobile Workers, 1933–1935 *

ON August 26, 1935, delegates from sixty-five American Federation of Labor locals in the automobile industry gathered in Detroit to launch the International Union, United Automobile Workers of America. Although many of the delegates thought that the A.F. of L. had unnecessarily delayed the convocation of this convention, they were no doubt mindful of the fact that an international was being formed in an industry where only a little more than two years previously unionism had been conspicuous primarily because of its absence.

When Franklin D. Roosevelt signed the National Industrial Recovery Act on June 16, 1933, only a few craftsmen in the automobile industry —principally pattern makers, molders, and metal polishers—were A.F. of L. members. The A.F. of L. had failed altogether to unionize the unskilled and semiskilled production workers who constituted the bulk of the labor force in the plants where automobiles were manufactured and assembled and where parts for automobiles were fabricated. The Carriage and Wagon Workers' International Union, organized in 1891, had, to be sure, demonstrated an organizational interest in the early years of the twentieth century in the rapidly growing automobile industry, but its ambitions had foundered on the rock of craft-union jurisdictional claims, and the union was expelled from the A.F. of L. in 1918. Reorganized as the United Automobile, Aircraft and Vehicle Workers of America, the union disintegrated in the 1920's, its surviving remnants being gathered into the Communist-controlled Auto Workers Union. The A.F. of L., for its part, decided at its 1926

* The preparation of this article was facilitated by grants to the author from the John Simon Guggenheim Memorial Foundation and the Horace H. Rackham School of Graduate Studies of the University of Michigan.

249

convention to initiate its own organizing campaign in the automobile industry, but this effort "failed to get beyond the verbal stage."[1]

The depression of 1929 and following, of course, made more difficult the task of organizing the automobile workers. The industry's average employment total of approximately 447,000 wage earners in 1929 was reduced by almost half by 1933, and total wages paid to employees during the same period were slashed by almost two-thirds.[2] A somnolent A.F. of L. was stirred to action, however, by Section 7(a) of the NIRA, which provided that codes approved under the statute should state, among other things, that employees were to have "the right to organize and bargain collectively through representatives of their own choosing" and were to be free from employer interference in designating their representatives or in "self-organization." Officers of the A.F. of L.'s national and international unions gathered in Washington on June 6 and 7, when it was clear that the NIRA was to be passed, and decided to launch an organization campaign in the automobile industry. President Green thereupon sent William Collins to Detroit to take charge of the drive.[3]

In directing the A.F. of L.'s campaign in the auto industry, Collins, who arrived at his post on June 21, was aided by organizers assigned directly to him, who operated principally but not exclusively in Michigan's auto centers, and by organizers in such places as South Bend and Cleveland, who devoted only part of their time to the automobile industry. Where A.F. of L. organizers were not available, the local city federation of labor or central labor union was expected to aid with the job of recruiting union members.[4]

[1] *Report of Proceedings of the Fifty-fifth Annual Convention of the American Federation of Labor, 1935* (Washington: A.F. of L., n.d.), pp. 739–40; John A. Fitch, "The Clash over Industrial Unionism. Exhibit A—The Automobile Industry," *Survey Graphic,* XXV (Jan. 1936), 41–42; William H. McPherson and Anthony Lucheck, "Automobiles," *How Collective Bargaining Works* (New York: Twentieth Century Fund, 1942), pp. 579–80; Selig Perlman and Philip Taft, *History of Labor in the United States, 1896–1932* (New York: The Macmillan Co., 1935), p. 587. In 1920 the A.F. of L. Executive Council asked each of several international unions to send an organizer into the automobile industry and offered to assign an organizer of its own. Nothing, however, came of this proposal. Philip Taft, *The A.F. of L. in the Time of Gompers* (New York: Harper and Brothers, 1957), p. 460.

[2] Bureau of the Census, *Biennial Census of Manufactures, 1935* (Washington: Government Printing Office, 1938), pp. 1150, 1156.

[3] Marjorie R. Clark, "The American Federation of Labor and Organization in the Automobile Industry since the Passage of the National Industrial Recovery Act," *Essays in Social Economics in Honor of Jessica Blanche Peixotto* (Berkeley: University of California Press, 1935), pp. 74–75; Green to Executive Council, June 21, 1933, Green to Collins, June 30, 1933, Green Letterbooks, A.F. of L.—CIO Archives.

[4] Collins to Green, June 23, July 22, 1933, Collins to Morrison, July 28, 1933, Collins File, A.F. of L.—CIO Archives; Green to T. J. Conboy, June 16, 1933, Green to Coleman Claherty, July 14, 1933, Green to Collins, July 24, 27, 1933, Green Letterbooks; W. Ellison Chalmers, "Collective Bargaining in the Automobile Industry," (Incomplete MS [1935]), V, 23–24.

Efforts were made to reach workers through general meetings and plant meetings, and the union message was also spread through hand-bills and by radio and, in Detroit at least, by sound truck. The workers were told that the higher wages and shorter hours intended by the NIRA could come to them only through organization, that Section 7(a) protected them in their right to organize, and that employers were forbidden to interfere with this right. The workers who responded to this message were placed in federal labor unions chartered directly by the A.F. of L. One federal union was normally set up for each plant, except in Toledo, where a single local served the city's numerous auto plants.[5]

Complaining, sometimes with exaggeration, that his annual earnings were altogether inadequate, that he was "forced to work at a speed beyond human endurance," that the methods of compensation employed in the industry were too complicated, that he was not always fully compensated for the time he spent at his job, that management ignored seniority in determining the order of layoff and rehiring, that workers over forty years of age found it difficult to keep their jobs or to secure employment in the industry, that female labor was being substituted for male labor, and that safety and health conditions in the automobile plants were deplorable,[6] the auto worker had grievances upon which organizers seemingly could have capitalized. Progress in organization at the outset was not, however, particularly impressive. Although six charters had been issued in Detroit by the end of July, Collins informed A.F. of L. Secretary Frank Morrison on August 5 that he had taken in but $1,300 in initiation fees—which represented perhaps one thousand members—and that he would not issue membership books or cards until the automobile code was approved because it was too risky to establish unions which could function openly.[7]

The result was that when hearings were held on the automobile manufacturing code on August 18, it was Green himself who argued

[5] "Cooperative Plan of the American Federation of Labor to Provide Collective Bargaining for the United Automobile Workers of America," handbill in Case 209, Records of the National Labor Board, National Archives, Record Group 25, Drawer 35 (henceforth, records in this group will be designated NLB); Collins to Green, July 15, Aug. 12, 1933, Collins File; Chalmers, "Collective Bargaining," V, 27–28, 32–33; Anthony Lucheck, "Labor Organizations in the Automobile Industry" (MS, [1936]), p. 46. In a few places, like St. Louis, a single local served both the Chevrolet and Fisher Body workers.

[6] The grievances of the workers are summed up in NRA, Research and Planning Division, "Preliminary Report on Study of Regularization of Employment and Improvement of Labor Conditions in the Automobile Industry" (Jan. 26, 1935), Appendix B, Exhibit 19.

[7] Detroit *Labor News*, July 21, 28, 1933; Collins to Morrison, Aug. 5, 1933, Collins File. The initiation fee for a federal labor union member was two dollars, but Collins did not insist that the full amount be paid at once.

the case for the automobile workers, and no spokesmen from the ranks of the new automobile unions were present to make statements. The National Automobile Chamber of Commerce, the trade association of the automobile manufacturers, submitted a code that called for a minimum wage of forty to forty-three cents per hour for male factory employees, that permitted most factory workers to labor as many as forty-eight hours per week (although their average employment during the life of the code was not to exceed thirty-five hours per week), and that excluded from even these hours limitations employees engaged in the preparation, care, and maintenance of plant machinery and of production facilities. The NACC also insisted that the code state explicitly that industry members should be permitted to operate an open shop, which was traditional with the auto manufacturers.[8]

Green attacked these proposals in vain. The code that was approved by the President on August 26 was little altered from the document Green had criticized, and it contained the statement that "without in any way attempting to qualify or modify" Section 7(a) by interpretation, "employers in this industry may exercise their right to select, retain, or advance employees on the basis of individual merit, without regard to their membership or nonmembership in any organization." [9] Although Green tried to assure Collins that nothing in the code qualified Section 7(a) and that the discharge of workers for union activity violated the code,[10] the so-called merit clause seemed at least to the more timid auto workers to be a warning that despite Section 7(a) industrial relations in the open-shop automobile industry were to remain unchanged.

Green was aware that the A.F. of L.'s inability to secure better terms for the auto workers was the result of its weakness in the automobile industry. Because the A.F. of L. remained weak in the industry and insufficiently representative of the workers, it also failed to secure any important amendments to the code throughout the life of the NIRA.[11] Indeed, despite constant effort, the A.F. of L. was unable

---

[8] For the code hearings, see NRA Release No. 366, Aug. 18, 1933.

[9] The NACC did agree to a change in the code providing that factory employees whom it had previously wished to exempt from all hours limitations should not exceed forty-two hours per week averaged on an annual basis, although they could work an unlimited number of hours in any one week. NRA, *Codes of Fair Competition,* I (Washington: Government Printing Office, 1933), 255, 256.

[10] Green to Collins, Aug. 28, 1933, Green Letterbooks.

[11] Green to Collins, Sept. 18, 1933, *ibid.* On Jan. 8, 1934, the basic thirty-five hour week provided by the code was increased to forty hours. Amendments to the code authorized on Jan. 31, 1935, provided for the fall announcement of new car models, stipulated that time-

even to secure a public hearing on the provisions of the code on any of the five occasions on which the life of the code was extended.[12] In view of these circumstances and of the fact that no other industry was permitted to include a comparable merit clause in its code, it is not surprising that organized labor came to regard the auto code as "as rotten an egg as was ever hatched by the Blue Eagle." [13]

The "industry" to which the automobile manufacturing code applied was defined as "the manufacturing and assembling . . . of motor vehicles and bodies therefor, and of component and repair parts and accessories by manufacturers and assemblers of motor vehicles." About 25 per cent of the workers in the automobile industry came under the code of the automotive parts and equipment manufacturing industry.[14] However, since the parts makers sold their products chiefly to the vehicle makers, they took their cue from the automobile manufacturers, and the standards for their code were largely determined by the terms of the auto code. The A.F. of L. consequently concentrated its attention on the code of the automobile manufacturing industry and paid relatively little attention to the automotive parts and equipment manufacturers' code.

"The need of the moment," Green advised Collins after the auto code was approved, "is organization, complete organization if possible, so that the chosen representatives of [the] organized automobile workers may speak with authority for the automobile workers." [15] Because the A.F. of L., however, failed to organize a substantial proportion of the automobile workers, it was unable to "speak with authority" for them during the years 1933–1935. For this failure of the A.F. of L. to achieve greater success in the automobile industry, there were many reasons. Some of the problems the A.F. of L. faced were the result of its use of the federal labor union as the means by which to enroll auto workers in the A.F. of L. In contrast to the trade autonomy which normally prevailed in the A.F. of L., federal labor unions were, in effect, "wards"

---

and-a-half was to be paid for hours above forty-eight per week, and confirmed and continued the terms of the President's settlement of the auto labor dispute of Mar. 25, 1934. *Codes,* XVI (Washington: Government Printing Office, 1934), 223–24; *Codes,* XXI (Washington: Government Printing Office, 1935), 203–04.

[12] When the code was extended on Nov. 2, 1934, the President ordered an inquiry into the problem of regularization of employment in the industry. This inquiry, which was directed by Leon Henderson, provided A.F. of L. auto workers an opportunity to air their grievances.

[13] Samuel Romer, "That Automobile Strike," *The Nation,* CXL (Feb. 6, 1935), 162. The Blue Eagle was the symbol of compliance with the NIRA.

[14] *Codes,* I, 253. For the A.P.E.M. code, see *ibid.,* II (Washington: Government Printing Office, 1933), 599–609.

[15] Green to Collins, Aug. 28, 1933, Green Letterbooks.

of the Federation, and although they could elect their own officers, the A.F. of L. exercised direct control over most of their other activities. This naturally raised the question of the rights of the rank and file, which plagued the A.F. of L. throughout the period.

Also, although federal labor union members paid dues of only one dollar per month, thirty-five cents of this sum was sent to the A.F. of L., whereas the international and national unions paid a per capita tax of only one cent per member per month. President Green might argue that the A.F. of L. performed "tremendous services" for its federal locals by seeking favorable code terms and favorable legislation and in other ways, but some auto workers felt that they received too little in return for their per capita tax. "We have fought our fight alone," Carl Shipley, the president of the strong Bendix local, complained to Green on April 14, 1934.[16]

Since the federal labor unions were free to accept any plant workers not already in an A.F. of L. union, they were, temporarily at least, of an industrial character. However, inasmuch as federal labor unions had generally been regarded as the recruiting grounds for the trade unions, the possibility remained that the craft workers in these unions might at some future date be parcelled out among the craft unions.[17] Although the relentless technological progress of automobile manufacturing had reduced the percentage of highly skilled workers in the industry and, as Green conceded, had "practically wiped out" craft lines, organizations like the International Association of Machinists and the Metal Polishers were jealous of their jurisdictional rights, and the IAM in particular persistently and vehemently opposed the inclusion of all workers in an auto plant in a single union.

The IAM claimed jurisdiction over machinists on machinery and equipment maintenance work and those building and repairing tools and dies and working on experimental work in plants where autos were built and assembled. It also insisted that parts plants operated independently of an auto plant and owned by a separate company were "entirely" under its jurisdiction. Although the IAM had failed almost completely to organize workers in these categories, President A. O.

[16] Chalmers, "Collective Bargaining," V, 33–34, IX, 10–11; Constitution of the A.F. of L., Article X, A.F. of L., *Proceedings, 1935*, xxviii; Green to Philip Johns, Aug. 9, 1934, Green to Shipley, Nov. 26, 1934, Green Letterbooks; Shipley to Green, Apr. 29, 1934, A.F. of L. Strike File, Local 18347, A.F. of L.—CIO Archives.

[17] The A.F. of L. plan for organizing the auto industry in 1927 provided that the workers were to be placed in federal labor unions but were to be transferred to international unions as rapidly as possible. Lewis L. Lorwin, *The American Federation of Labor* (Washington: The Brookings Institution, 1933), pp. 246–47.

Wharton and General Vice-President H. W. Brown protested bitterly the inclusion of such workers in the federal labor unions. They claimed that machinists and tool and die makers had been attracted to the federal labor unions only because their dues and initiation fees were lower than those charged by the IAM and that this had placed the IAM in an unfavorable light. Brown dismissed as "silly" Collins' claim that IAM interference with the federal labor unions would "seriously" damage the campaign of organization in the automobile industry.[18]

As president of the A.F. of L., William Green had no choice but to advise Collins and other organizers that the jurisdictional rights of the IAM and other national and international unions must be respected. Green was aware, however, that this was easier said than done. He informed Collins during the early months of the auto campaign that if auto workers could not be persuaded to join the union within whose jurisdiction they fell, they should be taken into the federal labor unions, and he advised Wharton that in some instances organizers were faced with "either organizing a Federal Labor Union or none at all." Annoyed by Wharton's constant complaints of his failure to co-operate with the IAM in the organization of the mass-production industries, Green retorted that it was not the A.F. of L.'s fault if the workers in these industries had become "mass minded" and suggested that "we ought to be broad minded enough to understand the situation." [19]

To the workers in the federal labor unions the possibility was always present that the craftsmen in their midst would be transferred to one of the national or international unions. Collins feared that his work with the Hudson local, virtually the only strong auto local in Detroit, would be frustrated by the IAM. Shipley informed Green that craft jurisdictional claims constituted "one of the greatest hindrances of organization" and warned that if the attempt were made to absorb auto workers into the craft unions, it would "kill" auto unionism.[20]

[18] Green to Max Hayes, July 28, 1933, Eric Peterson to Wharton, May 23, 1934, Wharton to Green, June 1, 1934, May 13, 1935, Brown to Green and Morrison, July 17, 1934, Green Letterbooks; William H. McPherson, *Labor Relations in the Automobile Industry* (Washington: The Brookings Institution, 1940), pp. 7–8; Brown to Wharton, July 27, 1933, Brown to Collins, Mar. 26, June 22, 1934, Wharton to Green, July 29, Aug. 8, 1933, IAM File, A.F. of L.—CIO Archives. For the jurisdictional worries of the Metal Polishers, see A.F. of L., *Proceedings, 1935*, pp. 743–45.

[19] Green to Collins, Oct. 18, 31, 1933, July 23, 1934, Green to Wharton, Nov. 14, 1933, Apr. 9, 1935, Green to Organizers, Feb. 19, 1934, Green to Dillon, May 21, 1935, Green Letterbooks.

[20] Collins to Green, Oct. 14, 28, 1933, Collins File; Shipley to Green, Apr. 29, 1934, A.F. of L. Strike File, Local 18347; Chalmers, "Collective Bargaining," V, 34–35.

The failure of the A.F. of L. to make an all-out effort in its campaign to organize the auto workers also helps to explain its relative lack of success during the years 1933-1935. During the entire period from July 1, 1933, to February 15, 1934, the Detroit headquarters of the A.F. of L. spent only $5,692 on organization work, exclusive of the salaries for regular organizers. Funds were never plentiful enough for the task at hand, and in October 1933 Collins had to eliminate some of the special organizers he was using and to reduce his distribution of literature. More funds were eventually made available, but even the $36,049 spent on the Detroit office between October 14, 1934, and June 29, 1935, was a small sum considering the magnitude of the job confronting the A.F. of L. and the opportunity the NIRA presented. The latter sum, incidentally, was less than the A.F. of L.'s income from the per capita tax for auto unionists during the same period.[21]

Not only were an insufficient number of organizers engaged for the task at hand, particularly during the early months of the campaign, but the A.F. of L. was also often disappointed in its expectation that the central labor unions would be of assistance. Collins found that the CLU in Pontiac had to be aroused "from its dead ashes," that the CLU in Muskegon was defunct, and that the Flint CLU was of little assistance. He complained that even "with all this so-called Labor Movement in Detroit," it was difficult to find anyone in that key city who could carry the A.F. of L. message to the auto workers.[22]

The A.F. of L. was particularly defective in the leadership that it supplied to the auto industry. The organizers it employed knew something of the "technique of joint relationships" but precious little about shop conditions. Collins' experience had been in the field of street railways, and Francis Dillon, who replaced Collins on October 15, 1934, as the A.F. of L.'s national representative in the auto industry, had gained his experience with the Pattern Makers' League. The men from the ranks who became officers of the new locals, on the other

[21] Collins to Morrison, Oct. 21, 1933, Feb. 16, 1934, Collins File; *Proceedings of the First Constitutional Convention of the International Union, United Automobile Workers of America, 1935* (Detroit, n.d.), pp. 22-24. The A.F. of L. received $47,000 in per capita taxes from the auto workers during the six-month period ending July 1, 1935. Green to George F. Addes, July 16, 1935, CIO Historical File, Reel 1, A.F. of L.—CIO Archives. For methods the A.F. of L. might have used to devote more funds to organizing, see James O. Morris, "The Origins of the C.I.O.: A Study of Conflict within the Labor Movement, 1921-1938" (Ph.D. thesis, University of Michigan, 1954), pp. 293-94.

[22] Collins to Green, July 22, Aug. 12, 26, Oct. 28, Nov. 7, 1933, Collins to Morrison, Sept. 22, Dec. 9, 1933, Collins File; Chalmers, "Collective Bargaining," V, 23-24.

hand, were usually without trade-union experience, were unskilled in collective bargaining, and were overly anxious for quick results.[23]

The A.F. of L.'s lack of militancy in pursuing its objectives in the auto industry also limited its effectiveness and its appeal to the workers. From the start the A.F. of L. made it clear that it was simply trying to aid the workers to realize the goals of the NIRA and that it had no intention of fomenting strife. It attempted to convince the employers at the same time that it was a "good" union and that both labor and management would benefit if recognition were extended. When the employers were not swayed by this appeal, the A.F. of L. did not seek to win the argument by a resort to its economic power but rather turned to government agencies for assistance. The strikes that developed during the period were called by the federal locals, often without the knowledge and generally without the advance approval of the A.F. of L.[24]

Conscious of its weakness in the auto industry and of the depressed state of the economy, the A.F. of L. hesitated to risk a showdown with the employers in the economic field. One can well understand the caution of the A.F. of L., but the A.F. of L. was too timid for its own good. It was, after all, a strike at the Bower Roller Bearing Company in September 1933 that put the auto locals on the map in Detroit.[25] It was strikes in the Toledo parts plants, at the Seaman Body plant in Milwaukee, at the Nash plants in Racine and Kenosha, and at the Hupp plant in Detroit that helped to entrench unionism in the affected companies. And, as we shall see, it was an unauthorized strike at the Toledo Chevrolet plant that gave the A.F. of L. its greatest victory in the auto field during the National Recovery Administration period. The A.F. of L. was wise to recognize the crucial role that government could play in the organization of the unorganized—it is clear that the NIRA, for example, was an important factor in the organization of the auto industry—but as the auto workers were themselves to demonstrate after they broke away from the A.F. of L., bold action in the economic field was a necessary supple-

[23] Collins interview, Feb. 4, 1957; Nicholas Kelley interview, Feb. 4, 1957; Leo Wolman interview, Feb. 4, 1957; Chalmers, "Collective Bargaining," VII, 24; Clark, "A.F. of L.," p. 79.
[24] Green to Collins, June 30, 1933, Green Letterbooks; "Cooperative Plan," Case 209, NLB Drawer 35; Detroit News, July 29, 1933; Edward A. Wieck, "The Automobile Workers under the NRA" (MS, Aug. 1935), pp. 33–36, 240–42; Chalmers, "Collective Bargaining," V, 31–32.
[25] Detroit Labor News, Sept. 22, 1933; Chalmers to William Leiserson, Sept. 17, 1933, Case 141, NLB Drawer 22.

ment to government assistance in winning the day for unionism against the giants of the auto industry.

The marked seasonality of automobile employment,[26] coupled with the very heavy unemployment as the result of the depression, further complicated the A.F. of L.'s task. With seasonal layoffs and outright discharge staring them in the face, automobile employees were reluctant to risk the displeasure of their employers by aligning themselves with a trade union. Fear, as Collins recognized, was one of the A.F. of L.'s greatest problems.[27]

The A.F. of L. faced a special problem in organizing auto workers in Detroit, not only because of its inability to appeal effectively to the large number of Negro and foreign-born auto workers in the city,[28] but also because of the poor reputation of organized labor in that stronghold of the open shop. The labor movement in Detroit, Collins informed Green, is "regarded as just a racket with no ideals and principles." There was, moreover, bad blood between Collins and Frank Martel, the president of the Detroit Federation of Labor. Collins had, as a matter of fact, been reluctant to accept his assignment in Detroit because he did not relish working with Martel. Martel, for his part, did not welcome Collins' presence partly because the Detroit F. of L. had launched its own organizing campaign in the industry before Collins arrived on the scene. It was thus not at all surprising that the Detroit F. of L. approved a resolution on August 1, 1934, asking Green to remove Collins from his post.[29]

The Communists, whether enrolled in the tiny Auto Workers Union or in the A.F. of L. federal locals, were a constant source of trouble to the A.F. of L. The Communists were few in number, but they had a disproportionately large influence because almost alone among the auto workers they had some experience in trade unionism. They were forever sniping at the leadership of the A.F. of L., at its

[26] Only one third of the auto employees in 1934 worked throughout the year, and 25 per cent worked less than six months. N. A. Tolles and M. W. LaFever, "Wages, Hours, Employment, and Annual Earnings in the Motor-Vehicle Industry, 1934," *Monthly Labor Review*, XLII (Mar. 1936), 521.

[27] Collins to Green, June 23, Nov. 4, 1933, Collins File.

[28] Collins to Green, Nov. 18, Dec. 15, 1933, *ibid.*; Chalmers, "Collective Bargaining," V, 26–27.

[29] Collins to Green, Nov. 18, Dec. 15, 1933, Collins File; Collins interview, Feb. 4, 1957; Richard Frankensteen interview, Apr. 10, 1957; Chalmers, "Collective Bargaining," V, 24–25; Detroit *Labor News*, June 16, 23, 30, 1933; Detroit *News*, Aug. 7, 1934; *Business Week*, Aug. 18, 1934, p. 16.

lack of militancy and its alleged collaboration with the employers.[30] Much to the annoyance of the A.F. of L. the Communists played an important role in some of the strongest auto locals, such as the Seaman Body local in Milwaukee and the White Motor local in Cleveland. Collins advised the federal locals to oust any Communists who were disrupting their work, and Dillon, with reference to the Communists in the Cleveland locals, informed Green, "There are certain individuals in Cleveland who must get out of those local unions and they are going to be put out." [31]

Finally, the A.F. of L. had to contend with the aggressive and implacable opposition of the employers to independent unionism in their plants. Discrimination, the company union, and espionage, the A.F. of L. charged, were weapons employed to this end. Collins, at the outset, regarded discrimination as his "biggest problem," but just how prevalent the practice was, it is almost impossible to say. Certainly, the A.F. of L. exaggerated the extent to which discrimination was practiced,[32] but the fear of discrimination on the part of the insecure auto worker was as important a deterrent to organization as discrimination itself.

Company unions had not been utilized by the automobile manufacturers prior to the passage of the NIRA, but Section 7(a) persuaded virtually all auto employers except Ford to establish employee representation plans in their plants to stave off the threat of auto unionism. Although Green regarded the company union as the A.F. of L.'s "greatest menace" in the auto industry, it is difficult to evaluate the A.F. of L.'s complaint. There is no doubt that the employers them-

---

[30] *Auto Workers News*, Dec. 30, 1933, Jan. 13, Mar. 10, Apr. 7, 21, May 5, 19, July 21, Aug. 4, 18, 1934; *Michigan Worker*, July 1, 1933; "Directives on Work within the A.F. of L. and Independent Trade Unions," *Communist*, XIII (Jan. 1934), 113-15. The AWU dissolved itself in December 1934, and advised its members and sympathizers to join the A.F. of L. if they were production workers and the Mechanics Educational Society of America if they were tool and die makers. *Daily Worker*, Dec. 25, 1934.

[31] Collins to Green, July 22, Sept. 9, 1933, Collins File; Dillon to Green, Aug. 18, 1934, Apr. 4, 1935, Dillon File, A.F. of L.—CIO Archives; Dillon to Green, Dec. 22, 1934, A.F. of L. Strike File, Local 19059; UAW *Weekly News Letter*, Aug. 25, 1934, Vertical File, A.F. of L.—CIO Library.

[32] Collins to Morrison, July 28, 1933, Collins File. While the Automobile Labor Board was functioning (Mar. 29, 1934–June 16, 1935), employers voluntarily reinstated 1,129 workers who brought charges of discrimination, and, in addition, the ALB decided in several cases that discrimination had been practiced. In its final report, however, the ALB stated that discrimination because of union membership was "not by June, 1935, a problem of any magnitude in the automobile manufacturing industry," and had not been for some months previously." "Final Report of the Automobile Labor Board" (Aug. 1935), pp. 15, 23.

selves initiated and supported most of the company union plans as alternatives to independent unionism, but how many workers were persuaded not to join the A.F. of L. locals as a result, it is impossible to say.[33]

The facts concerning espionage in the auto industry did not come out until the La Follette committee hearings of 1937. At these hearings Herman L. Weckler of Chrysler Corporation conceded that Chrysler used espionage reports as "the background on which we built our whole structure," and General Motors officials also testified to their company's use of detective services for labor espionage purposes. La Follette concluded that "perhaps nowhere" was the correlation between labor organizing activities and expenditures for spy services "more marked than in the automobile industry." [34]

Whatever the reasons, the Big Three in the automobile industry, G.M., Ford, and Chrysler, were on the whole able, particularly in Detroit, to resist unionism during most of the period 1933–1935. Independents like Nash, Studebaker, White, and Hudson, which were in a more precarious financial position, were not, however, so successful in meeting the union challenge, and the same was true of many of the parts companies, which could not afford prolonged labor strife lest they lose their business to their numerous competitors or to the main plants themselves.

During the autumn months of declining automobile production following the adoption of the auto code, organization work in Flint and Pontiac met with some success, but in Detroit, Collins ruefully reported to Green, membership increased at a snail's pace. Even when production began its upward climb in December and January, Collins continued to report "a let-down" in interest. The federal locals during these months were also meeting with little success in their efforts to establish a satisfactory relationship with the employers. The A.F. of L. charged that union members, particularly in the Chrysler plants and in the G.M. plants in Flint, were being discharged for union activity

---

[33] Green to Richard Byrd, Feb. 8, 1934, Green Letterbooks; Wieck, "Automobile Workers," pp. 42–47; Chalmers, "Collective Bargaining," V, 4–23; General Motors, "Labor Relations Diary," Sec. I (1946), pp. 20–22.

[34] Subcommittee of Senate Committee on Education and Labor, *Violations of Free Speech and Rights of Labor. Hearings Pursuant to S. Res. 266, 74 Cong. . . .*, 75 Cong., 1 Sess., Part 4 (Washington: Government Printing Office, 1937), pp. 1206, 1211–13, 1215; Part 5 (Washington: Government Printing Office, 1937), pp. 1621, 1690–93; Part 6 (Washington: Government Printing Office, 1937), pp. 1879, 1907, 1911, 1915, 1928, 1970–73, 2042–43; Senate Committee on Education and Labor, *Violations of Free Speech and Rights of Labor*, 75 Cong., 2 Sess., Sen. Report No. 46, Part 3 (Washington: Government Printing Office, 1939), pp. 23–24.

and were being discriminated against in layoff and rehiring. When the unions sought to present their grievances to their employers and to attain a measure of recognition, they were told to refer their complaints to the company union representatives or to supply a list of union members so that management would know for whom the union representatives were speaking. The unions retorted that the company unions had been imposed upon the workers and that the submission of membership lists would simply invite discrimination. The proper way to determine representation rights, they insisted, was through elections conducted by the National Labor Board, and in February 1934 the stronger unions, particularly in Flint, began pressing for such elections.[35]

The A.F. of L. took many of its complaints to the Detroit Regional Labor Board for determination, but Collins was hardly pleased with the results. He complained about the "lumbering processes" of the Board and criticized its handling of discrimination and representation cases. The Board did, as a matter of fact, rule in favor of the auto unionists in some instances, but the management of the companies concerned refused to abide by its decisions.[36]

Frustrated in their efforts to deal with their employers and with the Regional Labor Board and fearful that the production season would pass without material gain for their cause, the federal locals began turning their thoughts to strike action. Consequently, when the officers of the Michigan auto locals gathered in Lansing on March 4, they advised the strong A.F. of L. locals in the Buick and the two Fisher Body plants in Flint and in the Hudson plant in Detroit to wire their employers at once for wage and hour adjustments and to demand a reply in forty-eight hours.[37] Collins, however, actually had

[35] Collins to Green, Sept. 9, 22, Oct. 14, 28, Nov. 18, 1933, Jan. 6, Feb. 9, 1934, Collins to Morrison, Dec. 9, 1933, J. F. Anderson to Morrison, Nov. 12, 1933, Collins File; file of correspondence in Case 209, NLB Drawer 35; case files involving auto industry in Detroit Regional Labor Board Boxes 281, 282; Pontiac Fisher folder, Records of the NRA, National Archives, Record Group 9, Automobile Labor Board Drawer 4103 (henceforth, Automobile Labor Board records will be designated ALB; other NRA records will be designated NRA); Buick folder, ALB Drawer 3991; Chalmers, "Collective Bargaining," V, 37–42. The NLB was created by President Roosevelt on Aug. 5, 1933, to adjust "differences and controversies" arising out of the President's Reemployment Agreement. Its powers were subsequently enlarged by the President, and on Feb. 1, 1934, it was specifically authorized to conduct elections of employee representatives for collective-bargaining purposes. The NLB began establishing regional boards in the latter part of October 1933.

[36] Collins to Green, Jan. 6, 20, 1934, Collins File; case files involving auto industry in DRLB Boxes 281, 282; Buick folder, ALB Drawer 3991.

[37] Collins to Morrison, Mar. 3, 1934, Collins File; Chalmers, "Collective Bargaining," V, 42–49; Detroit *Free Press,* Mar. 5, 6, 1934. This was the fourth such conference called by Collins.

no intention of permitting a strike to be called. Believing that the automobile workers were too weak to stage a successful walkout, Collins, who for months had been insisting that the intervention of the NRA or NLB was necessary to stimulate organization, was using the threat of a work stoppage in this key industry to bring about federal intervention and a government-sponsored settlement that would improve employment conditions and give the auto workers courage.[38]

Collins, therefore, quickly called the threatening situation to the attention of the President and warned him that if the strikes were called against the four plants, there was a "serious possibility" that other plants would also become involved. Collins' warning had the desired effect. The NLB, at the President's behest, assumed jurisdiction on March 5 and by promising that hearings on the dispute would be held on March 14 was able to get the impending strikes postponed.[39]

The NLB hearings of March 14-15 gave Collins and the representatives of eleven different auto locals a chance to air their grievances, but the hearings were barren of result because G.M. and Hudson challenged the NLB's authority and made it clear that they would not co-operate in any plant elections the NLB might order. This persuaded General Johnson to intervene and to try his hand at arranging a settlement, but when his efforts also failed to break the deadlock, President Roosevelt on March 20 stepped into the dispute and persuaded the auto workers to defer strike action while he conferred with both sides in Washington.[40]

By this time the dispute had come to center on two issues:[41] the form that employee representation should assume and the question of discrimination. The A.F. of L. contended that the representatives of the majority of the workers in a given plant, as determined by an NLB election, should bargain for all the workers. The auto manufacturers, however, insisted that Section 7(a) required the employers to deal with the accredited representatives of all groups in the plant, re-

---

[38] Collins to Green, Sept. 9, 22, 1933, Collins to Morrison, Sept. 16, 1933, Collins File; Collins interview, Feb. 4, 1957; Chalmers, "Collective Bargaining," V, 43-44, 48-49.

[39] Collins to F.D.R., Mar. 4, 1934, Wagner to Collins, Mar. 6, 1934, Case 209, NLB Drawer 35; Chalmers, "Collective Bargaining," VI, 1-4; Detroit *News*, Mar. 6, 7, 8.

[40] NLB, Stenographic Report of Hearing. In the Matter of Buick Co. . . . , Mar. 14, 15, 1934, NLB Drawer 68; F.D.R. to Collins, Mar. 20, 21, 1934, Collins to F.D.R., Mar. 20, Official File 407-B, Box 18, Franklin D. Roosevelt Library, Hyde Park (henceforth, Official File will be designated O.F.); *The New York Times*, Mar. 17, 21, 1934; Chalmers, "Collective Bargaining," VI, 13-15.

[41] The wages and hours issue was blunted on March 13 when the NACC announced it had advised member firms to reduce the average work week from forty to thirty-six hours and to institute compensatory wage increases.

gardless of their size, and that individuals who desired to bargain for themselves also had a perfect right to do so. If an organization wished to establish its right to bargain for its members, it must submit a membership list to the employer.

As regards the issue of discrimination the auto magnates proposed that charges of discrimination should be brought before a three-man industrial relations committee appointed by the code authority, with its findings subject to appeal to a Board of Review composed of three men, not identified with the industry, appointed by the NRA. The A.F. of L., for its part, wanted the adjudication of discrimination cases entirely divorced from the code authority and vested in a government-appointed joint industrial-relations board whose decisions would be final.[42]

The terms of settlement of the auto dispute were announced by the President on March 25 after five days of negotiation in Washington. The employers agreed to bargain with "the freely chosen representatives of groups" and not to discriminate against union members. If there was more than one group in a plant, each bargaining committee was to have "total membership pro rata to the number of men each member represents." The government furthermore stated that it favored "no particular union or particular form of employee organization or representation" and that its only duty was "to secure absolute and uninfluenced freedom of choice without coercion, restraint, or intimidation from any source."[43] By accepting these terms the A.F. of L. surrendered the vital principle of majority rule in favor of the concept of proportional representation and also, in effect, conceded that the requirements of Section 7(a) could be met by a company union as long as the employees had not been coerced into joining it.

The settlement further provided that the NRA was to set up a board responsible to the President, composed of a labor representative, an industry representative, and a neutral. It was "to pass on all questions of representation, discharge and discrimination," and its decisions were to be final and binding on both sides. It was to have access to payrolls and lists of "claimed employee representation." In cases

42 Collins to Johnson, Mar. 20, 1934, O.F. 407–B, Box 18, F.D.R. Library; NACC to Johnson, Mar. 21, 1934, Roy Chapin Papers, Michigan Historical Collections; *The New York Times,* Mar. 14, 18, 19, 20, 1934.

43 The terms of the settlement and the President's amplifying remarks are given in full in *The New York Times,* Mar. 26, 1934. In his amplifying remarks, F.D.R. stated that he looked forward to the development of "a kind of works council in industry in which all groups of employees, whatever may be their choice of organization or form of representation, may participate in joint conferences with their employers. . . ."

where lists were not disclosed to the employer, there was to be no basis for a claim of discrimination, but no such disclosure was to be made "without specific direction of the President." The issue of lists was thus compromised. Apparently, although it was not specifically stated in the settlement, representation was to be determined by a comparison of lists and payrolls rather than by the elections the A.F. of L. preferred,[44] but this comparison was to be undertaken by a board responsible to the President rather than by the employers. Also, the lists used in discrimination cases were, in effect, to be protected by the President.

As regards the question of seniority, which was closely related to the problem of discrimination, the settlement provided that in reduction and increases of force, "such human relationships as married men with families shall come first and then seniority, individual skill and efficient service." After these factors had been taken into account, "no greater proportion of outside union employees similarly situated" were to be laid off than of "other employees." In his amplifying remarks accompanying the settlement, the President declared that "we have for the first time written into an industrial settlement a definite rule for the handling of reductions and increases of force."

Two days after the settlement had been agreed upon, the President announced the membership of the new Automobile Labor Board. The choice of the union delegation, accepted by the President, was Richard Byrd, secretary of the G.M. Truck local of Pontiac. The President also accepted the nominee of the employers, Nicholas Kelley, counsel for Chrysler, and appointed Leo Wolman to be neutral chairman. Wolman was a professor of economics at Columbia and the chairman of the NRA's Labor Advisory Board.[45]

Although some members of the union delegation claimed complete victory, Arthur Law of the union group was closer to the truth when he stated, "The settlement is not what the boys wanted originally."[46] It is true that the unions had made some gains with respect to discrimination and seniority and that a tribunal had been set up whose decisions the employers agreed to accept, but the union delegation, as noted, had capitulated on the key issue of representation and collec-

[44] *Ibid.*; Chalmers, "Collective Bargaining," VI, 19.
[45] *The New York Times*, Mar. 25, 28, 1934; Chalmers, "Collective Bargaining," VI, 25, 40.
[46] Detroit *News*, Mar. 26, 1934; Detroit *Free Press*, Mar. 27, 1934; *The New York Times*, Mar. 26, 1934; Flint *Weekly Review*, Mar. 30, 1934.

tive bargaining. The employers, however, had made it perfectly clear that they would not yield on this issue,[47] and thus the alternative was a strike or the acceptance of the settlement.

Green, like Collins, was apprehensive about a strike, believing that it would be "tragic in its effects and tragic in its results." Although the display of interest on the part of the Federal Government in the problems of the auto workers had proved, as Collins had hoped, a decided boon to union organization,[48] Green knew that the federal locals had only approximately thirty-two thousand paid-up members in March out of a total of 450,000 factory employees in the main and parts plants and that the organization was particularly weak in Detroit. The A.F. of L. strength in the industry was, to be sure, greater than the figure of paid-up membership might indicate, but Green felt himself unable to appraise the number of workers who would actually walk out if a strike were called and how they would conduct themselves under pressure. Under the circumstances, he preferred an imperfect settlement to the risk of losing all in a strike against the powerful auto manufacturers.[49]

An additional factor in persuading the union representatives to accept the settlement was their faith in President Roosevelt. The union men who spoke with F.D.R. were impressed with his knowledge of labor affairs, his sympathy for their problems, and his assurances that the law would be enforced. "He asked us to trust him," Byrd declared, "and we will."[50]

From the time it began its work on March 29 in Detroit until the NIRA was declared unconstitutional on May 27, 1935, the ALB was a major factor on the auto labor scene.[51] Increasingly, it became the object of A.F. of L. attack, and the A.F. of L. began to attribute its difficulties in organizing the auto workers to the influence of the ALB.

[47] Alvan Macauley to F.D.R., Mar. 21, 1934, O.F. 407–B, Box 18, F.D.R. Library; Macauley to Johnson, Mar. 25, 1934, Chapin Papers.

[48] Joseph Sherer to NLB, Mar. 9, 1934, DRLB Box 280; Flint *Weekly Review*, Mar. 16, 1934; Wieck, "Automobile Workers," p. 95.

[49] Green to Executive Council, Mar. 27, 1934, Green to Matthew Woll, Mar. 30, 1934, Green Letterbooks. The paid-up membership figures were supplied to me by the bookkeeping department of the old A.F. of L. on Aug. 17, 1955.

[50] Flint *Weekly Review*, Mar. 30, 1934; *The New York Times*, Mar. 27, 1934; Detroit *Times*, Mar. 27, 1934.

[51] The automotive parts and equipment manufacturing industry was brought within the jurisdiction of the ALB on Apr. 27, 1934, provided that both parties submitting a question to it subscribed in full to the March 25 settlement. *Codes*, IX (Washington: Government Printing Office, 1934), 936. The parts plants were otherwise under the jurisdiction of the National Labor Relations Board.

Differences between the ALB and the A.F. of L. became apparent almost as soon as the Board began to function. The A.F. of L. thought that the ALB should proceed at once to deal with the matter of collective bargaining, but the ALB assigned a higher priority to the settlement of the strikes then taking place in the industry and to the issue of discrimination. The A.F. of L. was further displeased that in dealing with the latter problem, the ALB did not quickly seek to ascertain which employees had been discriminated against and to order their reinstatement, but rather sought to persuade the auto companies to return to their payrolls voluntarily as many men as possible from among those who alleged discrimination.[52]

The ALB had actually told the auto employers soon after it took office to meet with the representatives of "all groups of labor in bona fide collective bargaining." Conferences began to take place coincidentally with the submission to the ALB by the A.F. of L. of the membership lists of some of its locals. At the conclusion of one of these conferences, at the Fisher Body plant in Cleveland, the federal local, confusing a mere meeting with the employer as recognition, announced that it had been recognized by the management. Antagonized by the union claim, E. F. Fisher insisted that the meeting had simply been "an informal interview." The ALB tried to smooth ruffled feelings by stating on April 16 that it had begun the process of verifying the lists submitted to it and that it was desirable while it was engaged in this task for the employers to grant conferences but with the understanding on the part of all concerned that the conferences were not to be viewed as involving the recognition of the union "as such," nor were the employee representatives to be regarded as representing any employees other than those whom it would be determined they represented according to the lists.[53]

Following this announcement conferences were resumed at Fisher Body in Cleveland, but failing to secure the terms it sought, the local went out on strike on April 23. Since the key Cleveland plant made body stampings for Chevrolet, Pontiac, and Buick, any prolonged strike there would have seriously affected G.M.'s auto production.[54]

[52] Collins to F.D.R., Apr. 9, 1934, O.F. 407–B, Box 18, F.D.R. Library; Wolman interview, Feb. 4, 1957; "Report of the Activities of the A.L.B. to Feb. 5, 1935," pp. 1–2; Chalmers, "Collective Bargaining," VII, 1, 12, 41–46.

[53] "Report of the A.L.B. to Feb. 5, 1935," p. 2; Cleveland *Plain Dealer*, Apr. 11, 13, 16, 1934; Wolman to Collins, Apr. 12, 1934, ALB Drawer 3999; statement of ALB, Apr. 16, 1934, ALB Drawer 4107.

[54] Cleveland *Plain Dealer*, Apr. 17, 18, 23, 30, 1934; *Iron Age*, CXXXIII (Apr. 26, 1934), 40; *ibid.* (May 3, 1934), 44; Chalmers, "Collective Bargaining," VII, 19.

The Cleveland strike was quickly followed by strikes at the Fisher Body plants in St. Louis, Kansas City, and Tarrytown, none of which involved A.F. of L. locals, and by deadlocked negotiations in other Fisher Body plants, which did involve the A.F. of L. Collins therefore informed the ALB on April 27 that the federal locals had failed in their efforts to bargain collectively with the local managements of the various Fisher plants and that the situation could be resolved only if the top Fisher management conferred with union representatives.[55]

Apparently troubled by the Cleveland strike, G.M. agreed to a conference but would not permit representatives of the Cleveland local to take part unless the Cleveland strike was first called off. At the insistence of the A.F. of L., which thought that more was to be gained by a conference with G.M. than by the prolongation of the strike, the Cleveland local reluctantly agreed on April 29 to return to work. The conference was held in Detroit from April 30 to May 2 in the presence of the ALB. The basic decision reached was simply that conferences should once again take place at the local plant level and that some of the higher officials of G.M. and such outside leaders as the locals desired should participate in at least some of the meetings. Because management insisted upon it and the ALB favored it, Collins reluctantly agreed that at least in Cleveland and Pontiac representatives of the various organizations in the plant, including the company union, should meet jointly with the management.[56]

Conferences were held at various Fisher Body plants, but the A.F. of L. was dissatisfied with the results. What was required to strengthen its position in negotiating with management, the A.F. of L. thereupon insisted, was for the ALB to certify that the A.F. of L. had enrolled a majority of the workers in the fifteen plants for which lists had been submitted. The ALB, however, found these lists to be relatively useless. Not only did the employers challenge the authenticity of the signatures on the membership application blanks, but the ALB also discovered that "a substantial proportion" of the claimed members had signed application blanks but had not paid initiation fees or

---

[55] Collins to ALB, Apr. 27, 1934, ALB Drawer 3990; Flint *Weekly Review*, Apr. 27, 1934. The Kansas City and St. Louis locals had seceded from the A.F. of L., but they reaffiliated shortly after the strike ended. The Tarrytown organization also joined the A.F. of L. after the strike.

[56] Cleveland *Plain Dealer*, Apr. 30, 1934; Green to Charlton Ogburn, May 9, 1934, Green Letterbooks; Wieck, "Automobile Workers," pp. 105–08; ALB, Stenographic Report of Hearing. In the Matter of: Fisher Body Corporation, Apr. 30—May 2, 1934, Michigan Historical Collections.

dues and that some of the alleged members belonged to more than one organization.[57]

As union membership fell off in the months following the March 25 settlement,[58] the A.F. of L. more and more saw the ALB and the settlement as the source of its troubles in the auto industry. It complained about the slowness of the Board in arriving at its decisions and about the unfairness of some of these decisions. It pointed out that even when the ALB found that a worker had been discriminated against, it did not order that he be returned to his original job and that he receive back pay. It felt that the ALB was insufficiently concerned with the alleged efforts of G.M. executives to promote company unions in their plants.[59] Increasingly, also, the A.F. of L. became antagonistic toward the labor member of the ALB, Richard Byrd. Since he had been nominated for his job by the officers of some of the federal locals, the A.F. of L. regarded him as its representative on the ALB, but the A.F. of L. discovered in June and July 1934 that Byrd was actually hostile to the A.F. of L. The A.F. of L. tried in vain in July to get Byrd to resign from the Board or to have him removed from his post, and Green wished Wolman to know that "under no circumstances can we cooperate with the ALB if Mr. Byrd is to remain a member." [60]

Above all, the A.F. of L. became displeased with the ALB and the settlement because it could not reconcile itself to the fact that collective bargaining in the automobile industry was to be determined on the basis of proportional representation whereas majority rule prevailed, at least in theory, everywhere else. Whatever the apparent fairness of the idea of proportional representation, Green pointed out, and properly so, that it represented "a division and a schism of that united front necessary to be represented by labor." Why should not the

[57] Cleveland *Plain Dealer*, May 7, 8, 9, 10, 17, 20, 1934; Chalmers, "Collective Bargaining," VII, 20–23; Wieck, "Automobile Workers," pp. 112–13; "Final Report of A.L.B.," p. 25.

[58] By June, 1934, there were only 18,244 paid-up members in the federal locals. This figure was supplied by the bookkeeping department of the old A.F. of L., Aug. 17, 1955.

[59] Collins to Wolman, May 23, 1934, and enclosed petition, T. Woody and G. Rymer to F.D.R., May 28, 1934, ALB Drawer 4105; Buffalo *Central Labor Council Herald*, May 25, 1934; Charles M. Schang to Wolman, June 7, 1934, ALB Drawer 3999; Collins to Green, Apr. 14, 1934, Collins File; Ogburn to Green, Oct. 26, 1934, NRA Box 657.

[60] Collins to Green, Mar. 31, 1934, Collins to Morrison, July 21, 1934, Collins File; Green to Arthur Greer, July 23, 1934, Green to Ogburn, June 28, July 23, 1934, Green to Collins, July 24, 1934, Green Letterbooks; Collins and Dillon to Wolman, July 26, 1934, ALB Drawer 4105; Wieck, "Automobile Workers," p. 188; Official Proceedings of First Session, National Council United Automobile Workers Federal Labor Unions, July 9–14, 1934, Joe Brown Collection, Wayne State University Library; Tracy M. Doll interview, Dec. 17, 1957.

President on the basis of Public Resolution 44, approved by Congress on June 16, 1934, establish a board for the automobile industry like the one he had appointed for the steel industry and order it, as he had ordered the Steel Labor Relations Board, to conduct elections on the principle of majority rule? The National Labor Relations Board, which the President had created on June 29, 1934, to replace the NLB, had decided in favor of majority rule on August 30, 1934, in the Houde case, which involved a federal local in a parts plant. Why, asked the A.F. of L., should this principle not be applied to workers in the main plants as well? [61]

The A.F. of L. charges against the ALB, although not entirely accurate, were not without some substance. The ALB did take a long time in arriving at its decisions, and in some cases insufficient protection was accorded to employees returned to work as a result of its rulings.[62] Byrd did behave improperly, even if the A.F. of L. was unjustified in thinking that he was to represent only its interests on the Board rather than the auto workers generally. Of course, the A.F. of L. complaint about proportional representation was a complaint against the settlement itself and not properly directed against the ALB, which was charged with implementing the settlement. But whatever the merits of the A.F. of L.'s brief against the ALB, it was in error in assigning its lack of success in the auto industry to the ALB. Its difficulties were of a more fundamental nature, and it would have been in trouble even if a board more to its liking had been established.

On September 11, 1934, William Green wrote to President Roosevelt to announce the withdrawal of the A.F. of L. from the March 25 settlement. He informed the President that Charlton Ogburn, the A.F. of L.'s counsel, had advised him that since the settlement was simply an agreement of "no fixed duration of time," the A.F. of L. could withdraw from it by giving notice to the President and the auto manufacturers. Through Secretary of Labor Frances Perkins, F.D.R. requested

[61] Ogburn to Wolman, July 7, 1934, ALB Drawer 4106; Green to F.D.R., Sept. 11, 12, 1934, and enclosed resolution of National Council, Aug. 31, 1934, O.F. 466, Box 7, F.D.R. Library. For an account of Public Resolution 44, the Steel Labor Relations Board, the NLRB, and the Houde case, see Lewis L. Lorwin and Arthur Wubnig, *Labor Relations Boards: The Regulation of Collective Bargaining under the National Industrial Recovery Act* (Washington: The Brookings Institution, 1935), pp. 258–61, 291–352.

[62] It was not at all unusual for three months to elapse between the time a case was filed and the decision rendered. For an analysis of ALB decisions, see "Report of the National Labor Relations Board on an Inquiry into Industrial Relations Boards" (Feb. 26, 1935), pp. 27–30, O.F. 716, Box 2, F.D.R. Library.

Green to withhold the letter from publication until he (Green) could discuss the matter with Perkins. Perkins, in turn, later asked Green not to release the letter until he had talked with F.D.R., but a subsequent conference with the President did not cause Green to change his mind.[63]

As a matter of fact the A.F. of L. soon found new reason to be displeased with the ALB. On December 7 the Board made public an election plan designed to provide each of the plants under its jurisdiction with a bargaining agency whose membership would be determined on the basis of proportional representation. The plan called for the division of each plant into voting districts. In the primary election, each voter was to nominate one person, who did not have to be an employee, to represent his district, and he could, if he desired, "indicate the group, if any, with which his nominee is identified." The names of the two persons receiving the highest number of votes in a district were to appear on the ballot for the final election along with their group affiliation, if any had been indicated. The tabulation of primary votes would determine the relative proportion of representatives on the bargaining agency to which each group containing "a substantial number" was entitled. Voters who expressed no group affiliation for their nominee were to be treated as a single unaffiliated group. If the representatives victorious in the final election did not provide the proportional representation to which a group was entitled on the basis of its primary vote, the ALB was to add to the bargaining agency a sufficient number of additional representatives from among the defeated candidates of that group receiving the highest number of votes.[64]

Quite apart from its attempt to implement a scheme of proportional representation, the ALB plan differed markedly from the election procedures then being employed by other government labor boards. Whereas nearly all other collective-bargaining elections originated in a complaint by a trade union that it was being denied recognition, the ALB elections were scheduled for all the auto plants, whether organized labor desired them or not. Normally, also, the elections involved a straight choice between a trade union and a company union, whereas in the ALB elections an individual could not vote for an organization

[63] Green to F.D.R., Sept. 11, 1934, Green to Alfred Reeves, Jan. 8, 1935, enclosed with Reeves to F.D.R., Jan. 14, 1935, O.F. 466, Box 7, F.D.R. Library; Green to Ogburn, Sept. 24, Oct. 8, 1934, Green Letterbooks.

[64] ALB Memorandum, Dec. 7, 1934, ALB Drawer 4019.

at all. Moreover, he was not, strictly speaking, to express his own affiliation, if he had any, but rather the affiliation of his candidate, assuming he knew what that affiliation was and was inclined to indicate it on the ballot.[65]

The A.F. of L. was displeased not only for the above reasons but also because of its objection to the whole idea of proportional representation, because the elections were to take place on company property, because the first elections were not held in the plants for which the A.F. of L. had submitted membership lists, and also because it had not been given ample opportunity to criticize the plan in advance. It must also have been apparent to the A.F. of L. that if the ALB bargaining agencies became the means through which bargaining took place in a plant, the auto workers would see no point in paying dues to a labor union. The A.F. of L., consequently, advised its members not to participate in the elections.[66]

In the first eleven elections, all held in Detroit, only 4 per cent of the voters indicated that their candidate was affiliated with the A.F. of L. The A.F. of L. picked up strength outside Detroit, however, and ultimately 8.6 per cent of the 163,150 voters in the nominating elections designated their candidate as affiliated with the A.F. of L. It should, of course, be noted that the elections were held only in plants under the automobile manufacturing code, and not in plants under the automotive parts and equipment manufacturing code, that elections were not held in the Ford plants, where the A.F. of L. was weak, or in the Nash, Studebaker, and a few other plants where it was strong, and that the A.F. of L. locals made no effort, in most instances, to win votes for their people.[67]

Not willing to delay the matter any longer, Green wrote to the Automobile Manufacturers Association (the NACC took this name on August 22, 1934) on January 8, 1935, to announce the A.F. of L. withdrawal from "participation in the work and decisions" of the ALB.

[65] Twentieth Century Fund, *Labor and the Government* (New York: McGraw-Hill Book Company, 1935), pp. 90, 94–95; Wolman, *Ebb and Flow in Trade Unionism* (New York: National Bureau of Economic Research, 1936), pp. 78–83.

[66] Green to Dillon, Dec. 8, 1934, Green Letterbooks; Detroit District Council of UAW Resolution, Dec. 10, 1934, Dillon to Wolman, Jan. 11, 1935, ALB Drawer 4105; Dillon press releases, Dec. 8, 18, 1934, Jan. 25, 26, 1935, Dillon File; House Committee on Labor, *Labor Disputes Act. Hearings on H.R. 6288*, 74 Cong., 1 Sess. (Washington: Government Printing Office, 1935), pp. 213–14, 245–46, 248, 253–54.

[67] "Final Report of A.L.B.," Appendices A and B; Wieck, "Automobile Workers," pp. 161, 164–68. The NLRB ordered elections in the Bendix and Kelsey-Hayes plants, but these orders were appealed by the employers to the courts, and before decisions could be rendered, the NIRA had been declared unconstitutional.

Acting on the advice of Frances Perkins, he stated that the A.F. of L. wished to meet with AMA representatives to agree on a new tribunal to replace the ALB. When the AMA refused to confer with him on the subject, Green on January 24 publicly announced that the A.F. of L. would have "nothing more to do" with the ALB.[68]

Green naïvely assumed that the announced withdrawal of the A.F. of L. from the settlement meant the ALB would "pass out of the picture,"[69] but nothing of the sort occurred. Since a new board was not created to replace the ALB, the A.F. of L. federal locals in the main plants thus found themselves after January 1935 without a government tribunal to which they could take their complaints against their employers.

While the A.F. of L. was having its difficulties with the ALB, steps were being taken which led ultimately to the establishment of an international union of automobile workers. The A.F. of L. leadership did not, however, move toward this objective with sufficient speed to satisfy some of the automobile locals, with the result that they themselves initiated efforts to hasten the formation of an international. Conscious of the lack of co-ordination among the various federal locals, the strong Bendix local sent out a call for a conference of locals to be held in Chicago on May 18, 1934. Unionists from eighteen different locals attended and resolved in favor of the establishment of an international. A similar conference, and with a generally similar result, was held in Chicago on June 3, this time at the instigation of the St. Louis Fisher Body and Chevrolet local.[70]

Collins' reaction to these unauthorized actions by the federal locals was to suggest the calling of a meeting of the auto locals to bring into the open the "underground discussion" of an international and to expose the persons involved and the methods being employed. Green, however, counseled him against this proposal. It would be better, he suggested, to call a national conference to discuss "a specific constructive program." The best way to convince the workers that they were not

[68] Green to Reeves, Jan. 8, 1935, enclosed with Reeves to F.D.R., Jan. 14, 1935, O.F. 466, Box 7, F.D.R. Library; Green to Ogburn, Oct. 8, 1934, Jan. 9, 1935, Green to Perkins, Jan. 12, 1935, Green Letterbooks; Detroit *News*, Jan. 25, 1935.

[69] Executive Council Minutes, Apr. 30—May 7, 1935, Auto Workers File, 1935–37, A.F. of L.—CIO Archives.

[70] Shipley to Green, Apr. 29, 1934, Shipley to John L. Lewis, May 27, 1935, A.F. of L. Strike File, Local 18347; Collins to Morrison, June 2, 1934, Collins File; entry for June 5, 1934, Minute Book of Local 19324 (UAW Local 95), State Historical Society of Wisconsin. The St. Louis local had been interested in establishing an international as early as December 1933. Collins and Paul Smith to Green, Dec. 6, 1933, Collins File.

yet ready for an international was to make them aware of the size of the organizing task before them.[71]

Following a meeting with Green, Collins began to lay plans for a conference of auto locals on June 23–24 for the purpose of setting up a national council to serve principally as an advisory agency to the national representative of the A.F. of L. in the auto industry. The council, as Collins envisioned it, would include eleven members elected by the delegates and apportioned among the locals on a geographical basis, would meet only at the call of the national representative, and would aid him in his organizing work. In advance of the conference, Collins worked out the bylaws of the council and the chief resolutions to be passed.[72]

One hundred and twenty-seven delegates representing seventy-seven locals gathered in Detroit on June 23 for the two-day conference.[73] The key question they considered was whether to accept Collins' plan for a weak national council or to resolve in favor of the establishment of an international. Those who were inclined in the latter direction were by no means agreed as to the method of reaching their goal. One group, which included the delegates from the powerful Hudson local, accepted the idea of a council but wanted it to appoint its own chairman and to develop a program for the establishment of an international at the earliest possible moment. The Hudson local was resentful of the tight control the A.F. of L. leadership exercised over its federal locals and feared that it would be ordered to surrender the skilled workers among its members to the craft unions. Richard Byrd was covertly associated with this group.

A second group, which included delegates from the South Bend and Fort Wayne locals, wished the A.F. of L. Executive Council to provide for the prompt establishment of an international. The third group, led by Communists and fellow travelers like Wyndham Mortimer,[74]

---

71 Collins to Green, May 26, 1934, Collins to Morrison, June 2, 1934, Collins File; Green to Collins, May 29, 1934, Green Letterbooks.

72 Collins to Automobile Workers, June 6, 1934, Collins to Morrison, June 19, 1934, Collins File.

73 My account of the conference is based on the following: UAW *Weekly News Letter,* June 27, 1934, Vertical File, A.F. of L.—CIO Library; *Daily Worker,* June 25–28, July 17, 1934; *Auto Workers News,* July 21, 1934; *The New York Times,* June 24, 25, 1934; Chalmers, "Collective Bargaining," IX, 1–13; Wieck, "Automobile Workers," pp. 126–28; Tracy M. Doll interview, Dec. 17, 1957; *MESA Voice* (July 1934). The delegates indicated their dissatisfaction with the A.F. of L. organizers by voting to take the privileges of the floor away from them.

74 Benjamin Stolberg described Mortimer as "a Stalinist from the very beginning." *The Story of the CIO* (New York: Viking Press, 1938), p. 164.

the president of the White Motor local and later a UAW vice-president, and taking a position which paralleled the Communist line, was openly critical of the A.F. of L. and called for the prompt establishment of an international, industrial union controlled by the rank and file.

William Green, who was present at the conference and was painfully aware that the auto locals at that time had only about eighteen thousand paid-up members, told the delegates that the A.F. of L. would set up an international as soon as the auto workers had created "a permanent, self-sustaining organization," but that at the moment "a slower approach" was needed. The resolutions committee thereupon recommended nonconcurrence with the various resolutions calling for an international, and this was accepted by the convention over the opposition of fifty delegates. The committee then secured the conference's approval of Collins' project for a United Automobile Workers National Council.

When this action was taken, about twenty-five delegates, headed by Arthur Greer, the president of the Hudson local, bolted the conference. This act of defiance took on added significance several weeks later when the Hudson, G.M. Truck, and Olds (Lansing) locals seceded from the A.F. of L. to form the Associated Automobile Workers of America. The AAWA complained about the "dictatorial" methods of the A.F. of L., its high dues, and its criticism of Richard Byrd, and insisted that an organization led by workers in the plants was more likely to succeed in the automobile industry than one dominated by "outside" leaders.[75]

The National Council created at the June conference met on only three occasions, and it did not play a particularly important role in the development of organization in the auto industry.[76] Certainly, its existence did not satisfy those auto workers bent on the early formation of an international, and particularly the leaders of the nine auto locals in Cleveland, which had formed the Cleveland auto council in good part to promote their desire for an international, industrial union

[75] Chalmers, "Collective Bargaining," IX, 13–17; Detroit *Free Press*, Aug. 4, 5, 7, 9, 1934; Detroit *News*, Aug. 5, 7, 8, 1934. Greer was later accused of being on the Pinkerton payroll and thereupon left the labor movement. Doll interview, Dec. 17, 1957; J. Raymond Walsh, *C.I.O.: Industrial Unionism in Action* (New York: W. W. Norton and Company, 1937), p. 110.

[76] The first session of the National Council (July 9–14, 1934) was mainly concerned with relations between the A.F. of L. and the ALB. Official Proceedings of First Session, National Council, Brown Collection. The chief interest of the second session (Aug. 28–31, 1934) was the renewal of the auto code. The Second Session of the National Council of United Automobile Workers Federal Labor Unions, Aug. 28–31, 1934, *ibid*. For the third session (Feb. 23—Mar. 2, 1935), see below.

under rank-and-file control. Although the Cleveland locals were by no means Communist unions, persons like Wyndham Mortimer, the president of the Cleveland auto council, exercised a conspicuously large influence in their deliberations.

The Cleveland locals, and especially those at the White Motor Company and Fisher Body, were primarily responsible for the convocation of three self-styled rank-and-file conferences to promote the development of an international. These conferences were held in Cleveland on September 16, in Flint on November 10, and in Detroit on January 26. Although the Cleveland leadership insisted that the movement was "*not* a split-off from the A.F. of L.," the calls to the conferences and the resolutions passed were critical of the "false policies of the top officialdom" of the A.F. of L. and particularly of the A.F. of L.'s cautious strike policy. The conferences all passed resolutions calling for the establishment of an international, industrial union under rank-and-file control.[77]

The A.F. of L. responded to this pressure by informing the auto workers that the conferences were called without the authorization of the A.F. of L. and were the result of Communist activity and by criticizing the "Communistic propaganda" that issued from the meetings.[78] The A.F. of L. might well have paid heed to the fact that whether Communist-influenced or not, the demand for a complete industrial jurisdiction for the auto-workers' union and for rank-and-file control struck a responsive chord among organized auto workers, the vast majority of whom were not Communists.

President Green, in particular, thought the demand for the prompt establishment of an international premature. He had insisted from the start that the creation of an international could not be considered until the workers had gained more experience and had developed effective leadership and until the A.F. of L. was assured that the organization would be "self-sustaining," conditions that in his opinion had not yet been met. He was particularly annoyed with those who thought that the mere establishment of an international would solve the organizational problems in the auto industry. With considerable insight into the shape of things to come, he wrote to Carl Shipley on November 26, 1934:

[77] *Daily Worker*, Aug. 22, Sept. 18, Nov. 15, 1934, Jan. 9, 30, 1935; Call to Conference on Jan. 26, 1935, Labadie Collection, University of Michigan; *Labor Digest*, Mar. 15, Apr. 5, 1935.
[78] Second Session of National Council, Brown Collection; Collins, Important Notice to All Automobile Workers, n.d., *ibid.*; Dillon to Auto Workers, Jan. 11, 1935, Dillon File.

You seem to think that the establishment of a national or international union among the automobile workers would solve all your difficulties and bring about a perfect, ideal state. Please accept this prediction from one who has had training in a wide field of organizing work. When a national or international union of automobile workers is formed, you will still find that the ideal state has not been reached; that condemnation will be indulged in by impetuous members, that serious internal problems will be presented, and fights of the most bitter kind take place between those who seek to secure and exercise control over the international union.[79]

The subject of an international union of auto workers received attention at the annual A.F. of L. convention of October 1934 in San Francisco. Resolutions were introduced by a delegate from the White Motor local importuning the convention to call a constitutional convention of the auto locals not later than December 1, 1934, to complete the formation of an international, and by a delegate from the Bendix local empowering the Executive Council to establish an international with complete industrial jurisdiction, directed by men selected from the ranks, and advised by and receiving the financial support of the A.F. of L. The convention, however, approved the report of its Committee on Resolutions, which directed the A.F. of L. to issue charters for internationals in several mass-production industries, including the automotive, with the A.F. of L. for a probationary period to direct their policies, administer their affairs, and designate their officers. The question of the jurisdiction of the auto union was inconclusively debated, although craft unions like the IAM made it clear that they expected their jurisdictions to be respected.[80]

The question of implementing the decision of the San Francisco conference as regards an auto international was discussed by the Executive Council at its meeting in Washington of January 29—February 14, 1935. A committee of three members of the National Council was present to recommend that a convention to launch an international be called during the slack season on a date set by Green. By a vote of 12–2, with John L. Lewis in the minority, the Executive Council instructed the president and the secretary to issue a charter "at once" for a national or international "to embrace all employes directly engaged in the manufacture of parts (not including tools,

[79] Green to Collins, Dec. 12, 1933, Green to Shipley, Nov. 26, 1934, Green Letterbooks; Green to Leo A. Powers, May 28, 1934, A.F. of L. Strike File, Local 18384.

[80] *Report of the Proceedings of the Fifty-fourth Annual Convention of the American Federation of Labor, 1934* (Washington: A.F. of L., n.d.), pp. 192–93, 214–15, 586–98.

dies and machinery) and assembling of those parts into completed automobiles but not including job or contract shops manufacturing parts or any other employe engaged in said automobile production plants." This left the projected union with only a semi-industrial jurisdiction and was hardly designed to satisfy auto unionists who thought their union should include all workers in and around the auto plants regardless of their craft. The Executive Council also stipulated, as the San Francisco resolution required, that for a temporary period to be determined by the Executive Council the officers to function under this charter were to be designated by the president of the A.F. of L.[81]

By the time the National Council convened on February 23 to hear the report of its three-man committee, the issue of a general strike in the auto industry had become intertwined with the question of the establishment of an international. The A.F. of L. leadership had actually realized for some time that there was no hope of persuading G.M. or Ford to bargain without a "show of force," but the same doubts lingered as to the ability of the auto locals to strike the giants of the industry.[82] The matter was given an added urgency at the close of January 1935 when the administration renewed the auto code without bothering to consult the A.F. of L. and, rubbing salt in the A.F. of L.'s wounds, included in the code a confirmation of the March 25 settlement.[83] This prompted the A.F. of L. to talk as though it would seek to gain by the exercise of its economic power what it had failed to achieve as the result of its political weakness.

When President Green arrived in Detroit on February 23 for the major address of a tour of the auto centers on which he was then engaged, he told reporters that a strike was not contemplated, but he intimated to the audience that heard his address that the A.F. of L. would not halt a strike if results could be obtained in no other way.[84] While in Detroit Green also conferred with the National Council and received its approval of the Executive Council's decision as regards an

[81] Dillon to National Council, Jan. 17, 1935, Dillon press release, Jan. 25, 1935, Dillon File; Michael J. Manning, Forrest G. Woods, Otto E. Kleinert to Executive Council, Feb. 1, 1935, Brown Collection; Executive Council Minutes, Jan. 29—Feb. 14, 1935, Auto Workers File, 1935-37.

[82] Chalmers, "Strike Plans. Sept. 1, 1934," Brown Collection.

[83] *The New York Times*, Feb. 1, 1935; Detroit *News*, Jan. 31, Feb. 1, 1935; Raymond Gram Swing, "The White House Breaks with Labor," *The Nation*, CXL (Feb. 13, 1935), 181; Swing, "Pursuing a Prevarication," *ibid.*, CXL (Feb. 27, 1935), 241; *Codes*, XXI, 204.

[84] Dillon to Auto Workers, Jan. 30, 1935, Dillon press release, Feb. 20, 1935, Dillon File; *The New York Times*, Feb. 18, 24, 1935; Detroit *News*, Feb. 23, 1935; Detroit *Labor News*, Mar. 1, 1935.

international. At the same time the National Council advised the Cleveland locals, which were pressing for a constitutional convention, that in view of the "tense situation" in the industry, the Council realized the need for A.F. of L. support and had therefore asked that the charter be held in abeyance for the time being.

The Council also discussed the question of a general strike and decided to designate the A.F. of L. as its bargaining agent and to authorize Green to represent it in negotiations with management. The federal locals were requested to grant Green similar authority and to take strike votes which would authorize him to call a strike through the National Council if the employers refused to accede to demands to bargain collectively.[85]

Green thereupon wrote to the AMA on February 27 requesting a conference to negotiate an agreement respecting wages, hours, and working conditions. Alfred Reeves, vice-president and general manager of the AMA, replied on March 7 that the AMA was not itself an employer and therefore had no occasion to bargain with workers or to arrange such conferences as Green suggested. The individual AMA members, he said, negotiated regularly with the ALB bargaining agencies and would also meet with other duly accredited representatives. Reeves quite correctly insisted that the A.F. of L. had "no just claim to be spokesman for the automobile workers generally." [86]

Green responded to this refusal by requesting conferences on behalf of their employees with the individual employers who made up the AMA, but in a typical reply, he was informed that insofar as representatives of "special groups" were "duly accredited" they could take up "suitable questions" with the management "in the regular way." The stage thus seemed to be set for a strike, and Dillon had already let it be known that all but a few of the 176 auto locals had authorized strike action. But Green had no intention of permitting a strike to be called. Ever conscious of the weakness of the auto locals, he had told the president of one of the locals as early as February 7 that a strike did not fit in with the A.F. of L.'s plans, and he later informed the Executive Council: "They wanted to engage in a general strike but I stopped that. I said, you are in no position to engage in a general strike." In the last analysis, the strike drive, as one auto

[85] Minutes of Third Meeting of National Council of United Automobile Workers Federal Labor Unions, Feb. 23—Mar. 2, 1935, Labadie Collection.

[86] Green to Reeves, Feb. 27, 1935, Green Letterbooks; Reeves to Green, Mar. 7, 1935, NRA Box 661.

executive stated, was simply an "A.F. of L. sales promotion campaign." [87]

Although the A.F. of L. itself was reluctant to call an auto strike, the powerful Toledo local, which had won a bitter battle against the major Toledo parts plants in April–May 1934, decided to test its strength against G.M. itself by calling a strike at the Toledo Chevrolet plant on April 23.[88] The plant was a key one since it was the only one in the G.M. empire that made Chevrolet and Pontiac transmissions. G.M. was able to transfer the manufacture of Pontiac transmissions to its Buick plant, but the stoppage of the production of Chevrolet transmissions, plus some sympathy strikes, soon resulted in the idling of thirty-two thousand workers over the country, mostly in Chevrolet assembly plants and in Fisher Body plants making Chevrolet bodies.

Dillon arrived on the scene on April 26, and from that date till the strike was called off on May 13, the A.F. of L. "ran the Toledo strike." The union was striking for a signed agreement and recognition as the exclusive bargaining agency for the employees. The militant strike committee, which included some delegates who were very far to the left, sought to encourage other G.M. locals to join the strike and to pursue a common strike policy, but Dillon held such key unions as the Buick local in line and then used every ounce of his influence to secure acceptance of a settlement in which G.M. agreed to deal with the union's shop committee and made other important concessions but which did not recognize the union as the exclusive bargaining agency and, above all, did not include a signed agreement. The Toledo local was antagonized by Dillon's action,[89] but nevertheless an important, if limited, victory had been won over a powerful antagonist.

The Toledo Chevrolet strike dealt a smashing blow to the prestige of the ALB, which had been excluded from the strike picture from beginning to end. It was clear, moreover, that no ALB bargaining agency was to be set up in the Chevrolet plant. Even the business press conceded that the A.F. of L. had staged a comeback in the auto

[87] Green to Chapin *et al.,* Mar. 18, 1935, John T. Smith to Green, Apr. 17, 1935, Green Letterbooks; *The New York Times,* Apr. 10, 1935; Green to Shipley, Feb. 7, 1935, A.F. of L. Strike File, Local 18347; Executive Council Minutes, Apr. 30—May 7, 1935, Auto Workers File, 1935–37; *Iron Age,* CXXXV (Mar. 7, 1935), 37.

[88] My account of the Toledo strike is based principally on the following: A.F. of L. Strike File, Local 18384; Dillon to Officers and Members UAW, May 17, 1935, Dillon File; G.M., Labor Relations Diary, Sec. I, pp. 54–63; *Strike Truth,* Apr. 26, May 7, 1935; Chalmers' analysis of the Toledo strike, Apr. 24, 29, May 16, 17, 18, 1935, MS in Brown Collection; Chalmers, "Collective Bargaining," XII, 1–42; Toledo *News-Bee,* Apr. 22—May 15, 1935; Toledo *Morning Times,* Apr. 23—May 15, 1935; Toledo *Blade,* Apr. 23—May 15, 1935.

[89] William K. Siefke to Green, May 24, 1935, Green Letterbooks.

industry when it appeared to be on the ropes. Moreover, the Toledo settlement led to further negotiations in May and June between G.M. executives and Dillon in Cleveland, Norwood, Atlanta, Janesville, and Kansas City, in which G.M. agreed to deal with the union shop committees. Dillon informed Green that G.M. had acknowledged the "fundamental fallacy" of the company union and had recognized the A.F. of L. as a "legitimate bargaining agency." [90]

The Toledo strike was a fitting prelude to the establishment of an international union of auto workers. Green, armed with an Executive Council authorization to the Federation's officers to form the international when in their judgment it was "appropriate and convenient," conferred with Dillon on the subject on June 17, 1935, following which Dillon announced that preparations would be made for a convention beginning August 26 to launch an international union. The replies to a questionnaire sent out by Green to the various auto locals on June 19 indicated overwhelming support for the idea.[91]

A portent of what was to come, however, if the charter approved by the Executive Council was applied to the auto workers, was revealed in a letter of May 27, 1935, to John L. Lewis from Carl Shipley, long an advocate of an international union with an out-and-out industrial jurisdiction. Dillon, he reported, had told him the craft unions would claim the skilled workers in the federal locals. "We say like h—— they will and if it is ever ordered and enforced there will be one more independent union." "If you have to follow through to a split which we don't want only as a last resort, I believe," Shipley accurately predicted, "it will be an easy matter to get the Automobile Industry, because now they are discontented. . . . Are they [Executive Council] going to loose [sic] this chance to organize America because of Craft Jealousies?" [92]

At the time the auto workers' constitutional convention opened in Detroit, the total paid-up membership in the auto locals was 25,769, short of the thirty thousand Green thought necessary for a self-sustaining organization.[93] The paid-up total was approximately 6 per cent

[90] *Business Week*, May 18, 1935, p. 9; *Iron Age*, CXXXV (May 23, 1935), 41; Dillon to Green, May 17, 23, 31, June 10, 1935, Dillon File.
[91] Executive Council Minutes, Apr. 30—May 7, 1935, Auto Workers File, 1935–37; Dillon press release, June 18, 1935, Dillon File. Only 28 of the 107 locals to which the questionnaire had been sent responded, but these locals represented 16,143 of the 35,228 paid-up members as of that date; 98.1 per cent favored an international. Green to Automobile Workers Federal Labor Unions, June 19, 1935, "Automobile," July 12, 1935, CIO Historical File, Reel 1.
[92] Shipley to Lewis, May 27, 1935, A.F. of L. Strike File, Local 18347.
[93] "Automobile Workers Unions Affiliated with the A.F. of L., Aug. 23, 1935," CIO Historical File, Reel 1; Executive Council Minutes, Apr. 30—May 7, 1935, Auto Workers File, 1935–37.

of the four hundred thousand workers then in the industry. An equal or perhaps larger number of workers, concentrated largely in Detroit, were enrolled in the so-called independent unions, the Mechanics Educational Society of America, the Associated Automobile Workers of America, and the Automotive Industrial Workers Association,[94] the latter two of which were to join the auto international in 1936. The strength of the A.F. of L. was almost entirely outside Michigan. There were only 1,455 paid-up members in the various Detroit locals and another 636 members in Michigan locals outside Detroit. The real power of the organization was concentrated in the White Motor local in Cleveland, the Toledo local, the Fisher and Chevrolet local in Norwood, the Studebaker and Bendix locals in South Bend, the Nash locals in Kenosha and Racine, and the Seaman Body local in Milwaukee.[95] These were, in the main, locals that were committed to a more militant policy than that pursued by the A.F. of L. and were determined to resist any raids on their membership by the craft unions. It was principally the delegates from these locals who formed the "progressive" bloc that led the fight on the floor of the drama-packed convention to extend the jurisdiction granted by the charter to encompass all auto workers and to permit the delegates to elect the new international's officers.

In the end, however, the charter remained intact, and Green, ignoring the expressed desire of a majority of the delegates, personally selected the officers, including Francis Dillon as president. The convention thereupon elected a committee of seven to go before the Executive Council and the next annual A.F. of L. convention to gain the right for the new international to organize any automobile workers and to elect its own officers.[96] The committee failed to win its points,[97] but by the time the UAW met in convention in South Bend in April 1936 it had been authorized to elect its own officers. To win the jurisdiction it sought, however, the UAW found it necessary, as Shipley had predicted, to leave the A.F. of L. It associated itself with

---

[94] The AIWA grew out of the ALB bargaining agency at the Dodge plant and then spread to other plants and particularly to other Chrysler plants. *Proceedings of the Second Convention of the International Union, United Automobile Workers of America, 1936* (Detroit, n.d.), pp. 138–44; Frankensteen interview, Apr. 10, 1957. The MESA was an organization of skilled tool and die makers, although it also included some production workers.

[95] "Automobile Workers Unions Affiliated with the A.F. of L., Aug. 23, 1935," CIO Historical File, Reel 1.

[96] For accounts of the conference, see *Proceedings of the First Constitutional Convention of the U.A.W., passim*; Edward Levinson, *Labor on the March* (New York: University Books, 1956), pp. 88–93; Detroit *News*, Aug 25—Sept. 1, 1935.

[97] A.F. of L., *Report of Proceedings, 1935*, pp. 95–96, 283–85, 729–50, 824–25.

the new Committee for Industrial Organization in 1936, and it was one of the unions expelled by the A.F. of L. in 1938. Thus, although the A.F. of L., however inadequate its efforts, had succeeded during the years 1933–1935 in making independent unionism an established fact in the automobile industry, the fruits of its organizing work were, in the last analysis, to be gathered by a rival organization.

SIDNEY FINE, *University of Michigan*

AFL Unions in the 1930s: Their Performance in Historical Perspective

CHRISTOPHER L. TOMLINS

T HE 1930s have been regarded as a pivotal period in the development of a modern organized labor movement in the United States. Historians have noted the rapid growth in membership of both old and new unions and the concomitant changes during these years in the political and economic environment of collective bargaining. In the course of their studies, these scholars have successfully analyzed many of the factors that played a role in that growth.[1] By concentrating primarily on factors peculiar to the 1930s, however, these scholars have remained within the dominant tradition of American labor history that has been organized around events and has emphasized the simple dichotomies they appear to illustrate. Thus, analysis of the rapid growth of unionism in the 1930s has concentrated largely on strikes, contracts, federal legislation, and the effects of the confrontation between two rival federations on the institutional structure of the labor movement.

Operating from within this tradition, historians have generally agreed that the 1930s saw the ascendancy of industrial over craft unionism.[2] The industrially organized unions of the Congress of Industrial Organizations (CIO) broke with the American Federation of Labor (AFL), established themselves as a rival federation, succeeded for the first time in organizing the workers employed in

Christopher L. Tomlins is a graduate student in the Department of History, the Johns Hopkins University.

[1] For example, see Irving Bernstein, *Turbulent Years: A History of the American Worker, 1933–1941* (Boston, 1969); Walter Galenson, *The CIO Challenge to the AFL: A History of the American Labor Movement, 1935–1941* (Cambridge, 1960).

[2] A craft union is defined as consisting of "workers requiring identical skill and training who can carry through to completion a particular whole process." An industrial union is defined as including "the skilled, semi-skilled, unskilled [workers] and the auxiliary trades and occupations engaged in the performance of a particular service or the production of a particular commodity." See David J. Saposs and Sol Davison, "Employee Organizations and Elections: The Structure of AFL Unions," *Labor Relations Reference Manual*, 4 (Washington, 1940), 1044, 1047.

1021

mass production industries, and initiated a period of sustained rapid growth in labor unionism. As a result, the craft unions affiliated with the AFL were forced to reconsider their role in the labor movement. In order to survive, they began to admit less-skilled workers. Traditional interpretations hold that, in so doing, the craft unions altered their long-established strategy of organizing only skilled workers and changed their institutional structures to accommodate the new masses. These changes in AFL unions are thought to have been necessary preconditions for their subsequent expansion, for before the rise of the CIO the organized labor movement is thought to have been weak and structurally obsolete, with the unions isolated from the strategic sectors of a modern industrial economy. After the rise of the CIO, with industrial unionism in the ascendancy, the movement became powerful, self-assured, and capable of playing an influential role in American industrial society.[3]

While the political and economic circumstances of the period offer much support to this view of labor history, they do not by themselves provide a suitable framework for interpreting the distribution of membership gains in the 1930s. Although the unions affiliated with the CIO fought many bitter strikes, overcame the open hostility of management in the manufacturing sector of the economy, and succeeded, by and large, in organizing permanent unions in important areas of industry, it was the supposedly unregenerate "craft" unions of the AFL that contained the bulk of the organized labor movement's membership throughout this period. The affiliates of the AFL experienced substantial growth between 1933 and 1934. This growth was sustained despite the split in the AFL's ranks in 1936. Although it lost 1,104,900 members between 1936 and 1937 as a direct consequence of the suspension of the CIO unions, the AFL's major affiliates recruited over 760,000 new members in the same period. As a result, the AFL lost only 340,000 members overall. Even when the CIO unions were leading some of their most militant organizing cam-

[3] For example, Walter Galenson writes: "The shock of the CIO was necessary to the rejuvenation of the AFL. . . . If it had not been for the intense struggle between the two organizations, the U.S. might have entered the war with its labor force largely unorganized." Galenson, *CIO Challenge*, 644. See also James O. Morris, *Conflict within the AFL* (Ithaca, 1958), particularly 248; Mark L. Kahn, "Recent Jurisdictional Developments in Organized Labor," *Industrial Relations Research Association Publications*, 21 (New York, 1959), 5–6; Sidney Fine, "The History of the American Labor Movement with Special Reference to Developments in the 1930's," *Labor in a Changing America*, ed. William Haber (New York, 1966), 105–20; Jack Barbash, "The Rise of Industrial Unionism," *ibid.*, 143–57; Milton Derber, *The American Idea of Industrial Democracy, 1865–1965* (Urbana, 1970), 300–01.

paigns, the AFL unions were able to achieve results little inferior.[4] Between 1937 and 1939 the CIO lost members, and entered a period of sustained growth only with the onset of the war boom in defense production. Over the same period the AFL quickly recovered from the split and expanded steadily. Between 1937 and 1945 nearly four million workers joined unions affiliated with the AFL. In the same years the CIO unions recruited slightly under two million.[5]

[4] The unions that left the AFL in 1936 to form an independent CIO were: United Mine Workers; United Mine Workers, District 50; United Textile Workers; Amalgamated Clothing Workers; International Ladies' Garment Workers; Mine, Mill and Smelter Workers; Iron, Steel and Tin Workers; Oil, Gas and Refinery Workers; United Automobile Workers; Fur Workers; Flat Glass Workers; Rubber Workers; Newspaper Guild. These unions had a total membership of 1,104,900. It is impossible to ascertain precisely how many future CIO members came from AFL ranks between 1936 and 1937, for a number of established AFL unions (such as the machinists and the carpenters) lost membership to the CIO, although the unions themselves did not change affiliation. If it is assumed that the CIO took more members from the AFL than those in the ranks of the major unions listed above, then the share of the CIO in the overall gain to the labor movement in dues-paying membership 1936–1937 will be smaller and that of the AFL correspondingly larger.

[5] Table 1: Membership of American Labor Organizations, 1933–1945 (in thousands)

	All organizations	AFL affiliates	CIO affiliates	Independent unions
1933	2,973.0	2,317.5	—	655.5
1934	3,608.6	3,030.0	—	578.6
1935	3,753.3	3,218.4	—	534.9
1936	4,107.1	3,516.4	(1,204.6)*	590.7
1937	5,780.1	3,179.7	1,991.2	609.2
1938	6,080.5	3,547.4	1,957.7	575.4
1939	6,555.5	3,878.0	1,837.7	839.8
1940	7,282.0	4,343.0	2,154.1	784.7
1941	8,698.0	5,178.8	2,653.9	865.3
1942	10,199.7	6,075.7	2,492.7	1,631.3
1943	11,811.7	6,779.2	3,303.4	1,729.1
1944	12,628.0	6,876.5	3,937.1	1,814.4
1945	12,562.1	6,890.4	3,927.9	1,743.8

* Estimate.

Table compiled from Leo Troy, *Trade Union Membership 1897–1962* (New York, 1965), Appendix 1-27 and Leo Wolman, *Ebb and Flow in Trade Unionism* (New York, 1936), 172–92. Both authors use the same criterion—the payment of dues—to establish the membership of each national union. The growth in AFL membership 1933–1936 is usually attributed to the activities of unions such as the UMW that later helped form the CIO. Unions that remained in the AFL, however, also began to grow in these years:

Table 2: Organizing Gains of AFL affiliates, 1933–1936 (in thousands)

	Future CIO unions	All other AFL unions	Total gains	Col. 1 as a percentage of Col. 3
1933–34	448.4	264.1	712.5	62.9%
1934–35	57.7	140.7	198.4	29.1
1935–36	111.9	186.1	298.0	37.5

(The 1933–1934 figure is distorted by the affiliation to the AFL of the previously independent Amalgamated Clothing Workers with 135,000 members. This union was later a founding member of the CIO. Corrected to exclude this "gain" the 1933–1934 figure for Col. 1 is 313.4, for Col. 3 it is 577.5, and for Col. 4 it is 54.2 percent.) See Wolman, *Ebb and Flow*, 172–92, and Troy, *Trade Union Membership*, Appendix 1-27.

These figures indicate the need for reevaluation of the performance of AFL unions in the 1930s. A new analytic framework is needed, moreover, to help explain both the particular pattern of membership gains and the reasons behind the AFL's success. Analysis of the histories of AFL affiliates—as well as of the actual results of their organizing campaigns in the 1930s—indicates that traditional historiography exaggerates the extent to which competition between AFL and CIO was responsible for causing changes of strategy and structure in the AFL's affiliates. From the time of their founding the major AFL unions had exhibited a tendency to alter both organizing strategies and institutional structures to accommodate changes in the industrial environment in which they operated.

A long term perspective on the institutional development of major AFL unions helps to explain their success in recruiting and retaining new members in the 1930s. Such a perspective views the 1930s from within the "emerging organizational synthesis" in American history and relies to some extent on conclusions suggested by Alfred D. Chandler's studies of corporate development.[6] In application this approach confirms that the use of a simple polarity of "craft" versus "industrial" unionism, of AFL versus CIO, does not materially contribute to an understanding of the growth and development of the organized labor movement in the 1930s and after.

The AFL was formed in 1886 by national unions such as the Molders and the International Typographical Union and by numerous independent local unions that were not coordinated into single national organizations. These "basic building blocks" were predominantly unions of skilled workers.

Since before the Civil War, skilled workers had sought to enhance their economic power in confrontation with owners and management by organizing at the national level. This sometimes resulted in their isolation from less-skilled and unskilled workers who lacked the bargaining power and job control that craftsmen

[6] Louis Galambos, "The Emerging Organizational Synthesis in Modern American History," *Business History Review*, XLIV (Autumn 1970), 279–90; Robert D. Cuff, "American Historians and the Organizational Factor," *Canadian Review of American Studies*, IV (Spring 1973), 19–31; Alfred D. Chandler, *Strategy and Structure: Chapters in the History of the Industrial Enterprise* (Cambridge, 1962).

had.[7] But the impact of technological change, particularly the mechanization of production, on the division of labor and on industry's skill requirements weakened the ability of the craft unions to control their job territory (jurisdiction).

Unions responded in several different ways. Some resisted the mechanization of the production process or sought to compete with machinery by lowering their piece- or wage-rates. Others tried to control the introduction of machinery and to widen their jurisdiction to include craftsmen working on the same or related production processes, thus preserving their influence by building one union of all the strategic workers in one industry or group of industries. They also began to include particular strata of production workers (other than the skilled nuclei) where the organization of such groups was necessary to the preservation of job control.[8] Attempts to adapt to technological change through the alteration of jurisdiction and organizing strategy led both to the amalgamation of related crafts and to cautious organizing among

[7] Lloyd Ulman, *The Rise of the National Trade Union: The Development and Significance of Its Structure, Governing Institutions, and Economic Policies* (Cambridge, 1955), 23–45, 49–52. The role of the skilled worker in the formation of the early unions is discussed in Benson Soffer, "A Theory of Trade Union Development: The Role of the Autonomous Workman," *Labor History*, 1 (Spring 1960), 141–63. The first part of this essay relies to some extent on the concept of the strategic worker. One definition of this term is a worker whose replacement would cost his employer more in lost production than the worker's wage demands. In manufacturing industries all skilled workers were strategic before the introduction of machinery. Less-skilled workers became strategic, as far as the unions were concerned, when mechanization gave them a role to play in the production processes previously dominated by craftsmen. Employers were able, however, to replace less-skilled workers much more easily than craftsmen, and where mechanization created an industrial labor force that was predominantly low-skilled—as in most of mass production—the unions had neither the power nor the inclination to organize. They only took in less-skilled workers where the division of labor resulting from technological innovations had split the job formerly performed by the craftsman into a number of related functions performed by "helpers," "assistants," or "specialists," without entirely displacing the skilled worker. The unions attempted to gain control of these new jobs so that they could preserve the wage-bargaining power of the craftsmen. In other cases the importance of particular jobs in an industry (for example, maintenance men in manufacturing firms) or the role of a particular industry in the economy (for example, trucking) made workers strategic and encouraged the unions to organize them. See Margaret Loomis Stecker, "The Founders, the Molders, and the Molding Machine," *Quarterly Journal of Economics*, XXXII (Feb. 1918), 304–08; Elizabeth Faulkner Baker, *Printers and Technology: a History of the International Printing Pressmen and Assistants' Union* (New York, 1957); Mark Perlman, *The Machinists: A New Study in American Trade Unionism* (Cambridge, 1964), 229–33.

[8] All three reactions are outlined in Ulman, *Rise of the National Trade Union*, 32–37. See also George E. Barnet, *Chapters on Machinery and Labor* (Cambridge, 1926), 139–61. The first two reactions were viable in the short-term only. In the long run unions that persisted in resisting or competing were severely weakened. See also Samuel Gompers, *Seventy Years of Life and Labor: An Autobiography* (2 vols., New York, 1925), I, 373.

selected sections of less-skilled workers.[9] As a result of these developments, by 1915 only 28 of 133 unions active in the labor movement, most of them affiliated with the AFL, could still be described as craft organizations. Of these, at least half were engaging in informal cooperation with other affiliates and were thus cutting across craft lines.[10]

The various AFL unions showed different rates of adaptation. Although the organized labor movement as a whole was directly and continuously confronted with the impact of technology on the organization of industry, different sectors of the economy were affected at different times.[11] Consequently, unions developed widely differing structures and jurisdictions.[12]

These varied responses by its affiliates in turn put great pressure on the federation itself, but for some years after the AFL was formed by the craft unions, its leadership continued to favor the creation of national unions of the pure craft type. Between 1886 and the early 1900s it encouraged the formation of as many autonomous craft unions as possible.[13] The jurisdictional boundaries between these small groups of skilled workers were frequently rather narrow—the Pocket Knife Grinders and the Table Knife Grinders were chartered as separate national unions, as were

[9] Theodore W. Glocker, "Amalgamation of Related Trades in American Unions," *American Economic Review*, V (Sept. 1915), 574–75. See also Elizabeth F. Baker, "The Development of the International Printing Pressmen and Assistants' Union," *Industrial Relations Research Association Publications* (Madison, 1958), 159–61; Robert A. Christie, *Empire in Wood, a History of the Carpenters' Union* (Ithaca, 1956), 117–18; Garth L. Mangum, *The Operating Engineers: The Economic History of a Trade Union* (Cambridge, 1964), 42–45, 59; Michael A. Mulcaire, *The International Brotherhood of Electrical Workers: A Study in Trade Union Structure and Functions* (Washington, 1923), 28, 56–60; Perlman, *Machinists*, 23, 33–34; Frank T. Stockton, *The International Molders Union of North America* (Baltimore, 1921), 43–45.

[10] Glocker, "Amalgamation of Related Trades," 554.

[11] Historians have recognized the importance of technology as a factor in the development of labor unions, and the first part of this essay is based almost wholly on secondary sources. When approaching the question of the development of the organized labor movement as a whole over time, however, historians have generally ignored the findings of studies of individual unions, and resorted to the events and dichotomies of traditional historiography. Studies of union growth are an exception, for they recognize technology as one of a number of important general factors influencing the growth of the organized labor movement. See John T. Dunlop, "The Development of Labor Organization: A Theoretical Framework," *Insights into Labor Issues*, ed. Richard A. Lester and Joseph Shister (New York, 1948), 163–93; and Julius Rezler, *Automation and Industrial Labor* (New York, 1969), 119. But the occurrence of growth is not by itself a reliable index of adaptability to technological innovation. Many AFL unions were more concerned to control their jurisdictions by selective organization than to attempt to recruit en masse. The lack of rapid growth before the 1930s does not, therefore prove the irrelevance of AFL unions to the modern American economy.

[12] Saposs and Davison, "Employee Organizations and Elections," 1042–48.

[13] Christie, *Empire in Wood*, 124–25.

the Watch Case Makers and the Watch Case Engravers—and the policy led to constant jurisdictional squabbling among the small craft organizations.

At the same time the policy of the federation's leadership proved increasingly unpopular with the larger, well-established, and imperialistic affiliates—for example, the International Association of Machinists (IAM) and the United Brotherhood of Carpenters and Joiners (UBCJ)—which feared the division of their own more inclusive jurisdictions among a host of splinter groups of craftsmen claiming commonality of specific skills and refusing to be included in a more diffuse organization. The carpenters' union, in particular, put great pressure on the federation's leadership to end the practice of chartering small splinter groups and proposed a new policy that would reflect its own interests. The union sought the organization of different groups of skilled workers under the jurisdiction of the paramount craft in an industry or trade. Acceding to the carpenters' demands, the federation ended the process of jurisdictional division and subdivision, encouraged the amalgamation of related crafts, and in 1911 approved the policy of chartering only one organization for one trade: "The action of the 1911 convention of the AFL marks a turning point in its history. . . . After a decade of running strife the Atlanta convention of the AFL declared soundly for the principle of organization by the paramount craft in an industry, rather than for craft autonomy."[14]

Henceforth, the AFL was formally oriented not to the encouragement of pure craft unionism, but to the development of single organizations containing all the strategic workers of a particular trade or industry. Although the new policy allowed for the continued existence of craft unions where feasible, its major purpose was to encourage the formation of "craft-industrial" unions, like the carpenters and the machinists, in those industries where technological developments had weakened the position of craftsmen and required the extension of the union's jurisdiction in the interests of the paramount "policing" trade or craft.

The new policy was further reinforced by the creation of separate and autonomous divisions within the AFL known as departments. All the unions claiming jurisdiction over workers in a particular sector of the economy were affiliated to the relevant department.

[14] *Ibid.*, 135–46.

The Building Trades Department, for example, contained all the unions claiming the right to organize workers in the construction industry. The departments gave unions that were active in a particular industry a structure through which they could coordinate their activities, and thus complemented the organization of all crafts in an industry around the paramount craft or trade. At the same time the formation of the departments turned the federation into a bureaucratically decentralized and multidivisional organization that could service highly differentiated affiliates.[15]

Even after altering its structure, however, the AFL proved far too weak to impose an ordered adaptation to technological change on its affiliates. The major unions had no intention of allowing the federation to impede their own particularistic responses to developments in their industries. The principle of national union autonomy that governed the federation's relations with its member-unions meant that the AFL could never be a structurally coherent body. It was always less than the sum of its parts. The developments of the first decade of the twentieth century had resulted from policy changes of its major affiliates rather than a conscious attempt by the federation's leadership to initiate policy. After the 1911 Atlanta convention, the federation remained committed to "one trade, one organization," but the responses of the major unions soon took them beyond the Atlanta Declaration—beyond craft-industrialism— and toward multi-industrial organization.[16]

Because the federation was unable to exert real influence on the behavior of its affiliates, its policies provide an inadequate guide to the evolution of the organized labor movement in these years. It is at the level of the national union that significant changes in organizational policy may most precisely be discerned and the reasons for such changes isolated, for at this level occurred the most direct confrontation between labor unions and potentially disruptive alterations in the organization of industry and production.

The history of the carpenters' union affords an excellent il-

[15] Ibid., 136. See also Albert Theodore Helbing, The Departments of the American Federation of Labor (Baltimore, 1931), 51, 121–34. The departments were the Building Trades Department, the Metal Trades Department, the Railway Employees Department, the Mining Department, and the Union Label Trades Department. Helbing concludes: "The affiliated unions are not looking toward the formation of single unions in the various industrial fields. In fact, it has been one of the chief concerns of the Department officers that the separate unions be kept intact. . . . The development of the Department idea provided the believers in autonomous national unions with a foundation on which to build if industrial conditions made local and national joint action necessary." Ibid., 134.

[16] Christie, Empire in Wood, 170–71, 182.

lustration of these points. Originally a craft union with a membership mainly of construction workers, the UBCJ had, by 1902, begun a process of adaptation that eventually resulted in its transformation into a multi-industrial organization. This process was a direct response to on-going changes in the woodworking industry. The union was concerned above all to safeguard the position of the skilled carpenter. To achieve this goal it expanded its jurisdiction to cover first "all that's made of wood," and by 1914 anything "that ever was made of wood."[17]

The former claim took the union fully into the woodworking industry, which it sought to control on industrial lines.[18] The latter claim led the union to attempt to organize workers in metal-fitting manufacturing firms where it clashed repeatedly with the unions affiliated to the AFL's Metal Trades Department. A further logical development, confined in its fullest extent to the 1930s, was to enter the lumber industry, a move that gave the union control of the basic raw material of many of the industries in which it was active. At the same time the union remained the most powerful of the AFL's building construction unions and also organized woodworkers in railroad repair and maintenance shops. Each adaptation of jurisdictional policy inevitably meant alterations in the union's structure. As Robert Christie has observed: "Each of these alterations in union structure met a threat posed by changes in the organization of the [woodworking] industry, in the extent of the labor market, or in the tools of production. Whenever any one of these three factors has changed, carpenters' unions have had to change or cease to exist."[19]

While successfully widening the scope of its control to include diverse occupations and industries, the UBCJ continued to organize only those strata of workers that were strategic in any industry or trade in which it was active. In common with most AFL unions at this time it felt no obligation to organize "en masse." The union's policy was to control an industry in the interests of its skilled members and to organize only those less-skilled workers who could add to its power to "police" that industry.[20] In woodworking, the mechanization of the production process had led to the employment

[17] Ibid., 106–19, 170–85.
[18] Frank Duffy, the Carpenters' national secretary, declared at the union's convention in 1904 that "every man employed in the woodworking *industry* . . . ought to belong to the United Brotherhood [of Carpenters and Joiners]." Quoted in *ibid.*, 117–18.
[19] Ibid., xvii.
[20] Ibid., 196–97.

of less-skilled and unskilled workers in numbers sufficient to weaken the bargaining power of the craftsmen. The carpenters' union was therefore obliged to attempt to extend its control over all workers in the industry through selective organization of less-skilled workers; the union thus came to operate on an industry-wide basis. In the construction industry, where a number of unions were active, the carpenters' union organized only the skilled carpenters and their apprentices—and thus acted as a trade union. Unskilled workers in the construction industry had their own organization, the Hod Carriers' Building and Common Laborers' Union.

A similar process of structural evolution characterized the early history of the International Brotherhood of Electrical Workers (IBEW), the largest of the AFL's construction industry affiliates after the UBCJ. Like the carpenters' union, the IBEW's membership was not limited to skilled construction workers; although originally a multi-craft organization of construction workers and telephone and telegraph wiremen, the IBEW became occupationally diverse, "an amalgamation representing more than thirty different branches of the electrical trade."[21] In common with other AFL unions, the IBEW attempted to control the industries and trades within its jurisdiction by organizing the strategic workers. It was prepared to admit less-skilled workers wherever technological change undermined the position of skilled workers. After 1912, for example, it had considerable success in organizing telephone operators, who were mainly unskilled women.[22]

Throughout its early existence the IBEW was pressed to keep up with the rapid technological development of the electrical industry and constantly widened its jurisdiction to cover new jobs. This meant that the IBEW had to find a way of controlling a great diversity of occupational groups, while admitting to membership only those workers who were strategic. It was evident, however, that an organization, the membership of which ranged from the erectors of telegraph poles to workers installing, maintaining, and repairing complex electrical equipment, could not have any definite national rules concerning membership. The union responded to this problem in 1903 by adopting a decentralized and multi-divisional structure.

[21] Mulcaire, *International Brotherhood of Electrical Workers*, 23.
[22] *Ibid.*, 34–37.

The union was divided into three basic administrative divisions with separate jurisdictions: "outside" (workers in telephone and telegraph installation and maintenance, and power generation and distribution); "inside" (construction); and "shop" (production and maintenance workers in manufacturing). A fourth division was added later to cover IBEW members employed by the railroads. Each division was responsible for advising the locals affiliated to it on the criteria they should adopt for determining the eligibility of potential recruits.

The multi-divisional structure "simplified the question of jurisdiction."[23] By allowing the locals (through their respective divisions) to control the admission of new members, the union did away with many of the causes of internal disputes between different occupational groups competing for the control of new jobs. In this way the IBEW organized workers from remarkably diverse occupational backgrounds.[24] These structural developments early in its history enabled the IBEW to adjust to the rapid extension of the use of electrical power, and by 1923 the union had claimed a particularly extensive jurisdiction.[25]

The Teamsters' Union was confronted with a similar situation in the trucking industry. Until the 1930s the union's membership had consisted mainly of local draymen and haulers organized into occupationally distinct local unions, such as the Milk Drivers' Local Union or Coal Haulers' Local Union, operating within particular cities or metropolitan areas. Confronted with the emergence of highway trucking in the later 1920s and early 1930s, however, the union was forced to make fundamental changes in organizing strategy. Because of the nature of the job highway truck drivers could not be organized into locals covering such limited geographical areas. To bring these workers into the union the teamsters had to adopt new organizing policies.[26] Because of the strong tradition of local autonomy in the union, these policies were not initiated at the national level but were developed by local leaders. The regions rather than the national office introduced

---

[23] *Ibid.*, 27.

[24] *Ibid.*, 23.

[25] IBEW claimed jurisdiction over all workers engaged in the manufacture, installation, maintenance, assembly, and operation of all electrical devices by which electrical power was generated, used or controlled. The bulk of its membership consisted of workers employed by telegraph and telephone, heat, light, power, and transport companies, the building trades, and the electrical manufacturing industry. *Ibid.*

[26] Robert D. Leiter, "The Relationship between Structure and Policy in the Teamsters' Union," *Industrial Relations Research Association Publications*, 20 (Madison, 1958), 150.

changes in strategy and structure.[27] By the mid-1930s organizing and administrative bodies intermediate between the national office and the virtually autonomous locals had emerged in the West (Highway Drivers' Council covering California and the Pacific Coast states) and the Midwest (Central States Drivers' Council).[28]

These developments were complemented in the later 1930s by the creation of the regional conference in the West. The Western Conference of Teamsters coordinated the local and district organizations of the union throughout the region; the conference served as a vehicle for the extension of teamster organization throughout a rapidly growing and increasingly diverse jurisdiction. Subsequently, the Western Conference served as a model for similar organizational innovations in the Eastern, Southern, and Midwestern regions (a process of adaptation that was substantially completed by the mid-1950s). By adopting the regional conference model, the Teamsters' Union was able to set up a multi-divisional structure and to coordinate on a national scale all of its members in different industries and occupations, including manufacturing and the retail trades.[29]

As these three examples demonstrate, AFL unions were capable of a significant degree of institutional flexibility. Other front-rank unions showed similar levels of "creative response" to changes in the industrial environment. The International Union of Operating Engineers, for example, responded to a widening product market in the 1920s and 1930s in the heavy and highway construction industry with a policy of centralization.[30] The Amalgamated Meat Cutters and Butcher Workmen (AMCBW), confronted with managerial hostility in the meat packing segment of its jurisdiction,

[27] Ibid., 150–51. See also Donald Garnel, The Rise of Teamster Power in the West (Berkeley, 1972), 180–89. On the historically decentralized structure of the Teamsters' Union see Leiter, "The Relationship between Structure and Policy," 148–49; and Ralph C. James and Estelle Dinerstein James, Hoffa and the Teamsters: A Study of Union Power (Princeton, 1965), 16–17, 128–40.

[28] Garnel, Rise of Teamster Power, 325–27; James and James, Hoffa and the Teamsters, 90–93.

[29] The Western Conference of Teamsters was established in 1937, the Southern Conference in 1943, and the Central States and Eastern States Conferences in 1953. See Leiter, "The Relationship between Structure and Policy," 151.

[30] Garth L. Mangum, "The Development of Local Union Jurisdiction in the International Union of Operating Engineers," Labor History, IV (Fall 1963), 257–72. Elsewhere Mangum comments: "The continuing mechanization of the construction process has been the most important determinant of the history of the International Union of Operating Engineers." See Mangum, Operating Engineers, 10.

responded by decentralizing and organizing retail butchers.[31] Finally, the IAM, originally a Southern-based organization of skilled railroad shop craft metal workers, early claimed jurisdiction over all skilled machinists, regardless of industrial boundaries, and from this base sought to control the industries in which its members were active. First developed during the presidency of James O'Connell (1893–1912),[32] this policy led the IAM in the early 1930s to organize industrially in those sectors where it had been granted an industry-wide jurisdiction by the AFL.[33]

Structural change thus occurred at many different times and involved a variety of AFL unions. The affiliates were each confronted with a particular technological and economic environment. Each faced alterations in the organization of the production process, in the extent of the labor market, in the "skill-mix" of the industry, and in relative factor prices. In some cases, as with the teamsters, innovation in the industry was fairly abrupt and demanded a swift and thorough institutional response. In others, a more gradual process of adaptation was sufficient to cope with changes in their respective industries. But all the major affiliates at one time or another came to terms with a complex and changing industrial environment.

This does not imply that AFL affiliates could deal effectively with all of the problems of industrial change which they faced. The AFL unions proved powerless to organize workers in those industries where the labor force was predominantly semi-skilled or unskilled—as throughout most of mass production. These industries remained unorganized until the unions that were to found the CIO grew tired of the vacillation of other AFL affiliates. The United Mine Workers (UMW)—a union determined to preserve its position in coal mining by extending its control to encompass steel, the

[31] David Brody, The Butcher Workmen: A Study of Unionization (Cambridge, 1964), 127. AMCBW's decentralized structure proved well-suited, after 1933, to the accommodation of the major development in retail food marketing of the 1920s and 1930s—the rise of the chain store. The union organized the chains by using its decentralized locals to apply boycott pressure to local chain store management, while at the same time approaching the centralized management of the large chains through its national officers. Ibid., 130, 135, 141–46.

[32] Mark Perlman writes: "O'Connell's administration saw the IAM grow from a quality-conscious organization into a 'pure-and-simple' type. It changed from a small railroad-craft-dominated organization to an industrial 'house of many mansions'. . . . [O'Connell's] eye was always on the facts of industrial development. Consequently, he steered a consistent and realistic course. He charted the IAM's development toward industrial control, while seeking to retain hegemony for the craftsmen." Perlman, The Machinists, 148.

[33] Galenson, CIO Challenge, 495, 506–09.

major industry using coal as a producer good—finally launched the Steel Workers' Organizing Committee in 1936.[34] The UMW also supported the organization of workers in the automobile industry, while the garment trades unions sought the unionization of textiles. The subsequent achievements of the CIO underline the failure of AFL unions in the major manufacturing industries. Because the affiliates relied on organizing strategic nuclei to maintain and extend their control of jobs in an industry, they were unwilling to organize in situations where no such groups of workers could be found.

This should not, however, obscure the more successful adaptation of AFL unions to changing conditions in other sectors of the economy. The unions were best able to achieve and maintain control where industry was organized on a small-unit basis with comparatively little coordination between firms beyond the locality or region. This was the case, for example, in the trucking, retail, and construction industries. Here managerial hostility, which had complemented the weakness of the unions' strategies in the major manufacturing industries, was less coordinated. The unions were better able to maintain their positions and to keep abreast of technological innovations.

The AFL affiliates were not blindly committed to the organization solely of craftsmen or to the craft union structure. Between 1915 and 1939 the number of craft unions affiliated to the AFL diminished to 12 (out of 102 national unions).[35] In 1939 these unions contained only 0.68 percent of the AFL's total membership. Rather than remaining committed to craft unionism, the affiliates showed a tendency to adopt the form of organization that best suited the nature of their industries and best preserved their general bargaining position.

Structure followed strategy as unions altered their organizations in response to new threats. They were hindered by the opposition of management, by the opposition of elements within their own ranks, and by their general commitment to an organizing strategy applicable only to certain sectors of the economy. Nevertheless, it should now be apparent that to analyze the 1930s in terms of a victory of "industrial" over "craft" unionism is misleading. It obscures the fact that, although the majority of AFL unions were not

[34] Ibid., 133.
[35] Saposs and Davison, "Employee Organizations and Elections," 1044. See also Benjamin Stephansky, "The Structure of the American Labor Movement," Industrial Relations Research Association Publications, 9 (Madison, 1952), 46.

"industrial" unions in the 1930s, they were certainly not "craft" unions either.

In the 1930s labor unions consolidated existing areas of strength and extended to new and important areas of the economy. The growing pressure to organize the unorganized exacerbated differences of ideology, strategy, and personality within the AFL. At the same time an important new factor affecting the structure and policies of labor unions appeared during this period, as the state began formally to intervene in collective bargaining.

In the case of AFL unions, quantitative analysis of their patterns of growth in the 1930s indicates that, until the war, the affiliates grew mainly in those areas of the economy—construction, transport and communications, and some of the manufacturing and service industries—where large-unit firms were comparatively rare. The factors highlighted by a long-term perspective on their institutional development thus continued to have a decisive influence on their performance, for it was on account of their decentralized wage-bargaining and administrative structures, adopted during the preceding era, that AFL unions were better equipped than the centralized CIO unions to handle the problems of organizing workers in these industries.

Traditional analyses of the growth of unionism in the 1930s tend, however, to underestimate the importance of AFL unions. Although historians have now recognized that the AFL grew faster than the CIO, they argue that the latter was more significant not only because its unions organized the center firms which set the general price and wage levels of the major manufacturing industries,[36] but also because the threat of a rival federation was instrumental in awakening the AFL unions from a state of "stunned inactivity" in 1936.[37]

The preliminary analysis of gross membership figures, earlier in this essay, has already disputed elements of this traditional view. Both federations contributed significantly to the "great leap forward" of the labor movement in 1936–1937. The campaigns of the CIO contributed a maximum of 53 percent of the total gains in membership experienced during this twelve-month period (886,000 of 1,673,000); those of the AFL unions at least 46 percent (768,000 of 1,673,000). This can hardly be called "stunned inactivity." Nor is it justifiable to imply that durable manufacturing

[36] "The growth of organization in the traditional AFL trades, more imposing numerically, was less significant from a strategic point of view than the CIO concentration in vital centers of American industrial might." Galenson, CIO Challenge, 592.

[37] Ibid., 587.

is the only strategic area of the economy. This ignores the importance of transport and trade in a consumer economy and takes no account of the important secular trends toward growth of employment in the service sector and relative decline in manufacturing. It also neglects the importance of the construction industry and the long-term stability of employment in that industry.[38]

The traditional view is also inadequate because it conceives of the latter part of the 1930s as a contest between two rival blocs—one of craft unions and one of industrial unions. This concentrates the historian's attention on the attitudes and policies of the federation's top leadership. There is undoubtedly some truth in a description of the federation's national officers as "stunned" following the split. The AFL, however, unlike the CIO, was not a centralized body but a loose decentralized organization of widely differing and autonomous affiliates. It was the activities, reactions, and organizing strategies of its member-unions that governed the AFL's overall pattern of growth. As the following analysis of their performance indicates, these unions met with considerable success.

The strength of the AFL in the later 1930s and 1940s owed much to the performance of its affiliates in industries outside manufacturing.[39] AFL unions in transport and communications

[38] See John P. Henderson, *Changes in the Industrial Distribution of Employment, 1919–59* (Urbana, 1961), 36–79.

[39] Table 3: Membership of American Labor Organizations by Industrial Division and Federation, 1933–1945 (in thousands)*

	Manufacturing		Construction		Transport & Communications		Services	
	AFL	CIO	AFL	CIO	AFL	CIO	AFL	CIO
1933	692.9		617.7		314.6		359.8	
1934	1,008.4		639.6		352.7		393.7	
1935	1,001.0		498.5		469.8		445.2	
1936	1,142.0	(518.2)*	565.0	—	527.6	(44.1)*	509.3	(5.8)*
1937	837.5	952.1	743.5	—	727.8	95.5	673.8	71.9
1938	952.0	1,081.8	817.8	—	765.2	111.6	761.0	82.0
1939	1,022.1	1,060.6	891.1	2.5	844.1	118.4	857.0	86.3
1940	1,277.5	1,308.6	980.7	2.5	897.0	112.4	923.0	98.6
1941	1,525.6	1,798.3	1,354.8	2.5	1,034.0	110.2	981.9	111.0
1942	1,869.1	2,136.7	1,841.8	—	1,101.3	116.9	952.4	127.5
1943	2,326.4	2,873.5	2,066.9	—	1,092.5	138.5	947.7	147.8
1944	2,481.5	3,414.5	1,823.0	—	1,181.1	187.9	1,012.9	162.5
1945	2,393.9	3,361.2	1,723.9	—	1,381.0	204.9	1,112.8	178.4

* Table 3 does not include details of extractive industries—mining and agriculture. The latter remained unorganized. The former was dominated by the UMW, a founder of the CIO but independent after 1942.

* Estimates.

Table compiled from Wolman, *Ebb and Flow*, 172–92, and Troy, *Trade Union Membership*, Appendix 1–27.

grew rapidly; 1,000,000 workers in these industries joined unions between 1933 and 1945. The teamsters accounted for over 50 percent of this growth, expanding in membership from 71,000 to 644,000. Although concentrated in the trucking industry, this union also organized groups of manufacturing and retail workers. By 1956 it had become the largest union in the labor movement, with over 1,300,000 members.[40]

The AFL unions active in the construction industry expanded membership to a peak of 2,000,000 during the war. These unions, particularly the IBEW and the carpenters, also organized significant groups of manufacturing workers. The major period of growth occurred during the construction boom in the early 1940s.

Neither the teamsters nor the construction unions faced any competition from the CIO. Similarly, AFL unions in the service sector grew in areas where there was little confrontation with CIO unions. AFL growth here was based on the performance of its affiliates in consumer service industries and in public services. The Hotel and Restaurant Workers' Union grew from 26,000 to 282,000 between 1933 and 1945; the Building Service Employees added 76,000 members over the same period (18,000 to 94,000); unions of public service employees grew collectively from 145,000 to 300,000.

AFL unions were also successful in the retail trades. The Retail Clerks' Union expanded its membership from 5,000 to 96,000 between 1933 and 1945. By 1956 this union had a membership of 300,000. In the New York metropolitan area it faced competition from the Retail, Wholesale and Department Store Workers-CIO but elsewhere the clerks' union was less affected. Nor was the clerks' union the only AFL affiliate recruiting retail trade workers. The teamsters and meat cutters were also active in this field.[41]

In the manufacturing sector, unions of both federations grew most rapidly during the war. After the split in 1936, AFL unions added 400,000 members before 1940 and 2,000,000 in the next

[40] "One of the most important single factors responsible for a revival of the AFL from 1933 on was the decision of the Teamsters Union to organize everything on wheels. It was during this period that the IBT became the most powerful union in the country." Robert D. Leiter, *The Teamsters' Union* (New York, 1957), 38.

[41] In many cases the teamsters proved to be of decisive importance in aiding the unionization of the retail trades. See Marten S. Estey, "The Strategic Alliance as a Factor in Union Growth," *Industrial and Labor Relations Review*, IX (Oct. 1955), 41–53; and Marten S. Estey, "Patterns of Union Membership in the Retail Trades," *ibid.*, VIII (July 1955), 557–64.

five years. Defense production and wartime labor shortages were clearly prime determinants of the growth of unionism in manufacturing, especially in the durable goods industries, where CIO strength was concentrated. In these industries CIO unions added 1,600,000 members between 1940 and 1945. AFL unions active here also grew substantially in the war years, but their rate of growth was slower than that of the CIO organizations.[42]

Outside durable goods the rates of growth of affiliates of the two federations in manufacturing were approximately the same. Between 1936 and 1937 the AFL lost 450,000 members in non-durable manufacturing industries when unions that had joined the CIO were suspended.[43] Thereafter, unions of both federations attracted approximately the same number of recruits overall, although the CIO lost members when the International Ladies Garment Workers' Union disaffiliated. This union rejoined the AFL in 1940.[44]

The non-durable goods industries were less affected by the expansion of defense-related production, and the overall rate of AFL union growth in these industries was approximately the same before and after 1940. By contrast, the CIO unions here enjoyed their greatest success after 1940. CIO membership rose by 400,000 between 1940 and 1945, with approximately 50 percent of the gain coming in textiles and in rubber and chemicals. As was the case elsewhere, unions of both federations expanded in areas where they

[42] Table 4: Comparison of the Memberships of Affiliates of the AFL and the CIO in the Manufacturing Sector, selected years 1933–1945 (in thousands)

	1933	1936	1937	1938	1939	1940	1942	1944	1945
A. Metals, Machinery, Shipbuilding (Durables)									
AFL	186.9	284.9	336.9	355.5	371.6	435.6	870.0	1,355.7	1,184.7
CIO	—	(67.0)*	415.4	460.8	530.2	717.1	1,390.5	2,478.7	2,340.9
B. Other Manufacturing									
AFL	506.0	857.1	500.6	596.5	650.5	841.9	999.1	1,125.8	1,209.5
CIO	—	(451.2)*	536.7	621.0	529.9	591.5	746.2	935.8	1,020.3

* Estimates.

Table compiled from Wolman, Ebb and Flow, 172–92, and Troy, Trade Union Membership, Appendix 1–27.

[43] Unions in these industries which remained affiliated to the AFL recruited 100,000 members over the same period. Actual losses were thus 350,000.

[44] Several other unions changed their affiliations between 1937 and 1945, thereby influencing gross membership figures. The UMW left the CIO in 1942; the International Typographical Union left the AFL in 1939 and rejoined in 1943; the Brewery Workers' Union left the AFL in 1942.

had previously shown strength and did not compete to any great extent.[45]

The CIO's expansion in the manufacturing sector was thus primarily a function of the success of its affiliates in the durable goods industries. These unions were responsible for 80 percent of the CIO's gains in all manufacturing industries between 1940 and 1945. Their activities were also crucial to the performance of the labor movement as a whole in the manufacturing sector. Although they were not securely established until after the expansion of defense-related production,[46] these unions had organized many of the major manufacturing firms by 1940. In the next five years they contributed 68 percent of all union growth in durable goods and 51.5 percent of all union growth in manufacturing as a whole.

While the CIO expanded rapidly in manufacturing, its affiliates did not contribute materially to the general growth of the labor movement elsewhere in the economy. In 1937 48 percent of CIO members came from manufacturing (952,000 out of 1,900,000). By 1945 86 percent of its members were in unions active in this sector (3,300,000 out of 3,900,000). The three major durable goods unions—United Electrical Workers, United Auto Workers, and United Steel Workers—together contained over half of the CIO's entire membership.

In contrast, the AFL's membership did not become concentrated in any one sector of the economy. Between 1933 and 1945 the AFL grew from 2,300,000 to 6,900,000 in membership. In 1933, 30 percent of its members were in manufacturing industries. In 1945, 35 percent came from these industries. Both in 1933 and 1945 the construction unions contributed 25 percent of the AFL's membership, and the service sector unions between 15 and 16 percent. Finally, the membership of unions active in transport and communications rose from 13.5 percent of the AFL's gross in 1933 to 20 percent in 1945.

As these figures indicate, AFL unions made major contributions to the growth of the organized labor movement in the 1930s and

[45] The major exception was the lumber industry where the carpenters' union competed with the International Woodworkers of America-CIO in the Pacific Northwest. Competition also occurred in the meat industry between the AMCBW and the Packing House Workers Organizing Committee.

[46] "The situation . . . was still precarious five years after the formation of the CIO." David Brody, "The Emergence of Mass-Production Unionism," *Change and Continuity in Twentieth-Century America—the 1930s*, ed. John A. Braemen, Robert H. Bremner, and Everett Walters (Columbus, Ohio, 1964), 221–62; Barbara W. Newell, *Chicago and the Labor Movement: Metropolitan Unionism in the 1930's* (Urbana, 1961), 145–56.

1940s. Between 1937 and 1945 AFL affiliates added 3,700,000 new members. Approximately 2,000,000 of these recruits came from non-manufacturing industries, representing 90 percent of all union growth outside manufacturing. AFL unions were thus crucial to the success of the labor movement in important sectors of the modern American economy: because they were spread throughout the economy AFL affiliates were able to consolidate their positions across an unusually wide range of industries and occupations.

Outside of some manufacturing industries, the growth of AFL unions cannot be attributed to the stimulus provided by CIO competition; throughout the period in question the membership of the two federations continued to come predominantly from different sectors of the economy. Indeed, throughout the economy, competition appears to have been the exception rather than the rule. Between 1938 and 1946 unions seeking the right to represent groups of workers filed 47,600 cases with the National Labor Relations Board (NLRB), of which 29,700 had to be decided formally by holding an election or card count. Of these only 3,900—13 percent—involved direct electoral competition between AFL and CIO unions.[47]

While analysis of these cases calls into question the importance of AFL-CIO competition, the volume of the cases clearly indicates the importance of another element stressed in the traditional viewpoint—the influence of new political factors on labor union organization. Every historian of the period has noted the impact of the Wagner Act and NLRB on union organization and collective bargaining, and some have concluded that federal labor legislation

[47] Broken into three 3-year periods, the percentages of all formally decided cases that involved competition are:
    1938–1940: 24%
    1941–1943: 12.5%
    1944–1946: 11%
Between 1938 and 1946, 8.1% of all representation cases filed—decided both formally and informally—involved competition. These figures are compiled from Harry A. Millis and Emily C. Brown, *From the Wagner Act to Taft-Hartley* (Chicago, 1969), 77 (Table 1—"Cases Filed and Elections Held"); Joseph Krislov, "Organizational Rivalry Among American Unions," *Industrial and Labor Relations Review*, 13 (January, 1960), 218; and *Third Annual Report of the National Labor Relations Board* (Washington, 1939), 50; *Fourth Annual Report of the National Labor Relations Board* (Washington, 1940), 54; *Fifth Annual Report of the National Labor Relations Board* (Washington, 1941), 7; *Sixth Annual Report of the National Labor Relations Board* (Washington, 1942), 37; *Seventh Annual Report of the National Labor Relations Board* (Washington, 1943), 88; *Eighth Annual Report of the National Labor Relations Board* (Washington, 1944), 95; *Ninth Annual Report of the National Labor Relations Board* (Washington, 1945), 85; *Tenth Annual Report of the National Labor Relations Board* (Washington, 1946), 86; *Eleventh Annual Report of the National Labor Relations Board* (Washington, 1947), 83.

played a more important role than CIO competition.[48] State intervention in collective bargaining, however, also had significant strategic and structural implications, for it permanently and substantially altered the environment in which unions operated. Increasingly, it was the NLRB rather than the union itself that defined the appropriate unit of organization and bargaining. By the 1940s, unions were constrained to operate in accordance with the board's criteria of efficient organization. They were no longer free to choose the strategy that best suited their particular industrial environment and their own institutional objectives.

The long-term structural implications of government intervention were noted in 1945 by President Paul R. Hutchings of the Office Employees International Union-AFL. Although recognizing that the Wagner Act had been a powerful stimulus to trade union growth, Hutchings criticized it for interfering with union autonomy:

Prior to the Act, unions were free to organize in whatever manner they found to be most effective. Frequently a union would build its membership in a shop by first organizing a small group of workers who had the fortitude to stand strong for the union. Upon the organization of such a group, certain job improvements would be obtained for them from management. And this working example of the gains to be achieved through organization frequently formed the most potent organizational appeal to other workers in the shop. . . . Now, trade unions must conform their organization to the appropriate bargaining unit patterns laid down by the [National Labor Relations] Board. They cannot organize and bargain for those workers in a plant who are interested in collective bargaining, they must organize and bargain for all workers within 'an appropriate bargaining unit.' The Board's measure of what constitutes 'an appropriate bargaining unit' is frequently far removed from what the union may recognize as the most propitious to protect its members and promote collective bargaining.[49]

As Hutchings observed, the passage of the Wagner Act added a new, and in the long term a crucial, political dimension to the environment in which unions operated. In the short term, of course, the major effect of federal labor legislation was to qualify the ability of management to oppose the spread of unionism. The extent to which AFL unions could take advantage of the opportunities that the Wagner Act presented was due primarily to their earlier creative responses to industrial change. In the long run,

[48] For example, Perlman writes that "the fact of the NLRB caused the change within the IAM—far more than the 'fact' of the UAW, the SWOC [Steel Workers Organizing Committee], or the rubber workers." Perlman, *The Machinists*, 92.
[49] Paul R. Hutchings, "Effect on the Trade Union," *The Wagner Act—After Ten Years*, ed. Louis G. Silverberg (Washington, 1945), 73.

however, the government became the chief arbiter of how the unions would adapt to future economic changes—a subject that perhaps deserves more attention than it has received to date from labor historians.

That subject, however, leads far into the postwar economy and beyond the scope of this essay. For the present, a new perspective on union growth in the period from 1930 through 1945 must suffice. An examination of that growth calls into question the traditional argument that the AFL's success depended on the structural transformation of its affiliates in the face of CIO rivalry. Historically, AFL unions had already shown a tendency to adapt to the challenge of a changing industrial and economic environment. Similarly, the pattern of labor organization in the 1930s indicates that unions of the two federations were expanding in different areas of the economy and adopted strategies best suited to the varying structure of industry in their respective sectors. It is misleading, therefore, to regard the CIO's emergence as an apocalyptic event that decisively altered the shape and strategies of the entire organized labor movement. It is equally misleading to regard industrial unionism as a panacea or as an ideal toward which all unions should necessarily strive. Indeed, the history of the modern labor movement after World War II tends to confirm that industrial unionism is merely one phase in a continuing process of structural evolution rather than the final outcome of that process.[50]

These conclusions suggest the need for a new perspective on AFL unions in the 1930s. In concentrating on the newsworthy events of those years and on conflicts between the leadership of the two federations, historians have failed to account for some of the most important aspects of the growth of labor organizations in the 1930s. The history of the AFL's affiliates and the nature of the industries in which they were active must be studied to find explanations of the federation's achievements. Until such a perspective is adopted, the performance of AFL unions in the 1930s will appear anomalous because it cannot be fully explained by any of the factors traditionally emphasized.

[50] See Arnold R. Weber, "The Craft-Industrial Issue Revisited: A Study of Union Government," *Industrial and Labor Relations Review*, 16 (April 1963), 381–404; Arnold R. Weber, "Craft Representation in Industrial Unions," *Industrial Relations Research Association Publications*, 28 (Madison, 1962), 82–92; Abraham L. Gitlow, "The Trade Union Prospect in the Coming Decade," *Labor Law Journal*, XXI (March 1970), 131–58; Kahn, "Recent Jurisdictional Developments," 21–23; Joseph Krislov, "Union Organizing of New Units, 1955–1966," *Industrial and Labor Relations Review*, XXI (Oct. 1967), 31–39; Joseph Shister, "The Direction of Unionism 1947–1967: Thrust or Drift?" *ibid.*, XX (July 1967), 578–601.